Conrad von Orelli

The Old Testament Prophecy of the Consummation of God's Kingdom,

traced in its historical development

Conrad von Orelli

The Old Testament Prophecy of the Consummation of God's Kingdom,
traced in its historical development

ISBN/EAN: 9783337245863

Printed in Europe, USA, Canada, Australia, Japan

Cover: Foto ©Lupo / pixelio.de

More available books at **www.hansebooks.com**

THE
OLD TESTAMENT PROPHECY

OF THE

CONSUMMATION OF GOD'S KINGDOM,

TRACED IN ITS HISTORICAL DEVELOPMENT.

BY

C. von ORELLI,

PROFESSOR OF THEOLOGY, BASEL.

Translated by

REV. J. S. BANKS,

HEADINGLEY COLLEGE, LEEDS.

EDINBURGH:
T. & T. CLARK, 38 GEORGE STREET.
1885.

TRANSLATOR'S NOTE.

THE following work aims at ascertaining the meaning which a certain section of Old Testament prophecy must have had for its first hearers and readers. The tendency of Christians has ever been to read the New Testament into the Old. However natural this tendency may be, it is not without injurious effects on the intelligent study of Scripture. Under its influence the difference between the two dispensations is overlooked; type and antitype, promise and fulfilment, childhood and maturity are confounded; ancient believers are credited with knowledge and ideas which go far beyond their circumstances; a weight of meaning is put upon Old Testament passages which they are too weak to bear. Evidently our first effort should be to ascertain what the earlier Scriptures meant in the age to which they spoke; and this is what Dr. Orelli tries to do in the present volume. While doing ample justice to the Christian fulfilment, he first considers every prophecy of the divine kingdom in its relation to speaker, hearers, and the general historical circumstances out of which it arose. The student is placed at the Old Testament standpoint, as far as this is possible to us. We need not fear the results of such an investigation. Even granting that on single points the author may have gone too far, and that some details of his exposition cannot be regarded as fully established, enough remains to demonstrate the divinity of Old and New Testament alike. Prophecy and fulfilment correspond as bud to flower. Neither is intelligible without the other. It is refreshing to note the energy with which the author, who certainly cannot be charged with ignorance or prejudice, maintains at his special standpoint the miraculous element in prophecy. In this respect the new method of interpretation is far preferable to the old. We do not need to read Christian ideas into prophecy in order then to bring them out again. Reduce the teaching of prophecy to its most literal form, and yet the image of the future undeniably shines through it. The unity of subject pervading the whole from first to last, the uninterrupted progress both in the form and matter of revelation, the correspondence between prophecy and fulfilment, are evidences of divinity which nothing can explain away.

I thought at one time of retaining the author's spelling of Jewish proper names. I found, however, that to do this consistently would give the pages a very repulsive look, at least to English readers, and the compensation would not be great. "Yahveh" is the only exception. This more accurate form of the word has now become tolerably familiar.

I only wish to note further that the term "authorities" is used in Part I. for the German *Quellen* (*sources*), to denote the original documents on which the early books of the Old Testament are supposed to have been based. Perhaps a better English term might have been found.

CONTENTS.

---o---

		PAGE
	INTRODUCTION,	1

SEC.
1. Biblical Prophecy, ... 4
2. Are Phenomena analogous to Biblical Prophecy found in Heathenism ? . 13
3. The Kingdom of God as the Subject of Biblical Prophecy, . . . 25
4. Influence of the Age on the Prophecy of God's Kingdom, . . . 31
5. The Office of Type in the Development of God's Kingdom, . . . 37
6. Are Phenomena analogous to the Prophecy of God's Kingdom found in Heathenism ? 41
7. Fulfilment in general, ... 50
8. Fulfilment in the New Covenant, ... 54
9. The Treatment of the Subject in Christian Theology, ... 62

FIRST PART.

THE PROPHETIC WORD HERALDING THE RISE AND ACCOMPANYING THE
DEVELOPMENT OF A NATIONAL KINGDOM OF GOD ON EARTH.

FIRST SECTION.—PATRIARCHAL PRELUDES OF PROMISE.

10. General View, ... 77
11. The Primitive Divine Capacity and Destiny of Man, ... 82
12. Man's Common State of Sin (the Protevangelium), ... 86
13. The Threefold Development of Mankind, ... 93
14. The Promises to the Fathers of the Covenant People, ... 104
15. The Leading Tribe, Judah, ... 115

SECOND SECTION.—MOSAISM.

16. The Law of Moses, ... 125
17. Mosaic Outlooks, ... 130
18. Balaam's Oracles, ... 134

THIRD SECTION.—THE LORD'S ANOINTED.

19. The Prophetic Testament to the Davidic Royal House, . . . 148
20. The Echo of the Prophetic Word in the Songs of the Anointed One, 158
21. Typical Significance of David, Solomon, and the Davidites, . . 167
22. The Dwelling of Yahveh on Zion, ... 186

SECOND PART.

THE PROPHETIC WORD AS THE HERALD OF THE NEW BIRTH OF GOD'S KINGDOM AND THE SECURITY FOR ITS FUTURE CONSUMMATION.

FIRST SECTION.—THE PROPHETS OF THE PRE-ASSYRIAN AGE.

SEC.		PAGE
23.	General Character of Prophecy in the Pre-Exilian Period,	191
24.	Obadiah,	196
25.	Joel,	204

SECOND SECTION.—THE PROPHETS OF THE ASSYRIAN AGE IN THE NORTHERN KINGDOM.

26.	Amos,	224
27.	Hosea,	228
28.	Zechariah ix.-xi.,	244

THIRD SECTION.—THE PROPHETS OF THE ASSYRIAN AGE IN THE SOUTHERN KINGDOM.

29.	Isaiah and Micah: The exalted Zion,	255
30.	Isaiah's Oracles of Immanuel,	264
31.	Further Oracles of Isaiah respecting Zion (chaps. xxviii.-xxxix.),	285
32.	Isaiah's Visions respecting the Gentiles and the World-Judgment, as well as the glorifying of the World from Zion,	295
33.	Micah, Nahum,	305

FOURTH SECTION.—THE PROPHETS OF THE DECLINE (CHALDÆAN PERIOD).

34.	Zephaniah,	314
35.	Habakkuk,	323
36.	Jeremiah's Prophecies of the New Covenant,	329
37.	Zechariah xii.-xiv.,	345

FIFTH SECTION.—THE PROPHETS OF THE EXILE.

38.	Ezekiel's Oracles and Visions,	361
39.	The Prophecies of the Servant of Yahveh, Isa. xl.-lxvi.,	376

SIXTH SECTION.—THE POST-EXILIAN PROPHETS (PERSIAN PERIOD).

40.	Haggai and Zechariah,	419
41.	Zechariah's Visions,	426
42.	Malachi's Sayings respecting the Herald of the Lord,	447
43.	Daniel's Apocalypse,	454
	CONCLUSION,	467

OLD TESTAMENT PROPHECY.

INTRODUCTION.

IN the whole of creation there dwells a profound longing after perfection, a noble instinct for completeness. By degrees nature has brought forth more and more perfect creatures upon earth. In considering the structures of past æons, when man as yet was not, we seem to see the creative spirit struggling after something perfect, without reaching it. And where the formative force has spent itself for a time, and the contradiction between the imperfection of existence and the perfect idea makes itself felt, the instinct for completion changes into longing for redemption. Whoever is able to catch the innermost tones vibrating through nature hears issuing from it sad, yearning voices, beseeching redemption from the burden of imperfection—a sighing of the creature, as the apostle calls it, more plainly in the plant-world than in inorganic nature, more audibly in the animal kingdom than in the plant-world.

Man, then, as the most perfect creature of earth, feels all the more powerfully the instinct for completion. The desire for likeness to God grows stronger in him, the nearer he stands to God, the nobler he is. This instinct is a mighty factor in history, impelling to the creation of new forms, when things are ripe for further advance. Although the passion for innovation is a morbid excrescence, it is still the caricature of something noble and divine in man; it testifies to a striving after completeness that is never satisfied. And when all the lauded, hardly-won steps in advance bring one no nearer to the goal, which rather seems to recede farther and farther away, the yearning after a better world arises among all uncorrupted peoples. Among many this yearning takes the form of lamentation over a far-distant happy past. Presages of the future also are heard, as if there were a golden age to come.

But as nations grow more rational and mature, such dreams are given up, and the completion which life fails to supply is sought in the region of art and idea. That both are powerless to satisfy the inmost craving of man's heart was confessed reluctantly by Goethe, the last of the Hellenes, who, if any one could, would have reconciled the contradictions of life by harmony of form. After he, in his masterwork, had pictured, but not really healed, the anguish of the human spirit in its utter impotence to compass perfection, the antagonisms became still fiercer, the discords more painful. Sorrow for the imperfection of existence is felt all the more keenly when the hope that has been placed in advancing culture turns out on the whole illusory in every field. Twenty years ago liberalism preached on every house-top its favourite dogma, man's capacity for eternal progress. To-day in the most advanced circles this is looked down on with scorn. An actual progress of real value is no longer believed in. The pessimism which in our days has gained so large a following, learned and unlearned, is itself a witness to the imperfection under which man groans. It yearns for release from the ban, without believing in a future consummation. Instead of redemption, nothing but a dissolution of existence will satisfy it, so strongly does it feel its burden. This, then, is the end of modern intellectual progress, as it was the end of ancient heathenism, even of buoyant-spirited, idealistic Hellenism—an unsatisfied turning away from the world with nothing to take its place, despair of reaching the ideal which man instinctively cherishes as his best possession. Are we nowhere to find any solution but this despair, which cuts the knot of fate and at the same time the sacred life-thread of humanity?

One *nation* in the human family felt this drawing to perfection, to God-likeness, in a peculiarly powerful way,—the nation of Israel, to which the true God revealed Himself. In the revelation of this God the goal of its effort stood clearly before its eyes —to be holy like God, to keep His commandments perfectly, and thus to be made partaker of the highest good—perfect peace. That the perfection, for which man's soul thirsts, has complete subjection to the holy *God* for its indispensable condition, and fellowship with Him for its essential contents, dominion over creation being the natural consequence,—the knowledge of this truth distinguished Israel from all nations of antiquity, and was not so much a fruit of its own musing and reflection as rather the result of the miraculous converse this nation had with its God, and of the legal discipline to which God subjected it above all other nations.

But while this nation was chosen before others to experience the blessing of the divine rule, it was also compelled to look deeper than any other into the abyss separating sinful man from the holy God. The divine law—that privilege of Israel—was also a thorn in its flesh. In the light of revelation it saw human imperfection in all its depth to be *sin*, sin in all its gravity to be deadly guilt, and all unhappiness in the creature to be punishment. Hence a yearning for redemption, for a complete transforming of humanity in God's service and of all creation, goes hand in hand with a desire for the establishing of the divine rule. The conviction is more and more definitely expressed, that no simple improvement of the existing can lead to perfection, but a total change must take place, a new creative act of God.

But what we find in Israel is more than a deep, holy longing for completion and redemption. It is the actual certainty that both *will be realized*. As the law presents itself to the nation with sovereign independence as God's demand, so the nation receives prophecy as a positive pledge, which with the seal of the divine veracity stands secure above the vacillation of ages and nations and the vicissitudes of circumstance. The prophecies are not ideals, such as men fashion for themselves to strive after but can never reach; they are ideas which God purposed to Himself to realize. What is it that gives us a right, nay, compels us, to assert the divine reality of these words of the future? The answer is simple.

In *one man* the perfection which prophecy sets before us has been actually realized, in a Son of man, who was also Son of God. Through Him also the felt need of reconciliation with God has found its full satisfaction. In these marvellous facts we have security that the divine rule thus founded will spread over the earth and thoroughly permeate the world, that through it redemption from evil, inward and outward, will be perfected, as announced already by the prophecies of the Old Covenant. Thus the sacred voices of the prophets are an answer, not merely to the inquiry of their people and age, but also to the noblest seeking and searching of man's heart, to the longing and sighing of the whole creation. They point to Christ, and proclaim to the world to-day what it may find in Him. They remind the Christian how wondrously in the long period of waiting the morning stars bore witness to the coming sun, until at last it rose. But they also point him beyond our days to the days of the consummation of that kingdom of God, to behold which is our deepest longing.

Let us then, before bringing forward these prophetic oracles of the Old Testament, take account of the source from which they spring, the peculiarity of nature and contents distinguishing them (in contrast with everything of a like kind presented by the extra-Israelitish world), of their fulfilment already accomplished or still future, and of the different attitudes which the Church and theology of Christian times have assumed to them and their fulfilment.

§ 1. *Biblical Prophecy.*[1]

Prophecy is the product of prophesying. In answering the question, What is to be understood by it on Biblical ground? we start from the definite, uniform statements of the Bible. According to these, prophesying is in general the speaking of individuals under the influence of the Spirit of God. And by the Divine *Spirit* we do not understand the general potency of life dwelling in all men and giving breath to living beings generally,[2] but the supramundane Spirit of God, who only comes on man exceptionally to qualify him for work beyond his natural powers, and only settles in permanence upon him extraordinarily, and, moreover, is clearly distinguished from man's natural life-spirit (note A).

In accordance with the free working of this Divine Spirit, prophecy is not bound to office and order. Even those who were not organs of God by their life-calling might be seized momentarily by Him, obtain glimpses into hidden things, and under the

---

[1] Cf. with this section especially: A. Knobel, *Der Prophetismus der Hebräer*, 1837. Fr. Köster, *Die Propheten des A. und N. T.*, 1838. Redslob, *Der Begriff des Nabi*, 1839. Hengstenberg, *Christology of the Old Testament*, vol. iv. p. 396. A. Tholuck, *Die Propheten des alten Bundes*, 1860. H. Ewald, *Die Propheten des alten Bundes*, 2nd ed. Bd. i. 1867. A. Dillmann, art. "Propheten," in Schenkel's *Bibellexicon*, 1872. G. F. Oehler, *Theology of the Old Testament*, 1873 (T. & T. Clark); cf. his art. "Prophetenthum," in Herzog's *R.-E.* H. Schultz, *Alttestamentliche Theologie*, 2nd ed. 1878, p. 187 ff. F. Hitzig, *Biblische Theologie des A. T. und messianische Weissagungen*, herausg. von Kneucker, 1880 (cf. also Hitzig's *Commentar zu Jesaja*, the Introduction). Kleinert, art. "Prophet," in Riehm's *Handwörterbuch des biblischen Alterthums*, 1880.

[2] Isa. xlii. 5; Job xxxiii. 4, xxxiv. 14 f.; Ps. civ. 29 f.; cf. Gen. ii. 7; Num. xvi. 22, xxvii. 16.

impulse of the same Spirit publish what they saw. In Genesis, for example, such illuminations are related of the patriarchs, especially before death. Prophetic words were uttered by Balaam the heathen seer, by David the king, and in the New Testament by Caiaphas the high priest. On the other hand, the Old Testament prophecies come as a rule from the lips of those who enjoyed in abiding converse with the Lord the gift of the prophetic spirit more frequently and served as His standing instruments.[1] Still they clearly distinguished their natural subjectivity from revelation, and even as to time believed they heard the word of the Lord and were empowered to speak in His name only in stated hours.

The work of the prophet in prophesying is twofold, as is expressed by his two most common appellations. He is called רֹאֶה (seer),[2] and נָבִיא (speaker) (note B). The first name implies the receptive, the second the productive side of his attitude.

On the former point Isidorus Hispal. (Etymol. viii. 1) says not amiss: "Qui a nobis prophetæ, in V. T. videntes appellantur, quia videbant ea quæ ceteri non videbant et præspiciebant quæ in mysterio abscondita erant." Their endowment consists chiefly in an extraordinary heightening of the perceptive faculty. Whether the sensuous organs are or are not concerned in this is primarily indifferent. But the essential element to be maintained in prophecy[3] is, that it *sees* its contents before announcing them, although as to time the two acts may be combined. For not merely where the contents take sensuous forms, as in the vision proper, but even where the more abstract medium of speech obtains, the Hebrew designedly uses חָזָה to express how the prophet came by

---

[1] Such an one is called אִישׁ הָרוּחַ, Hos. ix. 7; more generally אִישׁ הָאֱלֹהִים, 1 Sam. ix. 6.

[2] According to 1 Sam. ix. 9 his earliest popular name. This passage proves that the idea of רֹאֶה and נָבִיא is substantially identical. Synonymous with it is חֹזֶה, beholder. But the verbs רָאָה and חָזָה must be distinguished to this extent, that the former denotes simply the relation of the eye to an object which it sees, the latter the dwelling of the glance on the form of an object, therefore on an image. Accordingly, they are related to each other as our "seeing" and "beholding."

[3] We use the word "prophecy" in the more general sense, according to which it is not so much the product of prophetic activity as rather a designation of this activity itself. Both uses of the word are warranted linguistically. Cf. Rom. xii. 6, 1 Cor. xii. 10, xiii. 2, with 1 Cor. xiii. 8, and προφητεία (from προφητεύω) with ῥητορεία (from ῥητορεύω), the gift of rhetoric, then the artistic discourse itself. Thus we do not need to take refuge in Knobel's phrase "prophetism."

his knowledge.¹ The contents of prophecy are, consequently, not something thought out, inferred, hoped, or feared by the prophets, but something directly perceived. This explains the categorical certainty with which they announce their oracles. They know these oracles to be independent of their own subjectivity. The revelation comes before their gaze as something independent, nay, belonging to another.

It is God who discloses² these things to them—things withdrawn from human gaze ($\mu\nu\sigma\tau\acute{\eta}\rho\iota\alpha$ in N. T. language). The fundamental assumption always is, that the attitude of the genuine prophet to the contents of his discourse, if not passive, is primarily receptive.³ Only false prophets announce what they themselves have thought out or inferred on grounds of probability.⁴ The heathen wonder-workers or diviners are called חֲכָמִים or יִדְּעֹנִים—"wise men" or "experts," because they fabricate oracles by certain arts and devices.⁵

What has thus forced itself on the seer in direct intuition as divine certainty, he then feels himself compelled by the same power of the Spirit *to utter*. This divine causality, compelling the seer not merely to see, but also to tell what he sees, is pictured most vividly in Amos iii. 8: "The lion hath roared, who will not fear? The Lord God hath spoken, who will not prophesy?" Just as involuntarily as one starts in terror when the mighty voice of the king of beasts roars, must the prophet prophesy when God's revealing word comes to him.⁶ Only false prophets are led by outward human considerations to proclaim what pleases others or brings gain to themselves.⁷ But when a word has issued from that living stream of thought which the prophet plainly distinguishes from his own thoughts and feelings, he proclaims it not as his own conviction, but as a word of the Lord, demanding correspondent obedience and the trust due to

---

¹ Cf. the general headings, Amos i. 1 ; Isa. i. 1, ii. 1, xiii. 1 ; Micah i. 1 ; Hab. i. 1, etc.

² גָּלָה סוֹדוֹ אֶל, Amos iii. 7; in N. T. language, $\dot{\alpha}\pi o\kappa\alpha\lambda\dot{\upsilon}\pi\tau\epsilon\iota$ $\mu\upsilon\sigma\tau\acute{\eta}\rho\iota o\nu$. It is only another expression for the same circumstance to say, "God declares such things to them, the word of the Lord came to them," or to introduce their discourse directly with "Thus saith the Lord," or to accompany it with the clause, "the decree of the Lord is " י'י נְאֻם.

³ Cf. Isa. l. 4 ff. ⁴ Cf. Jer. xxiii. 31 ff.

⁵ Cf. Ex. vii. 11 ; 1 Sam. xxviii. 3, 9. ⁶ Cf. Jer. xx. 7, 9 ; 1 Kings xxii. 14 ff.

⁷ Cf. Micah ii. 11 f., iii. 5, 11 ; Ezek. xxxiv. 2, and elsewhere.

God. He is *God's speaker*, the organ through which the Invisible One speaks audibly to His people. This lies directly in the word נָבִיא, which is interchanged in Ex. vii. 1, iv. 16, with פֶּה (mouth), the organ of speech.¹

Whilst it is a necessary part of the character of the true prophet to be a seer and speaker of God in the way just explained, on the other hand it is not equally necessary that what he sees and announces should relate to the *future*. Even the historians, who illumined the foretime with the light of revelation, wrote prophetically, because they made known God's ways in the past. And what did not fall, locally or by its nature, within the prophet's natural field of vision, might be revealed to him in that way.² We may instance Ezekiel, who sees as present what is far distant in space, and also the deep insight of the prophets into their times and the hearts of their fellow-men.³ But, of course, not only is the prophetic word always significant for the future, because it announces divine truth, and because it has the kingdom of God for its subject, having reference chiefly to its future completion, but the divine mission of its bearers is proved to the contemporary world most obviously by the fact that they are able even to lift the veil of the future.⁴ The Deuteronomic law expressly proposes this criterion for discriminating true and false prophets, that the result should confirm the predictions of the former and falsify those of the latter.⁵ Undoubtedly the prophets, whose writings we still have, owed their high reputation in great part to the fulfilment of their oracles in reference to the future, while later prophets laid great stress on the fulfilment of earlier predictions.⁶

---

¹ Apuleius (*De mundo*, p. 288): Prophetæ deorum majestate completi effantur cæteris, quæ divino beneficio soli vident.

² Chrysostom (in Tholuck, *Die Propheten*, 2nd ed. p. 23): Οὐ μόνον δὲ τὰ μέλλοντα προφητείας ἐστὶν εἰπεῖν, ἀλλὰ καὶ τὰ παρελθόντα—ἔστι δὲ καὶ τὰ παρόντα προφητείας εἰπεῖν, ὅταν τι γένηται μὲν, κρύπτηται δέ.

³ Cf. 2 Kings vi. 12; 1 Cor. xiv. 24. Just as little does נָבִיא imply an express reference of the utterance to the future. Prophetic discourse (נִבָּא, הִתְנַבֵּא), which was ecstatic especially in more ancient times, was often more distinguished by this feature than by its contents from ordinary human discourse (cf. 1 Sam. x. 10 ff., xix. 20 ff.). The Greek προφήτης also denotes, not one who *foretells*, but one qui profatur, who expressed the obscure tones of the Pythia in the form of human language.

⁴ Cf. 1 Sam. ix. 6.

⁵ Deut. xviii. 22; cf. Jer. xxviii. 9, 14-17; Ezek. xxxiii. 33.

⁶ Isa. xxxiv. 16, xli. 21 ff., 26 ff., xlii. 9, xliii. 9.

If, then, we ask how this peculiar form of life which we call prophecy is to be explained and estimated, certainly in a formal respect the Shemitic-Hebrew disposition and temperament has much to do with it, and must have its due weight in the explanation.[1] To the Shemites (*i.e.* the Hebrews) and the tribes akin to them in race, language, and character, a certain directness of intuition is peculiar. While viewing a phenomenon in its isolation, they bring it into direct connection with the supreme cause dominating their thoughts. Whereas the Indo-Germans strive to analyse the object by reflection and inquire into its special nature, to subsume it under the next general idea and refer it to its proximate causes, the Shemite directly sees the divine in nature and history as well as in his own inner life, sees the absolute in the particular and finite, and has little taste for ideal abstraction and dialectic methods. His perception is intuitive, not systematizing. He does not distinguish universally valid truths from passing phenomenal forms; but the truth which (because it is divine, *i.e.* absolute) dominates him, seems to him the absolutely essential thing in the particular concrete form. Hence the undivided, undiluted certainty in a particular judgment, which is not disturbed by the remembrance of diverse dialectic cross-lines. This entire mode of thought, in comparison with that of Indo-Germans, is naive and childlike. This, however, does not lessen its worth in regard to the perception of the highest truths. The child that thinks it hears God's voice in the rolling of the thunder, hits the mark more easily and surely than the scientist, who must reason his way back through a crowd of physical second causes to a supreme one, and just here finds himself left in suspense by his infallible scientific method. But comparative psychology plainly teaches this much, namely, that the Shemites were more adapted by nature than other peoples—their equals or superiors in culture—to see the absolute in the finite, the working of God in nature, His action in history, and to hear His words in the inner spiritual life of individuals.

[1] Attempts to characterize Shemitism (or Hebraism) as natural genius, on the basis of which Biblical prophecy rises with more or less independence, may be seen in F. Hitzig, *Der Prophet Jesaja*, 1833, p. ix.-xxxiii., and in his *Vorlesungen über A. T. Theologie*. E. Renan, *Histoire générale et système comparé des langues sémitiques*, prem. partie: *Histoire générale des langues sémitiques*, Paris 1855, 4th ed. 1864. G. Baur, *Geschichte der A. T. Weissagung*, 1. Vorgeschichte, 1861, p. 33 ff. R. F. Grau, *Ursprünge und Ziele unserer Culturentwickelung*, 1875.

As the ethnological factor is to be recognised in explaining prophecy generally, so is the *personal, individual* factor in tracing the derivation of particular oracles. The prophet is not a blank mirror, on which divine images are cast that have no sort of existence in time and no connection with his peculiar character. Formally, revelation joins on to existing conceptions, and is partly determined in the shape it assumes by the temperament of the prophet, the liveliness and cast of his imagination, his mental training and calling in life. Dreams may serve as a comparison, where our own conceptions occur to us, without our being masters of them. Thus, Ezekiel sees the buildings of the temple, with whose circumstances he was most familiar. An Amos brings images from his shepherd-life.

But the question is, whether Biblical prophecy can be referred to this natural genius of nations and individuals, without an unexplained remnant being left. Even in a formal respect we must deny this. We may indeed be reminded, by way of explaining the conception of a divine agent in the prophet's consciousness of other mental circumstances and conditions which are derived from special divine causation, *e.g.* the melancholy of Saul, 1 Sam. xvi. 14 ff., which is natural, as shown by the remedies applied to it, and is yet said to be caused by an evil spirit sent by God,[1] or the natural wisdom of Solomon,[2] or the technical skill of Bezaleel.[3] But, to say nothing of the fact that the Hebrews would not ascribe these cases to nature, even measured by our standard, the prophet's inner relation to his revelation remains still a psychological enigma. It is not a question here of a peculiar state of mind or a permanent mental gift, but of particular previsions, which are distinguished to a hair's-breadth from the prophet's own thinking and feeling. Hebrew naïveté did not go so far, as one might suppose according to Hitzig's representation (*ut ante*, p. 24), that among this people "the spirit was still unconscious of its own internality (*Innerlichkeit*), and was still external to itself, so that it could regard its own products, purposes, and thoughts as something external and obtained from without."[4] The conscious, sharp severance between the prophet's human feeling and opinion on one hand, and his word of revelation on

---

[1] So Spinoza, *Tractatus Theologico-pol.*, cap. 1.   [2] So Spinoza, *ibid.*
[3] Ex. xxxi. 3; so Redslob, as above.
[4] Cf. his *Biblische Theologie des A. T.* p. 11 ff., 76 ff.

the other, is altogether inexplicable on this view. How differently Nathan is instructed by divine inspiration from what his individual opinion suggested, 2 Sam. vii. 3, 4! A factor is always lacking to the explanation of such discrimination and immovable subjective certainty. The insufficiency of the old rationalistic explanation, which made the prophet a man of distinguished gifts of head and heart, an observer of life, a friend of virtue and therefore of Deity, a predicter of bright or cloudy days through that sure gaze into the future which escapes the thoughtless worldling,[1] is self-evident. Moreover, the higher intelligence and feeling as explained by Knobel,[2] and the native conception, which Redslob makes the basis,[3] are here seen to be inadequate.

The clearer, in distinction from Shamanism, the intelligent consciousness of the prophets remains in receiving their prophecies, and the more their entire bearing is pervaded by moral, holy earnestness, the less can their assertion of the divinity of the word they announce be understood psychologically, unless a higher power is present in their consciousness. An analogy to such a power is furnished by the voice of conscience in its most emphatic utterances, and by the spiritual life in its inmost, purest converse with God. We are thus led to the explanation, which is the only one known to the Bible itself, the theory of a supernatural agent, who is the principle of prophecy. Of course from the Deistic standpoint a living intervention of God is negatived at once. The Pantheistic theory, it is true, does not cast doubt on the divinity of these spiritual transactions, but it regards them simply as products of heightened nature-power. Whoever, on the other hand, has mastered the Biblical idea of God, according to which an entrance of the Divine Spirit who transcends nature into the limits of finitude is the very essence of revelation, will discern in prophetic communication the form in which the living God made Himself known to His people in the preparatory age of the Old Covenant.

Certainly the decisive proof of the divinity of prophecy must always be sought in its *contents*. The value we put on these will determine whether we are compelled and disposed to refer prophecy

---

[1] Hufnagel; similarly Eichhorn, Griesinger. Cf. even Stutzmann in Knobel, *Prophetismus der Hebräer*, i. p. 184.

[2] *Ibid.* i. p. 179, 215 f.   [3] *Der Begriff des Nabi*, p. 18.

to a supernatural cause. Before entering on the spirit and contents of biblical prophecy, let us first search for phenomena of analogous form in the extra-Israelitish world.

NOTE A.—This current conception plainly follows from the expressions with which the *coming* of this prophetic Spirit *upon* a man is described: הָיָה עַל, Num. xxiv. 2; 1 Sam. xix. 20, 23; 2 Chron. xv. 1, xx. 14; or more violently נָפַל עַל, Ezek. xi. 5; and צָלַח עַל, 1 Sam. x. 6, of sudden piercing, penetrating. Because it is a power seizing man powerfully, often violently, יַד יְהוָֹה also stands instead of רוּחַ, 2 Kings iii. 15; Ezek. i. 3, iii. 14, 22, xxxiii. 22, xxxvii. 1, xl. 1. It is also said of this Spirit: He puts on (לָבֵשׁ), a man like a dress, thus making him His bodily veil (Judg. vi. 34; 1 Chron. xii. 18; 2 Chron. xxiv. 20). Along with this, נוּחַ עַל is found of the Spirit: to settle on one, rest on him (Num. xi. 26; 2 Kings ii. 15; Isa. xi. 2). In consequence of this the Spirit of God *is upon* a man (Num. xi. 25; Isa. lxi. 1). This expression points to a permanent state of inspiration, in which, however, its higher origin is also distinctly intimated. The dispenser of these extraordinary gifts is still more conspicuous, where it is said of God: He gives (נָתַן עַל, Num. xi. 29; Isa. xlii. 1) or pours out (Joel ii. 28 f.) this Spirit on men. Accordingly it is everywhere something new and higher that must come upon man if his words are to be divine. And even where this Spirit has become his permanent possession, this relation has taken its rise from a divine, creative act, which does not coincide with the imparting of the general spirit of life, either as a rule in regard to time, or in any case in regard to substance.

NOTE B.—The signification of the word נָבִיא cannot be obtained from the Hebrew verbal stem נָבָא, because of the latter only the denominative formations *niph.* and *hithp.* occur: to act or behave as a נביא. On the other hand, the *kal* of the nearly-related נָבַע occurs, at least in the participle (Prov. xviii. 4) נַחַל נֹבֵעַ, bubbling brook, which meaning is confirmed by the more frequent *hiph.* הִבִּיעַ, to make to gush forth, pour forth abundantly, sounds or words for the most part forming the object (Prov. xv. 2, 28; Ps. xix. 2, cxix. 171). With this agrees also the signification of the Hebrew and Arabic root נב, to rise, come to light, swell, with many variations. The question whether in נביא the form קָטִיל is active or passive in meaning has indeed been answered by most in the latter sense, because in Hebrew it is almost always passive; cf. קָלִיא אָסִיר, roasted grain, alongside קָלוּי; also פָּקִיד, overseer, properly, one appointed to oversee, alongside פָּקוּד. Accordingly Redslob interprets: one made to bubble (*der Angesprudelte*), namely, with God's Spirit, who is thought of originally as fine fluid,—*one inspired*. Similarly Keil (on Gen. xx. 7): the God-addressed or inspired. With this may be compared אַבִּיעָ לָכֶם רוּחִי (Prov. i. 23), although this very place shows that הִבִּיעַ means not to bubble, with accusative of person, but can only be joined with the accusative of the thing. Just as passively Köster: instructed, taught; he appeals to نبا, and Hupfeld. But such a passive derivation is plainly unjust to the sense of the Hebrew word, which may be most clearly seen by comparing Ex. vii. 1 with iv. 16. Also the compromises between the passive and active sense, attempted by Oehler and previously by Schultz, are unnatural. On the other hand, the matter assumes a perfectly simple shape when the active, or at least intransitive, signification of the form קָטִיל is recognised from the first. That this signification occurs in Hebrew, is proved by חָסִיל, locusts, properly *devourers*, חָסִיד, which Hupfeld wrongly interprets in the passive: *favoured*, פָּלִיט, *fugitive*, עָתִיק, *glistening*, synonymous with פָּלַט עָתֵק, Ewald, *Ausf. L. B.* § 149 c. Cf. also Hitzig on *Sefanja*, i. 11. *Katil* so intensifies the active participle as to make it express a permanent quality. In Arabic the form فَعِيل stands far oftener in the active sense (بمعنى الفاعل), and Fleischer (Delitzsch, *Comm. zu Genesis*, 4th ed. p. 551 ff.) has proved that especially the فَعِيل, exactly corresponding to our word, is to be so regarded. Cf. also Marti, *Jahrb. für protestantische Theologie*, 1880, i. p. 147. If there can no longer be any doubt respecting the active signification of this word (which is also acknowledged by Delitzsch, von Hofmann, Ewald, Dillmann, and now by Schultz), the question at most is, whether the word describes the prophetic discourse as breaking forth involuntarily, violently (*the bubbler*), in which case the peculiarity distinguishing the Nabi from other speakers would lie in the utterance itself, or whether we should be content with the meaning *divulger, announcer, speaker*, and then supply conventionally: of God and divine secrets. The latter is favoured by the Arabic نبا, as well as by the parallels quoted by Ewald (on *Jesaja*, p. 7): Sanscrit *vâdi* or *vâdica*, Latin *vates*, from *vad*, to speak, Moses = كلم الله and نطيق among the Druses = prophet. At all events, the Assyrio-Babylonian God Nebo, so called as the speaker, revealer, has his name from the same word. See Schrader, *Jahrb. für prot. Theol.* 1875, p. 338 ff.

§ 2. Are Phenomena analogous to Biblical Prophecy to be found in the Field of Heathenism?[1]

The possibility of Deity speaking directly to and through man is often assumed in antiquity outside the Bible. We find there a widespread opinion, that man has the capacity, in virtue of his spiritual nature, of hearing the voice of Deity.[2] And in particular, it is supposed that individuals are endowed with capacity for so doing, and enjoy closer converse with the gods, so that, initiated into their counsel, they are able to foreannounce it. This prescience of the future is not acquired through the intellect, but the soul is made directly aware of the future.[3] Such knowledge is the result of divine power and gift.[4] More precisely, it is the Divine *Spirit* who comes upon and fills man in order to speak through him, so that, possessed by a higher power, he is detached from his subjective thinking and feeling (note A).

Thus the main general conditions of prophecy seem present here also. Nor can it be asserted without qualification that this inspiration, in distinction from that of the Israelitish prophets, is one that completely annihilates the moral individuality of the recipient. Alongside such phenomena as are presented in Shamanism we find also the higher conception, approximating more

---

[1] Cf. with this section, especially: In Pauly's *Realencyklopädie der classischen Alterthumswissenschaft*, Metzger's art. "Divinatio," ii. p. 1113-1185 (1842). Nägelsbach, *Homerische Theologie*, 2nd ed. 1861, p. 149-194, his *Nachhomerische Theologie*, 1857, p. 157-191. Tholuck, *Die Propheten und ihre Weissagungen*, 2nd ed. 1860, p. 1 ff. G. F. Oehler, *Ueber das Verhältniss der A. T. Prophetie zur heidnischen Mantik, Glückwunschschreiben*, Tübingen, 1861. P. Scholz, *Götzendienst und Zauberwesen bei den alten Hebräern und den benachbarten Völkern*, 1877. Lenormant, *Die Magie und Wahrsage-Kunst der Chaldäer*, 1878, especially p. 421 ff.

[2] Cf. the beautiful passages in Ovid, the first describing rather man's relation to the transcendent, the second that to the immanent Deity: Est deus in nobis et sunt commercia coeli. Sedibus aetheriis spiritus ille venit (*Ars Amat.* iii. 549 ff.). Est deus in nobis, agitante calescimus illo. Impetus hic sacrae semina mentis habet (*Fast.* vi. 5 f.).

[3] Cf. Plato, *Phaedrus*, p. 242, c. 20 (μαντικόν τι ἡ ψυχή): Cicero, *De divinatione*, i. p. 1, 6. Plato calls such knowledge ἐπιστήμη προσδηλωτική ἄνευ ἀποδείξεως. Plutarch also remarks expressly: ἀσυλλογίστως ἅπτεται τοῦ μέλλοντος (*De def. orac.* c. 40).

[4] Θείᾳ δόσει διδομένη, Plato, *Phaedr.* 244. Cf. Cicero, *De divinat.* i. 6, ii. 63; *De Leg.* ii. 13.

closely to Israelitish prophecy, that man receives oracles with a certain personal independence, and these oracles are partly conditioned by his individual peculiarities.[1]

But, first of all, it is to be noted, that both the direct intercourse of the gods with men, and also their revelation through individual, spiritually illuminated seers, where these things occur, scarcely ever belong to historical times, but to that happier age when gods and men lived together in more intimate and unconstrained intercourse. Rich as the mythical period everywhere is in such intercourse, much as fable has to relate (*e.g.* among the Hellenes) of the elect favourites of the gods,[2] to whom it was granted to behold past, present, and future, these noble figures remain on the threshold of the nation's historical life. In Homer, the seer Tiresias, Calchas (*Il. a.* 69 ff.), Helenos (*Il. η.* 44 f.), Polydamas (*Il. σ.* 250), Amphiaraos (*Od. o.* 244 ff.), Halitherses (*Od. ω.* 451), still stand in high esteem; but already they rely in part on outward signs, which they have only to interpret (cf. Halitherses, *Od. β.* 157 ff.). And while traces of doubt respecting such divine gifts are found even thus early (*Il. ω.* 220 ff.; *Od. a.* 415 ff.), the seers sometimes appearing in historical times, who prophesied extempore in accordance with an inner spiritual communication, were regarded as adventurers, at least by the educated.[3] Apart from the spiritual import of the divine oracles, we see a fundamental antithesis in this respect to the Israelitish literature, where *the prophets, sustained by the bare power of the Spirit, appeared in every period of the classical history,* and were able to maintain their reputation in presence of a critical age.

And yet the whole of heathen antiquity thirsted for divine revelation, and listened and looked for every intimation of the Deity. Even the precarious substitutes sought and found in place of prophecy exercised incredible influence on the entire life of heathen nations, both cultured and uncultured. We have now to consider somewhat more closely the variety of means by which men sought to place themselves in contact with Deity.

The less a divinely superior power positively entered into consciousness, the greater the attention given in the heathen world

---

[1] See Plutarch's account, *De defectu orac.* 21, 22.
[2] Cf. as to the Chinese, in Victor v. Strauss, *Schi-king* (1880), p. 7, the words of the supreme God to King Wen.
[3] Cf. Nägelsbach, *Nachhomerische Theologie,* p. 174 f.

to such utterances as at least did not seem to be under the control of man's reflective consciousness. Involuntary, inevitable *presentiment* was regarded as a reflection of the divine will. Nor was it always illusory, but often inexplicably fitted in to the connection of events. So far as such feeling is of moral character, divine dignity cannot be wholly refused to it. Compare the δαιμόνιον of Socrates in its affinity with conscience. Presentiments at the moment of death seemed least deceptive,[1] since man was then all but released from bodily life and its limiting influences.

In particular, *dreams* were marked out by their relative independence of conscious thought as inspirations of a higher power. In ancient Egypt as in the Homeric world, among the ancient Romans as among the Germans, among the Babylonians as among the Chinese[2] (and where not?), they were often held of the highest importance.[3] Experience indeed showed that their reality could not be trusted without reserve. Already in Homer (*Od.* τ. 560 ff.) dreams are divided into such as issue from the ivory gate and befool men (as intended occasionally by the gods), and such as issue from the gate of horn and are trustworthy. No criterion by which to distinguish them is known. In dream a deity or a departed spirit may appear and speak to the sleeper, so that he receives intelligible information. But the dream-image is also often symbolic, needing interpretation, as in the Egyptian story in Joseph's life and the Babylonian in Daniel's. Hence an important branch of ancient mantism is always dream-interpretation, which, of course, degenerated into wilful trickery, unless a spirit possessing control over the system of nature inspired the interpretation as well as the dream (Gen. xl. 8, xli. 16). For the rest, the Bible, while placing dreams at God's service, draws a clear distinction between dream-vision and prophetic vision. Zechariah's night-visions are no dreams. The Arabs also keep the two apart, placing the dream, which always has something sensuous about it, far below the vision.[4]

The significance attributed to dreams led to express efforts to produce dreams by artificial means,[5] and to the setting up of

[1] Cf. Plato, *Apol. Socr.* 30.   [2] Strauss, *Schi king*, p. 11.
[3] Cf. *Il.* α. 63, καὶ γάρ τ' ὄναρ ἐκ Διός ἐστιν; β. 22. 56. *Od.* ξ. 495, θεῖος ὄνειρος. See especially Cicero, *De divinatione,* i. 29.
[4] Cf. Fleischer's remark in Delitzsch's *Biblical Psychology,* p. 332. T. & T. Clark.
[5] Cf. as to the ancient Egyptians, Ebers, *Ægypten und die Bücher Mose's,* i. 321 f.

dream-oracles.¹ We find this wilful inducing of an unconscious state, in order to obtain higher revelation, especially in *ecstasy*, which seemed all the more favourable to higher influence, because it was always regarded as a momentary possession by a higher power. Even the settled state of lunacy was explained by the sway of a demon, on which account lunatics were sacred, as they still are among the Bedouins.² But in temporary ecstasy the inspired state differed still more from the natural. Of course there are countless gradations in it, from the rational self-control which is laid hold of by inspiration, up to complete loss of self-control, where a real *alienatio mentis* intervenes. Cicero describes the *furor*, where the spirit, withdrawn from the body, is excited by divine impulse (*instinctus*), as a heightening of the presentient faculty natural to man.³ Elsewhere also with respect to this enthusiasm, which has something in common with the state of drunkenness, release from the ties of the body, unshackling the soul, is held to condition the revelation of the divinity slumbering within.⁴

The exalted state then (μανία) being regarded as a voucher for supernatural discourse, attempts were made to induce it by artificial means. Thus arose mantism (divination) in the proper sense of the word (μαντική, sc. τέχνη). Stupefying vapours, herbs, movements, conduced to this end. In this way a mysterious state was brought about, such as not seldom presents itself in the diseased human organism (somnambulism, etc.). What was said in this state was no longer under the control of reflection, and often went beyond the field of ordinary perception in a surprising manner.

1 Kings xviii. 26 depicts a dance designed to induce the state of madness, similar to the conduct of dervishes to-day. The opposite to this is beautifully seen in Elijah, who without artificial intensity of feeling, relying on bare faith in the living God, accomplishes more by his simple prayer than the whole crowd of Baal's prophets. It is true, even the נָבִיא is in a sense released from bodily life and the limits of his surroundings; nay, some

---

[1] See in Pauly, as above, ii. 1124 f. ; and as to the Babylonians, Lenormant, p. 404.
[2] Cf. v. Orelli, *Durch's heilige Land*, 2nd ed. p. 140 f.
[3] *De divinatione*, i. 31 f., and especially i. 50.
[4] So especially by Plato and Plutarch. Cf. the latter's utterance, *De def. orac.* 39 : ἡ ψυχὴ τὴν μαντικὴν οὐκ ἐπικτᾶται δύναμιν ἐκβᾶσα τοῦ σώματος, ὥσπερ νέφους, ἀλλ' ἔχουσα καὶ νῦν, τυφλοῦται διὰ τὴν πρὸς τὸ θνητὸν ἀνάμιξιν αὐτῆς καὶ σύγχυσιν.

hints in the older history show us prophets in a state of stupor, like that of possession (cf. the casting away of clothes, 1 Sam. xix. 24). But if inspiration took this violent form in the disciples of the prophets and in a Saul, this was not the case in a Moses, in Samuel, in an Isaiah or Jeremiah. Those indeed who had to convey the Word to men appear more or less in a state of unusual excitement and enthusiasm, which is seen even in the form of their written oracles. But the security for the divinity of their message does not lie in their speaking in a half-conscious or unconscious state, but they heard the voice of the Lord and saw His visions with clear consciousness.[1] Balaam is rather an example of a clairvoyant. The emphasizing of his state in his account of himself should be observed, Num. xxiv. 3 f. Nearly allied to this example is the Shamanism still flourishing among the Tunguse.[2] Here by outward incitements the physico-mental torpor is induced, which makes a man the channel of words, whose meaning he himself does not know.

Among the *Hellenes* also such artificial inspiration is found. The Pythian oracle has such an origin. Vapours rising from a rift in the earth were used to stupefy the Pythia, her words or sounds being then expounded by priests ($\pi\rho o\phi\hat{\eta}\tau\alpha\iota$).[3] Such interpretation gave still larger play to human influence. The interpreting priests were of necessity regarded as inspired by the Deity. But, in any case, something human inheres in the artificial character of every oracle, since the initiative belongs to man.

If, in a state of emancipation from the limits of reflection, such as occurs in dreams, lunacy, and at the approach of death, special disclosures were expected from man's spirit respecting what was concealed from it in the normal state, they were especially expected from the *spirits of the departed*, to whom of necessity insight was granted into the other world where the roots of earthly events lie. As the demons were supposed to know what was hidden from man,[4] so also the souls of the

---

[1] The LXX. rightly translate the Hebrew נביא invariably by προφήτης, never by μάντις.

[2] See Tholuck as above, p. 8 ff.

[3] Cf. Justin, xxiv. 6: Profundum terrae foramen, quod in oracula patet, ex quo frigidus spiritus, vi quadam velut vento in sublime expulsus, mentes vatum in vecordiam vertit, impletasque deo responsa consulentibus dare cogit.

[4] Cf. Dieterici, *Thier und Mensch vor dem König der Genien*, Leipzig 1879.

departed, to whom a demon-like existence was ascribed. Hence necromancy (calling up and questioning the dead) is found among the most diverse nations,—Babylonians,[1] Egyptians,[2] Canaanites (Deut. xviii. 12), Persians,[3] Thracians,[4] Greeks,[5] Etruscans, and Romans.[6] In the Old Testament this mode of ascertaining future events is not seldom mentioned, of course as a gross abuse altogether in opposition to the Divine Spirit. We thus see that this gift of summoning spirits was not a general one, but was only in the power of certain media who had a divining demon (note B).

The strict prohibition in the divine law, which directs all its severity against such over-curious arts that were held criminal even among the Babylonians,[7] was fully justified by their ungodly character. Not merely was the imposture connected with these things condemned, while the folly of the superstition is also emphasized,[8] but still more the guilty licence with which man transgresses the limits of the sphere allotted to him, in which divine revelations enough were granted. In 1 Sam. xxviii. we see that this art was not always ineffectual, but that occasionally it might lead man to knowledge, although never to salvation.

That conscious deceit played a part in these inquiries from the first and everywhere, is a quite untenable supposition. The wide extension and the high importance attributed to these oracles imply of necessity that, if nothing substantial lay beneath apparitions of the dead, the deception was originally at least a universal self-deception, in which even the media were involved. As in magic everywhere, art was resorted to afterwards, and so the superstition was purposely turned to profit. Ventriloquism often produced the voices; yet the beginning of the superstition is not to be sought in mere art. How far demonic influences were actually at work, is a question we need not examine here, and one which lies beyond the reach of scientific examination.

p. ٢٣ وكانت الجنّ توهم الانس انّهم تعلم الغيب (the demons persuaded men that they knew what is hidden).

[1] Cf. Lenormant, p. 508 ff.; Scholz, p. 89 ff.   [2] Cf. Isa. xix. 3.
[3] Cf. Strabo, xvi. 2.   [4] Cf. Herod. iv. 94 ff.
[5] Cf. *Odyss.* xi. 29 ff.; *Argonaut.* iii. 1030 ff.; Ovid, *Met.* vii. 240 ff.; see Greek oracles of the dead in Nägelsbach, *Nachhom. Theol.* p. 189.
[6] See on Etruscans and Romans, Lenormant, p. 512.
[7] Lenormant, p. 517.   [8] Isa. viii. 19.

In the case mentioned in 1 Sam. xxviii., a divine interposition is to be supposed, such as may occur also in dreams.

But the yearning of all ancient nations for living intercourse with the Deity, and inquiry into His will, early attached itself to other revelations than to *speech* springing from the human *spirit* in those of its emotions which were regarded as divine. As the Deity Himself was believed to be most directly known in *nature*, so His intimations were there most certainly apprehended. In lightning and thunder, in the flight of birds, in the rustling of the wind, in the state of the stars, divine voices, hints, and *signs* were recognised from the earliest days. Certainly special inner illumination was needed rightly to understand such τέρατα and σημεῖα,—and thus, in Homer, their interpretation was practised by the seers, or a definite class of seers, at least pre-eminently. Signs and interpretation were also often exposed to the attacks of scepticism by reason of their ambiguity and untrustworthiness.[1] And in this field mantism proper developed into a profession, observing and interpreting natural phenomena by certain rules of art apart from all inspiration.

But even where, in the noblest, because most direct manner, the secrets of Deity are discovered in the sighing of the wind, the rustling of the grain, the murmur of the fountain, something obscure, indefinite clings to such intimations, plainly distinguishing them from clear prophetic speech. An enigmatic character belongs essentially to such natural revelation as the Hellenes and Romans under Oriental influence personified in the Sibyl.[2] And where, as at Dodona or Delos, in some sanctuary of nature a standing oracle was established,[3] of necessity in the course of time purely rational observation, or even calculation that avails itself of any kind of help, and in the best case the moral consciousness, take the place of immersion in nature. Most of the oracles, even the one at Delphi,[4] although somewhat differently,

---

[1] Cf. Nägelsbach, *Homerische Theologie*, p. 177 ff.
[2] Cf. H. Ewald, *Abhandlung über Entstehung und Werth der Sibyllinischen Bücher*, 1858, p. 8.
[3] At Dodona the natural media of divination were the motion of the leaves in the sacred oak (φυλλομαντεία), the murmur of the spring, and the sound of the wind beating against the brazen cymbals; at Delos the rustling of the laurel.
[4] It is disputed whether at Dodona originally a personal medium was put into a state of mania, or oracles were constructed from the whistling of the outrushing wind.

appealed to the intimate union of man with nature, and were able long to maintain their reputation partly by this means, partly by the co-operation of the moral sense, which owes not a little to the stimulus of natural surroundings. Still men like Socrates, Xenophon, Plato (especially in the Timæus) speak in high terms of them, and the Stoics as well; whilst the Peripatetics, Cynics, Epicureans, and in the same way for different reasons a Lucian, Aristophanes, Demosthenes, hold them in little esteem. Even the symbolic obscurity, nay, ambiguity, of the oracular utterances gave little offence, from the right feeling that such features had their reason in the nature of the Deity. Occasionally the purpose was recognised of provoking the inquirers in this way to reflection, and so of appealing to the revelation in the human breast (Herod. i. 53, 55). But here an essential distinction is obvious between the groping and feeling after the Deity who reveals himself only in dim twilight, and the God who really *speaks like one spirit to another in clear speech.*

If a sort of inspiration by the spirit of nature underlies these mantic oracles, this inspiration fell into the shade the more that attention was directed to mere observation of the outward phenomenon. There were not wanting indeed, on the soil of heathenism, acute observation and research into nature, undertaken for the purpose of learning the divine will and work. Exact knowledge of the *stars* and calculation of their course grew out of the effort to discover the powers ruling in life, and to foresee what was to be expected from them. The *Chaldæans*[1] were the most successful labourers in this field, and won the fame among all ancient nations of the best and most systematic acquaintance with divination. By the priestly caste, which went by the name of "Chaldæans" among other nations, divination was carried on in higher style, in accord with their higher conception of nature and Deity. Philo[2] excellently characterized their theory of the world in saying that they identify God and nature, making everything to be determined by fate and necessity. Cf. Diodor. Sic. ii. 30: No phenomenon or event on earth is accidental or spontaneous, every one is determined beforehand by the gods. The system pervading the universe, according to their view, necessarily made it possible to discover natural as well as

[1] Cf. Lenormant, p. 421 ff.   [2] *De Migr. Abr.* 32.

human events from the indications given in nature. Continued observation might lead to some degree of certainty, *e.g.*, in weather-omens. It was especially the stars to which, as higher powers, a determining influence upon earthly events was ascribed, and from their state accordingly conclusions were drawn respecting the course of human transactions. The more systematic the observation of nature, especially of the stars, the more must the thought of law, instead of capricious chance, have occurred to man; only in subordinating human events to natural law the theory of the world became of necessity fatalistic.

Even where alongside this more scientific divination, and partly among the same nations, more *isolated* natural phenomena, having less of a cosmical character, were explained as presages, the basis assumed is the connection between visible nature and man's invisible, still unaccomplished destiny. If not a science, at least a fixed method was taken as guide, the signs having to be interpreted according to definite rules. Here comes in the interpretation of extraordinary natural phenomena, such as earthquakes, untimely births, etc., observation of the lightning and clouds, of the flight of birds, of the pecking of fowl,[1] inspection of entrails, all which auguries are found in specially elaborated forms among the Babylonians, Etruscans, Romans, and to some extent among the Greeks. To the same class belongs also the observation of tortoise-shells among the Chinese.[2] In all this men saw symptoms of the life of nature, from which, because of the intimate connection of the latter with man's life, conclusions might be drawn respecting that life, provided one understood the method to be followed, which soon became the business of a special guild (*e.g.* the Etruscan Lucumones) and formed the subject of a special sacred literature. At first, the unexpected flight of a bird seemed significant. Later, such observation was reduced to rule. At first men interpreted by the instinct of the moment, then by rules, last of all by a code of rules embodied in written tradition. In particular, the Stoic school, in order to justify the whole system of divination, pointed to the συμπάθεια binding the universe together, the *cognatio, concentus* or *consensus naturæ*,[3] in

---

[1] Cf. the Slavic horse-oracle in Rügen, Jul. Lippert, *Die Religionen der europäischen Culturvölker*, 1881, p. 99.
[2] Cf. Strauss, *Schi-king*, p. 10; Faber, *Licius*, p. 72.
[3] Cf. Cicero, *De divinatione*, ii. 14, 58, 60, 69; *De natura deorum*, ii. 7, iii. 11, 23.

virtue of which the individual being, and not least the animal, feels instinctively along with all nature, and has presentiments of much that happens.[1] But it is evident how easily popular consciousness might lose this connection and persist in blind adherence to single auguries, whilst philosophical speculation was of necessity just as easily led astray by this popular faith.

Next in order to this prophetic application of single natural phenomena comes the use of certain apparatus to arrive at unknown results. Such was the hydromancy of the Egyptians, prophecy by means of the water in a cup, whose rising bubbles were the material of interpretation, etc. The *lot* appealed more directly to the Deity. Here the ruling principle is, that what is not determined by man is determined by the Deity. The lot was cast with various instruments—dice, arrows, wands, etc., among the Babylonians,[2] Arabians,[3] and others. Of the lot, as of the dream, it is true that God may employ it.[4] On the other hand, he has not given man the right to consult Him at pleasure. Whether the Urim and Thummim was a special privilege of the people of God, a kind of lot, or whether the answer was read in the shining of the precious stones,[5] or the medium was of another kind, is matter of dispute. But the import of the answers given by this oracle is as different from O. T. prophecy as its character. It served an essentially different end from the standing institute. In it the will of God—of course the relation of God and the nation being in a normal state—might be ascertained in doubtful cases. It was a supreme court of appeal in grave decisions affecting the commonwealth. The answer was always a direction in reference to the particular case, without further explanation. No spiritual illumination of man was connected with it.

Let us return to the appliances of heathen divination. Like the primitive lot, *chance* also as a divine ordinance, and consequently the incidental circumstances of an action (especially a religious one), appeared presignificant to the piety of ancient times. Not merely meeting certain animals and meeting men, but a word addressed to one without intention, and the like, had

---

[1] Cf. the suggestive reasoning in Cicero, *De div.* i. 15, cf. 48, ii. 14, 34, 35, 72.
[2] Cf. Lenormant, p. 430 ff. ; Ezek. xxiv. 6 f., and Jerome on the passage.
[3] Cf. the details in Scholz, p. 75. Respecting the Slavs, cf. Lippert, p. 100 ; the Germans, p. 189.
[4] Cf. Jonah i. 7 ; Acts i. 24 ff.
[5] Cf. the oracle in the Libyan Ammonium, Diod. xxvii. 50 ; Curt. iv. 7.

the force of an omen. In distinction from auguries, these omens presented themselves unsought. Human caprice is the more evident in them as the individual might accept or decline the omen he encountered or even interpret it in his favour, if he only had the necessary presence of mind, which freedom Pliny (xxviii. 4) describes as a great prerogative bestowed by God on man. As the higher unity of nature is presupposed in the auguries mentioned before, so in these omens the presupposition is a unity of events that excludes chance. Thus it is wrong to speak of a "fetishism of chance" (de Wette) in the original teaching of religions, although adherence to single signs degenerated into this.

Let us sum up. The universal search of the nations for revelations of the Deity and indications of His will proves a vividly-felt need of self-revelation on His part, a need making itself directly felt in man as he stands with childlike simplicity in presence of God and nature. But although points of attachment were given to the nations in nature and history, intellect and conscience, in which they might discern the Deity, still the uncertain, superstitious, inquisitive, and insane feeling after divine revelations beyond the sphere in which God was pleased to make Himself known to them, shows how little these revelations could satisfy the natural man with his nature corrupted and power of perception weakened by sin. But great as was the error and selfishness of the course man took, it was the outcome of the noble hunger for God implanted in him and nowhere fully satisfied in heathenism. With this the revelation of the Lord to Israel stands in powerful contrast. He announces His ways, usually unsought, in clear speech, through His Spirit, who is essentially distinct from the spirit of nature,—a free, moral power,—and distinct also from the national spirit, a holy, chastening, and redeeming power of God.

This contrast loses nothing of its greatness when we take into account the nations bordering on and allied to Israel. No doubt a common spiritual inheritance is traceable among the Edomites, Arabians, Moabites, etc.; but whilst these tribes more and more blended the knowledge of God transmitted to them with heathenism, and thus became involved in the errors described above, in Israel alone a converse with God was maintained, worthy of the majesty and condescension of the Supreme

Spirit, and conducive to His further revelation. Of prophecy there is little sign in these tribes. The "wise men" are there the depositories of the knowledge of God, inherited from antiquity. Of a future plan of God they have nothing to tell. To say nothing of individual poets in Mohammed's age, almost the sole remnant of prophetic discourse is preserved to us in the Koran, which claims to be inspired by God. But although points of similarity even in form are not to be overlooked between the admonitions of the Biblical seers and those of the prophet of Mecca, the latter is destitute of the originality which must be postulated in an epoch-making prophet, and still more in a religious founder. The inspiration also is rather morbidly sought than one that bursts forth by inner constraint. At the same time, religious enthusiasm is not to be denied to Mohammed's discourses. Especially in the older Suras it is present in a high degree. But his language is related to that of the prophets pretty much as the confused tirades of a spiritualistic medium, made up of motley reminiscences, and held together by mere pathos, are related to the works of the spirits whom he professes to represent. Mohammed is throughout an *epigonus* of Biblical literature, and what he has of national character in common with the prophets of the Old Covenant is too little to raise him to the height from which they bear their testimony through the sovereign Spirit of God.

We come to the conclusion that no phenomenon analogous to Biblical prophecy, even in form, is anywhere to be found in the world of nations. It is true, all nations sought after special divine revelations beyond what reason and conscience taught them of the working of the Deity in nature and history, and expected to succeed by the intensifying of human susceptibility and by immersion in the unconscious nature-power. But such means of becoming acquainted with the divine, such morbid *self-enhancing* of the human spirit, artificially *enfeebling* it up to the point of unconscious surrender to the dominion of nature, is opposed to the true nature of God, and can only lead farther away from Him; whereas His Spirit reveals Himself in Israel by clear speech in keeping with His dignity.

NOTE A.—A *furor divinus*, a θεόπνευστος ὁρμή, overpowers the seer. Cf. Plato, *Timæus*, p. 71, 72 (also Lücke, *Offenbarung*

Johannis, i. 32 f.); Cicero, *De divin.* i. 6, 18, 49. *De natura deorum*, ii. 6; Livy, v. 15. More general expressions are *agitari Deo*, κατέχεσθαι τοῦ Θεοῦ. Hence, too, the name μάντις, from μαίνομαι (on the etymon, see Curtius, *Grundzüge*, i. n. 429), which expression is then certainly transferred to every kind of divination. In Cicero (*De div.* i. 6) we find a twofold *genus divinandi* distinguished, the first of which was artificial, the second natural. To the former technical class belong all mechanical observations of signs; to the latter, among others, mantism proper, in which the spirit is excited by higher power. Only the latter will bear comparison, to a certain extent, with Hebrew prophecy.

NOTE B.—Such a demon is called אוֹב or יִדְּעֹנִי, the Knower, minister of knowledge, yet not the same as كاهِن = diviner, cf. wise woman, etc. (Gesenius, Delitzsch), but originally (like אאב) applying to the spirit (so Fürst, *Concordance*) who conveys knowledge (cf. δαίμων, according to Plato = δαήμων, cf. πύθων), and then transferred to the בַּעַל אוֹב, 1 Sam. xxviii. 3, 9, and often. אוֹב is variously derived, from אאב, *to be hollow* (whence *skin-bottle*), then *to sound dull* (Gesenius, Delitzsch), because the departed spirit has a hollow, dull voice, speaking from the bowels of the earth. Cf. Isa. xxix. 4. On the other hand, according to Lenormant, 516 f., Scholz, 91: the Accadian *ubi*. In Deut. xviii. 11 the interrogating the dead is distinguished from the *ob* and *yid'oni*. Still, according to 1 Sam. xxviii. (cf. Isa. viii. 19), the two are so closely connected that the *ob* or *yid'oni* (*i.e.* the conjuring spirit) formed the medium through which its possessor could conjure up the dead at pleasure.

§ 3. *The Kingdom of God as the Subject of Biblical Prophecy.*

The material characteristics of Biblical prophecy are in harmony with the formal ones specified in § 1. If the prophet sees what the Lord reveals to him and speaks to men as God's organ, it is to be expected that his announcement will have the *will* of God for its subject, so far as God sees fit to make it known to His Church, but may also contain everything received by the Church as God's will. In point of fact, God's entire revelation to Israel is traced back to the message of prophets. This is the case above all with the fundamental Torah, by which God regulated and ordered the life of the nation in accordance with His will. Moses is first of all a prophet.[1] And all the

---
[1] Hos. xii. 13.

many-sidedness of the Torah, containing indiscriminately general ethical commands alongside judicial and ritual laws, precepts for personal life alongside public ordinances, finds its unity precisely in the principle of the theocracy, which is absolutely supreme over civil as well as religious life, over individuals as well as the community, over externals as well as over the inner life of every member of the sacred nation. As certainly as this legislation, traced back by the whole of tradition to primitive prophetic revelation, was regarded as an expression of God's will, so certainly must subsequent prophecy be based upon it and essentially agree with it.[1] Cf. Deut. xiii. 1-3: If a prophet, legitimatized even by miracles, set himself in opposition to the fundamental law of the theocracy, his word was to go for nothing. The will of God, who had planted His kingdom among this people, could only remain in force, reveal and realize itself more and more fully, by the Lord raising up through His Spirit further witnesses to the same, who should vivify, complete, and deepen the incomplete and often misunderstood law. Moreover, the rule of God was to prevail in a very different extent and intensity from what was the case in that establishment of the divine nationality which was always imperfectly carried out, and always to some extent remained an ideal. None but these speakers of God could discern and announce God's will beyond those limits.

As prophecy had God's previous revelations for its basis, so it had the glory of the Supreme and the carrying out of His will (*i.e.* His rule, His kingdom) for its goal. What is made known to the seers can never be knowledge devoid of this divine ground and aim.[2] A clairvoyance without such consecration, a divination[3] in the service of human curiosity or earthly gain, would be as different from Biblical prophecy as heathenism from God's kingdom. The Bible is so far from regarding all

---

[1] In reference to the relation of prophecy to the law, cf. C. J. Bredenkamp, *Gesetz und Propheten, ein Beitrag zur A. T. Kritik*, 1881.

[2] A certain overlooking of the specific cause and higher aim of the miraculous vision of the prophets might perhaps not seldom be found among the great superficial crowd; cf. 1 Sam. ix. 9. The same thing meets us in our Lord's miracles.

[3] Our phraseology distinguishes the "prophesying" that is the product of noble, divine inspiration from the mechanical "divining," that in any case is not inspired by any ideal power. This distinction certainly has no etymological ground; cf. Hofmann, *Weissagung und Erfüllung*, i. p. 12.

supernatural knowledge and power as truly divine that it is aware of demonic divining and diabolic miracles. But the same divine causality and purpose in prophecy that excludes everything having no reference to the rule of God, gives it also a breadth of action in correspondence with the absoluteness of its author. The prophet is able to receive disclosures respecting Israel and heathen nations, the past and future, nature and history, inasmuch as all space and time are under the control of his God. He can announce the general moral law obligatory on all men, as well as foreannounce the fate of a particular person. Thus in prophecy the outward is not severed from the inward, the spiritual from the physical, the particular from the general. As a rule, the general appears in the form of the particular, the spiritual in concrete embodiment. Events are foretold in definite form; their time and place are foredetermined.

Just these particular details in prophecy, inaccessible by inference from general principles or other rational means, have always seemed to apologists of special importance in proving the supernatural origin of prophecy. The predictions of single incidental circumstances seemed the most striking. Since Schleiermacher,[1] the course pursued has been different. He distinguishes in the O. T. prophesyings a prediction proper, which in its more or less definite statements possessed, now a higher, now a lower degree of accuracy, from the Messianic prophecy, in which the prophets had risen above the particular to set forth the universal, and in which the particular statements were more or less mere clothing. In the same manner in our days only the ethico-religious ideas and views are acknowledged as the real divine purport of prophecy, whilst the predictions, which cannot be deduced from these generalities, are supposed to have no theological worth, but rest at most upon an inexplicable faculty of presentiment.[2]

Now, except by an abuse of criticism, it cannot be denied that definite predictions, whose fulfilment was matter of fact, even as regards their supposed indifferent form, are frequently found in O. T. prophecy; and we have already seen that the authority of the prophets, their reputation as divine

---

[1] *Der christliche Glaube*, 4th ed. § 103, 3.
[2] Cf. *e.g.* H. Schultz, *A. T. Theologie*, 2nd ed. p. 231 ff.; A. Dillmann in Schenkel's *Bibellexikon*, iv. 613 ff.

speakers, depended as a rule on such fulfilment, even as they were also attested by miraculous signs. Examples of such concrete predictions are not merely to be met with in ancient times, when prophecy had " not yet purged itself of its magical elements," but run through the entire history of prophecy.[1] In the same way the prophets appear as miracle-workers, not merely in times "obscured by myths" (Moses), or in "narratives adorned with myths" (Elijah, Elisha), but also in the properly classical period of prophecy and in passages unassailable by criticism; cf. Isa. vii. 11, viii. 18.

The latter point concerns us no further here. On the other hand, in presence of the former fact we are confronted with the question: Can we in Hebrew prophecy distinguish two quite heterogeneous powers—first, the genuinely prophetic spirit resting on deep, ethico-religious conviction, and then alongside it a mantic faculty of presentiment having nothing to do with religion? Such a severance is impracticable, because to the prophetic seer the vision is thoroughly homogeneous. He has neither first of all settled by rational methods his general principles, nor received any information outside his ethico-religious fellowship with God. Instead, then, of resolving this unity into a dualism of inexplicable composition, it is in any case more pertinent to seek a higher unity between what seems to our modern modes of thought to belong to heterogeneous spheres. This unity is found in the God, who is not only the source of the truth, but also controls its realization in all its parts, the living God, to whom there is no difference of outward and inward, necessary and accidental, who just as much rules nature and history in their apparently accidental details as He is the legislator of universal morality, and the author of the inmost, holiest feelings. This unity is the vital condition of prophecy. On it rests the truth of its entire contents. For by no means is its aim merely to deduce general intellectual and moral truths from particular, and, in their form, accidental facts. But its main purport is to seek the realization in fact of the entire truth of God. The meaning of "the kingdom of the Lord" is, that He will prove Himself ruler in the whole domain of life,

[1] Cf. e.g. Moses (Ex. vii. ff.), Elijah (1 Kings xvii.), Amos (vii. 17), Isaiah (vii. 8, 16, xvi. 14, xxi. 16, xxxvii. 33, xxxviii., xxxix.), Micah (iii. 12, iv. 10) Jeremiah (xxv., xxvii., xxviii.), Ezekiel (xii., xxi.).

thoroughly penetrating and controlling His people and the world. In this process even the phenomenal form cannot be accidental.

But if the Bible is right in its position, that the contents of prophecy are not the result of merely finite factors, such as are found in the prophet as an individual gifted with intelligence and moral consciousness, but that a higher spiritual factor, not bound to human limits, fructifies him, it cannot be required that the inner unity of the phenomenal form of the divine kingdom shall be known to him. Certainly the divine dignity of a particular prophecy does not lie in its foreannouncing something beyond the reach of man's knowledge, just as little as the divine character of a miracle is proved by its violating natural laws. As the miracles wrought by God are no isolated, arbitrary violations of the earthly order of life, but have their internal grounds, in virtue of which they fit into a higher plan, so is it with the disclosures which prophecy makes about the future. They must be rooted in the supreme will, which expresses itself also in ethical laws and revelations. The mistake is only when this unity is postulated in the consciousness of the prophet, *i.e.* when everything that does not follow of necessity from those general principles and maxims in accordance with the prophet's human perception is disparaged as non-essential in the prophecy and accidental in the fulfilment. It is essentially the same mistake as when a particular miracle, for which sufficient internal reasons are not found, is critically rejected, as if its higher justification must always approve itself to our limited, subjective perception.

If, then, prophecy in general is an announcing of the divine will, and has the realizing of that will for its contents, it is clear that no sharp severance is practicable between past, present, and future, or between special and general, Messianic and other prophetic oracles. The theocracy, which comes into external existence with Moses, and which reached a provisional conclusion in the occupation of the land designed for it and the installation of the God-anointed king, is the subject of all prophecy. But, thanks to prophecy, its development never halts, but is always the goal of promise in still more perfect form. And although from the multitude of divine oracles, announcing the carrying out of God's will on the basis of the existing form of God's kingdom, a selection may be made of such as relate to the real building up of that kingdom, still the latter grow out of the former, because God's revealed will is one at every stage. For example, a single judgment by its inner unity is a member of the general one, and judgment in general paves the way for a higher revelation. And in virtue of this inner unity it is permissible to combine oracles that indicate an advance in the realization of God's kingdom or depict it in its future development and completion. These have usually been called "Messianic," because the Messiah (*i.e.* the anointed king of David's house) is the medium through whom the perfect state of this kingdom will be introduced. Certainly in this case one is compelled to give the word a more general meaning alongside the obvious one, since the person of the Messiah by no means appears in all the oracles, where the completion of God's kingdom is spoken of. For this reason we prefer the designation chosen in our title, "*The Prophecy of the Completion of the Kingdom of God.*"

As from the beginning the divine will encounters in the world resistance, which it has first to overcome in order to work itself out, this conquest forms an essential ingredient in the prophecy of God's kingdom. It is the *judgment* of the world. But as the proper end of the divine ways is the salvation of His people under His rule, every judgment can only serve as a means to make room for the *redemption* which from the beginning is the subject of the promise. Nevertheless, menace of judgment and promise of redemption are not so distributed that the former applies only to the heathen world, the latter exclusively and unconditionally to the chosen people. On the contrary, Israel, because of its actual state, falls more and more under prophetic condemnation, whilst at the same time the outer world, so far as it turns to the salvation of the God of Israel, is more and more definitely received into God's purpose of grace. The completion of the former era is summed up in the favourite phrase, "*Day of the Lord.*" This includes the perfect revelation of the Lord to the world, above all in His retributive justice; on which account the Day of the Lord is the reckoning-day for all nations, when their sins will be repaid them, while upon Israel also the righteous will of its Lord will be carried out in punishment. The goal of God's gracious purpose, which enters in close connection with that judgment-day, is expressed by the designation "*Kingdom of the Lord,*" or by the *dwelling* of Yahveh in the midst of His Church. The kingdom of the Lord is the full working out of His will in the world, the dwelling of God among His people in most intimate fellowship with them. Both coincide in so far as the ultimate aim of God's will is to live in fullest communion with His Church upon earth, into which all mankind destined to salvation have been received, and so to wield upon earth an undisputed sway.

§ 4. *Influence of the Age on the Prophecy of God's Kingdom.*

As the individuality of the prophet is not without a shaping influence on prophecy (p. 9), so also his prophecy clothes itself in conceptions common to him with his contemporaries. It bears the stamp of the age. While this is a limit to it on one hand, on the other it is the indispensable condition of the fulfilment of its design. Prophecy is meant in the first instance to serve God's will in the present, to contribute to its realization. But this is only possible if, and in so far as, it is intelligible to contemporaries. Thus it links its promises to existing circumstances and tendencies, sometimes to living persons, causing them to see God's kingdom through their own experiences. It serves its own age, although not exhausted in it, but stretching beyond it. Thus it pictures God's perfected kingdom still with national limits and colours. Mount Zion is the centre to which all nations journey to worship, because at the time God's kingdom was national and local in character, and in the first instance the chief point was that all nations should do homage to the God then worshipped on Zion. Just so the prophecy of the coming divine ruler attached itself in the post-exilian age (Hag., Zech.) to Zerubbabel as the actual Davidic ruler. The old hereditary foes—Egypt, Moab, Edom, etc.—are named as the foes who will fall before God's kingdom. Nor are these temporal forms to be regarded as a conscious accommodation of the prophet to his hearers; but they were the forms in which the future presented itself even to him. An artificial dress is nowhere found. On this point what was said in § 1 about the nature of prophetic perception should be recalled. The prophet sees the future generally, but not always, in visions. These are homogeneous figures, made up more or less of sensuous elements. But this fact necessitates the use of temporally given forms, with their inevitable limitation. Nor is it the way of these seers to add reflections respecting such visions and their significance. The very intensity, indeed, of the figure, too feeble to sustain its idea, points beyond it. And again, the limitation is supplemented and corrected by other views of the same thing, often granted to the same seer. The case is the same here as in the parabolic presentation of the kingdom of heaven in the New Testament. There one figure can only present the subject on *one* side, and needs to be supplemented by other figures. Thus, since the N. T. parables treating of the kingdom of heaven only exhibit it on one side, they must be put together if a correct view of the whole is to be obtained, When, *e.g.*, the kingdom of heaven (Matt. xiii. 47) is compared to a Fishing-net, in which at first good and bad fish are caught indiscriminately, the intended teaching is, that not merely those finally chosen partake in the kingdom at first. But it would be an error to think that the partakers in it are quite passive in receiving it, as might be concluded from following the figure out in a one-sided way. The correction is supplied by parables like that of the Banquet (Matt. xxii. 2 ff.), where we learn that all the invited do not obey the call. The case is similar with prophecy. According to Isa. xi. 14, Zech. ix. 13 ff., and many other passages, we might think that the perfecting of God's kingdom will be brought about by force of arms. But other visions, perhaps of the same prophet (Isa. ix. 6 f.; Zech. ix. 9 f.), which picture the Perfecter of the kingdom as simply a Prince of peace, show that these martial images denote the triumph of the power of the Divine Spirit. Thus these prophecies need to be combined, that they may supplement each other and even correct their own one-sided representations.

But in order to understand its concrete form, the visionary character of prophecy dwelt on in § 1 needs to be taken into account. Since the concrete form offered itself naturally to the seer in his presentation even of spiritual things, one may sometimes be in doubt how far he himself regarded his plastic description as symbolic, or unconsciously supplied a more sensuous conception as a substratum to the abstract idea. For example, in Zech. ix. 9, apart from the fulfilment, one might be in doubt whether the prophet really expected the Davidic king upon an ass, or consciously viewed this trait as a mere symbol of a King of peace. But, in general, it must be remembered that in prophecy proper reflection remained in the background. The prophet relates what he sees, without himself intending to distinguish between contents and means of presentation. How far what is described will literally be fulfilled, the event only can show.

In the same way, later times must show how far what is seen will take shape in the precise local or temporal unity in which it was presented to the prophet. Obadiah sees a complete devastation and destruction of Edom. Whether, now, this will take place in the special form in which he sees it, or whether only the idea is to be retained, that this hostile nation will utterly disappear, whilst imperilled Israel will live on,—on this point no information is to be expected from the seer. In the same way, whether the doom of annihilation will be executed at a blow, or distribute itself over a series of catastrophes,—a Persian, Maccabæan, Roman one,—the fulfilment only can tell. To the import of the message of retribution it is indifferent. The message becomes even more emphatic and effective when that which in reality spreads itself over a longer space of time is compressed into one picture.

Hence the so-called *perspective* character of prophecy. As the low-lying intervals are concealed from the bodily eye, only the heights of a district combining into a picture bounded by the highest peaks, so the seer beholds the lofty points of history in their harmonious connection, and indeed only up to a certain horizon, which represents the termination of the course of spiritual development in the midst of which the prophet stands. This horizon is called אַחֲרִית הַיָּמִים, not = the following age, the future, but = *the end of the days*, the last age. The idea relates rather to things than time: the termination of the course of things surrounding the prophet; for this reason also the "end" is nearer or farther according to the range of the motive engaging the prophet; but the prophecy is always exhausted within these limits. Now, in the prophetic picture nearer heights touch this highest peak of consummation; only when they emerge in history is it seen that an interval lies between them and the final consummation.

As, then, all the words and work of the prophets obtain their unity through their reference to the divine rule, so also the prophecies relating to the consummation in the future are bound together by the living idea of the *coming* of God's perfected rule. But this idea unfolds itself gradually out of seminal beginnings to more and more definite and rich, but also more pure, forms. Thus prophecy has a *history*, which implies two things—its progressive growth and abiding unity.

Not at once was the news of a future kingdom of God communicated to the believing people as a complete doctrine. To this the people would not have been at all receptive. But *that particular aspect* of the Messianic future was always disclosed to them which they needed to know, the discovery being in proportion to their sense of need. But the need was not always the same. The receptiveness, indicative of advance or growth, rose and fell from time to time, while the highest, boldest thoughts of God always had to make way for what could be understood by a generation of more limited spiritual culture.

Between the outward history of the nation and the development of its most sacred hopes an intimate connection existed, the two being bound up with the nation's spiritual life and ordered by the same God. Hofmann, indeed, goes too far in making the prophecy so dependent on the history, that the former is merely the interpreter of the latter—*i.e.* puts into words the knowledge which ought at any time to be gathered from God's historical revelation. On the contrary, prophecy, issuing freely from the Divine Spirit, is often far in advance of history, announcing really new things. But the outward experiences of Israel negatively prepared the ground for prophecy, and positively furnished it with material. Positively they enlarged its range of vision. As long, *e.g.*, as geographical and ethnological knowledge was narrowly limited, only a limited conception of the divine rule upon earth could be formed. But when the great world-empires—the Assyrian, Babylonian, Persian—came on the stage before the eyes of Israel, prophecy first really gained wings, and the future of God's kingdom, before which all this power and glory was to fade, shone all the brighter to the eyes of believers. In the same way, familiarity with nobler heathens like the Persians exerted a fructifying influence on prophecy, the hearts of the people now becoming more receptive to the thought expressed long before, that Israel had a lofty mission to discharge even to the heathen. In Israel itself the erection of the Davidic kingdom laid the historic foundation for a new upbuilding of prophecy. But every mighty act of God, every conquest, every conflict of deeper significance, served as a finger-post in the ways of God, broadening and facilitating the insight both of seers and hearers into His leadings and judgments.

Such events as made inroads on the wellbeing of the theocracy and community, or seemed to make an end of it, had negative effects, opening the way for prophecy. When the whole existence of the commonwealth was in question, and its destruction was certain to the enlightened after brief respite, prophecy was moved to its boldest utterances. The ruins of the old theocracy awakened painful longing for the building of the new one. Mourning over past glory turned into yearning for a glorious future. Moreover, the sense of inadequate fulfilment impelled to new hopes of a perfecting future—*e.g.* after the exile. Even the Christian Church is driven to the word of prophecy chiefly in times when it is made painfully conscious how little present conditions correspond to God's perfect will.

Under the joint operation of all these motives the prophetic voices spoke now louder, now softer—now more clearly, now more obscurely. But their discourses were not the work of the spirit of the age, but of the one Spirit of God. For the prophets were always conscious to themselves of carrying forward something begun long before, of developing further something existing. Hence they frequently resumed oracles of predecessors; and certain fundamental ideas—like the Day of the Lord, the Kingdom of God and His Coming—were transmitted from one generation to another, only gaining in significance with time. Thus a progress from indefinite to definite, from mere intimation to declaration, from sensuous to spiritual, is evident in prophecy. The promise is specialized; it is linked first to Shem, next to Abraham, then to Isaac, Jacob, the tribe of Judah, and finally to the Davidic royal house, and is last of all transferred to a particular scion of the same. According to Jacob's blessing the kingdom of God was still altogether external, distinguished by external power and external abundance at God's hand. But the idea of the future holy land and people, the city of Zion, etc., grew more and more profound, until the outward form became too weak to bear its weight, and the sensuously fashioned conceptions were no longer tenable. Such is the case in Isa. xi., where in the mountain of the Lord the wolf dwells with the lamb, etc., and (Isa. lx.) where it is said of the city of God: The sun shall no more be thy light by day, and the light of the moon shall no longer shine on thee, but Yahveh shall be thy everlasting light. Here the sensuous veil bursts under the spiritual glory streaming through it. So in many other visions. If we concede a progress to more perfect spiritual heights, we would not, on the other hand (like G. Baur, p. 27), describe it as progress from error to truth. As certainly as prophecy is a divine word, it always contains divine truth, so far as truth can and ought to be comprehended at the existing standpoint. All genuine pædagogy takes this course. It does not indeed teach the truth from the beginning in adequate form, but it never inculcates error as the initial stage of higher knowledge.

After what has been said on the inner connection of the development of the prophecy of God's kingdom with the outward history of the nation, it is of course to be expected that the great epochs of the nation's history will be epoch-making for prophecy, and that the several periods of the outward will be distinguishable in the inner development. In fact, the most suitable division of our subject is according to the chief phases of Israelitish history. First of all the long period of the forming of the people and kingdom is to be marked off, reaching a climax with the completion of the kingdom in the Davidic-Solomonic age. From this point the decline of the regal power begins. In prophecy these two periods are distinguished in the most marked way. In the former are found merely single oracles, addresses, songs of prophetic import, which sing and speak of a future glorious consummation—passages about whose date critics differ widely. In the second appear entire prophetic books, the kernel of which is Messianic prophecy. In the former period it is more the shaping and *completing* of the kingdom that floats before the gaze of the prophetic seers; while in the second *redemption* forms the bright background of the destroying judgment, which must precede the true consummation. In the earlier period divine deeds preponderate over divine *words;* the types are far more elaborate than the prophecy, the outer history has the advantage over the inner. In the later period the reverse is the case: prophecy is in advance of history; the types are more and more absorbed into the prophecy; word is mightier than deed.[1] The transition certainly is not sudden. *E.g.* Elijah and Elisha, although belonging

---

[1] Cf. Auberlen, *Jahrb. für deutsche Theologie,* iii. 4, p. 779 f.

to the period of the decline of the Israelitish royalty, are still men of deeds, not of words.

We thus distinguish two main periods. In the first the prophetic word inaugurates the origin and shaping of the concrete rule of God on earth. From the grey fore-time we catch patriarchal benedictions transmitted by tradition. In the Mosaic epoch we observe forward glances into the future of the theocracy. Then Samuel crowned his work in Israel by giving the nation the "Anointed of the Lord," whose prophetic significance is also reflected in many psalms. The second main period again divides itself according to political epochs. First, we have prophetic writings from the pre-Assyrian age, Obadiah, Joel; then from the Assyrian, Amos, Hosea, Zech. ix.–xi., Isaiah, Micah, Nahum. Zephaniah and Habakkuk form the transition to the period of the Chaldæan rule; then follows the time when the kingdom of Judah is in full course of decline. To this belong Jeremiah and Zech. xii.–xiv. Ezekiel and Isa. xl.–lxvi. speak in the exile. The dissolution of the sacred commonwealth again introduces a turning-point. From the beginning of prophecy in the stricter sense, that is, from the age which gives us entire prophetic books up to that catastrophe, the announcement of judgment stands everywhere in the foreground, the promise forming merely the bright background, since the redemption of God's people can only appear after the overthrow of the previous theocracy. On the other hand, after the catastrophe the promise emerges without anything to obscure it, forming the main subject of prophecy. So in the later visions of Jeremiah and Ezekiel, as well as in Isa. xl.–lxvi. After the exile the promise remains in the foreground (Haggai, Zechariah); still the earnest warning against the judicial severity of the "Day of the Lord" is not wanting (Malachi). The apocalypse of Daniel fills a special position, unfolding in grand perspective the triumph of the kingdom of God over the world-empires.

§ 5. *The Office of Type in the Development of God's Kingdom.*

Besides prophecies, types also bear witness in the Old Testament to the future completion of the kingdom of God on earth. Prophecy and type must be distinguished from each other. By *Type* (note A) we understand the inadequate presentation of a divine idea, which is to be more perfectly realized afterwards. The Spirit of God not only reveals Himself in definite words, which He suggests to consecrated seers. He also rules in history, shaping it with significant reference to the future.

In modern days natural philosophers have established in detail the designed connection in the structures of different periods. Thus the most perfect being—man—presents himself first in imperfect preformation in the animals which, the higher their grade, so much the more plainly prefigure the structure of man. Just so there are types in history. Not at once does an idea appear in complete realization. Hofmann says: "Every triumphal procession that marched through the streets of Rome was a prophecy" (in our view rather a type) "of Cæsar Augustus; for what the latter represented always, this the Triumphator represented on his festival-day—God in man, Jupiter in the Roman citizen. In according this pageant to its victors, Rome proclaimed as its future, that it would rule the world through its divinely-worshipped imperator."[1] This very example shows the essential distinction between type and prophecy. For a Roman rhetorician or poet to greet in such a triumphator the future ruler of the world on the Tiber, might perhaps be regarded as prophecy. But, dumb and unconscious as such a type is in reference to the very fact that it is a type, it lacks an essential mark which, according to § 1, cannot be wanting to prophecy. Not merely is speech, the proper element of prophecy, absent, on which account the type has been called concrete prophecy[2] in distinction from verbal prophecy (Kurtz); the profounder contrast lies in this, that the type is still unrecognised by contemporaries in its reference to the future, the necessity of a more perfect embodiment of the idea it contains not being declared. Utterances also may be typical, so far as their contents will only attain complete realization afterwards in a way unknown to the speaker.

Although now in human history such preformations are as little purely accidental as in the history of nature, they have yet deeper reasons in the history of redemption, according to what was said of its character in § 3. Of course it is a mistake to assume a type on the ground of mere outward similarity, as the ancient Church often did. Both phenomena—the typical and

---

[1] *Weissagung und Erfüllung,* i. 15.   [2] *Realweissagung.*

perfect—must have received from the same Spirit their distinctive character, by which they resemble each other, so that an inner relation obtains between them. And as certainly as the form of the Israelitish nationality was meant by God's will to present a preliminary reign of God, so an inner relation must exist between this still imperfect kingdom of God and the perfect one, which always remained future in the Old Testament. And this inner affinity will necessarily find expression also in the outer life of this nationality, so far as that life is determined by God. Not merely the ritual and polity of Israel, so far as they are ordered by God, its experiences also, so far as these befall it as God's people, will by inner necessity present beforehand what awaits God's perfected people, provided it is the same God who reveals His will, here preliminarily, there finally. Accordingly different classes of types may be conceived—archæological and historical, personal and national. To the *archæological* belongs in particular the whole complex of ritual types. The Israelitish ritual, as practised generally from the days of Moses, is predominantly symbolic. And as the symbol always expresses an idea but imperfectly, so it is here. But the ideas, partially veiled, partially announcing themselves plainly, are those of God's perfect revelation; a truth which cannot surprise us if we receive the testimony, according to which this form of divine worship was not of natural growth or arbitrary institution, but rested on divine revelation. Only the typical action did not necessarily give to human consciousness the thought of a future, more complete method of salvation. The idea of vicarious expiation is central to Christianity. It is imaged already in the O. T. expiatory sacrifice, of course but inadequately, inasmuch as animal life can be no valid substitute for man's. But the Levitical priest might long continue to lead his sacrificial animal to the altar, before becoming aware that his act was inadequate, having its justification only in something future to which it pointed. Israel's symbolic ritual is pervaded by such ideas, which had to acquire their full import afterwards. On the other hand, there is an *historic* type (*e.g.*) in the departure of Israel from Egypt, joined with the destruction of the hostile army, inasmuch as here the deliverance of God's holy Church from the yoke of the ungodly world-power is first presented. Moreover, *personal* types not seldom occur. David presents the idea of a ruler standing in filial relation to God and governing in His name. But the divine-human government of David is still a thoroughly imperfect realization of this lofty idea.

Such types are meant first of all in their imperfection to render familiar the idea expressed in them, and thus to prepare for their adequate manifestation. But a mediate stage between the beginning and completion is found when these types are seen in their prefigurative significance, and pass over into prophecy. Thus Isa. liii. 10 speaks of a sin-offering, and (ver. 7) of a lamb atoning for guilt by voluntary suffering. Here the idea of this sacrificial lamb is transferred to a more perfect bearer—the Servant of God. Just so prophecy often applied the departure from Egypt to the future, promising a final deliverance of the Church from bondage, and setting forth this divine act with the well-known features taken from the Egyptian days. Cf. the antitype of the Egyptian plagues, Rev. viii., ix. Finally, David was so well known as a type of the Messiah κατ' ἐξοχήν, that the prophets expressly call the king of the final perfecting age David, Hos. iii. 5 ; Jer. xxx. 9. Here therefore the type, lending a voice to the prophetic word, enters into our proper province. And as the express prophetic word had led the way in applying the past to the future, the thought of the Church felt itself called upon to understand the historic form of the God-anointed king in general typically, and to interpret his experiences as mirroring future experiences, turning his songs and words into prophecies.

NOTE A.—The expression is borrowed from N. T. phraseology, where it often occurs in this special application. τύπος, properly *blow* (from τύπτω), signifies primarily *the impression of a blow, mark* (John xx. 25); hence *definite stamp* (therefore also the *style* of a letter, Acts xxiii. 25 ; of a doctrine, Rom. vi. 17; *image, figure, copy, idol*, Acts vii. 43). Then especially *type*, and both (*a*) the ideal model, Acts vii. 44, Heb. viii. 5, and (*b*) the ethical pattern, type of virtue, Phil. iii. 17 ; 1 Thess. i. 7 ; 2 Thess. iii. 9 ; 1 Tim. iv. 12 ; Tit. ii. 7 ; 1 Pet. v. 3 ; but finally also (*c*) the historic type of something future, Rom. v. 14 ; 1 Cor. x. 6, 11 ; and according to these passages the design of the type is to prefigure the future, therefore to point to it as something more complete. The correlative idea to τύπος is τὸ ἀντίτυπον, *the antitype*, and may either denote a secondary copy of lower value, corresponding to the type (*a*) (Heb. ix. 24), or the more perfect counterpart to the type (*c*) (1 Pet. iii. 21).

§ 6. *Are Phenomena analogous to the Prophecy of God's Kingdom to be found in the field of Heathenism?*

Before going further, we raise this question, which is well adapted to give us a true conception of the difference of Biblical prophecy from all other literature. The ancient Church was fond of adducing the Sibyls of the heathen world alongside the prophets of Israel as witnesses to the future kingdom of God. Did mantism, then, really produce anything like the seers of Yahveh? On the contrary, the complete superiority of the latter is seen most plainly when we compare the products of their prophesying, the spirit and substance of their communications, with what the heathen oracles and prophets produced. Even the prevailing form of the oracle is indicative of the spirit of such revelation. No doubt it was a pious desire which the heathen felt for divine revelations. Their δεισιδαιμονία left them no rest until they had inquired into the will of the gods, and assured themselves of their assistance in every undertaking. *Sine divino numine nihil*—this principle ruled their hearts. But in the mantism current almost everywhere in ancient heathenism, as described § 2, the initiative significantly belonged to man; he asked whenever he pleased; he managed the communications of the deity; whereas the genuine prophets of Israel as a rule raised their voices unasked and unsought, and very often made themselves heard when and where it was least expected and desired, on the other hand always returning negative answers to questions of curiosity and impatience. As it is a general characteristic of heathenism, especially the Indo-Germanic, for the normal relation between God and man to be gradually inverted, what is divine being made subservient to human ends, so we find in the case of oracles. The entire oracle-system was far more serviceable to human, perhaps political interest, than to the deity, and readily became an instrument of mere political craft. And although in favourable circumstances it might be the minister of a healthy moral sense, as the Delphic oracle was for a long time, still it only represented the natural conscience of the people, not a spiritual power independent of this as Biblical prophecy did,[1] which against princes and peoples, and without respect of person and regard to ordinary interests, often assumed

[1] Jer. i. 17 ff.

an attitude to the questions of life incomprehensible to the natural order of thought. It did this, because it represented simply and solely the cause of God, whose organ it was. The utterances of these prophets often stand in boldest antithesis to the spirit of their age, to the moods of their people, nay, even of their own hearts. In appearance they withstand patriotism, the advantage of their country, the honour of their nation. They bow down before no human greatness, not before the most famous kings of the present and past, judging everything inexorably by a uniform standard loftier than the natural conscience of the nation. They are conscious of one aim which they all proclaim with one accord and immovable certainty in the most diverse ages and circumstances, despite all differences of individual inclination and gifts. "This unison," says Delitzsch,[1] "is the seal of divine revelation as the work of one and the same Spirit in the laboratories of many individuals." Criticism has the right and the scientific task of classifying these prophetic voices according to the character of the age and individual. But if it does not detect the grand elevation and unity of the spiritual force which set in motion all these tongues in the course of the centuries, it is dull and incapable of discerning the divine. Compared with this, what sort of products are offered by heathenism, which likewise boasts of divine revelations? What disorder and uncertainty, what a mingling of truth and deception meets us everywhere, directly we seek information respecting the divine! And how insignificant the little offered us as a specially memorable product of the Delphic god or Cumæan sibyl!

If all unprejudiced examination of O. T. prophecy proves its unique character, it may still be asked whether the Sibyl is altogether disqualified as a witness to the kingdom of God. Certainly what the ancient Church used under the name of the "sibylline books" as a witness of heathenism to Christ, was not a product of heathen mantism, but an almost worthless imitation of Biblical prophecy, such as was practised by Jews in the last centuries before Christ and then passed over to Christians.[2] At most, some remnants of the lost sibylline (*i.e.* heathen) oracles may be interwoven therein. Such an oracle is found in Virgil's fourth Eclogue, which will be spoken of afterwards. Moreover,

[1] *Comm. on Habakkuk*, p. 119.
[2] Cf. the article "Sibyllinen," in Herzog's *R.E.*

the other literature of heathen nations, distinguished by such great works, should be examined to see whether it can supply a substitute for what O. T. prophecy was to the Israelites and then to the Church of the New Covenant. Above all, the comparison may be made with respect to historians. If an unrivalled moral independence must be ascribed to the Biblical narrators, their style is also quite specially distinguished by the way in which they connect earthly things with the divine government. History to them, owing to the divine plan ruling in it, is really homogeneous, and moves towards a definite goal. An Herodotus, Plutarch, Tacitus, know indeed of a higher pragmatism than that of mechanical occurrence; they point out, each one in his own way, higher laws coming into play in history. But in how much loftier a style do the prophetic historians of the Bible write history! Here is found a uniform derivation of all human history from one origin, a uniform standard of judgment, here only the consciousness of a uniform positive progress in the whole course of the world's development. Whilst ancient Egypt in its monuments sought to deify the existing, and ancient India regarded the dissolution of existence as the highest goal of movement, thus seeking salvation in going back to nonentity, these prophets, who view the past as a revelation of the living God, proclaim that the future will see a consummation, to which all history will serve as the way to the goal.

If to-day we hear so much of a uniform progress of the human race and of its unceasing advance to a goal of perfection, we do not sufficiently consider that such knowledge and hope is no heirloom of classical antiquity, but a fruit of the prophetic spirit of the Bible. We also too little remember that this hope finds adequate security in supernatural revelation alone. Neither empiric reality, nor dialectic truth, nor æsthetic idealism can raise the hope to certainty. Plato, indeed, and Aristotle sketched a State, which floated before them as an ideal; but that such a relatively perfect condition would ever become fact, they nowhere taught on good grounds. Plato, in a well-known passage (note A), gave so striking a description of the perfectly just man, who as such must be tested by the heaviest sufferings, that the Church from the earliest days[1] saw therein a prophetic picture of the

[1] From Clemens Al. (*Strom.* l. v. 14, l. vi. 7) to Döllinger, who calls it at least a "presageful glance into the future" (*The Gentile and the Jew*, vol. i. p. 328). Such

suffering Son of man. But, passing by the fact that the entire conception of the Just One in Plato is essentially different from that given in the Bible, it must be conceded that some traits are drawn with great truth, and to some extent found a literal fulfilment in Christ. But it must be observed, to say nothing of the inner difference just mentioned, that at most we have here only a type, standing in a line with the type of the suffering, misunderstood Job. For Plato scarcely thought of such a just man ever appearing on earth, and in any case laid no stress on such appearing. His image of the perfectly Just One, or the sketch which the Stoics give of the true sage, according to their view loses nothing of its truth, even if such an one never[1] actually appears, or appears but once every 500 years (according to Seneca). On the contrary, prophecy stands or falls according as it does or does not find an adequate fulfilment. *The actuality of the fulfilment forms an essential element in its truth.* This is a distinction between the heathen ideal-world and Biblical realism that is not sufficiently considered. The element wanting to the former (the certainty that the perfection seen will appear in realization) prophecy possesses from first to last, thanks to the experience of God's self-revelation, which theologians again and again confound with conceptual knowledge; whereas the mere idea of a perfect Spirit is not equivalent to His " reign " in the Biblical sense, *i.e.* His adequate revelation in the finite world.

In comparison with Plato, the Stoic school certainly shows greater confidence in the realization of its ideas. Zeno does this first of all. He also gives his ideal State of the future a more comprehensive range, perhaps not without Oriental influence. This State was to unite all nations into one flock, governed only by the law of reason. This was the goal of the world's progress, after which wise men were to strive. Here a view is given, which we do not encounter elsewhere in Hellenic antiquity. On the other hand, a comparison of the Stoic ideal with what is promised by the prophets shows at once that in it justice is not done to the Deity in His distinction from every creature, while the

---

a glance, in far higher measure, is seen in the positive Chinese expectation of a "Holy One," who will restore complete harmony between heaven and earth. See Confucius, *Tchong-Yong*, translated by Plänckner, 1878. The entire translation has certainly been attacked (by Strauss, *Essays*, 1879, p. 109).

[1] Cicero, *Tusc.* ii. 22.

mere enhancement of the human ends in utopias. That the ideal, even apart from its realization, is inferior to the true perfection taught in the Bible, is evident directly we examine the Stoa as to its chief motive. Here it is self-righteousness, not the divine compassion and divine-human love, of which the wise man boasts, and by which perfection is sought (note B). History teaches that the goal will not be reached by this path, even if it is seen. How it is reached is shown by the New Covenant established in the way described beforehand by Biblical prophecy, which will be treated of afterwards.

But although since Justin Martyr's days Messianic prophecies and types have been often wrongly drawn from the heathen world by overlooking the essential distinctions in superficial similarities, that world is by no means without *presentiments* of the redemption that in God's counsel was to be imparted to it. As the reminiscence of a golden age of unruffled peace, like a beautiful dream, was preserved among the nations, so they cherished the hope that one day the vanished paradise would again open to them, and popular fancy painted to the best of its power a state in which this longing of man's heart would find rest. This land is either conceived as existing in some remote place (note C), or it is the special abode of the departed (note D), or the earth awaits a future glorification (note E).

Among all the religions of civilised antiquity, it is the *Parsi* which comes nearest to the Bible, owing to its serious conception of life as a far-reaching, ceaseless conflict between the good and the evil principle. According to the teaching of Zarathushtra, the good conquers in the end, after the evil in the last (fourth) world-age had gained the upper hand, and unfolded all its power and enmity.[1] Here, plainly, the moral postulate asserts itself, which elsewhere also moves human reason to demand a future reconciling of the contradiction between moral and physical relations. Like the heart that pines for redemption, so conscience also requires a state of loftier order and harmony than is to be found during the course of earth. On the other hand, in distinction from the Bible, Parsism with all its ethical character shows a physical taint in its dualism, and hence is unable to take as its goal the pure glorification of everything earthly by the good Spirit. But in general this whole doctrine

[1] Cf. Spiegel's art. "Parsismus," in Herzog.

rather gives the impression of an artificially elaborated system than of a living faith. These expectations by no means enter into the development of history and life with such real power as we find to be the case in Israel. Not Sosiosch, the expected "Saviour" of the seed of Zarathushtra, but the Redeemer of the seed of David, appeared to set up the divine kingdom. Still the eschatology of the Parsis remains a powerful witness to man's need of a revelation of righteousness in the world, and a noteworthy example of presentiment of future consummation.

If we turn to the land of the speculatively gifted Hindus, there the cheerful view of life, meeting us in the Rig-Veda, soon gives place to a pessimism which, as in scarcely any other religion, proclaims to us the pining of all creation for redemption from the burden of existence. But neither Brahmanism nor Buddhism was able to supply a positive redemption. Just here lies the great weakness of these religions, even of Buddhism, which is so much praised in our days. A morality so self-denying without faith in the God who is the supreme Lawgiver, a love of the creature so comprehensive, but without hope, can never conduct man's heart to true peace. And it is well known that a reaction against overstrained demands without corresponding reward and promise very soon followed in Buddhism, Buddha himself, in complete opposition to his teaching, being made the object of deification, and a paradise in the future being put in place of Nirvâna, of simple extinction. Buddha himself, as history describes him, to say nothing of legends, reminds us in several respects of the Rabbi of Nazareth; many traits, if we may so speak, are here typically prefigured. The king's son, by his mere preaching, which is addressed to all castes and designed for all nations, founding a new community of enlightened ones, who give themselves up completely to the service of others, is one of the most notable and glorious figures in all heathendom. But in order to speak of a real type in the Biblical sense, of a type of Christ, the spirit in which the one and the other came to redeem the world from its evils would need to be less divergent. Bringing no revelation of the heavenly Father and His love, Buddhism lacks basis and goal for its work upon earth. It points man, like Brahmanism, to the path of self-redemption; and the only fruit of this redemption it can promise him is dissolution. In its most ideal representatives it labours under this defect.

In the deifying of the person of Buddha we saw a testimony to man's longing for fuller union with the divine. The later development of Brahmanism is a proof of the same. Here we have, plainly under the influence of Buddhism, a series of avataras (incarnations) of the deity (Vishnu). The eighth of these, where Vishnu takes bodily form in *Krishna*, is here of special interest, because this genius, skilful in war and peace, is worshipped as the saviour of the Brahmans in the proper sense, and certain external points (such as the rhythm of the name with Christ, etc.) have often provoked comparison. It has seemed specially significant, that Krishna crushed the head of the evil serpent Kâliya. But on closer examination it appears that a cosmical, not ethical opposition is meant, and in certain particulars a borrowing from Christian tradition seems to have taken place. And this applies also to the treatise of the Indian sages showing most resemblance to Christian ideas, the Bhagavad-Gita.[1] If in many passages the freedom of the gospel is taught, in opposition to work-righteousness, the main thing is still wanting—the gospel itself. Here, too, in this late production, which has often been thought to exhibit the influence of Christianity, the old Indian spirit is to be perceived, presenting only a path of self-redemption.

In this place the Norse and German mythology, as contained in the Edda, also deserves mention, inasmuch as there not merely a state of glorious life is set forth in true German taste, but also the end of the present world-age is contemplated. It is a testimony to the depth of the German spirit, that it did not ascribe eternal duration to its gods, with their finite, physical character. At the end of the days there follows a "twilight of the gods," when even they are overtaken by the fate of the transitory. Nevertheless, on the destruction of the world, then occurring, follows its rejuvenescence. But the ideal state, then introduced, is only intimated in several features. All evil is banished, and the descendants of the Asen live in harmony with men under the rule of the gentle Balder. The All-father is supreme over all.

It would be easy to give illustrations from other religions of what we said at the beginning of this work of the universal

---

[1] Cf. the parallels, to be examined cautiously, which Lorinser gives in his edition, 1869.

longing for a better state of peace with God, and for the suppression of the world's evil. But the more closely we compare the hope of Israel with these poetical dreams or systematic teachings, the more striking appears the contrast,—here an uncertain seeking and groping, there a firm possession; here a vague, fickle surmising, there a firm, prophetic word; here the most diverse views of the goal and the way leading thereto, there the goal clearly described from the first and the way more and more clearly illuminated, until He came who described Himself as the Way and the Truth.

Examination of the import of Biblical prophecy, combined with its fulfilment, will always prove its higher origin and divine character to all who believe in Jesus Christ. E. Renan describes "prophetism" as an essential feature in the spiritual life of the *Shemitic* race, as the form in which all great movements work themselves out among the Shemites. Where then, we ask, are the Shemitic prophets whose productions can be placed beside the Bible, nay, who deserve to be called prophets beside the Biblical ones? Where are the oracles and books, coming from any other Shemitic race, that with any literary right could be added to the collection of O. T. prophecies which belong to such diverse periods? The Arabians, who are usually, and not unjustly, regarded as the unsophisticated, original type of the Shemitic nature—what have they to show that compares with the prophetic literature of the Old Testament? Compared with it, how little original, how poor and insipid, appears the one Koran, that secondary imitation of true prophecy! Moreover, the genuineness of this divine word is proclaimed not merely in outward excellences of style and living inspiration, but in its profound insight into the human heart and into the course of history, in its moral elevation above the stream of the age and current natural feeling, in its wonderful unity, binding into one products of such different persons, ages, and circumstances, finally in its fulfilment in that perfect revelation in Christ, which is seen to be the ripe fruit of this growing organism, because, although itself a gift to humanity from above, its way was unmistakably prepared for in those witnesses. Thus O. T. prophecy is a unique product among the works of the nations, and still less than faith in the one living God can it be derived from merely finite, national, and psychological factors.

It is more than the purest expression of the Shemitic nature, more than the noblest flower of the Hebrew national spirit—it issued from the fructifying of diverse human characters, which certainly had some elements in common, by the one Divine Spirit, who, while raised above humanity, has in the course of time brought His work to maturity in it.

Note A.—*De Repub.* ii. p. 361 s.: "Such being our unjust man, let us place the just man by his side, a man of true simplicity and nobleness, resolved, as Æschylus says, not to seem, but to be good. We must certainly take away the seeming; for if he be thought to be a just man, he will have honours and gifts on the strength of this reputation, so that it will be uncertain whether it is for justice's sake, or for the sake of the gifts and honours, that he is what he is. Yes, we must strip him bare of everything but justice, and make his case the reverse of the former. Without being guilty of one unjust act, let him have the worst reputation for injustice, so that his virtue may be thoroughly tested, and shown to be proof against infamy and all its consequences; and let him go on to the day of his death, stedfast in his justice, but with a lifelong reputation for injustice. . . . They (who prefer injustice above justice) will say that in such a situation the just man will be scourged, racked, fettered, will have his eyes burnt out, and at last, after suffering every kind of torture, will be crucified; and thus learn that it is best to resolve, not to be, but to seem, just." (Trans. by Davies and Vaughan.)

Note B.—See the careful treatise of Ed. Müller: *Parallelen zu dem messianischen Weissagungen und Typen des alten Testaments aus dem hellenischen Alterthum,* 1875, where also other passages of the classics, which one would fain regard as products of the Λόγος σπερματικός, are subjected to a necessary criticism. On p. 30 ff. it is shown how different the kingly, priestly, and prophetic office, which has been supposed to be found in the sage of the Stoa, is from the threefold dignity of the Messiah. When, on p. 66, Zeno's State, with its character of universal humanity, is contrasted with the particularism of the Messianic prophecies, we, on the contrary, are unable in the former to recognise a higher standpoint. We shall see that Isaiah, for example, includes all nations in the organism of God's kingdom, while salvation proceeds from Zion.

Note C.—Cf. *e.g.* the notions of the *Chinese* respecting such ideal lands and states, in Ernst Faber, *Der Naturalismus bei den alten Chinesen, oder die sämmtlichen Werke des Philosophen Licius,* 1877, p. 17.

Note D.—So in the *Rig-Veda,* where the departed in the

kingdom of Yama lay aside all imperfection and partake in divine enjoyment. Respecting the old *Egyptians* (*Germans, Parsis*), cf. Edm. Spiess, *Entwickelungsgeschichte der Vorstellungen vom Zustande nach dem Tode*, 1877. Also, according to the faith of many wild races, as the Indians, the departed reach the land of the blessed.

NOTE E.—Here comes in the fourth Eclogue of Virgil, where the poet, referring to an oracle of the sibyl of Cuma (of uncertain origin), announces the dawn of the last world-age as a blissful kingdom of peace, where strife among men and in nature will cease, as well as the wearisome tilling of the ground and perilous voyaging. Cf. Piper, *Evangelischer Kalender*, 1862, p. 55 ff.

§ 7. *Fulfilment in General.*

As prophecy rests on a historic basis, so it is an essential mark of its character to aim at a historic realization. Every true prophecy needs *fulfilment*, without which it would be a mere sound, not a word of the living God. In distinction from human ideals and hopes which may be genuine and noble without being realized, prophecy is spurious and a product of human ingenuity unless it is fulfilled; for God's counsel, such as the prophetic word claims to be, must be realized. Even the biblical expression "fulfilment" or "establishment" (note A) implies that something is lacking to the completeness of prophecy until it gains reality by the occurrence of what is foretold. If, in prophecy, the living God has pledged His word to history, He will redeem it by fulfilment. He is everywhere regarded as the real Fulfiller; men are mere instruments in working out His decree.

As relates to the mode of fulfilment, its diversity is grounded in the diversity of the prophecies. Where in the prophecy itself the chief stress was placed on the form of the outward occurrence, where *e.g.* the prophet expressly made this the criterion of the genuineness of his oracle, there, of course, the exact accomplishment of the events foretold became the "sign" by which his contemporaries recognised the messenger of the true God. If such a sign was not fulfilled, the prophet was convicted of imposture (Deut. xviii. 22; cf. Jer. xxviii. 9; Ezek. xxxiii. 13). (See *ante*, p. 7.) That such predictions of single historical events are found in the Biblical literature and also in the classical prophetic books proper, whose literal fulfilment is either expressly testified or must be assumed as an indispensable condition of the acknowledgment of the prophets in question, we have emphasized on p. 27. Here the view of prophecy maintained by H. Schultz [1] is certainly insufficient. Not merely is it impossible to foretell names and numbers from mere "ethico-religious conviction," it is also an illusion to suppose that the catastrophe of Sennacherib or the fate of King Zedekiah could have been suggested to the consciousness of an Isaiah or Ezekiel in the concrete definiteness, in which they were foretold by these seers and happened in history, by "the knowledge of the eternally valid laws of the divine nature." Now in all such cases which, with the best will, it is impossible to expunge, must we talk of divination—a descent from the height of pure prophecy? Such an explanation would be as perverse as it is audacious. We must take prophecy as it was according to the authentic testimonies of history, not as it ought to be according to abstractions of the present day. Nor do we see anything "magical" or "unnatural" in such coincidence, but a *super*natural manifestation of God, who thus revealed Himself as the sovereign director of history in the little as well as in the great.

But just because God is not a blind nature-power, but voluntarily assumes a reciprocal moral relation to men, His words are no unalterable fate; their realization depends on men's moral attitude to Him. In urgently summoning men to forestall the threatened judgment by repentance, and by faithful devotion to the holy God to fulfil the condition of participation in the promised blessings, the prophets plainly intimate that their threatening or promise is itself conditional; and where its fulfilment is wanting or postponed in consequence of men's changed attitude to God, its divine character does not suffer on this account. God's holy justice remains consistent with itself, for the very reason that it speaks in one way to him who defies its law, and in another to the sinner who bows in penitence to the divine will.[2] In this way God makes known His personal ethical freedom; no unalterable destiny, no physical system of nature guides the course of human history.

In such cases there can be no question of unfulfilled prophecy in the proper sense, because the divine utterance had its effect and exhibited its power, even though the prophet in human

---

[1] *A. T. Theologie*, 2nd ed. p. 230 ff.   [2] Cf. *ibid.* p. 243 f., 247 f.

weakness might regret the suspension of the carrying out of the divine decree. The latter case meets us in the classical example of Jonah. Jonah iv. 2 shows that the prophets often had like experiences of the divine mercy. In this case, indeed, the prophet precisely and definitely proclaimed the will of the Lord respecting Nineveh,—" overthrown in forty days,"—such as would have been realized if the city had persisted in its ungodly life; but the universal repentance, brought about by the preaching of judgment, restrained God's avenging arm. If the prophet understood his vocation, he rejoiced in such repentance, like Joel. Another example, in which the Lord repented of His word,—this anthropopathism is to be understood as above,—is mentioned in Jer. xxvi. 18 f. Cf. Micah iii. 12: the prophecy of Micah of the overthrow of Jerusalem was followed by Hezekiah's earnest repentance, and the fruit of this repentance was the remission of the judgment. In the same way, Ahab owed it to his repentance that the sentence threatened him by Elijah was only realized in his son (1 Kings xxi. 29). Where great guilt awaits vengeful expiation, the Lord, as the last example teaches, may be moved at least to delay retribution by the penitence of individuals. The retribution may strike other generations, other individuals. But at last everything must find its due punishment. The "Day of the Lord," as the day of general reckoning, may be kept back by God's mercy, but at last it strikes in with its universal judgment. Such a prophecy of doom, *e.g.*, respecting a nation like Edom, Moab, a city like Tyre, is first fulfilled when the guilt of these tribes and cities is revenged in their fate. But this doom may be delayed for centuries by God's compassion and their own conduct. And such an oracle as that of the Day of the Lord, which is to come upon these nations, is only finally fulfilled when there are no longer any of the kindred and confederate enemies of God, in whom it has not been realized.

Moreover, salvation as the subject of prophetic promise is bound, according to the definite statements of the Bible, to certain ethical conditions in regard to its realization. Where the individual or a whole generation proved unfaithful to God, God could not bestow the blessings promised to it. Failing the ethical disposition, the salvation promised to Israel could not

---

[1] Cf. the resumption of older oracles by later prophets.

appear, or could not appear as it would have done at the time described by the seer. Thus the prophets see the coming of the Lord or of the Davidic king in the form of a subjection of the foes of Israel to this people. The reasons why salvation did not then come, why when it came Israel did not attain this glorious position, nay, even remained in great part at a distance from the kingdom of God, at least for a time, are to be sought primarily in Israel's conduct, its lack of readiness and receptiveness for the salvation promised it. Of course this positive aim of the divine plan could not be frustrated by human guilt. All the oracles pointing to the blessed completion of God's kingdom must be fulfilled. They were fulfilled when their full import attained realization.

If, then, we combine what was formerly remarked on prophecy (p. 31), that it borrows the colours and forms with which it sets forth the future from the past and present, with what has just been said, that its realization depends in part on man's voluntary conduct, which may postpone, where it cannot prevent, the execution of God's purpose, we shall expect, not a mechanical, but an organic agreement between prophecy and history. The concrete image of the future, sketched by the seer in accordance with the inner and outer condition of the age, will be changed even outwardly, if an inner change occurs in those concerned, without its losing in true reality on this account. It will be fulfilled only successively and gradually, perhaps in other subjects and objects, which meantime have taken the place of the former ones in both an outward and inward respect.

Finally, we need not remark that it would be intolerable pedantry to say that the prophecies of Israel's dispersion among *all* nations of the earth are unfulfilled, because it cannot be proved that Israelites have lived among the Lapps or Patagonians, or to find fault with the saying of Luke xix. 41, because the Romans left some layers of stones standing in the south-west haram-wall. But it is not otherwise with many prophecies which are often described as unfulfilled, because no account is taken of the poetical style of expression peculiar to the East. The limits between form and contents, expression and import, are certainly not easily drawn. In many prophetic pictures the fulfilment only reveals how far they were apt prefigurings, how far inadequate shadows of the future, their outlines not squaring with the reality. But this we must maintain, that the realization itself is an essential element in prophecy. The rule for the relation of prophecy to fulfilment is: *A prophecy can only be regarded as fulfilled when the whole body of truth included in it has attained living realization.*

As to the *type*, the rule, as we have seen in § 5, is, that it is known as such only by the appearance of the antitype, in which it is fulfilled, except where it has been explained in its prefigurative significance by prophetic speech. It is fulfilled when the idea imperfectly hinted in it has found its adequate exposition in realization.

NOTE A.—The expression "fulfilment" is found, although more rarely, already in the Old Testament: מָלֵא piel, 1 Kings ii. 27, viii. 24 = 2 Chron. vi. 15 and xxxvi. 21. Occurring in reference to vows (Jer. xliv. 25), to counsel and prayer (Ps. xx. 4 f.), the word affirms that the prophetic word is without its full import until it has received that import through realization. In the New Testament, as is well known, πληροῦν is exceedingly common in this sense. Instead of it the Old Testament generally uses other designations, like בוא, *to come about*, Hab. ii. 3, Jer. xxviii. 9, or transitively, where God is the subject: עָשָׂה, *to carry out* what has been said (Num. xxiii. 19; Jer. xxviii. 6), בִּצַּע, *to accomplish* (Lam. ii. 17), but chiefly the specially expressive הֵקִים, *to establish, bring to pass*. In opposition to prophecy falling to the ground (נָפַל, Josh. xxi. 45, xxiii. 14; 1 Kings viii. 56), genuine prophecy is first called to life by fulfilment. This is implied in קוּם, of which the *kal* stands in this sense, Jer. li. 29, *piel*, Ezek. xiii. 6, but as a rule the *hiph.* (which is also used elsewhere of the performing of vows, Num. xxx. 14, Jer. xliv. 25, and commands, 1 Sam. xv. 11, 13; Deut. xxvii. 26, 2 Kings xxiii. 24; Neh. v. 13; Jer. xxxiv. 18, xxxv. 16; cf. the *hoph.*, ver. 14): Num. xxiii. 19; Deut. ix. 5; 1 Sam. i. 23; 1 Kings ii. 4, vi. 12, viii. 20 (= 2 Chron. vi. 10), xii. 15 (= 2 Chron. x. 15); Neh. ix. 8; Ps. cxix. 38; Isa. xliv. 26; Jer. xi. 5, xxviii. 6, xxix. 10, xxxiii. 14. In the LXX the word is expressed, not by πληροῦν, but mostly by ἵστημι and its compounds. It stood also in Ecclus. xxxvi. 20 (cf. Fritzsche, *Comm.* p. 201), where the Greek translation gives ἔγειρον. In the New Testament ἀποκαθιστάναι corresponds to it, Matt. xvii. 11 = Mark ix. 12; Acts i. 6; cf. ἀποκατάστασις, Acts iii. 21, out of which a "restitution of all things" has been wrongly made.

§ 8. *The Fulfilment in the New Covenant.*

The entire prophetic and typical prophecy of the Old Covenant, so far as it pointed to a perfect setting up of the divine rule upon earth after a previous judgment and redemption, found its essential fulfilment in the appearance of the Mediator of the New Covenant. Jesus of Nazareth presented Himself as the Messiah announced in the Old Covenant, who, according to prophecy, was to make this kingdom of God a fact; and in harmony with His own claim, the Christian Church has seen in Him the One in whose person all the lines of prophecy meet. In the *person* of the Son of God and Son of man the relation towards humanity which God has always been aiming at is purely and perfectly realized. In His *work* the service which God asks of the true Servant of the Lord is perfectly rendered, and thus the fundamental condition of the divine-human reign on earth fulfilled. In a word, *Jesus is the Christ*, in whom the central idea of the Old Covenant has been realized under every aspect. Law and prophecy are fulfilled in Him, and can desire no further extension of which He is not the ground and medium. On the other hand, of course, it ought not to be forgotten that this realization exists in perfect form only in His *person*, not in the world. The kingdom which He founded has not yet been revealed in its complete form. And as long as this is not done, according to the above canon, the oracles of the Old Covenant, which require that God's kingdom shall fill the whole earth with undisputed supremacy, are not satisfied; for the fulfilment cannot contain less than the prophecy. Only, these statements must not be referred to the future at once, without being brought into the light of Christ's revelation. But the several rays of prophecy, which without exception meet in the person of Christ as their focus, thence divide again in all directions. Christ Himself and the apostles again expressly resumed them. Thus prophecy of judgment and salvation opens anew. But such judgment is merely the outward effect of the inner attitude that has been and will be assumed by nations and individuals to the salvation offered in Christ's historic person. Cf. the saying of Christ, John iii. 18, xii. 48: "He that believes not in me is condemned already." And the salvation still future is merely the actual appearance of the blessed kingdom of God introduced in Christ and already virtually existing in the believer.

If the person and earthly work of Christ thus form the centre of its historical fulfilment, we cannot call it "accidental" that in His history prophecy has been realized not merely as to its ideas, but also in respect of its form, as in no other history. Prophecy, indeed, is not a mechanical copy of the fulfilment, in the way in which the artificial "sibylline" oracles narrate beforehand the history of Christ.[1] But innumerable undesigned coincidences, apparently of a merely formal kind, point to the organic connection of prophetic and typical prophecy with the life of the true Messiah,—divine hints indicating in the historic Jesus the long-promised Christ. We shall meet with many such traits, some expressly emphasized by the Lord, the apostles, and evangelists, and others made clearly evident in other ways. As modern rationalism stumbles at all such shaping of outward life according to divine counsel as it is unable to derive from general maxims, and it cannot here avail itself of *vaticinia post eventum*, while the supposition of mere accident does not satisfy reason, it here after the example of Strauss suspects the fulfilment of having copied the prophecies. And yet it is clear how differently a life of the Messiah must have turned out, if it had been arbitrarily sketched by the apostles according to their own Messianic conceptions.

In the fact that the fulfilment by Christ presents a wondrous agreement with the word of prophecy even in outward reality we see something more than *adminicula* for the weak, which is the utmost that some even believing theologians would allow such coincidences to pass for. We discern therein an intimation that "the end of the ways of God is corporeity." Even in outward form the Lord will at last reveal His glory. And while it is certain that we ought not again to transfer to the future any part of O. T. prophecy which the gospel has shown to be mere transient limitation, as is done to some extent by a too realistic theology, still, on the other hand, it is perverse to maintain that the only permanent elements in those oracles are certain abstract ideas, while the form has no enduring significance. As little as the agreement of the form with the appearance of the person of Christ was accidental, so little will it be unrelated to the shape of God's kingdom that is to come. Only this is certain, that the fulfilment will always contain something far higher than could be pictured with the aid of prophecy. Even the truest Israelites, who waited for the consolation of Israel, following prophecy, conceived the Messiah quite differently from

[1] Tholuck, *Die Propheten*, p. 146 f.

what He actually was when He came. But when they had come to know Him, they wondered to see how exactly everything was fulfilled in Him. In the same way, no doubt, all who under the guidance of prophecy have formed a concrete conception of the future kingdom of God have a very inadequate, and in part mistaken conception thereof. But this does not make it impossible that, when the kingdom shall appear, we shall be astonished at the wondrous coincidence between God's word and work even in outward details.

In considering more closely the attitude which *Jesus Himself* took to the O. T. revelation,[1] we see first of all that He placed Himself in subordination to it, because it contained His Father's will: "Think not that I am come to destroy the law and the prophets. I am not come to destroy, but to fulfil" (Matt. v. 17). He speaks thus in the very beginning of the discourse, in which He opposes to the commands of the old law a "But I say unto you," uttered in divine self-consciousness. For by that which He contrasts as His own demand and action with the old command, He by no means destroys the latter, but clearly brings out and perfectly realizes its full divine import.[2] But certainly in such a treatment of the Mosaic law is seen at once the claim, that He alone is called and empowered to disclose in its full truth and clearness the expression of God's holy will once given imperfectly by Moses, and at the same time to convert it into reality. Jesus puts Himself under the law so far as it is divine, above it so far as it is Mosaic. We find a similar contrast in the attitude of Jesus to prophecy. On the one hand, He subjects Himself completely to the course there prescribed to Him, and considers His life and death in all its details as something that *must* so take place, because it is so written in God's word; on the other hand, He views Himself as the culminating point to which the whole of prophecy, nay, the entire Old Testament was meant to lead. While He nowhere sets Himself in opposition to the letter of prophecy, as found at least formally in the law, He first gives the words of prophecy their true import (*e.g.* to ideas like "righteousness" and "God's kingdom"), and, indeed, such an import as of itself abolishes the formal limits of the prophetic

---

[1] Cf. Lechler, *Das alte Testament in den Reden Jesu, Stud. u. Krit.* 1854, Heft 1.
[2] C. J. Riggenbach, *Jesus Christus, der Erfüller von Gesetz und Propheten* (Vortrag, 1878), p. 4 ff.

oracles, their local and national boundaries. But the "sovereignty" of the Lord Jesus in relation to the prophets shows itself chiefly *in His making His own person the centre of what they foretold of God's kingdom, and treating it all as fulfilled in Himself.*[1] More than once He solemnly and expressly declared Himself to be "the Christ," the Messiah, and thus laid emphasis on the regal divine dignity belonging to Him as the true "Anointed of the Lord,"[2] and raising Him far above David and Solomon, Abraham, and the prophets from Moses to John.[3] But at the same time He alluded to His humiliation and passion as something belonging of necessity to His mission, since it was just as emphatically set forth in Scripture.[4] He thus applied entirely to Himself the two images of the glorious Son of God and the suffering Servant of God, ideas which in the Old Testament were merely tending towards unity in certain hints, and thus disclosed a deeper connection in Scripture little known to the ancients. But still more. From the first He declared His appearing to be a coming of the kingdom of God,[5] thus claiming for His own person also the prophecies that referred, not to the "Messiah," but to the "coming of Yahveh." He designated His forerunner John the voice which, in Isa. xl. 3, makes itself heard before Yahveh, or Elijah who comes before the day of the Lord to prepare everything.[6] The two lines of prophecy, one of which speaks of the coming of Yahveh, the other of a future ruler from David's house, thus blend in Him. And if everything great and essential that had been said of the completion of God's kingdom is combined in Christ, and only obtained its true greatness and essence in His person, it follows, of course, that the whole Old Covenant bore witness and pointed to Him, that the reign of God in Israel, viewed from a higher standpoint, aimed at this consummation, and that all God's previous revelations were but a prelude of the one given in His Son in the fulness of time. Here type reaches its adequate completion, just as prophecy its full realization. From the N. T. standpoint the two are not essentially different. Here

---

[1] Cf. Gess, *Die Souveränität des Herrn Jesu gegenüber von den Propheten* (Vortrag), 1879.

[2] Cf. His self-designation "Son of man," according to Dan. vii. 13, and especially Mark xiv. 61 f.

[3] Mark xii. 35-37; Matt. xii. 42; John viii. 58; Luke vii. 28.

[4] Matt. xii. 40, xvi. 21; Mark viii. 31; Luke xxiv. 45 f.

[5] Mark i. 15.   [6] Matt. xi. 10.

it is a subordinate question how far the reference to the completion in the future was present to man's consciousness. Even if David or any other man of God in the Passion-psalms spoke primarily of his own experiences and feelings, the idea of the suffering King and Servant of God is first realized in Christ; the words apply to *Him*, are fulfilled in Him, *i.e.* receive their full meaning first in the experiences of His life. We choose an example, in which the Lord Himself sees His death foretold: "Ye all shall be offended in me this night; for it is written, I will smite the shepherd, and the sheep shall be scattered" (Matt. xxvi. 31). The citation is from Zech. xiii. 7, where it is said: "Awake, O sword, against my shepherd, and against the man that is my fellow, saith the Lord of hosts: smite the shepherd, and the sheep shall be scattered: and I will turn my hand against the little ones." Even if this oracle applied to a pious shepherd of the prophet's days, to himself, or a king of his days, it was verified in an incomparably higher degree in Christ. He is *the* "Good Shepherd," who with full right and consciousness claims for Himself everything of this idea found in the Old Covenant. And as He can call Himself the "fellow" of God with incomparably more reason than all other shepherds, so also what is said of the violent end of the best Shepherd, causing such bitter woe to the poor flock, will have its most terrible fulfilment in Him and His disciples.

Only by pondering and appreciating in all its bearings the attitude which the Lord assumed to the Old Covenant in His witness to Himself, can we understand the exposition and application which the N. T. authors, *apostles* and *evangelists*, give to the prophetic word, and indeed to the Old Testament generally, as a prophecy of Christ. It is impossible to deny that the view of Scripture current in those days, the training of the authors of the Gospels and Epistles, as well as that of their readers, had some influence on the exposition,—more, indeed, on the remarks of the evangelists than on the discourses of the Lord,—in one form in the case of the author of the Hebrews with his Alexandrian culture, and in another in the case of Paul with his Rabbinical training. The Jews of those days were fond of a free application of Scripture, not always professing to be a proper exposition,[1] and even where it professes to be expository,

---

[1] Cf. the excellent treatise of Tholuck, *Das Alte Testament im Neuen Testament*

not always governed by the grammatico-historical principle. But such a reference to the subjective modes of conception in those days, which had their influence on the authors of the New Testament, or the supposition of an accommodation on their part to their readers, would not do justice to the facts of the case. The objective ground, justifying the messengers and witnesses of Christ in what they did, lies in the above-stated relation of Christ to the Old Covenant. Not only did the divine thoughts made known in that covenant first find their true expression in Christ, and in Him without exception, but the agreement between the form of prophecy and the appearance of Jesus Christ made an overwhelming impression on contemporaries, so far as they were enlightened by the Spirit of God, an impression which they strove by their testimony to impart to others. In the first and the fourth Gospel the aim throughout the story of the life of Jesus is to show that He is "the Christ," the promised Messiah. To those who saw with their own eyes, and handled with their own hands, the Word of life, no detail seemed accidental or insignificant. In the least, as in the greatest, they discovered a wondrous harmony with what God had said of old, and mention it when referring to the Old Covenant. They do so as those who stand entirely in the light of the new, and for whom the entire significance of the old lies in its bearing testimony to the new. In the full confidence that their Master is the Yea and Amen to everything God ever said and promised, they seize without anxious inquiry upon the wealth of the prophetic word, and place the entire garland on His head, careless whether single flowers and leaves are thus removed from the place that bore them,—they all grew for Him alone!

Finally, from what has been said the question will answer itself, whether and how far the N. T. fulfilment must govern us in discussing O. T. prophecy. In opposition to the course followed in the Church formerly, which will be treated of in the next section, preference is rightly given in our days to the grammatico-historical method, according to which every prophecy is to be first considered in the meaning which it must have had for its contemporaries, and which, therefore, the speaker himself intended. The N. T. authors by no means wish to exempt us from this

(1861), and the literature there given on Rabbinical hermeneutics and the relation of N. T. authors thereto.

scientific labour; their business lies elsewhere than in the historic indication of the original context and character of a passage. Hence we do not detract from their reputation by first inquiring into the human conditions of a saying, as to which they consider the absolutely divine import alone. It is easily possible for such a saying to go through a long course of development, only attaining a greater range of meaning at a higher stage of revelation.

But, on the other hand, it must not be overlooked that the single prophetic oracle is not a chance product of momentary circumstances and moods, but professes to come from the Divine Spirit; and that this origin is confirmed by the inner unity of prophecies originating in the most diverse circumstances and individuals, and separated by centuries; finally, that the revelation of Christ claims to be the one centre, in which all the arteries of this organism meet. Thus a mode of treating single oracles is demanded, which does not consider them as isolated atoms, but regards them in their inner connection. And since every organism can only be truly understood in all its members from the completion of its development, the connection and full significance of the prophecy of the Old Covenant can only be duly appreciated in all its members from its fulfilment in the New Covenant. We cannot content ourselves with the dualistic dismemberment we meet with in Riehm: "*The contents* of the prophecies—*i.e.* the sense in which the prophets themselves understood them, and would have them understood by their contemporaries—must be distinguished from the *reference*, intended by God and historically revealed, *to the fulfilment by Christ.*"[1] In many passages, indeed, the two things need to be distinguished. But, in general, the reference to the completion of the divine kingdom by Christ is part of the contents of prophecy, nay, forms its essential, although often veiled contents. It is to be noted that the prophetic word usually has an enigmatic remnant, a mysterious something, before which the consciousness of the prophet and of the hearers stands in hushed reverence. Therefore we must not merely reckon what was perfectly clear to the understanding of prophet and hearers as forming part of the contents of prophecy. Prophecy, as a rule, contains a mysterious germ, whose unfolding was only surmised, but which was nevertheless

[1] *Messianic Prophecy,* p. 151 (Eng. trans.) [Riehm criticizes the phrase "dualistic dismemberment," *Stud. u. Krit.* 1883, 4 Heft, p. 804.]

part of its contents. A satisfactory, though still historic, treatment will take account of this germ, and at least indicate its future unfolding. Thus will the organic unity with the N. T. fulfilment be spontaneously established. But the witnesses of the New Covenant show us only the ultimate goal for which we are to look. We must take our stand altogether in the age of the origin of these oracles, and simply make clear the way thence to the goal. In other words, the history of the fulfilment has indeed an essential influence on our consideration of prophecy, but a merely regulative one.

§ 9. *The Treatment of the Subject in Christian Theology.*

In Christian theology, one of whose postulates is the fulfilment of O. T. prophecy, the mode of treating this subject has been very different, according to the idea of revelation governing the writers, and their scientific skill in philological and historical research. Here we desire to point out merely the main lines that come to light as theology developes, remitting the reader to the more specific investigations of Tholuck[1] and Diestel.[2]

We have seen that Christ and the apostles, on the best inner grounds, transferred the divine ideas of the Old Testament and its divinely-ordered types into the New Covenant, in order in its light to show their complete realization. On the other hand, the *ancient Church*, from the first centuries down to the Middle Ages, almost ignoring the distinction of Old and New Covenant, imported the N. T. revelation directly into the Old Testament, and thought only of establishing the complete harmony of the two. The things wanting to an historic appreciation of the genetic process were—first of all, philological knowledge, the foremost Church Fathers, with the exception of Jerome, being unacquainted with the Hebrew tongue; secondly, the critical eye, able to distinguish what belongs to different periods; and, in general, the delicate historical sense, skilled to discern in that development the organic control of the Divine Spirit. The Fathers therefore sought references to Christ's life and teaching at random in the Old Testament, dwelling much on mere details.

---

[1] *Das Alte Testament im Neuen Testament.*
[2] *Geschichte des Alten Testaments in der christlichen Kirche,* 1869.

Even the arts of literal Cabbalistic symbolism were not despised,[1] the text being often wrested from its original meaning. Where it seemed quite impossible to obtain a Christian meaning, the allegorical mode of explanation was applied. In 1 Cor. x. 4, Gal. iv. 21 ff., Paul had apparently given authority for this. But, apart from the consideration that greater freedom belonged to the inspired witnesses of the N. T. revelation in applying the written word than to the later Church, and that the former passage does not impose a foreign meaning on the words, but alludes to a mystery hidden under the outward occurrence,— apart from this, the moderate, judicious way in which the apostle makes use of such interpretation was not taken for a pattern. The manifold sense of the letter was elevated into a principle, all secure ground for Bible interpretation being thus cut away. Still the ancient Church was not without more unsophisticated perception of the real facts of the case. Whilst the allegorical method, borrowed from the Hellenistic Jews, flourished in the *Alexandrine* school (Origen), far more important results were achieved for historic interpretation by the *Antiochian*, viz. by Diodorus of Tarsus and his greater scholar *Theodore of Mopsuestia*, who referred only three of the psalms, which were nearly all regarded as Messianic, to Christ, applying most of them to David, Solomon, Zerubbabel, Hezekiah, etc. He fought zealously against the Allegorists. On the other hand, he lays special stress on the *type*; he really includes even verbal prophecies under this idea; to him they are not germs of something future, but imperfect preformations, whose import is always transcended by the fulfilment. Here we have the beginning of a rational explanation of prophecy, which, of course, might degenerate into Rationalism. But this mode of view, like the freer method of handling Scripture in general, forthwith fell into discredit, and this corrective to the unhistoric spirit of the Church was soon lost. Moreover, Theodore knew no Hebrew or Syriac, and in his interpretation was not always faithful to his own principles. A middle position between the Alexandrians and Antiochians is occupied by *Chrysostom*, who filed off the edges of Theodore's hermeneutics, and knew how to turn Bible language to account in the most pleasing manner.

---

[1] Cf. the so-called Epistle of Barnabas, chap. ix., where the name of Jesus is read out of the 318 servants of Abraham. I = 10, H = 8, are the initial letters of 'Ιησοῦς; T = 300, has the form of the cross, etc.

He also busies himself much with types; only the Messianic prophecies proper are to him not merely typical, but directly Messianic.

In the earliest ages the interest felt in O. T. prophecy was very great. It formed a main argument of the Apologists against the Jews. *Justin Martyr* especially, in his treatises against the Jews, makes use of it, laying the greatest emphasis on the harmony between prophecy and its fulfilment (in Christ). He calls this harmony the μεγίστη καὶ ἀληθεστάτη ἀπόδειξις of Christianity. He describes prophecy as the kernel and chief import of the Israelitish religion. It states what will be done to Christ, through Christ and with Christians. But his interest in it is far less historic than apologetic. Thus the national element in prophecy is more and more ignored, and everything receives a Christian colouring. The allegorizing of an *Origen* achieved great things in this line. All oracles, for example, treating of Jerusalem, according to this Church Father are to be referred to the heavenly Jerusalem. The facts announced therein have no historical meaning, but denote supersensuous events. The oracles respecting foreign peoples apply to the souls of these peoples in heaven. Israel also is always to be spiritually understood. *Augustine* states his hermeneutic principles in reference to the prophets in *de civitate Dei*, l. xvii. chap. 3 : One class of prophecies applies to the earthly Jerusalem, another to the heavenly Church, to which all believers belong; a third species refers to both. In the same work Augustine is the first to give a systematic exposition of the development of prophecy, as well as a review of the prophets existing in literary form, l. xviii. chap. 27–35.

After the age of persecution was past, the attitude of the Church to prophecy changed in a marked way, its fulfilment being no longer looked for so eagerly. In opposition to the chiliastic expectations of the sects, the prophecy of the Old Covenant was regarded as finally fulfilled and done with. The canon of Jerome (on Isa. xl. 14) at once became current: Prudens et christianus lector hanc habeat repromissionum prophetalium regulam, ut quæ Judæi et nostri, immo non nostri, Judaïzantes carnaliter futura contendunt, nos spiritualiter jam transacta doceamus, nec per occasionem istiusmodi fabularum et inextricabilium juxta apostolum quæstionum judaïzare cogamur. Everything was held to be fulfilled, and where the language of prophecy accorded too little with the actual appearance of Jesus and His Church (as *e.g.* in the delineations of the Messianic kingdom), it was thought the expressions should be interpreted spiritually. Indeed, such a spiritual interpretation was attributed to the prophets, as if they had understood their oracles in no other way. The literal (*reale*) interpretation, that sees a preliminary but not yet fully revealed fulfilment in Christ's first appearing, and expects the perfect one at His second coming, was discredited by the extravagances of the chiliasts, and looked on as heretical. Just so this spiritualistic interpretation did not scruple to refer the promises, applying to the future of the people of Israel, to the Church as the spiritual posterity of Abraham according to Gal. iii. 7. But the prospect opened out by the same apostle (Rom. xi. 12), that by the conversion of the whole of Israel the prophecies will one day be fulfilled entirely, was ignored by the Gentile-Christian Church.

Thus we must say in general of the ancient Church, that it imported the New Testament directly into the Old, using in a one-sided manner the maxim of Augustine, correct in itself: *Novum Testamentum in Vetere latet, Vetus in Novo patet*, to bind the two Testaments closely together, and leaving out of sight the essential diversity expressed in the *latere*. That the prophecies and discourses of the prophets generally were full of references to their own age, was altogether overlooked (except by the Antiochian school). Characteristic is Chrysostom's view, that the prophets often spoke in appearance only of the past, and mixed historical matters in their discourses in order to veil their true meaning; for if they had put everything into plain language, they would have been slain by their contemporaries and their books burnt, as the example of Jeremiah proves. The conditions of the age which limited even the prophet's gaze are thus ignored. According to 2 Pet. i. 19, prophecy is like a lamp shining in a dark place. Instead of paying regard to this, the clear light of day was presupposed in the Old Testament.

No scientific treatment of the subject was possible until the Bible could be again read and examined in the original text. Throughout the Middle Ages the only uses of the Old Testament were the practical and the scholastic. Finally, Humanism and the *Reformation* took in hand philological study, and thus opened the way for an historical treatment. The important conclusion was arrived at, that the meaning of a passage can at bottom only be one. But the new path was entered on only gradually and not without many exceptions. It was in reference to the prophecies that historic interpretation was at its weakest, because here too great haste was made to reach the N. T. revelation. The Reformers took too little account of the difference between the two Testaments, borrowing from the early Church the common spiritualizing method in interpreting the Messianic prophecies. Yet here and there we see a freer view, acknowledging that the sense of an O. T. passage is not exactly the same which it receives in the New Testament. It was gradually seen that the idea in prophecy arises out of an historic ground. So Zwingle comments on the peculiar passage (Matt. ii. 18), which also gives us an example of the exceedingly free manner in which Matthew especially finds references in the Gospel history to prophecy. The passage in Jer. xxxi. 15, where Rachel, the mother of the deported tribe Ephraim, mourns over the loss of her children, is cited in reference to the slaughter of the Bethlehemite children, and indeed is introduced by the formula: τότε ἐπληρώθη τὸ ῥηθὲν διὰ Ἰερεμίου τοῦ προφήτου. Thus in this incident of the history of Jesus Matthew sees a fulfilment in some way of the prophetic oracle. On this Zwingle aptly remarks: Evangelista detorquet hæc verba ad Christum; omnia enim quæ in Vetere Testamento etiam sunt gesta, in figura tamen contigerunt et figuræ fuerunt, in Christo omnia consummantur et vere implentur. The *detorquet* should be noticed, plainly intimating that there is a certain violence in the association. Nor is the reason assigned incorrect.[1] Matthew, indeed, did not assume a direct prophecy wherever he speaks of a πληροῦσθαι. And as certainly as the mourning of Rachel was typical of the mourning of these mothers robbed of their children, so certainly everything in the Old Covenant was typical, and everything in the New had its type there.

Luther, who saw, like no one else since Paul the apostle, the

---

[1] It is better than Calvin's: Non intelligit Matthæus illic prædictum fuisse, quid facturus esset Herodes, sed Christi adventu renovatum esse illum luctum. Less happily Bengel on Matt. ii. 15, 18: Unius dicti sensui minor et major non unius temporis eventus respondere potest, donec vaticinium exhauritur,—a rule correct in itself, but more suitable elsewhere than here.

depth of the antithesis between law and gospel, had not, on the other hand, the historic sense to separate enough the Old Testament from the New. He is too eager to find Christ in the Old. The Psalms, *e.g.*, are to him "a little *Biblia*, because they speak so clearly of Christ's kingdom, death, resurrection, and ascension." In this respect Calvin, altogether the greatest exegete of his age, has indicated the right way. His first effort is to discover the sense which the author himself gave to his words, and he by no means lifts this sense at once out of its historical sphere by adducing its N. T. parallel, which is often rather an application or borrowing than an exposition. We take an example at random. Calvin refers Ps. xxii. to David, who is there speaking of his own sufferings, and then rightly observes: Minime vero dubium est, quin illo clamore palam ostenderit Christus, quamvis hic *suas* miserias deploret David, psalmum hunc tamen prophetico spiritu de se fuisse compositum,—therefore a divinely-ordered type, unknown to David, of words as well as of events.[1]

In Zwingle, Calvin, Œcolampadius, and the Reformers generally, we meet with the first attempts to do justice to the historic sense. The imperfection of their attempts cannot surprise us. In the following age of orthodoxy, alongside certain efforts to understand the history of redemption more thoroughly, we see many steps backward in consequence of dogmatic prepossession. The Reformed Church (and in it the Netherland portion chiefly) earned special merit by its research into the O. T. language and theology. Alongside Grotius, who with his fine humanistic culture did not enter thoroughly into theological questions, stood the school of *Coccius*, who tried to put the two Testaments into a right relation to each other. The latter divine founded a purely Biblical theology, which took for its aim the tracing the course of the redemptive history. *Theologia prophetica* appears henceforth as a special discipline. But the types were treated in preference to the Messianic prophecies proper. The rules laid down for typology were certainly insufficient to form an effectual barrier

---

[1] We have every reason to admire the historical acuteness and severe truthfulness of Calvin shown in this view, which diverges from the traditional one; and the Reformed Church especially cannot be thankful enough to him for it. Instead of this, Böhl reproaches him with historical prepossession (*Christologie des Alten Testaments*, p. 33 f.).

against subjective caprice in its treatment. Hence, although the teaching of the Cocceians contains much that is true and beautiful, the overgrowth of the typical element obstructs their vision. The highest place belongs to Campegius Vitringa, who attempts a middle course between Grotius and Cocceius. His commentary on Isaiah is one of the foremost achievements of Christian exegesis. He is careful first to leave the prophecies in their historical significance, and not to refer them directly to the time of Christ and the Christian Church. That, despite this correct insight into the nature of prophecy, he is often seen to be inconsistent in the application of these principles and infected with the failings of the theological theories of his age, cannot lessen his merit.

It was inevitable that the structure of dogmatics should first be shattered by the negative one-sidedness of rationalism before men could see how much of this structure was really built on the rock of truth. Even in the age of orthodoxy there were harbingers of this school of opinion. Standing outside the Church indeed, but exercising no slight influence on the science of the next age, B. Spinoza had treated the Bible from the naturalistic standpoint. In particular, he brought an acute criticism to bear on prophecy,[1] although without any intelligence for ethico-religious life. According to him, the superiority of Israel consisted, not in any special gracious relation of God to it or in any religious vocation, but simply in the fact that for a long time it abode happily in its country in a well-ordered commonwealth. Its relation to God was not different from that in which the Canaanites stood to Him so long as they possessed the land. The aim of the whole Mosaic revelation is *secure et commode vivere!* But within the Protestant Church a rationalistic tendency existed from the first, although not such naked naturalism. It originated in humanism. The attitude of Grotius († 1645), with his humanistic culture, and the *Arminians* towards prophecy and type was mainly negative; with overdone sobriety they dwelt exclusively on grammar and history. The Arminians early suggested that the Jewish authors also cited passages of the Old Testament very arbitrarily, without any justification from the sense and context of the passages. This tendency was the ruling one in the 18th century. The transi-

[1] *Tractatus theologico-politicus* (appeared 1670), cap. I.-III.

tion to the age of *Illuminism* is represented by a work of the Genevan theologian, A. Turretin (*De S. S. Interpretatione*, 1728), which expresses itself very freely respecting the N. T. citations; they are said to be *meri lusus ingenii*, and to rest on an accommodation to Jewish conceptions. The next age went farther. Rationalism strove generally to establish inconsistency between O. T. prophecy and the historic appearance of Christ, as well as the truth revealed in Him, by external historical interpretation, overlooking the internal development which joins the two Testaments together. If the mistake formerly was fondness for emphasizing the coincidence of prophecy and fulfilment in formal particulars, the aim of Rationalism now was to show these particular references to be futile and unwarranted, thinking that in this way it did away with supernatural prophecy itself, which was as offensive to it as miracle. The great religious ideas, of which those particulars are merely symptoms, were left unnoticed in the Old Testament. Still the early Rationalism was devout. As it sought to evade miracles, while leaving the dignity of Scripture intact, so it did with predictions. It made use of the accommodation-hypothesis already mentioned. J. S. Semler used it very extensively. For example, the parallel drawn by the author of the Epistle to the Hebrews between Christ and the O. T. high priest is to him merely an accommodation to Jewish readers. Not that the same idea of priestly representation lies in the two places, but the author desired all the more surely to emancipate his readers from this common idea by setting forth Christ as the true High Priest. So little intelligence was there for deeper religious ideas! One cannot wonder that less devout rationalists went a step farther (note A), and found in the apostles themselves (and in Christ), not merely in their readers, the ground of the illusion that led to the recognition of prophecy and fulfilment. The apostles were placed on exactly the same footing as other Jewish writers who so often quote the letter of the Bible without inner reason. A gulf was now made apparent between the grammatico-historical significance of those O. T. passages and the sense given them in the N. T., and no reasonable mode of explanation was seen. Men could no longer bring themselves with Hamann to sacrifice " the pet child " of the grammatico-historical sense in order to obtain the life-blood.

On the present century lies the task of rising above the rationalistic theory, and yet learning something essential from it in reference to the grammatico-historical character of prophecy. Schleiermacher, who is in general rightly regarded as the conqueror of Rationalism, remained entangled in many of the prejudices of that school in respect to his treatment of the Old Testament. We spoke before (p. 27) of his limiting the theological import of prophecy to universal ethico-religious convictions. The influence of this arbitrary abstraction is strongly felt in modern theology. The same is true of the theory of the world received from Rationalism, in deference to which supernatural coincidence is eliminated from prophecy by literary criticism, or, where the prophecy cannot be put chronologically after its fulfilment, is rendered suspicious by doubts cast on the fulfilment. Still even the bald rationalistic works of modern days have made certain valuable contributions to philological interpretation. Less in the wake of Schleiermacher than of J. A. Bengel († 1752) and Chr. A. Crusius [1] († 1775), the view has gained favour, that prophecy is to be treated as systematic and anticipating fulfilment, and thus the true reconciliation is to be found between the mere grammatico-historical and the pneumatic exposition. But certainly this problem is solved in very different ways.[2] Even among decidedly orthodox theologians the method of treatment is extremely different according to the view taken of the relation between spirit and form in prophecy. The spiritualistic tendency aims rather at indicating everywhere the eternally valid truths and laws of God's kingdom. This was done first of all, in opposition to the reigning rationalism, from the standpoint of faith in revelation, by Hengstenberg's *Christology of the Old Testament* (note B). In characteristic contrast to it stands Hofmann's *Weissagung und Erfüllung* (1841–44), where the organic interconnection of God's word and work, the uniform advance of redemptive history and prophecy, is emphasized so strongly, that really the latter merely expresses what the former always implies.

---

[1] Cf. F. Delitzsch, *Die biblisch-prophetische Theologie, ihre Fortbildung durch Chr. A. Crusius und ihre neueste Entwickelung seit der Christologie Hengstenberg's*, 1845.

[2] Cf. e.g. J. T. Beck, *Bemerkungen über messianische Weissagungen als geschichtliches Problem und über pneumatische Schriftauslegung*, in the *Tübinger Zeitschrift für Theologie*, 1831, Heft 3 (reprinted since), with H. Schultz, *Ueber doppelten Schriftsinn, Theol. Stud. u. Krit.* 1866, Heft 1.

Yet the two are by no means to be explained by finite, external factors, but in the greatest as in the least serve to delineate the plan of the divine kingdom. With all its one-sidedness, this grand conception was an admonition not to depreciate the historic growth of God's kingdom in the interest of dogma. This holds good in respect to the past as well as the future. The spiritualizing method, which would only retain ideas, easily infringes on the vital import of prophecy, whilst certainly the realistic method is in danger of repristinating in a Judaistic spirit what has long been consigned to oblivion.[1] The difference here is one of degree. The same holds good for the most part of the adherents of the school that criticizes the traditional canon. This criticism influences in a large, but still very unequal degree, the expositions of J. J. Stähelin (note C), G. Baur (note D), R. Anger (note E), H. Ewald (note F), E. Riehm (note G), H. Schultz (note H), F. Hitzig (note I), and Kuenen (note J). Others, again, more or less conservative in the exposition itself, accept the traditional canon as it is, and take up a negative attitude towards all literary criticism of it. So Hofmann (note K), Hengstenberg, Böhl (note L). On the other hand, Francis Delitzsch (note M) and G. F. Oehler (note N), while thoroughly maintaining the supernatural character of revelation, and rejecting the naturalistic criteria of the moderns, by no means assume the infallibility of the Jewish tradition of Scripture, and acknowledge the right to exercise criticism on the present form of the Bible in its own spirit. With these two theologians we are at one in this respect, despite differences in the application of principles in particular cases.

NOTE A.—To the gross rationalists, who denied all relation between prophecy and fulfilment, belonged, *e.g.*, Reimarus, the Wolfenbüttel Fragmentist. See his utterance in Tholuck (*Das A. T. im N. T.* p. 1): "So much every one sees, that, unless we assume the proposition, ' This oracle speaks of Jesus of Nazareth,' on trust from the New Testament, no single oracle proves anything; but, on the contrary, they naturally speak of quite other persons, times, and incidents."

[1] In a different form from Hengstenberg, theologians of free critical leanings emphasize the obsoleteness of the O. T. form of prophecy, after the ideas it contains have been fulfilled in Christ. Here, of course, all depends on how much is included in that form. Cf. E. Bertheau, *Die A. T. Weissagung von Israels Reichsherrlichkeit in seinem Lande, Jahrb. für deutsche Theologie,* Bd. iv. and v., and Riehm, below.

NOTE B.—E. W. Hengstenberg, *Christology of the Old Testament*, 4 vols. (T. & T. Clark), an epoch-making work, that courageously and successfully vindicated the divine character of prophecy, and did much towards reviving reverence for the Old Testament and the confidence in it which had declined in the Church,—a merit which the many defects of the work, only partially amended in the 2nd edition, ought not to obscure. See the excellent criticism on Hengstenberg and Hofmann in Delitzsch, *infra*.

NOTE C.—J. J. Stähelin, *Die messianischen Weissagungen des Alten Testaments in ihrer Entstehung, Entwickelung und Ausbildung*, 1847, endeavours with all critical freedom to establish an organic connection between the two Testaments.

NOTE D.—G. Baur, *Geschichte der A. T. Weissagung*, 1861, 1 Theil — alas, not continued. The investigation of the "Vorgeschichte," here treated of,—corresponding to the subject of our First Part,—leads the author, indeed, for the most part to negative results. But it seems as if the further development would have been more satisfactory. The exposition is distinguished above the majority of works of the kind by clearness and pleasantness, notwithstanding the abundance of material.

NOTE E.—R. Anger, *Vorlesungen über die Geschichte der messianischen Idee*, published after the author's death by Max Krenkel. Doubtless if the work had been edited by the author himself, this meagre summary would have been expanded in an instructive way.

NOTE F.—See his commentaries on the *Prophets of the Old Covenant*, 2nd ed., 1867–68. (Translated into English in 5 vols.)

NOTE G.—Ed. Riehm, *Messianic Prophecy, its Origin, Historical Character, and Relation to New Testament Fulfilment*, 1876 (T. & T. Clark), a treatise suggesting a third element alongside those to be gathered from Hengstenberg and Hofmann, namely, the unprejudiced critico-historical view, in which certainly the author seems to us to go too much into minutiæ. On the other hand, we miss in him the appreciation of the intuitive character of prophecy. His exposition gives far too much the impression of prophecy having arisen through dialectic reflection out of the fundamental ideas of the O. T. religion. But the fundamental ideas themselves, with their living energy, are a fruit of prophetic revelation. The treatment of the theocratic kingdom (p. 59 ff.) is perhaps the best part of the work. See p. 61, respecting our divergent view of the relation of prophecy to the N. T. fulfilment.

NOTE H.—Cf. his *Alttestamentliche Theologie*, 2nd ed., 1878.

NOTE I.—F. Hitzig, *Vorlesungen über biblische Theologie und messianische Weissagungen des Alten Testaments*, edited by J. J. Kneucker, 1880 (cf. his commentaries on Isaiah, Jeremiah, the

Minor Prophets, Psalms), while instructive by its acute philology and criticism, in theological respects gives nothing but arid rationalism.

NOTE J.—Kuenen's work, *The Prophets and Prophecy in Israel*, 1877, presents the logical working out of the modern critical principles which exclude the supernatural. In Bernh. Duhm, *Die Theologie der Propheten* (1875), there is in addition an active imagination, that substitutes a political pragmatism for all prophetic ideas.

NOTE K.—Cf. besides *Weissagung und Erfüllung* (1841-44), his *Schriftbeweis* (2nd ed. 1857-60). Everywhere original exegesis and striking combination, the latter, however, being subjective in many respects, the former often violent.

NOTE L.—Ed. Böhl, *Christologie des Alten Testaments, oder Auslegung der wichtigsten messianischen Weissagungen*, 1882. This latest discussion of the subject returns to abandoned traditional methods, not merely in its dogmatizing manner and conservative aversion for literary criticism, but also in detailed exegesis.

NOTE M.—See his commentaries, especially on Genesis, Psalms, Isaiah; also the above-quoted work, *Biblisch-prophetische Theologie*; finally, see his lectures, *Messianic Prophecies*. 1880 (T. & T. Clark), a free outline of the material, suitable for academic lectures; and of a like kind, *Old Testament History of Redemption*, 1881 (T. & T. Clark).

NOTE N.—See his *Old Testament Theology*, 2 vols. 1874 (T. & T. Clark), as well as his articles, "Messias," "Prophetenthum," in Herzog's *Real-Encyklopädie*.

FIRST PART.

THE PROPHETIC WORD HERALDING THE RISE AND
ACCOMPANYING THE DEVELOPMENT OF A
NATIONAL RULE OF GOD ON EARTH.

FIRST SECTION.

PATRIARCHAL PRELUDES OF PROMISE.

§ 10. *General View.*

IN the Pentateuch (or Genesis), lying before us as a whole, there meets us the remarkable phenomenon, that the word of prophecy accompanies the growth of the holy nation out of the common beginnings of human development, from one stage to another, and specializes itself as it advances, inaugurating, and always characterizing briefly and aptly, every new phase of the process. Even if we see in this nothing but a view of the origin of Israel's history that grew out of knowledge acquired later, to this organic mode of considering history, with its foresight of the goal, we must ascribe the palm among all the historical conceptions of antiquity. And as certainly as the goal which those oracles have in view is one raised above common, national aims, so certainly shall we concede higher prophetic dignity to the spirit by which later observers are supposed to have shed light on the beginnings of their nation. Nor can it be denied that if the goal, which these words assign to the history, was in truth divinely ordained, it must have been prior to the outward events. Behind the actual facts the enlightened mind of man discerns a *preceding* divine word, as *e.g.* the account of Creation shows, where each special work reveals to man's gaze, enlightened by the Creator, a creative divine word. Just so certain occurrences in nature and history bring to light divine thoughts conceived *before*, Gen. vi. 3, 5 ff., viii. 21 f. Still the narrative certainly claims something more for these prophetic words, namely, that they were audibly spoken to men before, so that at the initial points of these phases their significance was recognised as God's will by the rational representatives of the divine thought.

Generally speaking, there are two forms in which during this first period the divine will is declared. In the first place, God (or His angel) speaks directly to man, imparting to him blessing or curse, promise or penalty. In the Israelitish tradition, as among other nations, this immediacy of intercourse is one of the characteristic peculiarities of the primitive age. "Walking with God" in extraordinary intimacy is ascribed to Enoch and Noah.[1] Words of God to Adam, Eve, Cain, Noah, Abraham, Isaac, Jacob, words of an angel to Hagar, etc., are given.

But along with this, during the same period, the form of prophetic blessing (or curse) through the mouth of an ancestor is common. Whereas words of God specially appear where something quite new is to be created, the *patriarchal* blessing is the medium by which an inheritance already bestowed is transmitted. It is so first in the case of Noah; and then, within the line of promise, in the case of Abraham, Isaac, Jacob. When one of these men of God distributes the blessing among his sons, he thereby makes his mental and spiritual testament. In doing so, he disposes of blessings not in his possession externally, but of those which he has a claim to through his relation to God. But the most precious thing he has to bequeath is the special attitude in which he stands to God, and which again may pass over to one of his sons in special degree, along with the specific, gradually-unfolding promises linked with that relation. The most natural course was for the eldest, the first-born, to have the place of privilege in this respect also. But, on one hand, God sometimes arranged the matter otherwise, assigning this supreme blessing to another, as in the blessing of Isaac; and, on the other hand, the father (like Jacob, Gen. xlix.) might deviate from the order of nature, if the first-born had shown himself unworthy of the sacred privilege. But a decisive effect was always ascribed to such solemnly-uttered blessings of a progenitor, because no doubt was felt concerning his inspiration by the Spirit of God.

The course of development then is as follows. First of all, at the Creation, the thought of God respecting humanity is declared in unsullied ideality, Gen. i. 26: As God's image, man is to rule the earth in divine dignity. Next, in Gen. iii. 15 ff., divine words define the empirical state of the human race, as it has been since the sin of our first parents, to whom a certain lot

[1] Gen. v. 22, 24, vi. 9.

is announced, with special characteristics in the case of each sex; while a certain superiority over evil is held out to the hope of their posterity. Whereas these first oracles treat humanity collectively, a later one (Gen. ix. 25–27) characterizes it by the diverse developments of its several lines. Here among the sons of Noah, who after the Flood takes the position of universal progenitor, the divergent directions are characterized which the human race will take in its differentiation, while a divine privilege is assigned to the one main branch of humanity. In this race of Shem, Abraham is set apart in a unique position, since he is to stand in a peculiar relation to God, while he receives specific promises for himself and his posterity. The stream of these blessings is carried over to his son Isaac, and from him to Jacob. Finally, the prophetic blessing of Jacob inaugurates the existence of the organized nation in its twelve tribes, with their special spheres, privileges, and faults, while the place of leader is assigned to one tribe (Judah). Thus gradually things proceed by more and more specific designation towards perfection. The goal of this development is *the holy nation in possession of the holy land*, crowned by its God with various blessings.

But is not this harmonious progress of prophecy disturbed in its homogeneous connection by the *criticism* that resolves the "books of Moses" into various authorities, and thus refers the oracles under consideration to various hands? No doubt, if the current supposition that such oracles of blessing owe their origin to the author or redactor of the historical work in which they are found were proved, their historic value would be utterly gone. We should then have to see in them merely subjective reflections of these comparatively recent authors, although even then their inner harmony would necessarily point to an objective ground. But those oracles, as will be shown in detail, announce themselves as a legacy of the foretime, transmitted by tradition and given into the hand of the late narrator. It is only the setting of this legacy that has felt the narrator's influence in the way of arrangement, and at most of some formal redaction, where it was not fixed. Looked at closely, the value of this inner unity is enhanced by the fact that several members were not shaped and welded into a whole by one hand, but came to their present position from various authorities. Moreover, the question as to the age of these authorities, respecting which criticism is less than ever agreed, is for us of secondary importance, considering the above-stated circumstance, that their age does not coincide with that of the oracles of blessing contained in them.

Let us see how the prophetic oracles contained in Genesis may possibly be distributed among the authorities indicated in the Pentateuch, a process in which certainly conjecture has wide scope.

The account of Creation (Gen. i. 1–ii. 3), describing God's first plan in respect to humanity, it is self-evident, cannot be regarded in the light of a history handed down by contemporaries. Here Job xxxviii. 4 applies. Nor is there any trace of a prophetic revelation respecting the act of creation to one living later. But perhaps we have here a monument of what the earliest humanity, standing nearest to God and nature, read out of nature respecting its relation to God. That we have to do, not with a late didactic fiction, but with a primeval legacy of the world of nations, is shown by the parallels among other nations, especially by the closely-allied Babylonian version in the stone-inscriptions, beside which the Hebrew version in its simplicity looks so much more antique that a borrowing of the matter in the Babylonian exile is inconceivable. These traditions are older than the Hebrew nationality itself, which, however, does not preclude their having undergone a sifting and purifying in the spirit of the theocracy.

The oracle of Destiny (Gen. iii.) is so closely connected with the history of the Fall, related in that chapter, that it must necessarily be assigned to the same authority as the latter; and indeed it is the so-called Yahvistic authority (so named after the predominating use of the divine name יְהוָֹה, but in the present section יְהוָֹה אֱלֹהִים) that has narrated the primeval history and Israel's earlier history in prophetic style and spirit. Respecting the age of this redaction views differ widely, since this prophetic mode of thought continues in the nation down through centuries, especially from Samuel's days. But how mistaken it would be to think that the "myth" of the Fall could be invented in such an age, is proved by the connection of this history with the Babylonian inscriptions. True, no parallel has been found in the stone-inscriptions specifically to Gen. iii., as to the history of Creation or the Flood. But the entire material of the history of the Temptation confronts us so completely and unmistakably in those monuments, that there can be no doubt of a connection with the Babylonian mythology. The tree of life, the cherubim, the demonic serpent, Paradise—are plainly conceptions belonging to the primeval Babylonian circle.[1] This history, therefore, is not a didactic fiction, thought out in the prophetic age, but is borrowed from the store of traditions brought by Israel's forefathers from Ur Chasdim.[2]

In the same way the blessing of Noah, which the Yahvist also seems to have received into his work, is in no sense a creation of his, but was already found in existence by him. The attempts to derive this oracle from specific circumstances of historical times have fallen through.

Greater influence on the form of the oracles of blessing must be conceded to the authorities in the promises to Abraham, Isaac, Jacob; and here too variations are seen in each narrator. But the variants are of no importance for the contents. To the prophetic narrator (Yahvist) appear to belong: Gen. xii. 1–3, 7, xiii. 14–17 (xv. 1–7, 13–21), xviii. 17–19 (xxii. 16–18); Isaac, xxvi. 2–5 (xxv. 23); Jacob, xxviii. 13 f.; he also introduces Isaac's blessing, xxvii. 27 ff. On the other hand, Gen. xvii. 4–8 (15–21), addressed to Abraham, and xxviii. 3 f., xxxv. 11 f., to Jacob, are Elohistic. *Jacob's blessing* (xlix.) has a thoroughly original stamp. Chiefly on account of the oracle respecting Dan, applying to the judge Samson, criticism has transferred its origin to the later age of the Judges (Bleek, Tuch, Ewald, G. Baur, Steiner, etc.). On the other hand, in the oracle respecting Judah, Knobel, Wellhausen, and others see the Davidic epoch; others come still farther down. For the internal grounds on which the possibility of real prophecy is contested, see G. Baur, i. p. 219; H. Schultz (2 ed.), p. 666 f.: The blessing is too ecstatic for a dying old man; the prediction of the geographical and historical position of the tribes is too exactly defined (certainly only up to a certain limit of time), and also too unimportant, to be the subject of genuine prophecy; the transmission of such oracles through a space of centuries is inconceivable, and so on. On the other hand, it must be remembered that in the aged Jacob there was a twofold natural basis

---

[1] George Smith, *Genesis in Chaldaic.*
[2] Bredenkamp, *Gesetz und Propheten*, 1881, p. 75 f.

for such distant vision: first, he knew from many years' residence the land to which his hope was turned; secondly, a father's keen vision enabled him to see through the character of his sons. Modern theology, perhaps, may think that the geographical distribution of his sons in Canaan had no moral importance. But to Jacob the sight of the settlement of his children in the Promised Land was the necessary conclusion of his life. With it the promises made to him were fulfilled. Finally, as to transmission, no one will expect the words of Jacob to be protocolled with the precision of a notary. But such prophetic oracles were certainly handed down as a sacred legacy from generation to generation with great tenacity. The seriousness of the historical style of the Bible is security that they did not originate in the muse of a later poet, but were always handed down in the tradition of the race as an honourable inheritance. In confounding such productions of native power with the *vaticinia* of the Book of Enoch and Esdras iv., Schultz denies the difference between original and copy. Had there never been genuine prophecy and genuine oracles of blessing, artificial imitation would have been unknown. Moreover, it is certain that no historic time can be shown when the picture sketched by Jacob for the final age was fully realized, and when, therefore, the "fabricating" of this blessing might be understood. How, *e.g.*, would the portionless dismissing of Levi, the priestly tribe, which stood in high esteem even in the stormy days of the Judges, and still more after David's days, be explained?[1] In general, all these patriarchal oracles are so elementary in character, that they by no means give the impression of *vaticinia post eventum*, or of productions of an intellectually advanced period.

§ 11. *The Primitive divine Capacity and Destiny of Man* (Gen. i. 26–30).

Nature itself, if viewed with an eye open to what is noble, shows the high, exceptional position that God assigned to man among the creatures. The account, Gen. i. 1–ii. 3, given through divine illumination, and reading the Creator's ideas in the laws pervading nature and His words in the works of creation, has

[1] Cf. Diestel, *Segen Jacob's*, 1853. Oehler, *Theology of O. T.*, vol. i. p. 96.

sketched man's position in relation to God and the world with incomparable brevity and sharpness:—

Gen. i. 26: "Then spake God: Let us make (note A) men in the character of our image, after our likeness (note B). And they shall rule over the fish of the sea, and over the birds of the heaven, and over the cattle, and over the whole earth, and over every reptile creeping on earth."

This saying contains two things: Man's primitive God-created capacity and God-willed destiny, his God-likeness and world-rulership. Certainly the latter is virtually conferred on man in the former; but the two are not to be at once identified, as if the וְיִרְדּוּ specified the whole import of the preceding expressions צֶלֶם and דְּמוּת, and the outward superiority over creation constituted man's divine nobility. On the contrary, in himself, apart from his relation to the world, man bears in his attributes the image of God specifically distinguishing him from all lower creatures; just as it is peculiar to the plant in distinction from preceding inorganic structures to propagate itself by seed (ver. 12), and to the animal to have a "living soul," a sensitive life-focus, where all impressions meet, and whence all impulses flow. By the image of God, therefore, we are to understand the essence and sum of that which distinguishes man from the creation subject to him. It is impossible here to think of a mere corporeal attribute, since the divine *spirit* of life (i. 2, cf. ii. 7) must inhere in this image of God in special degree. Man's corporeity, indeed, is far from indifferent. It is so constituted as, like that of no other earthly creature, to express the divine spirituality inherent in man, forming, as it does, an unsurpassable harmonious whole, equally furnished with every organ for receiving divine impressions and every member for expressing volition, and at the same time by its erect build hinting the authority man is designed to exercise. But not merely in his outward appearance, still more in the fact that as an ethical, personal being, man deliberates and speaks and acts consciously like God, whilst plants and animals merely represent species without personality,[1] does the peculiar excellence of man expressed in those phrases —his affinity with God — come clearly out; and from this affinity follows his calling to rule on the earth like God. Despite the signs of comparative divine life visible in plants and animals,

[1] Cf. the מִין characteristic of them.

they are expressly subordinated to man (vers. 29, 30), who not merely gives glimpses of the working of divine powers in him, but whose being and work seem a reflex of the divine.

The fact that man's true essence, his specific peculiarity, is declared to be likeness to God, involves both his dependence on God and his elevation above the world. What he has more than the lower creatures he inherits from the Deity, as something in the highest degree peculiar to and essentially distinctive of the Deity. For that the image presents but a faint reflex of the archetype, is evident of itself. Only so far as man is and remains a reflection of God's glory does he possess his special dignity and his lordship on earth. But from the first this lordship is proposed as the reward of labour, the goal of a course of development. The summons of ver. 28 especially renders it certain that man will not become ruler of the earth apart from his own effort, although his patent of nobility, as old as the primal beginning, secures to him the right to this rule over the world. As men multiply gradually until they fill the earth intended for their dwelling-place, so by degrees they will attain more and more perfect power over it, while of course they are to seek their chief greatness in likeness to God. This is man's true destiny in the world: *He is to prove himself lord of nature by culture, and this culture is to be an all-sided reflection of his relation to God.*

It is impossible to express the significance of man more truly and profoundly than is done in the childlike words that announce the divine consultation respecting him. All that natural history teaches respecting man's relation to the universe confirms in full the account of Gen. i. First, the ground was prepared for him, his support and environment,—first his form was made ready in more imperfect structures, but structures gradually aspiring after perfection during entire periods, until in man this perfection was reached and the new creation ceased—in man, who, however, is not merely distinguished from the lower creatures in degree, but represents essentially a higher principle that finds expression in no other creature. But as man is the goal of nature, so in virtue of that higher principle the aim of his own efforts, as the history of civilisation proves, is everywhere and always to make the forces of nature more and more completely his subjects. And the history of religion shows how the fulfilling of his vocation in the world has always been determined by his relation to God. Although, in consequence of overlooking his dependence on God or of defacing the divine image, he has very often striven after an arbitrary, self-willed, and therefore impious rule over the world, still even this perverted effort, with its immense struggles, partial successes, and final miscarriages, is a witness to the primitive divine purpose, that man is to rule on earth as an image of his Creator. But the realization of this lofty aim was reserved for the history of redemption. For when corruption had penetrated into human nature, there was needed in order to this result the higher life-force bestowed on humanity in Jesus Christ, in whom the kingdom of God has come on earth, and by whom it will be perfected. Thus, on the first leaf of the Bible the germ of the end is contained; the first word of God respecting man involves His entire plan for humanity, which will be all the more gloriously realized the more numerous the hindrances in the way.

It is from the standpoint of this ideal primitive destiny that the *eighth* Psalm views man — the lord of nature, outwardly insignificant, but raised by God's grace above every earthly creature, ver. 3 ff.:—

"When I behold Thy heavens, the work of Thy fingers, the moon and the stars, which Thou hast prepared; what is man, that Thou thinkest of him, and the son of man, that Thou takest interest in him? And Thou didst put him little below divine beings, with honour and glory Thou crownedst him, thou madest him ruler over the work of Thy hands, all things didst Thou put under his feet," etc.

Clearly the psalm speaks of the dignity of ruler conferred on man generally in distinction from all visible creatures, having its root in God's relation of intimate communion with him (ver. 5). Since, however, the divine idea of humanity on both sides (in relation to God as well as to the world) has attained full reality only in one "Son of man," or awaits full realization through him, the author of the Hebrews (ii. 6 ff.) is fully justified in raising the psalm an octave higher, and referring it to the true, perfected Son of man.[1] Only the reference to the future Adam [2] must not be imported into the translation, as is done by Luther, who has also misunderstood ver. 5.

[1] Cf. also 1 Cor. xv. 47; Eph. i. 22.   [2] 1 Cor. xv. 45; Rom. v. 12.

NOTE A.—The plural נַעֲשֶׂה is neither to be regarded as *plur. majest.* (Knobel), nor as plural of resolve, self-summoning, reflection (Hitzig on Isa. vi. 8; Tuch, H. Schultz). Nor can the three persons of the Godhead be imported directly into the Old Testament, as is done by the exposition of the early Church. And the angels cannot be introduced, at least as working along with God. On the contrary, this plural is explained here as in the neighbouring אלהים (Dillmann). The Godhead in its fulness of distinctions comprehends many organs of service, activity, and revelation. These together with God form over against man a unity of a divine kind. Cf. Gen. iii. 22; Isa. vi. 8; Ps. viii. 5. After the image of this divine kind man was created.

NOTE B.—The patristic and then the ecclesiastical exposition attempted to draw an essential distinction between the ideas צלם and דמות, referring the former to the substance, the latter to the accidents, making the former denote the inalienable affinity of essence, the latter the likeness to God defaced by the Fall. It is true, indeed, that man's likeness to God was sullied by the Fall without being destroyed, as his lordship over nature was disturbed, without, however, coming to an end. But it is wrong to distribute this twofold reference between the two expressions which are substantially synonymous in Hebrew idiom, as Calvin rightly perceived. Cf. Zöckler, *Die Lehre vom Urstand des Menschen* (1879), p. 54–73.

§ 12. *Man's Common State of Sinfulness (the Protevangelium).*

Whereas in Gen. i. 1–ii. 3 the ordering of the Cosmos, of which man is the crown, is brought before us in an articulated series of daily works, at the conclusion of which man is appointed ruler over the earth, on which "everything is very good," the separate narrative ii. 4 ff. passes at once to the relation of man to the natural creatures as well as to God; and in a free order, determined simply by the necessities of the narrative, it depicts the contrast between the primitive state of blissful innocence and the common life of man in a state of sin and suffering closed by death. The state of paradisaic happiness was really the object of the Creator's gracious will. But as the existence of heaven and earth, the existence of plants, animals, and man each discloses a divine word, so the resistance of nature to man's labour, the suffering and death from which he will never be free, each discloses another. These woes, however, are not instituted by a primal word of God, coeval with the creative words of the beginning. What

God said at first brought forth life, and everything created was good. The evil, culminating in death and summed up in it, is at first only instituted by God conditionally (ii. 17); suffering and death first became a general law of nature through man's fall, through his presumptuous disobedience to God's ordinance; man is excluded from his primitive state of life-fellowship with God (iii. 22 ff.). This penal state, that has become man's common lot, is more precisely specialized (iii. 16 ff.) in accordance with the universal distinction of male and female. The suffering bound up with human nature dates from the divine judgment upon the original Fall of man. Hence spring the sorrow and dependence inseparably joined with the nature of woman; since only through suffering, in dependence on man, can she fulfil her destiny of motherhood, ver. 16 ; hence the passive resistance of nature, making man's work of tillage so burdensome (ver. 17 ff.), since the rule over the earth promised to him (i. 28) can only be won at the cost of constant toil. The destiny of man to till the earth remains, but the privilege has become a servitude.

If we cast a glance at the first of the three divine words referring to the serpent, iii. 14, 15, it seems natural at first sight to take this oracle in a purely physical sense:—

"Then spake Yahveh God to the serpent: Because thou hast done this thing, cursed art thou above (note A) all cattle, and above all beasts of the field. On thy belly shalt thou go, and dust shalt thou eat (note B) all the days of thy life. And enmity will I put between thee and the woman, and between thy seed and her seed. It shall crush to pieces thy head, and thou shalt crush his heel" (note C).

Is not the serpent's walking on its belly just as natural to it as it is to the woman to bring forth in suffering, or to the ground to bear thorns and thistles ? What is said further of the hereditary enmity [1] between the serpent and the seed of the woman might be supposed to refer merely to the natural aversion and enmity of the two races, in consequence of which they injure and destroy each other wherever possible. This interpretation would also perhaps include the fact that clearly in this struggle for life and death the serpent is worsted. Indeed, in this oracle the

---

[1] As here the enmity of the serpent and its seed is spoken of, the whole serpent-race being included, so the Arabs to-day practise charms against the bite "of the serpent and its brother" in this sense (v. Orelli, *Durch's Heilige Land*, p. 18).

serpent as the most guilty is said to receive the severest sentence. And in point of fact it is degraded to the dust, whilst man remains erect. The consequence of this is that he is able to crush its head, whilst at most it strikes his heel. Generally, the victory is assured to man, although not without painful suffering; defeat to the serpent, although not without revenge. Accordingly this subjection of the serpent to man, required by justice, finds its expression in the physical order of things. According to the literal words, therefore, the oracle in itself might simply contain the explanation of the strange fact that the serpent—so fair and clever, and abject beyond other creatures—is forced to go on its belly in the dust,[1] and is hateful and hostile to man as nothing else is. That the unhappy state resulting from this enmity will ever cease, there is nothing to indicate, but it would be first learnt from oracles like Isa. lxv. 25.

But the context would forbid our stopping at this singular natural fact, even if the Babylonian mythology did not put the demonic character of the serpent beyond doubt.[2] As the entire account is plainly not exhausted in the literal meaning of the words, as the trees and fruits of Paradise are embodiments of something spiritual, so is this especially the case with the creature condemned as a tempter (ver. 14: כִּי עָשִׂיתָ זֹּאת).[3] The poisonous serpent, with its glistening, rainbow colours, its tortuous windings, its duplicity and bewitching gaze, is the embodied temptation, as afterwards in its ignominious abasement and hatefulness it represents the embodied curse.[4] True, in the childishly naive representation so thoroughly in keeping with the conceptions of the first men, the demonic tempter is not yet distinguished from the sensible temptation; but the very fact that, in and with the animal, the power tempting man to evil, the power that has proved fatal to man, is at the same time abased to the dust, involves a promise. First of all it is significant that man is to be in constant conflict with this power; he is therefore destined to maintain a sterner conflict than the one for daily bread—the conflict with evil, against which he must

---

[1] Cf. the Sanscrit name for serpent: uraga, breast-goer.
[2] Cf. Smith, *Genesis in Chaldaic*.
[3] That the Hebrews did not understand this myth, coming to them from without, in a spiritual sense (Hitzig, *Bibl. Theol.* p. 141), is a daring assertion in view of the psychological truth and delicacy by which the Hebrew narrative is distinguished.
[4] Cf. Delitzsch, *Comm. zur Genesis*, 4th ed. p. 147.

be always on his guard, since otherwise it will cause him bitter woe; cf. Gen. iv. 7. Even this divinely-established hostility between him and the evil power is a blessing; for what would become of man, if he only knew the glistening serpent of temptation, working him constant ill, and did not also know the serpent under the curse? And in the struggle with this power of evil a certain superiority is conferred on him, so that he is able to conquer the foe, who has brought all sorrow on earth, although the victory is not won without grievous suffering. For he—the tempted one—remains erect, whilst the tempter must needs crawl at his feet. This implies that God designs him to prevail over the animal, and so over the power that robbed him of innocence and blessedness. Man's aim must consequently be, not merely to rule over the earth, to break its passive resistance, but in particular *to tread under his feet the evil* so perilous to him; cf. Gen. iv. 7.

From this point the interpretation of the early Church goes a step farther: The seed of the woman will bear off the victory, not merely in single conflicts, but, compressed into a personal unity, in a definitive decisive conflict. So the Jerusalem Targum. In this case the יָשׁוּף no longer predicts something merely customary and common to man; it foretells something historical, destined one day to happen. Here the explanation, looking from the standpoint of historical fulfilment, sees greater definiteness in the general language than is expressed therein or could be evident to the first hearers. It is not definitely said whether the prolonged conflict between the woman's seed and serpent's seed will ever find a conclusive, final decision in time. But it is implied in the language that, should such a crisis occur, the issue will be in favour of the woman's seed.

On the other explanation, greater definiteness is given to the word זֶרַע than belongs to it, according to the obvious meaning and context. The early Church understood it directly of the Messiah in the individual sense.[1] Calvin,[2] however, and the Reformed divines in his train, acknowledged the collective sense of זֶרַע as well as of הוּא; whereas the older Lutherans,[3] for the most

---

[1] Irenæus, Clemens Al., Cyprian; see C. Baur, p. 165.
[2] See Calvin on the passage: Generaliter semen interpretor de posteris.
[3] According to Luther, Flacius, the Formula of Concord. In recent days Böhl of the Reformed side advocates the view generally given up by the Lutherans. He

part, maintained the individual signification.[1] Of course the collective notion, which as such has also its mental unity (cf. Gal. iii. 16), does not preclude the abstract becoming a personal unity, or preclude posterity in a single person obtaining perfect victory over the power of evil. But all that is certain from the quite general terms of the oracle is, that if a single person should bring this severe struggle to a triumphant end, and so fulfil the destiny of the entire race, he will be a son of the woman. That all men will not be stedfast in this life-struggle and share in the victory, but many of them will succumb and even adopt the nature of the evil one,[2] is not as yet indicated in this universal promise.

Accordingly a real promise lies in the oracle, and with deep spiritual insight the Church has found in it the πρῶτον εὐαγγέλιον. Certainly the promise is not couched in the form of a blessing, but of a curse. The entire history of redemption takes its start from the Fall of man, and begins with a judgment governing his whole state of life. But a beam of grace towards fallen humanity shines unmistakably through the gloom of divine retribution. For—1. Man's wearisome labour is not without fruit for him, but is the way to the sustenance and enjoyment of life. 2. Woman's suffering is not without result to her, but the way to the perpetuation of life and the joy of motherhood. 3. The perilous, painful conflict against the power of evil is no hopeless, useless one, but the way to victory.

Here in the present passage is the first reference to the future development of the human species, to the woman's seed so full of hope. To the latter, not to the woman herself, is the real conflict and victory over the serpent assured. To the woman's *seed* belongs the future; whereas no higher development, no fuller energy, awaits the serpent's *seed*. Hence the old serpent itself remains the subject and object of the future conflict. Henceforth man's gaze is no longer turned backwards in longing after a lost Paradise, but is directed hopefully to the future,[3]

also revives the Messianic translation of iv. 1, which the facts make impossible: I have gained a man, *Yahveh* (instead of: with Yahveh's aid), where Eve is supposed to designate her first-born the God-man promised to her!

[1] The Catholics refer even the subject-pronoun to Mary, the Vulgate giving: "*ipsa* conteret," which Bellarmine earnestly defends, *De Verbo Dei*, ii. 12; whereas Calvin waxes wroth at this unwarranted interpolation.

[2] Matt. iii. 7, xxiii. 33; John viii. 44; Wisd. ii. 24.

[3] Gen. iii. 20, iv. 1, v. 29.

which in undreamed richness and variety will unfold the theme of man's conflict with the evil one, tending from the first towards a conclusion lying beyond human thought.

As regards the mode of the final redemption, we learn from the N. T. revelation that this divine word of the beginning, as yet undeveloped, carried in it the germ of the finally revealed salvation. The woman's seed was to find its consummation in one person — the Son of man, so called because in Him the idea of man is perfectly realized (see p. 85). By Him, who always victoriously trod the tempter under foot, the decisive victory has been won,[1] not without the victor being wounded by the serpent's bite, *i.e.* experiencing in fullest measure the death that is the bitterest import of the curse which is the fruit of sin. In Him, and with Him, men also are victors over the evil one,[2] and may be delivered from the entire curse descending from Adam to the race.[3] For the consummation of the state which He initiates will also bring to an end the resistance man meets with from the soil, the plant and animal world, as well as bring redemption from the doom of death (Rom. viii. 19 ff.). It is a noteworthy coincidence, that the serpent-conqueror was in special sense the *woman's* seed, born of woman, without being the offspring of a man. Here, too, it holds good: Where the transgression abounded, grace showed itself still mightier. As the woman was more accessible to the tempter than the man, so, being the weaker vessel, she showed herself more receptive to divine grace. As misery was brought into the world by woman, so the Redeemer also was born of her. In the same way from the perfect revelation in Christ a clearer light falls on the nature of the tempter embodied in the animal. The tempting power, encountered by the first human beings in sensuous shape, and to their thoughts inseparable from it, is there revealed in its spiritual nature and independence.[4] Herein lies the capacity of the visible creation for redemption. Thus the outlines of the divine plan of salvation glimmer through the veil of the first oracle. That oracle establishes not only all men's need of redemption, but also their capacity for redemption. For the evil inherent in all had not its primal seat in man; for which reason also the divine curse proper is

---

[1] 1 John iii. 8; Heb. ii. 14 f.; Col. ii. 15. [2] Rom. xvi. 20.
[3] Rom. v. 12 ff. [4] Rev. xii. 9, xx. 2.

not laid on him. The grand revelation implied in the fact that sin, suffering, and death are not set forth as something necessarily bound up with human nature, but something that came on man in consequence of his degeneracy, is all the more important as this universal need of redemption and its satisfaction are at first thrown into the background by a provisional realization of the rule of God in a portion of the sinful world.

NOTE A.—מִן is a particle of distinction, eminence. By its subjection to the curse the serpent is distinguished from all animals, marked off from all. Quite similarly it is said in Judg. v. 24: Blessed above women (מִנָּשִׁים)—blessed like none else. Cf. Deut. xxxiii. 24 and Gen. iii. 1. The word does not include other animals being cursed, but also does not exclude it. In any case they are not like the serpent.

NOTE B.—אָכַל עָפָר does not refer to the food of the serpent in the proper sense, but is an expression meant to picture vividly the humiliation involved in its mode of motion. Cf. Micah vii. 17 and our "to bite the dust." Hofmann (*Schriftbeweis*, i. 574): "Eating dust is joined to its prostrate position, and serves along with the latter to picture the state of abasement in which it is found in contrast to man who stands erect on his feet." Still it is not to be denied that many nations have believed that the serpent really eats dust, Bochart, *Hierozoicon*, t. iii. p. 245, ed. Ros. According to Isa. lxv. 25, in the future ideal state of peace the serpent is content with dust, and therefore no longer bites. For the rest, the narrative must not be pressed to mean that before the condemnation the serpent had another form of motion (Josephus, Targ. Jonathan, etc.). As man first perceived his nakedness after the Fall, so the serpent's mode of life first seemed an ignominious humiliation to it after the curse.

NOTE C.—The meaning *catch at, pursue after* (= שָׁאַף), is not sufficiently assured to שׁוּף by Job ix. 17, although the LXX. (τηρεῖν) and Onkelos give a similar sense. On the other hand, Jerome rejects *servabit* and prefers *conteret*. Hence the Vulgate has first *conteret* and then *insidiaberis*. Cocceius, Umbreit, v. Bohlen, Ewald, Knobel, Hupfeld, Dillmann, and others revive the association with שָׁאַף: *pant for, catch at, pursue after*, in which case it would express the bare *conatus*. Delitzsch, Hengstenberg, Tuch, Wright, G. Baur ("strike at"?), Keil, and others, after Rom. xvi. 20, and the Rabbins, with the Syriac (ܫܘܦ and ܬܫܘܦ) and Samaritan versions, adhere to the meaning secured to the root שׁוּף by the dialects (Syriac ܫܳܦ and ܫܽܘܦ, Aramaic שׁוּף, שָׁפָא שָׁפַף): *grind, bruise, crush*. Inaptly Lange: *grasp, lay hold of, hit.* The conjunction of the word with עָקֵב also makes no difficulty. It is explained first by the intended rhythm, and again by the custom of the Shemites to express such thrusts by verbs of striking. Cf. הִכָּה, Jonah iv. 7, the Arabic ضرب of the scorpion, and also the Latin *ictus serpentis, feriri a serpente*, Greek πλήσσειν, which the *Græc. Ven.* uses both times. Respecting the double accusative with the verb, see Gesenius, *Grammar*, § 139. 2.

§ 13. *The Threefold Development of Mankind (Noah's Blessing),* Gen. ix. 25–27.

The development of mankind, as might be expected from the oracle just examined, was interrupted by the breaking in of unnatural depravity, having for its consequence an extraordinary intervention of divine justice. After the human race had been checked in its extension by the judgment of the great Flood, it appears again, so far at least as it lies within the horizon of the Bible, comprised in a personal unity—that of the sole-surviving Noah.[1]

Noah, with his family, is placed by God in a *covenant relation*, ix. 8 ff. But the Biblical idea of "covenant" by no means implies equal rights, and in consequence of this similar reciprocal conditions, in the two contracting parties. בְּרִית denotes properly settlement, adjustment, solemn conditioning, arranging,[2] but especially a conditioning by which God puts Himself in a special relation to men, more closely specializes the relation existing already between Him and all men. On this understanding of the word and idea it is obvious that the initiative proceeds entirely from God, and we see why the obligations of men are not always expressly set forth as covenant conditions. God makes such an arrangement in sovereign grace, and only in the second place is the new relation to God to take shape in human life. Thus in vi. 18, ix. 11 ff., nothing is said of conditions to be observed by Noah. Rather it is a covenant of grace, in which God binds Himself by

---

[1] According to ver. 29, this name expresses the longing for a comforter under the divinely-inflicted weariness of tilling the land. Thus the human race, groaning under the curse of Gen. iii., to say nothing of the Flood, set its hope of alleviation on his divinely promised posterity.

[2] Cf. διαθήκη, LXX., testamentum. See Hos. ii. 20.

promise. Certainly in ix. 1 ff. a new order of life is enjoined, but the covenant relation is not expressly made dependent on the keeping of these precepts. In the rainbow God gives a covenant sign to remind both sides of the promise He had given.

The substance of the divine covenant made with Noah, and in him with all mankind, consists in the promise that God will not again bring a judgment of universal destruction on mankind after the manner of the great Flood. The Yahvist, also, while not using the form ברית, gives eloquent expression to this divine decree of love respecting rescued humanity, making the Lord say to Himself in response to Noah's thank-offering :—

"Henceforth I will not again curse the ground for man's sake, because the imagining of man's heart is evil from his youth,[1] and henceforth I will not again smite every living thing as I have done. As long as the earth endures, sowing and reaping, and frost and heat, and summer and winter, and day and night, shall not be interrupted," viii. 21 ff.

It is an exceedingly profound and true thought, that the normal succession of days and years, on which the existence of the earth and the welfare of man's life depend, and therefore the regular course of nature, by reason of the radical sinfulness of the human race, are no fixed and self-evident course of things, as is usually supposed, but a voluntary gift of divine grace. The continuance of creation in beautiful harmony, the unbroken development of the history of humanity, is a fruit of divine grace, which will not let God's glorious plan in reference to creation and humanity be frustrated by man's sin. And that gracious decree is linked to Noah's name. It was carried out in the sparing of Noah, and again especially in the unchecked growth of his posterity, which, though without Noah's disposition, and in great part inwardly estranged from God, was destined to fulfil outwardly the end of man's creation, and to spread without limit in space and time. God's grace does not deprive the world's history of its basis, but leaves it free scope.

In reference to the duration of this development of humanity,

---

[1] "כִּי יֵצֶר לֵב" does not belong to לֹא אוֹסִיף, but developes the בַּעֲבוּר הָאָדָם, belonging to לְקַלֵּל. Thus it is not a ground of palliation to pacify the Lord, but rather a reason that might move Him to destroy the creature, if His grace did not restrain strict justice.

the definitions לְדֹרֹת עוֹלָם (ix. 12, cf. 16, *Elohist*) and עַד כָּל־יְמֵי הָאָרֶץ (viii. 22, *Yahvist*) are synonymous. A time is meant of which no end is visible. No temporal limit of this covenant relation enters into view; which certainly does not mean that an end of this state is absolutely out of the question. The possibility of its duration being unlimited in a merely relative degree is even suggested by the last expression; and with this the usage of עוֹלָם is reconcilable, inasmuch as no positive limit of duration is within sight.[1]

Thus, after the divine covenant concluded with Noah, humanity was to go on developing without interruption. Noah's prophetic oracle then describes this development as threefold. Gen. ix. 25–27 characterizes the races of mankind, so to speak, according to their theological diversity, as the one in Gen. iii. does according to their natural unity. Noah's blessing speaks of a historical development, as the former oracle of a natural one.

Here also the oracle of blessing arises out of a curse on sin, but a curse having a reverse side of promise. This time, however, we have not an arrangement made directly by God, but a prediction of an inspired ancestor respecting his posterity, the outcome of prophetic prevision (cf. p. 78). This long vista opens before him on an occasion that gives him deep insight into the inner character of his sons; and their varied character will impress a differing stamp on the main branches of mankind. The fact that God's relation to all nations, as previously His attitude to all creatures, is here traced back to an ethical ground, forms a worthy introitus to the history of the world and redemption; in which God of His free grace will indeed choose a particular nation, yet not without the co-operation of ethical grounds, and not without the ethical conduct of this chosen nation reacting on the covenant relation.

The qualities which were conjoined in man generally, and in Noah specifically, found separate and characteristic expression in his sons. The evil which in the form of sensuousness had overcome even Noah, rose in Ham to shameless vice and flagitious, unnatural sensuality. Hence the curse of sin, encircling all

---

[1] Cf. on עוֹלָם, v. Orelli, *Hebräische Synonyma der Zeit und Ewigkeit*, p. 68 ff.; *ibid.* on עַד (properly "perpetuity of all the days of the earth"), p. 31.

mankind, smites him more directly. On the other hand, in the filial reverence and obedient love of his eldest son, Shem, Noah sees his own piety. To him, accordingly, he promises his best blessing, that of the divine friendship in higher degree. The middle son, Japhet, followed the pious initiative of his elder brother, thus showing true human feeling, and fulfilling his duty as a son. To him, therefore, the blessing promised to man generally is imparted in richest measure, Gen. ix. 25–27:—

"And he spake: CURSED be CANAAN! A servant of servants let him be to his brethren! And spake: Blessed be YAHVEH, the God of SHEM! And let Canaan be a servant to him! Wide room let God make for JAPHET! And let his dwelling be in tents of glory! And let Canaan be a servant to him!"

It is an aggravation of the divine displeasure, that in ver. 25 the divine curse is directly inflicted on a man (as first in Cain's case, Gen. iv. 11, differently from Adam's case before). But this is only done to a portion of mankind in distinction from the other portions to which the divine blessing is assured in different forms. The fact that Ham is not mentioned in the curse is strange,[1] seeing that "his brothers" plainly are not the brothers named in Gen. x. 6, but Shem and Japhet. Thus in some sense Canaan stands as representative of Ham and all his race, in contrast to Shem and Japhet with their posterity. But why this substitution? Certainly the chief consideration is that Canaan is the branch of Ham which came into most direct contact with the Israelites, and in which they saw the character of that progenitor most decidedly expressed, and the curse pronounced on him most openly fulfilled. Thus the curse was not executed forthwith on the progenitor, nor on all his posterity. But the rule of ignoble impulse, the absence of all nobler feeling, which showed itself in him, was in the course of history to develop on a large scale in a race given up to sensual sin, and this race will suffer the curse of slavery. So much is implied in this prophetic word of the patriarch.

Not all Ham's posterity show moral decay in the same degree,

---

[1] One might be tempted to read straight away אָרוּר חָם אֲבִי כְנָעַן, since the first member of the mashal seems too abrupt. In any case in the twice-recurring refrain, which there is no reason whatever to question (in opposition to Olshausen), Canaan appears as bearing the curse which should fall on Ham.

and not all fall an inglorious prey to slavery. Nimrod (Gen. x. 8 f.) was no עֶבֶד. Egypt long enjoyed independence before succumbing to Shem and Japhet, and owed its culture principally to the good moral discipline it maintained in comparison with many heathen nations. But certainly neither the bringing salvation to the world, nor rule over the world, was granted to a Hamitic people. And in the Phœnicians, whose descendants were the Canaanites (note A) previously inhabiting the Promised Land, the Israelites saw the full development of sin up to utter depravity, as well as God's severity in punishing it. These Phœnicians were proverbial in antiquity for their craft, effeminacy, cruelty, and licentiousness. On this account retribution fell on this people in fullest measure. Its sway was never great in extent, nor was it able anywhere to maintain itself long against its foes. With its trade and its inventions, its mission in the world was perhaps to be a *servile* people. As the Shemites, especially the Israelites, robbed it of its lands and reduced it to bondage, so, despite all the strength of its cities and all the heroism of its warriors, it succumbed in turn to the Persian, Macedonian, and Roman arms. The "fate of Carthage" was to yield, as that of Rome was to conquer.

That the Negroes of Africa are to be classed with the Hamites is contested,[1] but scarcely with reason. That the black races came very early within the horizon of the ancient Israelites may, in view of the abode of the latter in Egypt, be assumed with certainty. Obviously they were then regarded as Hamites. Nor, considering the representative position in which Canaan stands to Ham, can it be maintained that in any case they were not included under the curse falling on Canaan. Rather the negro tribes are among the very peoples who exhibit Ham's character in its most aggravated form, and on this account fall a prey to the hardest slavery. That this is no justification of slavery, with its dishonour to human dignity and its outrages, such as have been practised even by Christians, would scarcely need to be said, if the present oracle had not been appealed to in this sense.[2]

Then in ver. 26 follows the blessing upon *Shem*, who had given the real impulse to the act of filial piety in concealing the

---

[1] *E.g.* by J. G. Müller, *Die Semiten in ihrem Verhältniss zu Chamiten und Japhetiten*, 1872.
[2] See Diestel, *Geschichte des Alten Testaments*, p. 777.

father's shame. This may be inferred from his age, since he appears as the first-born, and agrees with the large reward that he receives.¹

Instead of blessing Shem himself, the aged father, with prophetic glance at Shem's future salvation, blesses (note B) Yahveh, the God of Shem, whom he sees in intimate union with Shem. The oracle of blessing is thus turned into praise of Him who is the source of blessing, and has proved Himself such.² Shem's highest happiness is that he has this God for his God. Here for the first time, as Luther notes, we find the genitival combination common afterwards: *God of a man, nation*, etc. For when humanity parts into different branches, the universal Deity also is specialized. To one portion of humanity the true, living God stands in a relation of mutual possession.

For God, thus making Himself known in living, special revelation, the passage uses the name יהוה as a proper name, whereas אלהים has an appellative significance. אלהים³ signifies the Deity in the rich diversity of aspect (hence the plural) in which He manifests Himself to man in the sphere of creation and history, claiming man's reverence. יהוה signifies the absolute God in His unconditional sovereignty,⁴ not as one intuitively known to all men from daily experience, but as one to be made known to a small portion of mankind by special revelation. It is thus evident that אלהים might with a certain justice be applied to the gods of all nations, since the elementary manifestations of the Supreme Being underlie all the heathen conceptions and representations of God; whereas, on the other hand, יהוה became necessarily the proper name of the God of revelation, who made Himself known only to a portion of mankind, and in all His greatness only to one people. Yahveh, indeed, is not a particular God; He is the alone true Being, of whom all אלהים are merely outbeamings or mutilated shadows; He is האלהים κατ' ἐξοχήν, but in a more

¹ Perhaps also the singular in וַיִּקַּח (ver. 23) alludes to this, so that וְ in וַיֶּפֶת would only express accompaniment. In any case, Shem stands first in this action.

² Gen. xiv. 20; Ex. xviii. 10; Deut. xxxiii. 20; 2 Sam. xviii. 28; 1 Kings x. 9.

³ From אָלָה, *to fear*, cf. اَلَ; cf. פָּחַד, Gen. xxxi. 42.

⁴ אֶהְיֶה אֲשֶׁר אֶהְיֶה, Ex. iii. 14. The *hiphil* derivation, preferred by many in recent days, "He who calls into existence," is in any case foreign to Hebrew thought, nor can it be verified on linguistic grounds. See Delitzsch in the *Zeitschrift für lutherische Theologie*, 1877, p. 593 ff.

glorious revelation of His nature than the latter name expressed. He is the God of the history of redemption, as the former is of the history of nature and the world. While it is said that the curse will be fully realized in a branch of the tribe of Ham (Canaan), there is no intimation of this kind in the case of Shem, because the progress of the patriarchal promise and history shows of itself that Yahveh's perfect revelation was granted to a particular people. Although we must repudiate the exaggeration of Renan, that the root of monotheism is to be sought in the peculiar temperament of the Shemites, the fact remains, that the specific Yahveh-religion of Israel was built up on the basis of a monotheism prevailing over a wider area, and already contrasting favourably with heathenism. Moreover, the three great monotheistic religions—Judaism, Christianity, Islam—issued from the tents of Shem.

Then the curse, which was at first put in the foreground, follows as the gloomy background, against which the blessing shines all the brighter: "And let Canaan be a servant to him,"[1] words which remind us chiefly of the ignominious extermination and subjugation (Josh. ix. 23) of the Canaanites by the Israelites.

Ver. 27. To the third son, *Japhet*, also a happy omen is given by way of reward. This is done with an allusion to his name, a favourite course in oracles of blessing,[2] as the name Canaan previously, suggesting meanness, stooping, humiliation, introduces the lot of slavery. The name יֶפֶת leads to the oracle יַפְתְּ, where, indeed, a verb of unusual form and signification is chosen for the sake of the rhythm: Wide room may God make (note C) for Japhet!—certainly an outlook rich in promise for his descendants. For wide room, in which it may spread, is to his race the condition of prosperous development, and also its consequence. As matter of fact, Japhet has extended in breadth. He has spread, not merely over an important part of Asia, but also over the distant, broad island-continent of *Europe*. And to this geographical extension correspond his conquests in the intellectual field. In all branches of culture he has borne off the

---

[1] לָמוֹ might perhaps refer as a plural suffix to the collective idea "Shem" (and his posterity, *Tuch*), or be an echo of לְאֹהָלָיו, but is rather to be regarded as a singular form=לוֹ. Cf. Gesenius, *Grammar* (23rd ed.), § 103, 2, note 2; Ewald, *Gram.* § 247 d. 1. 3.

[2] Cf. Jacob's blessing.

palm. The Indo-Germans have attained world-wide supremacy in the intellectual as well as physical sphere. This is the work of אֱלֹהִים, " the Deity to be feared," who has deposited His revelation in nature and human history, and even rewards the δεισιδαιμονία of the heathen with rich benedictions, which, however, are chiefly of a natural order. The fair flowers put forth in Hellenic civilisation owed their ideal consecration to the loving nurture of divine intimations in nature and human life, and quickly withered away on the entrance of moral corruption. Just so the matchless development of power in ancient Rome had the secret of its strength in pious reverence for the divine, and rapidly fell to pieces when this serious spirit vanished away.

But the second hemistich וְיִשְׁכֹּן בְּאָהֳלֵי־שֵׁם is difficult. The chief question in dispute is, who is to be considered the subject of וְיִשְׁכֹּן. Among moderns, von Hofmann, Baumgarten, H. Schultz,[1] after the example of Onkelos and other Jewish expositors and also Theodoret, have taken *God* as the subject, which would give an attractive and highly significant sense: Japhet gains the wide world, but Shem's distinction consists in this, that God dwells in his midst. שָׁכַן is used specially of the dwelling of God (Num. xxxv. 34). By the later Jewish theologians His gracious presence is called directly the שְׁכִינָה, a reminiscence of Onkelos. Nor is there any weight in the objection usually urged against this interpretation, that the parallelism requires Japhet as the subject in this verse, since Shem has been dismissed in the preceding one; for, just as the curse on Canaan recurs, so the blessing on Shem may recur, and we should thus obtain the pleasing arrangement: 1. Curse on Canaan; 2. Blessing of firstborn on Shem and its antithesis in the curse on Canaan; 3. The second blessing of the middle brother, with reminiscences of the higher blessing of the first and the curse on the third. Nevertheless, the majority of ancient and modern expositors give up the reference of וְיִשְׁכֹּן to God, as it seems to us rightly. For it cannot be denied that in the first hemistich the emphasis lies on the repeated יֶפֶת, not on אֱלֹהִים, on which account the harmony of style is best preserved by referring what follows to Japhet. An antithetical relation of the two clauses (*but He will dwell*) would of necessity have been noted in the language used.[2] More

---

[1] *A. T. Theologie*, 2nd ed. 677 f.
[2] See the form in Stäheliu and Dillmann, *Comm. zur Genesis*.

especially we should expect to find the name יהוה, seeing that God dwells in Shem's tents as Yahveh. The plural designation of place would also be strange, since God elsewhere always dwells in His אֹהֶל; yet this might perhaps be explained by the indefinite generality of the oracle. But supposing *Japhet* to be taken as the subject, his dwelling "in the tents of Shem"[1] makes no less difficulty. Some, not without anti-Jewish tendency, have after Justin M. (*c. Tryp.* 139) understood a hostile occupation of the Shemitic country,[2] which would introduce a quite incomprehensible infringement of Shem's birthright-blessing. Far more in keeping with the connection would be the interpretation to the effect that Japhet is to acquire a share in this birthright-blessing, entering into brotherly fellowship with Shem by peaceable residence with him, just as the two joined with brotherly feeling in the pious act to their father. But certain as it is that the historical fulfilment proves that Japhet was to be received into spiritual fellowship with Shem, and so to share as his guest in the highest blessings, still it is more than doubtful whether such a thought could be so expressed. The dwelling of this race in the tents of the former seems to give the impression, if not of conquest,[3] still of a crowding inconvenient to both in strange contrast with the יָפְתְּ. The use of the phrase to denote peaceful, hospitable relation cannot be proved. And even if this meaning were usual, the absence of all intimation of any blessing which Japhet was to seek and expect there, would be strange. Nor does the uniform refrain, in which the למו above was to be taken as a singular, favour any reference to Shem in this phrase. Accordingly, since the days of J. D. Michaelis many[4] have taken שֵׁם in ver. 27 as an appellative:[5] *renowned tents*, properly tents towering above space and time, of which *fama* tells far and wide, early and late. Certainly in this association the word אהלים looks very modest; still it harmonizes with the notions of primeval simplicity. The strongest objection that can be raised against this interpretation is the ambiguity occasioned by the double use of שם in vers. 26, 27. But precisely in this asso-

[1] LXX., Calvin, Delitzsch, Tuch, G. Baur, Hengstenberg, Dillmann, J. P. Lange, G. Fr. Oehler (*A. T. Theology*, i. 82).
[2] So Bochart, Clericus, Rosenmüller, and still Hengstenberg, Sörensen.
[3] The phrase is so used in 1 Chron. v. 10.
[4] Vater, Schott, Gesenius, de Wette, Winer, Stähelin, Schumann, Knobel, Anger.
[5] As in Gen. vi. 4; Num. xvi. 2; cf. 1 Chron. v. 24; Job xxx. 8.

nance, according to our view, lies the explanation of the surprising expression. As the oldest Hebrew *mashals* are fond of assonance, especially at the close of the strophe, so here not only is the refrain on Canaan purposely repeated with like sounds, but in בְּאָהֳלֵי שֵׁם the אֱלֹהֵי שֵׁם is echoed with very slight variation in sound.

Japhet is to have the lion's share, not only of the possession of the world, but also of the glory of history. Canaan can dispute neither with him, but on the contrary is subject to him. Shem's prerogative is more internal, intellectual, divine; he has indeed his כָּבוֹד, his special glory, but this is more than mere worldly renown (שֵׁם always refers to consideration in men's eyes, and has a profane character); its root is simply in his special relation to the God of revelation.

Thus a threefold development of humanity is foreseen in this oracle. One portion of it will be received into a specially intimate relation to God, who reveals Himself to it as Yahveh. It will be the depository of the history of revelation and redemption. Another will extend prosperously in the world and acquire lasting renown, by the favour of the God who makes everything go well with all who fear and honour him by right conduct. It will be the depository of culture, and the heroic race of history. A third for its ungodliness, in addition to the curse of the ground, will bear the curse of history, subjected and enslaved by its brethren, lowest in the world's history as in that of redemption, laden with the world's ban. These are the different attitudes which the several branches of humanity will henceforth assume to God. If these branches are here attached to the sons of Noah, it is not meant that all Shemitic nations will be united with Yahveh and all Hamitic nations laden with the curse, and still less that all individuals among these nations will assume their ancestors' attitude to God. This is opposed by the solitariness of Canaan in the curse, and still further by the solitariness of Israel in the blessing. But regarding history as a whole, we see that certain characteristics are hereditary, not merely in nations, but even in families of nations. On these leading types, which will be more or less reproduced in their posterity, blessing and curse are here pronounced. Thus this pithy oracle, whenever it arose and by whomsoever spoken, contains the grand programme of the development of mankind in its separate lines. The brief saying to Japhet opens out a wide prospect of a general history rich in external and intellectual results, while the still briefer one to Shem carries in its bosom the germ of the history of redemption.

The question from whom such an oracle sprang or received its present form, is one of extraordinary difficulty. It is clear from the above interpretation how great was the influence of the Hebrew language on the form of Noah's blessing, and of course the Hebrew language was just as little spoken by the patriarchs as by Adam in Paradise. In its contents also the oracle is conditioned by the revelation given to the people of Israel after Moses. Compare the emphatic use of the name Jahveh and the description of Canaan as cursed by the progenitor. On the other hand, it is out of harmony both with the spirit of antiquity and in particular with the moral earnestness of the Biblical authors, to invent such oracles of set purpose and publish them as words of an ancestor. Rather in this old Hebrew oracle we have to deal with a primitive tradition, the kernel of which reaches back beyond the Hebrew nationality, but which received its present form from the spirit of the Israelitish theocracy (as in the account of Creation). The greatness of its contents makes it certain that it was a prophetically deep and far-seeing seer who put down Noah's word as the Alpha of the world's history. Such a saying cannot be explained as a limited reflection of the view of a particular time, or as the product of certain political relations and moods (note D).

NOTE A.—כְּנַעַן, properly lowland, applies to the low tract on the Phœnician coast, and therefore quite properly denotes the Phœnicians, and next the Canaanites, who meanwhile had penetrated into Palestine. That this people was of Hamitic descent the Israelites had no doubt, despite the Shemitic language so called which it spoke. Cf. Kautzsch in Riehm's *Handwörterbuch*, art. "Phönizien." On the moral depravity of this people, see Münter, *Religion der Carthager*, p. 150 ff.; on their licentious worship, Scholz, *ut ante*.

NOTE B.—We have no verb corresponding to בֵּרַךְ under both its aspects, the best still is "bless." It has God for its object in the sense of praising as well as man in the sense of blessing, i.e. invoking God's good-will on one, conveying God's blessing. Only in the latter sense does Heb. vii. 7 hold good, that the less is always blessed of the greater. Cf. the Arabic صَلَى, properly the cross (صَل), *to bend*, hence *to pray;* moreover, of God it is said: *to bend graciously over* (عَلَ) *one, to bless him.* Cf. *Borhân ed-dîn. Enchirid. Stud.* ed. Caspar. p. ר, line 2 ff. of the Commentary.

Note C.—From פָּתָה (root פת, to be open), the hiphil means here: *to make wide, give wide scope* (not *allure, persuade,* like the piel with accusative, after which Calvin in the present passage accepts the meaning *alliccre, blande reducere;* with gentle voice God will allure Japhet to reunion with Shem, as has been done by the gospel). Cf. הִרְחִיב לְ, Gen. xxvi. 22; Ps. iv. 1. Because breadth of room to extend in was the first condition of prosperity in nomadic life, designations of happiness generally have been formed from this idea of space; cf. הִרְוָיָה. Yet it would not be in place in the present passage to generalize the meaning of הִפְתָה into that of making happy (Tuch, Hengstenberg).

Note D.—That an oracle so natural in character is not to be regarded as a mere expression of national hate and a justification of that hate (Tuch, p. 147), is self-evident. Of the aberrations into which the so-called scientific interpretation falls, which labours to find the roots of all prophetic vision and speech in historical occasions, a shocking example is given in the present passage, alas! by G. Baur (p. 176 ff.), who sees in Noah's blessing a political and indeed anti-Isaianic manifesto, written in favour of an alliance with the Assyrians, who are supposed to figure as Japhet! (Ewald here led the way in error, *Geschichte Isr.* iii. 643.) Such attempts at least show how hard it is to point out pragmatic motives for these oracles in the political history of the age. According to our interpretation of ver. 27, shared by most exegetes of critical skill, a noteworthy element is, that Japhet's fame in the world was far below that of Shem and Ham during the whole history of ancient Israel, and at all events first appeared on the horizon of the Jewish nation in unimagined greatness long after the composition of these sayings; and, indeed, in earlier days little enough indication could be seen of any subjugation of Ham, specifically of Canaan, by Japhet.

§ 14. *The Promises to the Fathers of the Covenant-Nation* (*Abraham, Isaac, Jacob*).

The promise given to Shem of a closer relation into which God will enter with him is further specialized[1] to the effect that

---

[1] Cf. in Isa. xxix. 22 the redemption and severance of Abraham from heathenism.

Abraham and his posterity specifically, more precisely the seed of Isaac, and still more definitely the seed of Jacob, will stand in this covenant, *i.e.* in distinctive relation to God. This is made known to the forefathers of Israel themselves by divine utterances. Whereas God's talking with men is presupposed in primitive days more generally, in the patriarchal period it has already become exceptional. The pious patriarchs themselves, although only in special solemn moments of their life, are deemed worthy of divine communications, and their spiritual greatness consists in their trusting this voice of God. Take away from an Abraham this believing trust in God's promise, which is the sinew of all his acts, and his spiritual significance is gone. The different authorities, distinguishable in the narrative respecting Abraham, agree in this, that he received from God special assurances respecting the future of his posterity.

The *form* of these revelations is subordinate. It is simply said: the Lord spake to Abraham, or: He appeared to Abraham and spake. Nevertheless the different authorities testify that the communicating of the promise was accompanied by a visible appearance of the holy God.[1] Other secondary circumstances are, that the revelation often takes place by night,[2] once also the covenant-promise is given in a dream,[3] and once (xxv. 22 f.) an oracle in reference to nations is given on an inquiring of the Lord, while it is not said in what way the answer was given. Of subordinate interest also is the more precise designation, met with occasionally, of the revealing Deity as מַלְאַךְ יהוה or מַלְאַךְ אלהים, *Angel* of the Lord.[4] For this difference is more one of form. God Himself speaks in and through the angel, so that the two subjects are constantly interchangeable— the subject who is the proper author of the revelation, and the one that is only its representative medium. See xvi. 7-13, where Hagar is sure she saw God Himself in the angel

---

[1] Cf. xii. 7, xv. 17, xvii. 1, xxvi. 2, 4.
[2] The still night is specially favourable to the reception of divine revelation; cf. Job iv. 13, xxxiii. 15; Zech. i. 8.
[3] Gen. xxviii. 12 ff. See p. 15. The dream as a form of revelation is usually regarded as a characteristic of the second Elohistic authority; but Gen. xxviii. is probably Yahvistic, at least the splitting up of the narrative is in the highest degree arbitrary.
[4] So in the Yahvistic authority, and the Elohistic closely allied to it; cf. xvi. 7, 13, xviii. 1 ff., xxi. 17, xxii. 11, 14, 15.

(cf. xxi. 17); just so the interchangeable relation between God and the three men, xviii. 1 ff.; further, xxii. 11, 14, 15, and xlviii. 16, where Jacob calls an angel the Saviour of his life. This interchangeable relation has its ground in the old conception of angels, according to which they only come into view as organs through whom God manifests Himself. Where God reveals Himself in time and space, this revelation may always be described as that of an angel (cf. too Gal. iii. 19). And it is noteworthy that the angel is first mentioned in the divine appearance to Hagar, not as if this favourite instrument of God appeared now in consequence of the making of the covenant, —in which, however, Hagar had no part,—but just here the mediateness of God's manifestation forced itself on the reflection. No doubt distinctions are made in certain narratives between one order of angels and another (Ex. xxxiii. 15 ; Isa. lxiii. 9), but not more than between the arm and the face of the Lord. The error of the opinion so much in favour in the Church, that among the angels one towers as an uncreated divine being above the other created ones, and that where מלאך ה״ stands, and the interchange of persons with God occurs, the covenant-angel is always meant, lies in this, that the individual angel is contemplated alongside or under God as an independent hypostasis in the style of a much later age; whereas for the Biblical books, especially of the earliest age, he comes into view simply in his working. The particular work or revelation of God shows a particular angel, who is its medium, and who in this special form and act sets forth God Himself.

Let us now consider the *contents* of the divine promises to the patriarchs.

The first one that meets us is that given to *Abraham* (xii. 1–3, 7), accompanying the divine summons to depart from his native land:—

"And Jahveh spake to Abram : Remove from thy land and acquaintance and father's house to a land, which I will show thee. Then will I make thee a great nation and bless thee and magnify thy name, and thou shalt be a blessing, and I will bless those who bless thee, and whoever utters imprecation on thee, him will I curse. And through thee all kindreds on the face of the earth shall be blessed."

The two main points, recurring uniformly in all the authorities, are *land* and *people*. The whole patriarchal history looks forward to the holy people in the Promised Land, a prospect already made known to the pious fathers themselves by divine illumination. The present saying to Abraham also looks in that direction, although he was the progenitor of a wider group of tribes. His intimate relation to God was transmitted in its blessed significance to a particular nation. First of all (vers. 2, 3) the divine blessing is attached to Abraham's person, of whom it is said expressly וֶהְיֵה בְּרָכָה — which by no means signifies merely that he himself will be blessed (Hitzig), or that his name will be a formula of blessing, but extols him as the medium and source of the divine blessing.[1] How Abraham himself, in virtue of his special relation to God, was a mediator of blessing to those about him, is shown in Gen. xx. 7; that his people in the same way were to convey the divine blessing, the dispensation of God's grace to the whole world, see in Isa. xix. 24; Zech. viii. 13. In the present passage the import of the brief saying is expounded in ver. 3, according to which God's relation to men depends on their attitude to Abraham (cf. xx. 7), and the Lord will deal well with those who wish well to him and do homage to the divine grace revealing itself in him; and, on the other hand, will make him feel His displeasure who despises and scorns one whom God has blessed. The singular number here is significant. It can only be single hardened sinners who so misunderstand one who is a source of blessing to all about him, as to contemn and hate him, and in him his God. The world, as a whole, will not withhold homage, and will therefore enjoy the benefit of this source of blessing. The latter is implied in the final words, which puts the crown on the promise, וְנִבְרְכוּ בְךָ כֹּל מִשְׁפְּחוֹת הָאֲדָמָה. But whether the subjective act of homage or the objective act of divine blessing lies in the niphal, exegetes are not agreed. That one involves the other follows, however, from the preceding words. The niphal, as is well known, is primarily reflexive. In accordance with this its original signification, which, however, mostly vanished in the idiom of later days, earlier Jewish expositors, not without a polemical interest, opposed the ordinary Christian interpretation (shall be blessed in thee, LXX., N. T.);

---

[1] Cf. Prov. xi. 25: נֶפֶשׁ בְּרָכָה, a soul that finds pleasure in blessing, from which accordingly streams of blessing flow.

and, according to Gen. xlviii. 20, only found therein the sense: All nations shall bless themselves in thy name, *i.e.* wish themselves thy good fortune.[1] Thus the niphal is said to be synonymous with the hithpael occurring in like connection in xxii. 18, xxvi. 4,[2] the seed of Abraham or of Isaac, however, standing as the means, whereas the niphal, again, is joined (xviii. 18) with Abraham himself, and (xxviii. 14) with Jacob along with his seed. We are certainly of opinion that the niphal here must have a meaning of its own, distinct from the hithpael.[3] In distinction from the piel (xlviii. 20) and hithpael, it expresses more the objective experience of the divine blessing. Only, even where the hithpael is used, the significant position of the word at the end of the promise requires even there more than a mere ceremonial honour to be meant. The distinction therefore is not material. The act of blessing is no mere formality, for which reason also the name of God or of a man used in it is of high importance. The former shows from whom the highest good is to be expected, the latter in whom it is to be found, and through whose mediation it may be attained. Therefore it is not something trifling that is affirmed, even in the reflexive sense. Not merely will Abraham's good fortune be proverbial throughout the world, but all nations of the earth will see that in Abraham the highest good is to be found; and thus he will be the priestly mediator of salvation between God and the world, since Abraham's blessing will bring to those farthest off the knowledge of the true God, and in praying for such blessing they will use the name of Abraham who prevailed with God. They would not do the latter (hithpael), unless the blessing and virtue of his person and name had been attested to them (niphal).

This promise was ratified to Abraham in important moments of his life. Such a moment, according to chap. xiii., was the agreement with Lot, the progenitor of the Moabites and Ammonites. After the proof of self-denying love of peace given by Abraham, the Lord spoke to him (xiii. 14–17), and assured him that his earthly blessing should not be less on this account,

---

[1] So Raschi (in G. Baur, p. 209), afterwards Clericus, and now the majority (de Wette, Gesenius, Anger, Stähelin, Hitzig, etc.).

[2] Cf. Ps. lxxii. 17.

[3] So also Tuch, G. Baur, Hengstenberg, Keil, Kautzsch, etc.

nay, would be measureless. Here also possession of land and a great posterity are the two chief points in the promise referring to the people of God; save that here the extent of the land is more definitely indicated, and a posterity countless (like the dust of the earth) is predicted for him.

Chap. xv. also, a section somewhat peculiar in the style of its narrative, moves around these two promises. The posterity of Abraham countless (like the stars of heaven) will appear, despite the fact that he has no proper heir; and he will take possession of the land from the brook of Egypt (not the Nile, but the Wadi el Arisch) to the Euphrates (ver. 18 ff.), although as yet he possesses not a foot's-breadth in it, and his posterity must first go into a strange land.

The Elohistic version of the promise given to Abraham is found in xvii. 1 ff., where we at once (despite the יהוה, ver. 1, which must spring from another hand) recognise the narrator, who in Ex. vi. 3 makes God say: And I appeared to Abraham, Isaac, and Jacob as אֵל שַׁדַּי, in the character and with the appellation of the "Almighty God," but in my name יהוה I did not make myself known to them. By the former name He calls himself God in fact: He is God as feared (אלהים, vers. 7, 15, 19, 23) by all nations as the strong One (אֵל); but as the true, alone mighty One, He enters into a special, distinctive relation to Abraham. Here, also, we find the divinely-established covenant בְּרִית,[1] as before in Noah's case (also in the Elohist), ix. 8. But whereas there God's gracious arrangement extends to all mankind, here a portion of mankind is marked off, Abraham and his seed (*i.e.* his posterity). At the same time this posterity is regarded, not under a physical aspect, but as a spiritual whole, and the crude, physical element is to be further sifted and cleansed. Since the race chosen by God is to bear a character correspondingly distinctive, the ברית has here a twofold aspect; it consists first and chiefly in God's choosing for Himself this tribe, and making known the election by His acts of blessing; on the other hand, it is an arrangement by which God determines how the tribe on its part is to give expression to this relation to its God. Accordingly the obligation contained in the terms of the covenant consists in the receiving

---

[1] See p. 93. The covenant-form, however, is not merely Elohistic, but is found most decidedly in a Yahvistic authority, Gen. xv.

of circumcision (ver. 9 ff.), the symbol of the purifying of man's nature from its innate impurity.[1]

The blessings promised to Abraham in this covenant-act are substantially the same as in the passages of the other narrators already discussed. They are, first of all, temporal, earthly blessings, in appearance not essentially different from those enjoyed by other nations. But the peculiarity from the first is this, that Israel owes these blessings to its special relation to the God who made the world. As the goal of God's gracious purpose appears chiefly (as before) the multiplication of Abraham (of which this name itself, a modification of Abram, is a reminder, ver. 5): "And I will make thee very fruitful and multiply thee into nations, and kings shall proceed from thee." Here is not merely the promise of a countless host of descendants (as before), but a number of nationalities and kings is distinguished therein. If this language suggests the thought of all the Arab nations in the line of Keturah (xxv. 1 ff.) and Ishmael, whose progenitor Abraham is, as well as of the Edomites, who according to xxxvi. 31 had kings even before the Israelites, in ver. 16 the horizon in the case of Sarah, to whom (her name also being modified) the like is promised, is narrower. This covenant promise is specialized to the effect that the son of Sarah represents the promised seed, xvii. 19, 21. And in xxxv. 11, in plain allusion to the present chapter, it is said to Jacob: "I am El Shaddai, be fruitful and multiply, a nation and a community of nationalities (קְהַל גּוֹיִם) shall proceed from thee and kings from thy loins." This passage shows, that even in the present chapter the promise refers to the Israelitish complex of nations and its kings; and also in xvii. 7, 8, which passes on to the second part of the promise, viz. the possession of the *land* of Canaan, there can be no doubt on this point. In xvii. 7 the inner nature of this covenant is revealed. The Almighty God will be specifically the Deity of this nation (cf. ver. 8 ff.). He puts Himself in a closer mutual relation to it. Of this the land, which He gives it for a possession, is an outward sign; a second, by which Israel will consecrate itself as God's elect to His service, is the symbol of circumcision, performed on the flesh of all male members of the nation.

This ordinance, like the whole act of the covenant, is expressly

[1] Herzog's *Real-Encyklopädie*, "*Beschneidung.*"

declared to be eternal (ברית עולם). Certainly it would not satisfy the emphasis of the divine saying to regard עולם[1] here simply as a hyperbolical designation of a time of indefinite length. עולם in prophetic speech signifies "long time," as little as אַחֲרִית הַיָּמִים "following time," instead of "final time." Rather it simply negatives the cessation of the covenant. Such cessation is absent from the speaker's as well as the hearer's thought. In the case of a promise or precept the word expresses the divine absoluteness, which pledges itself that its will is no mere momentary one. But of course this will, though not influenced by time, is influenced by the free conduct of man. According to the attitude of the people, the divine covenant is turned into blessing or cursing; it will unfold in unimagined fulness and more pregnant meaning. Unfaithful Israel, just because the covenant remains stedfast, will lose its land; faithful Israel will know its God more perfectly, and lay aside its natural impurity more completely than was done in circumcision. We see here that we ought not mechanically to transfer the initial form of the promise to a quite different stage of the divine economy, and without regard to the specific value of a promise to adhere to a particular chronology. Have we a right, without more ado, to infer from the present passage the future possession of the outward Canaan by Israel, while rejecting the perpetual observance of outward circumcision?

Compare, further, xviii. 18 (Yahvistic): "Since Abraham will certainly become a great and strong nation, and in him all nations of the earth will be blessed" (niph.).

xxii. 16–18: "By myself have I sworn, said the Lord: Because thou hast done this thing and hast not spared thy son, thine own (son), verily I will bless thee and multiply thy seed abundantly as the stars of heaven, and like the sand that is on the sea-shore, and thy seed shall occupy the gate of its foes. And in thy seed all nations of the earth shall bless themselves, because thou didst listen to my voice."

Here also, where the rewarding of Abraham's believing obedience is in question, a posterity countless (like the stars and sand) stands in the first line, and to this its victorious, awe-inspiring position is added. Finally, again, the highest reward of his

[1] Cf. p. 95, *Synonyma der Zeit und Ewigkeit*, p. 74.

trustful surrender to God is, that all nations of the earth will wish themselves the highest good in the name of his posterity. זֶרַע is here also a single, abstract idea, but not a personal one. That is, it is not expressly said that one particular individual among Abraham's descendants will be the channel of blessing to all nations. But if a son of man should discharge this highest function, in accordance with the promise he must be a descendant of Abraham.

In xxvi. 3–6 the entire blessing promised to Abraham is transferred to Isaac, and in xxviii. 13 f. is promised in a dream at Bethel to Jacob. Cf. also xlvi. 1–4, and especially the Elohistic revelation of xxxv. 9 ff.

Whilst the undivided stream of covenant-blessing is thus conducted to Jacob, in whose house it begins to attain its national breadth, the subordinate lines are plainly excluded. Much, indeed, of the blessing bestowed on Abraham passes over to them; but in the covenant proper, and therefore in the covenant land and people, they have no share. Thus in chap. xiii., Lot, the progenitor of Moab and Ammon, voluntarily separates from Abraham, to whom he gladly surrenders the rest of Canaan, choosing the rich Jordan valley. Abraham's son by Hagar, Ishmael, is excluded, not without an important future being assured to him, certainly of a mere earthly, profane kind, xvi. 10 ff. He too is assigned a countless posterity; but instead of being a blessing to all, he is the adversary of all, and of the land of promise he will have as little as he will be an heir of the divine covenant, xvii. 18 ff., xxi. 12. The real spiritual seed of Abraham, according to God's plan, is perpetuated in Isaac.[1] Isaac has two apparently equal sons; although very different individually, they are even twin-brothers. But here it was to be seen how it is God's free choice, following spiritual affinity, not physical descent, that qualifies for the inheritance. As divine appointment from the beginning (cf. xxv. 22 f., the struggle in the womb and the word of the Lord), and human adjustments in keeping with the character of the tribal representatives concerned (cf. xxv. 29 ff., the sale of the birthright-privilege), led to this result, so at last the patriarch, without his own knowledge and will, uttered his decisive oracle, to the effect that to the younger belonged the Promised

---

[1] Cf. xxi. 12: בְּיִצְחָק יִקָּרֵא לְךָ זָרַע.

Land with all its treasures, whereas to the older was left a mere shadow of blessing, in reality no blessing. To the former was also given the rightful dominion, to the latter only the possibility of freeing himself by rude force from the yoke of his heaven-favoured brother, chap. xxvii.

Since we have to do here, not with a new divine institution, but merely with the designation of the true heir to the promises of grace, Jacob is first of all designated by his father's blessing (the testament[1] of Isaac) as the depositary of the covenant-grace and the representative of the covenant-people. This oracle of blessing is diverted by the cunning mother to her favourite, not without deception of the blind father. Thinking that he has Esau before him, whose savoury food stimulates him (as outward things often do, *e.g.* the sound of a name) to prophetic utterance, he exclaims :—

"Behold, the perfume of my son is as the perfume of the field, which Yahveh blessed! God give thee of the dew of heaven and of the fatness of the earth, and fulness of wheat and wine! Let nations serve thee and peoples fall down before thee! Be a commander to thy brethren, and let the sons of thy mother do homage to thee! Cursed be they who curse thee, and blessed they who bless thee!" (xxvii. 27–29).

As the seer's gaze in such oracles rises prophetically above the ordinary horizon, so his language is loftier than usual.[2] The sustained harmony, rising in animation up to the close and culminating in the three pairs of clauses (ver. 29), corresponds to the import of the train of thought which ascends from vivid description of natural blessings to more and more extraordinary glory and distinction. Hence, too, the blessing on Esau, in import so much below this elevation, is far from exhibiting such inspiration of form. The oracle treats substantially of the heirlooms already familiar to us from xii. 2 ff. The land extolled in the present

---

[1] See p. 78.
[2] Cf. ver. 27, the *poetical* רָאָה for הִנֵּה (cf. ver. 39), perhaps also for the sake of the rhythm with רֵיחַ; further שְׁמַנֵּי הָאָרֶץ (pinguedines terræ), only found again in ver. 39, perhaps chosen in this passage also because of the rhythm with הַשָּׁמַיִם; further, הֱוֵה for הְיֵה, and גְּבִיר only here and ver. 37. Whoever objects that it is unusual to poetize in old age and in presence of death is to be pitied, as knowing neither prophecy nor true poetry.

ORELLI. H

passage is undoubtedly Canaan (in opposition to the barren land of the Edomites), which Isaac received from Abraham, although only in ideal possession. That Jacob will become a great nation is not actually said, but is as self-evident as that the description of Esau (ver. 40) applies to the nation springing from him. Only as a nation can he have a land richly blessed for his own, and occupy among the nations a position inspiring fear and respect. The lordship belonging to the covenant nation is emphasized more strongly here than previously (cf. xxii. 17). Although the indefinite עַמִּים וּלְאֻמִּים is not expressly equivalent to כֹּל מִשְׁפְּחֹת הָאֲדָמָה, still it makes Israel lord over the nations surrounding it, even over those of kindred descent (אַחִים). And the concluding sentence shows that the attitude of the nations to Israel will determine God's friendly or hostile attitude to them. What held good of the patriarchs personally (cf. xxvi. 26 ff.), that God would bless their friends and chastise their foes, so that every one courted their favour, was to be extended to the nations who favoured Israel for the sake of its God. Here is seen the objective side expressed in נִבְרְכוּ, and assumed in the hithpael. Respecting the way in which Israel will rule the nations, this glance into its spiritual power and the homage to be done it on that account, gives us at least some intimation.

By this oracle, the grey, blind father has plainly disposed of the entire blessing, one and indivisible, given to Abraham and devolving on himself as its heir by God's appointment. Because inspired by a higher spiritual power, such a blessing once uttered is no longer in the personal power of man to revoke. It is unalterable and irrevocable. This Isaac declares in ver. 33, after he perceives to his terror that a higher will has here crossed his own, and used him as an instrument in an arrangement not according to his own mind. Gladly as he would have done it, he can bequeath to his favourite Esau nothing more of the sacred heritage already disposed of. What he further gives Esau on his importunate urgency, is a mere shadow of the blessing already uttered, unworthy in comparison to be called a blessing:—

"Behold, without[1] fatness of the earth shall be thy dwelling-place, and without dew of heaven from above, and by favour

---

[1] מִן here privative, not partitive.

of [1] thy sword thou shalt live and serve thy brother. And it shall come to pass: as thou roamest there, thou shalt break his yoke from thy neck."

Even the land which Esau inhabits will form a sad contrast to Jacob's blooming fields. In point of fact, the mountain-range of the Edomites is extraordinarily bare and barren. If, then, he is to lack the abundance of the gifts of heaven and earth, which are God's gifts, he still retains his sword with which to make himself a living. Just so he can only win his independence by force; for his normal condition, fixed by God and reason, will be one of subjection to his brother, although, considering his native wildness and irrepressible passion for independence, it may be foreseen that he will break loose from the yoke of one who is his superior in spiritual dignity. What he wins, therefore, he will gain, not by divine right, but by right of might, in opposition to God's legal ordination and expressed will. To this resistance God will allow scope to a certain degree, the consequence of which to Israel will be, that God's people will only be able to maintain its position with trouble and hard conflict. To this extent a shadow rests on Jacob's blessing, and as matter of fact throughout the whole of the ancient history of Israel, Edom embittered the existence of its brother-nation.

§ 15. *The Leading Tribe of Judah (Jacob's Blessing,* Gen. xlix.).

Jacob also makes his testament at the end of his life. He, too, has Canaan to bestow. But in doing this, he does not hand over the land to one individual in unshared possession, while the others, like Ishmael and Esau, go empty away; but Jacob sees in spirit all his twelve sons settled in the land of promise, so familiar to him. We learn from this that the promise is not for the present more precisely defined, but all Jacob-Israel is to share in it. But each one of the twelve sons has a peculiar temperament, from which their father starts in foretelling what position they will take as members of the whole.

Gen. xlix. 1: "And Jacob called his sons and spake: Gather yourselves together, and I will declare to you what will befall YOU AT THE END OF THE DAYS." [2]

---

[1] On thy sword—*i.e.* putting it down as a basis, supported on it.

[2] Respecting this definition of time, see p. 33.

The dying patriarch does not refer his sons indefinitely to "after days" (Herder), but to "the end of the days," *i.e.* to the completion of the stage of development now proceeding. For Jacob the horizon, bounding his field of vision, lies where, according to the promise given him, his posterity has grown into tribes and taken up its abode in the Promised Land; for at this point the idea of the kingdom of God has reached its provisional realization, which again contains germs that ensure a higher development. Moreover, Jacob's blessing contains in the oracle respecting *Judah* a significant blossom that will further unfold itself.

On this point a distinction of rank is to be observed among the sons. One must have the primacy, but which one? According to Gen. xlviii., Joseph, the offspring of the beloved Rachel, the saviour of Jacob's whole family, was distinguished by the patriarch with a special blessing,[1] to the effect that his two sons were to be on a level with the sons of Jacob in the division of the land. The two grandsons are thus in a sense adopted by Jacob, while Joseph is honoured by a double share in the inheritance. On this account it is said in 1 Chron. v. 1, the right of first-born (בְּכֹרָה) passed to Joseph's sons. This can only refer to the double inheritance, for the chronicler adds, Judah became נָגִיד among his brethren, received the supremacy among them. But the supremacy was a chief part of the בְּכֹרָה; here, on the contrary, is meant thereby (as perhaps also in Gen. xxvii. 36) merely the larger (*i.e.* double) possession.

Gen. xlix. shows how Judah attained the leadership, which he possesses even in preference to Joseph, who certainly is called (ver. 26) the most noble (נָזִיר) among his brethren. In age, indeed, Judah is only fourth. But the three preceding him were declared to have lost the birthright by unpardonable transgressions, of which their father must perforce remind them even on his deathbed—Reuben on account of his dishonouring his father's couch (xxxv. 22), Simeon and Levi on account of their outrageous, cunning revenge on the Sichemites (xxxiv. 13 ff.). Instead of the expected special blessing, the eldest received severe rebuke. Jacob does not expressly curse them, but he solemnly

---

[1] xlviii. 14, 17 shows what outward gesture was usual in such patriarchal benedictions: Imposition of hands expressive of transference, which confirms what was said of the meaning of that act.

disavows their thoughts and ways. And now the stream of benediction gushes without check on Judah, who was not indeed without stain (cf. Gen. xxxviii.), but who had shown a noble, energetic character towards his father and brethren (*e.g.* in the history of Joseph), and whose moral energy became the abiding excellence of this tribe.

Israel has no reason for withholding the birthright from Judah. As he mentions his name, its high significance strikes him: He is not called "Praise"[1] in vain, his brethren shall praise him, as once his mother praised the Lord when she bore him (xxix. 35):—

xlix. 8-12: "Judah, verily thee thy brethren shall praise, verily thy hand (shall be) on the neck of thy foes, before
9 thee thy father's sons fall down! A lion's cub is Judah; from ravening, my son, thou hast ascended: he crouched, lay down like a lion, and like the lioness: who can arouse him?
10 The sceptre shall not depart from Judah, nor the general's staff from between his feet, until he come into his own, and
11 nations are subject to him,—who binds his foal to the vine-stem, and to the choice vine his ass's colt. He washed his
12 garments in wine and his apparel in grape-juice, his eyes dark with wine, and his teeth white with milk."

The meaning of the whole oracle is: Thanks to its prowess in offence and defence, Judah will be the real princely tribe, able to maintain its supremacy over its brethren as well as superiority over its foes. Thanks to the terror of its valour, it will enjoy undisturbed a land rich in milk and wine.

Compared with xxvii. 29, ver. 8 shows that Jacob's supremacy is transmitted to Judah. Among the kindred tribes it is the leader, whose moral worth and physical superiority they willingly acknowledge. Prepared for by ver. 8*b*, in ver. 9 the regal lion appears as Judah's emblem. After hunting his prey in the plains, this lion has ascended[2] to his lofty dwelling (alluding to the lofty situation of Judah's territory). There he now settles down comfortably; he knows, however, that no one will venture to disturb him in his rest or dispute his spoil with him. Ver. 10

---

[1] יְהוּדָה, a name formed from the impf. hoph. יָדְךָ also is similar in sound. The expression is taken from a beast of prey, which strikes its claws into the neck of the fleeing prey.

[2] עָלִיתָ, not: thou hast grown up (Luther).

speaks again of Judah's princely function. שֵׁבֶט, sceptre, and מְחֹקֵק, are synonymous; the latter here is not personal: *commander* or *lawgiver* (Hengstenberg), but according to Num. xxi. 18, *commander's staff, general's baton*, which insignia on sitting down are put between the feet.[1]

Leaving aside for a time the disputable words, ver. 10c and 10d, we cannot doubt that vers. 11 and 12 apply to *Judah*, and depict the rich abundance of his land, which he will enjoy as the prize of victory. The image of Judah, given in antique, poetic speech,[2] is in the highest degree picturesque. We see him binding his beast to the vine, which is the blessing of his land. The choice red sap flows for him in such abundance, that he has washed his garments in it, which therefore show the royal purple.[3] Nay, we only need look at him to see the profuse abundance yielded by his land. The dark fire, peculiar to wine, streams from his eyes,[4] the dazzling white of milk from his teeth; so that we see at once with what his land overflows. Wine and milk are so much the special pride and wealth of Judah's territory, otherwise not very fertile, that this characteristic is eminently in place,[5] and no reference of these words to Judah's Egyptian relations[6] is to be thought of. Thus the verses give the impression that Judah will secure rich spoil in lion-like conflict, in order then to enjoy its full possession in unbroken peace. In this connection, the clause עַד כִּי־יָבֹא שִׁילֹה cannot indicate the termination of Judah's influential position, but seems to denote the transition from the conflict for that position to its undisputed possession. But the reading and meaning of the word שִׁילֹה are

---

[1] To interpret with the ancients: "a ruler from thy loins," would be awkward. יָצָא מִבֵּין רַגְלָיִם denotes, indeed, in prosaic speech (Deut. xxviii. 57) the issuing from the mother's womb (cf. *Iliad*, xix. 110); but this local definition nowhere refers to paternal begetting. The Targum has סָפְרָא for מְחֹקֵק: the chancellor sitting at the king's feet.

[2] Cf. the forms אֹסְרִי, בְּנִי, Gesenius, *Gramm.* § 88, 3a; F. W. M. Philippi, *Wesen und Ursprung des Status Constr.* p. 11, 97, 101; further, עִירֹה and כֻּתֹּה, Gesenius, *Gramm.* § 91, n. 2; לְבֹן, § 93, 2. 1.

[3] Cf. Isa. lxiii. 2: blood-red as the colour of wine.

[4] חַכְלִילִי, dark (from חָבַל, to be dark) in the above sense. מִן is not to be taken comparatively in either instance, but states the cause from which his blooming appearance arises.

[5] v. Orelli, *Durch's heilige Land*, 2nd ed. p. 84 f.

[6] So Diestel, *Segen Jacob's*, p. 56.

questionable. As it stands, it seems most natural to take the word as the name of a place, as everywhere else,[1] and to translate: *until he comes to Shiloh*.[2] The "coming to Shiloh" would then denote the end of the journeying and conquest, during which Judah had held the leadership. Now in point of fact it is said in Josh. xviii. 1: "And the whole congregation of the children of Israel assembled together at Shiloh, and set up the tabernacle there; and the land was subdued before them." According to Delitzsch, the passage forms "a boundary-line between two periods in Israel's history." At that time, indeed, the conflict was not yet fought out, and Judah's championship was still only to begin in the true sense (Judg. i. 1). But the period of the great march in common was in fact concluded.

We confess, however, that this interpretation little contents us. Apart from the fact that, although the tribe of Judah led the van in conflict during the desert-march (Num. ii.), the sceptre and staff of command were quite wanting to it,—the tribe had no special relation to Shiloh; it did not there bind its foal to the vine; nor did it there receive any homage, either from the other tribes or from foreign peoples. The mention of this place therefore remains in any case enigmatical. But although one might accept under pressure the explanation given by Delitzsch, namely, that the aged Jacob in spirit saw Shiloh, known to him by name, as the resting-place of his people; on the other hand, from the "critical" point of view which makes these oracles later compositions formed in the time of the Judges or Kings out of history,[3] no reason is conceivable why the arrival at Shiloh should be regarded as the *terminus ad quem* of Judah's leadership! This long-past epoch could in no way be regarded as the satisfying conclusion "at the end of the days."

The embarrassment of the critics next led to a desperate "stroke of perplexity," as Diestel rightly calls it, first made by Hitzig,[4] and confidently repeated by Bleek, Tuch, Maurer, G. Baur, etc. עד כי is said here to mean, not "until," but "*as long as*" they come to Shiloh, which, spoken at a time when men resorted to

---

[1] Shiloh is the central place, where under Joshua the tabernacle was set up.
[2] Ibn Ezra, Teller, Herder, Rosenmüller, Eichhorn, Tuch, Ewald, Rödiger, Delitzsch, Diestel, *et al.*
[3] See p. 81.
[4] *Die Psalmen*, 1836, ii. p. 2, note; *Biblische Theologie*, 153.

God's tabernacle there, is said to signify: *for ever!* That עַד properly denotes "continuance of something," and hence may on occasion correspond to our "as long as,"[1] must be conceded. עַד כִּי certainly is never so found, and עַד שֶׁ־ (Sol. Song i. 12) cannot be quoted for the above interpretation. That parallel would rather require the interpretation: "as long as he shall be on the point of coming to Shiloh" (and therefore found on the way thither), which would give substantially the usual sense, but not: "as long as one usually comes thither." Moreover, that the latter was a proverbial phrase for perpetual duration, is preposterous. The tabernacle stood far too short a time in Shiloh to allow such an idiom to arise; in the thoughts of the Israelites its stay there was always something provisional; else the abode of the sanctuary would not have been changed without necessity.

But an important circumstance is that the form שִׁילֹה is relatively recent, and in any case שלה stood previously. It is true the name Shiloh was very frequently written defectively, but the word was early read differently. LXX., Aq., Symm., Pesch., Onk., Saady., read אֲשֶׁר לוֹ=שֶׁלֹּה=שִׁילֹה, which the majority took personally: He to whom it belongs, namely, the sceptre, the rule. Here Jews as well as Christians thought of the Messiah. Nay, to all appearance even Ezekiel took the שלה personally, and, indeed, of the Messiah. In xxi. 32, where the words עַד־בֹּא אֲשֶׁר־לוֹ הַמִּשְׁפָּט recall the phrase in question, he is referring to the time of redemption.[2]

Linguistically this translation is possible,[3] although very pregnant; theologically, not impossible. Let it not be said that such a sudden emergence of a future holder of national rule from the tribe of Judah goes beyond the limits of prophecy. These limits are not to be fixed on rationalistic principles. For the rest, the rationalizing view always has the resource of making the saying to have been spoken after David, to whom it would refer in the first case.[4] Unfavourable, on the other hand, to such

---

[1] Cf. in Latin *donec eris felix*, etc.
[2] Cf. Smend, *Commentar zu Ezech.* p. 147.
[3] שֶׁ־ for אֲשֶׁר is found in all periods of Hebrew literature, nor can it be maintained that it occurs merely in sections belonging to North Palestine. Cf. Judg. v. 7; Sol. Song i. 7; and also Gen. vi. 3; Job xix. 29.
[4] So Wellhausen, *Geschichte*, i. 375. He (and after him Stade, *Gesch.* i. 160)

an intrusion of a ruler into the general tribal blessing, is the fact that his relation to the tribe would not be indicated. True, the whole style of the oracle does not suggest that Judah's greatness is to come to an end with the coming of a greater ruler, but the עד כי points to the culmination and full realization of Judah's dignity as ruler. But one would then expect some such words as עד כי יצא מִמֶּנוּ שָׁלוֹ. Add to this, that the following words (ver. 11), depicting Judah's peaceful prosperity, only follow naturally, provided he is the subject in what precedes and וְלוֹ יִקְּהַת' applies to him.

These objections apply also, in all their weight, to every interpretation that would stamp the word שילה in any other way as a name of the Messiah. Not to speak of the rendering *qui mittendus est* (Jerome), which takes שָׁלַח as the root, שילה, derived from שָׁלָה, is said as a proper name to signify *rest-bringer, rich in peace* (Hengstenberg). At all events this is better than to take the word with the same derivation appellatively: *until rest comes;* or *until he comes to rest* (Kurtz, Hofmann)—which indeed would be very suitable to the context, but is forbidden by the fact that no formations of appellative nouns of this kind from verbs ל"ה or ע"י (שׁגּל) occur. On the other hand, the local name שילה (place of rest), shortened from שָׁלְמֹה,[1] שִׁילֹה from שָׁלְמוֹן, are found. As to form, therefore, it might in the present passage be a *nomen proprium* of a prince in a symbolic sense; but the context, as remarked before, is against this. Ver. 11 was only interpreted of the Messiah by means of such artificial allegorizing as robbed the forceful description of its meaning.[2]

The context on one hand, the oldest authorities in respect of the reading[3] on the other, conduct us to our translation. שֶׁלֹּה was the reading handed down from antiquity, and the LXX. render this neutrally: ἕως ἂν ἔλθῃ τὰ ἀποκείμενα αὐτῷ.[4] Instead of this abstract neuter subject we take the personal

---

would expunge וְלוֹ, thus spoiling the entire beautiful rhythm of the oracle. Also his critical attack on ver. 10 is no permissible means of escape from an exegetical difficulty awaiting investigation.

[1] Cf. Stade, *Hebr. Gramm.* i. p. 177.

[2] Clemens Alexandrinus applied the vine to the Logos, the ass to the nation. The washing of the garment in the blood of the grape required a reference to the suffering of Christ. [3] Ezekiel, LXX.

[4] According to a weakly attested reading, ᾧ ἀπόκειται, like the other versions in a personal sense.

subject predominating everywhere here, and render: *until he come into that which belongs to him*, therefore *into his own*, his possession described in the sequel. Cf. especially the blessing of Moses on Judah, Deut. xxxiii. 7 : וְאֶל־עַמּוֹ תְּבִיאֶנּוּ. As champion of the other tribes, he will display untiring energy until he has won his territory without curtailment ; and then not merely will the tribes of Israel do homage to him, but other nations also will bow to his rule. For the וְלוֹ יִקְּהַת עַמִּים¹ cannot apply to the Israelites merely, who already always followed Judah's sceptre and staff, but must refer to the more general national rule, which according to xxvii. 29 is part of Jacob's heritage, and will be Judah's special portion.

What then is the import of this oracle of blessing and prophecy respecting Judah ? At all events, according to the entire Jacob-blessing, the promise received by this progenitor passes in a certain degree to all his sons, who are to dwell together as brethren under the one God of their father (cf. xlix. 24, 25) in the Promised Land. But they need a leader, to whom they will willingly bow and the nations must perforce submit; and this leader, this head, will be *Judah*. To him therefore the quintessence of the blessing falls. As the land designed for him brings forth the noblest and richest fruit, the royal vine, so he himself is comparable in lofty energy to the royal lion, and as such he will bear the sceptre. Here plainly (whether שִׁילֹה or שֶׁלֹּה be read) two stages are distinguished in Judah's future, a stage of conflict and one of peace. In the conflict for the attainment of his high destiny he will be the resistless conqueror, in peace the ruler unsurpassed in glory. That a definite person is announced here as the perfecter of this victorious conflict or as prince of peace, we have not been able to find in the course of our exposition. But should one individual as Israel's chief lead it to final victory and peace, he must belong, according to the present passage, to the tribe of Judah.

History has brought the *fulfilment*. Not only was Judah in the van on the desert-march, not only was he the unwearied

---

¹ יִקְּהָה (still only stat. constr.) with dagesh dirimens, from יָקָה, after the Arabic وَقَهَ, وَقِهَةٌ, *to obey, obedience*. Jerome translates : "et ipse erit expectatio gentium," as though it were connected with קָוָה.

champion of the rest in the conquest of the land, but in other ways also he showed his lion-like superiority. The age of greatest triumph and glory was ushered in by David, the Judæan, when he assumed the sceptre and staff, which were no more to depart from his house, and went up in lion-like style to Jerusalem. Who is not reminded by the calmly couching lion of Solomon, under whom followed the most peaceful epoch of abundant prosperity as under a true שְׁלֹמֹה, Prince of Peace? This was the climax of Israelitish national life. The ideal, however, was not reached then, and still less afterwards. On this account prophecy speaks again and again of a new setting up of the tabernacle of David (Amos ix. 11), of a future David, to whom it belongs to administer the law (Ezek. xxxiv. 23), who will subjugate all nations and bring in eternal peace. This king will enter Zion riding on the animal of peace (Zech. ix. 9); and under him men will enjoy the abundance of the land undisturbed, sitting under their own vine and fig-tree (Joel iv. 18; Micah iv. 4, etc.). Not the least significant echoes of the present oracle are found in Isaiah, the prophet from Judah, a circumstance to which Herder has alluded.[1] The final fulfilment of this patriarchal saying we can only find, with the apostolic Church (Rev. v. 5), in Christ, who has overcome as "the lion of the tribe of Judah," and now extends His kingdom in undisturbed peace, and rejoices in its glory.

If we look back on the oracles contained in this and the previous paragraph, they all point to a concrete establishment of God's kingdom on earth. The seed (*i.e.* the posterity) of Abraham, set apart spiritually by divine election of grace, is to live in Canaan as the people of the true God, and so to form the centre of the world, this people being the medium of divine blessing to all peoples. The concrete form must not offhand be declared non-essential, as is done by Hengstenberg,[2] who finds in the call of Abraham nothing essentially different from what occurs in every divine call imposing self-denial on man. Little as we would deny that general rules of divine ethics and pædagogy are contained even in this history and its words of promise, still the significance of these events is not exhausted therein. It is a special design that God has in view in His dealings with this race, a unique relation into which He will enter

[1] *Briefe über das Studium der Theologie*, 1 Br. 5.   [2] *Christology*, i. 47.

with *this* people. Not merely will He enter into a peculiar spiritual relation to it, but its outward existence, its outward abode in the land of Canaan, will be a fruit of this covenant-relation. These externalities therefore are essential, inseparable from the spiritual. Here the bases are laid for a divine kingdom that is to have outward existence, as indeed its history is in fact confined, up to the end of the Old Testament, to the limits of one nation and bound to a definite territory. Hence the outward realization of this kingdom appears in these earliest oracles not as a mere means, but as an end and goal.

There shall be a people of the Lord, chosen by God's grace to be a blessing also to others. This conception would be of high significance even if we learned it as a divine thought first from its realization. But according to the many-voiced witness of tradition, it was not merely in God's counsel before its realization, but was known to men through divine revelation. The forefathers of the nation, who migrated from the east to Canaan and dwelt there as strangers amid many vicissitudes, obeyed on that journeying a higher voice, and during the sojourn on foreign soil were assured by the same voice of a future, when they should not only possess this land, but also in consequence of their unique relation to God occupy an extraordinary position in the world of nations. Thus they obtained in spirit a glimpse into the consummation of the divine work just then beginning. To this John viii. 56 alludes: Ἀβραὰμ ὁ πατὴρ ὑμῶν ἠγαλλιάσατο ἵνα ἴδῃ τὸν ἡμέραν τὴν ἐμήν, καὶ εἶδεν καὶ ἐχάρη. In genuine Johannine style the words rise to a climax: he exulted that he should see — he actually saw and rejoiced in it. What, according to the promise, he rejoiced in as future, nay, what the promise made present and visible to him, was in reality nothing but the day of Christ. Accordingly, what is meant is not a seeing with bodily eyes, as if the saying referred specifically to the birth of Isaac (von Hofmann), nor a seeing after Abraham's bodily life, but a glimpse of faith that gladdened Abraham. What he beheld present with this eye of the spirit, was the Day of Christ, *regnum Christi*, as Calvin interprets the passage. For in point of fact only through the coming of this kingdom did the gracious covenant with Abraham gain its true realization and completion, the Lord not allowing it to fall to the ground even through the unfaithfulness of His people (2 Kings xiii. 23).

SECOND SECTION.

MOSAISM.

§ 16. *The Law of Moses.*

AS we found that divine promise heralded the origin of a divine rule on earth, so now also a prophetic word brought about its realization, nay, begot the national kingdom of God. For *Moses*, the mediator of this covenant between God and the nation, was himself a prophet and a prophet first of all,[1] *i.e.* an organ of divine revelation in the sense stated in the Introduction (p. 4). If that covenant-transaction, along with the redemption of the nation preceding it, was really effected by a single person divinely called and illumined, then as matter of fact prophecy formed the beginning. "In the beginning was the Word" is true here also—the Word of God to an individual, and through him to the multitude. But in this potent beginning of the work of establishing the kingdom of God the creative act was joined with the word.

In word and deed Moses showed himself an instrument of the Lord, unapproached by any other. He was the prophet without rival in respect of his intercourse with God and of what the Lord did and revealed by him. Of Moses it is said more frequently than of all other prophets together: "God talked with him," or "God spake to him." He is not only called עֶבֶד יהוה, "Servant of the Lord,"—and, indeed, most frequently of all the men of God in the Old Testament,—and עבד אלהים, "Servant of God," a designation used of him exclusively;[2] but he is also called נָבִיא κατ' ἐξοχήν, the greatest among the

---

[1] Cf. Ewald, *History of Israel*, ii. 47: "He was indeed leader, lawgiver, and worker of miracles to his people, but all these additional attributes fade before the primary one of prophet; only as a prophet was he leader, lawgiver, and worker of miracles, and all his greatness belongs to him as a prophet alone."

[2] Cf. Knobel, *Prophetismus der Hebräer*, ii. 2. Herzog's *Real-Encyk.*, art. "Mose."

prophets on account of the intimacy and familiarity of the intercourse he enjoyed with God, and on account of the clear directness which in consequence distinguished the revelation given to him.[1] Moreover, his mission consisted, not merely in being a channel of the divine word, but in a unique, creative work—it was Moses who, through the divine word, introduced the divine rule in Israel.

The condition and means of this instituting of the theocracy was the deliverance of Israel from Egypt. This deliverance was accomplished through Moses the prophet. "By a prophet (נביא) Yahveh brought Israel out of Egypt, and by a prophet was it preserved," says Hos. xii. 13. Moses possessed no title to which he could appeal, before the heads of the people sojourning and enslaved in Egypt, but his divine call, the special revelation of the holy God imparted to him on the Sinaitic peninsula. By this divine word, attended with signs, he then set free his people. And when it was set free, he led it by that word and arranged its constitution.

Thenceforward the calling of the people was to serve the God who had appeared to Moses. Before this people He called Himself יהוה,[2] announcing Himself, indeed, as the same who appeared to the patriarchs—Abraham, Isaac, Jacob, but at the same time proclaiming a new name, which disclosed his nature on a new side and with greater depth, and was destined to be a sacred motto for the divine kingdom, whose first form was now seen in actual existence, Ex. vi. 3. It is true, certain traces are discernible, from which we might gather that the name יהוה was used even before Moses.[3] The Yahvist also says (Gen. iv. 26) that even in the time of Enoch men began to call on the name of Yahveh, which, of course, is not to be understood strictly of the name as such, since the Hebrew language did not then exist. The same applies to Gen. ix. 26. In order to reconcile the pre-Mosaic use of that divine name with Ex. vi. 3, the passage has not seldom been interpreted: "As to my name יהוה I was not made known to them," means, "As to the import of this name I did not reveal myself to them."[4] We adhere to the more natural exposition,

---

[1] Num. xii. 6 ff.; Deut. xxxiv. 10 ff.   [2] Cf. p. 98.

[3] Cf. the name of the mother of Moses יוֹכֶבֶד, which, if the analogy of so many other names is decisive, would be compounded of יהוה. But is it really older than the Mosaic revelation?

[4] Hence we might attempt to understand the name in the hiphil sense: *He who*

and believe that here we have a thoroughly exact tradition of the Elohist. Whilst the Yahvist, without hesitation, uses the name of the holy covenant-God from the time of the Creation, in which he is justified by the intrinsic unity of that God with the Creator (אלהים) or the mighty God (אל שדי), the other narrator uses the specifically theocratic name only from the point where it passes into the speech of his nation.

The name יהוה, with its explanation אֶהְיֶה אֲשֶׁר אֶהְיֶה, is certainly more pregnant in meaning than any to be found in any other language. Hereupon those who will endure nothing uncommon in the Bible, nothing towering above the "level of development" prescribed by them to the sacred history, at once reject the authentic interpretation and degrade the alone possessor of true being to a "Creator." But they do not in this way explain the other phrases moving on just the same height, such as Ex. iii. 14, a wonderful passage, considering how little gifted the Hebrews were in philosophy, and how plainly the thought here comes out, that the nature of God strictly taken can only be expressed by itself, every other definition detracting from it. There are other passages where God is called "He" simply, for the same reason.[1] It is poor comfort to the anxious worshipper of the development-process to say that these reflections were first made subsequently, an assumption incapable of proof, and which fails to explain the chief matter.

For the rest, we do not hold it altogether impossible that the form יהוה was introduced among the Israelitish people by Moses's mediation from the wisdom of the Egyptians.[2] Brugsch has found in Egyptian writings the formally analogous designation of the Deity, "nuk pu nuk"—"I am I" (*Die aegyptische Gräberwelt*, 1868, p. 38).

Such a formal borrowing in the history of revelation need not surprise us. If Egypt (of course not Hamitic, but Shemitico-

---

calls into existence, namely, what he has said; therefore the God who fulfils His word. But, as remarked above (p. 98), this interpretation is impossible; אהיה אשר אהיה can under no circumstances be read as hiphil.

[1] Deut. xxxii. 39; Isa. xliii. 10.

[2] Wellhausen and Stade certainly speak very slightingly of this supposition, which would show the Elohist to be specially trustworthy. But, to say the least, it is more justifiable scientifically than the arbitrary assertion of Stade, that Moses introduced among the Israelites the Kenite worship of Yahveh (*Geschichte Israels*, i. 2, 129 ff.).

Japhetic Egypt) coined for the revelation of the New Covenant the most adequate expression, of which John's Gospel first discerned the true application, is the evangelist on this account less original? At all events the word λόγος received its true import, not from Philo, but through the revelation of Christ. So the Egyptian formula, describing the Deity as the absolutely existing One, is only a shadow; Moses beheld the living God, the God to whom alone the name really belongs, seeing that He alone is a supernatural, absolutely sovereign Being.

Moreover, the God of the Egyptian priests was a mere abstraction, a theoretical notion. Moses beheld the absolute God as living—absolute, not merely in His metaphysical being, but just as much in His holiness; and to bring God into the life of His people was the aim of his whole work. The knowledge of the true Deity was not to be the secret treasure of a caste, but the common treasure of the whole nation; and not a mere theoretical possession, but the centre of all life. As Yahveh was to belong to this people, so this people was to belong only and wholly to Him, Ex. vi. 7.

The relation of possession, in which Israel stands to God, is described as one of childship, *sonship*, Deut. xxxii. 6. More precisely Israel is called significantly God's first-born son (Ex. iv. 22), which implies two things, God's universal proprietary right (the lofty significance of the word protesting already against the conception of God as a particularistic God), and His provisional, special appropriation of this people. But as God's property the nation is bound to *serve* Him. And because its king is God, the nation's service must be a *priestly* one, its character *holy*, Ex. xix. 6. How it was to be moulded after God's will, the law of Moses teaches.

Think as we may of the origin of the Torah in its present written form, it is impossible to deny that the nation always regarded the exodus from Egypt under Moses's divine leading as its birth-hour,[1] that in the covenant at Sinai it always saw the climax of divine revelation,[2] and gloried in having received through Moses's mediation a divine law (תּוֹרָה).[3] It is true that

---

[1] Ex. xv. 13, xx. 2; Hos. xi. 1, xii. 13; Mic. vi. 4; Jer. ii. 6 f.; cf. Deut. xvi. 1, etc.
[2] Judg. v. 4 f.; Deut. xxxiii. 2; Ps. lxviii. 7 f.; Hab. iii. 3, etc.
[3] Deut. xxxiii. 4; Mal. iv. 4.

originally תּוֹרָה has somewhat less of a juristic sense than our "law." The word signifies instruction generally. So in the Chokma literature it is used of general moral rule and discipline, Prov. vi. 23, xxviii. 4, 7, 9, etc. But in the theocratic sphere it always applies to a revelation of the divine will in the form of a norm and permanent rule. As sovereign, God is also lawgiver of His people. Hence the Torah is the theocracy in practice; it appears claiming immediate observance. It demands obedience from every individual, because the entire nation is subject to it à priori. Hence the legal character of this revelation. Moreover, its claims cover the entire life of the nation, putting everything in relation to the will of God. On this account, beside intrinsically ethical precepts there are found ordinances of civil and criminal justice, beside ritual laws those relating to public policy or domestic custom.[1] Precisely in the fact of its affecting the entire life, private as well as national, civic as well as religious, the character of the Torah is seen as a revelation of the ruling will of Yahveh, to whom everything relating to His people is to be subject.

Certainly in different parts of the legislation of the Pentateuch, now the ethical, then the juristic, again the ceremonial, character predominates; but this distinction is not absolute. Even the covenant-book, Ex. xx.–xxiii. 33, usually regarded as the oldest part, contains laws of each of the kinds mentioned. And just because the primal, fundamental law, that gave shape to the holy nation in every direction, sprang from Moses, no law whatever could afterwards be proclaimed in any other name than that of Moses. But Moses was simply the mediator, speaking in the name of the covenant-God.

Thus Mosaism exhibits an epoch-making advance in the development of the *kingdom of God*. The covenant made with the patriarchs is now, after the latter in accordance with the promise have grown into a numerous people, made in national form. Herewith the divine rule is seen in actual existence for the first time, since the whole life of Israel, so far as it is governed by the divine Torah, bears witness that Israel is God's

---

[1] Herzog, vii. 171. A particular Levitical direction is called תורה (Lev. vii. 37, xiv. 54; Hag. ii. 11, etc.; also the king's law, Deut. xvii. 18 f.) in the above sense, just in the same way as the whole Mosaic law with its general ethical principles (Ps. lxxviii. 5; Deut. i. 5, xxxiii. 4; 2 Chron. xv. 3, etc.).

people, and Yahveh is its God. The relation of the Lord to a national commonwealth necessarily found expression in more precise definition of holy places, times, persons, actions. In this externality lay a great defect. But so far as the divine rule appeared in a mighty, comprehensive, though still imperfect realization, Mosaism, which brought a nation under the rule of the true God, is the type of the future subjection of the world to God's kingdom.

§ 17. *Mosaic Outlooks.*

Through the covenant transaction at Sinai and the Mosaic law-giving, the divine rule entered on a state of direct, present existence. On this account references to the future retire into the background. The significance of Moses lay, not in prediction, but in exhibiting in preliminary form God's perfect kingdom. On this account we find scarcely any oracles of the future ascribed to him, the friend of God, except such as related to the conquest of Canaan immediately impending, and the arrangements to be made there. Even the song of Moses (Deut. xxxii.), echoes of which are heard throughout subsequent prophecy, has to do rather with the future issues of the Mosaic covenant, which despite all interruptions by the nation's disobedience will be indestructible. This is also evident from Lev. xxvi. 40 ff., Deut. xxx. 1 ff., where certainly repentance always appears as the condition of salvation. But nothing is said here of a perfecting of the covenant in after times. Almost the only respect in which the blessing of Moses (Deut. xxxiii.) adds to the picture beheld by Jacob (Gen. xlix.) is in the new lustre to be added to the priestly tribe of Levi. Only cursorily does the divine saying in Num. xiv. 21 open the prospect of the whole earth being filled with the glory of Yahveh, *i.e.* of the whole human world acknowledging Him, and so being incorporated in His kingdom. This thought, indeed, is a noteworthy index of the wide aim which the Lord set Himself. As Lord of heaven and earth He could have no other. But for the time the central-point of the sacred cause lies in the present work of revelation, the institution of the "royal priesthood."

Certainly the Mosaic form of the Church and of its intercourse with God greatly needed spiritualizing and perfecting, and so points to the future. Much in it is mere shadow, and seems to us at first sight essentially precarious, only intelligible as a means of setting forth an idea to be realized more perfectly afterwards. But in transporting ourselves back to that historical period we are not to suppose this reference to the future to be known. No single appointment of the Mosaic law is explicitly of a mere provisional character; they are ordinances eternally valid, belonging as they do to divine revelation. No detail of the cultus is ordained primarily as a mere symbolic sign; rather form and idea are not yet separated, they condition each other. This entire system is indeed typical, but it is not felt meantime to be a mere type of God's final kingdom on earth, but is contemplated as the intended form of His kingdom.

Therefore, however rich in meaning the system of symbols and types in the forms of life and worship established by Moses,[1] we must not, wherever the future has brought a greater perfection of what is here aimed at, ascribe offhand to Moses and his age a conscious reference to the future. For example, that the expiation of human sin is not accomplished satisfactorily by animal sacrifice, was for the time hidden from consciousness.[2] Expiation was really viewed as a fruit of these sacrifices. Also, the extension of God's kingdom over the whole earth at first fell into the background, men's minds being dominated by the actuality of the kingdom then existing. That the law could not permanently unite God and man in covenant, was not yet perceived. Rather in it was recognised the only sure bond between God and every Israelite. We must therefore guard against ascribing to Mosaism the conscious possession of what it carried in its bosom. Certain as it was that Mosaic law owed its origin to a higher, superhuman Spirit, man's spirit was not yet complete master of the divine truths deposited therein, and hence at first was scarcely conscious to itself of the inadequacy of the actuality.

It is, however, significant that the legally-ordained theocracy did not remain without an organ for its further development and transformation, nay, was possessed of power to entirely recreate itself. The prophecy that had given birth to Mosaism was still to remain a precious prerogative of God's people; its original intercourse with its Lord was never to end. If Moses himself did

[1] Cf. p. 38.
[2] Certainly the inadequacy is already intimated in the נָתַתִּי, Lev. xvii. 11, which expresses condescension on God's part.

not edit the law found in Deut. xviii. 15 ff., it was at least spoken quite in the spirit of Mosaism. After necromancy, divination, and the like have been strictly forbidden, it is there said: "Yahveh, thy God, has not so allowed thee. Rather a *prophet*, of thy brethren, like to me will Yahveh, thy God, raise up to thee out of thy midst. Him ye shall hear."

The early Christian Church (except Origen) found in this oracle a direct, personal Messianic prediction. So Justin M., Tertullian, Athanasius, Eusebius, Augustine, followed by Luther also and most of the older Protestants (not Calvin, however). The New Testament itself shows that in the days of Jesus the coming of a prophet of extraordinary greatness was expected on the basis of this passage, who, however, as a rule was *not* identified with the Messiah, John i. 21, vii. 40. According to John iv. 25, the Samaritans expected from the Messiah prophetic disclosures, and since they relied on the Pentateuch only, it is probable that this expectation depended chiefly on the present passage. (Soon after the destruction of Jerusalem the sectarian leader Dositheus gave himself out as the prophet promised in Deut. xviii. 18.) Hengstenberg collects a number of sayings, according to which Jesus professed to be this prophet, John v. 45–47, vers. 38, 43; John xii. 48–50; in the same way testimonies of the apostles in this sense, Acts iii. 22 f., vii. 37. To this Hofmann skilfully replies:[1] In John v. 46 the Lord does not mean a particular passage in the Torah, but the whole of it; what Moses wrote is a prophecy of Him, and whoever really believed in this prophecy would believe in Him in whom it was fulfilled. In Peter's discourse, Hofmann continues, vers. 22 and 23 are not Moses's testimony concerning the Messiah alongside that of the other prophets, but Moses's testimony to the prophets, to whose message a hearing is due. Finally, Stephen rebukes disobedience to the prophets who were commended by Moses.

Although there may be difference of opinion respecting the use made by Jesus and the apostles of this saying, there can be no doubt that the exegetical interpretation of Deut. xviii. 15 endorsed by Hofmann is the only right one. If the personal Messiah were here predicted, it would be strange for Moses to describe Him as like himself. Was not the Messiah to be greater than he? It may be said: The reference is to the special pre-

---

[1] *Schriftbeweis*, ii. 1, 138 ff.

rogative of the Messiah — like Moses as mediator of a new covenant; but according to the context the כָּמֹנִי applies not so much to the rank as to the nature of the divine revelation; it more precisely defines the prophet as such, in opposition to magicians and necromancers. And if we include the sequel, where the criteria are given for distinguishing true from false prophets, it is evident that the subject is just as little a single prophet as in the law of the king in Deut. xvii. the subject is a single king. It is out of the question to take the נביא as a collective,—nowhere is it joined with the plural,—rather it refers to the particular prophet whom the Lord will raise up from time to time, and thus indicates the Lord's ordinary mode of revelation. That according to later predictions[1] the Messiah will appear as prophet is true; but in the present passage the prophet does not yet figure as Messiah, and no one definite prophet is meant (note A).

Consequently the significance of this passage lies in the advance of divine revelation being foreseen, nay, certainly affirmed, by Mosaism; so that the theocracy was not to remain limited to laws of rigid finality, but living intercourse between the Lord and His Church was to continue. But here attention is directed more to the blessings of the present than to the greater blessings of the future.

Nevertheless we cannot get rid of the impression, that the apostolic citations (Acts iii. 22 f., vii. 37) really understood this προφήτης in the individual sense; and perhaps John v. 46 also refers specifically to the present passage. This application is explicable partly from the current acceptation of that age, which looked for a definite, extraordinary prophet, and therefore came prepared with this personal explanation; partly from the principles laid down respecting the relation of prophecy and fulfilment in the Introduction, p. 55, 59. The Lord was fully justified in describing Himself as the Fulfiller of the saying of Moses, because in Him the revelation announced by Moses culminated; and the apostles had the more reason to appeal to the passage, because many were startled by the appearance of their Master being more of a prophetic than kingly hue.

[1] Especially Deutero-Isaiah, where, however, the personal union between the Davidic King and the prophetic Servant of the Lord is scarcely present to consciousness.

NOTE A.—As a parallel to this oracle of Moses, Ed. Müller (*Parallelen zu den Messianischen Weissagungen*, p. 7) adduces the presentiment of Socrates, to the effect (*Apology*, c. 18) that after his death the Deity would send the Athenians another teacher to rouse them from slumber. But, to say nothing of the profound difference between the sage with his stimulating, disturbing influence on commonplace natures and the prophetic dispenser of divine utterances, there is a vast interval, felt also by the author, between the confident promise of Moses and the altogether hypothetical prospect sketched by Socrates as scarcely probable, since he rather impresses the Athenians with the idea that they will hardly again obtain another like him.

§ 18. *Balaam's Oracles.*

Whereas elsewhere in the Mosaic age the prophetic spirit was more occupied with organizing the actual theocracy than with looking forward to an ideal future, one oracle has come down from that age, which, falling from the lips of a stranger, is well adapted to make us feel the glory of the theocracy, and at the same time give a glimpse into its future; it belongs to the last days of the desert-march. Resting from its victory over the powerful Amorites, Israel encamps in the fields of Moab over against Jericho, but according to divine direction (Deut. ii. 9) without encroaching at all on that people. However, Balak, son of Zippor, is uneasy at seeing these strange guests on his soil. He is sensible of a divine superiority in them, and knows not how to deal with it. The Midianites, who are on good terms with him, advise him, as it seems, to paralyse this divine power by demonic might. *Balaam*, son of Beor,[1] a sorcerer dwelling on the Euphrates, and, according to Num. xxxi. 8, in alliance with the Midianites, credited, moreover, with the power to bless and curse effectually, is summoned by the Midianites from his home to render the divine strength harmless by the ban of his sorcery. But although this man, dwelling in the native home of magic, does not disclaim the heathen arts of the soothsayer,[2] still he has long been acquainted with the power of Yahveh,[3] and anxiously avoids opposing it; on the

---

[1] Num. xxii. 2 ff.; cf. Deut. xxiii. 4 ff.
[2] Josh. xiii. 22: הקוסם; cf. p. 16.
[3] Num. xxii. 8, 13. He even calls Him with ostentation יהוה אלהי; neverthe-

other hand, he is reluctant to forego the rewards of the king of Moab. This inner contradiction having come to light in a characteristic way, he so acts that in the moment when he is about to utter the curse agreed on, the Spirit of the Lord comes upon him and changes his curse into blessing.

FIRST ORACLE OF BALAAM, Num. xxiii. 7–10.

"And he lifted up his oracle (note A), and said:

From Aram Balak brings me, — Moab's king from the mountains of the East:

Go, curse me Jacob — and go, to chide Israel.

How should I curse him whom God does not curse — and how chide him whom Yahveh does not chide?

For from the summit of the rocks I see him — and from the heights I perceive him:

Behold a nation that shall dwell by itself alone — and among the nations is not reckoned.

Who counts the dust of Yakob — and reckons up[1] the fourth part of Israel?

Let my soul die the death of the just — and let my end be like his!"

The nation which he is forbidden to injure by a higher power than that of Balak, whom he would fain please, will "dwell apart" and not let itself be numbered among the other nations. This concrete expression speaks, in the first place, of its isolated abode; but the separate spiritual position, of which the former is merely the outward side, is forthwith emphasized: In virtue of its peculiar character, Israel will not be ranked among the other nations. This is the first feature which the clear-eyed heathen finds strange in it—a feature remaining peculiar to Israel still. On the inner excellency that makes this isolation a distinction this first oracle does not yet touch. On the contrary, in ver. 10a it mentions a second outward excellency, which every heathen nation would envy Israel—its immense numbers, which means, of course, not the numbers of the people at present encamped in the desert, which it needed no seer to estimate, but the far greater increase awaiting it in the future. These numbers

---

less his business falls under the ban, Deut. xviii. 10, just because it was a business. A similar divided state of heart is seen in Simon Magus, Acts viii. Cf Hengstenberg, *Geschichte Bileams*, p. 15.

[1] Instead of וּמִסְפָּר read וּמְסַפֵּר, or better וּמִי סָפַר.

are expressed by a metaphor used already in the patriarchal promise (Gen. xiii. 16), but without verbal reference to that passage.

Ver. 10*b* gives a first example of a heathen blessing himself by this nation, *i.e.* wishing himself the prosperity and salvation peculiar to the nation in virtue of its special relation to God, who rewards pious, sincere service, in life and in death.[1]

Oehler observes:[2] "And just as little is Num. xxiii. 10, 'Let my soul die the death of the righteous,' a testimony to belief in eternal life (for which the passage was formerly often taken). The meaning of these words is rather that Balaam wishes he might be allowed to die after a life as richly blessed as was the case with the righteous in Israel." This explanation, however, is not just to the literal meaning, which lays the chief stress on the manner of dying, nay, is quite silent about the blessings of life, supposed by Oehler to be chief. Rather the speaker is here thinking of his soul's welfare, and can wish nothing better for himself than that his soul may fare in death as the souls of these pious ones (he makes no distinction within Israel). Certainly it is here signified that in his opinion man's relation to God is revealed in death, piety rewarded, ungodliness punished—a faith so widespread among the heathen that it may rightly be ascribed to this seer. Instead of cursing the people, in this first oracle he has intimated how distinguished above all peoples Israel will become, not merely in rank and numbers, but above all in piety, so that for his soul's well-being one could wish nothing better than to belong to it.

SECOND ORACLE OF BALAAM, Num. xxiii. 18–24. Balak is naturally dissatisfied with the first oracle, nor will he listen to what the seer says respecting the power of the greater Lord, to which he is subject. On the contrary, he thinks the great multitude of Israel has influenced the seer too much. He therefore leads him where merely the end of the Israelitish camp was visible, for to be able to see something of it seemed necessary to effectual cursing. How runs the oracle now?

---

[1] For to a heathen the entire physiognomy of this nation must seem one well-pleasing to God. With יְשָׁרִים comp. the name יְשֻׁרוּן, used in the Mosaic song and blessing (Deut. xxxii. 15, xxxiii. 5, 26), found elsewhere only in Isa. xliv. 2.

[2] *Theol. of Old Test.* i. 253.

"Arise, Balak, and hear — hearken to me, thou son of Zippor.[1]
Not a man is God that He should lie [2] — nor a son of Adam that He should repent.[3]
Should He speak and not perform it — or say, and not bring it to pass?
Behold, to bless I have received — and He has blessed, I cannot prevent it.
No iniquity is discerned in Jacob — no oppression is seen in Israel.
Yahveh his God is with him — and the jubilation of a king is in him.
God it is that brought them out of Egypt — He has horns [4] like the antelope.
For there is no divining in Jacob — and no oracling in Israel.
At the (right) time it shall be announced to Jacob — and to Israel what God performs.
Behold, a people, like a lion rising up — and a young lion raising itself.
He will not lie down until he has devoured the prey — and drunk the blood of the torn."

This oracle pierces deeper into the inner life of the Israelitish people, and describes the blessings accruing to it from the divine rule and intercourse with the living God. אָוֶן and עָמָל are not found there.[5] No one sees in Israel those things which are inevitable among heathen peoples: wickedness and oppression. אָוֶן is moral laxity of spirit, and especially the unhappy delusion of superstition; עָמָל is wrong inflicted on the weak. The latter is the consequence of the former; for reckless oppression and plunder of men is the fruit of the dark superstition and unprincipled unbelief that knows not the true God. Both vices

---

[1] Here, too, the language is extraordinary in several particulars. On בְּנוֹ, cf. Gesenius-Kautzsch, *Gramm.* § 90, 3*b*. הָאֲזֵן seldom stands with עַד.

[2] Ewald, *Ausf. Lehrbuch*, § 347.

[3] וְיִתְנֶחָם. On the vocalization, see Stade, *Gramm.* i. p. 76, 280.

[4] תּוֹעֲפוֹת might be derived from עָיֵף (*to be weary*), in the sense of *fatigues*, forced toils (*Parforcetouren*); then the sense would be: He is unweariable as the antelope. But the other passages in which the noun occurs, especially Ps. xcv. 4, suggest that it comes from יָעַף, *to be high*, referring here to the lofty horns (symbols of strength and honour, LXX. δόξα) of the gazelle.

[5] Cf. the combination of the two, Job iv. 8, v. 6; Isa. x. 1.

are inseparable marks of heathenism. Israel owes its freedom from both to the hallowing presence of its God, in whom it exults as its king.[1] What honour, to have Him as commander and ruler in the camp! He leads the people safely in its wanderings, and under this leading it is strong and proud as the lofty-horned antelope. In ver. 23 a new excellency is mentioned, accruing to this people from its intimate relation to God, and especially striking the eye of the heathen seer: There no נַחַשׁ and קֶסֶם are found, no conjuring and magic art, *i.e.* artificial soothsaying (of which two kinds are here named), such as was common among the heathen, but, as Balaam well knows, often most deceptive.[2] Israel need not have recourse to such evil, uncertain, futile arts, because what God purposes to do is announced to it in plain, unmistakable words. This costly privilege belongs to God's dear covenant-people. Moreover, this close union with God gives His people unconquerable strength towards the world without. Its victorious superiority over its foes is symbolized by a second animal figure—the twofold lion, already familiar to us from Gen. xlix. 9. It is pictured to us as just risen up to fetch its prey. It will not lie down to rest until it has won rich booty. Just so stands Israel, ready for battle, on the threshold of the promised land.

Thus this oracle depicts the source of Israel's peculiar happiness, which is to be sought in its exceptional relation to God. Thanks to the divine law it is a holy, thanks to divine revelation an enlightened, thanks to God's royal leading an unconquerable people, for whom a glorious future is reserved.

THIRD BALAAM-ORACLE, xxiv. 3-9. A third time Balak attempts to draw from the seer an oracle hostile to Israel. He chooses a new standing-ground for him,—this time Mount Peor, —with the idea that locality most powerfully influences the import of the oracle. But Balaam, who, as is remarked, now knew God's intention, forbore this time to go for the נְחָשִׁים, *i.e.* the voices or signs that were to inspire him. On the contrary, he directed his gaze directly to the tents of Israel spread out before him to draw inspiration from the sight, and took up his mashal and said:—

---

[1] In תְּרוּעַת מֶלֶךְ, therefore, the second word is the genitival object: the joyous tumult, jubilant acclamation, with which a king is greeted.

[2] Cf. p. 14, 20, 23.

"Thus speaks Balaam, Beor's son[1] — the man speaks, whose eye is closed (note B).
Thus speaks he who hears God's words — who beholds visions of the Almighty,
Falling down, with eye unveiled —
How lovely are thy tents, Jacob — thy dwellings, Israel!
Like brooks stretched out[2] — like gardens by the stream!
Aloes that Yahveh planted — like cedars by the water!
Water drips from his buckets[3] — and his seed is in many waters.
And loftier than Agag let his king be[4] — and his kingdom on the increase.
God it is who brought them out of Egypt — He has horns like the antelope.[5]
He will consume nations, His foes — and gnaw their bones, and crush his loins.[6]
He has couched, lain down like a lion — and like a she-lion: who will rouse Him up?[7]
Blessed they who bless thee — and cursed they who curse thee!"[8]

As the seer looks on Israel encamped in the order of its tribes, the Spirit comes upon him, and by an inner sense he beholds the tribes in the promised land—that region which in comparison with the desert-abodes of Moab, Midian, and Edom was a very garden. There stretch, like brooks, the long lines of Israel's tents, planted in fact by fresh waters, vers. 6, 7. The thirsty eye of the Oriental rejoices in nothing so much as in water. Where this is, there is life, growth, wealth, joy.

[1] בְּנוֹ בְעֹר, form as in xxiii. 18.

[2] נִטָּיוּ. The niphal נָטָה is used of a measuring-line stretched out (Zech. i. 16); here of the tents or dwellings forming a long line, like brooks in the valleys.

[3] His water-buckets are full to overflowing, in contrast with the dearth of water among the surrounding peoples.

[4] וְיָרֹם; the passive is not quite equivalent to the indicative (against Gesenius); rather: let his king become higher than Agag.

[5] Ver. 8a like xxiii. 22.

[6] חִצָּיו יִמְחָץ, *He breaks his arrows*. The suffix refers to the foe. But in accordance with the Syriac translation חֲלָצָיו is to be read: *his loins*, as the seat of strength along with the bones. Otherwise LXX., Kimchi: *with his arrows* (acc. instr.).

[7] Ver. 9a like Gen. xlix. 9; there merely רָבַץ instead of שָׁכַב.

[8] Ver. 9b like Gen. xxvii. 29.

Hence this blessing of God is promised in fullest measure to Israel, which in consequence will grow up like most stately trees. From this peaceful prosperity ver. 7 then passes to the power of military expansion dwelling in the people, by which it will be raised above the mightiest nations. Even Agag will be put into the shade by it. An Amalekite king of this name was taken captive by Saul (1 Sam. xv.) and killed by Samuel. Many consider this humbling of Amalek by Saul as the event here referred to *post eventum*. But according to ver. 20 the oracles spring from a time when Amalek still held a position in the van of the nations, and just for this reason Agag is named here; this was probably a common name of the Amalekite princes, as Abimelech among the Philistines, Pharaoh among the Egyptians (so also Winer). According to xxiii. 21, one might be inclined to refer מֶלֶךְ and מַלְכֻּת here to God and the divine rule founded in Israel. But the jussive form and the tense תִּנַּשֵּׂא require us to think of a future human dynasty, since the superiority of the divine king above Agag could not be represented as in course of growth. This physical superiority in attack and defence will be shown (as the fourth oracle will expressly state, here it is only intimated) when the nation has a king of its own. Here, too, the superiority is set forth by the image of the lofty-horned antelope (verbatim as before) and the majestic lion. In the latter comparison a verse of the blessing pronounced on Judah (Gen. xlix.) is exactly reproduced; just as in the expressive closing saying we have an important part of the patriarchal blessing (Gen. xii. 3, and especially xxvii. 29, etc.), according to which this people will be the mediator of the blessing or displeasure of God to other nations, according to the attitude these assume towards it. See p. 107, 114.

FOURTH BALAAM-ORACLE, Num. xxiv. 15–24. King Balak would now fain check the stream of blessings which the seer is pouring out on enviable Israel. But he cannot arrest the spirit he has called forth. Balaam, dismissed in anger, says to him, ver. 14: "And now, behold, I will go to my people: come, I will inform[1] thee what this people will do to thy people in the end of the days." The end of the days, which to Jacob was the time when his sons would grow into tribes

---

[1] יָעַץ, elsewhere *to give counsel*, here *information about the future* (cf. Isa. xli. 28).

and dwell peacefully in Canaan,[1] to this heathen seer is the time when the whole heathen world shall feel the powerful superiority of the kingdom of Israel.

"And he took up his oracle and said:
Thus speaks Balaam, Beor's son — thus the man, whose eye is closed:
Thus speaks he who hears God's words — and knows of the knowledge of the Most High,[2]
Who sees visions of the Almighty — falling down with unveiled eye:
I see Him, but not now — I perceive Him, but not near:
There goes a star out of Jacob — and a sceptre arises out of Israel,
And it crushes the sides of Moab — and the crown of all the sons of revolt.
And Edom shall be for a conquest — and Seir shall be a conquest, his foes,
And Israel does valiantly — and out of Jacob one comes to destroy the remnant out of the city."

This oracle, in which Balaam's prophecy culminates, is a true example of the language of seers. Everything is concrete, as presented to the senses; for at first even the inner sense sees in the outlines and form supplied by the outer senses. A star proceeds from Jacob; respecting the meaning of this the parallel leaves no doubt: a sceptre rises aloft from Israel. Among the most diverse nations the star is a common symbol of ruling greatness and glory. Hence the prevalent faith in the ancient world, that the birth or coronation of great kings is announced by the appearing of stars, to which belief Matt. ii. 2 alludes. In xxiii. 21, where a king in the camp of Israel is spoken of, we must understand God dwelling in its midst. The present passage, on the contrary, speaks, like xxiv. 7, of the rise of a human dominion, which, it is true, must stand in close relation to the divine one. The question, whether by this star and sceptre is meant a single king or a whole dynasty, goes beyond the horizon of the seer.

[1] Cf. p. 115, and on the idea in general, p. 33.
[2] In this introduction, otherwise pretty literally the same as in xxiv. 3 ff., there is an additional member which plainly affirms that the seer knows of things otherwise known only to the omniscient God. It is not impossible that this member has dropped out of the former passage, since there the symmetry is defective by a half-verse.

He sees but one star, one sceptre, which does not preclude the possibility of several persons being prefigured by this symbol, but in this case they must form a united power.

That star Balaam sees in sure ascent, but still far off in time, and not near in space. Thus the seer himself shows the consciousness of a distance between what he sees and its realization. The kingdom, promised in the patriarchal oracles, but which had not begun to be realised in the Mosaic age, is reserved for the future. Only when it arrives will Israel's full power be displayed in the evil fate of its foes. It is characteristic of the heathen conception ruling in these oracles, that the only effect of the ideal kingdom described is the hostile one on surrounding nations. This is primarily its exoteric bearing. It will then fare ill with the rebellious hordes of the Moabites, Edomites, and with all of whatsoever name who ought in the name of God and right to submit to Israel,[1] but who are never quiet, and always ready for revolt.[2] That sceptre smites them heavily on both sides and on the crown (note C). Their land will become a conquered province. The remnant of their hostile population will be rooted out of their cities.

But the seer does not stop here. He holds a fatal review of the nations, in which it appears that they are all devoted to destruction.

Ver. 20. "And he looked on Amalek, and lifted up his oracle and spake:

First-born of the nations is Amalek,—and his end inclines to destruction."

Amalek presents itself full of pretension as the first-born (properly "beginning" in the abstract[3]) of the nations; it can boast of high rank and age as no other can; what does that avail it! Its end is to be destroyed,[4] *i.e.* its ultimate fate is to pass away, leaving no trace behind (אֹבֵד).

---

[1] Cf. Gen. xxvii. 29; respecting Edom especially, Gen. xxvii. 40, p. 115. שֵׂעִיר, *the rugged land*, is the bushy, hilly land of Edom. The Edomites always belonged to the "sons of revolt;" hence they are mentioned next to Moab.

[2] For this reason they are called בְּנֵי־שֵׁת, which is to be explained by the related passage, Jer. xlviii. 45, which calls the Moabites בְּנֵי שָׁאוֹן, *sons of tumult*. Thus שֵׁת is for שְׁאֵת from שָׁאָה.

[3] Cf. Job xl. 19.

[4] The participle stands where we should expect the infinitive, as in xxiv. 24.

Ver. 21 f. "And he looked on the Kenites,[1] and lifted up his oracle and spake:
Thy abodes last for ever, — and thy nest is hidden in the rock.
But Kain[2] awaits devastation. — How long? when Asshur leads thee captive!"

As the Kenites form a branch of the Midianites, probably they here represent them. With a play on the name the seer praises their impregnable mountain-nests, defying the teeth of time (אֵיתָן). But these will not avail them for ever; their days also are numbered. Until when? How long will it last? Until Asshur lead thee captive. Whereas the mountain-nests rather suggest the Kenites dwelling in the rocky south-land of Judah, who, like the Edomites, had their strong cities on steep heights (1 Sam. xxx. 29), the carrying away by Assyria suggests that a branch of the tribe was also settled in the north of Palestine (Judg. iv. 11). But this branch in any case played too slight a part in the deportation by Assyria for the oracle to have arisen *post eventum* (in reference thereto). The chief emphasis lies on the thought that the great power, Assyria, will bring to an end the independence of these tenacious small tribes. Then the prospect before the seer assumes large dimensions, as he sketches in a few faint strokes the decline of the next great world-power.

Ver. 23 f. "And he lifted up his oracle and spake:
Woe, who shall live before that which God brings about?[3]
And ships (arrive) from the parts of the Chittites,
And oppress Asshur, and oppress Eber,
And he too leans to destruction."

Assyria's star also the seer sees wane. It is outstripped by a mightier empire coming by ship from the west, from Chittim, *i.e.* Cyprus;[4] but it is not said, ships of Cyprus come, but a fleet comes from that direction. Thus it is a Western power, the island of Cyprus having always played a special part in voyages from the West into the East and the opposite. This Western power,

---

[1] According to an exceedingly common Hebrew idiom in such mention of nations or tribes, the singular is used, as in our own popular language it is said: the Frenchman stands on the Rhine, Gesenius, *Gr.* § 109.

[2] The tribe is also called Kain in Judg. iv. 11.

[3] אֵל כְּמִשֻּׂמוֹ, properly before the fact that God does it. But שׂוּם is not *to intend, determine* (cf. שׂוּם עַל לֵב, τιθέναι ἐν φρεσί), but applies to the carrying out of a determination; its realization; cf. Ex. x. 2.

[4] Cf. the later usage, which applies it to Macedonia, 1 Macc. i. 1.

emerging without name or more precise indication, humbles the entire East, and first of all world-ruling Assyria, as well as Eber subject to the latter, by which is meant the cis-Euphratic Shemites (Israel, Edom, Moab, etc.). Then follows the oracle of doom: עֲדֵי אֹבֵד וְגַם־הוּא, recurring as a refrain, since it states the lot of all heathen nations. We might be tempted to refer this הוּא to Assyria, this world-power having been just mentioned; but in this case עֵבֶר would come awkwardly between. Moreover, in this oracle Assyria is already in decay, and the mysterious Western power rules. But even the latter (designedly indicated by הוּא) tends to destruction. Then with this fact of the final world-power going the way of all flesh the seer's fatal review closes, as it ought. Heathenism nowhere has permanence. The great powers dissolve in rapid succession, their mere physical might makes no stand against the judgment of time. Along with this perception of the frailty of his own power and greatness, which this heathen here betrays, just as remarkable is the presentiment of the Eastern seer, that the dominion will fall at last to the West, which fills him with special horror. Who will endure to live, when the most gigantic power of the East is cast down by a still mightier power from the West? This catastrophe took place under Alexander the Great. But the subjection of the East to the West became more enduring with the conquests of the Romans. The oracle as little distinguishes Macedonia from Rome as Assyria from Babylon; it sees only a great Eastern and Western power. History has brought the more precise distinction in what is seen here in general outlines (note D).

Reviewing these oracles, we see that they materially enrich the patriarchal benedictions, while also partially coinciding with them. That Balaam knew of those promises to Abraham and Judah (Hengstenberg), is not indeed to be supposed. As he did not speak in Hebrew, his words in any case have been put here also into a Hebrew dress. Oral tradition for a long time perhaps moulded these oracles, while written redaction settled their formal shape. But is this fourfold blessing simply a later Jewish product? This we must expressly deny. Their whole substance bears witness to the unusual source from which these mashals spring. First and chiefly, we have an original and circumstantial sketch of the exoteric development of God's kingdom, such as no Israelite, even of the age of Isaiah, could foresee without extraordinary revelation. We can understand how a heathen seer, coming from the Euphrates,[1] followed the political effects of the divine kingdom with special interest. Elsewhere a similar panorama is first found in Daniel. Again it is to be observed that, in opposition to the prophetic discourses of every age, a bright picture without shade is here given of Israel. The explanation is that the speaker is not an Israelitish prophet but a heathen, who sees before him not the empirical people whom he had to admonish and chide, but Israel—the people of God, the depositary of revelation, in opposition to the heathen world. Just the Mosaic age, when this people was in the promising beginning of its mission and gave the first proofs of its divine strength, must have produced the strongest impression of its superiority over the heathen world.

The enrichment of the patriarchal benedictions in the Balaam oracles consists precisely in what Israel had become through the Mosaic covenant at Sinai. We see there the people countless in numbers, in a fruitful land, thanks to the covenant with Yahveh, who brought it out of Egypt, and continually dispenses His revelation in its midst. This sacred nationality stands there—an impregnable, victorious power, full of blessing, unfolding into true royalty, whilst every worldly power and force is sinking into dust.

NOTE A.—This oracle is named מָשָׁל, chiefly on account of its symmetrical form and beautiful finish, which comport well with its lofty inspiration. The language is peculiar and antique. Cf. (ver. 7) the poetic הַרְרֵי, אר=אָרָה with *He paray*. from אָרַר, like זְעָמָה for זָעֲמָה, and קָבָה (as in xxii. 11, 17) for קָבַב from רָבַב. See Gesenius, *Gramm.*, ed. by Kautzsch, § 67, Anm. 2; Böttcher, *Ausführliches Lehrbuch*, i. p. 160; Ewald, *Ausf. Lehrb.* § 228*b*; B. Stade, *Lehrb. d. Hebr. Gramm.* i. p. 324 (explains אָרָה and קָבָה from ־ being pronounced like ô).

NOTE B.—The man of "closed eye" is he whose bodily eye is withdrawn from the sensuous, whilst from his inner one the veil is lifted, which hides secrets from human vision. Hence he is also

---

[1] Such an one might certainly in the Mosaic age be acquainted with Asshur, which conquered Babylon about 1270 (Maspero, *Geschichte der morgenländischen Völker im Alterthum*, 1877, p. 275). His foresight of the future greatness of this Eastern empire is not more wonderful than his prediction of the final rise of a Western empire.

called גְּלוּי עֵינָיִם. To this נֹפֵל adds a still stronger feature: He who falls down unconscious in the manner of the Shamans, in order then to speak in a clairvoyant state. Herder recalls the unmistakable similarity in the case of Balaam to the modern Shamans. As this state marks a lower stage of prophecy (see p. 17), so in general the air of ostentatious mystery, with which Balaam puts forward his own person, contrasts with the unconscious manner in which the Israelitish prophets act. These use the form נְאֻם יהוה. On the other hand, the last solemn oracle of David agrees in form with Balaam's mashal, 2 Sam. xxiii. 1.

NOTE C.—פֵּאֲתֵי, dual from פֵּאָה (cf. Stade, *Gramm.* i. p. 139), properly *facies*, then the side of the body. The *crown* comes in as the centre. Jeremiah (xlviii. 45) read קָדְקֹד instead of קַרְקַר; so in the present passage also Köster, Ewald, Gesenius, Baur, etc. Considering the great similarity which already existed in the ancient Hebrew writing between ד and ר, a confusion is easily conceivable. It is true, the present reading has the greater difficulty in its favour; but this קַרְקַר (reduplicated stem from קוּר, to bury), which is said to signify "to disturb" (LXX. προνομεύσει, *to plunder*), does not really suit the object and has the context against it.

NOTE D.—The rationalistic *Criticism*, which will hear of no prediction, but would infer the date of the oracles from the things predicted, finds itself here in no slight perplexity. That these oracles sprang from the age of the early kings, may be rendered plausible by xxiv. 7, 17 f. (cf. xxiv. 9 with Gen. xlix. 9). But on those principles the mention of Assyria (xxiv. 22) would compel us to descend (G. Baur) to the Assyrian age (8th cent.), when the ideal description of Israel and the picture of its superiority to all heathen nations would be in sorry keeping with other prophetic announcements. But what shall be done with xxiv. 24, the oracle of the fall of the East under the dominion of the West? Yet the existence of Balaam's oracles in the age of Micah (vi. 5) and Jeremiah (xlviii. 45) is beyond all doubt. That the oracle in xxiv. 24 is an addition from the age after Alexander, the three preceding utterances respecting the heathen world on the other hand being very ancient (Köster), is far too arbitrary, and inconsistent with what is admitted as to the age of the entire Pentateuch. Respecting the embarrassment of de Wette and Bleek, see in Tholuck, *Die Propheten und ihre Weissagungen*, 2nd ed. p. 102 f. No better than the expedient of these scholars, who would fain refer the agreement of the oracle with its incalculable, grand fulfilment to chance or later interpolation, is the evasion resorted to by Ewald and Hitzig to make the words intelligible. The former (*Hist.* i. 109) adduces a passage of Menander, preserved in Josephus (*Antiq.* ix. 14. 2), according to which the Cyprians in Salmanassar's days had rebelled against the Tyrian king Elulæus, just at the time when that Assyrian ruler invaded Tyrus. What has this to do with Balaam's oracle? Ewald thinks a piratical fleet must (!) then have visited the Hebrew (= Canaanite - Phœnician!) and the Assyrian (= Syrian!) coasts. Of such a fleet Josephus and Menander know nothing (on the contrary, they say the Tyrian fleet went to Cyprus); and yet this visit of the Phœnician coast is the event under the fresh impression of which the oracle arose! By this fleet, not worth naming, Assyria's power was put in the shade, whereas in Ewald's own opinion "Salmanassar wished to use this quarrel in his own favour in the war against Tyrus."

This makeshift is so precarious that it has found no favour. And the same may be said of the somewhat more popular explanation of Hitzig, which is just as pretentious as Ewald's. Hitzig avails himself of a passage in the Armenian *Chronicon Eusebii* (ed. Ven. p. 21), according to which Sennacherib hurried to Cilicia to repel an attack of the turbulent Greeks, which he succeeded in doing, not indeed without loss, so that he had a monument built there to immortalize his name. Von Lengerke, v. Bohlen, Knobel seize eagerly on this Cilician expedition, of which the rich prophetic literature of that period, for intelligible reasons, takes not the least notice. And this is the catastrophe so perilous to Asshur and Eber, which an Israelite scarcely hoped to survive! Plainly the prophet is credited with the most pitiable shortsightedness, instead of a gaze stretching far beyond the common horizon. But the meagreness of these explanations is too patent to expose anything but the perplexity here falling on rationalistic criticism.[1]

[1] Cf. also Schultz, *A. T. Theologie*, ed. 2, p. 681 : "The peculiar obscurity of the section makes it hard to say when the poet wrote—certainly in an age when Asshur stood in the foreground, and European buccaneering hosts figured in the history of Hither-Asia" (!).

THIRD SECTION.

THE ANOINTED OF THE LORD.

§ 19. *The Prophetic Testament to the Davidic Royal House.*

AS Jacob's blessing held out before the tribe of Judah the prospect of eternal dominion in the land of God, so now this dominion is promised to a single family. Meanwhile in Israel the monarchy had taken shape, late indeed, but all the more longed for by the people. The theocrats, it is true, received it at first reluctantly, regarding it as an infringement of the theocracy; and the motives for its introduction were also of a lower character than the great Mosaic ideas of God's direct rule, which the commonwealth was meant to realize. But this breach with Israel's sacred prerogative of having no king but God was designed, as His prophets saw afterwards, to pave the way for a loftier plan of the Lord, and to conduct the divine kingdom to a higher stage of consummation.[1] Even Saul receives his kingdom from a prophet's hand, and by anointing with oil; he is therefore called מְשִׁיחַ יהוה.[2] His dignity was the gift of God's grace; hence its reception was a consecration as in the case of a priest,[3] who was also anointed, and in the case of a prophet, who also received this symbol.[4] The pure, golden, gently flowing oil, where used in worship, is in general a symbol of the Divine nature and Spirit. In the regal consecration, it

---

[1] In opposition to the notion that the contradiction in Samuel's bearing is to be traced to different, mutually exclusive accounts, of which one regarded the monarchy as a purely beneficial advance, while the other regretted it as a purely lamentable relapse (so Wellhausen, *Geschichte*, i. 265 f.), see Riehm, *Messianic Prophecy*, p. 62 ff.

[2] 1 Sam. xxiv. 6, 10, xxvi. 9, 16, 23; 2 Sam. i. 14, 16.

[3] Ex. xxix. 7, 21; the high priest is called "the anointed priest," Lev. iv. 4.

[4] 1 Kings xix. 16. But here מָשִׁיחַ is perhaps used only for the sake of uniformity, since in ver. 19 another symbol of consecration is mentioned.

sets forth the unimpeachable divine majesty transferred to the person of the anointed one. Only the king is called absolutely "the Lord's anointed,"[1] and, indeed, the king of Israel, of God's people.[2] As certainly as God stood to this people in a special covenant-relation, must its rightful king stand in nearer relation to Yahveh, being the depositary and representative of divine majesty. Certainly we have here a complete contrast to the deification of kings, such as we often meet with on heathen soil. Israel's king is never the personification or incarnation of Deity, but always remains accountable to his God, and is called to account by God's messengers, since this God is holy, and gives living revelations of Himself.[3] The Lord who conferred this dignity can also take it away again, but of course only He.[4]

This Saul was forced to learn, as he became less and less content with the position of a mere servant of the Lord, and fell into ruin through the heathenish self-exaltation to which he was prone. Already during his life another was set apart by anointing; and from the prophet's lips he had to hear the sentence of rejection, which God Himself confirmed in due time by the course of events. It was *Samuel* who was the instrument in the Lord's hand in assigning to the king in Israel his true position, his divine and human vocation. He then sought out the "man after God's heart" (1 Sam. xiii. 14), who was fitted to understand and realize this vocation—*David*, the son of Jesse the Bethlehemite. Only in such a ruler could the divine idea unfold itself more richly. This was carried out by the prophetic words, which bound the future of God's kingdom to David's house.

[1] By transference in Ps. cv. 15, the patriarchs are called מְשִׁיחָי, *my anointed, consecrated*, as they are also called נְבִיאָי.

[2] King Cyrus also as a divinely-called ruler (Isa. xlv. 1 ; cf. 1 Kings xix. 15). Subsequently the word became the name of the great Davidite from whom the completion of God's kingdom was expected; so especially in Aramaic מְשִׁיחָא, Targum of Onkelos on Gen. xlv. 10 ; Num. xxiv. 17; Targum of Jonathan, Hos. iii. 5, and elsewhere; in the New Testament either ὁ Μεσσίας, John i. 42, iv. 25, or translated ὁ Χριστός, i. 20, 25.

[3] Cf. *e.g.* the Egyptian conception of king, the product of pantheistic blending of divine and human being, where in truth the power of nature is adored, while the divine holiness is ignored. See Brugsch-Bey, *Gesch. Aegyptens unter den Pharaonen*, 1877, p. 82 f., 124 f., 481 f.

[4] That in Israel the regal dignity must depend on the choice of the sovereign God, is determined by Deut. xvii. 15 (see the opposite of the kingdom by God's grace, Hos. viii. 4), and is strongly emphasized in the history of Saul and David.

It is true, such a testament was not entrusted to that house at the anointing of David by Samuel. At first he was only chosen for himself, like Saul previously, to be ruler in God's place over Israel. But on the occasion related in 2 Sam. vii., a promise extending to his race was given him, a hereditary monarchy being thus established by God's grace. With this act the promise pointing to the realization of God's kingdom in Canaan comes to a conclusion. For when the people of God has His law, possession of His land, a permanent prophethood and monarchy, and finally, a local centre where God dwells, what more does it need? Then a new stage of development opens. Outwardly a far-reaching world-mission lies before this divine kingdom, inwardly a great task of refining and spiritualizing. In its actual state it is unable to fulfil either task without first undergoing the doom of dissolution.

This testament, dictated by the prophet, was made over to King David when he formed the pious, magnanimous resolve to erect a fixed temple to the Lord instead of the provisional pilgrim-tent,[1] 2 Sam. vii. 1 ff. = 1 Chron. xvii. 1 ff. The prophet Nathan, one of those true servants of God who discharged the prophetic office in Samuel's spirit, and perhaps came from his school, judging by human rules, could not conceive other than that the Lord would give His blessing to the resolve. But he was soon taught differently by the word of the Lord, which came to him the same night, and told him to announce to the king that the carrying out of the glorious work was reserved for his posterity. God the Lord needs no princely dwelling, and never sought one, but bestowed His high favour on David of free grace. Still his self-denying spirit and ardent desire to see the Lord dwelling abidingly with him shall not go unrewarded. Instead of the king building a house for Yahveh, Yahveh will build an abiding house for the king, 2 Sam. vii. 11*b*–16 :—

"And the Lord commands to tell thee, that the Lord will prepare thee a house. And it shall come to pass[2] when thy

---

[1] Respecting the time in which that resolve and the message of Nathan are to be put, see Herzog *R.E.*, 2nd ed. iii. 520. The genuineness of this oracle cannot reasonably be disputed. Even Anger (p. 30) describes it as "having arisen probably from true tradition."

[2] וְהָיָה is to be read before כִּי, after LXX. ; 1 Chron. xvii. 11. So also Wellhausen, *Text der Bücher Samuel*, p. 171.

days are fulfilled and thou art laid to sleep with thy fathers, I will make thy seed arise after thee, who shall go forth from thy body, and will make his kingdom to continue. He shall build a house to my name, and I will make the throne of his kingdom endure for ever. I will be a father to him, and he shall be to me a son; so that, when he does wrong, I will chastise him with rods of men and blows of the children of men,[1] but my favour shall not depart from him,[2] as I withdrew it from Saul, whom I made give way before thee. And thy house and thy kingdom shall be unchangeable before thee[3] for ever. Thy throne shall endure for ever."

It is very significant that the gaze is here directed from the present to the future, nay, the establishing of the kingdom of God is there seen. Not David himself, but his posterity, will carry out the work of temple-building. Thus Yahveh will obtain a fixed house, but David's own house will be still firmer. For God promises that his posterity will inherit the throne of David for ever. Consequently the monarchy will be hereditary; the Lord Himself guarantees the inheritance. Thus the top-stone is put upon the former promises, and at the same time the foundation-stone is laid for the subsequent promises, the Messianic in the stricter sense. The seed (זֶרַע) is here a homogeneous but collective idea. What is said of the temple-building was fulfilled in Solomon; but the "unchangeable mercies of David" (Isa. lv. 3: חַסְדֵי דָוִד הַנֶּאֱמָנִים), first assured in this testament, point much farther. They are indestructible, on which account the suppliant in Ps. lxxxix., in a time of heavy misfortune, with good reason takes the Lord at His word, reminding Him that, according to His testament, He cannot cast off the house of David for ever.

But the present oracle makes us see still deeper into the בְּרִית עוֹלָם (2 Sam. xxiii. 5), made by Nathan's revelation between God and the Davidic house. According to ver. 14, David's seed is to stand in the relation of *son* to God : "I will be to him a father,

---

[1] That is, not with destructive judgment, but with rods such as men use on their children.

[2] The better reading of the LXX. is אָסִיר instead of יָסוּר, as in 1 Chron. xvii. 13. Saul's name was perhaps not mentioned in the original text as in LXX.; it may have run as in 1 Chron. xvii. 13: מֵאֲשֶׁר הָיָה לְפָנֶיךָ ; so also Bertheau, Wellhausen.

[3] לְפָנֶיךָ is the better reading, after LXX. and Syr.

and he shall be to me a son." This is the most intimate relation of possession conceivable, and for this reason inalienable. One may be angry with a son, and a wise, just father, especially a holy one, like God, will not let his son's ill-conduct and perverseness go unpunished; but one cannot deny a son, nor will one kill him, but in chastising will always keep his well-being in view. Thus God will not so give rein to His holy wrath as to consume David's house, but will only afflict him in the same degree and with the same purpose as a human father his son.[1]

Now the relation of sonship in which David's house is placed to God is no new one. The whole of Israel was already placed by the Mosaic revelation in this relation to God.[2] But, like Israel among the peoples, so the regal house within this people is God's accepted, acknowledged child. It thus appears that this idea, in which divine revelation expresses men's most intimate belonging to God, is narrowed in order to be deepened; it is made personal in order to be perfected. Not merely the house collectively, but each single ruling Davidite stands in this relation of son to God; he sets forth in more intense potency what Israel in union with God is in general. Ver. 14, indeed, along with this lofty divine idea, contains a strong reminder of the fact that, in consequence of the human sinfulness of David's seed, this relation will not be without disturbance, which must needs mar its purity and perfection.[3] Nor is it expressly said that a single Davidite will realize purely and perfectly this lofty idea of divine sonship. But if in the future one person should ever fully verify that relation, and should rule as God's son over Israel, according to this divine oracle it must be a son of David.[4]

---

[1] On the application of this divine decree, cf. 1 Kings xi. 34.

[2] Ex. iv. 22; Deut. xxxii. 6; cf. Hos. xi. 1, etc. See p. 128.

[3] The chronicler, who abridges the oracle somewhat, has left out this feature, because in his time the monarchy, with its weaknesses and sins, no longer existed; but for him David's kingdom came into view—in past and future—merely in its greatness. For the rest, the feature is characteristic of the true religion. Compare how differently heathen kings were regarded in their character as sons of the gods.

[4] That with the declarations respecting the collective seed of David (ver. 13) a declaration is joined applying personally to Solomon (Wellhausen would expunge the verse, were it not for 1 Kings v. 18), is a direct proof of the age and genuineness of the oracle, since, to the speaker's view, the temple-building pertained still to David's posterity, not to himself. In addition, Keil, with Hengstenberg, reminds us

THE ANOINTED OF THE LORD.   153

A second prophetic message to David, more richly unfolding the glory of the covenant made with him, is contained in Ps. cx. The most accurate explanation of this remarkable song is that of Ewald,[1] who makes it a kind of oracle (נְאֻם יהוה) addressed by a prophet to David, perhaps when he came with offerings to the sanctuary at the beginning of a war :—

"A song of David :
Thus speaks Yahveh to my ruler : Sit at my right hand
Until I put thy foes as the footstool of thy feet !
The staff of thy power will Yahveh stretch out from Zion :
Rule in the midst of thy foes !
Thy people is (full of) willingness on thy army-day.[2]
With holy ornament [3] — from the womb of the dawn thy youth [4]
    arises to thee.
Yahveh has sworn — and He will not repent :
Thou art a priest for ever — after the manner [5] of Malki Zedek !
The Lord at thy right hand — shatters kings on the day of
    His wrath.
He will judge among the heathen — it is filled with corpses
    — he shatters the head on a broad field.[6]
From the brook in the way he shall drink, Therefore shall he
    lift high the head."

The heading, as we believe, is historically right, since the psalm is in fact Davidic, *i.e.* springs from David's time, and its

---

that the building of the temple also waited for its real execution until Christ, and consequently formed a part of that mission of David's seed which outlasted O. T. history, John ii. 19.

[1] *Dichter des Alten Bundes*, i. 2, p. 39.

[2] = on the day when thou marchest forth ; then thy people comes of free impulse, without force.

[3] בְּהַדְרֵי־קֹדֶשׁ, *with holy ornament* (cf. הֲדְרַת קֹדֶשׁ, Ps. xxix. 2, xcvi. 9 ; 2 Chron. xx. 21). Thus it is no profane army, but a priestly people.

[4] מִשְׁחָר is related to שַׁחַר like מֶחְשָׁךְ to חֹשֶׁךְ. The dew of thy youth, of course, is not to be understood of the king's youthful age, but יַלְדוּת is *abstr. pro concr.* The *juventus* denotes the youthful manhood appearing suddenly in the freshness of morning, comparable to the dewdrops that glitter in countless numbers, born of the womb of the dawn.

[5] עַל־דִּבְרָתִי, not "*on account* of Malki Zedek" (Hupfeld after a later idiom), but, "in keeping with the relation or state of Malk Zedek."

[6] רַבָּה may contain a play on the hostile metropolis of Ammon, Rabba (2 Sam. xi. 1). But in any case by אֶרֶץ רַבָּה, "the broad land," is meant the battlefield where the Lord holds judgment.

contents refer primarily to David's person. On the other hand, we cannot persuade ourselves to accept the *lamed auctoris*, and to consider David as the prophet speaking, on which view another higher ruler would be addressed by him, namely, the perfect Messiah to come.[1] Such a conscious distinction between his own person and the true Messiah, to whom David was so constantly subject that he could call him his ruler, finds no sufficient support either in 2 Sam. xxiii. or in any other psalm. This view would scarcely have been adhered to so tenaciously, if the proof adduced by Jesus to the Pharisees for the superiority of the Messiah over David did not presuppose this distinction and subjection on David's part.[2] But the presupposition of Davidic authorship, universal then, cannot give the law to our historic understanding of the psalm. Looked at closely, the appeal thereto is merely the form in which Jesus brought home to the scribes the incomparableness of the true Messiah, well attested in the Old Testament. In distinction from the account of Nathan which announced a vision received by night, this psalm, with its solemn form and enigmatic, abrupt ending, is to be regarded as an oracle bursting directly from prophetic inspiration. It may have been by Nathan himself. But it may also possibly spring from another seer of that age, struck with the divine greatness of the new kingdom on Zion, and depicting it in prophetic tones. This panegyric, just because it is prophetic, applies not to the earthly ruler as such, but to the sacred dignity and glory conferred on him by God. This glory is so great that the most renowned monarchy (that of David) is but a weak vessel, scarcely able to contain it. But it was such a vessel. God would have His condescension in dwelling beside David on Zion regarded as His Son taking the place of honour at His right hand. David's victorious campaigns would display the power of God that would fight for him against all foes. Nay, God acknowledged him, the pious singer of Israel, as *priest*, his care for and management of the sanctuary being shown in many ways. Although his priesthood was not realized, yet God's word and oath promised him one. The completed monarchy would not fall behind the one that Melchisedek once possessed in David's city, who wore the priestly fillet along with the crown. And like his kingdom, his

---

[1] So still Hengstenberg, Delitzsch, v. Hofmann (in his last statement).
[2] Matt. xxii. 41-46; Mark xii. 35-37; Luke xx. 41-44.

priesthood should be *eternal*. The psalm closes with images of war and triumph. Ver. 3 exhibited the divine king as he marched forth, voluntarily attended by countless hosts of youthful, priestly warriors, and ver. 4 hinted how he himself, the devout suppliant, did not disdain to draw near to God as priest before going to meet the foe; and at the close, where God Himself fights by his side (ver. 5), we see him victoriously ruling on the blood-drenched, corpse-covered field, and, after sharing every toil with his warriors ("of the brook in the way he shall drink"[1]), victoriously lifting up his head.

How far this picture of victory and triumph through God's power was realized in David, Ps. xviii. = 2 Sam. xxii. shows, where he sings to us how by God's help he leaped over walls, and the Lord made his foes the footstool of his feet. But just as clearly we see the incongruity between God's oracle and the actuality, when we compare the lofty Ps. cx. with the entire government of David. That government is far from being the glorified priestly kingdom pictured in the song. With all its victories it falls far short of the utterances of the prophetic singer, so that we have to choose between two views: Either we have here an enthusiastic idealization dealing in hyperboles and above criticism, or David's greatness and dignity had in God's eye a significance that went far beyond its empirical form. The latter supposition alone is worthy of a prophetic oracle. It is confirmed by the further development of Messianic prophecy, the life and sinew of which is just this, that divine thoughts, realized at first imperfectly, must reach complete development. Instead, therefore, of "idealizing" actuality, this oracle utters a creative word of God, which reveals the Anointed of the Lord in His heaven-willed glory.

There he sits beside God in abiding fellowship, sharing in God's honour. Consequently all his foes must become subject to him (vers. 1, 2). And His own people does not serve him by constraint, but in pure willingness; it offers itself in a moment, countless and fresh as the dew of morning, clad in holy, festal attire. It is not a common army that is in question. The whole host is made up of ministers and priests, holy like its Lord, ver. 4. Let us note how the priestly dignity elevates the king. He has no common conflict to wage. God Himself

[1] See David's fatigues and marches as in 2 Sam. xxiii. 17.

vanquishes his foes; but he bears the consecration conferred by the presence and high service of God. Thus his triumph is certain, in God's strength he inflicts judgment on the heathen—the hostile nations around, and his voluntary abasement becomes the path to greatness.

Thus this prophetic oracle adds something of high import to what was said of the Davidic monarchy in 2 Sam. vii. It unfolds what is implied in the divine sonship conferred there, on one hand in reference to its power which no foe can resist, and on the other in reference to its relation to God. To the king on Zion a double crown is promised, a double sacred dignity—secular as well as religious supremacy, dominion as well as priesthood. As the nation, nay, all nations, are in this king to honour the ruler set in God's place, so God will acknowledge in him the priestly representative of the nation, nay, of the whole world. And like the Davidic monarchy according to 2 Sam. vii., so according to Ps. cx. the Davidic priesthood[1] is to have eternal existence. This does not preclude the possibility of the Davidic king for a time forgetting his priestly dignity, and, as far as he himself is concerned, losing it; but on God's part the arrangement is irrevocable (לֹא יִנָּחֵם) and matter of solemn oath, as the Epistle to the Hebrews emphasizes (vii. 21). He will not definitively detach this dignity from his person. According to our explanation, the psalm does not indeed expressly say that only a future Davidite will perfectly realize the divine decree of a priestly monarchy on Zion, and maintain this dignity in His own person for ever. Only the power of the divine decree and the fact of human imperfection involve of necessity that a greater than David should verify this utterance. But if a ruler from David's house should answer perfectly to God's word of promise, he must—so the psalm determines—unite the high-priestly with the kingly dignity; and his people must not only be voluntarily subject to him, but also render to God priestly service.

The psalm is not merely typical, but prophetic, since it speaks expressly of the future. On the other hand, David, through the medium of whose person the psalm beholds the future, is a type.

---

[1] But observe that in this psalm not David's house, but only himself (or, the reigning king) is spoken of. He himself will rule for ever as priest. This personal strain corresponds to the ideal character of the oracle.

The high theological import of the psalm would not be materially lowered, even if the promise were given to a later Davidic ruler as the temporary representative of the Davidic monarchy. But in point of fact it is not easily conceivable that the union of royalty and priesthood was seen, at first typically, in any other than David who stood nearer to God than any one else, and presided over the sanctuary. And the whole language breathes a high antiquity. We here follow Ewald, who remarks : " Since the language also offers no opposition, it is to be regarded as certain that the king is David, for king and kingdom appear here still at the highest stage of greatness and glory."

The *fulfilment* of this psalm in its highest significance was claimed by Jesus in the passages quoted above as something raising Him above David. And certainly as those expressions were inspired by the Spirit of God, they first found their fulfilment in David's perfect Son. Him has God exalted above everything earthly, making Him sit down " at His right hand." The latter phrase, common in the New Testament,[1] originates in the present psalm. Expressly citing the words of this psalm, the Epistle to the Hebrews asserts the super - angelic majesty of the Son of God (i. 13) and the eternal High Priest (v. 6, vii. 17, 21, viii. 1, x. 12 f.). If de Wette, Hupfeld, *et al.*, think that the king who crushes heads and fills the land with corpses cannot be the Christian Messiah, Christ Himself and His apostles judged otherwise. In the wondrous prophetic picture they saw the divine-human head of God's kingdom on earth. And this with good reason. The image goes far beyond the actuality of the Old Covenant, glorifying its brightest forms with unwonted, loftier splendour. On the other hand, the N. T. Christology does not lack the wealth of realistic revelation which modern theology despises. As matter of fact, the powers of the outer world are at the service of the exalted Christ. And the bloodshed and fields of corpses of which history tells, are in truth divine judgments designed to place everything at last at the feet of His Anointed One.

---

[1] Acts ii. 32 ff., v. 31, vii. 55 f.; Rom. viii. 34 ; Eph. i. 20 ; Col. iii. 1 ; 1 Pet. iii. 22 ; cf. Acts iii. 21.

§ 20. *Echo of the Prophetic Word in the Songs of the Anointed One.*

In the poetry of the psalms generally we hear a hundred-voiced and yet harmonious lyrical echo of the acts and words of divine revelation. The prophetic messages to the Lord's Anointed, just noticed, found a many-voiced echo in these songs, proving that the import of the oracles was received into the understanding of king and people. But all the more must this be the case in the Psalms, as David, the chosen ruler, was, according to unanimous tradition, also the creator of this class of song.[1] From his lips also we first hear the sound of thanks and sacred rejoicing for the salvation vouchsafed to him. The first, most direct feelings of profoundly humble thankfulness, which the oracle of Nathan (2 Sam. vii.) awakened in David, find expression in the *thanksgiving* (ver. 18 ff.), in which the king acknowledges as the last and greatest, unmerited benefit of the Lord, that God spoke with him of the far future, and promised an eternal kingdom to his house after him.

Another royal song, namely, *Ps.* ii., a loftier outburst of the prophetic spirit, must be regarded as an echo of the divine messages in 2 Sam. vii. and Ps. cx., whether it was the direct sequel of such a prophetic oracle or the fruit of an inner revelation, which gave the king closer and deeper insight into the meaning of the divine covenant. The Messianic King here declares the import of the divine Sonship conferred on Him, and that in reference to His relation to the world: As God's Son He claims rule over the world. Thus we assume that the Messianic King is Himself the singer. At all events His divine, kingly feelings find expression here. And although, as in Ps. cx., the significance and worth of the song do not depend on the ruler of that house under or by whom it was sung, still the consciousness of the divine-human greatness conferred on him is so vigorous that it is hard to ascribe it to a later king of Judah after the division of the kingdom, when the heir of David did not even reign over his own land. Ewald suggests Solomon; Hofmann, still better, David himself. The absence of לְדָוִד is the less to be urged against this view as the heading of this psalm seems lost altogether. Whether, then, the song is by David himself or some

---

[1] 2 Sam. xxiii. 1 ; cf. Amos vi. 5 ; 2 Sam. xxii., etc.

one afterwards, at all events it speaks of the divine adoption conferred on David and his house. And whereas the thanksgiving in 2 Sam. vii. 18 ff. rather takes into view the eternal continuance of David's *house*, this psalm illustrates the divinely-established filial relation of the *person* of the reigning Messiah.

"Why do the peoples rage — and the nations meditate vain things?[1]

The kings of the earth take stand[2] — and the rulers consult together — against Yahveh and His anointed

'Let us rend asunder their bonds and cast from us their cords!'[3]

He that sitteth in the heaven laughs — the Lord derides them.

Then will He speak to them in His wrath — and in His fury He will terrify them:

'Yet have I established my king — on Zion my holy mountain.'

I will make announcement concerning Yahveh's decree:[4] — He spake to me:

'My son art thou! — I have to-day begotten thee.[5]

Demand of me and I will give peoples to be thy inheritance — and the ends of the earth for thy possession.

Thou wilt dash them in pieces with iron sceptre — like a potter's vessel wilt shatter them.'[6]

And now, ye kings, be prudent — be instructed, ye judges of the earth.

Serve Yahveh with fear — and exult with trembling.

---

[1] By רָגַשׁ, *to bluster, roar*, is meant the stormy unrest, tumult, which announces revolt; by הָגָה, properly *to hum, buzz*, and then *to muse*, when one murmurs to himself half-aloud — the unhappy mood which bespeaks evil designs, which, however, as רִיק says beforehand, will be in vain.

[2] הִתְיַצֵּב, defiantly to offer battle, challenging to enter the lists, as in 1 Sam. xvii. 16.

[3] Only the plural מוֹסְרוֹת (and מוֹסְרִים, Ps. cxvi. 16) occurs, from a singular מוֹסֵר=מַאֲסָר from אָסַר, cf. Ps. cvii. 14. Observe the sonorous poetical suffixes.

[4] סִפֵּר with אֶל is *to make announcement* in regard to a thing (as in Ps. lxix. 26): "circumstantially and therefore solemnly" (Delitzsch). חֹק, statute, fixed decree.

[5] יְלִדְתִּיךָ, see vocalization in Gesen. *Gramm.* § 44, 2.

[6] תְּרֹעֵם from רָעַע, *to break*; on the other hand, the LXX. (ποιμανεῖς αὐτοὺς ἐν ῥάβδῳ σιδηρᾷ) read תִּרְעֵם from רָעָה, which, however, in view of the parallels must be rejected. נָפַץ, allied to פּוּץ, signifies: *to scatter, burst, rend asunder*.

Kiss the Son (note A), lest He be angry — and ye perish in the way!

For soon His wrath will burn — Well for all that trust in Him."

The poet sees the princes and peoples around him in commotion. The newly-arisen, divinely-founded monarchy on Zion stands in their way. True, they will be quickly vanquished and taken captive, but they already roar and rage like the ocean at the rising of a storm. The keen eye of the enlightened poet sees that the great ones are preparing for rebellion and planning alliances, and the nations only wait for the signal to break out in open revolt against the Lord, whose anointed representative is the king on Zion. Already is heard here and there the wild cry for deliverance from his rule as an unworthy yoke. But with the first words judgment is passed on this mad spirit of rebellion. In vain is all this consulting and arming, for really the enmity that would set aside God's chosen ruler is directed against the God of heaven and earth. As the king looks out upon this wild tumult a feeling of holy pride comes over him, whereas in God's presence he was overcome by the sense of his own lowliness and nothingness. Looking at these worldly kings, he learns who *he* is and who *they* are. Why, for what end—cries he to the blinded rebels—do they rage and brood over empty, vain things? With like confidence Isaiah (viii. 9 f.) addresses the heathen nations: " Equip yourselves, but tremble; form a purpose, and it shall be broken! take counsel, and it shall not come to pass!" To disclaim obedience to the Lord Himself and try to get rid of His bonds is a desperate undertaking.

The reply to this declaration of war is right worthy of the divine King: "He that sitteth in the heavens laughs." It is the laughter of divine irony, smiting the senseless bearing of the weaklings who act as if they would storm heaven; cf. Ps. xxvii. 12 f. But this laughter is the forerunner of the divine wrath, and is therefore terrible. "Then will He speak to them in His wrath." This אָז—often answering to "now," often to "one day"—fixes a definite moment, here the hour beheld by the inner eye as near, when He will reckon with them as a judge and avenger, whereupon all their courage will collapse. Without preface His decree strikes into their talk; to their obstinacy He simply opposes His sovereign will: " And *I* have established *my* king on Zion, *my* holy mountain." Here it stops.

In ver. 7 the king himself speaks, which is most natural if he is the singer. To all the world he proclaims the decree of God made known to him by revelation. Yahveh has spoken to him in solemn asseveration: "*My son* art thou; to-day have I begotten thee." In these words He has acknowledged him as belonging most intimately to Himself, investing Him even with personal kinship to God. The "I have begotten thee" suggests still more strongly than the simple "My son art thou," that the Messianic king has received a higher life from above. The conferring of this dignity was bound in the speaker's case to a definite point of time. The "to-day" was his Messianic birthday, whether on this day he first entered outwardly on his office, or its inner greatness was then revealed to him by prophet's message or personal inspiration.

In virtue of his new divine dignity everything is virtually subject to him, as certainly as heaven and earth belong to his Father. Everything also will fall to him, when he desires it of his Father. In his mediatorial position he is lord of the world. With sovereign authority he rules at pleasure in the world of nations, as ver. 9 says in drastic style. His power is to that of worldly kings as iron to clay.

In such circumstances (עַתָּה) these kings are exhorted for their own good to give up their resistance, ver. 10 f., and to submit willingly to Yahveh, because their own welfare demands it. "Rejoice with trembling!" is the charge to those doing homage. This charge, like the following kiss of homage, implies that not only fear, but inclination also, should lead them to submit to this lofty God and His great vicegerent. The feeling meant is the mixed feeling of shrinking and delight awakened in mortals by the glorious revelations of the holy and merciful God, Hos. iii. 5, xi. 10 f. Subjection to the Lord is at the same time subjection to His Messiah; nay, the service required by God consists in obedience to the latter. Therefore "kiss the Son," that "He," namely God, who requires this, "may not be angry." That God Himself, not the Messiah, is the subject in the last words of the song, is evident from the חוֹסֵי בוֹ, which is a standing phrase for taking refuge with the Lord.

It is high time to anticipate the divine wrath, since the measure will soon be full[1] that will bring about its outbreak. But the

---

[1] This is the meaning of the כִּמְעַט. Little more is needed for His wrath to burn. Hence the element of time also lies in the expression.

psalm closes in cheerful tones. Happy they who, instead of proudly building on their own counsel and on fleshly power, seek their strength and refuge in the Lord! The greatest benefit for the world is the rule of God and His Anointed, against which it strives.

The view taken of this psalm as a whole differs among expositors. As with Ps. cx., modern writers (Hengstenberg, Oehler) suppose that David spoke of another, ideal personality,— more precisely, spoke here in his name. But this view, as well as that of Hupfeld, according to which a later writer personated David in thought in order to set forth the bare idea of Messiahship, is refuted by the direct vividness of the piece, which points plainly to the attitude of earthly princedoms towards an actually visible king on Zion,[1] so that except with violence we can only think of the present King-Messiah, and in any case of the Messiah. That the state of the world set forth in the song fits no part of David's reign, cannot be maintained. David's early government was encircled by foes, who only submitted to his authority on compulsion (see Ps. xviii. 42 ff.). After Solomon's time few princes and rulers can be named who were subject to the Davidic king. To think, with Ewald, of Solomon's anointing on Zion, is needless. For, apart from the consideration that the anointing in Solomon's case did not really take place on Zion, it is not expressly spoken of.[2] We therefore prefer the Davidic to a later date, David giving utterance to his joyous rapture in these inspired words either immediately after Nathan's oracle respecting his house, or — which is more probable — after a revelation respecting his own person such as Ps. cx. contains.

In any case, the Messianic dignity peculiar to the heaven-chosen king of Israel is here set before our eyes in its intrinsic grounds and outward significance. In both respects it is altogether extraordinary. The peculiarity distinguishing the Messiah from all other men and princes is this, that he is to be called and to be God's Son. How great the range of this dignity, appears from the fact that the right of universal rule is promised him. It is thoroughly out of keeping with the seriousness of such intimations of the Divine Spirit to speak of mere poetical hyperboles or extravagances which, falling from

---

[1] Cf. H. Schultz in the *Theol. Stud. und Krit.* 1866, p. 29 f.

[2] נְסַכְתִּי does not signify: *I have anointed*; נָסַךְ is rather: *to pour, pour out*, hence here: *to establish, instate*.

the lips of a singer friendly to the king, did not agree with the reality, and so were made by a later age into an ideal, whose realization was expected in the future. No, every word here is well considered; divine utterances form the basis; hence the great idea is worked out to its boldest consequences. But its representative is meanwhile imperfect. That a future king will realize it fully and completely, we do not find expressly foretold in the psalm. But if One in the future shall exhibit this divine kingdom in complete fashion, according to this psalm He must be God's Son in a unique sense; and in consequence, dominion over the whole earth must fall to Him to the earth's advantage.

In whom these divine words found their true *fulfilment*, has never been matter of doubt to the Christian Church. One alone could call Himself in the deepest and fullest sense " Christ, the Son of the living God " (Matt. xvi. 16), a dignity raising Him, as Heb. i. 5 asserts, above the angels.[1] In Him alone person and Messianic dignity were completely one, a pure effulgence of God, so that He was the true representative to the world of the Father in heaven (John xiv. 7, 9). To Him, then, belongs dominion on earth, Matt. xxviii. 18 ff. But as in Ps. ii. the Lord's Anointed becomes the object of hostile sentiment on every side, so also Christ, as Acts iv. 25 ff. reminds us, became the object of hate to Jews and Gentiles. While this was the case even during the time of His earthly walk, after His exaltation to God's right hand His rule on earth is still a mark for fierce assaults and ever new storms (Luke xix. 14). Not merely kings and nations seek to shake off this yoke. Princes in the intellectual realm have also not seldom given the signal, the thoughtless crowd taking it up: " Let us cast away their bands ! " Through struggles meant to serve the cause of progress and freedom there shrieks not seldom the watchword, springing from stubborn, rebellious hearts: " We will not have this man to reign over us ! Let us shake off their bands," *i.e.* God's holy government revealed by Christ in its perfection. This passion for rebellion is foolish, the real folly of the world. Against the Mighty One, whose throne is in heaven, this storm-flood of earth's strong ones avails nothing. The foes of God prepare their own destruction, because, instead of sub-

---

[1] In Acts xiii. 33, also, Ps. ii. 7 is quoted to confirm the divine Messianic dignity, according to Codex D as a saying of the *first* Psalm, because Ps. i. was regarded as an introduction to the book, and was therefore not numbered.

mitting to God's Son as Prince of Peace, they become His prey as Judge. In particular this world-spirit is foolish, because it takes so little account of its own welfare, which would be secure in the service of this much-hated prince. "Blessed are they who submit to Him from love!"

Further, a kind of answer to the victory-promising oracle of Ps. cx. is given in the unquestionably Davidic thanksgiving after victory, Ps. xviii. = 2 Sam. xxii., which also at the end makes reference to the covenant-promise remaining to his seed.

The "*last words*" *of David*, 2 Sam. xxiii. 1–7, with a reference to 2 Sam. vii., also relate to the bright future of his house,—an oracle mysteriously introduced, prophetic in form, and so far similar to Balaam's oracles,—for the rest, like those oracles of original, antique speech, and unimpeachable authenticity. These last words run :—

"Thus speaks David, Jesse's son ; — thus speaks the man placed on high,[1]
The anointed of the God of Jacob — the lovely one in the anthems of Israel :[2]
The Spirit of Yahveh has spoken in me[3] — and His word is on my tongue.
The God of Israel said to me — the Rock of Israel spoke :[4]
A Ruler over men, just — a Ruler in God's fear—
And it is like morning-light, when the sun rises, a morning without clouds ;
By sunny brightness, by rain verdure (springs up) from the earth!
For is not my house thus with God ?[5] — for an eternal covenant He has made for me:

[1] עַל, properly substantive: *height* in the local accusative, stands here in pausal form עָל, as in Hos. vii. 16 ; cf. Hos. xi. 7. הֻקַּם for הוּקַם, see Stade, *Gramm.* i. p. 234.

[2] Properly, *the lovely one, the charmer of the songs*.

[3] Ver. 2 announces generally *that* he has received divine revelations ; ver. 3, on the other hand, proclaims *what* was told him by inspiration. דִּבֶּר בְּ is used properly of the "divine suggestion" (Keil), which must precede the prophetic announcement, Hos. i. 2. בְּ in such cases is not merely בְּ *instr.* (= בְּיָד), but denotes : (to speak) into one.

[4] Ver. 3, לִי is to be joined with אָמַר, contrary to the Masoretic division.

[5] כִּי לֹא וגו׳, according to the context, is to be understood interrogatively, just as at the end of the verse כִּי לֹא יַצְמִיחַ ; therefore לֹא for הֲלֹא.

Well furnished with everything and made sure; for all my
    welfare and all satisfaction, should He not make it
    spring forth?
And the good-for-nothing — like thistles, which one shuns, are
    they all [1] — for one seizes them not with the hand,
And if one touches them, he arms himself with iron and spear-
    shaft — and with fire they are consumed just where
    they abide." [2]

It is owing to the solemn form of this testament of David that vers. 3*b* and 4*a* have no verbs, nor is the logical relation of the two sentences indicated. On this account the beginning has been variously understood. Many complete ver. 3 thus: "A ruler over men *will be* or *come*," etc., "*then shall it be* like light of the morning," etc. (Hengstenberg, Keil, Tholuck, Oehler, *et al.*). The ellipsis would be strong, but not impossible in so pathetic an oracle. In this case the oracle would announce a ruler in future days (of course from David's house, ver. 5), in whom justice, fear of God, and power over the world would be perfectly united, so that his empire would be greeted as the welcome dawn of divine light. In support of this prophetic interpretation appeal is made to the solemnity of the entire oracle, which must perforce contain a significant look into the future. It might also be thought that if David did not during his life consciously contrast the true person of the God-anointed one with himself, at least at his death he attained the higher knowledge that the true and real kingdom of God and its king belonged entirely to the future. But decisive against this interpretation of the first verses, in our opinion, is the antithesis of vers. 6 and 7, which describe how the wicked who do pure harm inspire pure aversion, and so will be destroyed root and branch. This mashal-like oracle requires just as general a meaning to be given to vers. 3 and 4, which are then aptly followed by the great, definite

---

[1] בְּהֻלָּם, the ancient, uncontracted form, of which כֻּלָּם is a contraction. Gesenius, *Gram.* § 91, 1, 2.

[2] Vers. 6 and 7 describe in a few drastic touches how one avoids even coming near the ungodly, the bad (בְּלִיַּעַל, opposite of just and God-fearing). Even while seeking to exterminate, one cannot touch them. One burns them on the spot where they dwell (בַּשָּׁבֶת), so as not to spoil other places with seeds of thistles and thorns. According to Wellhausen, indeed, בַּשֶּׁבֶת has crept in from the following line.

example, ver. 5. We therefore complete the sense thus (like Ewald, Thenius, Bunsen, *et al.*): "*If a* ruler over men is just, a ruler in God's fear," or "If one rules justly over men, God-fearing, then is it like morning light, when the sun rises;" *i.e.* from his government pure blessing and satisfaction proceed; it is like a promising daybreak, when the bright rays after refreshing rain gloriously lure forth every green thing. This general rule, a testament worthy of the great king, in whom it was proved most gloriously true, is then confirmed by his own example, ver. 5: "Is it not so with my house?" What holds true generally on earth (cf. the general בָּאָדָם) is shown most palpably in his government. Moreover, the house of him who is ever intent on justice and God's fear has been glorified by God for all future time, and made sure by an "eternal covenant." Or, must not in fact all well-being and satisfaction spring up for him in the future from his house, according to the promise of the Lord? The true servant of God, the man after God's heart, thus declares when dying, that fidelity brings rich reward, and that from justice and the fear of God pure blessing springs beyond hope and understanding. Here, certainly, his gaze is directed to the future. What he leaves behind is a crop full of promise, which has yet to grow; for now when he, the old king, is departing, the sun is not going down, but the morning is only breaking in undreamed-of splendour. The salvation assured to him by God's grace will yet blossom.

If, indeed, מוֹשֵׁל צַדִּיק were understood of a future ruler announced by David, the reference to the future would be more definite and personal. We should then have the considerable advance that, as Oehler puts it, "the knowledge of the idea of monarchy advances to the individualizing of an ideal." Nay, a definite ruler would be announced, marked by justice and piety in fullest measure, in whom all the glory of his house would be unfolded. On the other hand, according to our more general interpretation, we do not find in the words any more personal view than in 2 Sam. vii. But David's gaze rests when dying, like Jacob's, on the future, where first the salvation will spring up, which he has only seen in germ, but which is secured to him by God's inviolable promise. The gaze also of the good among his people is henceforth fixed hopefully on the future days of the house of David, which, built on such firm ground, promises to culminate in greater glory than now belongs to it.

NOTE A.—בַּר, standing absolutely, applies to the Son of Him who is spoken of in the other words: "that He be not angry," etc. The solemn isolation of the word intimates the loftiness of the idea it contains. On the etymology of בַּר=בֵּן (in Hebrew again, Prov. xxxi. 2, also poetic), see Gesenius, *Handwörterbuch*, newly revised by F. Mühlau and W. Volck, *sub voce* בַּר. נָשַׁק (*kal* and *piel*) with personal accusative means nothing but *to kiss*, Sol. Song i. 2. The kiss of homage is meant (1 Sam. x. 1); and, indeed, the word is used chiefly in reference to the homage done to divine beings, 1 Kings xix. 18; Job xxxi. 27. The other acceptations of the passage proposed (cf. Hupfeld, *Comm. zu den Psalmen*) are unsatisfactory; so, too, the impersonal acceptation of the בר as adverb, *purely, sincerely* (Aq., Symm., Hier.), and the reading בּוֹ (Hupfeld): *unite yourselves to Him*, a construction without linguistic warrant.

§ 21. *The Typical Significance of David, Solomon, and the Davidites in Prosperity and Adversity.*

Although David exhibited the Messianic idea in his person and kingdom but imperfectly, and Solomon realized the hopes at first set upon him yet more imperfectly, still their reign formed the zenith of the Israelitish kingdom, and no kings were so worthy as they of the high dignity with which they were invested. Hence their life and songs, especially those of David, were afterwards regarded as typical of the greater Messiah to follow. Thus a series of psalms became in a manner prophetic, although in themselves they contained no reference to the future. These are the properly *Typical Psalms*. On one hand, in the life of those princes or the later Davidites there are conspicuous epochs (coronation, marriage, victory, deliverance) well suited to cause their divine dignity to be celebrated in songs which were afterwards interpreted of the future; while, on the other hand, there were dangers, assaults, and persecutions calculated to bring vividly out the hostility of the world to the Lord's Anointed, the sufferings of the elect saint and the divine help and exalted honour bestowed on him after humiliation. The latter picture, alongside the pictures of Messianic glory, bore abiding witness to a mysterious necessity of suffering in the supreme Servant of God, which suffering also pointed to a purer consummation of the idea of the Servant in the future. Finally, David—the devout suppliant and Psalmist—became a type of the sincere, believing souls who stand in living intercourse with their Lord and pour out their inmost thoughts before Him. On this account his name has been assigned to many songs of this class. And not a few sayings of such songs seemed afterwards to be a prophecy of the greater Son of David, who was to exhibit still more perfectly than His ancestor the ideal of true saintliness.

We have seen that the *Messianic idea*, traceable in its root to the revelations imparted to David and unfolded in the songs first sung by the Anointed one, is as follows. The Davidic king stands in most direct relation to Yahveh, who in virtue of His covenant is really king of this people. Chosen and appointed by the Lord, he represents before the people, nay, before the world, the almighty, sovereign ruler of heaven and earth. But at the same time the vocation of the holy people to be at once God's servant and son culminates in his person. Thus before the Lord the Davidic king represents his people in priestly fashion. The national form of the covenant-idea here becomes personal, without the thought of the national kingdom of God being given up; for the person thus intimately one with God is the national king, the mediator between God and His people.

It is self-evident that this idea was bound to make itself heard in the songs and other utterances of the *Church* under prophetic stimulus. This is the case in the so-called *Regal psalms*, where the Davidic kingdom is celebrated as God-chosen, or the Lord is invoked on its behalf, or on behalf of the reigning king (cf. Psalms like xx., xxi., xlv., etc.). But the ideal element of the Davidic kingdom was especially prominent where any epoch in the government of special lustre set its divine dignity in bright relief. Possibly Ps. xx. was sung on going forth to war, Ps. xxi. on the king's birthday' (Ewald). Ps. xlv. is, in any case, a song extolling the ruler on the day of his marriage with a king's daughter, who is led to him in festal procession. What prince is here celebrated cannot be made out with certainty. But the prophetic style of the hymn and its reception into the Canon perhaps requires us to think of a Davidite.[1]

---

[1] This against Hitzig, who would refer the psalm to the marriage of Ahab with Jezebel, and de Wette, who would refer it to a Persian king, as well as against Ewald, who suggests Jeroboam II. Ewald's inference from ver. 8, that the kingdom must have been an elective kingdom, where the king was merely the first among equals, is completely refuted by ver. 17. Since the fathers of the king reigned previously,

Since בַּת־צֹר (joined with דַר) cannot be an address, it is not said that the bride was Tyrian (so Hupfeld, who supposes a daughter of Hiram, of whose union with Solomon history says nothing). The entry of the well-known Egyptian consort of Solomon might be the subject of the song, whose reference to the Solomonic kingdom there is much to favour, if ver. 17 did not presuppose a line of reigning ancestors of the king which does not suit Solomon. Delitzsch regards the marriage of Joram of Judah with Athaliah of Israel as the occasion of the song.[1] In this case the exhortation to the queen to forget her people and father's house would get all the deeper significance; the pious marriage-wishes were, of course, not fulfilled; the hortatory praises[2] addressed to the king and queen were not laid to heart.

The near relation to God implied in Ps. xlv. 6—a Messianic echo of the prophetic sayings considered in the last sections—should be observed. Still in ver. 6 the personage celebrated is addressed directly as אֱלֹהִים, which is not a forbidden apotheosis, only because in virtue of his dignity he stands in God's place. Even the judges of the people of Israel represented God; to come before the judge is to come before God.[3] But here more is affirmed. It is said:—

"Thy throne, O God, endures for ever and ever; a sceptre
of straightness is the sceptre of Thy rule."

Here a certain identity with the Deity is ascribed not merely to the actual bearer of the office, but to the person of the king, or to his house, his dynasty, so that it will rule for ever (like God); cf. vers. 16 f., 2. As this rule, in virtue of its divine character, far exceeds all other earthly powers in age, so its splendour is immeasurably extended in space. The nations cannot withstand this glorious prince (ver. 5); foreign kings seek his favour

---

the divine anointing with the oil of delight, distinguishing the king from his companions, cannot be the call to the regal office, but refers to the salvation and prosperity with which God distinguished him above his fellow-rulers.

[1] See the reasons in his Commentary.

[2] Cf. the Egyptian custom of exhorting kings by daily eulogistic intercessions for them.

[3] Ex. xxi. 6, xxii. 8, 9, 28; cf. Ps. lxxxii. 1 ff., where even unjust judges are solemnly so named by the Lord (ver. 6). Jesus adduced this passage (ver. 6) to the Jews to prove that His claim to divine Sonship was no blasphemy, since He could boast of Deity with far more right than they to whom it was ascribed in a certain sense in the law (in Holy Writ).

and send to him their daughters (ver. 9); the treasures of the richest cities are offered to him and to his consort (ver. 13), who will gladly exchange the glory of her native court for the higher glory of David's. The sons will rule as gloriously as their predecessors, and as sub-kings will represent everywhere on earth the majesty of the house until they come to reign, ver. 16. This at all events supposes a vast enlargement of the modest Israelitish domain; for, limited to Israelitish territory, especially when divided, the שָׂרִים בְּכָל־הָאָרֶץ would be ridiculous. Even in adverse days the Davidic king makes lofty claims (Ps. lx.). Moreover, looking at Ps. ii., viii., and lxxii. 11, these boundless hopes of glory in the future are by no means unwarranted. But, of course, they can only be understood on the supposition that to the singer's consciousness the kingdom celebrated had a glory superior to every earthly power. Thus a brilliant epoch in the history of the Davidic house was sung; the after-world has referred this song of a king surrounded with god-like *doxa* to the future ruler on David's throne, who would be warranted in claiming Deity with greater right (cf. Isa. ix. 5).

Ps. lxviii.,—the great hymn of war and triumph, which sees in Israel's contests against the hostile kingdoms of the world the Parousia of God, as on Sinai and in Deborah's conflict,—a sort of expansion of Ps. cx., owed its origin to a solemn moment of another kind. The uncertainty of its date has become a proverb.[1] But whether it originated under David or later, it has found a well-merited place in the psalm-book for all time, as a testimony to God's victorious kingdom in Israel, which out of Zion made all nations feel its greatness.

The development of concrete Messianic glory culminates in a psalm bearing Solomon's name (Ps. lxxii.). In it the Church speaks, not the ruler himself. If, then, we wish to retain the Solomonic authorship in accordance with the heading, we must suppose that the wise, poetic (1 Kings v. 12) king, at the beginning of his reign so full of promise,[2] put this prayer into the mouth of the people. At all events the character of the song throughout suits Solomon's days and person. Whereas the

---

[1] Cf. E. Reuss, *Der achtundsechzigste Psalm, ein Denkmal exegetischer Noth und Kunst zu Ehren unserer ganzen Zunft*, Jena 1851.

[2] See prayers composed at the installation of a pre-Solomonic ruler of China in the *Schi-king* (translated by V. v. Strauss), p. 483-489.

Davidic psalms, cx., xviii., lxviii., ii., etc., have to tell of conflict and victory over menacing hostile powers, it is a broad kingdom of untroubled peace that floats as an ideal before this ruler. Instead of martial valour, his most brilliant virtue is the justice which gladly succours the just and defenceless (cf. 1 Kings iii. 5 ff., 16 ff.). The blessing of such peaceful government falls on the land like God's fertilizing rain (2 Sam. xxiii. 4). To this peaceful ruler spontaneous homage is done by Tarshish and the isles of the West, brought near to Solomon by his alliance with the Phœnicians; and in the same way by the kings of Sheba and Seba, with whom he is allied by trade, on the south (Ophir, 1 Kings ix. 28, x. 22), as well as by literary commerce (x. 1 ff.). Thus the divine blessings in nature join with the tribute (gold, ver. 15; cf. 1 Kings x. 10) brought by the farthest nations to make his land the most fortunate in the world. But the king's best reward is found in the intercessions of his subjects, who owe their being and well-being to his justice and gentleness.[1] His fame brightens as long as the sun shines and the moon endures.[2] In his name all nations bless themselves (with ver. 17, cf. Gen. xxii. 18, xxvi. 4; p. 107, *ante*), so that in a special sense he will be the heir of the supreme patriarchal promise!

"May his name endure for ever — as long as the sun shines
                      may his name put forth shoots;
And let them bless themselves in him — all nations call him blessed."

This, too, Solomon was permitted to experience in a certain measure (1 Kings x. 9, 24 f., v. 14). But no doubt even his kingdom remained in extent and glory far behind what this psalm wishes him as the heritage belonging to God's anointed.

---

[1] Ver. 15: "And so he (the one delivered) will remain alive and offer to him what is better than Saba-gold, and make intercession for him continually, bless him at every opportunity." This strangely misunderstood verse is plain enough, directly the מִן in מִזָּהָב is taken as the comparative, in which sense it also elsewhere stands before nouns expressing specially a pre-eminent quality.

[2] In ver. 5 it is disputed whether God is addressed (so *e.g.* Calvin, Delitzsch) or the king (*e.g.* Hupfeld, Hitzig); but the latter answers better to the context. Thus the Messianic character of the king appears, owing to which he remains to all generations an object of grateful reverence. עִם (Dan. iii. 33) and לִפְנֵי (cf. ver. 7) are temporal, not: *as far as the sun shines*. In ver. 17 the imperishable is more definitely separated from the mortal personality of the king.

After the rapid decline of Solomonic glory this psalm also was regarded, with complete justice, as a prophecy awaiting its fulfilment.

Here, too, is the place to mention the *Song of Solomon*, which, according to our opinion explained elsewhere,[1] celebrates originally the noblest, purest love of this king, but on account of Solomon's Messianic dignity was soon understood of the most sacred love with which the Lord woos His Church, and of which the prophets, especially Hosea, had spoken so gloriously. Little as the view of the synagogue and early Church, according to which this poem originated in allegorical intent, corresponds to its vivid, natural freshness, still the reference to the loving relation between the Lord and His Church is so far justified in that, according to unvarying prophetic and apostolic teaching, pure bridal love is an image of God's love, and Solomon is a type of the greater Messiah. Of this conception also the true Son of David brought the consummation, exhibiting the most profound condescension on the part of the heavenly King, and establishing the most intimate and living fellowship with His Church on earth. As, therefore, the marriage-song—Ps. xlv.—points typically to the completion of God's kingdom, so often set forth in the New Testament as a marriage-solemnity, so also is it with this song, which chants the Messianic king and his peerless bride, and illustrates still more strongly the tender love binding the two together,—bridal love with its longing and hoping, seeking and finding, the chaste affection which as a divine flame brooks nothing impure, and ignores all earthly disparity.

Among the typical songs we have to name in the second line the *Passion-psalms*. In keeping with God's wondrous redeeming plan it was typical of the Messiah in high degree that David rose to glory only through the heaviest persecutions, and was forced during the course of his eventful life to drink the cup of affliction to the dregs. Of the sufferings he had to undergo in his persecution by Saul and by Absalom a series of unimpeachable psalms speaks. Many early Christian expositors thought that David is not here always singing of his own sufferings, but occasionally of those of the future Messiah. But these songs spring so plainly from personal experience of affliction, that the

---

[1] Herzog's *Real-Encyk.*, 2nd ed. vi. 245 ff., especially p. 249. In this we follow Delitzsch, *Comm.*

view which makes the poet transport himself into another's soul is altogether excluded by the directness of feeling exhibited. David sings of suffering and sorrow, anguish and distress, actually experienced. Out of woe and peril he struggles upward in prayer to God. But this suffering saint, familiar with the Lord like none else on earth, and yet so beset by heavy affliction, was intended to set forth beforehand a divine decree, which was only to be completely realized in the perfectly Just One, who endured the hardest treatment. No conscious reference to the future lies in these songs, so far as they complain of suffering; they are all but without the prophetic stamp, which cannot be mistaken in Ps. cx., ii., etc.; but in the objective divine plan certainly there is a connection between the imperfect types in which the divine purpose is barely hinted and the complete image which was yet to appear. Later prophecy (*e.g.* Deutero-Isaiah) then recognised such a connection, took up the features of the martyr-image sketched in the psalms, and embodied them in its perfect image of the future. But on many points, where the language went beyond existing facts, the actual fulfilment brought a literal fulfilment. The *hyperbolical* character adhering to the suffering of the Old Testament saint was to *become fact*.

In this class of psalms their prophetic significance does not essentially depend on the question whether they originate with David himself, or with a later heir of his crown, or issued from the Church. The divine idea of the suffering saint might also be exhibited beforehand in another; as in fact Job and Jeremiah, although no Davidites, were typical of Christ's sufferings, and were so used by Deutero-Isaiah. But in any case it was of essential significance that the same *David*, who in the unique consciousness of his divine kingship could boast of a relation to God inconceivably close, was also obliged, beyond every one else of his age and nation, to complain of unmerited, malignant suffering. In his person we see united the two figures which to later Jewish thought fell apart in dualistic fashion—the image of the glorious king and the image of the mysterious martyr.

That David's troubles and persecutions gave rise to psalms, in which he poured out his inner misery before God, and at the same time fought his way to firm trust in the answering, delivering God, is also proved by the fact that later songs of this kind were referred to David, the bold suppliant in distress. By way of example we name as psalms which undoubtedly spring from him, and show how in bitter assaults from men he was conscious of his close relation to God, Ps. iii., iv., vi., vii., xi. xvii., cf. the opening of Ps. xviii. Ps. xli. we also assign to this class, and indeed to the time when Absalom's rebellion and the treachery of his best friend pressed heavily on the king suffering from sickness. That it is a person politically powerful, a king, who in these circumstances comforts himself with his God, is clear from vers. 5, 7, 10. How typical this sharp anguish was of the greatest Sufferer, the latter himself emphasizes, John xiii. 18: ἵνα ἡ γραφὴ πληρωθῇ· Ὁ τρώγων μετ' ἐμοῦ τὸν ἄρτον ἐπῆρεν ἐπ' ἐμὲ τὴν πτέρναν αὐτοῦ. Of course David is depicting his own experience: Ahithophel, whose counsel was to him like God's oracle, has basely betrayed him and secretly made common cause with the foe, as he well sees. Yet it is not a perfect saint who prays this psalm. Despite the confession of sin in ver. 5, he is hated without right and reason; in the last resort he is so attacked on account of his piety; compare the declaration of his innocence, ver. 12. For this reason his suffering is typical. And the bitter experience of faithless betrayal by a trusted favourite could not be wanting in the cup of Him in whom the full measure of sacred endurance for God's sake was to be seen. This feature is also found in the suffering image of other Old Testament saints; so Ps. lv. (vers. 12–14, 20 f.), which we do not regard as Davidic (see ver. 14).

Because it was David who in deepest tribulation first struck his harp in such a way that its tones became prophetic beyond his dreaming and understanding, men thought they heard his voice in kindred songs of other devout, sorely-tried suppliants, and sought in his life for occasions which might have given rise to particular songs. In the case of Ps. liv., lvi., lvii., lix., indeed, no valid objection can be raised against the view that they originate, as the inscriptions state, in the days of Saul's persecution. On the other hand, the Davidic origin of Ps. lii. (cf. ver. 10), despite a similar statement, is very unlikely.

Ps. xxii., the most notable of the Passion-psalms, is scarcely by David himself, as the inscription states and Delitzsch tries to prove. But the author was an eminent leader of the theocratic Church.[1] At present he seems banished or rather a prisoner, utterly

---

[1] Hitzig suggests Jeremiah.

helpless, given over to hate and scorn. This undeserved suffering, having its ground essentially in the suppliant's close relation to God (ver. 8), at last humbles him to the lowest point. He feels himself no longer a man, merely a worm (ver. 6). Even if, like Delitzsch, we call to mind the time of severest affliction which David passed through (1 Sam. xxiv. 15, xxvi. 20), and at the same time take into account David's sensitive temperament, which felt enmity and affliction in keenest measure, no adequate reason for the special wails of the psalm readily offers itself. At the time of Saul's persecution David was no broken man, such as the suppliant of the psalm seems to be. Thus we have to suppose a saint perhaps of the next age, who experienced suffering in the severest degree. In him David's sufferings appear in aggravated form, and just so the consciousness of martyrdom, *i.e.* of a good confession as the reason of the hostility of men.

He begins at once with the memorable words: "My God, my God, why hast Thou forsaken me?" in which a strong contradiction is evident between the devotion of one who can call God *his* God and his fate, which is that of one forsaken by God. As is well known, Jesus on the cross made this saying His own,[1] intimating that this intrinsic contradiction was realized in Him in highest measure—Him, the Son of God, abandoned by God to the most ignominious of deaths! If the Psalmist could only address God as his in a limited sense, our Lord could do this with fullest justice. And what the former complains of in mere figurative, though highly-coloured terms, befell the Son of God in veritable fact. This applies to several statements in the psalm, which are not to be pressed literally, but were literally fulfilled in Christ. Herein we see the objective connection established of set purpose by God's Providence, which so framed even the phrasing of the pious prayer that without knowledge of the suppliant it became prophecy, and again so controlled even what was outward, and seemingly accidental, in the history of Jesus, that the old prophetic oracles appear incorporated in it.

As ver. 1 furnished the words in which the Lord in His mortal agony gave expression to His feeling of deepest dismay, so ver. 6 ff. seem to describe the situation and surroundings of the Crucified.

---

[1] Mark xv. 34; Matt. xxvii. 46, the latter of which gives the old Hebrew wording, the former the Aramaic, Palestinian country-speech, in which the prayer on the cross was uttered.

With ver. 7 cf. Mark xv. 29; with ver. 8, Matt. xxvii. 43; with vers. 13–15, the exposure of the worn, anguished sufferer, especially John xix. 28. In ver. 16 the reading is uncertain.[1] But the Masoretic reading כָּאֲרִי is utterly impracticable despite ver. 21, and perhaps arose out of the latter. Hence, apart from all dogmatic prepossession, which Hupfeld holds alone capable of taking our view, the verbal כָּאֲרוּ of the versions is preferable, which afterwards ceased perhaps to be understood. כּוּר = כָּאַר, *to dig, dig through.* It seems to refer to the ill-treatment of a prisoner who, robbed of his clothes, and nailed fast by hands and feet, is abandoned to the derision of the rabble surrounding him. That the suppliant literally suffered this extreme outrage, is perhaps not to be supposed; his animal metaphors also show that he paints his desperate situation in drastic colours. But all these features were to find their realization in the martyr-form on Golgotha—the exposure of the victim, the painful nailing of hands and feet, His nakedness,[2] the division of His garments and casting lots for His cloak (Matt. xxvii. 35; cf. Mark xv. 24; Luke xxiii. 35; John xix. 24). The oracle is one of those which were fulfilled even in the seemingly accidental form of the Hebrew parallelism, where one member differs scarcely perceptibly from the other, as the fourth Gospel especially points out, where also Ps. xxii. 18 is expressly quoted.

From ver. 22 onwards the urgent prayer, to which the previous complaints lead up, passes into confident praise of the delivering grace which the suppliant is confident of experiencing. But the manner in which he describes the public thanksgiving for his deliverance is no less noteworthy than the picture of his sufferings. Not only will he, like a David, Hezekiah, and other pious kings, pay his thank-offering before all the people, so that they who fear God may enjoy this sacramental feast; the conclusion of the song, vers. 27–31, speaks even of the heathen coming from the ends of the earth and worshipping the Lord; "for the kingdom is the Lord's, and He will rule among the heathen" (ver. 28). Nay, it seems that the deliverance of this sufferer and his praise of

---

[1] The Hebrew MSS. almost without exception give כארי, not כארו. The LXX., on the other hand, have ὤρυξαν, and therefore read כארו; just so Syr. Vulg. Jerome. See particulars in the commentaries of Hupfeld and Delitzsch.

[2] Ver. 17a seems, on account of ver. 17b, to apply to this feature, which does not preclude the "counting of the bones" being at the same time a sign of emaciation in consequence of great anguish.

the Lord will bring about this conversion; cf. יוֹפְרוּ, ver. 27, to which תְּהִלָּתִי is to be supplied. As he invites his own brethren, in accordance with his vow, to a great sacrificial feast, so too he expects the heathen there as guests.

As, then, the beginning and middle of the psalm are typical, so the conclusion is prophetic. And it is just the prophetic conclusion which proves that we have before us here, not an imaginary type, but one that is the work of the Spirit. The suppliant was an intelligent leader of the Church; his prayer ends with an oracle of prophetic illumination; thus even in his bitter complaints he was directed by a higher Spirit, and not unworthy to be a prophetic type of *Him* who by His unique martyrdom founded the kingdom of God over the world.

Presumably Ps. xl. springs from the same author[1] as Ps. xxii. It also has the appearance of being a prayer of an eminent saint of the Church, perhaps a king; and stands related to the previous song of complaint and prayer as a grateful response after deliverance from the greatest distress and danger.[2]

Pondering, then, what thank-offering is most acceptable to God, the lofty suppliant comes to see that all words of gratitude are too little to praise the Lord's wondrous grace (ver. 6), while no sacrifices can really satisfy God. The only true, God-pleasing sacrifice is the surrender of one's own person in complete obedience to God's will revealed in word and writing.

Ver. 6 ff.:—

" In slain-offering and dedicated gift Thou hast no pleasure —
        my ears Thou hast digged!
Burnt-offering and sin-offering Thou requirest not — then I
        said: Behold, I am ready — in the roll
        of the book it is written concerning me!
I delight to perform what pleases Thee — and Thy law is in
        my inmost heart."

The sentence " my ears hast Thou digged " is not introductory to a disclosure afterwards made to him by God, but in contrast with what precedes: God prefers an obedient servant who listens to His voice, to one who brings many offerings. Just so ver. 7 is to be explained as an expression of complete readi-

---

[1] Cf. especially בְּקָהָל רָב, xxii. 25, and xl. 9 f., as well as in the related Ps. xxxv. 18.

[2] Cf. xl. 3, 9 f., with xxii. 22, 25.

ness to observe the divine law. To take this also, with Hupfeld, as merely introductory to the public praise of the Lord, as if all obedience consisted in this, does not agree with the emphasis of the words in ver. 8; although, certainly, according to Ps. lxix. 30 f., public thanksgiving is the best sacrifice, and the most pleasing to God. Against this view ver. 9 f. also tells, speaking as they do plainly of the past. Thus "אָז אָמַרְתִּי הִנֵּה־בָאתִי וגו'" applies to the writer's resolve to place himself, his own person, completely at God's disposal. As the servant, when his lord calls him, says הִנֵּנִי (1 Sam. iii. 4), so here the delivered saint: "Lo, I am come to do what Thou wishest." How he knows the Lord's wish the further sentence tells: "In the book-roll it is written concerning me; there it is prescribed to me what I have to do" (2 Kings xxii. 13). For the rest, this sentence gives the impression that it is an eminent personage who speaks thus (which is already evident from ver. 3), nay, one of whom the book of the divine law specifically treats. It is a king, so we must conclude, one whose conduct was there specially described, not merely in "the law of the king" (Deut. xvii. 14 ff.), but in all that is said in the Torah respecting government and judgment. Ps. li. 17 would naturally suggest David himself,[1] where the latter has spoken in similar terms of the value of sacrifice, in exact correspondence with the great principle uttered by his paternal friend Samuel, 1 Sam. xv. 22 f., according to which *obedience* is better than sacrifice. We shall, however, see presently in the case of Ps. lxix. that it is rather a later confessor, jealous for his Lord's honour, who sung these songs. Moreover, the antithesis between sacrifice and obedience is not an absolute one, as if God had no pleasure at all in sacrifice, and in no case required it. On the contrary, the harsh form of the contrast is to be explained by the Shemitic idiom, which prefers absolute to relative modes of expression. In 1 Sam. xv. 22 is found the relative mode of speech, which explains the present passage.[2]

Although the worst danger is escaped for the time, the devout suppliant is by no means out of all danger. On the contrary, the conclusion of ver. 12 shows that much still threatens him, against which he would fain assure himself of the Lord's abiding

---

[1] So most recently, Bredenkamp, *Gesetz und Propheten*, p. 59 ff.
[2] Cf. Marti in the Jena *Jahrb. f. protest. Theologie*, 1880, p. 309 ff.

help. The psalm which had begun with the thanksgiving of one delivered, concludes with request for further protection. But we should be just as little warranted in cutting it in two on this account as in the case of Ps. xxii., where the certainty of being heard turns complaint into joyous thanksgiving.

If, then, Ps. xl., rightly understood, forms an unquestionable unity, of course we have no right to refer the passage quoted above (ver. 6 ff.) to any other subject than the one who everywhere else in the psalm describes his painful and elevating experiences, and in ver. 13 confesses that his afflictions are not undeserved. The speaker everywhere is a saint, closely united indeed with God, yet humanly imperfect. When the Epistle to the Hebrews applies Ps. xl. 6 ff. to Christ, this is only right, because such an one might, of course, be a type of Jesus, even if he was not David himself. Especially the passage in which he describes his full surrender to obey the Lord as the true sacrifice, makes him well adapted to serve as a type of the obedient Sufferer, who came to fulfil the whole law implanted deeply within Him, and into whose mouth therefore, as into no other's, these words might be put, as is done in Heb. x. 5 ff., " on his entrance into the world." [1]

In a line with Ps. xxii. and xl. stands Ps. lxix., which, like Ps. xl. especially, refers to the person of the suppliant, and touches on the circumstances of his suffering, the tenor of his thoughts, and his mode of expressing his feelings. Here the cause of his sufferings and their nature come out still more plainly. It is fidelity to God, zeal for the house of the Lord, that has drawn on the sufferer the bitter hate of many foes, and estranged his neighbours from him (vers. 6, 7 ff.).[2] His mourning for the decline of godliness has exposed him to the grossest mockery (ver. 10 f.). His suffering, therefore, is that of a stedfast confessor who, although not free from wandering and sin in God's

---

[1] The citation is marked by exact adherence to the LXX., even where the LXX. deviate from the Hebrew text. Instead of "my ears hast Thou digged," the Epistle to the Hebrews puts the more general σῶμα δὲ κατηρτίσω μοι, which acquires a special sense in its context. So its author read in the LXX., who did not understand the Hebrew phrase, and found it too hard. Hence they generalized it, referring it to the forming of man's body in general. Hupfeld, de Wette, Bleek take a different view. They think that a clerical error ΣΩΜΑ, instead of Σ ΩΤΙΑ, crept in. But the κατηρτίσω, which is also a generalization, tells against this view.

[2] Ver. 9: "Zeal for Thy house consumed me, and the revilings of those who reviled Thee are fallen upon me!" Cf. John ii. 17.

sight (ver. 5), is yet unjustly[1] persecuted by men for his piety and stedfast testimony. They have no sympathy with him, but unmercifully aggravate his torments. "And they offered me poison for my food, and for my thirst gave me vinegar to drink"[2] (ver. 21). Still he does not despair, but, as one who waits for *his* God (ver. 3 ; Ps. xxii. 1), builds on the help of the Lord, and in spirit sees himself again exalted ; whereupon he intends to glorify God's name in song, which is an offering more acceptable to God than high-horned bullocks (cf. Ps. xl.). That it is David who so prays, as the inscription says, is not directly confirmed in the psalm. For David could not well speak according to the terms of vers. 8, 9 ; ver. 33 also implies an actual imprisonment. This may also be decisive against the Davidic authorship of Ps. xl. and xxii. On the other hand, the author must, as is true too of Ps. xxxii. and xl., be a conspicuous member, if not the head, of the believing Church (lxix. 6, 32).[3]

On p. 167 we have described even the personal relation of David in his capacity as a devout believer, apart from the high position assigned him by God and the humiliation and trial through which the Lord led him, as possessing a typical character which was to be consummated in David's greater Son. This relation between God and the soul inseparably one with Him and happy in Him, certainly finds expression often enough in the lofty regal songs that sing of the Messiah's dignity; in a remarkable way, with special intensity and vigour, it is expressed in the Passion-psalms of David and his like-minded companions in suffering of a later day. But along with these the songs are significant, in which David bears testimony, more as a man than as a king, to his salvation in God, without such testimony being wrung from him by distress and tribulation. A glorious example of this kind is Ps. xvi., in which David commends the happy lot that has fallen to him, the blessedness of which consists, not in any earthly greatness or outward fortune, but in fellowship with

---

[1] The citation John xv. 25, ἐμίσησάν με δωρεάν, refers to ver. 4 ; the saying is also found in the similar psalm, xxxv. 19.

[2] Cf. John xix. 28 ff. ; Matt. xxvii. 34, 48 ; Mark xv. 23, 36 ; Luke xxiii. 36.

[3] Several features suit the imprisoned Jeremiah (Hitzig), as in Ps. xxii., xl. Vers. 2, 14 (cf. xl. 2) might be an allusion to the miry pit in which he was imprisoned (Jer. xxxviii. 6), but no inference can be drawn from this. Vers. 12 and 22 do not agree with the position of Jerusalem then, nor ver. 26 with Jeremiah's fate.

Yahveh. It is not a cry for deliverance from special affliction, but a prayer for preservation from such evil as may befall any mortal. In the Lord he knows himself safe from this, even from the danger of death, Ps. xvi. 8-11:—

"I have set Yahveh ever before me;—for at my right hand
(He stands); I shall not totter!
On this account my heart rejoices and my glory exults—my
flesh also dwells in security.
For Thou wilt not abandon my soul to the underworld—nor
give up Thy saints to see the pit.
Thou wilt make known to me the way of life—fulness of
joy is before Thy face—blessednesses
in Thy right hand for ever."

It is true, the New Testament may easily lead to our reading something more definite in this testimony than it originally affirms. A prophecy of the resurrection of Christ, who "cannot see corruption," uttered *expressis verbis*, is obtained at best on the scarcely tenable assumption of the LXX., that שַׁחַת here denotes corruption,[1] and that the keri חֲסִידְךָ (sing.) is to be preferred; even then a resurrection from the grave would not necessarily be spoken of, but rescue from the state of death generally. But, on the other hand, to find in the passage merely the hope of long life does not do justice to the words. Observe the categorical form: "*Thou wilt not*[2] forsake my soul, that it should fall victim to the underworld; *Thou wilt not* give up Thy saints, so that they should see the pit." Would it be doing justice to these words to make them mean: The good shall live longer than others? Is it not said directly: They shall not fall a prey to the underworld, shall not see the pit? It is a word of bold faith that we have here, as in Ps. lxxiii. 23 ff. In closest fellowship with God,[3] David is conscious of triumph over the grave and death. For whoever is inseparably one with the Most High, over him death has no power. With the Lord he ever finds life and bliss. *How* the Lord will preserve His familiar friend from the power of death and grant him eternal

---

[1] So certainly Böttcher, *Ausf. Lehrbuch*, i. p. 419, who distinguishes this שַׁחַת as masc. from the fem. coming from שׁוּחָה, and attributes to it the meaning "corruption, destruction." The ת would then be radical.

[2] לֹא, not אַל, is used.

[3] Cf. Hupfeld on Ps. xvi. 10.

life is not declared; this does not trouble one united with God and joyfully certain of his heritage. In another psalm (xlix. 15) the same confidence appears in a more definite form: God will rescue the pious one, even him who in appearance falls a prey to the underworld, from its power, and prepare for him another dwelling. Ps. xvi. 10 f. gives no indication of the mode in which God will save His people from the bitterness of death. But that He will do it the singer is certain from his intercourse with the living God. For one who has chosen God for his portion to fall a prey to the world of shades (observe the ל in לִשְׁאֹל) and taste the destruction of the grave (רָאָה שָׁחַת), would be an impossible abandonment on God's part (עָזַב), an act of forsaking (נָתַן) irreconcilable with God's faithfulness.

As certainly, then, as Jesus is the Christ, of whom David, the Messiah of his age, was the inadequate type, as certainly as the ruling feature of this psalm—heartfelt union between God and the soul of one whom God has chosen and who has chosen God—was perfectly realized in Jesus, so certainly must the conquest of death and the grave attain complete realization in Him. The passage is one of those, even apart from its quotation in the Acts, which would convince any one enlightened by God's Spirit of the intrinsic necessity of Christ's resurrection, and by which the Lord proved the resurrection to His disciples. A fuller examination of the passage is found in the Pentecost-discourse of Peter (Acts ii. 25 ff.) and in the synagogue-discourse of Paul at Antioch (xiii. 34 ff.). It is evident from these two citations that the passage was a principal authority in the proof of Jesus' Messiahship before Israelitish hearers. And according to what has just been said, rightly. The variation of wording in the LXX., suggesting a still more definite reference to the resurrection (from the grave) on the third day, is a secondary matter; the argument of the apostles by no means stands or falls with it; apart from this point, they are quite in the right when they mention the imperfection of David, seen in the fact that he died and was buried, whereas according to David's own words the perfectly Just One should not be given up to the underworld. It is just as pertinent when they point out Christ as the one who verified the saying of David. And Peter's description of the saying of the Israelitish king as prophetic, as spoken in foresight of the true Messiah and His resurrection, is well justified by ii. 30,

—God's standing in so intimate a relation to David was a preparation for the far more intimate one of David's Son; what David beheld in moments of elevated devotion was a foresight of what God would afterwards reveal of His grace and truth. Thus this psalm-word was prophetic, awaiting a future fulfilment of unimagined glory, even if the suppliant was not aware that another only instead of himself would enjoy perfect religious fellowship, and prove it by perfect conquest over death.

If we look back on the typical psalms, their common mark is, that the reference to another person than that of the suppliant is not present in the latter's consciousness. They treat of the Messiah not expressly but implicitly, so far as in the singers, or in those sung of, the future Messiahship has already acquired life and provisional shape in its different aspects. True, the specifically prophetic cannot be entirely severed from the typical element, inasmuch as these songs not seldom speak consciously of things which will only obtain perfect shape in the future. Moreover, even in O. T. days these psalms had a *history*. The more that experience showed the human fragility of the typical Messiahship, the more loudly and definitely that the prophets spoke of a future perfect shaping of the divine ideas, so much the more certainly must these announcements have seemed prophetic to the typical representatives of these ideas; the superabundant import detached itself from their persons, and found its unity and the security for its realization in the person of the Messiah expected in the future. Schultz calls this transforming of the typical into the prophetic a fruit of the Church's thought.[1] No doubt it was still more a fruit of the prophets' thought. But the main question is, whether this reference of the testimonies of the suppliants to the future was predominantly subjective or was thoroughly justified on objective grounds; in other words, whether the ideal blessings that became afterwards the possession of the Church were arbitrarily clothed in past forms, imported into the old sayings, or whether those types and their utterances

[1] *Stud. und Krit.* 1866, p. 42, *Ueber doppelten Schriftsinn*. This title is misleading, since it suggests the notion of a second sense superposed without organic connection; whereas the prophetic sense grows organically out of the historico-psychological one, its germ lying already in the latter. For the rest, even the author acknowledges (p. 12) an inner relation, an essential affinity between the import of such psalms and what happened to Christ; in such a way, indeed, that the words gained their full sense and import, their deepest significance, first in Christ.

were meant by the will of the Spirit, whose work they were, to point to the perfect future. Only one who knows the living Spirit of God that, raised above human consciousness, controls human existence, thinking and speaking, and designedly moulds them into one vast system—only he will recognise prophecy in these songs of a David, Solomon, Jeremiah, as Christ and the apostles did. Moreover, only this view of history can lay claim to the name of *Christian*.

With Ps. xvi. a saying of the Chokma, prophetic in a certain sense, may be combined. We mean Job xix. 25–27. As in that song the popular conception of a state bordering on non-existence in the kingdom of the dead is transcended by the consciousness of blessed fellowship with God, so here that negative theory of a deeply unfortunate man is seen to be vanquished by the certainty that an adjustment of the contradictions of this life must ensue after death.

"But I am certain that my Redeemer is living, and as Afterman (*Nachmann*) He will arise upon the dust.[1] And after my skin which is there destroyed,[2] and free from my flesh shall I behold Eloah, whom I shall behold for my good, and my eyes shall see Him, not another's."[3]

As modern philosophy (Kant's *Kritik der praktischen Vernunft*) asserted immortality as a postulate of justice, so the Israelitish Chokma, from its knowledge of the living God, came to postulate an adjustment after death of the moral contradiction found in the temporal destinies of men. Such a case is that of the unutterably afflicted, pious Job, who is falling victim to death apparently without remedy, misunderstood and condemned for his misfortune even by his friends. He knows the just God too well not to be sure that his innocence and upright disposition towards God will come to light after death, if not before, and

---

[1] God Himself arises as גֹּאֵל, Vindicator and Afterman, upon the dust, under which the one unjustly condemned lies buried. יָקוּם in the *Kal* cannot signify *raising up*, but intimates the new vital power arising on the scene of death.

[2] אַחַר, not of place: *behind*, but time: *after* my skin. This requires fuller explanation, which is given in נִקְּפוּ־זֹאת. מִבְּשָׂרִי must be parallel with this; therefore not: *out of my flesh* (recovered or risen again), but *free from it*.

[3] Others explain: not as a stranger, but as a friend shall I behold God. But עֵינַי requires the antithesis above. He himself will enjoy the satisfaction of seeing God as his avenger and vindicator; not merely will others be forced to see God's revelation in Job's favour.

indeed in such a way that he himself will be present in personal vitality. We see here how the certainty of a life after death is born out of painful conflict. What in xiv. 13 ff. was mere longing desire, in xvi. 18 took the shape of bold demand, and in xix. 25 has become joyous certainty, namely, that even death cannot bury the right. In ver. 23 f., Job wished that his words (*i.e.* the assertions of his good right) were graven in stone, so that he might appeal to after ages. But there is no need of this; he has another, higher confidence. Even if he dies, a Goel will maintain his right after death. Since xvi. 18 speaks of blood innocently shed, in this Goel we have to think first of a blood-avenger. Still this expression, like the blood-shedding, is figurative. It is his Vindicator, who after death redeems him from the unjust ban pressing heavily upon him. This Goel is none else than Eloah (xvi. 19), his seeming opponent. Thus he has a representative who is *living*, *i.e.* not subject to death.[1] And the satisfaction which God grants him is, that he will behold Him after death—the God who now hides Himself from him and will not suffer him to approach Him. Then the dark riddle is solved and the ban broken. The greatest bliss a believer can conceive is this beholding of God.

Grand as is this inward conquest of death through the certainty of righteousness in God's sight and fellowship with Him, still the passage does not contain a direct Messianic prophecy, as has been often thought, the raising of the flesh by the Redeemer in the N. T. sense having been expressly found here.[2] The function of the Chokma in general is not the further prophetic development of the revelation received, but its application to practical life. But a weighty consequence, which we encounter also in prophecy, is here drawn from the knowledge of the true God. If, as Job shows, God's truth and justice do not find expression in individual life in this world (which constitutes a demand for a revelation after death), then prophecy brings the certainty that God's glory, which otherwise would lack complete manifestation on earth, will be revealed even to the dead. And if Job, the pattern saint and also pattern sufferer, mis-

---

[1] This reminds of the living God, from whom Jesus proves the resurrection of the dead, Mark. xii. 26 f.

[2] Also Hölemann's attempt (*Bibelstudien*, v. p. 178) to consider Job himself as the afterman and Goel rising up on the dust, must be rejected.

understood by every one, because he seems condemned by God Himself, whereas his suffering is martyr-suffering, by which God refutes the Accuser—if Job was a type of the alone really Sinless One, who had to suffer the more in virtue of an obscure but blessed decree of God, then in the latter also, who went to death unvindicated, the power of the holy, living God will be most gloriously revealed, since God could not leave His most faithful Servant in the dust of death. Thus the intrinsic necessity of the resurrection of Christ follows in point of fact from passages like the present one, although it does not speak consciously of the resurrection of One to come. The New Testament nowhere expressly brings this saying of Job into association with Christ, although it may have found its place in a pneumatic "opening of the Scriptures," such as is told of in Luke xxiv. 44–46.

§ 22. *The Dwelling of Yahveh on Zion.*

When the God of redemptive history bound Himself to the Davidic house by His covenant with it, thus giving His kingdom on earth a human and personal centre, His rule on earth at the same time gained a *local* centre. Part of the mission of His Anointed One was to build a house to the Lord (2 Sam. vii. 13), part of his dignity to be a priest for ever at Jerusalem (Ps. cx. 4). It is thereby declared that the gracious presence of God among His people, promised to them ever since the making of the Mosaic covenant, is to receive an abiding character. The Lord chose Zion[1] to be His holy mountain, where the idea of God's Church is to acquire full and complete form.

Ps. xxiv. celebrates the entry of the Lord into the proud gates of the citadel of Zion, probably on the transference of the ark to the residence of David, 2 Sam. vi. 12 ff. (vers. 7–10), and also directs how the people are to behave to the "holy mountain" now rising in their midst (vers. 1–6). The two halves of the song form a unity. To the dwellers in Jerusalem and the neighbourhood it is something new to have Yahveh

---

[1] The exceedingly frequent mention of *Zion* as the residence of the Lord is aptly explained by the opinion recently come into favour, that by it is meant, not the broad south-west hill of Jerusalem, as tradition would have, but the *temple-mountain*, so that the rare name Moriah then merely designates the rib of Zion supporting the sanctuary. See my journal, *Durch's heilige Land*, 1879 (2nd ed.), p. 91, 98.

dwelling within their walls; on this account they are reminded of the sacredness of the spot. True, the God who takes up His abode here is the Lord of heaven and earth, to whom everything belongs that He has made (vers. 1, 2). But He has chosen for Himself a hallowed spot, where He desires to be visited by a sanctified Church, and to bestow on it special blessing. The sanctity He requires is not mere Levitical purity, but purity of hands, heart, and lip. After such a Church is gathered on the mount of the Lord, Yahveh can make His entry, and the hoary, venerable gates are summoned to lift up their heads, even their lofty lintels being too low to admit so lofty a Lord, "the King of glory," "Yahveh of hosts," so called as God of the heavenly legions.[1]

Henceforth, therefore, the Lord of the world has His seat in an extraordinary sense on Zion, whence He judges the whole world (Ps. cx. 2) and bestows wondrous blessings on His people and Church; on which account Jerusalem is celebrated in so many psalms as the city of the great king, *i.e.* of God.[2] If Sinai was the mountain where divine majesty proclaimed amid the terrors of God's appearing over the people an inviolable law, Mount Zion, on the other hand, represents His gracious presence *within* His Church,—a view whose influence is felt in the New Testament (Gal. iv. 24–26), the idea of Zion, the city of God, no doubt growing more and more spiritual. But we believe we ought, in opposition to modern criticism, definitely to assert, that even in the Davidic-Solomonic age unique significance was ascribed to the temple on this hill, because it was regarded as the dwelling of the God of redemption, as David and his successors were regarded as the Anointed of Yahveh. Not first in the age of Isaiah did Zion rise before the prophetic vision above all mountains, although certainly then prophecy asserted its eternal significance with special emphasis. Even the pre-Isaianic prophets (Obad. ver. 17; Joel iii. 16; Amos i. 2) presuppose this local centre of the

---

[1] If in the divine name—Yahveh *Zebaoth*—the hosts of Israel were meant, the latter name would probably be found. Of course Israel may be called "the hosts of Yahveh" (Ex. xii. 41), since He is pleased to call Israel His Zebaoth, Ex. vii. 4; cf. Ps. xliv. 9=lx. 10, cviii. 11. But it would be too trifling to honour God by calling Him God of hosts in the sense: *God of our army*. The heavenly army no doubt as a rule stands in the sing., as in Josh. v. 14; but see Ps. ciii. 21 (cf. 20), where the plural occurs (certainly not with fem. ending).

[2] Cf. Ps. xlvi., xlviii., lxxxvii. (of which afterwards), xciii., xcvii., xcix., etc.

theocracy, this starting-point of judgment and salvation; thus confirming the testimony of the Davidic psalms, according to which at the same time when He chose David's person and house, He was pleased to take up His abode on Zion for ever. Even the prophecies which do not speak expressly of the Davidic Messiah, but describe God's perfect condescension to His Church and His dwelling in it, represent the Lord as throned on Zion. The New Testament first strips off this local dress (John iv. 21), while verifying the substance of the O. T. Zion-idea in all its completeness and purity.

SECOND PART.

THE PROPHETIC WORD AS THE HERALD OF THE SECOND BIRTH
OF GOD'S KINGDOM AND THE PLEDGE OF ITS
FUTURE CONSUMMATION.

FIRST SECTION.

THE PROPHETS OF THE PRE-ASSYRIAN PERIOD: OBADIAH, JOEL.

§ 23. *General Character of Prophecy in the Pre-exilian Period.*

WITH the founding of the Davidic monarchy and Solomon's temple-building, the divine rule — the subject of the previous promises — had reached a provisional conclusion in its course of development. The Messiah, *i.e.* the reigning monarch of David's house, was the ruler representing God upon earth, to whom all nations must in time submit, and the high priest representing the people before God. God had what He had long aimed at: He dwelt in the midst of a people which, according to His law and testament, did Him priestly service as His servant and also His son. One might now expect that from this point prophecy would limit itself to the further developing of this divine rule, and therefore merely announce its extension over the whole world. This claim of God is grounded in His nature, and from the first was intimated in His word as His goal; it was also declared with full consciousness by His Messiah as we saw in his psalms. The historically-existing kingdom of God, even in its greatest extension under Solomon, was still capable of vast local expansion, and in fact such expansion constantly appears henceforth in the programme of the prophets.

But from the first the divine idea of God's kingdom was of far too great ethical depth to allow the prophets, flattering the national feeling, to direct their gaze to a mere extension and perfecting of the empirical divine rule, and to predict a progressive enlargement of the existing divine rule and aggrandizement of God's people. On the contrary, God's faithful speakers were obliged first to rebuke the inner apostasy of Israel from its God, and from that time to foretell the dissolution of the present form of God's kingdom. Here, too, it is said: " Judgment must begin at the house of God" (1 Pet. iv. 17). Nay, it began at David's house, distinguished as it was above all the people. For how little the existing national kingdom of the Lord corresponded to God's will, was shown most glaringly in the Messiah Himself — king by divine grace. The flash of the menacing prophetic word smote David himself, and only by immediate and humble submission to that word was he able to soften the penalty into one of a temporary character. Solomon, whose response to the voice of conscience was persistent obstinacy, brought on the revolt of the northern tribes from the house of David, which soon saw itself reduced to the one tribe of Judah.[1]

This event was of high significance for the development of prophecy. Not without effect was a prophet obliged to foretell this dismemberment,—the beginning of the ruin of the kingdom,—which seemed to contradict every promise and hope. At one blow the entire realization of God's great plan seemed to be compromised, or at least postponed for a long period. The people and its king had shown themselves not only incompetent, but unworthy to take the lofty position assigned them by God; and the Lord showed His holy severity, which will not let itself be trifled with, least of all by His own people. The Lord cannot and will not renounce the lordship which He reserved to Himself in His law. Therefore He Himself overturns what He had built up. Nor did this overturning judgment stop at the dismemberment of the kingdom. In view of the still increasing corruption of the people, prophecy foretells their banishment for centuries, first that of the northern, then also of the southern kingdom. We here see how deep-seated to the eye of the prophets the evil is; the entire national life is corroded by it, so that the political nationality must first be broken utterly to pieces before any healing of Joseph's wound can be thought of. Notwithstanding all God's grace and favour, the sinful king and people cannot be spared a doom bordering on annihilation.

But God's decree is not frustrated by such guilt. The covenant of promise made with Abraham and affirmed to David is too firmly based to render a complete and final rejection of the people of Israel and the house of David conceivable. The

[1] 1 Kings xi. 13, 32, xxxvi. 12, 20; cf. Herzog, vii. 184.

inexorable severity and incorruptible truthfulness of the prophets are not of more divine sublimity than the confidence with which, despite the storm of judgment directly impending, they expect the appearing of a glorious salvation. Thus, up to the Babylonian exile (*i.e.* up to the complete dissolution and destruction of the visible theocracy) the promise of salvation forms the bright fringe on the dark judgment-cloud, which the host of prophetic seers saw hanging over Israel-Judah.

Thus, at the time of the division of the kingdom, we stand at an epoch-making crisis of religious development, after which an essentially new phase of prophecy begins. In the Introduction (p. 36) we briefly indicated the formal and material distinction existing between the stage of development considered so far and the one now opening. True, it is incorrect to date prophecy generally from the ninth or eighth century, or even to make the Messianic idea merely appear first at this period. The very origin and outward evolution of the Israelitish commonwealth took place under the auspices of the prophetic word. And the idea of the Anointed of Yahveh, as we have found, after being announced in the form of intimation long before, was uttered with divine sublimity already in David's days. But what had been heard hitherto of the glory of Israel and its king referred still to immediate realization and applied to the nation as it was, to the kingdom in its actuality, in its representatives at the time. Now a far-reaching crisis intervened more and more in the consciousness of the prophets themselves between promise and consummation. It was declared with increasing definiteness, that the people of God will first be dissolved in the crucible of judgment, and then, redeemed therefrom, fulfil its true destiny. Instead of a perfecting of the present divine institution, the true seers announced more and more inflexibly its approaching end, which would of course be followed by a new creation, the making of a new covenant.

In closest connection with this fact is the modification which prophecy underwent as to its form. True, even after the division of the kingdom we see Elijah and Elisha in the northern half acting directly and intervening in the political condition of the theocracy. On this account their history is the essential thing: their speaking is occasional rather than a testimony reaching beyond the present, though telling powerfully on events. Longer discourses of theirs are not given us. Elijah represents in person the divine judicial power, which once more confronts the rebellious people, restrains them with wholesome violence from the abyss, and brings them back to the one true God. Hence prophecy (Malachi) makes him appear again before the final judgment; and, in point of fact, the N. T. fulfilment presents the form of the preacher of repentance terrifying and arousing the whole nation. In Elisha we see the man of God in the main dispensing blessing at a time when the people had repented. Thus in his kindly bearing and acts he was in high degree typical of the Saviour Himself, in whom was revealed all the love and grace of God, given to all who trust Him in time of need. But the work of the prophets who come next, whether we assign Obadiah and Joel, or Amos and Hosea to this period, bears another character. Their element is not outward action, certainly of deep inner significance, but rational speech, certainly not merely theoretical, but practically effective in high degree. And since this speech of theirs, more and more giving up the present, appeals to the future, it is readily understood why greater importance is laid on its being fixed in writing than formerly. The prophetic preachers also attend to the recording of their testimonies. Whole prophetic books appear and are carefully preserved.

The *contents* of prophecy during this period have been indicated in general in what has been already said, and the discussion will furnish special details. Still we may refer to certain main conceptions mentioned cursorily in the Introduction, which emerge in this period and govern the prophetic field of view throughout. Above all, it is the rule of God, the *kingship* of Yahveh, which these prophecies contemplate, p. 30. Even in the Mosaic age this idea had found realization, although imperfectly; in the Davidic it had presented itself in new shape. Now it became the subject of oracles pointing to the remoter future.[1] The entry of God's perfected rule is denoted both by a temporal and local designation. The first is the "*Day of the Lord,*" the second the "*Coming of the Lord.*" The former denotes, as stated before, the point of time when the Lord will reveal Himself to all the world in the righteousness characteristic of Him. It is therefore the day of final judgment, when God's enemies, with everything evil, will be given over to

[1] Cf. even Ex. xv. 18.

destruction, at least to retributive punishment, whilst the good, the true Israel, will be saved. But it is the former conception, that of judgment, which is predominantly connected with the phrase. It is the day of reckoning, when the time of divine forbearance and human caprice comes to an end, when the contradiction between demerit and destiny is done away, when the will of God, hitherto only contained in word, is put in perfect harmony with actuality. The idea is plainly more positive, more definite in contents than that of אַחֲרִית הַיָּמִים (see p. 33), but has this in common with the latter, with which as to fact it often coincides, that the essential thing in it is not the temporal form, but the temporal contents. Hence we ought not to press the phrase to mean that these things must be transacted within twenty-four hours. The prophet sees the totality of the final judgment within the framework of a day. But the conjunction is more in contents than time, just as prophecy generally sees together things conjoined in contents, whilst in the outward reality they may be spread over different periods of time. When the judgment of God enters, the final judgment draws nigh, the day of the Lord, for the former is a herald of the latter. But although the final reckoning may at first fall only on a small fragment of mankind, it still forms a portion of the great general reckoning which concludes the present course of the world.

While the heathen are principally affected by this judgment-day, Israel-Judah also must pass through the fire of judgment, and that first; if and so far as it has not then repented, it also falls victim to the final judgment. But to purified Israel a promise is given, in a phrase borrowed from space, of a revelation of God's grace in highest perfection: He will *come* to take up His *abode* anew on Zion and dwell there for ever in all the fulness of the manifestations of His love. His dwelling in the midst of His people was always one of the ruling aims of the divine dispensations. "He has made His dwelling on Zion." To Israel this is the highest boast and ground of confidence. But the more that ungodliness gains the mastery there, the more the Lord withdraws from His temple and land. His glorious return to a blessed dwelling in His Church will take place when judgment has cleansed the place.

As these ideas generally contemplate a new, a more spiritual and holy consummation of the kingdom of God, the properly *Messianic* idea also enters on a new stadium. Even in the outward dissolution of the monarchy this idea is still retained, and assumes a purer and more ideal form the more it becomes the object, not of sight, but of faith and future expectation. As the nation itself must be again gathered from captivity that God's plan concerning it may be realized, so too David's house, though sunk into a shattered hut, must be again built up. And as in the prophetic founding of the monarchy a personal head was created in order to immediate contact of the nation with its God, so the later promise of salvation reached its climax in the announcement of a coming ruler of David's house, who would perfectly realize the Messianic dignity. Still here also the pyramid is built up gradually. There are prophets in whose oracles, so far as they are preserved to us, the hope of the future does not take this personal character, but dwells more on the national restoration in general; those also who, keeping more to the theological side, promise the day of the Lord, His taking up His abode on Zion, without touching on the human mediation that was to embody itself in David's son. But, starting from the human as from the divine side, the promise tends towards a personal union in the Son of David and Son of God.

How the prophetic writings of the pre-exilian period group themselves chronologically according to the world-powers dominant at the time, see p. 37.

§ 24. *Obadiah.*

The older prophetic writings preserved to us proclaim still more strongly their origination out of the living prophetic word. They were perhaps written down directly after their oral delivery. At all events their rhetorical, poetical style betrays an inner, natural mobility, such as is characteristic of the true seer. Among the earliest products (belonging to the pre-Assyrian age) we reckon the oracles of *Obadiah* and *Joel*, whose near relationship in point of time is beyond doubt, whatever the answer given as to the date of the two (note A).

Obadiah's Prophecy of the Day and Kingdom of God.—In the vision of Obadiah the seer beholds, in the first place (vers. 1–9), the divine judgment on *Edom*, to whose execution the Lord summons the nations. Its pride is humbled to the lowest point, its riches thoroughly plundered, its craft ignominiously baffled, its defensive power utterly broken. Thus its treachery, its love of wrong, its sordid selfishness, the bloodthirsty hate it showed against Judah-Jerusalem in its day of misfortune, are revenged (10-14). But from ver. 15 the seer's gaze expands into a view of the general judgment. Vengeance must come to Edom, for the *Day of the Lord, i.e.* of retribution, draws nigh for all nations alike.

15 "For near is the day of the Lord upon all nations: like as thou didst, it shall be done to thee. What thou didst
16 perpetrate shall return upon thy head. For as you drank on my holy mountain, all nations shall drink perpetually,
17 and drink and gulp and become as if they were not. And on Mount Zion shall be a community of deliverance, and the
18 house of Jacob shall conquer its possessions. And Jacob's house shall become fire, and Joseph's house flame, and Esau's house stubble, and they encircle them and consume them, and there shall be no escaped one from the house of Edom,
19 for the Lord has spoken it. And they of the south capture the mountains of Esau and the plain the Philistine's land, and they (of the mountain) capture the fields of Ephraim
20 and the fields of Samaria, and Benjamin Gilead, and the captives of this army of the children of Israel what belongs to the Canaanites up to Zarephath. And the captives of Jerusalem dwelling in Sepharad conquer the cities of the
21 south. And redeemers rise up on Mount Zion to judge the mountains of Esau, AND THE LORD'S SHALL BE THE KINGDOM."

As Edom has made itself like the heathen, it shall receive no better treatment from the Lord than they. Like them, it shall experience the retribution of the Judge on the day of the Lord. We find the phrase "Day of the Lord" (p. 30, 194) here for the first time in prophetic literature.[1] Not that it was newly coined by Obadiah. Still the context in him brings out the proper significance of the day as the day of reckoning and retribution with special force. It is the day of requital for all the iniquities committed by the nations in the world's history (ver. 15), especially for those perpetrated on the people of the Lord, and consequently on Himself. The Nemesis, as depicted in the case

---

[1] According to Ewald also, it belongs to the older oracle of Obadiah (the time of Uzziah). It is found also in striking passages in Joel i. 15, iii. 14.

of Edom, gives an example of the way in which every nation, when the divine justice is carried out, is punished with what constituted its sin. Especially does punishment overtake the nations for the indignities committed on Zion. As they have drunk there without limit, in gross indulgence disregarding the sanctity of the place, so in the same place they shall drink to excess until they lose their senses. This is a well-understood euphemism for the bloody end awaiting them. Whether this doom strikes them on the mountain itself, is not to be learnt from the passage with perfect certainty, but it is doubtless the author's meaning. We see this idea taken up afterwards. In Jer. xlix. 12 is found only a figurative drinking of the cup of God's wrath, a trope which had become familiar at that time (after Hab. ii. 16). The thought in Obadiah is independent of this.

In contrast with this destruction of the nations an escaped community [1] stands on Zion as a positive result of the "Day of the Lord." Zion (= temple-mountain, p. 186) figures as the centre of the divine kingdom, impregnable henceforth, because set apart by and for God. No vengeful foe, no unclean heathen shall again tread it. This divine seat is certainly narrow in extent. But the divine sway will extend itself over all the possessions belonging by right and promise to the house of Jacob and Joseph. These are the provinces mentioned vers. 18–20, which were but partially ruled by David and Solomon, and afterwards were all lost. This description does not seem to be based on any direct verbal promise; the extent is rather indicated freely by the prophet himself.

Then, when the old divine energy revives in every part of the nation, the retribution on Edom comes, ver. 18 ff. In ver. 18 the co-operation of the house of Jacob [2] (= the kingdom of Judah) and the house of Joseph (= the kingdom of Ephraim or Israel) in the judgment on Edom does not seem to agree with the following verse (19), according to which Joseph's territory itself must first

---

[1] פְּלֵיטָה, not, lik קֹדֶשׁ, referring to place : *asylum*, but according to the usage elsewhere (cf. especially Joel iii. 5 and Isa. xxxvii. 32, where it is parallel with שְׁאֵרִית) : *body of escaped ones, escaped remnant*. The word implies the unity, interconnection of those escaped from the judgment, in distinction from פְּלֵטִים, which denotes escaped individuals. Cf. Böttcher, *Ausf. Lehrbuch*, § 663, 3. Observe also the antithesis, ver. 18 : לֹא יִהְיֶה שָׂרִיד.

[2] So also Amos ix. 8.

be conquered by Judah.[1] But each supplements the other. The new expansion of the kingdom of God will start from Zion, extend first over the ancestral possessions in Canaan, and then also beyond the limits of the Promised Land, where hostile peoples, who have no part in this kingdom, are to be subjugated, nay, annihilated. A punctilious collation might also show a contradiction between ver. 1 and ver. 18, all nations being there summoned against Edom, here Jacob and Joseph appearing as avengers. The judgment is to be inflicted by both parties, by the heathen friendly to Edom and the Jews who suffer from it.

As the kingdom of God has its centre and starting-point in Zion, so it embodies itself first of all in Judah-Benjamin, the house of Jacob; its several parts extend themselves—(1) The Negeb = south of Judah, conquers the adjacent *mountains of Edom;* (2) The Shephela, the plain of *Judah,* conquers the *Philistine-country* on its border; (3) and in common[2] they conquer the territory of *Ephraim and Samaria;*[3] (4) Benjamin, Judah's faithful comrade (wrongly taken by LXX. as object), occupies *Gilead,* the name of a part standing for the east-Jordan country generally; (5) Ver. 20, "and this captive Israelitish army (conquers) what is *Canaanite-country* as far as Zarephath" (note B); (6) Finally, the captive Jerusalemites in Sepharad conquer the *cities of the south* (note C). Thus the kingdom of Yahveh rounds itself off on every side, even those driven into banishment contributing to bring the alien or disobedient territory into subjection to Him. God so orders it that the very dispersion of Israel must help to restore His rule. What shape this rule will take is intimated merely by a few touches in ver. 21. The phraseology here reminds strongly of the age of the Judges: "deliverers shall hold the judgment," human מוֹשִׁיעִים, exercising the office of

[1] So Ewald, *Propheten*, I. 491 (2nd ed. 1867).

[2] But probably, with Ewald, הָהָר is to be inserted as subject after the second וְיָרְשׁוּ; the mountain-land of Judah, the chief seat of the tribe, attacks Ephraim on its northern border. The LXX. seem to have read the lost word τὸ ὄρος, but to have referred it wrongly to Ephraim.

[3] No. 3 might seem to countenance a later date of origin, when Ephraim-Samaria was in hostile hands. But at all events it was alienated from the legal king, and must therefore first be reconquered. Moreover, the hostile attitude of the two kingdoms led to constant wars from the time of 1 Kings xv. 6 f., 16. Ver. 18 also intimates the division of the two kingdoms, which is one day to give place to the opposite. According to this verse, they both seem to be in existence, but in a depressed condition.

שֹׁפְטִים, as in the age before the erection of the monarchy the "Judges" with divine energy delivered the land from the enemy's oppression, thereby proving themselves God's organs, further judicial authority over the land being given them on that account. They establish their seat on Zion. For there is the centre of the divine rule, whence Edom also is judged. *And Yahveh's shall be the kingdom*, is the significant close of the oracle. Here the goal of prophecy is reached. The final purpose of God, according to these words, is not the rehabilitation of Israel, but the rule of God Himself. This is the end of all history, the goal of all judgments; this the destiny of Israel and the whole world: to become and be God's. It is true the divine rule in this oracle, with an allusion to the old promise, is still confined to narrow local limits; but the oracle by its nature is designed to undergo spiritualization; cf. vers. 15, 17, 21. Its few lineaments tend of themselves to grow into an outline of the divine world-plan.

As to the *fulfilment*, it leaves nothing to be desired in reference to the doom of annihilation threatened to Edom and to be carried out by heathens and Jews. After Edom, without laying to heart the prophet's warning, had filled up its measure of iniquity in the overthrow of Jerusalem, 588 B.C. (Ezek. xxxv. 5, 10; Lam. iv. 22; Ps. cxxxvii. 7), on which account Obadiah's prophecy is taken up anew by Jeremiah (xlix.) and Ezekiel, its punishment followed, probably at the hands of the Chaldæans. At least Mal. i. 3 presupposes a righteous devastation of Edom, and also announces that if they build again the Lord will again cast down. This, too, happened. It is known from history how the Maccabees, the last successful heroes who drew sword for the national theocracy, real מוֹשִׁיעִים and שֹׁפְטִים, waged a war of victorious revenge against Edom, 1 Macc. v. 3, 65; Joseph. *Ant.* xii. 18. 1. Judas Maccabæus vanquished them; then, according to *Ant.* xiii. 9. 1, John Hyrcanus completely subjugated them, even compelling them to receive the law (circumcision). Alexander Jannæus brought the remnant of the Idumæans under the yoke, *Ant.* xiii. 15. 4. In the conflicts of the Zealots against Rome the tribe utterly perished, *Bell. Jud.* iv. 9. 7.

Thus were the prophetic threatenings realized. Only, they combine in one picture what history splits up into different periods and events. But according to Obadiah, all peoples who war against the temple on Zion will fare like Edom. This general threat, as well as the bright side of promise in the oracle, takes us far beyond the time of the Edomite conflicts. According to the oracle, Israel's superiority to the hostile kindred nation and all the heathen has its roots in the dwelling of God in its midst. At the general judgment of the world a saved community remains on Zion, from which judgment and dominion go forth over the lands. The fulfilment of this has taken a form of unimagined greatness. In Jerusalem deliverance from the divine judgment was revealed. Salvation went forth from the Jews. Among them arose the true מושיע and עשׂוּי. Not that circumcision was forced on the heathen, but that they received the gospel from the Jews, is the true Israel's supreme triumph. And the extension of this divine rule has also surpassed all conception. The kingdom of the God who dwelt on Zion, the kingdom viewed by the prophet, in keeping with the horizon and vision of his time, as a kingdom of Israel with enlarged limits, in virtue of the spiritual might inherent in it, necessarily burst all limits, extended towards every quarter of heaven, and spread over all nations in a way quite different from what it was permitted him to see or necessary for his contemporaries to know. But as he surmised, it was allotted to the Jews scattered throughout the world to bring all nations into subjection to their God.

NOTE A.—As relates first to *Obadiah's date*, it is plain enough from his oracle that he vents his displeasure on the Edomites in lively indignation at their conduct in a catastrophe which befell Jerusalem. The most obvious course seems to be, to refer this "day of Jerusalem's calamity" to the overthrow by Nebuchadnezzar (588 B.C.), in which the Edomites in fact took an active part, Lam. iv. 21 f.; Ezek. xxxv. 1 ff., especially ver. 5; Isa. lxiii. 1 ff.; Ps. cxxxvii. 7; 1 Esdr. iv. 45, 50. But to this is opposed the fact that Jeremiah's oracle against Edom (xlix. 7 ff.), written to all appearance in the fourth year of Jehoiakim, and in any case before the overthrow of the city, seems to be a copy of Obadiah's oracle. See especially the detailed proof in Caspari, *Der Prophet Obadja*, 1842. Obadiah's oracle is original, homogeneous, characteristic; in Jeremiah the bold turns of speech are smoothed down: he starts again and again, whereas his original is struck off at one blow. The analogy also of the other Jeremiah-oracles against foreign nations favours this relation of dependence. Cf. especially how Jeremiah's oracle against Moab (xlviii.) leans on Isa. xv. xvi.; also Jer. xlix. 1–7 (against Ammon) on Amos i. 13–15; xlix. 23–27 (against Damascus) on Amos i. 3–5. In consideration of this state of the case, Ewald has distinguished in Obadiah's oracle two authors, an older one speaking in Uzziah's days (where he wrongly refers Obad. ver. 1 ff. to the past), whom Jeremiah took for a pattern, and whom some one still later, after the overthrow of Jerusalem, enlarged by adding Obad. vers. 11–14, 16, 19–21.[1] We rather hold by the outer and inner unity of the passage, recognising in the very fact of the prophet first seeing the judgment in clear lines as if it lay before his eyes, and only then bringing himself to speak of the well-known crime of which Edom had been guilty,[2] a sign of his high poetic afflatus. Moreover, exegetical considerations are here decisive. The question is, whether Obad. ver. 10 ff. *must* refer to that overthrow of Jerusalem, whether ver. 20 f. *can* refer to the Babylonian exile. In the latter passage, indeed, a great body of exiles is presupposed in the north among the Canaanites (= Phœnicians), conquering the territory of the latter up to Zarephath, and one in the west (Sepharad) capturing the cities of the south. But any exile in the east (Assyria, Babylon) or fugitives in Egypt are as little mentioned as a judgment on the Babylonians. For the land סְפָרַד, in which the captives of Jerusalem pine, according to the stone-inscriptions, where it figures alongside Jauna, Greece, is to be sought in the *west*, and, indeed, perhaps in Asia Minor (according to others = Sparta).

On the other hand, the catastrophe witnessed by Obadiah is without doubt the same that Joel has in view (chap. iii.), where Philistines and Canaanites are accused of having plundered Jerusalem and sold its inhabitants to the distant בְּנֵי יְוָנִים, and (ver. 19) Edom is specially marked out for judgment. Insolent carousings of the victors took place in Jerusalem, according to iii. 3 as according to Obad. 15. The difference is merely this, that whereas the last-named prophet has these misdeeds directly before his eyes, in Joel they lie farther back, although the recollection still burns as an unhealed wound, and the captives are still dwelling afar. That Joel speaks after Obadiah also appears from his citing Obad. 17 in ii. 32.

The most attractive view is that of von Hofmann (also Delitzsch, Kleinert), that the event referred to is the plundering of Jerusalem under Jehoram (2 Chron. xxi. 16 : 896–884 B.C.), since the later ones under Amaziah and Ahaz (2 Chron. xxv. 23, xxviii. 5) were the work, not of foreigners, but chiefly of Israelites. The former, again, are נָכְרִים or זָרִים, Philistines and Arabians, whom the designations suit, just because of their indefiniteness, better than they suit the Chaldæans. With them are joined the Edomites, who also, according to 2 Kings viii. 20 f., 2 Chron. xxi. 8 f., took advantage

---

[1] Cf. also Graf, *Der Prophet Jeremia*, 1862, p. 558 ff.
[2] To refer ver. 10 ff. to future crime (Caspari, *et al.*) is too artificial.

of Judah's weakness to revolt. Amos also (i. 6, 9, 11) has the same or like circumstances in view, which must therefore have transpired long before the Babylonian overthrow. Looked at more closely, moreover, the complaint (Obad. 10 ff.) contains nothing pointing of necessity to the Babylonian catastrophe. There is no mention at all of an overthrow of the city or temple (quite otherwise in Ps. cxxxvii.), only of a capture and plundering with insulting excesses,[1] and especially of deportations to various countries (cf. Joel iii. 2). In Obad. 18, also, the houses of Jacob and Joseph seem to be in existence side by side, although in a state of weakness and mutual variance. The promise exhibits them again united, and indeed around Zion as the centre, but says nothing of a rebuilding of the temple.

NOTE B.—We take חֵל to be a defective form of חַיִל, *power*, *army* (ver. 11). It is the captive *élite* of the children of Israel, and refers either—this is the most probable, according to ver. 11—to the captive soldiery of Judah in contrast with the captive inhabitants of Jerusalem, or to a deported army of the northern kingdom. At all events this army was taken northward; on its return thence it captures the Phœnician country, which as far as Zarephath (lying south of Sidon, somewhat inland, at present Sarafend) is added to the kingdom of Israel. הַזֶּה does not prove that the prophet was among the deported soldiery, but perhaps that this crowd of captives was in every one's thoughts, their carrying away was vividly before the eyes. We take אֲשֶׁר־בְּנָעֲנִים (like Hitzig) as object to וְיִרְשׁוּ to be supplied from the previous verse; the latter is first repeated in the following clause.

NOTE C.—The inhabitants of Jerusalem, carried away at the capture of the city and dwelling in the west, conquer the south, as the former army the north. They are perhaps to be thought of as removed to Egypt or Philistia. Sepharad, where they sojourn at present, is not Spain (so the versions and Rabbins), which is only suggested by the sound, but is perhaps like Javan (Joel iii. 6 in the same connection), a land in the *west*. For the inscriptions of Darius mention often a land Çparda alongside Jauna = Greece (used indefinitely). It must be a country in the vicinity of Greece, either in Europe or Asia Minor. After Silv. de Sacy had combined Çparda with our סְפָרַד, it was more precisely identified with Sardes (in native speech Çvarda, Lassen) or Sparta, a name to which the Jews, of course, would attach

---

[1] Volck (Herzog, art. "Joel") objects Joel iii. 2, which, however, applies better to deportation of captives by different countries and annexation of portions of territory by the same than to the Chaldæan catastrophe. Obad. 11 : "They cast lots upon Jerusalem," may, in accord with the parallel sentences, be understood of the seizure of what the city contained.

just as indefinite a notion as to "Ionia" (Hitzig, Delitzsch, Kleinert). In any case, it refers to the districts of the Mediterranean, whither the Phœnicians sold their captives. Cf. Schrader, *Keilinschriften und Altes Testament*, p. 284 f., who certainly would rather find the district in Babylonia. See, on the other side, Steiner in Hitzig's *Comm. zu den kl. Proph.* (4th ed.), p. 168.

§ 25. *Joel* (note A).

The occasion of Joel's prophecy is a terrible public calamity, namely, a desolation of Judah by swarms of locusts repeated, perhaps, for several years (i. 4, ii. 25). The devastation thus caused, which turned the smiling land into barrenness, the prophet describes in impassioned words (i. 2 ff.). He saw it before his eyes—a present fact, not something future. Only, a fresh swarm seems just to have come; hence the terror that has fallen on prophet and people.[1] It is perverse in any case to interpret these locusts allegorically (note B), to refer them, *e.g.*, to heathen armies, as though the destruction of all growth by those destructive insects were not terrible enough to move the prophet to the cry of alarm (ii. 1): "Sound the trumpet on Zion, raise a cry on my holy mountain, *for the day of the Lord comes, for it is nigh*,[2] a day of obscurity and darkness, a day of cloudiness and thick gloom;[3] a terrible day, such as none can endure" (ii. 11). This day of general retribution spoken of already by Obadiah is imminent. The Lord is coming to judgment. This wild army, darkening the heavens (ii. 10), is in a certain sense His terrible vanguard (ii. 25). Judah's fields are being utterly ravaged, and the strength of the land consumed. Still there is hope that the Lord may be moved to relent when He finds a penitent people, seeking His mercy, "rending its heart, not its garments" (ii. 13).

---

[1] Cf. on the different stages of hatching, Credner, *Comm. zu Joel;* Bochart, *Hierozoicon*, iii. 251 ff.; Thomson, *The Land and the Book*, p. 416.

[2] Cf. i. 15. The בָּא, which might be taken as perfect: "It is here!" would be easily misunderstood and seem strange; hence, by way of explanation, the more precise: *namely, it is near.*

[3] אֲפֵלָה = אֹפֶל, a more uncommon word, strengthening חֹשֶׁךְ; in the same way עֲרָפֶל, a poetic addition to עָנָן; עֲרָפֶל, in Ex. xx. 21, is the impenetrable cloud-darkness covering Yahveh at the lawgiving on Sinai. Cf. the dismal twilight on the day of the Lord (Zech. xiv. 7). Travellers compare the gloom caused by a swarm of locusts (cf. Ex. x. 15), and colouring the picture in the present passage, to an eclipse of the sun.

Not in vain does the prophet preach this. His word finds response; and in view of the general penitence and prayer of the Church, he is able to assure it that the Lord will by a double blessing abundantly make good all it has suffered (ii. 18–27). At the close of the promise allusion is made to the spiritual ground of this blessing. In the abundance of wheat, wine, and oil, produced by the long-needed, fruitful rain, Israel is to learn that Yahveh, its God, the only true one, dwells in its midst, just as in the desolation of nature it was forced to recognise the anger of its God. But the prophecy does not stop here. It is in special degree the manner of this prophet to rise from nearest to highest, from the outward and earthly to the spiritual and divine, and to view particular occurrences in immediate connection with the aim of the whole historic development. As he considered the plague of locusts in the light of its inner meaning as God's judgment, and therefore looked at it as an immediate forerunner of the final judgment, so behind the temporal, earthly blessings promised for the near future he discerns a fulness of heavenly blessing; on the natural he sees a spiritual, more heavenly rain follow, one still more refreshing, and making the nation bear fruit to the Lord:—

ii. 28 f.: "And it shall come to pass after this, I will pour out my Spirit upon all flesh: And your sons and your daughters shall prophesy; your old men shall dream dreams, and your youths see visions. And even upon the servants and upon the maids in those days I will pour out my Spirit."

The heavenly gift of the Spirit is well distinguished from the earthly, physical blessing both in its nature and time;[1] it follows later, crowning the work of the Lord in Israel, and also introducing the end of the world's history.

Of course, although Joel sees the necessity of an inner reformation of the people, he may think of it as near (in distinction from later prophets). A revolution in the outward and the spiritual atmosphere may bring it about.

To wish to refer ii. 28 ff. and chap. iii. to a different author from chaps. i. and ii. (M. Vernes) is totally to overlook the mode

---

[1] אַחֲרֵי־כֵן, indeed, leaves the duration up to the second epoch indefinite (cf. Isa. i. 26); still the prophet is not thinking merely of "the immediate future" (Anger), since a time of quiet prosperity (chap. ii. 26) precedes the world-crisis introduced by ii. 28.

of viewing the mundane and supramundane in intimate connection characteristic of this prophet, as already mentioned. On the contrary, the rain sent by the Lord of nature leads to a higher, diviner one, by which He will fertilize His Church. The natural rain suggests the expression, "outpouring" of the Spirit,[1] so well adapted to intimate the rich fulness of this heavenly gift. Here is something new, unheard before. Hitherto the Spirit of God came down on individuals, seizing and filling them; but an outpouring, in which all must needs share, as in a shower of rain, has never been. And yet this is the meaning, as the כָּל־בָּשָׂר more precisely states, "upon all flesh."

On the one hand, this בָּשָׂר certainly suggests the sensuousness and frailty of the human creature in contrast with the Divine Spirit (cf. Ps. lxxviii. 39; Job xxxiv. 14 f.; Isa. xl. 6; also Num. xvi. 22, xxvii. 16). The divine life-spirit does not dwell in the human creature by necessity. On the other hand, this כָּל־בָּשָׂר is always used to express a sense as comprehensive as possible. Sometimes even animals are included (Lev. xvii. 14; Gen. vii. 21), which, of course, is not the case in the present passage.[2] As a rule, the whole of mankind is meant (Gen. vi. 12 f.; Ps. cxlv. 21, and often). In the present prophecy, the extent is determined by what precedes and especially by what follows, where the general statement is specialized: "*your* sons and *your* daughters," etc. Consequently, all the inhabitants of the land (not of the earth) are meant.[3] The prophecy is therefore limited in the first instance to the covenant-people; only no emphasis of any kind rests on this national limitation; the stress lies on the universality within the nation. There every one without exception will be filled with the Spirit of God, young and old, the free, and even the slaves, who in great part might not be of Israelitish blood, on which account they are declared with special emphasis to be included.

---

[1] After Joel it became common (Isa. xxxii. 15, xliv. 3; Zech. xii. 10). To assert that the prophets took the Spirit for a fine fluid, is just as unwarranted as to infer from the N. T. phrase of the blowing of the Spirit that Jesus and the apostles represented it as a stream of air. How can one set forth the operation of the Spirit without sensuous expressions, or even speak of it? The mobile water and the unseen yet perceptible air are well adapted to give a conception of the nature and working of the Spirit (cf. His attributes, Wisd. vii. 22–24).

[2] In opposition to Credner.

[3] That such a limit may be assigned to כל בשר by the context, is proved by Jer. xii. 12; Ezek. xx. 48.

The *Spirit of God* certainly dwells in every animate creature as a breath of life (Ps. civ. 29 and elsewhere, see p. 4); but here a higher potency of the Spirit is meant, in comparison with which animated man, despite the divine breath, is still בָּשָׂר: not the Divine Spirit that since the creation dwells in every creature, nor that which characterizes men, but the superhuman Spirit of God, destined by God's gracious decree to become immanent in the Church. It is the Spirit who conveys the Lord's special revelations to His servants and handmaids, and is designated (ii. 28) by this fruit of His operation. "Your sons and daughters shall prophesy."[1] Whereas this refers to the utterance of divine revelation, the following expressions refer to its reception: "the young see visions, the old have dreams," in harmony with imaginative youth and slumber-loving age. Thus, what Moses mentioned as a scarcely attainable ideal (Num. xi. 29) will be actually seen: the entire people will participate in this high gift of grace. All its members, not excepting the least, will stand in as immediate relation to the Lord as the prophets, so that no mediation will be necessary for them. It will be a nation not merely serving the Lord as priests, but also testifying of Him as prophets—a Church of the Lord grown to maturity. This will be the consummation of the Church of God on earth, when it has become the body in which God's Spirit dwells, filling and animating every member, so that its God will no longer stand over against it distant and alien, but in accordance with His true nature will enter and dwell in it.

But this consummation of the Church is withal the inauguration of the end of the world. For in the world two developments run side by side, that of God's Church issuing in perfect divine fellowship, and that of God-estranged humanity tending to the final judgment—redemptive history whose fruit is salvation to the called, and the world-history whose goal is the world-judgment. Judah, in its present state, must necessarily be put to shame in the day of the Lord; but repentance there effects a spiritual change which, produced from above, creates a new Church which supplies a refuge in the judgment. In the same way from this Church goes forth before the judgment a warning prophetic testimony, which in union with the tokens in heaven and on earth announce to the world the approach of the

---

[1] נִבָּא, denominative niphal: *behave and bear oneself as* נָבִיא.

judgment-day. For the form in which the Spirit is made known in ii. 28 is not unconnected with the mighty convulsions impending. When the Church is filled with the Spirit, its eyes are opened to the great things coming on all the world. Hence the close conjunction of ver. 30 ff. with the foregoing:—

ii. 30 f.: "And I show[1] miraculous signs in heaven and on earth, blood and fire and vapour of smoke.[2] The sun shall turn into darkness and the moon into blood, before the day of Yahveh comes, the great and terrible day."

The approach of the judgment-day will be announced by all kinds of fearful signs; one of these has just been witnessed, other mightier ones will follow. There will be phenomena of such form as involuntarily to remind of the terrors of the divine judgment: heaven and earth will be fiery, blood-red, dark. The several phenomena are not to be more closely defined. At all events our prophet brings these natural phenomena into intimate connection with the divine action and human history. Darkenings of sun and moon are events of a kind best adapted to shatter men's security and fill them with horror. In the New Testament also they appear among the heralds of the final judgment, Matt. xxiv., Rev. vi. 12 f. How this "changing" of sun and moon is to be brought about, is quite indifferent. Enough that the clear daylight is turned into its opposite, and the gentle moon is to be seen terrible, blood-red. Perhaps earthquakes and tempests, volcanic outbursts and great conflagrations flitted before Joel's mind. Nor was it mere superstition to recognise an inner connection in such phenomena. With perfect justice, childlike faith sees therein divine hints pointing to the judgment on all creation.

Thus the judgment-day (ii. 1 ff.), once again turned aside by Judah's repentance, must yet one day come. But the Church of God, blessed in those days with the fellowship of the Divine Spirit, has no reason to fear the messengers of terror in the heavens, the conflagrations and wars on earth:—

[1] נָתַן, also in Ex. vii. 9 with מוֹפְתִים, *miracula, astounding phenomena*, by which God calls men's attention to His working, and here paves the way for His judgments.

[2] תִּמָרוֹת, from a sing. תִּימָרָה, but only occurring in the plur. in conjunction with עָשָׁן (Cant. iii. 6), and denoting lofty *columns* of smoke. The more correct writing according to the Massora is that with י; תִּימָרוֹת, thus from the stem יָמַר = אָמַר, *to rise aloft*, whence also תָּמָר (תֹּמֶר, *palm*, etc.), a secondary stem.

ii. 32. "And it shall come to pass: Every one that calls on the name of Yahveh shall escape. For on Zion-hill and in Jerusalem shall be a Church of deliverance, as Yahveh hath said. And among the escaped (they) whom Yahveh calls near."

This verse shows that the Jewish country is not safe in itself; but deliverance, or belonging to the Church of deliverance, is personally conditioned. Whoever in the universal *krisis* puts his trust in Yahveh, the true God, shall be delivered.[1] From Abraham's days invocation of Yahveh's name is also a confession of the true God in distinction from the many gods of the heathen; cf. Gen. iv. 26, but especially xii. 8, xiii. 4, xxi. 33, etc.; Micah iv. 5. "For where Yahveh makes His abode shall be an escaped host, a Church of safety (p. 198), as Yahveh said." Plainly an earlier divine oracle is cited; what other can it be than Obad. ver. 17?[2] "And among the escaped (they) whom Yahveh calls." One might separate these words as an independent sentence: "and among the escaped shall be those whom Yahveh calls." Then the שְׂרִידִים might be identical with the פְּלֵיטָה, adding by way of supplement to the forementioned condition of salvation, that he who is to be delivered shall not merely call on Yahveh, but also be called by Him. But the right view rather is, that the idea of the פליטה, at first confined to Jerusalem-Judah, is extended to the individuals whom the Lord calls near, as being still far from His Church. The prophet is scarcely thinking of the exiles who need to be summoned by Yahveh's powerful voice before the state of the Church reaches its completion, but of the *heathen*[3] who escaped the judgment.

This brings to mind the political visitations which the land suffered some time before, and the scars of which still burn. The shameful injustice inflicted on it by the heathen nations

---

[1] נִמְלַט, properly *to slip away*, LXX. σωθήσεται. From such prophetic passages σωτηρία (so LXX. in Obad. ver. 17 for פְּלֵיטָה, whereas in Joel iii. 5 it has ἀνασωζόμενος for this) becomes a positive fundamental idea of the New Testament. The positive O. T. phrase for this is תְּשׁוּעָה.

[2] Merx (6, 16) finds Isa. ii. 4, Micah iv. 1, Isa. iv. 2, x. 22, "cited" here—in fact an "unconstrained" form of citation!

[3] The כִּי (iii. 1) is to be connected with שְׂרִידִים: only individuals escape besides, for Yahveh will judge and destroy all nations in the Valley of Jehoshaphat, cf. Zech. xiv. 16.

gives occasion to describe now the *judgment-day itself*, when the Lord will reckon with them according to Obad. ver. 15.

iii. 1 f. "For behold in those days and at that time when I shall bring back the captives of Judah and Jerusalem,[1] then I will sweep together all nations and bring them down into the Valley of Jehoshaphat, and there try issue[2] with them respecting my people and my inheritance, Israel, which they scattered among the nations, dividing my land," etc.

The bringing back of the scattered Israelites will be accompanied by the instituting of the great judgment on all nations, set on foot by God, who guides the thoughts of the princes and peoples, and to their destruction incites them to assemble together against His city,[3] all which is set forth in detail in ver. 9 ff. The *Vale of Jehoshaphat* is named here and in ver. 12 as the place where the Lord will enter into judgment with His foes. That this valley is a mere fiction of the prophet[4] is not probable, considering the realistic character of his prophecy. Since Ibn Ezra's days, many with more right have thought of the valley where, according to 2 Chron. xx. 16 ff., the noble king Jehoshaphat won a glorious triumph over the confederated foes of Judah by God's miraculous help, almost without drawing sword. But that valley is called עֵמֶק בְּרָכָה, "valley of praise," from the anthems of the victorious people, and the name belongs to it to this day. A ruined site, Bereikut, has been found west of Tekoa. Accordingly, the place did not lie in the immediate vicinity of Jerusalem, where one must conjecture it in Joel's prophecy along with Obad. ver. 16, but farther south (halfway, perhaps, to Hebron). Hence we surmise that in Joel's days a valley between that scene and the capital bore Jehoshaphat's name in memory of his famous campaign, which took place about fifty years before. The later tradition, first appearing in Eusebius, has perhaps not gone far wrong in giving this name to the Valley of Kedron. The prophet

---

[1] The apodosis first begins in ver. 2. For the chief emphasis rests now on the general judgment of the nations. In itself certainly one might also, with Wünsche, take ver. 1 independently, as Zech. viii. 23 shows. The *keri* unnecessarily substitutes the *hiphil* for יָשִׁיב, for the *kal* also may be transitive.

[2] *Niphal*, because perhaps both parties put forward their claims at law. Cf. in ver. 4 ff. how the Lord pleads with them.

[3] Judg. iv. 7.

[4] Credner, Winer, *et al.* Kleinert also (in Riehm, *Handwörterbuch*, p. 759): "To Joel the name is not geographical, but the name of the great king."

was led to choose the place, first, by its nearness to Zion, which the hostile armies intended to besiege; and secondly, by its name, which inevitably recalled God's great act in inflicting a similar judgment, although on a smaller scale, on the combined foes of Jerusalem, without His people lending a hand.

The guilt of these heathen nations having been recalled to memory, and an apostrophe to them interposed, there follows, ver. 9 ff., a description of the way in which they are brought into the valley by a divine summons, there to fall a prey to the gory harvesting of the warriors of God.

9 "Proclaim this among the nations: Sanctify a war! Wake up the heroes: let all men of war draw near and come up!
10 Beat your ploughshares[1] into swords, and your pruning-hooks
11 into spears. Let the weakling[2] say, I am a hero! Hasten[3] and come, all ye nations round about, and assemble yourselves
12 —thither bring thy heroes down, Yahveh! Let all nations bestir themselves and come up to the Valley of Jehoshaphat;
13 For there will I sit to judge all nations round about. Put ye in the sickle, for the harvest is ripe![4] Come, tread, for the wine-press is full. The vats overflow, for great is their
14 wickedness! Heaps on heaps in the threshing-waggon vale.[5] For the day of the Lord is near in the threshing-waggon
15 vale! Sun and moon grow dark, and the stars restrain
16 their brightness. And Yahveh roars from Zion, and from Jerusalem He makes his voice thunder, that heaven and earth quake. But a refuge is Yahveh to His people, and a guard
17 to the children of Israel. And ye shall learn that I am Yahveh your God, dwelling in Zion, my holy mountain.

[1] אִתִּים or אֵתִים, from אֵת, according to the versions = *ploughshare*. As in 1 Sam. xiii. 20, מַחֲרֵשָׁה is distinguished from it; many prefer the meaning "hoe, mattock" (so Symm.). Cf. Credner here.

[2] חַלָּשׁ, only here, opposite of גִּבּוֹר, from חָלַשׁ, *to be flaccid, weakly*.

[3] עוּשׁ, only here = חוּשׁ, *festinare; festinate et venite = festinato venite*. Not so well LXX., Syr.: *assemble themselves*. This occurs first in וְנִקְבְּצוּ, which is not imperative, but perfect of the third person, into which the summons passes.

[4] בָּשַׁל, properly *to seethe, boil well*, then *to ripen in the heat of the sun*.

[5] חָרוּץ, explained usually: *something cut off*, then *a divinely-determined decree, fatum*, cf. Isa. x. 22—thus *valley of destiny*. But as the word here concludes the harvest-figure, it is far more natural to take it like כְּמוֹרַג חָרוּץ (so already Calvin): *the sharpened threshing sledge*, for which חָרוּץ alone occurs elsewhere (Isa. xxviii. 27; Amos i. 3).

And Jerusalem shall be a temple, and strangers shall pass 18 over it no more. And it shall be on that day, the mountains shall drop with new wine,[1] and the hills shall stream with milk, and all the valleys of Judah flow with water. And a fountain shall go forth from the house of Yahveh and water 19 the acacia-dale. Egypt shall be a desert, and Edom a waste steppe, because of the outrage on the sons of Judah in 20 shedding innocent blood in their land. But Judah shall remain for ever, and Jerusalem from generation to generation. 21 And I will cleanse them from their blood, from which I have not cleansed them; and YAHVEH DWELLS IN ZION."

Delitzsch remarks that the destruction of the locusts finds its full counterpart in the destruction of the enemies of Jerusalem, chap. iii. And, in fact, ii. 20 especially shows that those insects are not described by the prophet without a side-glance at the nations. The judgment upon them is brought about by a divine summons issued to the heathen, for to them the words of ver. 9 ff. are addressed. The Lord commands them, because He is the real author of this movement. He causes them to give vent to their hate against the city of God, really against the Lord Himself, by a general rising to war against Jerusalem. That it is the enemies of the Lord whom He commands, does not conflict with the challenge: "Sanctify a war," for קַדְּשׁוּ מִלְחָמָה means: "Prepare for war by ceremonial consecration," which was usual also among the heathen.[2] Accordingly it is not said that it is really a holy war in the Lord's service. Still the phrase is used of set purpose, because this war, unknown to the heathen, is arranged by the Lord, who is thus bringing on His judgment-day (cf. Isa. xiii. 3; Jer. xxii. 7).

An unusual martial enthusiasm, the work of a higher power, now seizes on the heathen world. Everything fit for war is set in motion. Not merely are the valiant heroes roused for the decisive blow, even peaceful rustics are seized by battle-rage, and beat the implements of their livelihood into deadly weapons. Even the feeble and cowardly gather themselves together, take courage, and play the man. Micah iv. 11 f. gives a commentary

---

[1] Hitzig presses these expressions most unpoetically to mean: "The new wine of the vineyards will pour so abundantly into the grapes that it will burst the skins; the cattle will have so much milk that it will run out involuntarily."

[2] Cf. Baudissin, *Studien zur semitischen Religionsgeschichte*, ii. 66 f.

on the passage. A daimonic excitement impels the nations to march against Jerusalem. But their martial eagerness against the city of God is kindled by the Lord Himself, who thus calls them to judgment.

The seer beholds this wildly-raging sea approaching the limits of the Holy Land on every side. "Come on!" runs his challenge, "Press close together!" "Thither," he cries next, turning to God, when he surmises what the Lord's purpose and wish is, "Thither, where the hosts are all thick together, bring down Thy heroes, Yahveh!" The passage recalls Judg. v. 13 (cf. ver. 23): ה׳ יְרַד־לִי בַּגִּבּוֹרִים. "Yahveh (Himself) came down to me among the heroes!" This parallel would suggest that by the "heroes" whom Yahveh is to lead we should understand the Judæans, who must rush down from Zion as the Israelites once from Tabor. The final judgment would then be conceived as a decisive battle between Judah and its foes, the Lord's intervention, of course, being the decisive factor. In Obad. vers. 18–21 also, we see God's people and their (human) leaders executing judgment on the heathen. But in the present passage heavenly avengers are meant, commissioned by God for the work, so that the people need lend no hand, as in Jehoshaphat's victory and other great deliverances, *e.g.* the destruction of the Egyptians in the Red Sea. The phrase הַנְחַת, properly: *let down*, does not suit a human army; also the suffix: "*thy* heroes," points to celestial warriors; cf. Ps. ciii. 20.

Again, in ver. 12, as in ver. 2, the valley is named to which God provokes the enemies to gather. The calm majesty lying in אֵשֵׁב: "There will I *sit* to judge," is in fine contrast with the excited multitude which, without suspecting it, presses before the judgment-seat of the Most High. Ver. 13 contains the judgment in the form of a command for its execution. God tells His גִּבּוֹרִים to put in the sickle, because the harvest is fully ripe, to tread the wine-press, because it is overflowing—a stately, twofold image of the general judgment used here for the first time. It applies to a harvest that comes after long waiting, when full ripeness has arrived. That which has to ripen is wickedness; of this the last words leave no doubt; cf. Matt. xiii. 30. The harvest-image, in itself so lovely and peaceful, is here full of terror. The sickle reminds one of the sword, the overflowing wine-press of streams of blood. This horrible harvest and vintage appears again in Isa. lxiii. 1 ff., Rev. xiv. 15, passages modelled upon this one.

The fateful command of the Lord is uttered in ver. 13. Next it is to be carried out. Meantime the throng becomes greater and greater in the "valley of the threshing-waggon," ver. 14. And the heaven above grows dark, ver. 15. Yahveh's thunder-voice is heard out of Zion. Now the tempest of judgment bursts on the heathen. But it is veiled in gloom from the gaze of the seer. There is no use in seeing or describing such judgments. God Himself draws over it the veil of night. All the brighter shines on the prophet the deliverance and safe hiding of God's people (close of ver. 16), which sensibly experiences the Lord's preserving care; cf. ii. 27. For Zion in truth has shown itself an inviolable sanctuary, and hereafter will be desecrated by no hostile foot. As in Obad. ver. 17, קֹדֶשׁ applies here to impregnability respected in the future.[1]

This terrible judgment-day becomes to the Church of God a mere storm clearing the air. Now every fount of blessing streams stills more richly than after the locust-plague, ii. 21 ff. In ver. 18 ff. the seer's gaze dwells with pleasure on the exuberant wealth of wine and milk then seen in Judah (cf. Gen. xlix. 11), and especially on the abundance of water vouchsafed then in distinction from the present. The most parched-up wadis in the broken country of Judah stream with water. And in particular a fount, springing from the temple, will water the acacia-dale. However one may stumble at the precise form of the symbolic dress, the image before the eyes of the seer is concrete. He is here also a realist, inasmuch as a physical basis for the spiritual is indispensable to him. As the natural rain is really meant, ii. 23, while at the same time it is a symbolic type and pledge of the spiritual (ii. 28 ff.), so a glorified Judah after the judgment really presents itself to him as well-watered in the significant way, that its source is found in the temple. The spiritual counterpart to this in a certain sense is seen in ver. 21. The outer aspect of the land will then fully correspond to its spiritual condition.

The "acacia-dale," whither the temple-spring sends its waters, is in any case a waterless wadi, the acacia (*acacia vera*), especially at home on the Sinai-peninsula, occurring just on dry, sandy soil. The locality named after this kind of tree in Num. xxv. 1 ff. is not to be thought of in this passage, because it lies east of

[1] Baudissin, *Studien*, ii. 48.

the Dead Sea, and the flowing of the temple-spring thither is inconceivable. Credner thinks the Kedron-vale intended, and there is no question that the seer contemplates this deep valley —waterless, mostly barren, lying near the temple-hill—as in the first instance watered by the temple-spring. But perhaps in his day the name "acacia-dale" rather belonged to the farther course of the valley toward the Dead Sea, perhaps a part of the present Wadi en-Nâr. With this agrees the description in Ezek. xlvii. 1 ff., which clearly adds further details to the above prophecy.

Whereas Judah then is cleansed and fertilized by a fountain springing up in its temple, Egypt, a land so rich in the arts of irrigation, is destitute of this blessing; it is bare and barren as hostile Edom. The former is mentioned as the old hereditary foe, whose land had drunk much innocent Israelitish blood (cf. for Rehoboam's time, 1 Kings xiv. 25), Edom as the kindred people that had proved so faithless in later days. To both, but chiefly to Edom, the justifying accusation applies: "because of the outrage to the sons of Judah[1] in shedding innocent blood in their land." Here the worst thing is selected with which Edom was to be reproached. In the rising of the Edomites under Jehoram, to all appearance the Judæans settled among them were slain. The innocent blood shed in these lands makes them from this time unfruitful. Judah and Jerusalem will never more be disturbed in their rest, Amos ix. 15. The judgment having been carried out, nothing more threatens the security of the place where God dwells. What? Is there not even in Judah the curse of innocent blood? To this the last verse replies: "I will cleanse their blood which I have not cleansed" (note C) = cleanse them from their blood-guiltiness, provide them means of expiation to cancel such guilt as hitherto I could not regard as cancelled. Even the Holy Land needs purifying before it can become God's permanent dwelling-place and partake in all His blessings. The temple-fount is the physical expression for this expiating of the land's guilt as well as for the blessing of the soil. In the former sense Zech. xiii. 1, in the latter xiv. 8, allude to the present oracle. "And Yahveh is dwelling on Zion!" As Obadiah closes with the sentence: "Yahveh's is the kingdom," so Joel stamps on his

---

[1] The same word with genit. obj. as in Obad. ver. 10. Where Joel speaks of Edom he falls back on Obadiah's words.

prophecy the seal of completion with this saying, a promise of the Lord's permanent presence in His Church, now hallowed and glorified.

This third chapter then foretells a general rising of the world (which certainly figures, in a historically limited view, as an alliance of the nations hostile to Israel) against the Holy Land and city, really against the Lord Himself. This conspiring of powers hostile to heaven leads straight to their destruction, which overtakes them near the sanctuary which they are invading, the Lord causing His avenging hosts at last to reap a bloody harvest; whereas Judah, secure in the guardianship of its God, who has cleansed and fertilized His land by opening a new fount of grace, will be henceforth His inviolable abode.

If chaps. i. and ii. picture the coming day of the Lord more from the view-point of nature, chap. iii. presents the completion of salvation more under a national and political aspect; for both stand in intimate union with the plan of the divine kingdom. Like the entire life of nature,—vegetable, animal, sidereal,—so political life must serve its ends. To bring about the rule of God and the consummation of His Church all the forces of heaven and earth are set in motion. For His judgment plant-world and animal-world, stars equally with the human world, must co-operate, even as they are all affected by it. And like the judgment, so also the divine salvation is seen in every sphere of the phenomenal world. There is nothing purely spiritual, and also nothing grossly material; nothing physical that is not animated by God, and nothing divine that is not revealed in nature. Whoever thus contemplates creation and history in connection with the kingdom of God is able to prophesy, *i.e.* to announce the destiny of nature and the goal of history!

Let us again recall the main thoughts which Joel, under the illumination of God's Spirit, reads in the occurrences of nature and the incidents of history.

1. There comes a Day of reckoning on God's part with all lands, when He will make known His terrible supremacy over nature. But for His people He will prepare an asylum on Zion, chaps. i. ii.

2. Along with the approach of the world-judgment the

Church of God is consummated, and that by an outpouring of the Spirit filling all its members, chap. iii.

3. The history of the world will issue in a universal rising of the nations against the people of God. In thus uniting in conflict against the Lord, the world-power delivers itself into the hands of the Judge, iii. 9 ff.

4. Meanwhile a sacred paradise blossoms around Zion, where the Lord dwells amid His own; while reconciliation and blessing stream forth thence upon ransomed heathen.

It is true these world-embracing ideas wear in many respects a form of national limitation. But this does not injure their universal character. To the prophet, Zion is the central spot of the history of redemption and the world. Against it, against God who dwells there, the whole world unites. There is the origin of the world-judgment, as well as the source of purity and grace. Instead of interfering with the range of these oracles, this local unity is itself of eminent significance,[1] all the more so that the prophet does not soothe himself with the illusion that people and land in their present state are fit for the kingdom of God. As the people needs sifting, spiritualizing, and sanctifying in all its members, so the land needs cleansing and glorifying, before God can take up His abode in it for ever. Thus we have here a mighty advance in prophecy. It gives us, indeed, no personal Mediator, but the divine action on the Church by which the Church will be completed is here definitely sketched. While this Church is not yet set free from national limits, the Church of the future is plainly distinguished from the present national one. First of all, it must be fertilized by the Spirit's regenerating power from above, before it corresponds to what it is meant to be, a God-filled people; and again, the salvation which preserves from the final judgment is made to depend on God's personal relation to the individual and the individual's to God.

As regards the *fulfilment* of Joel's prophecies, we know how the Apostle Peter (Acts ii. 16) has described Pentecost as the fulfilment of the close of Joel's second chapter.[2] That no

---

[1] Cf. Goethe's well-known saying: "The real, sole and deepest theme of the history of the world and man, to which every other is secondary, is the conflict between belief and unbelief."

[2] The oracle is there cited freely after the LXX. Instead of the μετὰ ταῦτα, which the LXX. have in conformity with the Hebrew text, he puts ἐν ταῖς ἐσχάταις ἡμέραις,

reference can be meant to any universal outpouring of the Spirit in the previous history is clear. But there in fact the youthful Church, consisting of Jews and associates of Jews of every kind, was fertilized by a shower of the Divine Spirit such as had never been before in the world, so that henceforth God's gifts of grace ($\chi\alpha\rho\acute{\iota}\sigma\mu\alpha\tau\alpha$) dwelt in it. Henceforth God's Holy Spirit was the heritage of the Church. Since receiving the Spirit of divine adoption and fellowship, the Church has attained maturity. It no longer needs human mediation and representation before God by prophets and priests; it hears for itself the voice of God and receives His revelation. This Spirit is not bound to a particular order or age or generation; He is the property of every living member of God's people, made such by personal faith, so that in the highest matters they have all equal standing and rights. Certainly this people of God, this mature Church of saints, only extends as far as the influence of the Divine Spirit reaches, so that the well-known axiom of Irenæus holds good, not indeed of Christendom, but of the true Christian Church as it has existed since Pentecost, although not in local and constitutional unity: *Ubi ecclesia ibi et Spiritus Dei, et ubi Spiritus Dei illic ecclesia et omnis gratia.*

It may seem strange that Peter also in his discourse makes the menaces of judgment (Joel ii. 30 ff.) follow immediately on the above words of promise. But this is done in harmony with the purpose of the prophet and the course of things. In the fact that the Church now received its full consecration, and was to be brought to its perfect state, the apostle recognised that now the other development, that of the world-power, was approaching its end—the judgment. And for the Israel, which had decided for this world, the two events fell very close together. A few decades after the shower of the Spirit had shaken the disciples' house at Jerusalem, the city burst into flames; not perfume of sacrifice, but vapour of smoke rose from the temple to heaven; fire and blood strove together. The doom of annihilation, foretold by the possessors of Christ's Spirit, and announced by many fearful tokens in heaven and on earth, was come.[1] Through this judg-

---

a phrase not without warrant, since even according to Joel the previous event introduces the conclusion of history.

[1] Cf. Josephus, *De Bello Jud.* vi. 5. 3, which narratives show at least that the consciences of the people were wrung—not without reason!

ment the Lord preserved to Himself—certainly by unforeseen means—a Church of deliverance. This Church was formed, the nation having been sifted, of all individuals who "called on the name of the Lord," *i.e.* took refuge in the Lord revealed in Christ. The fact that Joel lays down (ii. 32) such a purely personal, not national, condition of salvation, Paul (Rom. x. 13) knows well how to appreciate, for which of course he must submit to be taken to task by Dr. Aug. Wünsche! Here without doubt a reason is given to justify the reception of the heathen into God's kingdom, whether Joel is here precisely thinking of the heathen or not.

But although in the founding of the Church of Jesus Christ this prophecy was initially realized, its evolution, extension, and spiritualization are not concluded. The Church of God, to which many from all peoples have been called, is still by no means spiritually mature, and intimately one with its Head in all its members. When the work of the Spirit approaches completion, and the Church, filled with the Spirit, is fully prepared for the dwelling of the Lord, then also will the world-judgment, already provisionally accomplished on the Jews and the heathen, advance to its conclusion. From a universal war of extermination waged by the powers of this world against the Church, the Church will issue saved, purified, and hallowed. Then also the Lord's dwelling in His Church on earth will be realized outwardly. How far the picture sketched by Joel of this kingdom on Zion is an adequate likeness, how far a miniature outline, of what is to be, only the future can show. In any case, the outer will correspond to the inner glory of the Church.

NOTE A.—*Joel's Age.* Joel, too, belongs to the southern kingdom (Judah), like Obadiah, and the contemporaneousness of the two prophets seems to us beyond doubt. What elements, then, may be gathered from Joel's oracles in confirmation of this date? The natural occurrence to which his preaching refers—the locust-plague—cannot be fixed chronologically from other authorities. On the other hand, in the latter part of Joel's prophecy a clear political horizon comes into view. There appear as Israel's foes neither the Chaldæans nor Assyrians (as from Amos's days), nor the Syrians, but Philistines, Idumeans,[1] Phœnicians, just as in

---

[1] According to iii. 19, these especially have shed innocent blood, which seems to refer, like Obadiah's accusation, to the revolt under Jehoram (889 B.C.), 2 Chron. xxi. 16, 2 Kings viii. 20, which was avenged by Amaziah (825), 2 Kings xiv. 7. The

Obadiah. Along with these, Egypt, the old hereditary foe, is mentioned. Without doubt Joel iii. speaks of the same marauding inroads of the heathen on Judah as Obadiah. According to Joel also, Jerusalem was plundered, and the inhabitants made captive, carried away, and sold to the distant Greeks. These occurrences are still painfully remembered, nor does the בָּלָה or שְׁבוּת dwell afar off; but clearly in Joel that calamity lies farther back than in Obadiah's lively indignation at Edom's treachery. To all the misfortunes mentioned by the latter, a new one meanwhile is added, which fills up their measure; not from men, but from God Himself a new plague has come, not an army of heathen, but God's fearful host—the locusts.

(The oracles of *Amos* present a point of time still more advanced. In him, indeed, also the Philistines, Phœnicians, and Edomites appear as the foes who have invaded Israel, but in addition in the first line the Syrians, who meanwhile have become troublesome. How far Amos i. 6–11 has the same events in view as Obadiah and Joel may be disputed, seeing that Amos brings together, in his list of sins, occurrences of various periods. Amos also, like Joel, speaks of the sale of captive Israelites by Philistines and Phœnicians; and as regards Edom, cf. i. 11 with Joel iii. 19. On the other hand, in Amos i. 6, 9, the captives are handed over to Edom; whereas in Obad. ver. 14, Edom hands them over to others, and according to Joel they are sold by the Phœnicians to the Greeks. For בְּנֵי יָוָן (Joel iii. 6) are not a south-Arabian people (Hitzig); cf. B. Stade, *De Populo Javan*, 1880. Thus it is probable that at least in the Phœnician slave-dealing, Amos was thinking of an occurrence lying nearer to him. They were, perhaps, Israelites or Gileadites who were sold by the "Canaanites" in crowds southward, to Edom.)

If Obadiah is rightly put in the time of Jehoram, the time of *Joash* (877–833 ?), the second successor of Jehoram, would present itself as that of Joel. Since, as already remarked, in Joel's discourses the Syrians are not mentioned, who from 850 (2 Kings xii. 18) pressed hard on Judah, this circumstance points us to the first period of Joash, when this king was justifying the best hopes, while the monarchy was inferior to the priesthood by which it was held in tutelage, 2 Kings xii. 2; 2 Chron. xxiv. Credner first vindicated for the prophet so early an age (870–865); similarly Winer, Delitzsch (c. 860), Hitzig (870–860), Kleinert (875–850), Wünsche (860–850), Steiner.[1] In the same way Ewald puts forward internal reasons for the great age of the book. The attitude

oracle then arose before this point of time; cf. also Joel iii. 4-6 with 2 Chron. xxi. 16.

[1] Hengstenberg and Bleek bring the oracle somewhat lower down, namely, to the time of Amos, therefore c. 800.

of Joel to nature, to the people and cultus, points to an early time (Ewald, *Propheten*, i. 89). For his view one may appeal to Joel's language, and his simple, grand, luminous style. In point of form his tractate belongs to the most perfect we possess in the Old Testament. Prophecy and poesy so interpenetrate that separation is impossible.

Finally, frequent allusions to *Joel* are found in the prophetic literature. Amos adopted certain words of Joel. In i. 2 he borrows his phraseology from Joel iii. 16; cf. Amos ix. 13 with Joel iii. 18. Amos also speaks of the heavy plague, present to Joel, as past (iv. 9), where גוי is a designation of the locusts, occurring elsewhere only in Joel (i. 4, ii. 25). In Amos v. 18, 20 the warning against the Day of the Lord, addressed to those sick of the world who, in their self-righteousness, longed for that catastrophe as if they had only good to expect from it, implies that the expectation of that day was current among the pious, which certainly was in the main a fruit of Joel's oracles. In the time of Amos this prophetic truth was an object of abuse. That the Zion-oracle, found both in Isa. ii. 2–4 and Micah iv. 1–4, was originally Joel's (Hitzig, Ewald), is, on the other hand, an unproved conjecture. On the other side, Isa. xiii. 6, 9 f. leans on Joel i. 15, ii. 1 f., 10. And Zeph. i. 14 is, perhaps, dependent on Joel ii. 1 f. Joel iii. 18 is further expanded by Ezek. xlvii. 1 ff. Cf. also Ezek. xxxviii. 17, xxxix. 8, with Joel iii. 9 ff.

Thus, in modern days, despite the objections of Vatke[1] and Hilgenfeld,[2] who assign Joel to post-exilian times, we are pretty generally accustomed to see in Joel the oldest prophet whose oracles are preserved in literary form. On the other hand, more recently, several critics[3] have joined the two just mentioned in assigning Joel's oracles to post-exilian times. Duhm states the reasons, p. 275. They do not, however, seem to us weighty enough to rebut those on the other side. That this brief oracle does not mention the kingdom of Israel, is explained by the fact that the prophet has his dwelling in Jerusalem, and his work is limited to Judah, to which also the eschatological future belongs. That the monarchy is not referred to, while the priests are specially prominent, is readily explained by the circumstances of the first period of Joash, when, in fact, the priests were the real fathers of the nation. The real reason, however, why those critics push the oracle down to post-exilian days is something else: it contradicts too openly a hypothesis regarded in recent days by many as the unavoidable result of science. Were Wellhausen right in his

---

[1] *Biblische Theologie*, p. 462.
[2] *Zeitschr. f. wiss. Theologie*, ix. p. 412 f.
[3] Seinecke, *Der Evangelist des Alten Testaments*, p. 41; Duhm, *Theologie der Propheten*, p. 275 f.; Merx, *Die Prophetie des Joel und ihre Ausleger*, 1879, p. 1 ff.

assertion that only from Isaiah's days could the temple at Jerusalem lay claim to be the central sanctuary of the whole land, nay, Yahveh's sole dwelling-place, how could a pre-Isaianic prophet view Zion as the centre of the revelation of judgment and salvation, as Joel does?[1] Were it true that the pre-exilian prophets thoroughly disparaged sacrifice and declaimed against it, how would Joel, who complains of nothing so much as the forced interruption of the sacrificial service in the temple, agree with them? Thus this "little, unimportant book," as Duhm calls it, stands most inconveniently in the way of the Graf-Kuenen-Wellhausen theory as to the development of the Israelitish cultus and civilisation. For this reason it must be set aside, and the feeling of astounding originality and freshness impressed on the unprejudiced reader is dismissed with a phrase like the following: "Why should not an *epigonus*, gifted with great talent for form, and not troubled with much thought, by careful imitation of the best models, write a good style?" (Duhm, p. 276). Whereas all unprejudiced examination will allow priority to Joel iii. 16 over Amos i. 2, the inverse relation must be asserted,[2] etc.! But we will not, in the interest of a critical hypothesis, which at best is still infected with much error, and forced to support itself by so much arbitrariness, degrade so vivid a prophecy into the artificial product of an age of *epigoni*. See also Steiner in Hitzig's *Comm. zu den Kl. Proph.* 1881, p. 73 f.

NOTE B.—The four kinds of locusts are mostly referred to four kingdoms. So already the Targum of Jonathan, and after him nearly all Church Fathers, who differ, however, in interpreting the four kingdoms. Still Jerome and Theodoret declare the proper, natural acceptation not inadmissible. This acceptation, really his only admissible one, was maintained in the Middle Ages by Ibn Ezra, Raschi, David Kimchi, and was approved in the Reformation age by Luther and Calvin. Bochart ensured its victory in his *Hierozoicon*. He is followed by Credner, Hitzig, Ewald, Delitzsch, Keil, Wünsche, and most moderns. On the other hand, Hengstenberg, Hävernick, Hilgenfeld, Merx, *et al.*, have returned to the artificial allegorical or symbolic exposition.

NOTE C.—Gesenius, *et al.*, instead of the first נִקֵּיתִי, would read נִקַּמְתִּי, after the LXX. ἐκζητήσομαι. But the two words are not synonymous at all, but are opposite in meaning. נָקָה signifies "to declare pure," *insontem declaravit*, synonymous with הִצְדִּיק, elsewhere with

---

[1] See p. 187.

[2] Of course we do not mean that even thus Amos i. 2 suffices to refute the Wellhausen account of the late acknowledgment of the temple on Zion as the only true sanctuary (*Gesch.* i. 23 ff.). Still in this passage Amos already assumes as self-evident that Yahveh dwells on Zion, and from Zion judges the world; cf. Ps. cx. 2.

personal object, here with that of the offence. דָּמָם, according to Num. xxxv. 27 (cf. Deut. xxi. 8), is the blood lying on Judah, blood-guiltiness, for which the plural is more common, Ex. xxii. 1, and often. Merx explains differently (p. 26 ff.). He supposes that, "I declare (make) their blood נִקֵּי, pure, which (before) I did not hold נִקֵּי," means, as in Jonah i. 14, Deut. xxi. 8, Jer. xxv. 29: "I will let it not be shed with impunity, declare it inviolable." Even on this acceptation an expiation, a purifying, and that of persons, is presupposed. But ver. 19 favours the former explanation. Also the meaning assigned by Merx to this *piel* (*to declare inviolable*) cannot be confirmed by example.

SECOND SECTION.

THE PROPHETS OF THE ASSYRIAN PERIOD IN THE NORTHERN KINGDOM: AMOS, HOSEA, ZECHARIAH IX.–XI.

§ 26. *Amos.*

THERE follows a trio of prophets, Amos, Hosea, Zechariah ix.-xi., all belonging to the northern kingdom, at least doing their work there, and that at a time when the kingdom was on the decline. The oldest of them, Amos, a born Judæan (of Tekoa, i. 1), was called from his herd to prophetic preaching amid the idolatrous "house of Israel," by the Lord's imperative command, under the strong, prosperous rule of Jeroboam II. Growing up in severe simplicity, a speaker in the spirit and power of Elijah, he had to expose without fear the evils of the land, glossed over with glittering tinsel, and to announce the approaching judgment. He sees the judgment on the nations, not like Joel in a comprehensive picture, but in a cycle of single judgments. While he knows of the "Day of the Lord," his proclamation of judgment is more historical than eschatological. And since he cannot promise a future to the northern kingdom, the proper object of his menaces, the prophecy of the completion of God's kingdom with him falls into the background behind the announcement of the work of destruction which Yahveh purposes on Israel. The first half of the book in weighty discourses (i.–vi.), the second (vii.–ix.) in brief, simple, but pregnant visions, contains the judicial sentence on a faithless nation bewitched by wanton image-worship and forgetful of the most elementary moral duties. The nation will be scattered among all lands, nay, completely carried into exile, at which point the prophet sees *Assyria* rise before him, which was beginning to appear threateningly on the horizon.[1]

---

[1] The whole historical field of view shows close affinity with that of Joel, but as remarked, p. 220, is considerably in advance.

But although the present course of things can only lead to judgment on Israel (not merely the heathen, as mainly in Joel), instead of salvation, the book is not quite without bright features. Here also—and here in special degree—applies what we said (p. 193) of the contents of prophecy during this whole period: The threat of judgment stands in the foreground, the promise of salvation forms merely the bright fringe of the judgment-cloud then ascending. Precisely in Amos judgment like a storm-cloud makes the round of the nations to descend most heavily on Israel; and only through its last fringe does there appear a ray of divine grace, in whose light a happy future opens.

In the fifth vision (ix. 1 ff.) the prophet has seen God's house in Israel, the sanctuary of the northern kingdom, fall to pieces, and the nation buried under its ruins. The Lord intends a radical destruction of this sinful kingdom; only He will not utterly destroy the house of Jacob (=kingdom of Judah, ver. 8). As this limitation of the judgment recalls the patriarchal promises, so the oracle recalls the inalienable mercies of David:—

Amos ix. 11 f. "In that day will I set up THE COTTAGE OF DAVID that is fallen to pieces, and will repair its rents and set up its ruins, and build them as before,[1] that they may take in possession the remnant of Edom and all nations, over which my name has been proclaimed, says Yahveh, who performs these things."

Whereas to the northern kingdom, powerful and vigorous as it seems, the prophet can hold out no hope, God's covenant with David will as little fall to the ground as the one concluded with the fathers of the nation. The house of David is certainly at present in a ruinous state, really no longer fit to be called a house, but a mere hut (Isa. i. 8); soon it will tumble down altogether. Not long before, Jeroboam II.'s predecessor, Joash, had vanquished the Jewish King Amaziah; the fame of the Davidic dynasty seemed gone for ever. But despite this appearance of things, the incorruptible, fearless prophet proclaims to the Ephraimite land, that only this despised "cottage," i.e. the kingdom of Judah, the soul of which is the race of David, has a bright future before it, since God will restore its power to as glorious

---

[1] The sudden change in the gender and number of the suffixes in ver. 11b is strange. The suff. fem. plur. in פְּרָצֵיהֶן seems not to refer to the cities of Judah, but to a גְּדֵרוֹת lying in the verb; הֲרִיכֹתָיו to the בַּיִת lying in סֻכַּת; וּבְנִיתִיהָ refers to סֻכַּת.

a state as it had ever enjoyed. Disobedient Edom[1] must again bend under its sceptre along with all the countries already claimed for the Lord. This promise does not hover in the far distance, but keeps within local limitation, at least as to the sense it must have had for the hearers of Amos. The past greatness of Judah floats before the prophet's eyes, as ver. 11 f. shows, as something reappearing hereafter. As Jeroboam II. had just again restored the limits of the northern kingdom according to the prophecy of Jonah, son of Amittai (2 Kings xiv. 25), so according to the oracle of Amos a like restoration of power in yet fuller measure was to be granted to the house of David. Not merely everything which David and Solomon actually possessed, but everything already claimed by the Lord as His property[2] was to serve it hereafter. To this head belongs in the strict sense, *e.g.*, even Phœnicia, which was never an Israelitish possession. In the wider sense one might certainly remember that universal dominion has been virtually promised to David as the Lord's Anointed, God's son (Ps. cx. 2 and others); but the concrete conception of David's future kingdom is still ruled here by the past (just as in Obad. ver. 17). The evolution and expansion of the theocracy takes place in this form, that the lands previously designated to its service are all actually subjected to the house of David. This is said and sealed by Yahveh, " who performs these things." How this is to come about, is meantime incomprehensible; enough *that* at last it will so come to pass.

Then God's people and land have rest, peacefully enjoying the blessings which the Lord has bestowed on them. In exactly the same way as Joel, Amos closes with the joyous prospect of a covenant-people in Canaan enriched by God's grace with abundance of gifts and undisturbed by judgments:—

13   " Behold, days come, saith Yahveh, when the ploughman

---

[1] Cf. i. 11. Edom alone is named here, as the foe most hated, on whom the house of David must wreak satisfaction, which agrees excellently with Obadiah and Joel.

[2] The explanation: "All nations over whom the name of the Lord has been proclaimed" = preached, is contrary to idiom. According to Deut. xxviii. 10, נִקְרָא שֵׁם יי' עַל, the name of the Lord is *proclaimed over* a nation in the sense that He takes possession of it, makes it His property. But the *perf.* is not to be interpreted as *fut. exactum*: "all nations, to which I (the Lord) shall have proclaimed a right of possession;" rather what has been already promised to the house of David is meant. The LXX. obtain a much more general sense by reading אֶת־שְׁאֵרִית אָדָם.

overtakes the reaper, and the grape-treader the seed-sower: and the mountains drop with new wine, and all hills melt.
14 And I make the captivity of my people Israel return home, and they build again the desolated cities and dwell therein, and they plant vineyards and drink their wine, and plant
15 gardens and eat their fruit. And I will plant them upon their soil, and they shall no more be plucked up out of their soil, which I gave them,—saith Yahveh, thy God."

The physical blessing is depicted (ver. 13) in much the same language as at the close of Joel's prophecy (iii. 18), with a phrase, however, which points back to the Torah. The normal state of agriculture, described in Lev. xxvi. 5, according to which threshing-time is to reach to vintage and vintage to sowing-time, is surpassed in the prophetic description of the happy future: the plougher overtakes the reaper, etc. One will scarcely be done with ploughing when the crop will be ripe, and with treading grapes when the sowing will have to begin, which bespeaks just as wonderfully rapid growth as an exuberant wine-harvest. Almost all the year through reaping and grape-treading will go on. To this is added the same hyperbole as in Joel: the "dropping," nay, "melting of the hills," which abound in wine (and milk). Then strikes the hour, when the deported ones, whom we have already seen in Obadiah and Joel (cf. Amos i. 6, 9), but who are far more numerous, according to the view of Amos, after the whole of Israel has been "sifted" among the nations (ix. 9), shall return (Joel iii. 1) at the Lord's instance, to enjoy with their nation in undisturbed peace the fruit of their labour which the Lord has blessed; whereas at present, in consequence of the absence of His blessing, what has been built and planted with bitter sweat falls a prey to strangers.

Thus we see that the prophecy of Amos only at the end turns into a prophecy respecting the divine kingdom, setting forth its future establishment, like Obadiah and Joel, under historical, local, and political limitations. If Joel is richer in the historical breadth and spiritual depth of his prophetic views, Amos, on the other hand, on account of the scene of his labour, excels him in insistence on the truth, that the divine promise given to David cannot fall to the ground.[1] He does not, indeed, expressly attach the

---

[1] That "the entry of the Davidic monarchy into the circle of the Messianic prospects stands in causal connection with the new and promising beginning which

hope of future salvation to a particular ruler of David's house ; but he calls attention to the promises bestowed on this house, which can as little be abrogated by the sin of the nation and its rulers as those given to the patriarchs. Both together assure the continuance of the nation, at least of a vigorous remnant, right through the judgment, as well as its future imperial glory amid Davidic splendour.

The *fulfilment* of the promise of Amos does not admit of such palpable proof in the following age as that of his threatenings against Israel. Although under Uzziah an invigoration of the southern kingdom took place, this does not satisfy the language of Amos ix. 11 ff., if one keeps the kingdom within such historical limits. The setting up of the Davidic kingdom, as later prophets plainly show, was to take place on a grander scale, and the addition of the heathen to it was to assume far wider dimensions than the contemporaries of the herdsman of Tekoa were able to conceive. In this wider and higher sense the Apostle James (Acts xv. 16 f.) proclaimed the programme of God's kingdom in the words of Amos, his kinsman in spirit (following the LXX.), after the appearance of the Son of David, whom the synagogue after the present passage had called Bar Nafli (בר נפלי),[1] because he was to raise the cottage from its depth of degradation into a world-ruling empire.

§ 27. *Hosea.*

In the oracles of *Hosea*, a younger contemporary[2] of Amos, as different from the latter in temperament, in his mode of viewing and stating things, as he is one with him in the aim and nature of

---

the monarchy took after the accession of Uzziah—a king as pious as he was energetic, and adorned with every kingly virtue" (Riehm, *Messianic Prophecy*, p. 121)—is not to be asserted. Prophecy has proved that it can dispense with such pragmatic supports, since it drew the Messiah-picture most completely and confidently in the reign of Ahaz. (This seems also to be Riehm's view, according to the English translation.)

[1] Sanhedr. 76b. Fr. Delitzsch, *Messianic Prophecies*, p. 59.

[2] The Book of Hosea collects together discourses delivered throughout a long space of time. The first of them were spoken without doubt under Jeroboam II.'s rule, the later (vii. 7) describe the anarchy that arose after his death ; and his work in any case extended to about the time of Menahem. On the other hand, it can scarcely be supposed that he was still active under Hezekiah, as the inscription states and x. 14 has been thought to prove.

his prophecy, we encounter in still more triumphant form the confidence that the Lord will at last turn everything to the good of His people, after they have drunk the cup of judgment to the dregs. If Amos is a rough herald of the righteousness of the Lord (of course not without priestly sympathy for the judgment falling on his people, as vii. 2, 5 shows), Hosea is the impassioned singer of the Lord's love for His people. Even Hosea, indeed, is obliged to deal mainly in rebuke, doing this without human regard and indulgence. He is obliged to disclose still worse things, if possible, than Amos; for moral corruption, vice, and godlessness have made rapid strides. The judgment must soon and terribly be inflicted on Israel and its rulers; nay, Judah also, as the seer more and more perceives, will be involved in it.[1] This insight into the nation's heinous inner corruption, joined with the prospect of impending judgment, makes the lyre of this loving singer quiver with tragic, Jeremiah-like sadness. But he has seen just as deeply into God's *bottomless* compassion. On this account often, after language of rebuke, the most glorious promise bursts forth without any introduction. Despite all appearance to the contrary, he knows that the Lord will do good to His people at the end, and will verify His promises.

This prophet also, like Amos, is far from intending to introduce a higher, more spiritual religion, as has recently been attributed to him. The new element he brings is rooted in the old revelation made to the people through Moses, but fallen, as he bitterly complains, in his days into oblivion and neglect. But certainly Hosea gives more profound glimpses than any one before him into the mystery of the love of the God who brought His people out of Egypt under Moses. The designation of Israel as God's first-born son is Mosaic (Ex. iv. 22),[2] as well as the application of the marriage-relation to the covenant existing between Yahveh and His Church (Ex. xxxiv. 15 f.; Deut. xxxi. 16). But Hosea developed the latter analogy more elaborately and spiritually than had been done before, nay, made it the soul of his preaching, thereby suggesting a deepening of the covenant, the full importance of which was only revealed to the N. T. Church. Marriage is a love-bond, not tied merely by nature (like that between father and son) without regard to individual assent; it rests on a mutual choice, which again is determined

[1] iv. 15, v. 10 ff., vi. 4, 11, xii. 2.   [2] P. 128.

by sympathy of disposition. It is true that this element is not made so prominent in the Old Testament as in the New—first, because in antiquity the position of woman was still subordinate, she was unconditionally dependent on the favour of man; and again, in harmony with this, because the Church itself was not yet free, had not come to maturity. Hence in the passages touching on this relation the Old Testament chiefly emphasizes the absolute dependence of the woman on the man, of the Church on its Lord and Master, its duty to submit wholly to Him; its first and best virtue is obedience, chaste fidelity to Him. The relation (as in the Old Testament use of paternal right and filial duty) is more legal than in the application of filial and bridal love in the New Testament. But Hosea, if any one, is a precursor of the love-song echoing in the New Covenant. He has a high, intense ideal of the tender bond which, according to God's will, was to attach the Church to its Lord; he insists unceasingly that this relation must be exercised in *reciprocal* love, and gives a certain prospect of the realization of this divine ideal in the future. In this way, without doubt, he has contributed not a little to the application of the songs, extolling the love of the Anointed One, (Ps. xlv.; Canticles,)[1] to that love of God for Israel which was to form the crown of the future Messianic salvation, and withal its innermost sanctuary. The present time sets before the prophet's eyes nothing but the opposite of this blessed union of the Lord with His people. The more tender and sacred to the prophet the covenant into which the Lord entered with His people, the more painfully he felt the shocking disturbance of this fellowship by the gross sins of the people. But in order that the people also, despite their dulness, may feel how glaring is their unfaithfulness, Hosea was compelled to set this bad state of things before their eyes in his personal household life. The people's double-mindedness in God's service, their dalliance with Canaanite nature-worship, is nothing but adultery (iv. 12, 15, v. 3 f., 7, vi. 10, ix. 1). Thus in chap. i. ff. we see the prophet involved in heavy domestic misfortune. His wife is untrue to him, she runs after strange paramours; his children are children of whoredom. How far the prophet relates actual experience, how far he merely uses a didactic form, can scarcely be made out with certainty. To us it appears most probable

[1] P. 172.

that Hosea really suffered from unfaithfulness in his wife, and afterwards learnt that he (God's prophet and representative) must needs endure this unhappy lot by God's will, in order that by his domestic σκάνδαλον, which only too surely drew the people's attention to him, he might be able to hold before their eyes a mirror in which they should learn how they stood to the Lord and the Lord to them. On the other hand, it seems as if, after the prophet and the Church had become used to that parallel, the account of the third chapter were freely sketched by the prophet in order to exhibit a particular element of the prophecy. The three children of the adulteress (chap. i.) seem to be the prophet's actual children, meant by their names (like those of Isa. vii. 3, viii. 3) to remind the people of the misery and doom that would ensue from their unfaithfulness. On the other hand, in ii. 1 ff. the prophet is thinking of the children of the Church, *i.e.* its several members who suffered under the burden of its guilt, and were called to protest against its sinful conduct.

As the gloomy, vivid picture held by Hosea before the people's eyes is almost strong enough without words to impress even a race without conscience and insensible to divine things with a sense of its *guilt*, so it serves also vividly to depict the *chastisement* which the Lord purposes to inflict on His unfaithful people. He will take away His help from His unfaithful Church (ii. 6, 9 ff.) and withdraw His benefits, for which she thanks only false gods, and thus by want and affliction bring her to reflection; He will also, as chap. iii. pictures, shut her up in a place where intercourse with her paramours will be cut off, *i.e.* lead her into exile, where she can no longer practise the Canaanitish abominations attached to local conditions. Moreover, the purpose of these punishments is to be made clear in the example of the adulteress. The divine pædagogy leads her into exile as into a new Egypt, and into the wilderness as to a second sojourn at Sinai, in order to correct her and win back her love, to reawaken her longing for salvation. There she will repent, *i.e.* change her mind so as to desire to return to her former lord whom she faithlessly forsook, ii. 7. There in the time of punishment the Lord desires, as once in the wilderness,[1] to seek anew her love (ii. 14, what unfathomable condescension is implied in this repeated wooing of Israel's love by the Lord!); and when, as in the time of her first

---

[1] Cf. also ix. 10, xi. 1 ff., xii. 10.

love, she joyfully responds to Him, He will restore to her the promised land (ii. 15). Or, as it is said in iii. 5: "Afterwards (when under the stress of exile they have come to reflection) the children of Israel shall return and seek Yahveh their God and David their king, and shall tremble at Yahveh and His goodness in the end of the days." They shall return to the legitimate ruling-house, to "*their king David*," as well as to the legal sanctuary. By this (as in Ezek. xxxiv. 23) is not meant the deported king, but the ruler of David's house at that time representing his rights and mercies. Nothing more precise, indeed, is said of this king. But at all events under his sway extraordinary salvation will be revealed in the last days. The passage has in view rather the Davidic house than the person of the king, like Amos ix.; but it is far nearer the personal concentration of the Messianic promise than Amos. The mixture of feelings filling the returning penitents is beautifully described: Irresistibly drawn by fond desire, and yet trembling with a sense of their own unworthiness (cf. xi. 10), they will draw near to the Lord and His salvation, to the revelation of His goodness.

Moreover, the final state of happiness is more fully described by the help of the comparison with the human marriage-covenant as one of complete inner and outer harmony between heaven and earth, God and His people. When the Church's first love to her God is again revived in the time of her purifying in the wilderness, she will call Him her consort (ii. 16 f.), not her Baal (lord). The name of Baal will not again be heard from her lips. Thus in delicate modesty she will avoid everything offensive to the Lord. Her heart belonging exclusively to Him, she will also study delicacy of speech, avoiding the ambiguity in the name given to God which has so often proved the bridge to apostasy. "My Baal" has an unsuspicious and reverent sound, but it may easily become a cloak of unfaithfulness. "My husband, my consort," expresses devotion as trustful as it is unreserved; it excludes all dalliance with the multiform heathen "lords," and implies a bliss such as no heathen god can give. This bliss is expressed even in the outward aspect of the land and the people's life:—

ii. 18. "And I make a covenant with them in that day, with the beast of the field and the birds of the air and what creeps on the earth; and bow and sword and war I will break out of the land, and will make them rest in safety."

The peace, the secure rest, vouchsafed to the people that belongs wholly to its Lord and God, is described on two sides. It will enjoy happy rest from beasts and men. For God commands the beasts, which may prove destructive to sinful men, to spare His own. This is expressed thus: "I make with them a covenant on behalf of men," *i.e.* a regulation which they must observe.[1] Three classes of beasts are named: wild beasts without, to which beasts of prey belong; the birds above, among which also are many birds of prey; and reptiles beneath, which include the cunning serpent.

But as the Lord forbids the powers of nature to inflict injury, so also He wards off the attacks of men from His sanctified people. War will have an end in the land.[2] God Himself shatters bow and sword and implement of war, and casts them out of the land.[3] Thus, in contrast with the perpetual readiness for war necessary at present, one will be able to give himself to the calm enjoyment of peace. This physiognomy of the final kingdom of God, according to which it is distinguished by a truce of nature and truce of nations, is further elaborated by Isaiah some decades later, in Isa. ii. 2 ff., ix. 4, and elsewhere, truce of nations; in xi. 6 ff., truce of nature.

But this outer harmony of the last days has its inner ground in the sacred covenant of love then established by the Lord between Himself and His people, and become truly reciprocal.

ii. 19 f. "And I will marry thee to me for ever; and will marry thee to me in righteousness and judgment and love and compassion, and will marry thee to me in stedfastness, and thou shalt know Yahveh."

The true love-covenant belongs only to the future. The Lord as Bridegroom will *marry*[4] the Church as bride, of which He thrice gives assurance with solemn repetition. And this New Covenant shall not again be broken after brief duration; it shall not be a merely outward one; it shall no longer remain one-sided; the

---

[1] Cf. Job v. 23 and p. 93.
[2] That the apparently heterogeneous מלחמה is to be taken thus, is proved by Hos. i. 7.
[3] Used pregnantly: *frangam e terra* for *frangam et ejiciam e terra*.
[4] אֵרַשׂ is said of the man who marries a woman (accus.), Deut. xx. 7, xxviii. 30.

spiritual fellowship into which the Lord enters with His Church in imparting to it His own attributes secures to this covenant its inner truth and inviolable permanence.

The divine attributes mediating the covenant, by the Church participating in them, are righteousness (צְדָק) and love (חֶסֶד). The former is exercised in judgment (מִשְׁפָּט), right utterance and normal action, the latter in displays of mercy (רַחֲמִים). Both are attributes pertaining to God in the highest and fullest sense (note A), but cannot be wanting to His people, if His people are to be entirely one with their God. The two attributes are also so chosen that they describe what must adorn the Church as the Lord's bride, whereas in the Israel of the present their absence is conspicuous. They are God's communicative virtues, by which His union with the Church is effected.[1] At present Israel lacks these fundamental virtues of righteousness and love,[2] because it stands in no spiritual fellowship with the Lord, no "knowledge of the Lord"[3] belongs to it. But then those divine attributes will be reflected in the Church,[4] by which the most intimate fellowship with Him is conditioned and indicated. Finally, this New Covenant is made בֶּאֱמוּנָה in stedfastness. Unchangeableness, that ring holding together God's attributes, will also conclude the covenant with His people and secure its eternal duration. In sincere, immovable fidelity will God join His people to Himself, and this fidelity will be mutual. The description of this divine bridal-love reaches its climax in the clause: "Thou shalt *know* Yahveh." Knowing God is the chief condition on which the people can keep the covenant; and at the same time such knowledge, as the mention at the close shows, is the highest fruit of obedience to God rendered from love. This verb יָדַע elsewhere also denotes, as is well known, far more than a mere intellectual apprehending. It has been called a *nosse cum affectu et effectu*. It expresses the inner appropriation of something, and when a person is the object, appropriating insight into him, loving assimilation. So God knew Israel long ago (xiii. 5); when, now, on its part it knows the

---

[1] Nowack: "The gifts introduced by בְּ are so to speak the bridal gifts, which Yahveh makes over to Israel, His wife, on the making of the New Covenant," is not quite pertinent. These attributes are not conceived as a gift by which the Lord would acquire a right to the Church.

[2] iv. 1 f., v. 11, vi. 4 f., x. 4, 12, xii. 7.   [3] iv. 1, v. 4.

[4] Cf. Ps. lxxii. 1; Jer. xxiii. 5.

Lord, it receives Him into its inmost heart.[1] Here, then, the end is reached, which God had in mind from the first in covenanting with sinful man—perfect fellowship of life and love between Him and His Church on earth. Then begins complete harmony between heaven and earth.

ii. 21 f. "And it shall come to pass in that day, when I shall answer, saith the Lord, I will answer the heavens and they shall answer the earth, and the earth shall answer the wheat and the new wine and the oil, and they shall answer Jezreel; and I sow them to me in the land and have mercy on those without mercy, and say to those not my people: 'My people art thou!' And it shall say: 'My God!'"

This harmony is in contrast with the present, when disorders of various kinds appear in the economy of nature. Here one thing demands the other. Fruits demand sap from the earth, the earth rain from heaven,[2] the heaven clouds from God. So, finally, the asking and sighing of all creation turns upward to the Lord of life. When He is in the covenant, blessing streams upon all. His goodness makes one creature answer the demand of another (ענה), and thus no prayer remains unheard. Again, the glaring dissonances of the present turn into the opposite. The name Jezreel, which Israel had received (i. 4), in ominous recollection of Jehu's bloody deed, becomes of good omen, and signifies its new implanting in the Promised Land; instead of Lo-Ruhamah, as another child of the prophet is called, also representing Israel, this people will then be called the Favoured one, to whom special compassion has been shown; finally, the third will again receive the name עמי, "my people," properly belonging to Israel, but at present denied to it. God will again call Israel His people, and Israel, (here also the reciprocity is to be observed,) with full knowledge of what it says, will invoke Yahveh as its God. Already in the Pentateuch under Moses, God had defined

---

[1] The expression "to know the Lord" in this profound sense is a favourite phrase of this profoundly inward prophet and herald of divine-human love.

[2] The importance of rain in order to prosperity in the East is well known. W. M. Thomson, *The Land and the Book*, p. 91: "In the East is a deep sense of uncertainty and of entire dependence for their daily bread on the showers of heaven, delayed nearly every year until much painful solicitude is felt by all classes. Very often there is a universal cry from man and beast and bird and burning sky and drooping fields, ere the Lord hears the heavens and the earth, hears the corn and wine and oil."

the relation into which He will enter with this people thus: "It shall be to Him a people, and He will be to it a God" (cf. p. 128). In the time of consummation, this relation of possession shall be perfectly realized on both sides.

Already in i. 10 the prophet has quite abruptly appended to the foregoing sentence of rejection a similar promise. Only afterwards comes the physical (ii. 6 ff., iii. 4) and ethical means (ii. 2, 7, 14, v. 15), by which the transition from a state of enmity to God to one of covenant with Him is brought about. In this unlooked-for announcing of the promise (i. 10 ff.) appears the unfathomable mercy of God, which is the real ground of salvation.

In the former passage the promise has more of a political character.

i. 10   "And the number of the children of Israel shall be as the sand of the sea, which cannot be measured and numbered. And it shall come to pass instead of it being said to them, 'Ye are not my people,' one shall call them 'Sons of the living God.'
11 And the sons of Judah and the sons of Israel shall assemble together, and shall appoint themselves one head and go up out of the land; for great is the day of Jezreel."

ii. 1   "Say to your brethren, 'My people,' and to your sisters, 'Favoured.'"

Despite all guilt and punishment, what God promised to Abraham remains sure, namely, the promise of a countless posterity (Gen. xxii. 17, xv. 5; cf. xxxii. 13). And as it was promised to the Father of the faithful that in his seed all nations should be blessed, this people cannot always remain a witness to the divine curse. As it now bears the stamp of estrangement from God, so shall it unmistakably bear the stamp of divine sonship. The Pentateuchal declaration, that God has received the whole people into the place of a son (Ex. iv. 22; cf. Hos. xi. 1), is here individualized: individual Israelites are sons of the God who by His revelation proves Himself living.

The political consequence of this gracious act will be the ceasing of the present division of the Davidic kingdom[1] and the willing union of all the tribes under one head, of course under a prince of the heaven-chosen royal house[2] (iii. 5). God's people, countless as the sand by the sea, united under one head, will then go up from the land to Jezreel. By this march a military

---

[1] Zech. xi. 7, 14; Ezek. xxxvii. 15 ff.   [2] Cf. Amos ix. 11; Ezek. xxxiv. 23.

advance is meant. The people will take position in the great plain, so often the scene where the fates have come to a bloody issue, and where, in particular, in the time of the Judges, Deborah and Gideon, the Lord by His hosts smote to the ground the superior might of the heathen. In this sense the day of Jezreel here is the day of reckoning with the heathen, when Israel will finally conquer, thus approving itself the people anew received into God's favour.[1] Thus the members of the nation shall then be greeted as belonging to and favoured of the Lord[2] (ii. 1).

Hosea sees this glorious exaltation as something that can only follow on judgment and a protracted time of suffering (iii. 3), for the people were then quite incapable and unworthy of it. But he does not predict judgment as an unalterable fate. If the people repented, the Lord would certainly call them back to life from the death that had already partially overtaken them. Then the prophet (vi. 1 f.) dictates to them a healing, penitential prayer. As Joel summoned the Church to turn aside the approaching day of doom by sincere, inward sorrow (ii. 12 f.), so also Hosea here and in xiv. 2 ff. points out the way of salvation, waiting to see whether his people will take to heart his words, or whether those words will only be received afterwards by a Church judged, exiled, slain; cf. the summons (Isa. ii. 5).

vi. 1 "Come, let us return to Yahveh, for He has torn and He will heal us. He has smitten and He will bind us up.
2 He will make us live within two days, on the third day
3 He will raise us up, that we may live before Him. And let us know—hunt[3] after knowing, the Lord: Certain as the dawn is His rising,[4] And He will come to us as the rain-shower, as the latter rain which sprinkles the earth."[5]

---

[1] Without warrant, Hitzig specializes the prophecy, urging the local expression. He understands it as if the prophet expected a great battle in the above valley against the Syrians, which did not happen.

[2] Here also the suffix in עַמִּי refers to God, not to the speaker greeting his brother as a countryman, which would amount to a mutual acknowledgment of Judah and Ephraim.

[3] The Greek διώκειν, like this רָדַף, is a favourite word of Paul in the New Testament (Rom. ix. 30 f. and elsewhere).

[4] His rising (cf. צֵאת הַשֶּׁמֶשׁ) is "fixed"—i.e. His appearing is as positive as that of the dawn; Ps. lxxxix. 37.

[5] Ver. 1. We would use the hypothetical form: "Has He torn? then will He also heal; has He smitten?" etc. The omission of the copula in יְחַיֵּ is strange, but

If the people turned its thoughts back to God,[1] and sought Him zealously and heartily (ver. 3), He would as certainly set aside the judgment as He brought it about, and, what is more, make Himself known, appear with His revelation of grace as certainly and uniformly as the most regular phenomena of nature occur. But of special importance is the truth uttered in ver. 2: Israel must *die* in order to live; really it is found at present in a state of death, and can only be rescued from it by a creative act of God. We find this idea developed more copiously in Ezekiel (xxxvii.), in whose time, indeed, its state of death was far more obvious, the bones of the Church lying scattered on the earth. And as there God's omnipotence is dwelt on, which is able to make even the dead live again, so in the present passage, where it is expressed by the confident assurance יְחַיֵּנוּ, and especially by the indication of time, which is clearly meant to be the shortest space conceivable. Within two days[2] it will come to pass in unexampled fashion that divine life will come again into the people, so that on the third day by God's gracious working it will rise again to a holy, blessed life in God's sight. It is not really a rising of buried bodies that is meant, but a work according to the prophet's conviction no less miraculous than this, and possible to omnipotence alone: The raising a people from spiritual death, and from a bodily state no better and really no other than death,[3] to true life through God and before God, a life having its spiritual roots in God, and drawing from Him its outward success.

For the rest, the discourses of Hosea (chaps. iv.–xiv.) give no essentially new information about the future of God's kingdom. They expound more fully the contents of chaps. i.–iii. Above all, the hopeless corruption of the people in its unfaithfulness to Yahveh is laid bare, from ix. 10, with elegiac glances at the period of first love. Having shown itself incorrigible, Ephraim-

---

was necessary to preserve the perspicuity of the periods. In ver. 3 also the first words give hypothetically the presupposition of the sequel: "If we hunt after His knowledge, His rising is certain."

[1] "שׁוּב אֶל ה or עַד יהוה, xiv. 2, or with בְּ, xii. 7, is like the N. T. μετανοεῖν. xi. 5 complains that this repentance did not take place.

[2] מִן in מִיָּמָיִם is partitive. A distinction is made, chiefly indeed a formal one, in the vivid description, between the making alive which falls on the second, and the raising from the grave which falls on the third day.

[3] Cf. xiii. 1, Ephraim, the most powerful tribe, *died*, said in reference to the time of the Judges.

Israel goes into exile to Egypt and Assyria,[1] the lands with which it carries on dalliance, promising itself help from them.[2] Still the Lord in His unfathomable mercy cannot resolve to give them up to the doom of destruction for ever, as once the cities of the vale of Siddim, xi. 8 ff.

xi. 8 "How should I give thee up, O Ephraim, surrender thee, O Israel? How should I make thee like Admah, set thee as Zeboim? My heart turns within me, my compassions are
9 excited together (note B). I will not execute my fierce wrath, nor again destroy Ephraim. For I am God, not man,
10 holy in thy midst, and will not yield to passion. They shall go after Yahveh as after a roaring lion; for He will roar, and the children from the sea shall tremble, they shall flutter as birds from the land of Egypt, and as doves from the land of Assyria, and I will settle them in their houses."

Divine grace reaches beyond the judgment; here also behind the exile the prophet's gaze sees his people returning home. From the midland sea, therefore from Javan, where many prisoners are already found (Obad. ver. 20; Joel iii. 6), from Assyria and Egypt, whither soon many will be led, the Lord will call and bring them home. His call will be so powerful, that those alien to Him both outwardly and inwardly, will be irresistibly drawn by it, and will render obedience, partly from fear of the terrible might He displays, partly from joy at His salvation and the love breathing in it, and moving Him to seek His people again. This mixture of feelings (as in iii. 5) is expressed in the beautiful figure of the migratory birds and wandering doves, flying from distant lands to their native seats, at first anxiously fluttering, and then gaining confidence and nestling in their former haunts.

The difficult passage (xiii. 12 ff.) affirms that Ephraim will actually die, and yet the Lord will cherish thoughts of grace towards it (cf. vi. 1 ff.). The trial of Ephraim is closed. The judge is about to pronounce the fatal sentence. In the case of a hardened, unwise people a passing visitation is useless. Figuratively expressed: When the pains of one in travail overtake Ephraim, he is an unwise son who does not present himself at the opening of the womb. By this obstinacy he makes a happy, easy birth impossible. So the people in its sufferings

[1] viii. 13, ix. 3, 6; cf. x. 6, further xi. 5, 11.   [2] vii. 11, viii. 9, xiv. 3.

is compared to one in travail; while in so far as it frustrates a salutary result of its sufferings, it is like a child refusing to come to the birth. Thus pain and suffering fail to bring about a saving repentance. The people must fall a prey to death.

xiii. 14. "From the hand of the underworld I will deliver them, from death redeem them. Where are thy plagues, O death? where is thy sting, O underworld? Repentance is hidden from my eyes."

If the first two clauses of the verse are read interrogatively, the passage is all rebuke, condemnation without hope. "Should I deliver them from the power of Hades? Nay, forward, ye powers of death, I have no mercy!" But the interrogative acceptation is without support and little probable in point of form. As to meaning, it is in contradiction to the character of Hosea's prophecy, which always behind judgment discloses a prospect of redemption. The sense, therefore, rather is: "Only from the underworld will I redeem them." For this reason also שְׁאֹל stands here before מָוֶת. That God will redeem His people at last is certain to Hosea. But it is clear to him that no mere passing, remedial suffering must come first, but the radical judgment of death. Thus only from the realm of the power to which it is now handed over will the Lord redeem His people. The following apostrophe: "Where are thy plagues, O death?" might perhaps be understood by the analogy of ver. 10 as meaning, "Where, then, remains thy power? Thou wilt have none over them when I redeem them." But this does not suit the close of the verse and the connection with what follows; for the rendering, "Death shall hide in penitence from my sight, death shall grieve for having attacked my people," is not good sense.¹ Rather the phrase "to hide from God's sight" means, in reference to a decree, that it does not find favour with Him, is not acceptable to Him, is not to His mind. נֹחַם, "repentance," is formed from the niphal in meaning, it is used of God in Gen. vi. 6. God's fatal sentence is irrevocable. To its execution the plagues of death are summoned, *i.e.* those which deliver men to death; the "sting of the underworld" is the means by which it brings men into its realm; thus they will strain every nerve to extinguish the prosperity of Ephraim. Only this extinction is not a hopeless one, since, according to vi. 2,

---

¹ Just as little the reading of Hitzig, נֶחָם, instead of נֹחַם.

the Lord both can and will raise His people even from a state of death. He *will* one day do it, because His love cannot finally depart from His people (xi. 8). And according to vi. 1 ff., He would do it without delay, if His people only turned to Him sincerely. Hence at the close of his book the prophet once more, as in chap. vi., addresses it in winsome tones, putting in its mouth right, God-pleasing desires, xiv. 2–4. Let it heartily turn to God, and, beseeching forgiveness, look for salvation and help from Him alone, and He will "heal its backsliding," and be to His people a fertilizing dew, that will breathe into it new life, making it fair as the lily and firm as Lebanon. Then only will it experience God's eternal truth and goodness. Still, the last verse reminds us, wisdom and docility are necessary, if God's ways are to be understood to one's own salvation.

This truth escaped Hosea's people. Superficially regarded, his work was a failure. Ephraim had to descend into the jaws of the underworld. But all the more precious was and is the testimony left behind by him, drawn from the depths of the Spirit who spans time and eternity. The fate of the nation has stamped on his word the seal of attestation. The Lord cast it off, to seek it again and win back its love. The return which Hosea promised after the exile fell short of the prophecy. Judah was indeed really cured of idolatry; but the conversion which then took place was not of the inner character meant by the prophet. Even in outward respects the people could not attain the glory promised. The Davidic monarchy blossomed no more; the ban was not wholly abrogated, nay, it soon became the universal lot of Israel and Judah, and lasts to this day. But to the Israel that truly turned to the Lord His salvation (טוב) was revealed out of David's house (iii. 5) in undreamt-of blessedness. And still we are not at the end of the days. The call of God's unwearied grace to this people continues. With the apostle (Rom. xi.) we await the day when, after long blindness, it will come to itself, and, making Hosea's motto (vi. 1 ff., xiv. 2 ff.) its own, do homage to its lawful King.

Hosea's profound gaze saw that the present form of the theocracy must be dissolved in judgment and the nation pass through the ordeal of death before God's true kingdom could find place. But the Lord will call His Church to life from a state of death within "three days," as soon as the right attitude of heart to Him is present. To this alludes the saying of Jesus

(John ii. 19), which also does not apply in the first instance to a buried human body, but to the temple standing before the eyes, the embodiment of the O. T. Church of God. The sign given by Jesus to the Jews is that, when they in their blindness shall soon give up this temple to destruction, He Himself in the briefest space will recall to life the Church of God and rebuild the temple in purer and truer shape. Yet the evangelist is not wrong in remarking (ver. 21): "He said this of the temple of His body." For between the body of Christ and the Church of God there is an inner and outer connection. Christ's body was the perfected temple, in which God had taken up His abode. In laying hands on this sacred body, the Jews devoted their own temple and nation to destruction. And when Christ arose bodily on the third day the new Church of God was raised to life; for its Head was alive. This connection is indicated symbolically by Christ rising just on the "third day" and thus literally fulfilling the saying in Hos. vi. 2. For not merely Jonah's type (Matt. xii. 40), but certainly also this oracle of Hosea belongs to those sayings of Scripture, according to which the Messiah was to rise precisely on the third day as Jesus Himself taught.[1] We see here again the literal fulfilment of a declaration seemingly accidental in its particular form, something which seemed a figurative utterance passing into outward actuality. For there obtains here an intimate connection between details, that excludes chance, and a mighty action and reaction of the spiritual and the physical, such as forbids their separation.

But Hosea not merely saw *that* by God's infinite mercy a new Church of the future must be miraculously called into life, he was also granted a profound glance into the hidden glory of this future Church of God. To him, the "Minnesinger among the prophets," as Delitzsch once called him, that unfathomable mercy appeared the deepest mystery of God's ways; the blissful love-communion between the Lord and His Church, adorned in bridal beauty and wholly and solely devoted to him, appeared the ultimate aim of those ways. In this issue only will God's decree be fully and purely realized; thus only will full harmony between heaven and earth, nature and man, be brought

---

[1] Matt. xvii. 23, xx. 19, xxvii. 63; Mark viii. 31, ix. 31, x. 34; Luke ix. 22 xviii. 33, xxiv. 7, 46.

about. We know who changed this promise into glad tidings. No fanatical audacity led the prophet to such lofty utterances, a bright ray of the coming sun illumined him. The Son of God, in whom the love-communion between God and man is seen in perfection, is security that such is the aim of God's ways with mankind. And the world's history will not end until this aim is reached.

NOTE A.—As Kautzsch (*Die Derivate des Stammes* צדק *im A. T. Sprachgebrauch*, 1881) has proved, the root meaning of the word צָדֵק is that of conformity to norm, righteous character. Used of man, it denotes agreement with the norm given by God, and is therefore from the first broader than the juristic idea of righteousness. Still the latter is, of course, included, and stands in the foreground where the matter in question is national life and government and מִשְׁפָּט is spoken of. When the word is used of God, the meaning cannot be that He is subject to a moral norm, since this would be opposed to the absoluteness of the O. T. idea of God. Where God's צדק is praised, it refers to the agreement of His action with the norm established and revealed by Himself. But God's normal root-relation to man is that of goodwill, the goodness of the Creator to His creature (not merely to Israel). This does not seem sufficiently taken into account in the treatise referred to in explaining passages like Isa. xli. 2. Certainly in presence of sin this righteous character of God must become judicial righteousness; the latter is a specification of the idea. In reference to the covenant-people (or the good man) that divine "conformity to norm" again becomes grace, because the disorder is abolished, the normal relation restored, to which, of course, God appears as one who acts in harmony with His proclaimed covenant. In the present passage, then (cf. Kautzsch, p. 35), צדק and משפט are by no means synonymous with חסד and רחמים; nor do they refer merely to God's punitive righteousness, either in the form of a purifying judgment on Israel or a punitive judgment on its foes; but they apply to God's inalienable righteousness, which He will preserve, nay, first fully reveal, in this covenant. God will join Himself to Israel in accordance with His true nature, which is grace; but He will endure—this lies in צדק and משפט in distinction from חסד and רחמים—no violation of His holiness.

NOTE B.—The root meaning of this נכמר is perhaps: *to kindle, become hot;* cf. Nowack (*Comm.* p. 208). The נחומים, *emotions of sympathy* (like רחמים, Gen. xliii. 30), swell into burning pain when a father or mother sees a child suffer. This is here transferred to God, who cannot bear to look on the suffering of His people. The prophet, who sees God's union with His people under the figure of holy love, does not shrink from anthropopathy. How such transferences of human affections to God are to be justified according to the Bible itself, ver. 9 shows. God's love and holiness can forgive and forget, for it is free from all passion even in its wrath.

§ 28. *Zechariah* ix.–xi. (note A).

The prophecy of *Zechariah* ix.–xi. (issuing from a prophet who appeared in the northern kingdom not long after Hosea) also announces judgment in general terms, in such a form, however, that the promise of a future, brought about by God and rich in grace, forms the bright background. Gradual advance is to be observed in the prophecy. The first discourse (chap. ix.) announces the divine judgment to the nations of the world—hateful neighbours; whereas the glorious sun rises on Israel in Jerusalem, whither the seer would fain turn the gaze of the whole people. But before the true king can come to rule there, the Lord must first hold judgment upon Israel's kings and leaders, and in His visitation carry them away into exile among the heathen (chap. x.). Finally, in chap. xi. the prophet relates how his efforts to gather under his leading the community of the quiet in the land, the last remnant worthy of preservation, miscarried in consequence of their obstinacy and fickleness. Then he gave up the two ends he was seeking, the wellbeing of the Church and the fraternizing of Judah and Ephraim; whereupon at once the divine ban compelling the nations to spare Israel was cancelled. But even this manifest visitation, confirming the power of the prophet's words, only led the sheep of his flock to make him an unworthy return, on which account a cruel shepherd shall rule over them instead of the Lord.

If much in this prophetic passage will always remain obscure in consequence of our defective knowledge of the history of the times, an incontestable importance is secured to it by its Messianic import. If our chronological view is correct, it is the first passage, at least among extant prophetic writings, in which the future human representative of the divine kingly dignity is described in his personal characteristics; whereas in Amos and Hosea he was presented only under a dynastic aspect. This is done in the glorious description of chap. ix., which is brilliantly set off by its contrast with the heathen world under condemnation. Whilst amid universal astonishment wealth vanishes from Tyre, its king from Gaza, their inhabitants from Ashkelon and Ashdod, the destined king enters Zion with all the insignia of peace, of divine favour and human homage.

ix. 9 "Exult greatly, daughter of Zion! — Shout, daughter of Jerusalem![1]

Behold, thy king comes to thee[2] — just and having salvation is he,

Lowly and riding on an ass — and on a colt, the foal of she-asses.[3]

10 And I will exterminate the chariot-team from Ephraim and the steed from Jerusalem,

And the battle-bow is exterminated—and He will proclaim peace to the nations,

And His dominion shall go from sea to sea—and from the river to the ends of the earth."

Zion may justly appear in jubilant chorus like a festive virgin. For *her* King comes, no strange conqueror, but her native lord, evidently of David's house; the true ruler destined for her by God, whom she has long missed, *comes*. He comes with every virtue belonging to the Lord's Anointed, a *perfect* son of David. Foremost among his beneficent attributes stands righteousness, as the cardinal virtue of a ruler, and the chief condition of his acceptableness to God, and also of the welfare of the people he has to judge, according to Ps. lxxii. 1 ff., cf. Isa. xi. 5. As a just ruler he enjoys God's salvation and help, which tends again to his people's good. Such is the meaning of נוֹשָׁע, not active, σώζων (LXX., Targ., Pesch., Vulg.), which must have been expressed by the hiphil, as God Himself is called צַדִּיק וּמוֹשִׁיעַ, Isa. xlv. 21. The participle niphal means one who *experiences deliverance, help*,[4] namely, constantly from God; to him is given what the hosanna invokes from God for the Messianic King. Receiving the divine salvation, he also dispenses it to his people, to whom he condescends in gracious humility.

[1] בַּת־צִיּוֹן is genitive of apposition. By a personification common in Eastern lands the city herself is represented as a female, here as a daughter, elsewhere as a mother. Thus the population is perhaps not distinguished from the city as its daughter.

[2] לָךְ = אֵלַיִךְ, not dat. commodi.

[3] The seer's gaze rests with emotion on the animal, hence the second pleonastic parallel hemistich: *on a colt, the foal of she-asses*. The latter is the plural of species: "a foal such as she-asses bear."

[4] The Arabic ناصر, *victorious, fortunate* (Steiner), is analogous.

This is seen in his outward appearance, his entire bearing, which is described as עָנִי, properly "bowed," hence usually "lowly, mean, mournful, wretched," applied to subjects suffering under oppression, Ps. lxxii. 2 f.; Zech. xi. 7. This one word characterizes in a remarkable way a ruler making a triumphal entry. Forswearing royal pomp, he puts himself, in his humility and meekness, on a level with the meanest subject.[1] A feature of this condescending modesty of bearing is further indicated: He makes his entry into the royal city on an ass. The ass indeed is not a contemptible animal in the East; in the time of the Judges, nobles rode on it in peace and war; but since Solomon's days the warlike horse had taken its place, and no king was ever seen entering his capital otherwise than on a proud steed or steed-drawn chariot.[2] For the most renowned of kings, true to the saying of the ancient law, to make his entry on a lowly, peaceful colt, is something unheard of, but of pregnant meaning. He will not acquire reputation by outward splendour and might of arms, but will win hearts and gladden Zion by lowliness and condescension. Nor will he gain victories abroad by shedding blood like David, or buy martial glory with his people's lives, but will conquer the earth by the power of the Divine Spirit, and with weapons of peace erect an empire of peace. That the ass here (cf. Gen. xlix. 11) is to be regarded as an animal of peace, is clear enough from ver. 10, where the destruction of horses as animals of war is announced. Instruments of war are to vanish altogether. This is promised in Isa. ix. 3 also. But what the present passage, from which Micah v. 9 perhaps arose, specially points out is, that Ephraim and Judah-Jerusalem will be weaponless. Not with fleshly arm will its king take the field, he will rule the nations by peaceful words. דִּבֶּר שָׁלוֹם is not to "command" peace (Hitzig), which דִּבֶּר never means, but to "proclaim, speak peace." His simple word suffices to establish and preserve peace; cf. Isa. ii. 4. As Messianic prophecy here rises to the height of consummation in reference to the spiritual

---

[1] The relation of עָנִי to עָנָו usually is that the former applies to a state of abasement, the latter to the disposition answering to it ("still, modest innocence, gentleness"). In the present passage also the first denotes the outward habitus, while the second gives security for the corresponding disposition.

[2] Cf. Jer. xvii. 25, xxii. 4.

nature of the means by which that royal power will be set up and guided, so also as regards extent a universal kingdom of the Son of David is foretold. This is also implied, as we saw, in the idea of a divinely-anointed covenant king, current since David's days. He will reign "from sea to sea, and from the river to the ends of the earth." This definition of limit, taken from Ps. lxxii., is meant to abolish all limits, as plainly appears from Ps. lxxii. 11, 19. The sea (Mediterranean) was the western, the Euphrates the eastern, limit of the Solomonic kingdom. From the existing western limit it will extend to the sea again (the Hebrews conceiving the earth as encircled by seas), and from the extreme eastern limit then in force to the ends of the earth westward, where the earth is lost in the archipelago. But what in Solomon's days was a pious wish, fed by the prophetic Messiah-idea, grows now in the prophet's mouth into a categorical prediction in relation to the perfected Messiah of the future.

But if his rule brings peace and salvation to all nations, much more will it do so to the covenant-people, whose captives then return and receive double recompense for all the wrong they have suffered, ix. 11 f. Their redemption is effected "through the blood of thy covenant." The gracious covenant made at Sinai and solemnly sealed with blood secures to the people of God that their captives, dwelling far off (cf. x. 8 ff.) but not abandoned, nay, called by a beautiful turn "prisoners of hope," shall regain freedom. The Lord Himself will lead His people to victory against their foreign tyrants (cf. x. 5 ff.), the latter being neither Assyria nor Babylon nor Persia, but the children of Javan, as in Joel iii. 6; cf. Obad. ver. 20. The Lord will set free the flock of His people and guard like the crown-jewels glittering on His territory, so that a period of joyous security and prosperous growth in the sacred land is granted it.

The transition from the oppression of Israel by the heathen to this state of peace (ix. 13 ff.) is set forth, with a boldness rare even in the prophets, as a bloody conflict, the Lord Himself, armed with Judah and Ephraim as bow and quiver, storming along as champion, hovering over the warriors of His people, and causing them to trample down all weapons and drink blood in full draughts. We have here a characteristic proof that the prophetic oracles are to be adjusted together and are mutually complementary (see p. 32). The prophet who in the same chapter gives so peaceful a picture of the final conqueror and ruler cannot mean that the earth will be subjected to the Lord by the martial exploits of His people. But a fearful conflict must be fought and streams of blood must flow before the world's resistance is subdued. The Lord will fight out this conflict victoriously and tread down all the enemy's power. This prospect is a necessary complement to the one disclosed in ix. 9 ff.

As relates to the latter prospect, a word is required about its *fulfilment*, not merely because Matt. xxi. 4, 5 and John xii. 14–16 say that this oracle was fulfilled in a specific incident, but because it is well adapted to illustrate the connection of prophecy and fulfilment. The ideas here put forth Jesus Christ realized in a perfect manner, coming as He did in unique dignity and lowliness to set up His Father's kingdom among His people, and transforming the world by word alone, a word bringing true peace. The great paradox lying in the outward lowliness of this supreme monarch has been already hinted by the prophet. But is the form of his description non-essential, fortuitous?[1] The N. T. fulfilment teaches us otherwise. The lowliness and dignity, mysteriously interlacing in this oracle, are no less strangely blended in an event of the life of Jesus, which gives the speaking counterpart of this figurative language: in His entry into Jerusalem when the people did homage to Him as their king, whilst He entered on the modest animal of peace, not without bearing the woe of His people. Here, too, while the literal coincidence is not the chief thing, just as little ought it to be disregarded. It is a divine thought uttered in the prophetic word and finding embodiment in the after history. The exact coincidence is meant by a higher divine intention to make known the unity of the divine plan. In the present case this agreement is also a revealing of the consciousness of Jesus. In choosing this form of entry the Lord made Himself known with all possible plainness as King, and thus received on His way to most shameful suffering the homage due to Him alone.

The New Testament has also found a Messianic prophecy in Zech. xi., which, although not immediately, yet by means of types, stands in real connection with the Messiah. After the Lord had announced in chap. x. that the time of victory and free-

[1] See p. 32.

dom for Israel could only come when He had assumed the lead and arranged the government of the nation altogether after His mind, we learn in chap. xi. that He was beginning in fact to exercise the office of shepherd (ix. 16), that He set aside in brief space bad rulers by the word of His prophet, and gave the latter charge to assume the guidance of the people in His name. It seems that the prophet exercised this guidance a long time, in what form we do not know. At all events the poor and defenceless, the quiet in the land, joined themselves to him, having acquired confidence in his word. He tended the sheep committed to him with two staves נֹעַם and חֹבְלִים,[1] "delight" and "confederacy"; the former denoting the wellbeing and happiness of the people, which this good shepherd had in view, whilst bad shepherds cared only to despoil them,—the latter, according to ver. 14, denoting the brotherhood, the close union of Ephraim with Judah—the brother-kingdom, which this theocratic policy strove after in order to conduct the whole nation back again to the legitimate house of David. At all events this original representation of his work by two shepherd-staves intimates more than a political programme which he had followed. He acted with prophetic inspiration and authority. The staves are symbols of the power he wielded in his capacity of God's representative; hence the breaking of the staves (vers. 10, 14) had a perilous consequence partially understood at once (ver. 10). It meant that the prophetico-theocratic government was not of long duration. Shepherd and flock were weary of each other, so that he no longer felt called to guard them from destruction. When he sought his release from the Church, he put it to the Church whether it thought his service worthy of reward or not. It then weighed to him thirty shekels of silver. This seems to refer to an actual incident unknown to us. The Church professed to be fulfilling all righteousness in thus paying God's prophet and dismissing him. "Then said the Lord to me: Cast it to the potter, the valuable price at which I was valued by them." It is clear, according to this passage, that the Lord considers Himself dismissed by the people in the person of His representative, and regards His own merits, nay, His own person, as thus estimated. The הַשְׁלִיכֵהוּ intimates with what contempt the "glorious price," ironically so called, is regarded by God. It was the sum paid for a slave (Ex. xxi. 32)!

[1] Plural of abstraction.

Even without the evangelist's express declaration, Matt. xxvii. 9 f., to every one who believes in a divine connection in the great as in the little events of sacred history, what here befell a prophet not more fully known to us is a significant type. For it was just the fate of Him who could call Himself *the* Good Shepherd, and who like none else had tended the little ones of the people in God's stead with loyal devotion and divine authority. In Him as in none else Israel rejected God Himself, and even *His* price was assessed at thirty silver pieces. But Matt. xxvii. 9 alludes to a second detail in the history which recalls the prophecy, and so must cast light on the import of the treachery.[1] It is the phrase אֶל־הַיּוֹצֵר. The meaning of the Hebrew phrase is certainly open to dispute. If the word is read participially and understood as elsewhere of a potter, it probably means that the money is to be used indeed for divine worship,—the Lord claims the reward as His own,—but for its lowest offices, namely, for providing the earthen vessels used in the neighbourhood of the temple in great numbers for cooking the sacrificial meals. With this Matthew connects the peculiar circumstance, that Judas' reward came "to the potter," *i.e.* was paid for a piece of land called a "potter's field," which was applied to the meanest service, the burying of strangers. This parallel assumes the correctness of the reading and the reference of אל היוצר to a potter. Matthew, translating freely, has more closely determined this indefinite statement, εἰς τὸν ἀγρὸν τοῦ κεραμέως. Another ancient interpretation, with which most moderns agree, in any case deserves all attention: "The word means rather the temple-treasure or treasurer."[2] According to the context of the Hebrew passage, this is neither impossible nor improbable. The casting into the treasure, by which, of course, the temple-treasure is to be understood (as the prophet himself adds: "I cast them into the *house of the Lord*, into the treasure"), would declare in the strongest manner that the Lord regarded the reward as given to Himself. The

---

[1] In thinking that the parallel must be limited in the sense of Matthew to the purchase of a potter's field, Steinmeyer (*Leidensgeschichte*, p. 106) too much isolates the parallel between prophecy and fulfilment. This local detail, taken along with the amount of the price, is rather meant to suggest *who* was here sold for money.

[2] So the Targum: אֲמַרְכְּלָא, *treasurer;* Peschito: ܐܳܘܨܪܳܐ, *treasury;* Kimchi: אוֹצָר = יוֹצֵר, *treasurer.* Others take it as another form of אוֹצָר, *treasure,* or a copyist's error arising out of the latter.

confusion in sound of א with י in היוצר for האוצר between two vowels is easily comprehensible.¹ This confusion would then early bring about the exchange as if the word came from יָצַר, *fingere*; so already in the LXX., who translate εἰς τὸ χωνευτήριον, " into the smelting furnace." What especially favours this view is the circumstance that the phrase, " to the potter," would almost necessarily require some explanation or reason in the context. Matthew follows the text as it was understood in his days, finding in it an outward sign for his contemporaries. While we ought neither to stumble at this outward detail, nor overvalue it, the citation in Matthew otherwise reminds us of the human imperfection of the sacred letter; for this prophecy is ascribed to Jeremiah instead of Zechariah, perhaps in confusion with Jer. xviii. 1 ff., where the potter plays a different part. Thus it is questionable whether we have to do here with an inexact citation of the evangelist or an error of a copyist, or whether the statement arose in some other way.² Although, according to the more probable reading, an outward handle by which the evangelist takes hold of this oracle and seeks to make it intelligible to his generation falls away for us, Zech. xi. remains a prelude of the rejection of the Good Shepherd, in whose person the Lord Himself fed His people; and instead of ascribing the Judas-reward, with Strauss,³ to fiction, we see in the thirty silver pieces an outward sign stamped, not by the evangelist, but by the finger of God, on the sacred history (note B).

NOTE A.—A section of the book, now united with the post-exilian Zechariah, and probably owing its origin to a younger contemporary of Hosea in the Assyrian period, has many points of contact with Hosea's book. We therefore treat of it here. In favour of separating these oracles from the post-exilian Zech. i.–viii., we appeal less than others have done to the difference in style and outer prophetic dress, or in the circle of conceptions and ideas, in which the parts of the book in question move. On the other hand, decisive importance seems to us to belong to the pre-exilian impress marking the circumstances of the prophet, ix.–xi. Among the menacing foes of Israel rebuked by the prophet appear (as in Joel and Amos) Syria, Phoenicia, Philistia, whose almost autonomous

---

¹ Cf. הדיג for הדואג, 1 Sam. xxii. 18.

² On this point Luther expresses himself more freely than some modern theologians, as Kliefoth, Böhl. See Köhler, *Sacharja*, ii. 166 f.

³ *Leben Jesu*, 1836, ii. 395 f.

cities (Damascus, Tyrus, Sidon, Ascalon, Gaza, Ekron, Ashdod) are in opposition to Jerusalem. Egypt and Assyria are mentioned as lands whither God will send His people into banishment (x. 9 f.), exactly as in Hos. xi. 11, cf. Isa. vii. 18 ; Javan, as the land where many captives already pine at a distance from home, ix. 13, as in Joel iii. 6. See p. 203, 219. As consequently the outer political situation appears much more that of Hosea than post-exilian, so the inner one is the same.¹ Chap. ix. 8 does not necessarily imply the destruction of the temple; it applies much better to such plundering of the temple as had often occurred even before the Assyrian age. But not merely the southern, even the northern kingdom, Ephraim, seems still existing. For not merely is it remembered as in Zech. viii. 13, to which Hengstenberg appeals, or a future assured to it as in Ezek. xxxvii. 15–28, but passages like ix. 10 (13), x. 6 f., and xi. 14, assume the existence of this kingdom as a present power. There are already many captives in the far heathen country, while a more general exile only impends, x. 2, 9. The heathen pest of oracle-gods (Teraphim), soothsayers, and interpreters of dreams (x. 2) is still in full force as in Hos. iii. 4, whereas after the exile the nation is seen to be cured of it. That the prophet moves artificially in an "archaic schematism," describes the foes of God's kingdom with pre-exilian names, characterizes the sins of later times metaphorically as "idolatry," are unsatisfactory suppositions, by which some have tried to render the post-exilian origin possible.²

If asked what was the occasion of the oracle ix.–xi. having been ascribed to the post-exilian Zechariah, we should point especially to the similarity of ix. 9 to ii. 10. Still Berthold's conjecture, that the author of chap. ix.–xi. may also have borne the name Zechariah and been identical with the one named Isa. viii. 2 (cf. 2 Chron. xxvi. 5), does not deserve the contemptuous dismissal it received

---

[1] In face of these instances the proofs of the dependence of this prophet on Ezekiel, Micah, Jeremiah, etc., which Stade has recently tried to make good (*Zeitschr. für A. T. Wissenschaft*, 1881, Heft 1), seem to us unconvincing. On the contrary, we think the origination of the oracles Zech. ix.–xi. in such patchwork, as Stade supposes, impossible.

[2] The post-exilian origin is maintained by Jahn, Köster, Stähelin, Umbreit, Hengstenberg, de Wette (in later editions of his *Introd. to the O. T.*), Hofmann, Köhler, Keil, Kliefoth, Delitzsch (*Messianic Prophecies*, p. 99 ff.), Stade, *Anfang des dritten Jahrhunderts vor Christo*, etc. (similarly already Vatke, Gramberg). On the other hand, the second part of Zechariah (ix.–xiv.) is regarded as pre-exilian (to some extent with a further distinction of the authors of ix.–xi. and xii.–xiv.) by Bertholdt, Rosenmüller, Hitzig, Knobel, Maurer, Ewald, Bleek, v. Ortenberg (*Die Bestandtheile des Buches Sacharja*, 1859), Schrader (*Einleit. von* de Wette, 8th ed.), Riehm (*Messianic Prophecy*, p. 129), Steiner (Hitzig's *Kleinen Propheten*, 4th ed.), H. Schultz (*A. T. Theologie*, 2nd ed. p. 198), E. Reuss (*Gesch. der heil. Schrift des A. Testaments*, i. 266 f.).

from Ewald. It is especially favoured by the circumstance that that friend of Isaiah also had a Berechiah for father. Cf. Bleek's conjecture (*Einleit. in das A. T.*, 4th ed. p. 449). This prophet, according to his prophecy very probably a Judæan who, like Amos, had betaken himself to the northern kingdom for the sake of his work there (x. 4 ff.), must in this case have returned to Jerusalem and reached a great age. His oracles testify to a movement, due to prophetic impulse, which had gained ground in the northern kingdom amid the sanguinary confusion of the eleven years' anarchy that intervened after Jeroboam II.'s death (783), but was of short duration. The bad shepherd, who is announced in chap. xi. to the nation that despises the guidance of its God, is probably Menahem.[1] The three shepherds, whom the prophet set aside by divine authority in a month, were three rulers or pretenders of the anarchical period, most probably Shallum, to whom only a month's government is ascribed (2 Kings xv. 13 f.), his predecessor Zechariah, and a third, unnamed, who had acquired a momentary position of authority.

NOTE B.—Before leaving the prophets who laboured in the kingdom of Ephraim during the gradual rise of the Assyrian power, we mention also the prophet *Jonah*, of whom a highly pregnant story is told us, whilst no epoch-making prophecies come to us from him. We only hear (2 Kings xiv. 25) that he foretold the restoring of the limits of Israel, which took place under Jeroboam II.; cf. Obad. ver. 17; Amos ix. 12. In time, therefore, he belonged to Obadiah and Joel. But the significant thing in him is his relation to the Assyrian capital. In the highest degree noteworthy (*i.e.* when we combine therewith what Obadiah, Joel, Amos, etc., said about the heathen world) is the mission of Jonah to the heathen city Nineveh. This mission the Lord carries through with the utmost energy (following the prophet in the storm, preserving him by means of a sea-monster), and it has an unheard-of result. Although the present Book of Jonah may have been written considerably later and not without didactic purpose, several features pointing to an exilian or post-exilian composition, such a mission to Nineveh was certainly contained in the tradition coming from this early period; and this, as Delitzsch remarks, involves a miracle, when we compare with it the particularism of divine salvation even in the prophetic writings. We have here a weighty precedent for communicating the divine revelation to the heathen world and for its reception by the latter. In the centre of the world-empire the message of the true God was heard and believed; the city repented, and experienced merciful forbearance.

This history was *typical* in high degree of God's ways in the New Covenant. As the Lord (John ii. 18 f.) proposes the sign of

---

[1] Hitzig compares xi. 2 f. with 2 Kings xv. 10.

His raising up the temple in three days (in allusion to Hos. vi. 2), so in Matt. xii. 38 ff. (xvi. 4) and Luke xi. 29 ff., He proposes the sign or miracle of Jonah; which, however, ought not to be limited to mean that Jesus like Jonah was to remain three days in the bosom of the earth, which here is merely an attendant circumstance, of course a significant one. We have especially to consider the wonderful occurrence exclusively emphasized by Luke, that the heathen accorded faith to the prophet sent to them by divine grace and certainly accredited before them by the miracle. Thus this *typical* prediction supplements the prophetic one of Hosea. The latter promised the revival of the Church by God's act; the former at least gives hints of the raising of a new Church out of the heathen world by God's word and act. But the next prophet to be spoken of announced this plan of God in reference to the heathen world, not merely in typical form, but with full prophetic consciousness.

THIRD SECTION.

THE PROPHETS OF THE ASSYRIAN PERIOD IN THE SOUTHERN KINGDOM: ISAIAH, MICAH, NAHUM.

§ 29. *Isaiah and Micah: The Exalted Zion.*

IN the period of the highest splendour of the Assyrian power, which was preparing an abrupt end for the northern kingdom, great prophets were at work in the southern one, the greatest of whom once more held the ægis of the divine word over threatened Jerusalem. While *Isaiah*, by thus defending God's city, which in human opinion was lost, against the arrogant world-power, proved to his and our contemporaries the wonderful greatness and force of God's revealed word, the supreme value of the revelation given him lies in what he was permitted to see of the future divine kingdom which was only to enter after judgment. What he sees is supplemented by the oracle of *Micah*, his somewhat later contemporary. Both prophets speak of the future Messiah, Isaiah in particular depicting the rule of the future Son of David more clearly and vividly than all who came before and after him. In both, Zion is the glorious centre of the divine rule, the significance of which Isaiah especially puts in the clearest light.

The present Book of Isaiah may, we admit, very naturally be regarded as a collection made up of different, even heterogeneous, parts. But the Messianic prophecies in the proper sense, as well as the great Zion-oracles, belong without doubt to the prophet, under whose name they stand, and with whose personality they are inseparably bound up. Isaiah, the son of Amos (אָמוֹץ), a prophet labouring in Jerusalem, according to the heading which is confirmed by the contents of the book, from the time of King Uzziah to that of Hezekiah, spent a long life in this ministry; and Judah's being once more spared in the Assyrian judgment was due in large measure to his persistent toil. Isaiah, indeed, knew from the day of his call to this office (in the year of Uzziah's death, chap. vi.), that his preaching would not thoroughly cure the deep infatuation of his people or permanently turn aside the doom of exile impending over it (cf. vi. 11 f.). For this reason also his preaching is primarily an announcing of judgment, accompanied by severe, unsparing exposure of the moral corruption which no forms of worship could conceal (chap. i.). But like Hosea he sees a return from the exile. Although but a remnant, the Church of the Lord will at last experience a wonderful salvation. This salvation proceeds from David's house, and already in the presence of the prophet the Lord gives that house unmistakable signs of His favour and protection. Such was the case according to the prophet's prediction under the worldly-minded Ahaz, who is delivered from his foes, Syria and Ephraim, certainly not without his feeling the danger he incurred by his alliance with Assyria; and again gloriously in Hezekiah, the pious king, under whom Assyria's ascendancy comes to an end before Jerusalem's walls. The prophet is conscious of the complete superiority and glorious future of the Davidic house in conflict with these world-powers; he sees the renown to be conferred on this house and nation when its true heir appears. But certainly his call to repentance, the reception of which would at once secure God's favours and remove the misery of the times (ii. 5, i. 18 f.), finds as little intelligence and obedience as the analogous one of Hosea. Judgment must first refine even Judah (i. 25), exile swallow up the nation, and thus the glorious Messiah grow up out of the deepest humiliation of His house and people. Thus in Isaiah we see in especially striking fashion a contrast between insight into the deep corruption of his people on its way to dissolution, and rock-like certainty that a future, divinely brought about, will realize in actual life the mission which the Lord entrusted to the nation in an ideal form through His prophets.

The glorious final state, that will see God's plan realized, is described in ii. 1 ff. as a theocracy, having Jerusalem (or the temple of Yahveh) for its centre, from that point drawing all nations into its sphere, and thus bringing in universal peace.[1]

Isa. ii. 2. "And it shall come to pass at the end of the days:

[1] On the question of the origin of this passage, see afterwards in Micah.

the mountain of the house of Yahveh shall tower up at the head of the mountains,[1] and shall be exalted above the hills, 3 and to it shall all the heathen walk. And many nations shall go and say: Come, let us go up to the mountain of Yahveh, to the house of the God of Jacob, and He will instruct us in His ways,[2] and we will walk in His paths. For from Zion shall law go forth and the word of Yahveh 4 from Jerusalem. And He shall judge between the nations, and impart instruction to many peoples, and they beat their swords into ploughshares,[3] and their spears into vintage-knives. Nation lifts not sword against nation, nor do they practise war any more."

In the phrase "at the end of the days"[4] the seer strikes beyond the nearer future. At present neither Israel nor Judah can be saved from the judgment, scarcely the temple itself. Directly before proclaiming again this oracle of Isaiah, Micah at least says (iii. 12), Zion must be ploughed into arable land, Jerusalem turned into a heap of stones, the temple become a wooded hill.[5] But the history of the people and temple chosen of God cannot conclude with this well-merited judgment. The end must be a quite different one. Zion, at present oppressed and despised in its abasement, shall then tower above every proud mountain and hill. The dispute whether this is meant in a physical, topographical sense, the nature of the ground undergoing a mighty change, in order that Zion, now encircled by higher hills, may tower above all, or in a purely religious sense, the value of the mountain for worship coming exclusively into view, is an idle one. As seer the prophet actually *saw* Mount Zion, the site of the temple,[6] higher than all the rest, just as in fact he saw the nations journeying to this centre of the world under God's rule, or discerned Zion overshadowed with divine cloud and flame (iv. 5 f.); and it was not his business to convert such concrete

---

[1] Not "as head of the mountains;" בְּ is strictly local. Only, the meaning still less is that it is placed on the top of the other mountains; but it rises at their head, towers above their head; the conception therefore is quite parallel with that of the following clause: "exalted from the heights," therefore above them.

[2] מִדְּרָכָיו, partitive מִן.

[3] See on Joel iii. 10, p. 211.   [4] See p. 33, 194.

[5] Cf. a literal fulfilment, 1 Macc. iv. 38.   [6] Zion = Moriah, see p 186.

intuitions into abstract thoughts. But he must have been well aware of the spiritual import presented in and served by such representations. According to our Christian consciousness this import is the essential thing; what shape it will assume in the final fulfilment, is an open question. At all events the revelation of the God dwelling on Zion must be acknowledged by all nations, and the world's whole physiognomy even in outward respects will assume a shape in harmony with this subjection to Yahveh.

If Joel has shown us the negative end of the heathen world, here as in Zech. ix. 10 we have a significant prospect of the positive future of that world, when it becomes aware that salvation consists in willing subjection to Israel's God. The nations will all betake themselves to the Lord and receive instruction (תּוֹרָה) from Him, *i.e.* the revelation of His will. Thus their life will be governed by His word. In particular, their quarrels will be settled by His judicial decision. With the words כִּי מִצִיּוֹן the prophet's own discourse begins again. Zion-Jerusalem will be the source whence divine revelation goes forth to all lands, so that from this loftiest mountain spiritual waters will water the whole earth. Then, too, nations numerous and strong (עַמִּים רַבִּים) will acquiesce without resistance in the divine direction, instead of asserting their rights by force. Thus war ceases of itself, universal peace begins, and there appears the true converse of what Joel saw among the heathen (iv. 9 f.). There, they turned all implements of tillage into weapons against God and His people; here, they change all weapons of war, which they once used against each other, into instruments of peaceful, life-preserving toil. In God's kingdom on earth labour will not cease, but will be hallowed by Him and therefore fruitful. And the peace, everywhere promised to God's people for the last days (Zech. iii. 10), is here promised to the whole world (Micah iv. 4).

This prophecy belongs to the most glorious treasures in the world of human thought. Really it contains what human thought held and still holds impossible, but what is certain truth to God's seer. What supernatural confidence was necessary, in the very age when God's true servants were compelled to announce ruthless judgment on the temple, and it seemed as if everything ever said of God's kingdom in Israel was a beautiful dream lacking confirmation, to promise such a position in the world to this very temple! What consecration of the Spirit it bespeaks, when at the very time that all nations were whetting their swords to make God's people feel their edge, the seers of God proclaimed to these very heathen that they will one day grow weary of this sanguinary game and flock to Zion to obtain light and right!

Here also we have a confirmation of what was said about the prophetic oracles necessarily supplementing each other. In Zech. ix. it is the Messiah who sets up the kingdom of peace in the world. In the present oracle He is as little mentioned as in Micah iv., and yet it is Isaiah and Micah especially in whom the glory of God's final kingdom is concentrated in His person.[1] The opposite representations of the end of the heathen world in Joel and Isaiah-Micah are one-sided views, which are only contradictory in appearance. Isa. xxiv.–xxvii. exhibits their combination. The judgment and the conversion of the nations have been fulfilled and will be further fulfilled. For the latter is by no means complete. Zion, the city of God celebrated by countless peoples, from which light and salvation have gone out to all quarters of the world, has witnessed unexampled triumphs. The watchword: "To the holy mountain of Yahveh! Let us there learn the revelation of the Lord!" has been the watchword of all important nations and races for centuries. They have fetched their law thence and confess the doctrine there preached, a doctrine establishing peace on earth and God's goodwill to men. But certainly the realization of this doctrine remains to-day far short of what the prophet depicts. Does the fault lie in revelation? Or is it not powerful enough to abolish national differences? We Christians know the opposite. Although the worldly kingdoms that have become "Christian" still engage in strife, and the learning of war still exhausts most of the forces of civilised States, we know a divine spirit-power proclaimed to us from Zion which overcomes the world, and which, when fully developed, will dictate universal peace. The end must include such a peace even according to our observation. And it can only heighten our reverence for the prophetic word,

---

[1] In presence of such facts it seems to us premature for Riehm to remark (*Messianic Prophecies*, p. 129), that because Messiah is not found here, Isa. xxiv.–xxvii. must have been written at a time when the idea of the theocratic monarchy had lost much of its importance in the consciousness of the devout.

when we find that to-day, after all our boasted advances in culture and humanity, mankind, because it has not more sincerely and completely taken to heart and reduced to practice the teaching from the holy mount of grace, has not yet risen to the height of the goal that stood before the eyes of God's holy seers more than twenty-five centuries ago. Contemplating words of living truth, to which such age-long compass belongs, we shall not stumble at the local form demanded by the Old Testament mode of view. If Zion was the chosen seat of God's temple, the submission of the nations to God could not be more strikingly set forth than in the beautiful picture of the prophet, who sees all nations pilgriming thither. That Zion is wherever God's people are found, could only be taught in the New Testament, with its purely spiritual principle of fellowship with God. For the rest, the New Testament also teaches that God's kingdom must take visible shape; only when this takes place will the oracle of our seer altogether give place to its fulfilment.

If the oracle just considered shows us the world as God's kingdom of the future, Isa. iv. 2-6 describes the God-filled Church that will form the centre of that kingdom. It also forms a transition to the prophecies of Isaiah treating of the personal centre of the Church of those days, the Messiah of David's house. This second oracle, again, is a glance at the shining height in which the way of God terminates, although leading through judgment. It forms the brief conclusion of a long, fearful discourse of judgment (ii. 6–iv. 1). Judgment goes forth on Judah and Jerusalem so thoroughly, that everything on which in their fleshly mind they put confidence—their gods, their princes, their priests and prophets, their power and wealth, everything which exalts and is precious in their eyes—is smitten down and carried off, the Lord alone remaining exalted (ii. 11, 17). On that day, when against the false, wanton Zion judgment shall have gone forth, the holy Zion of God shall be revealed.

iv. 2. "On that day shall the plant of Yahveh be for ornament
    and honour, and the fruit of the land for pride and pomp to
3 the escaped of Israel.[1] And it shall be, whoever remains in
    Zion and is left in Jerusalem shall be called holy, every
4 one written among the living in Jerusalem, when the
    Lord shall have washed away the filth of the daughters of

[1] See p. 198.

Zion, and cleansed the blood-stains of Jerusalem from its midst, by the spirit of judgment and the spirit of cleansing. 5 And Yahveh creates on every spot of Mount Zion and on her assemblies a cloud by day, and smoke and blazing fire- 6 radiance by night; for over all glory shall be a vault. And there shall be a habitation for a shadow from the heat by day, and for a refuge and covert from tempest and rain."

Ver. 4 shows the close antithetical connection in which this promise stands with the preceding threatening. The glorifying of Zion must be preceded by a cleansing, which purges away what it now regards as its ornament and pride. Also in the expressions used in ver. 2 (תִּפְאֶרֶת, גָּאוֹן, כָּבוֹד, צְבִי) the antithesis to that which Zion now glories in is unmistakable. Not that with which they now in carnal vanity adorn themselves, but that *which the Lord makes to sprout* will suffice to be an honour and ornament to the Church brought safely through the judgment. What is the meaning of this 'יְ צֶמַח? In any case not the aftergrowth of the nation,[1] or its then existing remnant.[2] This comes afterwards in the dative. Rather one might understand the blessing of nature, which the Lord makes to sprout and the earth bears as fruit.[3] Hofmann says (*Schriftbeweis*, ii. 2, p. 542 f.): "What Jehovah makes to grow and the land brings forth the prophet opposes to the thousand products of human art, with which the vanity previously rebuked, especially in the women, adorns itself." But Hofmann and Schultz (*A. T. Theologie*, p. 730 f.) both acknowledge that in this context we cannot be satisfied with the mere blessing of nature, such as is contained in the products of the soil. Rosenmüller rightly remarks: *huic interpretationi obstat totius sermonis magnificentia* (cf. Delitzsch, *ad loc.*). Is then the "Sprout of Yahveh" the Messiah simply, and is He also described as the fruit of the earth, so that, as in Micah iv. 1, He would be contemplated in His divine and earthly origin?[4] As matter of fact, the Messiah is afterwards called a Sprout, or directly "the Sprout,"[5] and there can be no question that these passages lean on Isaiah's. But this does not imply

---

[1] Grotius, Gesenius, Knobel.   [2] Eichhorn.
[3] So most moderns, even Hitzig, Diestel. Cf. Joel iii. 18; Hos. iii. 5; Zech. ix. 17; Isa. lxi. 11.
[4] So Hengstenberg, Delitzsch, *et al.*
[5] Jer. xxiii. 5, xxxiii. 15; Zech. iii. 8, vi. 12.

that the word here has the same personal force as later on, when it had become a proper name of the Messiah. Considering the general character of the present passage, this is improbable.[1] What Yahveh causes to sprout and the earth brings forth will be a glory to the preserved nation. Altogether extraordinary displays of grace are meant, as ver. 5 also speaks of miraculous phenomena; but the Son of David is not exclusively referred to, since צמח had not yet become a fixed designation for Him. The expression, intentionally left in such indefinite mystery, corresponds to the טובו of Hos. iii. 5. The land will sparkle gloriously with the divine gifts which the Lord of His grace and power there causes to spring up and the earth produces. Since, according to the following chapters, the Messiah is the mediator of these benefits, nay, He Himself grows up the greatest, most mysterious among them, it is easily intelligible how the later prophets applied this צמח to the living, personal centre of these blessings in the last days, coining this word, so finely expressive of God's wondrous dealings, into a symbolic name for the expected King, whose existence would be a pure gift of divine omnipotence, a miracle of grace. In the present passage the chief emphasis lies on the thought, that the future glory will be altogether a work of God, on which account also Yahveh Himself is called the glory of the Church, xxviii. 5. The Church itself, issuing in safety from the judgment, is described (ver. 3) as holy in all her members. After the sifting, to use a Christian phrase, the visible coincides with the invisible Church. Whoever is entered as living in the burgess-roll of Jerusalem (cf. Ezek. xiii. 9),[2] bears also the mark of belonging to the Church of God, and this mark is holiness. But the question

---

[1] Nägelsbach also wrongly: "Growth of Jehovah and growth of the land are opposed to each other; the former denotes conscious personal life (as a fruit of God), the latter impersonal bodily life as a product of the earth." Untenably, too, Schultz respecting צמח: "It is meant to describe the spiritual fruit of the land, the life of the last days springing from God, that is to adorn the Israelites." This limitation of the promised glory to the spiritual is just as unwarranted as its exclusive reference to the material.

[2] The idea of a burgess-roll, like that of Zion, is capable of being spiritualized. In Ex. xxxii. 32 we find the notion of a covenant-book which the Lord keeps; so again in Dan. xii. 1. But in Isaiah, the emphasis lies on the fact that the city-book and the Lord's book coincide; every one entered on the list of inhabitants is also an actual member of God's holy Church. In Ps. lxxxvii. this burgess-roll is enlarged in an extraordinary manner.

is, on what element of this attribute the emphasis here rests. In our view it is not moral purity, which certainly according to ver. 4 is presupposed, nor official qualification as fitness and authority to serve God, though, in fact, this side is of course included, and the entire citizenship of Jerusalem in the last age forms a ἱεράτευμα ἅγιον ("Israel's national calling (Ex. xix. 6) is thus personally and universally realized," Delitzsch). But the statement of this verse is meant rather to ascribe inviolableness to this priestly community, morally purified and consecrated to Yahveh's service. Every one will be regarded as consecrated to the Lord, which implies that the Lord Himself acknowledges him as His elect possession.[1] Thus the citizen of Jerusalem, secured against all injustice, thanks to his uncontested priestly dignity, is miraculously guarded by God like the temple itself; for, according to ver. 5 f., by a creative act the Lord will put the Church that serves Him in a position to do so without interruption day and night, summer and winter. As the pilgrim-Church in the desert (Num. xiv. 14) was visibly accompanied by God's presence, shaded by day and illumined by night, so the Church of Zion, in which the Lord has taken up His dwelling, will be guarded in such a way, that no part of the temple will be unprotected, the oppositions of day and night, summer-heat and winter-rain, will cause no disturbance in the unbroken worship of the Lord. The fire-radiance is the outbeaming of the glory of the Lord, the smoke-cloud its veiling. It forms a חֻפָּה, a baldachin, over all His glory that dwells in Zion. Already in Ex. xiv. 19 f. the pillars of cloud and fire formed a protecting wall against the foe; now it shields the city of God against all violence of the elements. Men no longer do it hurt. But the glory of the Lord is represented as immanent in the Church, more than was the case in the desert marchings; cf. p. 188.

Whilst, then, ii. 1 ff. presented to us the whole world as an extended forecourt of the heathen, chap. iv. gives us a glance into Yahveh's sanctuary in Zion itself, where every member of the population shares in the dignity and inviolableness of the holy place, and God's majesty guards itself and its dwelling against all changes of time. Here for the first time the perfected Church is more precisely described as a glorified Jerusalem, an idea recur-

---

[1] Cf. אָמַר לְ in Hos. ii. 1. The name expresses the state of things.

ring again and again up to the Revelation of John. What the Davidic Jerusalem represented typically in empirical imperfection, will be realized, according to Isaiah, hereafter in its full ideal import. In a spiritual sense this prophecy is already fulfilled, a wondrous " Sprout of the Lord" having grown up, and by His mediation sifted the Church and clothed every member of it with priestly dignity, while this community has been made safe against all the storms of the world. But the Johannine Apocalypse again pushes the final fulfilment of our vision into the future, because the outer and inner consummation of this Jerusalem is not accomplished even in the New Covenant, but is only prepared for. The sifting of the Church still continues; and only when its outward condition corresponds to the divine ideal will it be raised above all assault, and its glory revealed to the world.

§ 30. *Isaiah's Oracles of Immanuel.*

The "Sprout of the Lord" of the previous oracle, left indefinite and general, is unfolded in chap. vii.–xi. in personal distinctiveness. A Sprout will the Lord cause to grow up from David's house, which as divine Head of the Church will bring it to completion. Chap. vii. 1 ff. tells us the historical occasion on which the prophet first alluded to the future Immanuel. In the critical moment of Judæan history, when the confederate kings of Syria and Ephraim, Rezin and Pekah (about 741 B.C.), advanced against Judah to put an end to the rule of the Davidic house,[1] and all hearts in Jerusalem were shaking as the trees of the wood before the wind, the prophet Isaiah[2] appeared before king Ahaz with the categorical prediction that nothing would come of this project, and summoning to calm, immovable confidence in the Lord: "Unless ye believe, ye shall not remain!" In support of a faith so opposed to probabilities he offered Ahaz a sign, which he might freely choose from Hades below or heaven above. By this is meant a sign occurring suddenly, of the kind referred to in chap. xxxvii. 7, a phenomenon by which the invisible God, to whom not only the earth, but also the world above and beneath is subject, would have verified His

---

[1] Cf. 2 Kings xv. 37, xvi. 5.
[2] Cf. Isa. xxx. 15.

power and purpose. Of course the citation of a spirit of the dead from Sheol[1] would have been as illegal as it was unprophetic (viii. 19). The matter in question here is not the consulting of such a spirit, but a miraculous sign *from the Lord*, which points rather to earthquakes and the like, and in the heavenly sphere to astral phenomena, lightning, etc.

But king Ahaz, really an unbeliever, expected little from Yahveh's help. On the contrary, he put his confidence in the support of Assyria, which he was secretly seeking (2 Kings xvi. 7 ff.), and cleverly evaded the fanatic (whom he took the prophet to be, like our modern theologians) by the courteous disclaimer, which seemed superficially more religious than the prophet's daring faith : " I will not request it, nor tempt Yahveh." Then the prophet answers sharply : The God whose patience they, the members of the royal house, were trying so severely, will give them a sign unasked :—

vii. 14. "Therefore the Lord Himself will give you a sign :
  Behold, the virgin conceives and bears a son, and she
15 calls[2] his name IMMANUEL (God with us); buttermilk and honey will he eat at the time when he knows to despise the evil and choose the good."

As this is to be a sign, it must contain a public act on God's part. It cannot, indeed, be as directly visible as in xxxviii. 7, and according to the purpose in view (vii. 11), cannot be the same. According to ver. 16, it extends over several years,[3] and yet, according to the same verse, over only a few years, reckoning from the present. The הִנֵּה הָעַלְמָה הָרָה may, indeed, apply to something future, whereas in the passage, Gen. xvi. 11 (analogous in point of syntax), Hagar has already conceived, but something immediately impending is to be thought of. The analogy of that passage, however, suggests that the chief emphasis lies on the child's name. The name Immanuel shall be given to the child, because God's assistance is visibly experienced at the time

---

[1] שָׁאֳלָה, ver. 11, according to the parallelism, is a second pausal form for שְׁאֵלָה (Ewald, Delitzsch), not imper. from שָׁאַל (Targum, Hupfeld, Nägelsbach).

[2] וְקָרָאת, 3rd pers. fem., from קָרָאת; cf. Gesen. *Gram.* § 74, note 1.

[3] The stage when moral consciousness begins separates innocent childhood from boyhood, when moral responsibility already exists. The limit of time in viii. 4 does not go so far. Isaiah's sign, xxxvii. 30, stretches analogously over several years.

of his birth. Ver. 16 assigns the reason of the name, for before the boy shall understand to avoid the bad and choose the good, "the land shall be forsaken, whose two kings thou abhorrest." Ver. 17, on the other hand, gives the reason for the 15th verse. In the boy's conscious age there will be nothing but buttermilk and honey to eat in the land.[1] "Yahveh will bring on thee, and thy people, and thy father's house, such days as have not been since the day when Ephraim fell away from Judah—will bring the king of Assyria," etc. According to the statements of these and the following verses, the sign given to this generation is of a political kind. In the period within which from the present time a virgin shall conceive and bear a son, a complete revolution shall take place in the circumstances of the world. His name will be called Immanuel, as a sign of glorious help experienced, and of perfect confidence. But when he arrives at years of reason, Judah itself is devastated by a worse foe —the Assyrians,[2] from whom good is at present expected. Thus, in this at first somewhat enigmatical dress, which, however, as a real sign must have been imprinted on the memory, a prediction is given, definite in point of time, of the course of political events, the prophet himself supplying the interpretation in clear words. It is a sign which that generation for the most part soon saw;[3] and here, as in the case of Isaiah's oracle, which afterwards foretold the fall of the Assyrians before the walls of Jerusalem, it is impossible to escape with a mere reference to the prophet's political sagacity, or his religious insight, or his bold faith. It would have been abominable arrogance or fanatical superstition thus to sketch the ways of God beforehand, and stake the faith of others on the occurrence of the events pro-

[1] That is, in consequence of the devastation, agriculture and vine-culture will be unknown; only cattle-keeping will be left, ver. 20 ff.

[2] The אֶת מֶלֶךְ אַשּׁוּר forestalls the following verse in a suspicious manner, and may be a gloss from viii. 7. Substantially the point is indifferent, as Isaiah does not leave it in doubt what foe he expects.

[3] After a few years followed the campaign of Tiglath-Pileser against Damascus, ending with the capture of the city, and the death of Rezin the king (732?), 2 Kings xvi. 9; cf. Schrader, *Keilinschriften und Altes Testament*, p. 152 f. Pekah also was at that time conquered by Tiglath-Pileser, and many people were deported, 2 Kings xv. 29; Samaria itself fell somewhat later (722 B.C.). The prediction of the ceasing of Ephraim in sixty-five years (Isa. vii. 8), attacked on critical grounds, refers not to the destruction of the capital, but to the settling of foreign colonists in the land, 2 Kings xvii. 24 ff.; Ezra iv. 2.

phesied, unless the prophet had been under the immediate influence of a higher power giving him certain knowledge, not only of ethico-religious truths, but also of the outward course of history. That naturalistic criticism has a hard position to maintain in face of this chapter, which is unassailable on literary grounds, is self-evident in relation to vii. 7, where it has to take the side of the king and his worldly policy.

But although the oracle of Immanuel, according to the further explanation, is meant primarily to inform the hearers of Judah's fate in the impending months and years, we have still to ask, whether it is exhausted in this application, whether the growth of a child is chosen as a measure of time only by chance, and whether a particular child and his mother are used for this purpose. In the latter respect it is said definitely הָעַלְמָה, *the virgin*. The word denotes a marriageable maiden, a virgin ripe for marriage (from עָלַם, *to be strong sexually*); on the other hand, the emphasis in this passage does not lie on the negative element of virginity. If the sign to the hearers consisted in a virgin conceiving without aid of man,[1] בְּתוּלָה must have been used. But still less could עַלְמָה be used of the prophet's wife, as asserted by many,[2] who point to the fact that Isaiah's children bore significant names, meant as signs to remind him and the people of the chief import of his preaching.[3] The prophetess (הַנְּבִיאָה, mentioned viii. 3), who had been a mother several years, since her son Shear-Jashub accompanied his father to the king, can never be described again as הָעַלְמָה; and to suppose her to be dead, in order to be able to foist a young maiden on the prophet as his wife, is a foolish makeshift. Moreover, it would have been unbecoming for the prophet to proclaim in such grand terms a sign to David's royal house taken from the circle of his own family.[4]

---

[1] So still Bredenkamp, *Vaticinium quod de Immanuele edidit Jesajas*, 1880.
[2] Gesenius, Hitzig, Knobel, *et al.*; even Tholuck, *A. T. im N. T.*, p. 43, *Proph.* p. 170; and J. P. Lange, *Genesis*, p. 89.
[3] Isa. vii. 3, viii. 3, 18.
[4] How great the perplexity attending the rationalistic explanation is shown by Knobel's difficulty, that Isaiah certainly could not know that his pregnant wife would bear a son; which he solves by supposing that the name Immanuel would also suit a girl, the prophet in his oral announcement perhaps speaking simply of a child, and *post eventum* interpolating the more definite son! This is verily: "I am no prophet, nor a prophet's son!"

It would be much more likely to take העלמה quite indefinitely in the sense:[1] "When now the virgin (*i.e.* any virgin) conceives, she will have reason after the birth has taken place (*i.e.* in nine months) to call her son Immanuel," according to the ordinary custom of naming children after domestic or public circumstances happening at the time of their birth. In this case the child along with its mother is nothing but a clock-finger in Judah's history. But one must concede that on this explanation the very opening of the oracle does not seem natural. That opening seems to point to a birth full of promise, despite all adverse circumstances. And the following chapters are decisive in this sense. When in ix. 5 the prophet exults: *A child is born to us, a son is given us,* meaning thereby the Messiah of David's house, we cannot avoid the impression, that it is he of whose conception and approaching birth the present passage speaks so circumstantially. And were any doubt left, it would be removed by viii. 8, where it is said: "Thy land, O Immanuel;" consequently the son of the עלמה is addressed as the prince of the land; cf. viii. 10. And whom would this name suit better than the Messiah, in whom God's presence is given most directly to the Church?

But although the Messianic dignity of the boy utterly excludes the notion that he may have been Isaiah's son, we cannot perhaps assume that the prophet alluded to a definite woman, belonging to David's Messianic house, as the mother of the Messiah. This is as improbable as that in ix. 5 he alluded to a particular new-born child. It would be preferable to refer to the son of Ahaz, the devout Hezekiah, whose mother Abi, daughter of Zechariah, is mentioned in 2 Kings xviii. 2. But this old Jewish interpretation[2] does not suit chronologically, as Hezekiah must have been already nine years old at the time when Isaiah spoke to Ahaz. Altogether unhappy is Nägelsbach's suggestion, according to which an unmarried princess is supposed to be denounced as pregnant by the prophetic saying. Rather is הָעַלְמָה (just as general as יֹלֵדָה in Micah v. 2), not indeed the house of David (Hofmann), but the elect Church, from whose womb the Messiah proceeds. The prophet discerns in its

---

[1] So Stähelin, recently also Reuss (*Gesch. d. heil. Schr. A. T.*, 1881, p. 303).

[2] The idea of the Messiah was, in several ways, brought into connection with the person of Hezekiah. F. Weber, *Altsynagogale Theologie*, p. 341.

present affliction the pains of a pregnancy, which will not be unfruitful, like those of the house of Israel, Hos. xiii. 13, but from which the Messiah will proceed. In the abasement and devastation now impending, He will grow up. This is parallel to the statement of Micah, that He is to go forth from Bethlehem. This prospect of the glorious fruit that will grow up, in mean circumstances, in the time of impending calamity, forms the bright obverse of the oracle, whose hard, dark upper side would be more intelligible to its hearers. There is something mysterious in the appellation of the mother of the Messiah. Whether it is the house of David, or Zion, or the community of the devout, or Judah, in any case she is a virgin; she is not here called the Lord's wife, as in Hosea, but a virgin in the sense above mentioned,[1] as one who was destined to be a mother, but had not yet fulfilled this destiny. The Church of the Lord is destined to conceive something quite new, divine; she will conceive it amid the tribulation now beginning. The rendering παρθένος (LXX.), according to the idiom stated above, is more in the right than certain tasteless modern ones;[2] and Matt. i. 22 f., who refers it to the virgin birth of the Lord, does not do this without intrinsic right. For the oracle implies that the Messiah will come into the world through a new miraculous influence of the Lord on the Church, and just the same is shown in the history of the fulfilment in relation to His mother.

We find, then, in the present oracle two chief thoughts intertwined: 1. Before a child now conceived is born, the foes are judged, Jerusalem delivered; before the child becomes a youth, Judah also is laid waste. Herein, in this rapid, unexpected sequence of political events, lies the sign for the present generation, *i.e.* a public testimony to Yahveh's conscious, almighty rule in the world's history. 2. In these pains the birth of a child, of Immanuel, is made known. In the extraordinarily unhappy state in which the land is placed, the Messiah grows up.

But the question, How are these two thoughts related to each other? is difficult. Did the prophet expect the Messiah's birth and the setting up of His kingdom in the time immediately impending? We would not contend against such a view on

---

[1] Hofmann rightly observes: "She only could rationally be called marriageable (*mannbar*) who was capable of knowing, but had not known a man."

[2] Cf. even Segond: *Voici, la jeune femme deviendra enceinte!*

dogmatic grounds, if it were exegetically established. But, first of all, Isaiah everywhere,[1] like his contemporary Micah, presupposes a judgment and sentence of exile on Judah-Jerusalem, and a near approach of the glorious Messianic age would be in contradiction to this. Again, one cannot mistake that in ix. 5 he speaks of a child that does not belong to contemporary history, but is only present to his seer-vision. Here also we must distinguish between the prophet's picture and his reflective thought. In the former, Immanuel is actually born in the Syrian-Ephraim tribulation, and grows up in the Assyrian trouble. But this does not imply that the event also took this shape temporally in the consciousness of the reflecting Isaiah, for other visions cut him off from the hope of witnessing such an epoch. Intrinsically regarded, however, the form of the prophecy is not without reason. The sufferings which then befell Judah were, in fact, the beginning of the end, of the judgment by which the old kingdom would be dissolved and give place to a new one; and in the degradation, in which people and monarchy were found after the Assyrian period, the new ruler grew up. But, at the same time, the superiority of Judah, such as was gloriously displayed in the days of Ahaz and Hezekiah, had its deepest reason in the fact that it was God's people, the mother of the Messiah. Hence God's wondrous way could not be more graphically described to that generation than was done in this oracle, where the Messiah, bringing comfort after its humiliation, was held up before its eyes as a token of what lay before it.

As in Isa. vii. so in Isa. ix., the promise rises as a light out of the night of doom; only that here the light, at least for a moment, quite pushes back the dark shadows. In the discourse principally in question (chap. viii. 5 ff.) the entire import is still condemnatory, until in ix. 2 a morning-ray suddenly shoots up: Uncomprehended and unheard, the seer stands there with his children, who are the living tokens of the message of doom. The nation seeks counsel in forbidden quarters instead of from the living God, and refuses to assent to the motto: "To the law and testimony!" *i.e.* will not bow before the divine Torah and accept the testimony of judgment and promise. Hence it is encircled by comfortless night, which grows darker and darker. The most natural explanation of the difficult ver. 20 seems to us to be this:

---

[1] Isa. iii. 1 ff., v. 1 ff., vi. 11 ff., vii. 20 ff., viii. 1, etc., xxxix. 6.

If they do not say, To the law and testimony, they are such as have no morning-dawn,—a desperate state of God-forsakenness expounded in ver. 21 f. Chap. ix. 1 joins on to this, assigning the reasons. It indicates why the opposite happy condition is to be expected in adherence to the law and the testimony. This testimony contains the wonderful promise:—

ix. 1. "For the district, where tribulation is, does not remain dark; at the first time He humbled the land of Zebulon and the land of Naphtali. And in the last time He brings to honour the way by the sea, the land beyond Jordan, the region of the heathen."

The portion of country in the east and north (2 Kings xv. 29), most exposed to foes, has according to God's decree a glorious future. The tribe of Zebulon and Naphtali is named, whose northern portion bore the name "district of the heathen," because the latter here always outnumbered the Israelitish population. To this tribe also belonged "the way by the sea," *i.e.* the west side of the sea of Tiberias (Rashi), finally, the strongly paganized Gilead. These districts had always been regarded by the sacred history with stepmotherly feelings, and now under Tiglath-Pileser were about to become altogether the prey of the heathen. But just here the prophet in a notable manner sees the light shine earliest and brightest. In his wondrous righteousness God has it in mind to bring just this despised portion of His inheritance to special honour. For a prophet of Jerusalem to speak thus is wonderful. Here also the fulfilment requires us with the evangelist (Matt. iv. 13 ff.) to acknowledge the working of God, who has fulfilled this saying literally, making the true light first to shine and the world's morning-dawn to break in Galilee, so that this despised country became partaker in the highest honour. On the ground of the present passage, without doubt, Galilee is regarded by the Jews as the place where the Messiah will emerge.[1]

The discourse shows us further the blessed metamorphosis that comes over the unhappy people, as well as Him who brings it about:—

ix. 2. "The people that walk about in darkness see a great
    light. They who dwell in the land of the shadow of death,
  3 upon them light beams. Thou multipliest the nation which

---

[1] Eisenmenger, *Entdecktes Judenthum* (1711), ii. 747.

Thou madest not great (note A). The joy with which they rejoice before Thee is like the joy in harvest, like as men 4 exult when they share spoil. For the yoke of its burden[1] and the beam of its neck, the rod of its driver Thou hast 5 broken to pieces as on the day of Midian. For every boot of the booted in the tumult[2] (of battle) and garment rolled in blood 6 —this shall be for burning, for fuel of fire. For a child was born to us, a son was given us. And the rule came on His shoulder. And His name is called: Wonder of Counsellor, 7 Strong God, Eternal Father, Prince of Peace, for the increase[3] of the government, and for peace without end,[4] on David's throne and on his kingdom, to establish and support it by law and righteousness, henceforth for ever and ever. The zeal of the Lord of hosts will perform these things."

In bold antithesis to the present time the prophet describes how the unhappy people, sunk in the gloom of God-forsakenness (and he understands by the people now no longer particular tribes, but the whole of degenerate Israel), will be made partakers in divinely-given freedom and joy. The nation, at present diminished by foreign conquerors, will be abundantly multiplied by God's blessing. To set forth its happiness the prophet chooses the joy of harvest, the purest and most blessed, in which the feelings of men are enhanced by the sense of God's goodness, which does not leave hard toil unrewarded (Ps. cxxvi. 6). Nay, it is a jubilee as after victory won, when men share the booty

---

[1] From סֹבֶל, *burden*, is formed סֻבְּלוֹ as a secondary form of סָבְלוֹ, with *Dagesh dirimens* סֻבְּלוֹ, or on account of the fainter sound סֻבְּלוֹ.

[2] סְאוֹן, according to the Syriac and Chaldee, *boot*, *soldier's boot*, not *equipment* (Knobel). בְּרַעַשׁ refers not directly to the tumult caused by the boots, but to the din of battle, where men go booted.

[3] מַרְבֵּה, a verbal noun (according to the form מַעֲשֶׂה), in the meaning, "to multiply" (רָבָה). The *Mem clausum* in this word springs from an incorrect but rather old reading: (רַבֵּה) לָם רַבֵּה, where לָם was taken for לְהֶם, as Elias Levita states. According to the Jewish Midrash, the *Mem* is said to have been closed when Hezekiah did not answer to the Messianic hopes cherished respecting him!

[4] לְמַרְבֵּה and לְשָׁלוֹם do not depend on אֵין־קֵץ ("of the greatness of the rule and prosperity there is no end," Knobel), but on the facts implied in the preceding verse. The ruler born suffices, in accordance with the attributes lying in his name, for increasing the government, and for peace without end. He is also the subject of the declarations: "On David's throne, and on his kingdom, to establish it," etc.

after hard conflict (Judg. v. 11). For the Lord has brought about a complete deliverance from the hand of the heathen world-power, as on the day of Midian, when the harsh tyrants who had degraded the whole people into bond-slaves were vanquished by Gideon, and their yoke was shattered at a blow (Judg. vii.). A simple victory over foes, however, is not to be thought of.[1] The exultant joy of the saved and freed people can only be compared to the joy of harvest and victory. When the world-power, built on blood and iron, has fallen, every implement of war is laid aside as something impure which is to vanish from the face of the earth, and is committed to the fire like condemned spoil (Deut. xiii. 16), with every soldier's boot and bloody mantle—an allusion to the faultless military equipment of the Assyrians, whose rigid bearing imposed not a little on the Israelites.

It is a grand thing for the seer just now, amid the turmoil of preparation and the clash of weapons, now when the invincible world-power is emerging with its armies, to promise that all this will be swept away for ever. What gives him such confidence? According to ver. 6, the birth of a child! The same without doubt from which (chap. vii.), although it was not yet born, a ray of hope shot through the whole oracle of judgment. Now the seer beholds it born, hence his triumphant joy. For God's gracious presence, of which this child is the pledge, is mightier than the whole world. The next moment the prophet sees the child clothed with the government; and already from his work and rule it is plain who he is. But no name will suffice to express this. The name Immanuel, given even before birth as a pledge to the mother, expands here into a plurality which, without exhausting itself in its terms, suggests more than it expresses. Four pairs of words[2] describe this ruler as towering divinely

---

[1] See x. 26 f. The divine lash, which the Assyrians felt, was different from that which fell on Midian.

[2] Quite unnatural are all the explanations which, referring some of the predicates to God, apply only the remnant to the Messiah. Thus, *He who is wonderful as Counsellor, the strong God, the eternal Father calls his name Prince of Peace;*" or so that even עַד אֲבִי would still be joined with שָׂרִ־שָׁלוֹם as a name of the Messiah. So the majority of the Rabbins, following the Targum of Jonathan. Moreover, פֶּלֶא must not be separated from יוֹעֵץ, so that five names would arise: *Wonderful, Counsellor*, etc. (Delitzsch), since the analogy in form of the following appellations is against this, and יוֹעֵץ after פֶּלֶא is too weak to stand alone.

above all others, and exuberant in blessing to his people. The first pair calls him: *Miracle of Counsellor*.[1] The word פֶּלֶא, *miracle*, denotes what goes beyond human power of comprehension, divine acts and leadings, which confound human wisdom, Isa. xxix. 14. God is the מַפְלִיא עֵצָה, *one who deals in wonderful counsel*. The miraculous is a mark of divine being and action; cf. Judg. xiii. 18. When in the first name a miraculous, divine character is ascribed to the ruler in his capacity of counsellor, planning for his people's good, this is saying more than that his wisdom far exceeds that usual among rulers; it is affirmed that his wisdom is related to the human as divine. Just so the second predicate attributes to him energy in action. He is called אֵל גִּבּוֹר, *strong God*, not merely *divine hero; a god of a hero*;[2] for גִּבּוֹר is an adjective, and the phrase cannot be understood differently than in x. 21, where it is used of the Lord Himself. In this second name also, doubtless, a definite expression of his dignity, one side of his working, is taken into view, namely, his divine energy in action, as in the first the superhuman grandeur of his counsel; but his person itself is thereby raised to divine greatness. He is called *strong God* in a way that would be inapplicable to a man, unless the one God, who rightly bears the name אל נבור, were perfectly set forth in this his Anointed One. In such passages the Old Testament revelation falls into a self-contradiction, from which only a miracle has been able to deliver us, the Incarnation of the Son of God. Elsewhere it draws the sharpest limit between the holy God and the sinful child of man, and its superiority to heathen religions depends in great part on this limit. Prophecy gradually lets this limit drop in proof that the aim of God's action is to transcend it, and to unite himself most closely with humanity. In such oracles we Christians find no deification of the human, such as is the order of the day on heathen soil. Otherwise prophecy would

---

[1] פֶּלֶא (to be so pointed, according to the text of Baer and Delitzsch, p. 68) is *status const.* (not acc. of obj.), after the analogy of פֶּרֶא אָדָם, Gen. xvi. 12 (Ewald); יוֹעֵץ frequently stands substantivally (Job iii. 14, etc.) for the minister as counsellor of the king, with whom as such he takes part in the government.

[2] Still less: *Strong Hero* (Gesenius, de Wette), as no adjective אֵל, *strong*, occurs, and such an adjective must have stood after the noun; the current idiom אֵל גִּבּוֹר has another meaning. This idiom also forbids Luther's separation: *strength, hero;* similarly Aquila, Symm., Theodotion.

be a retrogression from the teaching of the law into naturalism and heathen idealism. But in such oracles we find a clear proof, that even in the time of the Old Covenant the Spirit of God was consciously striving after the goal that we see reached in the New.

Of the last two names: *Eternal Father* and *Prince of Peace*, the first one creates difficulty. The word עַד occurs as noun in two very different significations, according to the choice of which the interpretation here differs very widely. Hitzig, Knobel, Diestel translate "Booty-Father," which is perhaps capable of defence linguistically[1] and in its import. In ver. 2 sharing of booty was spoken of (certainly only by way of comparison). Was not the Messiah meant to be described in this oracle as the deliverer of His people, who after wise counsel smites down the foe with heroic action as Gideon did the Midianites, so that after his victory rich booty would be enjoyed and a government of peace follow?[2] With respect to the first attributes, with which the Messiah is adorned, we have seen that they far surpass the measure even of the consecrated heroism of a Gideon or David, and amid names of such divine dignity "Booty-Father" would look too freebooter-like. Nor would full justice be done to this predicate were it limited to a single victory, and did it not, like the other names, denote an attribute permanently active. But "Booty-Father" cannot be a permanent attribute of the Messiah because of the following "Prince of Peace;" for the latter plainly affirms, that He is able without drawing sword to maintain His reputation at home and abroad, a true Solomon, not bloodstained like David, and yet a hero greater than he (cf. Zech. ix. 9 f.; Micah v. 3). We believe, therefore, we ought to hold fast by the common interpretation of עַד, according to which here as in Gen. xlix. 26, Hab. iii. 5, Isa. lvii. 15, it denotes uninterrupted duration.[3] Only by the translation "Father of eternity" one must not *per se* attribute to this definition of time a substantiality not belonging to the Hebrew עַד, and altogether foreign to the ancient Hebrew mode of conception. The genitive noun expresses pure quality. Even the paraphrase "Possessor of eternity," suggested

---

[1] The word is so used Gen. xlix. 27; Isa. xxxiii. 23; Zeph. iii. 8.
[2] Cf. Gen. xlix. 8-12.
[3] See more respecting עַד in this sense in my dissertation on *Die hebräischen Synonyma der Zeit und Ewigkeit*, 1871, p. 86 ff.

by the Shemitic employment of names of affinity, would be consonant to Arabic,[1] but not to old Hebrew thought. It is true that even in Hebrew we find this use of *father, brother*, etc., where an attribute is meant to be described as inseparably joined with the person in question, and it would be perverse in proper names, like אֲבִיחַיִל, אֲבִינֹעַם, etc., to lay specific stress on the relation of producer.[2] But עַד is too dependent an idea to allow אבי to be taken by such an analogy as a mere word of relation (possessor of something). We therefore follow Delitzsch in laying the chief substantive emphasis on אבי (after xxii. 21): "He is a father to his people for ever," one who will never leave them without fatherly counsel and helpful act. And as every individual has in Him a father, especially the poor, according to the description of Ps. lxxii., so the nation and the whole world (cf. ii. 3 f.; Zech. ix. 9 f.; Micah v. 3 f.) have in him a Prince of Peace.

In virtue of these attributes made known in his name He suffices for enlarging the government as a true augmenter of the kingdom, and at the same time for peace without end. The 6th verse also proves that the enlargement of dominion is not conceived as taking place through sanguinary wars such as other conquerors wage, but that this Immanuel, thanks to his divine superiority, makes the nations submit to him by more rational means. He will use the power he has as David's heir, first thoroughly to set up his kingdom, and then to support it for all time by the weapons of *law* and *righteousness*. These are the pillars on which he founds his dominion, Hos. ii. 21. His superiority then maintains itself and works by moral means. If Solomon's wise and righteous policy secured him the homage of distant princes and nations, this Anointed One of the future, who must be infinitely greater than Solomon, will bring the earth into subjection to himself by displaying a higher, divine righteous-

---

[1] The Arabs have a time-god, whom they call أبو عوض, with which Movers compares Isaiah's expression. See my dissertation, p. 107.

[2] In Arabic there are innumerable cases to prove that language here acts more freely. The jackal is not called "father of howling," but "son of howling" (ابن أوى); milk, "father of whiteness" (أبو الإ بيض), not because it produces whiteness, but because whiteness is distinctive of it; the husband, "father of the wife," because she belongs to him (أبو الرعة).

ness. "The zeal of the Lord of hosts will perform these things." The reference is to the zealous love for his people that removes all barriers standing in the way of the consummation of his kingdom.

Thus the name Immanuel assigned to the child of the future has unfolded itself. Divine wisdom, divine strength, paternal love faithful as God's, divine righteousness and peace, are ascribed to him, in such a way, indeed, that his person also appears divine; he perfectly exhibits God to the world, consequently his dominion is really God's dominion on earth. Certainly Nägelsbach on this passage rightly remarks that we must distinguish between the Old and New Testament standpoint: Considered from the former, the language did not possess the full dogmatic definiteness in which it appears to us who stand in the light of the fulfilment. But every Judaizing and rationalizing attempt to adapt the insignia conferred on the Messiah here to a man of our nature degrades them, and with them the Spirit who framed them. One alone could claim them as his, and for him they were already designed.

Did Isaiah then think that the perfect Son of David promised was already born at the time when he uttered these words? Had he in view a young scion of this house, like Hezekiah? This cannot be inferred from ver. 5 with any sort of right. If the passage were relating what had taken place, then also the government must already have come to the child of promise. Rather the preterites belong to just the same category as those of ver. 1. The prophet announces what he sees in spirit. But that he actually expected the dawn of the Messiah's glorious kingdom in the next age, is a supposition running counter to all his other predictions of judgment. No doubt the Messianic salvation finds points of attachment in the age of the prophet. He contemplates it from the horizon of his age; but the image of the Messianic salvation is so sharply severed from the images which his discourses unroll of the present and future of his contemporaries, that it is impossible to combine them in time. He was far from holding out hopes to his contemporaries which could not be theirs, and the failure of which would have ruined his influence for ever. Not the *when*, but the *that*, was immovably certain to the prophet in regard to the coming of the divine rule on earth through the perfect Davidite. But in any case a radical judgment must first go forth on the nation, only a remnant of which, the prophet unceasingly insists (x. 21 f.), will be converted to the Lord and share in His salvation. For even to the arrogant heathen whom the Lord uses as a rod, the Assyrian, a day is set, when the Lord will reckon with him. He falls before the walls of Jerusalem, as a miraculous vision informs the prophet (x. 28 ff.). And from rescued Judah, from the humbled house of David, grows up the world-wide power of the future, painted in xi. 1 ff. in new colours.

xi. 1. "And there comes up a twig out of the stump[1] of Jesse,
2 and a shoot from its roots bears fruit. And there rests upon him the Spirit of Yahveh, the spirit of wisdom and of understanding, the spirit of counsel and of strength, the spirit
3 of knowledge and of the fear of Yahveh. And his delight he has in the fear of Yahveh, and not according to what his eyes see does he speak judgment, and judges not according
4 to what his ears hear. And he pronounces judgment in righteousness to the needy, and passes sentence in equity for the defenceless in the land; and smites the earth with the staff of his mouth, and with the breath of his lips he slays
5 the wicked; And righteousness shall be the girdle of his hips,
6 and faithfulness the girdle of his loins. And the wolf dwells with the lamb, and the panther lies down beside the kid, and calf and lion and stalled ox together, a little boy driving
7 them. And cow and bear pasture, their young lie down
8 together. And the lion eats straw like the bullock. And the suckling plays by the hole of the otter, and to the basilisk's
9 hole the weaned one stretches its hand.[2] They hurt not and destroy not in all my holy mountain; for the land is full of

---

[1] גֵּזַע, the stump left standing after the tree is felled; from גָּזַע, *to cut off, fell*. Cf. Job xiv. 8 f., and Pliny, xvi. 44: *Inarescunt rursusque adolescunt, senescunt quidem, sed e radicibus repullulant.* Of the whole nation only such a root-stock is left, according to vi. 13.

[2] שִׁעֲשַׁע, a *pilpel* form (from שָׁעַע, *to stroke*), in the sense: *to dandle, play*. מְאוּרָה is probably, as the parallelism suggests, *a hole,* properly *light hole* (cf. מְנֻהֲרָה, Judg. vi. 2); following the Targum, on the other hand, Delitzsch prefers the meaning: "pupil of the eye," with which Prov. xv. 30 may be compared. הָדָה, only occurring here, "to stretch out," is found in the Arabic and Syriac in the sense "*to lead;*" cf. *manum ducere.* צִפְעֹנִי is a serpent name (so called from hissing); according to Aquila, βασιλίσκος; Vulg. *serpens regulus,* a small but very poisonous kind of viper.

the knowledge of Yahveh like the waters which cover the sea."[1]

While Assyria's power lies prostrate, judged by the prophetic word, slowly and at first insignificantly there rises before the seer's eyes a new power out of the house of David, which also like Assyria lies under judgment and deeply humbled. It is no longer a royal cedar; of the felled tree only a root-stock is left, but this strikes out again; and it is on a lowly twig from this tribe which has fallen back into the old pre-Davidic obscurity, a tender sprig from the remaining root, that God's entire good pleasure rests. From it the nation is to expect all salvation, and the world a divine rule such as has never been seen. The lowliness of the Messiah's beginnings, already intimated in vii. 15, and according to that passage connected with the judgment bursting over Judah and its royal house, is here explained much more definitely. The regal power no longer exists, when its true heir grows up out of humble soil. How true Isaiah's knowledge on this point was, we know from the history of the fulfilment, where the Son of David, scarcely known as such, grew up among the least of his nation, and, on a far mightier scale than David, traversed the path from unnoticed lowliness to highest honour.[2]

For it is not a fresh growth, a new upcoming that is promised to David's house, but the appearance of a particular branchlet, the production of which was the divine destiny of the whole tree from the beginning. The twig, the shoot of the 1st verse, as the 2nd verse proves, is meant in an altogether personal sense.[3] Without doubt it is the same person as in vii. 14 f. and ix. 5 ff. But whereas in the first passage only his significant Immanuel-name and his growth amid the affliction of his people were told, while the second unfolded his power based on right and aiming at peace, this third time, where his form appears, the prophetic eye lingers on the intrinsic character of his personality, and describes first of all, not his relation to the world, but his relation

---

[1] As a verbal noun רעה here governs the accusative; כָּסָה stands with dative: *to furnish covering*.

[2] The lowly roots of the stem of Jesse had strayed as far as despised Galilee (see before on viii. 23). In the fact that Jesus must be a "Nazarene," Matthew (ii. 23) sees a literal fulfilment of the present passage, where he is called a Nezer, *a twig, a branchlet*. In both at least His lowliness is indicated, so that the phonetic type has an inner point of support.

[3] It is the Messiah, who is also called Sprout.

to God. As we saw there how the true God appears to the world in his person, so here the Messiah appears as true man, perfect in godliness and fulfilling the highest destiny of the human race. As man he is distinct from God, but the Spirit of God has settled upon him. In this lies the mystery of His fellowship with God. "Resting upon him is the Spirit of Yahveh." This verb, especially when it stands in the participial form,[1] implies that the Spirit of God does not come on him intermittently, but has taken up his abode permanently with him and become his higher life-principle (p. 4). That the Bible by this Spirit denotes, not a mere potentiation of creaturely life, but a supernatural life, which, however, may and will enter into man, we have seen in the Introduction (p. 4). This Sprout of David is seen to be thoroughly penetrated and fertilized by the Divine Spirit. All his attributes and capacities are fruits of this Spirit, and through the one Spirit who confers diverse gifts he unites all the virtues adorning a ruler in God's sight and salutary to His people. Here follows the enumeration in pairs. The series is opened by wisdom and understanding, both together forming Solomon's high pre-eminence (1 Kings v. 9 f.), which he besought from God as the highest good (iii. 5 ff.). Whilst חָכְמָה denotes generally rational insight and knowledge, ethical in its grounds and aims, בִּינָה more specifically is the gift of discrimination, judgment, which distinguishes between good and evil, an aspect of the faculty of knowledge especially important to a king in his judicial duties.[2] As he is thus divinely qualified to be a judge, so the same Spirit supplies him with the insight in counsel and energy in action so requisite for a ruler; see ix. 5: פלא יועץ and אל גבור. But such wisdom and power as he exercises in the world come to him from the fact that Yahveh Himself is the goal of his life and effort. The spirit of the knowledge and fear of God fills him. The דֵּעָה, to which יהוה belongs as object, here and in ver. 9 as in Hosea, is not merely intellectual, but refers to deep spiritual fellowship with the Lord. And to this is added reverence for the Lord, the piety which was not faultless in David, but in Solomon was altogether lost. Here plainly the Messiah is not half-Deity or deified man, but true man, taking in all respects the position befitting man in God's presence. And just because he fulfils all God's will, he

---

[1] Otherwise in Num. xi. 26 ; 2 Kings ii. 15.
[2] Cf. the use of נָבוֹן, הָבִין, along with חָכָם, 1 Kings iii. 9, 11, 12.

stands far above the most religious kings who sat on David's throne, and bears worthily the divine dignity bestowed on him. Thus the Divine Spirit parts in a sense into three pairs. Delitzsch compares the רוּחַ יי to the shaft of the seven-branched lamp, from which three pairs of branches project. In any case the number seven, the number of divine perfection, does not occur here by accident.[1]

How this heaven-inspired king treats his subjects is told in ver. 3 f. As he is himself the impersonation of the fear of God, so also such fear in them is to him a perfume[2] in which he delights. And since he is wisdom and judgment in embodied form, he does not give sentence according to outward appearance, often so deceitful, or according to mere hearsay, often so unfounded, but reads the heart and detects the true state of things, even where it is not obvious. He will help to their rights those without influence and without means of obtaining any, the friendless poor and the defenceless or harmless (עֲנָוִים, see p. 246), who lie at the mercy of their foes, whereas otherwise they are always worsted, Ps. lxxii. 2, 4; for the righteousness that knows no respect of persons is the only rule by which he judges. On this very account all wickedness must receive its sentence from his mouth. His Spirit-filled mouth is in a sense the royal staff, with which he smites the earth; the breath going forth from his lips slays the reprobate. Consequently it is a spiritual authority by which he establishes, extends, and maintains his power (cf. ix. 6), namely, his spotless righteousness. His weapon is his word (cf. Zech. ix. 10), which suffices everywhere to secure victory for righteousness and execute judgment. Ver. 5 concludes the portrait of Jesse's great Son: "the girdle about his hips," *i.e.* always encircling him,[3] in a certain sense holding together his glorious armour, endowing him with firm, energetic mien, is righteousness, fidelity, stedfastness. In this latter virtue—immovable fidelity to God—the best rulers of Israel at times showed themselves wanting. Only to One does the description apply, to Him who, growing up in the deepest lowliness, showed unexampled love to the poor and needy, while from His mouth goes forth a two-edged sword (Rev. i. 16), that judges

---

[1] Cf. Zech. iii. 8; Rev. iv. 5, v. 6.

[2] הָרִיחַ with בְּ, in the same meaning as in Amos v. 21.

[3] Cf. the trope, Job xxix. 14.

all wickedness on earth. The רֶשַׁע here is quite general. No doubt, according to the N. T. revelation,[1] all wickedness also will be concentrated in one person, the Antichrist, who opposes himself to the Messiah. And to him Paul applies this term, 2 Thess. ii. 8.

The future ruler having been thus described, the peaceful state under his rule is pictured; the sequence of thought is therefore here the reverse of what it is in chap. ix. There, first the abolition of war was promised, and the birth of the Messiah assigned as the cause; here, first the Messiah is described, then His peaceful kingdom. And how is this done? Not political peace, as in chaps. ii. and vii., but a truce of nature is depicted. Wolf and lamb, panther and kid, dwell together; the lion lets itself be driven to pasture between calf and stalled ox, and is satisfied with the fodder of the bullock. Even from the most deadly serpent a venturesome child has nothing to fear. Thus the most dangerous beasts of prey have become harmless; the nature of the most ravenous beasts is completely changed in the holy mount of Yahveh, *i.e.* in His holy territory, which, according to ver. 9, embraces the whole land.

This passage, the rival of ii. 1 ff. in simplicity and grandeur, reminds first of Hos. ii. 20,[2] but is more than an enlargement of that promise, according to which the animal world is to be put under a divine ban to do no harm to God's people. The detailed account of the good understanding prevailing among the beasts, the most feared being no longer terrible, the weakest being no longer the prey of the strong, implies that the peace proceeding from this ruler will be shared in by the whole of nature, from which, of course, calm and security accrue to men. No hurtful, destructive powers are found in the land, so richly will it flow with the knowledge of the Lord, so permeated will it be by the Divine Spirit, who dispenses life and love. The conclusion (ver. 9) leaves no doubt that the human world is included in the divine peace proceeding from the blessed transformation of nature, and what is to be seen most vividly in the animal world will appear above all in men. They need an analogous transformation. For human, like animal life, supports itself commonly by a conflict for existence. Men have by nature something animal in them; and this reinforced by sin provokes them against each other. All

---

[1] Cf. the Book of Daniel.   [2] Cf. the opposite, Hos. ii. 14. See p. 233.

the world's civilisation does not abolish this animal nature; it simply clothes its immoral struggle for existence in finer garb, and furnishes it with more intellectual weapons, but at last makes the baseness of its aims come out all the more nakedly.[1] There is but one power that miraculously lifts men above this inborn selfishness, that is, the revelation of God, spiritual fellowship with Him. If man is not transformed into divinity, he sinks into bestiality. And the miracle of this transformation is quite as great as for the lion, whose teeth and jaws are intended for eating flesh, to feed on straw. But the miraculous takes place when God's kingdom is established. There the selfish nature gives place to a higher spirit, and thus peace comes on earth. Not without reason, therefore, has the Messiah in the New Covenant laid down a complete new birth as the condition of partaking in His kingdom. Moreover, He has been true to His promise. The Spirit whom He promised conquers in point of fact the most stubborn and powerful, the most selfish and interested natures, producing in them the fruits enumerated in Gal. v. 22.

But if in this description of Isaiah its reference to the human world and its inner as well as outer transformation forces itself irresistibly on us, was the oracle meant to exhaust itself in this reference, and only to speak allegorically of the irrational creation? Or did the prophet expect also a metamorphosis of the latter? It is true here as in Joel, that in the prophet's vision there is an interpenetration of concrete and abstract, nature and spirit, human world and earthly creation, which the prophet does not analyse by a process of reflection, but gives in conjunction, just as he saw it. And no explanation is perfectly satisfactory that does not yield this unity. Until the destructive nature-powers really become harmless, and the sad struggle for existence comes to an end in the whole of nature, this prophecy stands as a hieroglyph pointing to the future of God's ways. When once the divine rule is firmly established in the human world, then creation also, which is designed to be man's servant, will be redeemed from the ban of baleful conflict and death

---

[1] Think only of the modern science that treats men as mere animals. According to what has been said before, there is much truth in this view. But the fearfully immoral consequences of such a theory are as yet rightly apprehended by few, although those are not wanting who shamelessly avow them, and would erect animal egoism, according to which the strong are to destroy the weak, into the principle of private and civil life.

burdening it, as the apostle, resuming Old Testament prophecy, teaches in Rom. viii. 19 ff. Then only does the bite of the serpent cease to be deadly to man, as is promised here and in Isa. lxv. 25, not without a backward glance at Gen. iii. The woe which the world inflicts upon the sinner terminates. The world itself has become new.

True, the beatifying of God's Church is extended in the oracle just considered to the irrational creation, always with a local limitation to the holy mountain of God, as the land of Canaan is here called in a wider sense. Only so far as the rule of the Messiah goes can there be peace, and only where He dwells can the entire glory of God's grace be revealed. But this glory will be so great that the nations will set out thither to enjoy it.

xi. 10. "And it will come to pass in that day: the root-sprout[1] of Jesse, which stands as a banner to the nations,—the heathen will seek after it.[2] And its resting-place will be glorious."

Thus the banner, the signal, is the Davidic shoot, visible to the nations around; it beckons them to Zion, whither they eagerly journey to partake in the saving blessings there dispensed. Of what nature these are is more fully stated in ii. 1 ff., which passage, however, receives its necessary complement from the present one, inasmuch as we are told here that it is the divinely unique Davidite who is the occasion of the pilgrimage of the nations, and through whom the whole world receives God's law and judgment by peaceful means. By the resting-place, which is glory, honour, *i.e.* altogether glorious and honourable, is of course understood, not his grave, as the Vulg.[3] renders (giving the Romish Church a welcome handle for worshipping the Holy Sepulchre), but the residence of this much-sought king, which will be more stately and glorious than that of Solomon.

Finally, in Isaiah also the return of the exiles is not wanting as an essential feature in the picture of the Messianic future. From all lands they are gathered, ver. 11 f. Then the saved "remnant" of the people will sing a new song to the Lord, which in chap. xii. forms the harmonious conclusion of the cycle of

---

[1] Here שֹׁרֶשׁ stands briefly for this. Also observe here the contrast of lowliness and dignity in שֹׁרֶשׁ and נֵס.

[2] אֶל דָּרַשׁ, not: *to inquire* (Knobel), but: *to seek after*, certainly for the purpose of obtaining counsel and direction, as in Deut. xii. 5.

[3] *Et erit sepulcrum ejus gloriosum.*

Messianic oracles. The Book of Immanuel ends with this choral echo from the bosom of the ransomed Church.

NOTE A.—The correct division of the words is seen neither by the Masoretes nor expositors. Hence many incorrectly prefer the *keri* לֹו. שִׂמְחוּ is a relative sentence (Knobel), but not: "Thou increasest to him the joy, which they rejoice before thee," where the rhythm would entirely vanish. Also Studer's emendation (*Jahrb. für prot. Theol.*, 1881, i. 160 f.): הַגִּיל for הַגּוֹי, is unsatisfactory. The antithesis of הָרְבִּיתָ and לֹא הִגְדַּלְתָּ is the same as in ver. 23 : between the poor, wretched present and the glorious future. הַשִּׂמְחָה is not acc. obj. (so Masora, Steudel, Delitzsch, Gesenius, Ewald, Nägelsbach), but nominative. One would certainly expect here אֲשֶׁר as after determined nouns. It may, however, be absent in Hebrew even after such nouns (otherwise in Arabic), Ewald, *Gram.* § 332a. *Gaudium gaudere*, says the Hebrew, like קִנֵּא קִנְאָה, Zech. viii. 2.

§ 31. *Further Oracles of Isaiah respecting Zion*, chap. xxviii.-xxxix.

The series of oracles considered in the last section presents in personal setting the theocratic Davidic monarchy emerging safely from the judgment, and shows how it will pass from the humiliation of the age of punishment into glory never before seen. A further series of genuine Isaianic oracles comes to us from the days of Hezekiah, in which not the personal, but the local crystallizing-point of God's kingdom is most conspicuous. God's dwelling in *Zion*, inseparably joined with David's Messianic royalty, will be indestructible as that royalty, and despite all judgments will but assume a more divine and perfect form. The divine arrangement revealed in David's time had two sides, the raising of a human royal house to divine honour, and the descent of God to dwell for ever in an earthly place (pp. 148, 186). The significance of the one as of the other trait for the future was seen by Isaiah in new grandeur. He was led by the circumstances of the time to proclaim the divine dignity and significance of Zion, inasmuch as this abode of God was threatened by the Assyrians with the destruction which had actually overtaken the neighbouring Samaritan adulteress. The miraculous preservation of Zion, foretold by our prophet, from this overwhelming foe, was to be a sign to all the world of the power of Yahveh, who had taken His seat on the holy hill of

Jerusalem. But as the sayings respecting Immanuel, despite their comforting nature, presented a keen edge to the present generation, so the Zion-oracles are not without severity for the Jerusalem of the day, which must pass through judgment before God's dwelling there in His Church can be consummated. It is true, Isaiah promises to the city God's gracious protection in the impending Assyrian catastrophe, but the judgment on its inhabitants, formerly announced by him and also threatened under Hezekiah, will not fail. The prophet at last foretells this judgment in definite form as a deportation to Babylon, to which, however, he adds the promise of return, the true Church of Zion being imperishable.

Isa. xxviii., uttered in the first years of Hezekiah's government, while proud Samaria was yet standing (therefore before 722 B.C.), announces the abrupt end of the latter (due to the Assyrians); yet here the rebuke turns against the great at Jerusalem, as in chap. vii. against Ahaz. As the latter trusted secretly in Assyria instead of in the true God, so the nobles trusted in an alliance secretly and illegally made with Egypt.[1] In such false trust in a worldly power they abandoned themselves to wanton lust, disregarding and violating right in the teeth of the prophet's admonitions and the divine judgments announced by him, fancying that they were secured against death and Hades by their covering of lies and shelter of deceit.

xxviii. 16. "Therefore thus speaks Yahveh, Lord of all: Behold, I have founded[2] in Zion a stone, a stone of trial, a corner-stone, precious, in founding well-founded.[3] Whoever
17 trusts shall not need to flee. And I make right the plumb-line and righteousness the level, and hail sweeps away the covering of lies, and waters wash away the shelter."

Thus the worldly power, the human place of refuge, built up of lies and deceit, will furnish no shelter against the judgment

---

[1] With xxviii. 15, cf. xxix. 15, xxx. 2 ff., xxxi. 1 ff.

[2] Construction as in xxxviii. 5.

[3] פִּנַּת is to be taken, with Delitzsch, as the beginning of a new phrase (not joined genitivally to what precedes). After being called a touchstone, the stone is called a "corner of precious quality," *i.e.* *precious corner-stone*. The preciousness is characteristic of it, it is a gem (1 Kings v. 31); and at the same time it is adapted to be the corner-stone by reason of its firmness, which is especially emphasized by the repeated מוּסָד (the former a noun, the latter *part. hoph.*), properly "precious corner-stone of well-founded founding."

raining down from above, its foundation cannot resist the down-rushing flood of doom; but the foundation laid in Zion by the Lord Himself does this—that immovable foundation-stone and corner-stone, on which all adverse power is broken and judgment on Zion's foes is executed. By this stone, whose firmness and divine preciousness the seer cannot find words enough to praise, is not to be understood the city or citadel itself,[1] for, on the contrary, the dwellers in Jerusalem are to be shattered in their false confidence, nor the temple (Ewald), which is just as little a foundation, but the beginning of the divine rule on this mountain, which bore the citadel of David as well as the temple. We understand the divine act of foundation, not of the divine decree passed long ago, but of its historical realization (as in Ps. ii. 6), which belongs in Isaiah's eyes to the past, because it falls within the Davidic epoch. That one divine act, to which Davidic monarchy and Solomonic temple owed their origin, alone was an irrevocable foundation-laying, on which all the Lord's further work would rest, and by which all men were to be guided, if their building and work were not to be condemned in the final judgment. Thus not Jerusalem in itself is impregnable, nor the Davidic royal power in itself unconquerable, nor the temple indestructible; but the decree of the divine election of Zion, made known long ago by prophetic word, forms the imperishable beginning of the dwelling and rule of God on earth, which must needs be completed. Well then for those who base their trust *thereon*.

This stone is called a stone of trial, touchstone, *i.e.* not one that is itself chosen, tested, but by which everything must be tested and tried, according to viii. 14, where the Lord Himself is called a stone of stumbling and rock of offence, etc.; whereas here the stone denotes His revelation and personal work in the world. Thus the oracle, like the sign of Immanuel, has a double aspect: Something immovable is set forth as the object of true confidence, but also as a contrast to every other refuge having no permanence. Ver. 17 deals further with both sides, but points especially to the negative side: The Lord continues building on His stone, His line being straightness and His level righteousness. The conduct of the men who are to share in the salvation of the God who dwells on Zion, must, as already taught in Ps. xxiv. 3 ff., agree with the ethical character of His fundamental revelation

---

[1] Hitzig, Knobel, Reuss, *et al.*, after xiv. 32.

(Isa. xxxiii. 15). Else they are rejected along with their work. Whatever proves not straight when measured by that line and level His judgment sweeps away,—a result described further after the analogy of the general Flood: Torrents of rain congealed into hail from above, billows from beneath, the prophet at the same time alluding (ver. 21 f.) to such divine judgments as the national history furnished in the victories of a David and Joshua over the heathen.

But the disposition forming the main condition on man's part of God's favour and help, according to the last words of xxviii. 16, as well as vii. 9, xxx. 15, is *believing trust* in the God of salvation, who has already laid His foundation-stone, on which we may and should build. It is early said of Abraham (p. 105), Gen. xv. 6: "He believed, trusted (הֶאֱמִין),[1] and God reckoned it to him for righteousness" (צְדָקָה). While such a believer is not perfectly righteous in every respect, the normal disposition towards God is seen in such trust in the divine promise. Afterwards Hab. ii. 4 especially emphasizes this, and again the New Testament most effectively. That faith, as full inward surrender to the Lord, is on man's side the condition of salvation—this fundamental part of evangelical truth was already revealed to the prophets of the Old Covenant, and Isaiah in particular proposes such faith as the mark of the genuine Church of Zion that cleaves to the divine foundation and outlives the judgment.[2]

Isaiah's discourses xxix.-xxxiii. unfold further the theme given (chap. xxviii.) in the divine foundation-stone on *Zion* and the relation of the inhabitants to it; xxxvi.-xxxix. give the application of this revelation to the great events transpiring under Hezekiah. Moreover, chaps. xxxiv. and xxxv. must not be denied to be the prophet's. They form the indispensable key-stone of his prophecy of the city of God.

As the Lord took up His abode long ago in Jerusalem, so now, in the age of the prophet, the energy of His gracious presence on Zion is at work—a power superior to all the world, and guarding

---

[1] אָמַן, *to be* or *make firm*, forms a *hiph.*, expressing firm disposition in relation to something, *firm faith* (cf. part. niph. נֶאֱמָן, *faithful, stedfast*), like the Arabic اَمِنَ; hence the LXX. rightly rendered it by πιστεύειν.

[2] See afterwards the preliminary fulfilment of the oracle of Isa. xxviii. 16, celebrated in Ps. cxviii. 22 ff. after the exile.

His own city, provided its inhabitants, especially its princes, are filled with confident faith and observe the divine law. For this reason the prophet exhorts to immovable confidence in the promise of divine protection, and protests above all against seeking refuge in the world-power (Egypt). The invisible power dwelling on Zion is the sole rock of salvation. It will prove itself all-sufficient. Although Isaiah sees in spirit the city[1] girdled by countless foes, they will come to shame before it. So xxix. 1–8. The Lord will descend, like a lion that fears not a crowd of shepherds, to fight for His holy mountain against the besieging heathen. He will hover protectingly round Jerusalem, like a bird round its brood, xxxi. 4 f. Assyria will fall by the sword, but not by that of a man (ver. 8). If Isaiah spoke so confidently even before the invasion of the Assyrians, he could do so still more boldly after the fearful danger had come home to the minds of all, inspiring wholesome terror, chap. xxxiii. The message he sent to Hezekiah on the appearance of the Assyrians before the walls of the city is told in xxxvii. 6 f., 21-35. What is meant by the protection of Yahveh and the revelation of His salvation in behalf of His chosen city, the God-trusting Hezekiah was permitted to experience in wondrous fashion, when in those days Sennacherib's army succumbed to an invisible power before Jerusalem's walls.

But as already in chap. xxviii. the unbelieving, unrighteous generation at Jerusalem was threatened with the inexorable justice of the Lord, so also this threat runs through the Hezekiah-discourses of Isaiah, becoming more and more definite in form, until finally, when the good Hezekiah also gave way to worldliness, it passed into an unambiguous prediction of the *Babylonian exile*. See xxix. 9 ff., xxx. 1 ff., xxxi. 1 ff., xxxii. 9 ff., especially xxxii. 13, 14, and finally, xxxix. 5 ff.

But it is impossible for such a judgment to be the end of God's ways in relation to His city. The divine foundation-stone on Zion was laid irrevocably and immovably. As the prophet

---

[1] אֲרִיאֵל it is called xxix. 1 f., which according to xxxi. 9 (xxxiii. 14) and Ezek. xliii. 15 f. is to be explained: *hearth* of God (not: *lion of God*); cf. Arabic ارل, to burn, whence ارل, *focus*. Jerusalem is God's *fire-place*, where His altar burns, thus His native abode.

looks (xxix. 9 ff.) on a nation blind and deaf to his glorious promises, the certainty grows on him that the Lord must deal with it in strange fashion before it will understand his revelation for its own good. But the time of conversion will come, xxix. 17 ff.

17 "Is it not yet a little, and Lebanon is turned into a fruit-garden, and the fruit-garden is esteemed a forest?
18 And in that day the deaf shall hear the words of the book, and out of obscurity and darkness the eyes of the blind shall
19 see, and the lowly shall increase in joy in Yahveh, and the poorest of men rejoice in the Holy One of Israel," etc.

A blessed transformation of the Holy Land and people is here promised. Ver. 17 (like xxxii. 15) is not a proverbial phrase to express the exalting of the low and the humbling of the high, but like xxx. 26, a prophetic hyperbole, to picture the divine fertilizing and glorifying of the land. Lebanon is changed into a fruit-bearing orchard; and what is now called an orchard will be regarded as a mere forest in view of the enhanced fertility then witnessed. But side by side with this divinely-caused metamorphosis of the land will go a corresponding one of the people. Now it is dull and unreceptive to the book of prophetic revelation, then the deaf shall hear and the blind see. And the divine mystery of salvation, to which they are then receptive, will make the lowly, the poor, the harmless, defenceless and destitute in the world, rich in joy; while the mockery of unbelief is silenced, and the oppression of injustice put down. Then God's people, seeing the work of the Lord in its midst, is saved for ever, vers. 22-24.

In this description of the removal of grievous human infirmities (where xxxii. 3 f. and xxxv. 5 f. are to be taken into account), spiritual blindness, deafness, etc., are first considered. But in these chapters, as in the similar ones in Deutero-Isaiah, physical and spiritual again pass into each other very conspicuously; in xxxv. 5 f. especially, bodily defects are not excluded.

Christ did this gracious work for His Church by opening the eyes and ears of men, that they might know God's revelation. But not only did He enlighten them spiritually, but gave living expression to this redemption of His by the bodily healings which quite specifically constituted His miraculous activity. By these miraculous deeds, which were not merely works of mercy, but in the intention of Jesus were meant to be "signs," He also in a spiritual sense opened the eyes and ears of the people that knew the Scripture, making known to them who He was: namely, He by whom God's people was to be consummated.[1] But it is important that the fulfilment should show in the work of Christ the same interblending of spiritual and physical that the prophecy does. Christ by no means brought a merely spiritual truth presented by O. T. prophecy in a more external form, but, as comparison with the present passage shows, he realized the letter of prophecy still more completely than was meant. For man is not mere spirit; if he is to be completely redeemed, he must be saved body and soul. And the God of the Bible works not merely in the ideal, invisible sphere, but just as much in the outward and real.

The "lowly and poor," who under the existing unjust government cannot get their rights, have special cause, according to Isa. xxix. 19, to exult over the revelation of the gracious God. By these is not meant merely a certain social class, but one ethically disposed in a special way to receive salvation,[2] the class of the meek and poor *in spirit*, as Matt. v. 3, 5 calls them; whilst Luke vi. 20 is content with using the O. T. phrase אֶבְיוֹנִים. Even outward poverty belongs, according to prophecy and fulfilment, to the qualities disposing favourably to God's kingdom. As Jesus performed most of His deeds on the lame and blind, so He mostly gathered His Church, to which He promised the kingdom of heaven, from the poorest of the children of men.[3] But in doing the latter, and that from the beginning of His ministry, He made known unmistakably that He had brought about that completion of God's kingdom, to which the prophets bore witness. Thus the Sermon on the Mount in its very first words is of pre-eminent Christological significance.

In Isa. xxx. 18–26 also a blessed future of Zion is promised, the range of which extends beyond the deliverance of the city

---

[1] Matt. xi. 4 f.; Luke vii. 22. In John ix. 3, Jesus declares (cf. ver. 39) what He wished to make known by the healing of the man born blind. Cf. on the symbolic meaning of the several miracles of Jesus, Steinmeyer, *The Miracles of our Lord* (Clark).

[2] On עָנָו, cf. p. 246.

[3] Cf. also 1 Kings i. 26 ff.; Jas. ii. 5 f.

from the Assyrian army first treated of. By the Lord's mercy, safety and wellbeing will follow on tribulation, when the nation has learnt to mark the teachings of revelation, and to set aside idolatry. There follows a state of peace and abundance (described as in Joel iii. 18; Hos. ii. 23, etc.), after the bulwarks of the land, on which fleshly confidence relied,[1] have fallen, and a sanguinary judgment has gone forth on its martial power:—

25 "On every high mountain and every lofty hill there shall be brooks gushing with water, on the day of the
26 great carnage, when the towers fall, and the moonlight shall be as the light of the sun, and the light of the sun shall be sevenfold as the light of seven days, on the day when Yahveh binds the breach of His people and heals its scars."

Whilst heaven and earth are thus glorified for God's purified people, according to xxx. 27 ff. the Lord comes to judge the heathen with a mighty revelation of His wrath, whereas joyous festal songs echo in Zion. As often as the rod descends on Assyria (the world-power), there drums beat and harps play.

In xxxii. 1 ff. also a bright picture is unrolled of God's future people, in which, in contrast with the present time, just rule on the part of the great and docility to God's revelation on the part of the people, form the chief features. Because things are now so utterly different, the doom of desolation and captivity must first come (vers. 9–14).

15 "Until the Spirit is poured out on us from on high, and the desert becomes a fruit-garden, and fruit-garden is
16 reckoned a forest, and right takes up its dwelling in the desert, and righteousness takes its seat in the fruit-garden;
17 and the gain of righteousness will be peace, and the wages
18 of righteousness rest and security for ever. And my people shall settle in peaceful pasture, and in secure dwellings, and cheerful resting-places."

The end then cannot be the overthrow and humbling of the Holy Land and God's city,[2] but an exalting and glorifying of the abode of God's people, such as Joel promised. The latter's prophecy of a physical and spiritual rain (Joel ii. 23, 28)

---

[1] Cf. Isa. ii. 15; Micah v. 9 f.

[2] Ver. 19, like ver. 13 f., is to be referred to Jerusalem. A protracted desolation of the city will precede the new birth from above.

explains the above passage, where the two features, the physical and the spiritual glorifying of the land, are combined as the effect of one dispensing of the Spirit. Judgment and righteousness form the soul of this landscape, in a sense possess it as inhabitants and cultivators. Hosea especially foretold this as the blessed final state (Hos. ii. 21 ff.).

Also the glorious description of Zion in chap. xxxiii., which refers primarily to the deliverances from the Assyrian crisis,[1] speaks of an imperishable glory of the city of God, that will first dawn when God has cleansed it from sin and sinners. A prelude of this the city enjoys at present, unbelieving frivolity having been banished by severity of suffering, and sinners confessing the holiness of the God who rules among them.

xxxiii. 5. "Exalted is Yahveh, for He dwells in the height, He fills Zion with judgment and righteousness. And there shall be stedfastness of thy[2] times, a store of experiences of salvation, wisdom, and knowledge; the fear of Yahveh, it is its treasure."

The cleansing that proceeds from the holy fire dwelling in the city, therefore from God revealing Himself in His holiness, according to ver. 14 will so purify the Church that it will assume the character prescribed in Ps. xxiv. Then dishonour of the king and beleaguerment are no longer known.

xxxiii. 17. "Thine eyes shall behold the King in His
20 beauty,[3] they shall look upon a land of breadths.[4] Behold Zion, the city of our assembly:[5] thine eyes shall see Jerusalem a cheerful home, a tent that wanders not, whose pegs are never drawn out, and none of its ropes are broken.
21 Rather is Yahveh there glorious for us in a place of streams, canals broad on both sides:[6] No rowing-vessel may
22 go thereon, nor any stately ship sail over it. For Yahveh is our Judge, Yahveh our Captain, Yahveh our King: He

---

[1] On the date of this oracle see the Commentary of Knobel and Diestel.

[2] The suffix, like that of אוֹיְבָי, applies to the nation.

[3] Cf. Ps. xlv. 3.

[4] A territory of broad, free expanse, in opposition to the present state of beleaguerment.

[5] Technical term for a holy festal gathering; cf. xxx. 29.

[6] Yahveh takes the place of the streams and canals guarding other great cities, especially Nineveh and Babylon. On such a stream no warship ventures. Jerusalem is therefore unapproachable by the foe.

24 will deliver us. And no inhabitant shall say: I am sick. The people settled in it is freed from guilt."[1]

Here, too, the local city of God remains the comprehensive framework for the perfect Church of the future. But its earthly character has been greatly spiritualized. It is guarded, not by walls and towers, but by the Lord Himself, who surrounds it like an impassable stream. And no inhabitant is without forgiveness, so that the sickness that is a penalty of special sin, and that so disturbs the normal course of life, no longer exists.

The revenge inflicted on the world, on all nations, and chiefly on Edom, for the injury done to Zion, is described in chap. xxxiv. It is in harmony with the unique dignity of the city of God, that the *world-judgment* comes on its account (from which it alone is spared, according to xxviii. 22); it is therefore the spiritual starting-point of God's judicial work on earth, cf. Joel iii. And this judgment is so universal that even the heavens, as belonging to the visible creation, are drawn with their starry host into sympathy.

xxxiv. 4. "And the whole army of heaven moulders away and the heaven is rolled up like a book, and all its army withers as a leaf withers from the vine and withered leaves 5 from the fig-tree. For my sword revels in heaven," etc.

The latter passage refers not to a preceding judgment of the nations, but to one on heavenly powers, as xxiv. 21 proves, to be spoken of afterwards. Chap. xxx. 26 already hinted at a new creating of the heavens.

Finally, chap. xxxv. speaks of the *return* of those banished (to Babylon) through the desert *to Zion*. Then when the Lord appears in the desert to lead His people back to Canaan, as once before, the desert shall bloom with beauty. *Then* the healing announced before of all the ills of the people will take place, ver. 5 f.; here spiritual and bodily ailments are not distinguished; *then* a sacred pilgrimage will be made to Zion, whither none that is impure journeys.

xxxv. 10. "And the redeemed of the Lord will return and come to Zion with shouting, with eternal joy on their head. They obtain gladness and joy, and lamenting and complaining have given way."

Chapters xxxiv. and xxxv. are often denied to be by the

[1] Properly "removed from guilt," *i.e.* its guilt is removed.

prophet Isaiah. In point of fact they show close affinity to Deutero-Isaiah. This, however, is not decisive, since their connection with xxviii.–xxxii. is as close as possible, and they form a necessary conclusion to the series of Isaiah's Zion-oracles. As this prophet most emphatically announced the immovableness of the city of God, and as undeniably predicted the overthrow of Jerusalem and the banishment of its inhabitants (xxxii. 11–14, xxxix. 6), his prophecy must necessarily conclude with the return of the Church of Zion and its elevation above the world.[1] Here Isaiah gave the theme which a later prophet expanded further (chaps. xl.–lxvi.), who for this very reason seemed to be no other than Isaiah himself, but in reality built on his oracles, unfolding their import, which events were beginning gloriously to confirm, before the eyes of his banished contemporaries.

§ 32. *Isaiah's Visions respecting the Nations and the Judgment of the World, as well as respecting the glorifying of the World out of Zion,* chap. xiii.–xxvii.

Between the discourses of Immanuel (from the time of Ahaz) and the oracles about Zion (from the days of Hezekiah) there is interposed in our present Book of Isaiah a collection of Isaianic oracles about foreign nations (chaps. xiii.–xxiii.). Since these for the most part only contain elements of a subordinate character for Messianic prophecy, we need not discuss the critical attacks on several of them, which are denied to be by Isaiah. Here naturally the negative side of the divine rule predominates. Judgment prepares the ground for it, going forth on all proud world-powers. But judgment also leads the heathen, as Isaiah shows, to the knowledge of the true God and even to incorporation in His kingdom. In the oracle against *Babylon* (xiii.–xiv. 23), which as we saw came within Isaiah's horizon as Judah's last and most dangerous foe, nay, conqueror, the "Day of the Lord" that will come on this world-power is described in allusion to Joel[2] as a dark judgment-day, when all the nations will fall on Babylon, above which the heavens gather blackness.

---

[1] See the literary and critical proofs in favour of the Isaianic composition of chap. xxxiv. and xxxv. in Delitzsch's Commentary (3rd ed.), p. 356 f.
[2] Cf. xiii. 6, 9 f., with Joel i. 15, ii. 1 f., 10 (Amos v. 20).

Chap. xiv. 24–27 announces to *Assyria* the judgment of the Lord of hosts, chap. xiv. 28–32 to the *Philistines*, where the imperishable and mighty future of the Davidic rule is made prominent despite the humiliations suffered under Ahaz from the Philistines (2 Chron. xxviii. 18 f.). Although the people of God are poor, they stand under God's protection. And the shattered sceptre of David will grow to unimagined strength: From the root of the serpent a basilisk will come forth, and its fruit will be a flying dragon. In the oracle against *Moab* (chaps. xv., xvi.) xvi. 1 ff. are noteworthy. Deeply humbled and sorely afflicted, Moab submits to the judge throned in David's tent, who has won its confidence and homage by humanity and righteousness; whereas the ravaging world-power only drove it to despair, since it found no help in its god against that power. Chap. xvii. pictures the visitation coming on Damascene Syria and Ephraim in alliance with it, the result of which will be that Jacob, turning its back on false gods, will again look to the Holy One of Israel. According to the remarkable oracle in chap. xviii., even the *Ethiopians*, brought to the knowledge of the true God by the impending overthrow of the greatest world-empire (Assyria), will bring gifts of homage to Mount Zion. By these presents are not meant scattered Israelites, as in Isa. lxvi. 20. The far-stretching, smooth Ethiopian people itself seems to be offered as a gift to the Lord, whereas in Zeph. iii. 10 it offers gifts.

If thus already in the oracles about Moab and Ethiopia we see God's plan to bring these heathen by the now imminent world-judgments to acknowledge His greatness, in the oracle about *Egypt* (chap. xix.) this fact comes out with wonderful clearness. There is no sufficient reason for denying this oracle to be Isaiah's, since his authorship is confirmed from every quarter.[1] The judgment falling on Egypt by Assyrian invasion is a visitation of Yahveh, the God of Judah, who foretold it (see chap. xx.), and proves Himself alone superior to the conqueror. Hence a sacred terror will come on the Egyptians at the thought of what they have witnessed:—

xix. 16. "In that day shall the Egyptians be like women and tremble and shake at the swinging of the hand of
17 Yahveh, that He swings against them, and the land of

[1] See Caspari in the *Luth. Zeitschrift*, 1841, Heft 3.

Judah shall be a terror to Egypt. As oft as one mentions it before it, it shall quake because of the decree of Yahveh of hosts that He makes concerning it. On that day shall five cities be in the land of Egypt, speaking Canaan's language and swearing to Yahveh of hosts. Ir-ra-Heres shall one of them be called. On that day an altar to Yahveh shall stand in the midst of the land of Egypt, and an obelisk on its border to Yahveh. And this¹ shall be for a sign and testimony to Yahveh of hosts in the land of Egypt; when they cry to Yahveh against oppressors, He will send a deliverer and a champion who will save them. And Yahveh makes Himself known to the Egyptians, and the Egyptians know Yahveh on that day, and they serve Him with slain-offering and meat-offering and vow vows to Yahveh and perform them. And Yahveh smites Egypt, smiting and healing, and when they turn again to Yahveh He lets Himself be entreated for them and heals them. On that day a street will run from Egypt to Assyria, and Assyria comes to Egypt and Egypt to Assyria, and Egypt serves along with Assyria.² On that day will Israel be the third to Egypt and to Assyria, a blessing in the midst of the earth, so that the Lord of hosts blesses it, saying: Blessed be thou, my people, Egypt! and the work of my hands, Assyria! and mine inheritance, Israel!"

Terror at the judgment will drive Egypt to do homage to Yahveh. The five cities speaking the language of Canaan are placed by the prophet in the north-east of the land, where many Shemites had always been settled. The friendly Israelites also will be able to settle there and serve their God undisturbed, thanks to the reverence paid to Him. One of the five is the ancient, renowned Heliopolis, otherwise called אֹן, also עִיר הַחֶרֶס, here modified into עִיר הַהֶרֶס, *city of pulling down*, as a sign that the stately sun-temples and sanctuaries there will be previously destroyed by the ravagers. Instead of these an altar dedicated to the God of Israel will stand in the centre of the land, and at its entrance obelisks will bear witness to Him. Monuments of

---

¹ These two memorials (אוֹת refers to the altar, עֵד to the obelisk) will remind the Egyptians whom they are to invoke in affliction. They will not invoke Yahveh in vain.

² אֶת cannot be taken as *nota acc.*, since it is impossible for any subjection of Egypt to Assyria to be meant. עָבְדוּ has rather the same sense as in ver. 21.

Yahveh's deeds will remind the Egyptians, from whom their plagues and deliverance came, so that in the future they may turn to Him under the oppression of foes. If they do this in penitent spirit, they will be heard by Him, just as Israel has been for centuries. He will send them a rescuer, saviour (מוֹשִׁיעַ), a deliverer of the land,[1] and so will heal the wounds He has made. On that day (*i.e.* in Isaiah's usual style : in that epoch when, as ver. 21 still more definitely says, not merely a great number of Yahveh-worshippers will dwell in Egypt, but the Egyptians themselves will serve Him in consequence of the revelation of the true God made to them), friendly intercourse will take place between the two great powers, which at present would devour each other. A nation-uniting road will invite Egypt and Assyria to visit each other, and one service will unite the rulers of the world : The service of Yahveh dwelling on Zion. Thus Israel, His favourite people, comes between the two on equal terms. If hitherto, hemmed in between and equal to neither of its mighty neighbours, it had to suffer from both, now in virtue of its divine dignity as the central-point of Yahveh's revelation it will be a source of blessing on both sides. In fulfilment of the primeval patriarchal promises[2] it will be "a blessing," *i.e.* mediator of the divine blessing ; for its God will so bless it that the gifts of salvation bestowed on it will stream from it on the countries of the earth. This is made plain in the benediction put into the mouth of Yahveh, ver. 25, in which Egypt bears the name long since given to Israel, "my people," and Assyria is called affectionately "the work of my hands," whilst Israel, in a certain sense Yahveh's mother-country on earth, is called His "inheritance" as before.

The way in which the Old Covenant puts all nations on equal footing before Yahveh is among its most wonderful features. Prophecy here gazes on the height of the New Covenant with uncovered face. When the prophet shows us the specific representatives of the world-power—Egypt, Israel's hereditary foe, and Assyria, the chief heathen foe against whom Isaiah's word had to contend—united alongside Israel in the service of Yahveh as members of a great league of peace and blessing,

---

[1] שָׁלַח is to be noticed. It is not said הָקִים, as if the Lord would raise up the deliverer from among the Egyptians themselves.

[2] Gen. xii. 2 f., xxii. 18, xxvi. 4, etc.

it would be folly to stop at the formal limits of this programme. When these deadly foes are reconciled to each other by knowledge of the true God, the whole earth has become the Lord's, and the goal is reached that was afterwards proclaimed by angel-tongues to the world: "Glory to God in the highest, peace on earth, good-will towards men!"

Whereas chaps. xxi. and xxii. threaten single judgments on certain cities and lands (Babylon, Tyre, etc.), the section chaps. xxiv.–xxvii. forms an apocalyptic whole, in which the *world-judgment*, also announced in xxviii. 22 and chap. xxxiv., especially in connection with the city of God—presents itself under every aspect to the gaze of the seer. It is not by accident that this passage stands at the close of the single oracles of judgment on the nations. It forms to these, as Delitzsch says, a grand finale, where all the trumpets of judgment peal together, proclaiming the *dies iræ, dies illa* of the whole world; while at the same time the salvation issuing from God's kingdom even for the heathen under judgment is here unveiled in the most glorious manner. On account of the universal character and lofty ideal tenor of this prophecy its historic basis is less clearly seen than in the Isaianic oracles previously considered. The critics also refuse to ascribe this brilliant vision to the great prophet in whose book it is found, assigning it to the most various periods. We cannot follow them in such a course. Apart from the many formal references to Isaiah's prophecy, we hold, with Maspero,[1] that the Assyrian invasion under Sennacherib forms the historical scenery to xxiv. 1 ff. Those movements of the Assyrian empire exhibited a more comprehensive sweep than any former conflicts of the nations. Hence here the Day of the Lord, when He reckons with all, presents itself before the prophet's gaze. Certainly we cannot think, with Gesenius, Knobel, and the majority, that הָאָרֶץ in this section (vers. 1, 3, 4, 5, etc.) refers to the land of Judah. Such a view should have been precluded by the parallel תֵּבֵל of ver. 4. Ver. 5 also refers to earth-dwellers generally, because they have changed the divine commands and laws, broken the eternal ordinances. These expressions, intentionally general, point to the statutes embodied in primitive tradition and hallowed by their age and divine origin, to which even the conscience of the heathen bears witness (Rom. ii. 14 f.). The judgment of God

[1] *Geschichte der morgenländischen Völker*, 1877, p. 402.

comes on the heathen, because they have forsaken and violated this moral basis of their existence. Therefore not merely particular lands are affected by the catastrophe, but all are ravaged, depopulated, and judged, until only a remnant of inhabitants exists (ver. 13). Nay, the judgment is so universal that it moves even the heavenly hosts to sympathy. Not merely does the earth reel as a drunken man, but it is said at last:—

xxiv. 21. "And it shall come to pass, on that day Yahveh will visit the host of the heights on high, and the kings of
22 the earth on the ground. And they are confined, as captives are confined[1] in prison, and shut up in custody and visited
23 after many days. And the moon blushes and the sun grows pale, for Yahveh of hosts becomes King on Mount Zion and in Jerusalem, and before His elders is glory."

Thus the heavenly powers are judged like the earthly. It is clearly supramundane beings that are here contemplated, not, however, in their divine, but in their creaturely aspect. They form a portion of the world related to man, as the firmament with its stars to the earth. As creaturely beings they are not faultless in God's sight (Job iv. 18). Nay, perhaps a connection exists between them and the sinful powers of earth; hence they are judged together. Such a connection is at least apparent in the Book of Daniel. In the present passage, as in chap. xxxiv., where (ver. 4) the visible host of heaven, the stars, are meant, while in ver. 5a living powers also are hinted at, the emphasis lies simply on the fact that the whole sphere of creation is affected by the judgment, the highest powers being humbled and indicted like common criminals. After long waiting they receive their sentence, which is pronounced on them by the God throned in Zion and His glorious judicial assembly. Sun and moon lose their brightness in token of the divine displeasure. The opposite befalls the saved Church of Zion, according to xxx. 26.

But as the storms falling on Israel in the Assyrian period, the first of a really world-historical character, were in our opinion the occasion of Isaiah's painting at full length the Day of the Lord on all nations in the train of Joel's hints, so at the same time the preserving of Zion in that tempest promised by the same prophet, the wonderful deliverance of the sanctuary from the flood of the

---

[1] We should expect אֱסֹפָה to be in the *status constr.*, but in the case of a verbal noun the object may also stand in the accusative.

heathen, and the honour done it by the heathen nations on this account, became to him the pledge of a far higher and more glorious preserving of the Church and unfolding of the kingdom of God from Zion. Chap. xxv. 4 speaks of the preserving of the poor people of God (cf. iv. 6), ver. 6 ff. of the unspeakably rich salvation to be prepared for all nations on Zion after it has outlived the judgment:—

xxv. 6. "And Yahveh of hosts prepares for all nations in this mountain a feast of fat morsels, a feast of wines of strength,[1] of fat morsels full of marrow,[2] of wines of strength that have
7 been refined. And He destroys in this mountain the extended veil veiling all nations,[3] and the covering with which all the
8 heathen are covered. He swallows up death for ever, and the Lord, Yahveh, will wipe away the tear from every countenance, and make the shame of His people depart from the earth, for Yahveh has spoken it."

The Lord prepares a joyous banquet for all nations in Zion, where He entertains them sumptuously. The rhythm of the sixth verse sounds like accompanying music. The surprise is truly divine. At a stroke the Lord takes away the covering that has too long veiled the eyes of the nations,[4] so that they knew not Him, their God, and saw not what belonged to their peace. When this veil falls, they see themselves invited to the divine feast in the city they had despised and abused. Although the covering was not without fault on their part, still their eyes being holden implies a certain excuse for their conduct. God will suddenly and entirely remove this covering, and in consequence they will know Him as the author of life and grace. This is implied in the feast prepared by the Lord in His temple. It is a sacrificial feast (like the שְׁלָמִים), at which the Lord entertains men, and thus expresses the fellowship into which the Lord admits them by

---

[1] שְׁמָרִים, properly *dregs*, here *wine of dregs*, i.e. wine left on the dregs to give it greater strength and colour. Afterwards it was filtered.

[2] מְמֻחָיִם instead of מְמֻחִים for the sake of the rhythm; cf. Gesenius, *Gram.* § 93, 3, note 3. The force of the *piel* (or *pual*) here is not privative: "deprived of strength," but "endowed with strength."

[3] פְּנֵי הַלּוֹט. The word פָּנִים here, as in פְּנֵי הָאָרֶץ, applies to a broadly extending surface, namely, that of the veil spread over the nations. The second הַלּוֹט stands for הַלָּט for the sake of the rhythm, Gesen. *Gram.* § 72, 1.

[4] Cf. the similar covering over Israel, 2 Cor. iii. 15.

His bestowal of grace. The teaching of Christ also avails itself in word and symbolic action of this idea of a banquet to portray the communication of salvation, of life through God and in God.

Ver. 8 adds a further glorious trait. Just as energetically and thoroughly as He abolishes the covering of ignorance, does the Lord abolish *death* and all the sorrow condensed and culminating in death, everything finding expression in tears, therefore all sorrow and suffering. Complaining comes to an end for ever. Accordingly, in the time of consummation even the curse is abolished that burdens the entire human race, making mortality part of its nature (Gen. iii.). The power of sin and consequently of death is altogether set aside. Here again Isaiah's prophecy sees with certain gaze the final goal of God's dealings with humanity, a goal the path to which has been revealed in the New Covenant, but which has not been reached even yet, a fact the apostle confirms, citing (1 Cor. xv. 54) this passage before Hos. xiii. 14 to show what is still lacking to a blessed consummation.[1] Death is abolished (xv. 26) as the last foe, who has ruled over humanity from the beginning. Rev. xxi. 4 is in perfect harmony with this teaching.

What distinguishes this prophecy is the synthesis of two views hitherto found apart: Judgment on the heathen, and their introduction into God's kingdom. It was intimated and prepared for by what was announced in detail respecting Moab (xvi.), Ethiopia (xviii.), and especially Egypt along with Assyria (xix.). Of the whole heathen world we now hear that it will be sifted by judgment until only a remnant is left, but that this remnant will be brought to reflection by judgment and healed of its blindness by the Lord's gracious revelation on Zion. Thus two stages of divine knowledge are described, corresponding to the law and the gospel. Every nation that has rejected the teaching of the divine law given to it (xxiv. 5) must first pass through the judgment so fearfully carried out in the world's history, before the grace of God is revealed to it, the invitation to the divine banquet and fellowship. Every nation must first attain knowledge of the righteous God through a certain legal discipline, before it can be received into full communion of salvation and spirit with the holy God; cf. xxvi. 2, 9 f.

---

[1] Κατεπόθι ὁ θάνατος εἰς νῖκος, Paul translates freely and independently, taking נצח in the Aramaic signification "victory." Cf. v. Orelli, *Synonyma der Zeit und Ewigkeit*, p. 95 ff.

The hymn (chap. xxvi.) pictures Zion with indestructible walls, to whose gates the nation of the just and upright journeys. Its inhabitants have again become numerous. The sufferings it has endured are forgotten. But one thing is still wanting to the Church. Death, indeed, no longer thins its ranks, xxv. 8. But it *has* thinned them; it has swallowed up many of the faithful (xxvi. 14), who did not deserve the universal lot of death. Hence amid its devout prayer the Church confidently exclaims:—

xxvi. 19. "Thy dead ones become alive, my corpses will rise again! Wake up and exult, ye that dwell in the dust! For thy dew is dew of the lights, and the earth will spontaneously give up the shades."

"*Thy* dead ones" are God's dead ones (Böttcher, Oehler), who sleep in Him, and for this reason may also be called by the true Church "*my* dead ones." They are not given over to destruction (ver. 14), for their God is a God of life. This is expressed by the poetic and mysterious "dew of the lights is thy dew." The dew is God's fertilizing gift from heaven, eliciting the riches of the earth. Here the quickening energy that issues from Him is called with special emphasis "dew of the lights," to remind of its heavenly origin and miraculous operation. Coming down from the lights of heaven, which as such are viewed in close relation to life, God's energy bedews the earth, so that the earth in consequence gives forth the shades, *i.e.*, the souls of the departed which it hides. God, "the Father of lights" (Jas. i. 17), is also the giver of every good gift, and especially of life that is in affinity to light. God's miraculous, life-giving energy is security that *His* dead ones will rise again.

We see that as deliverance from death is necessary to perfected fellowship with God (xxv. 8), so the return of those already swallowed up by death is necessary to the perfecting of God's Church. This is definitely and clearly the sense of this prophecy of Isaiah. Whereas in the passage of Hosea formerly considered (vi. 2) and Ezek. xxxvii. the resurrection can only be taken improperly as a quickening of the aggregate of the Church, without any rising of its buried members being thought of; here plainly enough the reference is to the dwellers in the dust, whom the earth has swallowed up, but must again restore.[1]

---

[1] הִפִּיל, properly *to cast*, used also in other languages at least of animals. Cf. the *kal* in the corresponding sense, ver. 18.

Looking back on Isaiah's oracles, we see that on the basis given in the former prophets, from the foundation-laying in David's age, the building has gone vigorously on. Through the humbling of Israel and the judgment of the world the path will lead to the establishment of a divine rule, having the converted nation for its mother-Church, Zion for its local centre, and a unique scion of David's house for its personal mediator, and not merely subduing all nations, but also making them partakers in its divine blessings and saving privileges. *Psalm* lxxxvii., a song of the children of Korah, is like an echo, issuing from the Church, of Isaiah's prophecy of the universal extension of God's kingdom. Zion is addressed in it:—

Ps. lxxxvii. 3. "Glorious things are spoken about thee, thou
4 city of God. 'I will name Rahab and Babylon as those who know me, behold, Philistia and Tyre along with Cush—this
5 one is born there.' And to Zion it will be said: 'Each one[1] is born in her,' and he himself upholds her, the Most
6 High; Yahveh will count, when registering the nations:
7 'This one was born there,' while they sing as in chorus: 'All my springs are in thee.'"[2]

According to the correct interpretation given by Delitzsch and Hupfeld (the latter except in ver. 7), this song sung in honour of *Zion* declares, that it will be the mother city of all nations. God will mention Rahab (that is, Egypt, Isa. xxx. 7) and Babylon as numbered among those acquainted with him, will say of Philistia, Tyrus, Cush: "This one is born there," namely, in Zion, the residence of Yahveh. Thus "man by man," *i.e.* here nation by nation (for in ver. 4 also the nations are personified), they will be considered as natives of Zion. When the Lord registers His subjects He will enter them as springing thence. And they will confess exultingly that all their life-springs are in this city. The ever-recurring "This one was born there" intimates that the nations will not only receive citizenship there as belonging to Zion, but that they will receive there a new existence, experi-

[1] Cf. Esth. i. 8.

[2] חֹלְלִים from חוּל, thus *part. pil.* for מְחֹלְלִים. In מַעְיָנַי the pointing is not to be changed, as Hupfeld supposes: מְעִינַי (or מְעִינָי, *my indwellers*), by which he obtains the meaning: "All that dwell in thee sing and spring." For this שֹׁכְנֵי must have been used. According to the usual reading, the main thought recurs at the close with much more emphasis, and, indeed, now as a thankful confession.

ence a new birth. The divine springs flowing in the city (ver. 7) impart to them a new life (cf. Isa. xii. 3), so that henceforth with joy they ascribe their origin to the place whence they have received salvation.

§ 33. *Micah, Nahum.*

Another Jewish prophet, *Micah* the Morasthite, was at work, contemporaneously to some extent with Isaiah (note A).

As Isaiah foretold the judgment of exile and devastation on Judah-Jerusalem in the most definite terms, so his younger contemporary Micah still more definitely predicted the desolation of Zion with its temple, iii. 12; cf. iv. 10. But are the great outlooks opened in prophecy before this place to be regarded on this account as wishes, pious indeed, but far too bold? On the contrary, Micah makes the boldest oracle of Isaiah follow directly on the unmistakable sentence of punishment just mentioned, in token that he was not merely, like that great prophet, a servant of a higher Lord, but that the path to the exalting and glorifying of the temple lay right through the destruction foretold.[1]

Like Isaiah, but in greater detail, he adds an exhortation to his people to walk in the name, *i.e.* in the light of the revelation, of its God. Then its captives and its dominion will return in due time.

Micah iv. 6. "On that day, saith the Lord, I will gather that which limps,[2] and that which is cast out I will collect, and
7 that which I treated ill. And I make that which limps a remnant, and that which is far removed[3] a great nation, and Yahveh will be king over them on Mount Zion henceforth
8 and for ever; and thou, tower of flocks, hill of the daughter of Zion, to thee will it come,[4] and the former

---

[1] This judgment is represented (i. 3 ff.) as a descent of God from heaven, a parousia analogous to the one at Sinai, to which appearance also the prophetic picture of Hab. iii. 3 ff. (besides Judg. v. 4 f.; Ps. xviii. 9 ff.) alludes.

[2] *That which limps, is cast out,* etc., stands collectively, not of a single sheep.

[3] הַנַּהֲלָאָה, peculiar *niphal* formation from הָלָא (Amos v. 27): *that which is thrown far away*; thus the הַנִּדָּחָה above recurs in a stronger form.

[4] From the accentuation (*athnach* with תֵּאתֶה) it has been erroneously inferred that בַּת־צִיּוֹן is the subject of this verb. This is rather found in the second half of the verse. Luther: "Thy golden rose shall come," thinking of עֶדְיֵךְ, *ornaments*.

sovereignty will come, the kingdom to the daughter of Zion."[1]

"*On that day*" points with emphasis to the epoch described in ver. 1 as the end of the days. In this indication of time lies the difference between a divine oracle and the otherwise similar talk of false prophets, ii. 11 f.[2] What carnal hope expects prematurely comes only, according to God's word, at the end after purifying judgment. The human heart is always inclined to forestall the glorifying and ignore the judgment of the world. Also the " henceforth " (מֵעַתָּה at the end of ver. 7) refers, of course, not to the present, but to that time contemplated prophetically (יוֹם הַהוּא).

With ver. 8, as with v. 2, a new paragraph begins. If iv. 1 ff. referred to Zion as the seat of the temple, ver. 8 f. contemplates David's citadel on Zion, the Davidic rule (v. 2 ff.), and again still more distinctively the true Davidite. The Tower of flocks here is the local representative of the Davidic sovereignty, and belonged presumably to David's stronghold on Zion. " Hill " of the daughter of Zion is perhaps added to distinguish it from other towers of this name.[3] Moreover, this עֹפֶל was a conventional proper-name of a particular height on Zion (probably on the south-east edge). This royal residence will again behold the former glory of David and Solomon, of course not in the immediate future. On the contrary there await it, as vers. 9 ff. describe, pure anguish and pain, beleaguerment, deportation to Babylon, profound humiliation of the ruling house. But these are the pains of a travailing woman, and so not without fruit. Out of all these sufferings the future glory will grow, such as is shown in v. 2 to ver. 5a in a more definite and personal Messianic prophecy.

v. 2. "And thou, Bethlehem Ephratah,[4] small to be counted

---

[1] Not: *upon the daughter of Jerusalem* (Hitzig, after Num. xxii. 4), but according to Zech. ix. 9, which the passage resembles, לְ here indicates direction.

[2] Like Hofmann, Kleinert, *et al.*, we believe, in opposition to most expositors, that ii. 11 f. describes how the false prophets, audaciously copying oracles like Hos. i. 11 ff., promise speedy victory to the people. On the other hand, Hitzig would put ii. 11 f. after iv. 8.

[3] Gen. xxxv. 21.

[4] אֶפְרָת, "fruitfulness, fruit-field," agrees with the appellation בֵּית לֶחֶם, *house of bread*, as well as with the fertile situation of the village in barren surroundings (v. Orelli, *Durch's hei'ige Land*, 2nd ed. p. 154). The forms Ephrath and Ephratah

(note B) among the country-towns of Judah, out of thee comes forth to me [1] he who is to be a ruler in Israel. And his goings forth are from the foretime, from days immemorial.
3 On this account he gives them up until the time when she that travaileth has brought forth, then will the remnant of his
4 brethren return to the sons of Israel. And he stands and pastures in the might of Yahveh, in the majesty of the name of Yahveh, his God, and they have rest, for now [2] will he be
5 great unto the ends of the earth. And he shall be PEACE."

The וְאַתָּה, v. 2, corresponds to the וְאַתָּה, iv. 8. Alongside the Tower of Flocks, the proof of Davidic glory, appears the place of Davidic lowliness, that had seen a shepherd's son rise to a throne. For a Son of Jesse will again traverse the path from obscure lowliness to lofty glory. Out of Bethlehem, with scarcely the rank of a country-town, will come forth One whose name is here mysteriously suppressed, only the dignity that awaits him being mentioned. He it is who is destined in God's plan to be ruler in Israel. The name of the entire people, whom, like David, he is to unite under his sceptre, is intentionally used. Moreover, the next mysterious feature forms a significant contrast to the obscure birthplace of the Messiah: "His going forth from the gray foretime, from days immemorial." Does this only mean that His extraction is traceable to the earliest age, that He is thus of good race, as in fact (Ruth iv. 11 ff.) David's ancestors are traced back to Perez, son of Judah? Although it must be conceded that עוֹלָם in poetico-prophetic discourse has not always an unlimited range (cf. Amos ix. 11), it would yield here a very tame sense, especially to the Hebrew, to think only of physical descent from Jesse the humble ancestor, or from Judah. The descent of every genuine Israelite even from Jacob-Abraham was understood as matter of course. Or does this weighty description, containing a twofold, far-reaching definition of time, teach the pre-temporal existence of the Messiah, so that we should have here, as in John i. 1 ff., viii. 58, an irrefutable testimony to Christ's pre-existence? The

---

are found Gen. xlviii. 7 ; cf. xxxv. 19. But there the ה— indicates direction. On the other hand, in the present passage the second, more solemn form stands absolutely, as in Ruth iv. 11.

[1] The saying: "will come forth *to me*," implies that he comes to fulfil a divine plan.
[2] The reference to Ps. ii. 7, lxxii. 7, here is beyond doubt. What in that passage was still ideal has now become reality.

expressions קֶדֶם, עוֹלָם, and the general conceptions of the Israelites, are too little metaphysical to warrant such an inference. Moreover, strictly speaking, a premundane existence is not affirmed, but a coming from time immemorial. In Micah vii. 20, קדם is used in reference to the patriarchal promises. We therefore do most justice to the statement by taking it to mean that the future ruler from Bethlehem is he who has long been in God's view in the development of things. Because from the beginning of redemption everything tended to him, he was in course of coming from the beginning. His beginnings are rooted in God's primeval redeeming plan. The prophet is thinking not merely of pedigrees of genealogy, but just as much of those of prophecy. We agree with Hofmann when he remarks: "The ruler who at last will come forth from Bethlehem proceeds and is in course of coming from times of inconceivable length. For since it is he who is the goal of the history of humanity, of Israel, of the Davidic house, all advances in that history are beginnings of His coming, goings forth of the second son of Jesse." That our prophet usually takes into view the whole history of God's redemption and kingdom back to the early period of preparation of which Genesis treats, is shown, for example, in v. 6; cf. iv. 10. The fulfilment, indeed, has carried still farther this coming from of old, this going forth from the beginnings of history, disclosing the supramundane and premundane origin of the Messiah beyond primeval history, and in this way discovering the profoundest reason of the fact that the whole history of creation tends towards Him.

To the features literally realized in the fulfilment belongs also the rise of the Messiah out of Bethlehem, a fact which Matthew emphasizes with perfect right (ii. 6). This is not the place to discuss the credibility of the account of the birth of Jesus in David's city. On the other hand, we must differ from Hitzig when he denies that the prophet thought that the Messiah would be born in Bethlehem. The prophet sees the glorious Prince of Peace issuing, not out of David's stronghold on Zion, but out of the obscure shepherd-town, from which the first David was called by God to the throne. And we have no right to convert this vivid intuition into an abstract thought, as if such a thought were the *prius* to the seer, and the concrete form in his consciousness a mere dress. The fact that he did not see the thought of the supreme ruler's ascent from the obscurest lowliness otherwise than in and with the local form in which it was realized, is a proof, to those who do not ascribe everything to the arbitrary fetish of chance, of the express control of God.

Therefore, ver. 3 proceeds, because the coming of the true ruler over Israel is still future, the casting away of this people can only be temporary, continuing up to the definite point of time when its grievous sufferings issue in a blissful birth. According to the connection with vers. 2 and 4, he who is born to bring the suffering to an end can only be the ruler from Bethlehem. But who is the travailing mother? Since iv. 9 f. speaks of the pains of Zion, and in v. 3 even the dispersed Israelites are called the brethren of the Messiah (to whom the suffix in אֶחָיו points back), it is intimated that the Church, at present in grievous affliction and expecting still more grievous, is to be regarded as his mother; and with this Hos. xiii. 13 and Isa. vii. 14, according to our interpretation, agree.[1]

The fact that then even the remnant found among the heathen returns, shows how what is said in iv. 6 f. is brought about by the Messiah, whose rule is further described in v. 4: Divine power and gentleness are united in Him. "He stands and *pastures* in the power of Yahveh, in the majesty of the name of Yahveh." The expression "He pastures," without the addition given to it in Ps. ii. (בְּשֵׁבֶט בַּרְזֶל), is uncommonly peaceful in sound. He will be altogether a shepherd, a prince from Bethlehem, even as His ancestor grew up amid the flock. Yet He is strong and beautiful with the divine glory, the majesty of the name of Yahveh. Thus in Him the Lord reveals Himself in His essence. Then will His people "be settled," enjoy rest; for His greatness is then acknowledged over the whole earth; cf. Ps. ii. 8, what David there says virtually of himself will be realized in the Messiah; only that in the present passage the peaceful side of His rule, there the terrible side towards rebellious princes and nations, comes into view.

It is said, in the last place: *And He shall be peace.* This puts the seal on the description of the Son of David. He is *peace, i.e.* peace is concluded in Him, so that not only does His coming bring peace on earth, but His whole being is peaceful, and works peace. He is thus the means by which that pacification of the world is effected which was spoken of in iv. 3 ff. as a divine

---

[1] So after Calvin many moderns, like Kleinert.

work. Such a word as שָׁלוֹם is capable of unlimited intensification, and has found it in the Bible. Only the completed revelation has disclosed all its depths of meaning. In the Hebrew language שלום was an everyday word, a common greeting, a trivial wish. It denoted whatever any one desired for himself and wished for any one with whom he was on good terms: freedom from harm and disturbance, peace, rest, wellbeing. Among the peace-loving Orientals peace was and is, in the profane sphere of thought, the highest good. And in the religious life the sum of salvation may be comprised in it. When prophecy promises peace in the time of consummation, and calls the Messiah Peace absolutely, it means peace in inner and outer perfection, man being completely at one with God, and men having become through His revelation one with each other. This will be the Messiah's gift. Such peace, in fact, the Prince of Peace from Bethlehem brought to the world, only far more gloriously than human heart could conceive under the Old Covenant. And in the sense in which He established peace, it is also the highest good to the Christian. Hence everything we have in Christ may be summed up in the word borrowed by the apostle from our prophet: $αὐτός ἐστιν ἡ εἰρήνη ἡμῶν$ (Eph. ii. 14).

Even in this prophet, who so strongly emphasizes the peaceful character of God's kingdom, there is not wanting at the same time a warlike picture of the superiority which the Messianic Zion will display among the nations. Already in iv. 11 ff. Micah foretells the judgment of the nations: According to the Lord's plan (Joel iii. 1 ff.), the heathen will assemble against Jerusalem to desecrate the holy city, but will be gathered there like sheaves on the threshing-floor to be threshed.[1]

iv. 13. "Arise and thresh, O daughter of Zion; I will make thy horn iron and thy hoofs brass, that thou mayest crush to pieces many nations; and I consecrate their spoil to Yahveh, and their property to the Lord of all the earth."

A type of this final catastrophe to the heathen was given in the fall of the Assyrian army before Jerusalem. Also in v. 5 ff., where in a similar way the victorious might of God's people is seen by Micah, it is the Assyrian, the mighty world-conqueror, who first passes before him. Seven, nay, eight victorious princes will encounter him, and they will waste his land

[1] Cf. the harvest figure, Joel iii. 9 ff.

with the sword. The power of feeble Israel will thus be sevenfold superior.[1] And in v. 8, 9 f. again the double aspect of God's kingdom comes out, its human form, the Israelitish Church, being compared, on the one hand, to the fruitful dew, and on the other, to the most terrible beast of prey. Under both aspects the world of nations will come to know the people of God.

> v. 7. "And the remnant of Jacob shall be amid many nations as the dew from Yahveh, as dropping rain on the grass, that 8 waits for no one, and tarries not for children of men.[2] And the remnant of Jacob shall be amid many nations as a lion among the forest beasts, as a lion among the flocks of sheep," etc.

The first of these figures, viz. the dew, suggests not merely the idea of countless numbers, but also, as in the second figure, the effect produced (which certainly here is exceedingly beneficent), and at the same time the idea of higher origin. As the dew falls from heaven without being dependent on any man, so God's people comes on the world as a blessing of unworldly origin, and also with the irresistible power peculiar to the kingly lion above all beasts. If a sufficient corrective to the carnal and sensuous view of vers. 8 and 9 were not contained in iv. 1 ff., v. 2 ff., it would be found immediately in ver. 10, where, as we found in Zech. ix. 10, the setting aside of martial power is foretold (pp. 245, 247). Even the strong cities, in which false confidence had hitherto been placed, will vanish, for the Lord Himself will be the bulwark of His people (Zech. ix. 8). But before that time comes (vii. 11) Jerusalem must undergo judgment; and before the nations draw near to do homage to the Lord mighty judgments will fall upon them, vii. 12 ff., such as befell Egypt, so that trembling with terror and dumb with shame (vers. 16, 17), they will at last come to do reverence to the true God. Thus here also, as in Isaiah, the path of Israel, as of the heathen world, lies through judgment to salvation and peace.

The oracle of *Nahum* the Elkoshite takes us to the close of the Assyrian period. It also was spoken under King Hezekiah,

---

[1] The number seven is again transcended, after the manner of oracles of number (Amos ii. 1, etc.), by eight.

[2] This is not to be inverted, as if it meant: "For which no one waits," as though the unexpected, unhoped-for coming of the dew were meant; but: "The coming of the dew is dependent on no man," whereas conversely the children of men are very dependent on its coming and await it with anxiety.

but after Sennacherib's departure; in any case, before the fall of Nineveh, against which it is directed. Still, filled with indignation at all the outrage the Assyrians had inflicted on the land, the prophet foretells, in the name of the God who is jealous for His inheritance, the approaching overthrow of the imperial city. The obverse of this judgment is comfort for God's people, who hitherto could not keep their feasts without trembling before the overwhelming foe. Hence the good news of its fall is heard in Jerusalem with rapture. This evangel is indeed chiefly negative, banishing anxiety and solicitude in presence of the world-power. Paul has applied the oracle, Nah. ii. 1, to a far more positive message of peace. But see also Isa. lii. 7.

NOTE A.—According to the heading, Micah's work likewise belongs to the time of Kings Jotham, Ahaz, and Hezekiah. The latter date is confirmed by Jer. xxvi. 18; for when Jeremiah was accused of high treason in foretelling the fall of Jerusalem and the temple, the elders defended him by appealing to Micah's example, who, under Hezekiah, had done the same without molestation. There Micah iii. 12 is plainly alluded to; but to make the passage in Jeremiah a strict proof that the discourse of Micah iii. was composed under Hezekiah is to attribute too great critical value to it. In any case Micah spoke in great part before the fall of Samaria (cf. especially chap. i.). But after a long term of labour he put his oracles together in book form, so that they read like a work struck off at one blow (especially chaps. ii.–v.).

In Micah we find (iv. 1-4) almost literally the same oracle of the exalting of Mount Zion and the peaceful pilgrimage of the nations thither, that we read in Isa. ii. 2 ff. Only, at the end Micah has an addition (ver. 4): "And they shall sit, every one under his vine and his fig-tree, none frightening them; for the mouth of Yahveh of hosts has spoken it."

This second form of the oracle is held by many to be the original one (Hitzig, Caspari, Keil, etc.). They appeal especially to the fact that the oracle is not disconnected from the context as in Isaiah. This would imply that Micah spoke under Jotham, and Isaiah borrowed from him (Caspari,[1] Keil). This, however, having little probability, since the historical horizon in the context of Micah is that of the latest prophecies of Isaiah [2] (e.g. xxxix. 6 f.), others suppose that the oracle springs from an earlier prophet (Hitzig, Ewald: Joel), and was reproduced by Isaiah and afterwards by Micah (by the latter more faithfully). This hypothesis deserves notice, but

---

[1] C. P. Caspari, *Ueber Micha den Morasthiten und seine prophetische Schrift*, 1851.
[2] Cf. also Jer. xxvi. 18 ("in the days of Hezekiah") with Micah iii. 12.

is neither capable of proof nor necessary to explain the facts. That Micah repeats an oracle already given, he perhaps intimates in the sentence: "For the mouth of the Lord hath spoken it." But he has rounded off the oracle and woven it into his book with most beautiful antithesis. On the other hand, there seems to us no cogent reason for refusing to assign it to Isaiah, who sets it before us abruptly in the manner of a divine vision suddenly received.[1]

NOTE B.—צָעִיר, *masc.*, referring to בֵית, is usually taken as predicate; but then we should expect צָעִיר אַתָּה and a copula before מִמְּךָ. It is rather in apposition to the apostrophe, so that the sentence proper only begins with מִמְּךָ. Hitzig requires the article הַצָּעִיר, and takes over the ה from אֶפְרָתָה. But לִהְיוֹת does not rightly suit such determination of the adjective. Nor is the article necessary in such a qualitative apposition. For the rest, it is not said מִהְיוֹת: *too small to be able*. Bethlehem was really the centre of an אֶלֶף, the seat of an אַלּוּף, *country prince* (Zech. ix. 7, xii. 5 f.), but small even for this subordinate position, as we say: *small for a kingdom*. Matthew cites (ii. 6), with some deviation from the LXX.: καὶ σὺ Βηθλεέμ γῆ Ἰούδα οὐδαμῶς ἐλαχίστη εἶ ἐν τοῖς ἡγεμόσιν Ἰούδα, ἐκ σοῦ γὰρ ἐξελεύσεται, which is not essentially different from the original text.

[1] B. Stade (*Zeitschr. für A. T. Wft.* 1881, i. p. 161 ff.) would also assign the grand oracles, Micah iv. 1-4, 11-14, v. 2-4, 7-15, to a post-exilian "epigon," and affirms that hereafter Micah of Moresheth, Isaiah's contemporary, has no rôle to play in the history of the Messianic idea! No wonder if by such epigon-like abuse of the most venerable writings even lawful criticism falls into discredit.

FOURTH SECTION.

THE PROPHETS OF THE DECLINE (CHALDÆAN PERIOD): ZEPHANIAH, HABAKKUK, JEREMIAH.

§ 34. *Zephaniah.*

THE prophets who come next, of whom Jeremiah is chief, differ in a marked way from those considered in the last section, of whom Isaiah is the chief representative. If the latter sketched a brilliant picture of the ruler growing up from Jesse's root, now that picture, as well as the figure of Jerusalem preserved and glorified, retires again into the background. Scarcely any room is left for language of promise, since even Judah, to which comfort might still be offered in the Assyrian period, is now advancing rapidly to the Chaldæan judgment, and the prophets themselves are forced to deny it all hope for the nearer future. Yet the age gives all the more occasion for a new proclaiming of the world-judgment. The Day of the Lord is pictured. And in the same way confident hopes of a glorious end are afresh promised to the remnant of Judah, and the narrow way of repentance and humble trust is pointed out to it. The conception of the city of God is spiritualized and refined in the fires of judgment.

Zephaniah, whose tractate, according to the unimpeachable heading, belongs to the period of Josiah (note A), is among the most eloquent heralds who announce the Day of the Lord as the day of general reckoning, such as Joel already more precisely described. But Zephaniah emphasizes far more strongly than Joel the universality of the judgment, foretelling the conversion of the nations as its salutary fruit. In this twofold respect he has a place beside Isaiah, whose oracles[1] he to some extent

---

[1] So especially the oracles discussed in § 32, Isa. xiii., xxiv.-xxvii., also chap. xxxiv.

guards against the criticism of to-day, not merely by points of contact in words, but by coincidence in the main thoughts, which are thus shown to be the fruit of the Assyrian period.

Zephaniah forms a transition from the Assyrian to the Chaldæan period, still like Nahum threatening Nineveh (ii. 13 ff.), (which consequently has not yet succumbed to the Chaldæans), but having new foes in view and no longer able to promise Jerusalem gracious preservation. As on the appearance of this prophet everything within the land lies in the wicked one, so also near movements announce themselves to the prophet's gaze in the world of nations, movements going beyond ordinary limits and preparing for a general divine judgment. It has been rightly remarked that about this time the Scythians were moving from the north through Hither-Asia towards Egypt.[1] These northern barbarians, grazing the borders of Palestine, made a deep impression on the Israelites, as we see from Jeremiah, and especially from Ezekiel's description of "Gog from the land of Magog," taken line by line from those hordes. The Scythians treated the Philistine country at that time with special harshness. The rapid fulfilment in this way of Zephaniah's threats against these cities may have founded or greatly enhanced his reputation. But he has far more comprehensive events in view. He begins his oracles at once with the saying (i. 2 f.):—

"I will carry away, sweep away[2] *everything* from the surface of the earth—is the oracle of the Lord; will carry away man and beast, carry away the birds of the heaven and the fish of the sea, the ruins[3] along with the evil-doers, and exterminate the men from the surface of the earth! is the oracle of the Lord."

כֹּל stands first with emphasis: "Everything,"—more fully illustrated by the following words, where man (just as universal) comes first as the real sinner, on whose account judgment goes forth on every earthly creature. To him, as the chief object in view, ver. 3 recurs. But it is especially surprising that ver. 4

---

[1] Herodotus, i. 103 ff.

[2] With אָסֵף (*hiph.* from סוּף) is joined the infin. abs. אָסֹף, akin in sense and derivation, for the sake of the fuller rhythm. Just so Jer. viii. 13. Böttcher, *Ausf. Lehrbuch*, § 988, 1.

[3] הַמַּכְשֵׁלוֹת, not synonymous with מִכְשׁוֹל, σκάνδαλον, in which case it would have applied to the idols, but according to Isa. iii. 6: *tottering ruins*. All dwellings are mere tumbling ruins, which God easily sweeps away along with those dwelling in them.

turns specifically against Jerusalem, which is therefore not spared, on the contrary is first smitten by the judgment, and that without exception. Both those who practise heathen worship (Baal-worship, star-worship, etc.) without shame, and those who carry the holy name of Yahveh on their lips, fall a prey to judgment. Consequently, alongside the dwellers of the city engaged in heathen practices without disguise, there were those who at least maintained the name and ritual system of the Old Covenant-God, thus securing for themselves some good. But between the two parties, who in appearance differed to some extent from each other, the prophet can scarcely make a difference. His words show that God cannot be bribed by such partisanship in His cause, and the genuine prophet has to announce the judgment with equal severity to all parties, even to those who would fain stand well with the true God, if the service of God and the life of true holiness are wanting.

Already the Judge approaches, before whom the whole world must be dumb with reverence :—

i. 7. "Be still before Yahveh, Lord of all! For the day of Yahveh is near! For Yahveh has prepared a slain-sacrifice, has hallowed His invited ones."

This passage, alluding to Isa. xiii. 3, speaks of the judgment-day as a sacrificial feast, where blood will flow copiously. The sacrifice is already prepared; the invited guests are ready, or as it is said in sacrificial language, hallowed. These guests are the wild foes whom the Lord will summon against His people. The people are the sacrifice to be slain, as the following verses show, where in particular the princes dressed in friendly garb (ver. 8), the priests acting like heathen (ver. 9), the unbelieving and thoroughly materialistic triflers (ver. 12) are censured, while everywhere the population of Jerusalem is thought of. The capture of the city is described with a picturesqueness (ver. 10 f.) which, as Jerome early notices, vividly recalls the actual fate of the city (A.D. 70) as depicted more at length (than the Chaldæan catastrophe) by Josephus. The description of the judgment-day, i. 14 ff., is based on Joel ii. 1 f.; Amos v. 18, 20. It smites the whole earth, as the close of the chapter again insists.

Humility, penitent submission to God alone can save from the universal judgment.

ii. 1. "Press and crouch together,[1] O people, that despairs
2 of nothing, before what is decreed comes to the birth—
time flies past like chaff—before the burning wrath of
Yahveh comes upon you, before the day of Yahveh's wrath
3 comes upon you. Seek the Lord, all ye humble of the earth,
who have done His law, seek after righteousness, seek after
humility; perhaps ye shall be hid in the day of Yahveh's
wrath."

The judgment is a thing already settled, needing only to come
to light (to be born). Hence "the nation of the insolent"[2] should
know better than to behave arrogantly. The time before the
execution of the judgment flies as rapidly as the chaff before the
wind. And only the modest, the humble before God, who have
submitted obediently to God's commands, can then hope to be
spared. Thus the nation of the "humble of the earth" (ver. 3)
is opposed to the hardened nation of the insolent (ver. 1). Both
designations apply to men, inhabitants of the earth according to
their disposition, without regard to race; thus they include Jews
and heathen.[3] For even of the latter it may be said, that they
know God's law and do or neglect it. Here, too, Zephaniah is
in accord with Isa. xxiv. 5 (p. 299). But it is significant that
even those (whether Jews or heathen) who have been diligent in
observing God's elementary precepts must first inquire after
righteousness which God will accept on that day, and especially
seek the true humility that is alone susceptible to grace. The
judgment will terribly punish the arrogance of the world, in
particular of the heathen world, that is antagonistic to God's
people; and in consequence the worship of Yahveh will extend
over the whole earth:—

ii. 11. "Yahveh makes Himself terrible upon them; for He
makes all the gods of the earth vanish, and they pray to Him,
every one from his place, all the isles of the heathen."

---

[1] קוֹשְׁשׁוּ is *verbum denom.* from קַשׁ, *to gather stubble*; hence the rendering "to assemble." But it is stronger: *press, stoop together.* Instead of spreading out as now, they are to "crouch together," since the judgment rushes over all, infallibly striking all who stretch out their neck.

[2] In נִכְסָף the insolence of the people is hinted, and still more in the phrase: "that loses not heart," *i.e.* is not terrified in any of its evil acts. The nation of the insolent dwelling on the earth are meant, not a national people, as Judah.

[3] Otherwise Hitzig: "Pious of the land." But the prophet speaks here universally as in i. 2, 18, and then at once goes on to speak to the surrounding lands.

In Isaiah first we found[1] the pædagogic significance of the general judgment for the heathen to be a leading thought of prophecy, especially in Isa. xxiv.–xxvii., on which visions Zephaniah plainly builds. The latter, looking to the west, first names the "isles of the heathen" as an immeasurable territory which, though at present sunk in idolatry, will do homage to Israel's God. The isles and coasts of the Mediterranean are meant (cf. Isa. xxiv. 15). The world was conceived as projecting without limit into the ocean in this direction. The fact of the "isles" playing so prominent a part here, and again in Deutero-Isaiah, (they occasionally represent the less known heathen world), seems like a presentiment of the truth, that the moral centre of the heathen world is found in the nations of the west dwelling round the Mediterranean (cf. Num. xxiv. 24). But it is especially noteworthy that Zephaniah affirms of these island-dwellers that they will pray to Yahveh "*every one from his place*," a statement by no means, with Keil and Kleinert, to be supplemented to the effect that they will resort to Yahveh's temple in Jerusalem for worship, but hinting at most that in their prayer they will look from their place toward Jerusalem. The emphasis lies just on the fact that in their place, where they are at home, they will pay adoring homage to the Lord. We have here a notable effort to break through the localized conception of God's kingdom. This view, indeed, is so far from being in essential contradiction to the pilgrimage of the nations to Zion, Micah iv. 1 ff., that on the contrary the same Zephaniah also in spirit sees that pilgrimage, iii. 10, since according to him the farthest nations bring meat-offerings to Jerusalem;[2] but a weighty supplement to the thought, that everything must bring tribute to the God dwelling on Zion, is given in this glimpse of the farthest heathen praying reverently to Yahveh in their yet scarcely discovered lands (ii. 11). In Isaiah also we found such a hint of the latter view, to the effect that in the heathen lands themselves the name of the true God will be invoked, xix. 19 ff., alongside the pilgrimage of the nations, Isa. ii. 2 ff. The latter therefore is simply a way of contemplat-

---

[1] Pp. 295, 302.

[2] Even the Israelite prayed everywhere to Yahveh, which did not preclude his bringing offerings to Jerusalem. The idea of the altar, Isa. xix. 19, more clearly transcends the ordinary views, just so Mal. i. 11.

ing something that points beyond this figure. But this expressive figure was suited to the existing power of apprehension, and the defect inherent in it is only gradually remedied by such complementary revelations. After the exile the great thought, dawning in the present passage as in Isaiah, is still more definitely expressed, Mal. i. 11; but it is only to be read in perfect clearness in John iv. 23, and that from the lips of Him who most emphatically declared that salvation is of the Jews (iv. 22), thus fully acknowledging the necessity for all nations to journey to Zion, where alone salvation is to be found. This salvation, indeed, will not remain bound to the place, but to the person of Him in whom every promise belonging to Zion is verified. Through Him it was revealed that the kingdom of God on earth will be universal, while retaining a historical, personal centre.

Zeph. iii. explains more fully how through the general judgment the world will become God's kingdom, and Jerusalem God's city. The accusation in iii. 1 ff. is specially directed against Jerusalem, whose princes and judges are ravenous beasts, its prophets windbags and buffoons, its priests guilty of sacrilege; whereas the Lord is clearly and truly revealed in its midst by His word, and mightily revealed among the heathen nations around by His judgments. Because Jerusalem refuses chastening, the judgment long threatened and hitherto held back by God's long-suffering must actually come, ver. 7. Since it is no better than the heathen, it will not be spared from the universal judgment (ver. 8). But that judgment will turn all the nations into the Church of God; it is only a means to a blessed end.

iii. 8. "Therefore wait ye for me, saith the Lord, on the day when I rise up to testify.[1] For my decree is to gather nations, to sweep together kingdoms, to pour out on them my wrath, all my fierce anger; for in the fire of my zeal the
9 whole earth shall be consumed. For then will I turn on the nations purified lips, that they may all call on the name of
10 Yahveh, serve Him with one neck. From beyond the rivers

---

[1] לְעֵד, the reading according to the LXX., Syr. According to the Masora, followed by Keil, Kleinert, the reading is לְעַד, which would have to be rendered: *to the spoil*. But according to the following words the matter in hand is a judicial act, in which Yahveh is both witness and judge, and His "sentence" also intimates the mode of execution.

of Ethiopia my worshippers, the Church of my scattered ones, bring my offerings."

The judgment of the nations has here a direct missionary aim: to purify the language (properly the lip) of the nations, hitherto defiled by the names of strange gods. Henceforth they shall all invoke the name of the true God and serve Him together. Their yoke being the same, it is said, they will bear it with one shoulder; an intimate brotherhood of the nations is the natural consequence of their serving one Lord and God. The prophet here turns his gaze to the farthest south. Even in the mysterious land of the sources of the Nile, south of Ethiopia, Yahveh will have His worshippers, a *diaspora* of worshippers, who, to testify that they belong to Him, bring gifts to Jerusalem, for this is the goal of their homage. The passage alludes to Isa. xviii. 7 (p. 296), and speaks like that passage of the worshipping of Yahveh by the heathen, who in these remotest zones will form a daughter of scattered ones, *i.e.* a widely scattered Church.

Vers. 11–13 turn to the mother-Church at Jerusalem, which has also undergone a purifying.

iii. 11. "On that day thou shalt no longer need to be ashamed for all the transgressions thou hast sinned against me, for then will I sweep away from thy midst thy arrogant revellers, and thou shalt no longer be haughty on my holy mountain,
12 And I leave in thee a people humble and little, and they
13 hide themselves in the name of Yahveh. Those left of Israel shall do no wickedness and speak no lies, and in their mouth no tongue of deceit is found. For they shall graze and lie down, none making them afraid."

In the happy state of those preserved from the judgment the sense of guilt, that brings shame and pain, ceases (Isa. xxxiii. 24). Accumulated sin is forgiven; and by removing the proud the Lord has taken care that His Church shall not sin again, and especially shall not again draw down His judgment upon them by their haughtiness and arrogance. Only one Church is left, in the world's eyes mean and poor, which puts its confidence not in fleshly power and earthly greatness or worldly wealth, but in God's great revealed name, and therefore has peace with God and man. They lead a peaceful, harmless shepherd-life, really the flock of the Good Shepherd, which no foe dare touch. As it was said of these poor and humble ones in Isa. xxix. 19

(p. 291), that their joy and exulting is in God, so the prophet continues:—

iii. 14. "Exult, Daughter of Zion, shout, O Israel! Rejoice and be glad with all thy heart, Daughter of Jerusalem!
15 Yahveh has removed thy judgments, cleared away thy foe. As King of Israel Yahveh is in thy midst; fear no more
16 evil! On that day they call Jerusalem: 'Fear not,'
17 Zion: 'Let not thy hands be slack.'[1] †Yahveh, thy God, is in thy midst, a Hero who is a Saviour. He rejoices in thee with delight, is silent in His love, He exults over thee with shouting!"

The holy joy of the city of God is for the grace bestowed on it, because its sins are cancelled, and consequently its foes have no cause of revenge; while its God, the true King of Israel, can and will dwell in it without offence.[2] Then will the Church be fearless and full of energy (ver. 16). But its bliss culminates in the fact that God is able to feel unalloyed pleasure in His people, nay, an unshared joy, peculiar to Himself.[3] This relation of cordial goodwill formed between the mighty, holy God and His poor Church of the last days recalls Hosea. The Lord also has His heart's delight in it, He is silent in His love,—the latter a deep touch, not merely meaning that God does not chide, as He had hitherto been compelled to do, although it were a great thing for God's accusing voice to be no longer heard, but pointing to the most intimate fellowship of spirit, such as cannot be put into words and needs none. As the moments of most loving intercourse between human spirits are passed in silence, so when man is joined most closely to God he hears only the gentle breathing that indicates His presence. But this silence passes involuntarily into loud jubilee: "The Lord exults rapturously over His Church"—one of the boldest, most wondrous sayings of the Old Testament, which is not presumptuous only because the seer was vouchsafed a glimpse into the unfathomable decree of love revealed in the New Testament.

Finally, like the earlier prophets, Zephaniah inserts in his picture of the future Church the return of the scattered, captive

---

[1] אמר in the same sense as in Hos. ii. 1: The name expresses the state. In the second member, instead of the dative, an apostrophe seems to be used.

[2] Cf. Num. xxiii. 21, p. 138.

[3] Isa. lxv. 19. Deutero-Isaiah often alludes to Zephaniah.

Israelites, iii. 18-20, where it is intimated that these very exiles will cause Yahveh to be acknowledged in the lands of their sojourn,—a peaceful reversal of the martial outlook of Obad. ver. 19 ff., whose limits withal have of necessity given place to a far more comprehensive view of God's kingdom.

If Zephaniah has not spoken of the human mediator of the days of redemption, who was to spring out of David's stem, he bears witness all the more powerfully to the divine aim, which even the Messiah must serve, viz. the future blessed rule of God, which according to him also will have its centre on Zion, while dispensing life and blessing throughout the world. God Himself in the midst of the purified Church as its King, its Hero, its Saviour,—joined to it in blessed fellowship of love,—this, in fact, is the climax of the consummation, the goal of the divine ways. The range of the divine plan, the universality of the judgment which must subserve that plan, the universality of the redemption aimed at, are dwelt on by Zephaniah with special emphasis; and the necessity of an inward purifying, sanctifying, and in particular humbling of the Church by the fall of the outward city of God is here declared with a definiteness that shows progressive insight into the deep corruption of the nation. Zephaniah has not the originality and wealth of an Isaiah; but his visions move around the summits of Isaiah's prophecy, illumining them from fuller consciousness of the range they command.

NOTE A.—This indication of time is certainly elastic, since Josiah reigned thirty-one years. The main question is, whether God's word came to Zephaniah before or after the king's reformation of the worship of God, which, according to 2 Kings xxii. 3 ff., took place in his eighteenth year, on the basis of the newly-found Book of the Law. But 2 Chron. xxxiv. 3 shows that Josiah was engaged in restoring the pure worship of Yahveh before, and indeed from the twelfth year of his reign, although not with such thoroughness and severity. Now Zephaniah's oracle was scarcely spoken after the king's eighteenth year (Delitzsch, Kleinert), since the sentence of rejection on Jerusalem and its priests is universal, and nothing is heard of a salutary crisis and a praiseworthy effort of the leaders of the people. It fell, more probably, between the twelfth and eighteenth year (Hitzig, et al.), and most probably of all in the early part of Josiah's reign, when the king, beginning to reign at eight years of age, had not as yet time and strength to carry out his good intentions (so also Ewald, Schrader).

We do not take "the remnant of Baal" (i. 4) as implying that Baal-worship was already reduced, but probably, as in Amos i. 8, ix. 12, the phrase = "Up to the last remnant." Just so, in the same verse, שֵׁם is used in the sense: "Even the name of the priests I will destroy along with them" (Ewald).

§ 35. *Habakkuk* (note A).

Habakkuk, like Zephaniah, speaks of the coming judgment, which must first smite Judah, but will next reach the victorious world-power also, and gives direction to the true servants of the Lord as to how they may outlive this judgment. If Zephaniah preached lowliness of spirit, humility, as the chief condition of experiencing divine grace, Habakkuk demands stedfast faith, which, as Isaiah insisted before, is likewise indispensable if the Lord is to save. But the two are intimately connected. Habakkuk also denounces judgment on the pride that springs from inner untruth, and contrasts with it the sincere faith that sustains in life.

Habakkuk's book gives in most beautiful style a dialogue between God and the prophet, the lyrical expression of the subjective disposition of the latter alternating with the objective divine revelation imparted to him. So in chap. i. the prophet complains of the flagrant unrighteousness prevalent in Judah (vers. 2–4), and receives the answer of God: "I bring up the Chaldæan!" (vers. 5–11). He then laments over the desolation which in spirit he sees the arrogant destroyer perpetrating (vers. 12–17). In the second chapter the answer to this comes in a fivefold woe on the powerful criminal (vers. 2–20). The conclusion is the choral echo of chap. iii., as an anthem of praise to the God who comes to judge and save. The soul of the whole is found in the middle. After the prophet has betaken himself to his watch-tower to see what reply the Lord will give to his complaining protest against the triumph of a foe still more unjust than the people he is to punish by God's will, he receives the answer:—

ii. 2. "Write down the vision and engrave it on tables, that one may read it running; for the vision continues until the 3 set time,[1] and it pants[2] for the end and deceives not. If

---

[1] Properly: "Continuance (remaining) of the vision until the end."
[2] פוח, *hiph.*, properly : *to puff, pant*; here : *to hasten*.

it delays, wait for it; for it certainly comes, it fails not.[1]
4 Behold, puffed up, his soul is not honest in him. Yet the righteous man, through his fidelity of faith he shall live!"

The importance of the following oracle is indicated by the direction to write it down, nay, engrave it on stone tables, so that it may not only stand plainly before all eyes at present, but that its very words may be preserved, and bear testimony in future days to divine revelation, after the oracle has been fulfilled.[2] But, contrary to expectation, the oracle that follows does not show us the Chaldæan's fate, but lays bare his inner character, because thereby his fate is already sealed. In i. 11, at the close of the description of the Chaldæan's unbroken triumphant march, it is said: "Yet he is guilty, whose strength is his god." In this carnal, self-glorifying disposition of the world-power that puts itself in God's place, its destruction is already wrapped up. Just so the central oracle (ii. 4) gives a glimpse into the inner nature of the antithesis between the overweening foe and the righteous servant of God, which forms the ground of their different destiny. The Behold! calls attention to the hidden matter that turns the scale in God's eyes, and in which, therefore, the fate of men is to be read. Ver. 4a says of the world-conqueror: "Puffed up,[3] his soul is not straight in him." Inflatedness stands here in opposition to honesty. For arrogance, in which man makes himself God, always involves an untruth, deceit[4] towards God and one's self, the soul puffing itself out to a magnitude not belonging to it. Such hollow self-exaltation has been from the time of Gen. iii. a mark of a world estranged from God, and has its root in ethical impurity; it is therefore obnoxious to punishment. Whilst the first half of the verse implies this punishment, without expressing it, the second, on the contrary, promises life to the righteous man.

---

[1] The LXX., who are followed by Heb. x. 37, inexactly make God or the Messiah the subject: ἐὰν ὑστερήσῃ, ὑπόμεινον αὐτόν, ὅτι ἐρχόμενος ἥξει καὶ οὐ μὴ χρονίσῃ. Rather the vision is meant, whose import certainly is a manifestation of God, as chap. iii. shows.

[2] Cf. Isa. viii. 1, xxx. 8; Job xix. 24.

[3] Cf. עָפַל, *swelling*, *hill*. The *pual* accordingly signifies: *to be swollen*, here with arrogance and conceit.

[4] Cf. ver. 5, where wine in this sense is called a deceiver, seducing men into such arrogance; and i. 13, where the foes themselves are so called as to their disposition.

Those meant are the righteous in the nation, for whom the prophet made intercession, and in whose name he said, with divine confidence, in i. 12: "We shall not die!" The righteous shall abide in life despite the terribleness of the judgment, therefore escaping the latter (cf. Num. xxiv. 23).

But the chief emphasis of this central oracle lies on בֶּאֱמוּנָתוֹ. The word, indeed, is not to be joined with צַדִּיק, but with יִחְיֶה.[1] Substantially, however, the difference is unimportant. For when it is said through [2] what quality the righteous man receives the reward of righteousness (life), it is also declared in what element of his character the essence of his righteousness lies in God's view. The word אֱמוּנָה signifies properly *firmness*,[3] and is used of physical (*e.g.* Ex. xvii. 12), but mostly of moral firmness, on which one may build, therefore *trustworthiness*, especially in reference to promises and pledges; thus in daily trade and commerce: *conscientiousness, honesty, fidelity* (Prov. xii. 17); but especially of the fidelity of God, the Rock (Deut. xxxii. 4), whose word may be trusted without reserve. In the present passage it cannot refer to civic integrity, the antithesis requiring a disposition towards God. As a counterpart to the false inflatedness of the heathen, humble fidelity and uprightness is to be thought of. As the heathen are characterized in their inner nature as deceivers, so the righteous are characterized as upright and faithful. But prophetic usage and the connection of thought give the expression here a still more definite stamp. According to Gen. xv. 6, believing trust (הֶאֱמִין) was the condition of Abraham's righteousness (צְדָקָה). Here we have plainly the same correlates, the אמונה, corresponding to the *hiphil*, as elsewhere to the *kal* and *niphal*.[4] This is abundantly con-

---

[1] On the *tiphcha*, which is not opposed to this conjunction, see Delitzsch, *Comm.* p. 50.

[2] בְּ introduces the efficient medium of the preservation of life, as in Ezek. xviii. 22.

[3] From אמן, *to be firm, make firm.* Cf. p. 288, and Gesenius, *Thesaurus*.

[4] The *hiph.* properly expresses more than "to deem true," namely: *to show or attribute firmness*, hence *to hold firmly by something*. Cf. the Arabic form آمَنَ, which as to meaning = أَمِنَ, I, only stronger, but is to be explained in the *hiphil* sense. See Fleischer, *Allgemeine Hall. Literaturzeitung, Ergänzungsblätter*, 1838, p. 152. The אמונה, therefore, inheres in the מאמין, not merely in the thing in which he believes. Hence Abraham is called נאמן, Neh. ix. 8.

firmed by Isaiah, who, as we saw p. 288, unceasingly preaches confident faith, sincere trust in God's miraculous help, as the condition of salvation and protection from divine judgment, Isa. vii. 9, xxviii. 16, xxx. 15. Consequently human אֱמוּנָה as the correlate of the divine is meant; to the faithfulness of God that verifies His word corresponds that of man, which trusts God's word unwaveringly, despite all appearance to the contrary. This constancy of faith will, in a miraculous way, ensure safety in the fearful world-judgment.

Consequently the LXX. rendered the word by πίστις with entire fitness. Only they wrongly read בֶּאֱמוּנָתִי as if it referred to the divine fidelity: ὁ δὲ δίκαιος ἐκ πίστεώς μου ζήσεται, against which the necessity of antithesis[1] and again Ezek. xviii. 22 are decisive. From this reading the one found in Heb. x. 38 has come. On the other hand, Paul renders the passage correctly in Rom. i. 17; Gal. iii. 11. Moreover, his use of the passage corresponds to its meaning. The antithesis to the works of the law established by the passage in the Galatian Epistle is certainly not the prominent one in the prophet. But it may be obtained from his words, for plainly Habakkuk describes disposition, stedfast, undivided surrender to God, trust in His grace, as the soul of the righteousness on which at last everything turns. The vital question for the righteous man is, whether he has immovable confidence in God; for his righteousness itself is measured by this. The condition of salvation laid down by the prophet is thus essentially the same as is announced in the New Covenant: a faith that reveals the inmost character of the heart; a childlike, humble and sincere trust in the credibility of the divine message of salvation, the contents of which were certainly elementary and therefore mysteriously indefinite in the Old Covenant.

Thus Habakkuk joins hand with Zephaniah in teaching the docile and well-disposed among his people what was necessary in the time of crisis. If the latter intimated (Zeph. ii. 3) that even they who had done right must still zealously seek, in order to find, the Lord, true righteousness and right lowliness, and so be safely hidden on the day of judgment, Habakkuk names in one word[2] the condition of salvation that constitutes true righteous-

---

[1] This certainly does not apply to the LXX., who already were plainly mistaken in the first half of the verse.

[2] Even the formalistic synagogue felt the central truth lying in this utterance.

ness and is inconceivable without sincere humility. It is faith in the deep Biblical sense of the word, unreserved trust in the Lord's salvation.

On the *mashal*-like principle, Hab. ii. 4 is followed by an exposition of the threatening contained in it in the form of a fivefold woe on Babylon. The gigantic exertions of this world-power labour only for the fire; for another power will possess the earth, ii. 13 f., where Isa. ix. 1½ is taken up, but applied more generally. The whole earth will be filled with the glory of the Lord (cf. Num. xvi. 21), must therefore do homage to Him and no other. Everything men have built for their own fame or for the honour of false gods must vanish. Therefore let all the world be reverently silent before Him that reigns in heaven. Like Zeph. i. 7, this "Be silent!" announces His approach.

Chap. iii., the "prayer of Habakkuk the prophet, in dithyrambic style," forms the lyrical answer, not to what was seen in chap. i., but to what was seen in chap. ii., to the announcement of the approach of the Lord, who will cause His glory to be seen throughout the world. It is a prayer uttered in the name of the nation, as ver. 14 shows; but as the suppliant broods on the decree of God which he heard before, that decree grows more vivid and real to his soul, and so he becomes the prophet who depicts the parousia of God. God comes in power to take possession of the earth, casting down the foes of His people and of His Anointed.

iii. 2. "Yahveh, I have heard Thy tidings, I am terrified—Yahveh, Thy work in the midst of the years call to life, in the midst of the years make it plain. In wrath Thou wilt remember mercy."

The "tidings" is that the Lord will come to execute the world-judgment which falls, indeed, on the heathen world-power first of all, but fills every citizen of earth with trembling. For who can bear the approach of the holy God and see His glory unscathed? Yet the seer calmly utters the wish: "Thy will be done, Thy kingdom come!" Only, as a genuine priest he stipulates that

---

In the Gemara (Makkot, f. 24a) it is said: "David condensed the 613 Sinaiti commands into 11 (Ps. xv.); Isaiah into 6 (xxxiii. 15); Micah into 3 (vi. 8); Amos (v. 4), or rather Habakkuk, into *one:* "The just man shall live by his faith." It is also worthy of notice, that later Judaism takes אמונה altogether in the sense above stated. See Delitzsch, *ut ante*, p. 53.

in the midst of wrath God will not forget mercy, *i.e.* towards those who are free from pride and faithfully wait for Him. The grand picture of the appearance of the Lord, ver. 3 ff., borrows its features mostly from the theophany on Sinai which formed the basis of the entire Old Covenant. As He then showed Himself to His people, so He will now show Himself to all the world, in which manifestation certainly His fearful majesty brings destruction on the "house of the transgressor," by which the world-empire is meant; whereas to the covenant-people that has previously passed through the fire of judgment (chap. i.), and to His Anointed One, this manifestation brings redemption and victory.[1] The Anointed of the Lord is not Jehoiakim, who was unworthy of such distinction, but had to be swept away by the judgment (Jer. xxii. 18 f.), and just as little the nation itself (Hitzig, Ewald, Kleinert, according to a reading of the LXX.), but the more worthy king who, as Isaiah and Micah sufficiently show, will outlive the judgment. Of his character Habakkuk does not speak more in detail, being quite absorbed in contemplating the divine glory of Yahveh. Therefore, despite all the terrors and all the devastation that God's judgments must bring, the nation in whose name the prophet speaks is able to exclaim confidently at the close:—

18 "But I will exult in the Lord, I will rejoice in the God
19 of my salvation. Yahveh, the Lord of all, is my strength, and makes my feet like the hinds, and upon my high places He makes me to walk."

NOTE A.—The date of Habakkuk's prophetic oracle is not indicated. At all events he foretells the invasion of the *Chaldæans* as taking place immediately, "in your days," i. 5. But in the same verse this event is described as scarcely credible. This certainly does not preclude the appearance of the oracle a few years previously under the reign of *Jehoiakim*,[2] who soon witnessed the judgment; for we see from Jer. xxxvi. 29, that in the first years of this king up to the battle at Carchemish this prediction of the prophet was still regarded as absurd. To go back to Manasseh's days, when according to 2 Kings xxi. 10 ff. certain prophets threatened the land with like suffering, is forbidden by בִּימֵיכֶם,

---

[1] Cf. Judg. v., Ps. lxviii., where also an appearance of God, in some degree analogous to the one on Sinai, is celebrated.

[2] So the majority: Knobel, Ewald, Hitzig, Schrader, Kuenen, Kleinert, Kamphausen, *et al.*

which has in Hebrew a limited meaning of twenty to thirty years at most. Nor can the oracle be placed (with Delitzsch[1]) under Jehoiakim's predecessor Josiah, in whose days Zephaniah spoke. In all probability the reform in worship had been carried out long before the appearance of the oracle; Habakkuk has not, like Zephaniah, to complain of idolatry. And according to 2 Kings xxii. 20, the prophetess Hulda promised King Josiah that the land should be spared during his life. Consequently we must place Habakkuk's sayings, in accordance with the current view, under King Jehoiakim (609–599 B.C.), and in any case before the year 605, the year of the battle of Carchemish; for after that battle it was almost self-evident that the Chaldaean on his victorious march against Egypt would also visit Judah, which was in a state of complete dependence on the latter kingdom. Habakkuk accordingly is later than Zephaniah. The order in the canon furnishes no trustworthy chronological sign. The dependence of Zeph. i. 7 on Hab. ii. 20, insisted on by Delitzsch, cannot be proved. The relation may be the reverse, although Zephaniah borrows more than the more original Habakkuk. Nor can priority be inferred from the more compressed and forceful style of the latter; they are so nearly contemporaneous, that this difference must rather have its reason in subjective character.

§ 36. *Jeremiah's Prophecies of the New Covenant.*

Jeremiah lived in the same period as the prophets last discussed. He laboured a much longer time amid continued attacks and outrages, his period of activity extending from the thirteenth year of Josiah to beyond the overthrow of Jerusalem. Thus in this sad time of decline Jeremiah was the chief representative of prophecy before prince and people. Superficially regarded, the reformation of Josiah seemed to promise a future of divine blessing to the land. But the true prophet could not be deceived by a superficial improvement that made no change in the inward disposition of the people; and under the Kings Jehoiakim, Jehoiakin, Zedekiah, he repeated with increasing definiteness his testimony to the impending destruction of the whole commonwealth. All vain hopes, especially excited and fed by false prophets, he inexorably denounced. Since the nation would not forsake its sin (unrighteousness, immorality, idolatry), nor the princes their treacherous policy, it was settled in God's decree that Judah-

---

[1] Fr. Delitzsch, *Der Prophet Habakuk*, 1843. On the other hand, this scholar has recently put him in the time of Manasseh (*Messianic Prophecies*, p. 77).

Jerusalem should drink the cup of suffering to the dregs, and of the theocracy hitherto existing not one stone should be left on another.

While Jeremiah's office was predominantly one of rebuke, while he was forced to complain, accuse, pull down continually, he still directed his gaze to the future completion of God's Church. Although his call to repent like Hosea's dies away unheeded, yet in the end God's mercy breaks through as in Hosea. The divine plan in the election of this nation must yet be accomplished, Jacob's seed must dwell as God's people in the land of Canaan under a just ruler of David's house.[1] Moreover, this prophet, who leans in a striking degree on his predecessors, is not lacking in new, original features, partly arising out of his special charism, partly occasioned by the circumstances of the age. Salvation in him still more than in Isaiah bears the character of *redemption*, the penal state having meantime begun or at least seeming to the prophet palpably near. But redemption as deliverance from judgment, and the consequent establishment of the true divine rule, while not seen by Jeremiah in the same brilliant grandeur as by Isaiah, are seen in deeper *inwardness*.

This spiritualization is a fruit of the prophetic spirit that has been ripened in the glow of judgment. The inner disintegration, which Jeremiah had to feel in Judah still more vividly than his predecessors, raised to certainty in his mind, not merely the imminence of external dissolution, but also the necessity of a more spiritual foundation for the future building. He was forced constantly to fight against the carnal overvaluing of the outward theocratic form, in which a corresponding disposition was wanting. He saw his contemporaries trusting with perilous infatuation in the outwardly accepted covenant with Yahveh, in the outward covenant-sign of circumcision in the flesh;[2] in the outward temple, as if after the preservation of Zion in Isaiah's days no calamity could again befall it, although the temple looked more like a murderer's den,[3]—in the outward sacrificial service, which yet, as former prophets had already insisted, could only be offensive apart from holiness and inward surrender to God;[4] in the outward possession of the divine Torah,

---

[1] Cf. iv. 27, xi. 5, xxxi. 35, 36, xxxiii. 17, 26, xlvi. 28.
[2] Jer. iv. 4, ix. 24 f.   [3] Jer. vii., especially vers. 4, 10, 11, 14.
[4] Jer. vi. 20, vii. 21 ff., xiv. 12. Cf. Isa. i. 11 ff.

which, however, was falsified by the pen of false erudition and not observed in its true meaning;[1] finally, in outward prophecy, that apparently promised good things under divine inspiration and in reality merely aped God's genuine messengers and clothed the thoughts of its own heart in the garb of solemn oracles, in order with such welcome preaching to deceive a credulous nation.[2]

In opposition to all unholy confidence in the outward form of the theocracy and its means of grace, Jeremiah proclaims that man can only attain salvation through a complete change of mind ($\mu\epsilon\tau\acute{a}\nu o\iota a$), and that only in virtue of His forgiving mercy, by a complete remoulding of His relation to His people, can the Lord realize the true purpose that He has always had in view for them. Already in the days of Josiah, when the prophet is still uttering unceasingly the call to repent,[3] the notable passage is found (iii. 12 ff.), in which it is urged as a motive to repentance, that on sincere repentance God will receive His people again into a child's place, and acknowledge it as His bride, while He will so glorify Jerusalem, as His seat before all the world, by His presence, that the *Old Covenant shall no longer be remembered.* The oracle is addressed primarily to the Israelites of the northern kingdom already in exile, whom the Lord will bring back, so that no tribe or city may be lost; if ever so few of them obey the call, they will multiply in the land in the days of grace.

iii. 16. "And it shall come to pass, when you shall be multiplied and fruitful in the land, in those days, saith the Lord, they shall no longer say: 'The ark of the covenant of Yahveh,' and it shall no longer come into mind, nor shall they remem-
17 ber it or ask after it, nor shall they prepare it. At that time they shall call Jerusalem: 'Throne of Yahveh,' and all nations shall assemble to it, for the name of Yahveh, for Jerusalem, and shall no longer follow the hardness of their evil heart."

When, therefore, after the judgment the original blessing of creation (Gen. i. 28) anew displays its energy amid a rejuvenated people, the temple also will be remade, and shine in unimagined glory. No longer will the Lord's covenant be attached to the

---
[1] Jer. viii. 8.
[2] Jer. v. 31, xiv. 31 ff., xxiii. 9 ff., xxviii. 1 ff., xxix. 8 ff., 15 ff.
[3] Cf. especially Jer. iv. 1 ff.

wooden ark, which has meantime vanished,[1] hitherto the sign and pledge of the covenant, often enough indeed abused by the self-deceit of a superficial mind; but God's living presence will be so plainly discernible, that what the symbolical ark with the cherubim had hitherto been, viz. God's mercy-seat,[2] that Jerusalem will be to the whole world. And this immediate presence of God in His Church will be so much more glorious than the presence of which that symbol was the medium, that the latter shall no longer be even remembered, to say nothing of its being missed or again set up.

In this brief statement about the most holy palladium of the Mosaic covenant, sentence is passed on the entire concrete outwardness of the latter. It is seen to be something that only imperfectly hints and mediates God's gracious relation to His people, hence only appointed for a limited time, namely, until the Lord's full revelation becomes matter of experience. "We have before us here the announcement of a complete destruction of the earlier form of God's kingdom, but of such a destruction of its form as is also the supreme consummation of its essence, a decay like that of the seed-corn which only perishes to bear much fruit, of the body that is sown in corruption to rise again in incorruption" (Hengstenberg). In contrast with the Church of his own age, possessing only the empty sign of God's presence, the prophet here sees the Church of the last days, in which the Lord will be so vividly revealed, that the sign will no longer be needed. The full realization of what is here promised is found first in Rev. xxi. (cf. ver. 22). But the inwardness and immediateness of God's self-revelation and self-communication postulated by the prophet has only come into force since there has been a Church of the Lord which no longer misses the covenant ark, and knows of a revelation far more glorious than that of Sinai.

According to iii. 17, even the *heathen*, drawn by the glory of God's revelation, will gather to Jerusalem, in the sense of Isa. ii. 2 ff.; Micah iv. 1 ff. "They walk thither for the name of Yahveh, for Jerusalem," *i.e.* to partake in the glory of the Lord

---

[1] This feature shows that judgment will have gone forth upon Judah also, sweeping away even its holy things. That the covenant ark was destroyed by Manasseh (Ewald, *History*) is neither to be inferred from 2 Chron. xxxiii. 16 nor the present passage, and is altogether improbable in view of the silence of the historians on the point.

[2] Ex. xxv. 22; Num. vii. 89; Ps. lxxx. 1, xcix. 1.

there manifested. The name of Yahveh in such passages is His revelation, Yahveh Himself, so far as He has made Himself nameable, and therefore knowable. Meanwhile, over the heathen impends a similar judgment to that which Israel-Judah has passed through; but afterwards in like manner they will experience the grace of the Lord,[1] becoming then receptive to His revelation.

Just in the later saddest time, when the judgment, as he knew, was going on its way unhindered, and he himself had to undergo the most painful martyrdom, under the reign of Zedekiah, Jeremiah was often raised to the ideal height of the glorious future, of which formerly he was permitted to speak but seldom. An oracle of this kind is found in xxiii. 1 ff., where even the specifically Messianic outlook—that of the Lord's perfect Anointed One—is disclosed. Here a rebuke of the bad *shepherds*[2] (*i.e.* kings), who destroy and scatter the flock, turns into the promise, that the Lord Himself will collect His scattered flock and appoint it shepherds after His own mind. But on this more general promise (xxiii. 4, as already in iii. 15) there follows a new commencement, in which the climax is reached.

xxiii. 5. "Behold, days come, saith Yahveh, when I raise up to David a *righteous Sprout*, and he shall rule as king and act
6 wisely and do right and righteousness in the land. In his days Judah shall experience deliverance and Israel dwell securely. And this is the name with which he shall be named: *Yahveh, our righteousness.*"

In both these verses unquestionably a single, unique Davidite is spoken of, who rises to power, and rules as king by divine arrangement; in his days, and by means of his wise and just government, the once divided, but then again united kingdom, will reach inner as well as outer perfection. The relation of the good shepherds (iii. 15, xxiii. 4) to the king is not, that his posterity are combined with him in this plural designation, although in xxxiii. 17, 22, the indestructibleness of the Davidic rule is expressed by saying that David's posterity will be numberless, and one of them will always possess the throne. Rather the plurality (iii. 15, xxiii. 4) stands generally in contrast with the bad shepherds who at present oppress the people, popular leaders at work contempo-

---

[1] Cf. Jer. xii. 15 ff., xlviii. 47, xlix. 6, xlvii. 39.
[2] Cf. Zech. xi., xiii. 7; Micah v. 3.

rancously being referred to.[1] But One towers incomparably above them, who, springing from David's stem, is perfectly righteous, and does justice and righteousness faultlessly, so that in his days the united kingdom of Israel-Judah has peace and rest. The oracle is so brief, because it seeks in a single word to awaken the remembrances of the promises about the glorious Davidite given long before. The mysterious צֶמַח springs from Isa. iv. 2, but is now defined personally like the similar names in Isa. xi. 1; it recalls all the glorious things uttered by that prophet (Isa. vii., ix., xi.), as well as Micah, respecting the Sprout. Jeremiah describes him in his main inner attribute by the word צַדִּיק, thereby recalling what had been said since Solomon's days respecting the true bearer of this kingly virtue, and in particular the prophecies since Hosea's time; cf. Zech. ix. 9. This ruler will proceed wisely, implying subjective wisdom as well as objective success, and finally, in a way pleasing to God, will convert long-missing justice into fact.[2] And in consequence of his sound government the united[3] kingdom will enjoy rest and peace at home and abroad.

Moreover, in this oracle there is not wanting a word designed to deepen and spiritualize the existing Messianic hope. It is the brief but pregnant יְהֹוָה צִדְקֵנוּ, "the Lord our Righteousness," a characterizing proper name and the watchword of the Messianic age. To whom the name is given, may be open to dispute. Ewald, Graf, Nägelsbach refer the suffix in וְיִקְרָאוֹ to Israel, appealing to the similar language in xxxiii. 16, where the same name is given to the city of Jerusalem of the last days. But considering Jeremiah's fondness for variations, the latter passage is not absolutely decisive here; and since the chief stress in the present oracle lies on the righteous Sprout,[4] the majority rightly refer the sentence to it. As the Messiah is called in Isa. vii. 14 "God with us," so here "Yahveh our Righteousness." Whether this view be accepted or not, the gravity of the word remains the same. Its significance does not lie, as the interpretation of the early Church thought, in the fact that the Messiah would

---

[1] The relation of the one righteous twig that perfects the kingdom to the good shepherd is not expressly indicated. These are different prophetic glimpses, which are not placed in outward relation to each other. See below on xxxiii. 14 ff.

[2] Cf. Hos. ii. 19, p. 233.   [3] Cf. Hos. ii. 2; Zech. ix. 10, 13, xi. 7, 14.

[4] Cf. also ver. 6: "*in his days*," whereas in xxxiii. 16 it is said "in those days." The allusion also to the name Zedekiah (2 Kings xxiv. 17), undoubtedly intended, favours the reference to a personal ruler.

be called Yahveh, who is our Righteousness. The two words are not to be joined appositionally, but the name consists of a sentence expressing, like Immanuel, the relation of God to the Church. Its great wondrous import, however, is that the righteous character, the moral life of the Church, has its ground not in any outward institution or law, or in an outward action, but in Yahveh, the merciful God Himself, on which Ezek. xxxvi. 25 ff. especially gives a commentary. צדק is not equivalent to salvation (Graf),[1] but "righteousness of character, good conduct." As, then, this normal state, when affirmed of God, carries with it goodness and favour towards men,[2] so when promised to men it brings with it salvation and wellbeing. But, our oracle teaches, it does not lie in man's power to put himself into the righteous man's relation to God, and to keep himself permanently therein. The need of redemption felt by the most pious is met by Jeremiah with the comforting assurance, that hereafter the Lord Himself will establish and preserve the righteousness of His people, a promise involving as well grace to forgive and justify as to sanctify and help in holy living.[3] When, then, in xxxiii. 16 Jerusalem is called "Yahveh our Righteousness," this plainly means that the Church[4] there will be acknowledged as one whose righteousness has its ground and permanence in the Lord; and when in xxiii. 6 the Church calls the Sprout of David by this name, it is implied (in a sense analogous to that in Isa. vii. 14) that the Church sees in him the one through whom a divinely-wrought righteous relation is brought about. He is the personal centre and head of the Church, in whom divine righteousness is presented most directly, and from whom it proceeds into every member.

Perhaps one may say that this name, with which the prophet salutes the period of the great Son of David, contains the N. T. evangel *in nuce*: The New Covenant will be a state of righteousness in the Church, its salvation a fruit of its right relation to God, and this relation will have its root in the Lord Himself,

---

[1] Kautzsch rightly remarks (*Ueber die Derivate des Stammes*, צדק, p. 39), that to put the consequence in the place of the *causa efficiens* is perverse.

[2] So Isa. xli. 2. In the name Zedekiah also the צדק is perhaps so meant, *i.e.* to express the favour of Yahveh. Jeremiah points to a profounder idea.

[3] On the former, cf. l. 20, xxxi. 34, Dan. ix. 24, where צדק is to be observed; on the latter, Jer. xxxi. 33; on the two, Ezek. xxxvi. 25 ff.

[4] Cf. Jer. xxxi. 23.

being constituted and guaranteed by Him. The Lord Himself is this state, conveys it to the Church, and that through the incomparably wise and righteous king of Israel's house of whom the prophets spoke long ago.

The promises of coming redemption and of a New Covenant between God and His people are found in special abundance in the "consolation-book" of Jeremiah, chaps. xxx.–xxxiii., which unless chaps. xxx. and xxxi. are of earlier origin,[1] which cannot be proved, likewise fall within the few years of Zedekiah's government, and therefore within the time of the greatest affliction of Jerusalem and the grossest attacks on the prophet. That Jerusalem indeed must fall, and the people of Judah, like that of Ephraim, go into exile, is so certain to the prophet, that he assumes it as a completed punishment; and it has even been supposed that these sections have been interpolated by an exilian prophet (Deutero-Isaiah).[2] But Jeremiah here raises the song of redemption in all the more comforting tones in days of foreign domination and exile.

This we find to be the case immediately in xxx. 1 ff., where deliverance from foreign yoke is proclaimed as an act of God, by which He will conduct His people to its true destiny:—

Ver. 9. "And they shall serve Yahveh their God, and David their king, whom I will raise up for them."

As in Ps. ii., the Lord's Anointed appears here in immediate conjunction with the invisible king; it is one and the same government they carry on. Yahveh rules through His Anointed, who is called David,[3] because he not only springs from David's seed, but also perfectly executes David's mission. He is the true David, in whom will be seen in perfect form what the Lord had in mind in David's election, namely, perfect mediatorship between God and His people. Of course this "King David" is identical with the "righteous Sprout" of xxiii. 5, xxxiii. 15; so that no return of the dead David is to be thought of in the sense in which the Germans expected the return of their Barbarossa, the Portuguese their Sebastian.[4] How this David is

---

[1] So Ewald, Nägelsbach: under Josiah; Stähelin, Graf: Jehoiakim.

[2] So Movers, de Wette, Hitzig.

[3] Hos. iii. 5 was the first to give this name to the king of the last days. But afterwards the idea became more concentrated and individual through what Zech. ix., Isaiah, Micah said.

[4] So von Ammon, D. Strauss, and in the analogous passages in Ezek. xxxiv. 23 f.,

to be raised to unique familiarity of intercourse with the Lord, chap. xxx. 21 says in a few weighty words:—

"And his (the people's) governor shall come from him, and his ruler proceed from his midst; and I make him approach and he draws near to me. For who is he that would pledge his heart[1] to draw near to me? saith Yahveh!"

It is not a slight thing that then a mighty and honoured ruler of the stem of this now enslaved people again bears the sceptre (cf. Micah v. 1 f.); but the most glorious feature in his kingship is his high privilege to come before God in priestly dignity, nay, to draw nigh to God as none else could do.[2] The close of the verse dwells on the greatness of this distinction. To pledge his heart to approach God means: "To draw near to God of his own impulse," supported by a good conscience. Thus it stands in contrast with the divine call: "*I* make him come near to me." But the oracle affirms still more than that the prince will share the privilege of the priests in not coming before God uncalled. The emphasis of the words as well as the spirit of Jeremiah's prophecy compels us to think of a more intimate approach even than that of the high priest, who was admitted into the Holy of Holies, namely, of a drawing near to God, for which no man can have confidence enough, but which is reserved for Him who sits at God's right hand and as true High Priest represents the people before the Lord in accordance with Ps. cx.

If the Head is so closely joined to God, the Church also will belong to its heavenly Lord, and He to it. "Ye shall be my people, and I will be your God." This destiny,[3] already stated in the days of Moses, will then be first really fulfilled, as Hosea foretold and Jeremiah again and again repeats.[4] But to this end nothing less is necessary than a reshaping of the basis of the holy nation, the making of a *new covenant*, as is revealed in chap. xxxi. The prophet first gives us a glimpse into the

---

xxxvii. 24, Hitzig also. The הקים, so frequently used in Jeremiah, nowhere means in such a connection: *to raise from the dead*, but: *to raise to power*, as already in 2 Sam. vii. 12.

[1] ערב is to be explained after Neh. v. 3: *to pledge, stake*.

[2] הקריב is taken intentionally from the priestly language, in which *kal* and *hiph*. are used of drawing near to God with sacrificial gifts. נגש affirms still more: *an approaching so as to touch*. It is used, e.g., of Moses, Ex. xxiv. 2.

[3] Ex. vi. 7. See p. 128.

[4] Cf. Hos. ii.; Jer. xxiv. 7, xxx. 22, xxxi. 1, 33. Cf. Zech. xiii. 9.

"goodness of the Lord,"[1] prepared in His imperishable *love* (xxxi. 3, 20) for the nation after its return into the Promised Land. In this picture, painted *con amore*, chap. xxxi. 22*b* forms a peculiarly mysterious feature. There the exhortation to the rebellious, stiffnecked daughters of Israel to return to their salvation is based on the prospect of some new thing, something hitherto unheard on earth which the Lord will do. This new state or new divine work is described by a laconic mashal, incapable of reproduction with the same indefiniteness. So much is certain, that the Hebrew expressions make the emphasis fall on the distinction of sex, and accordingly a reversal of the ordinary relation is to take place; whether generally, or in a specific case, the oracle leaves formally open. We shall not translate תְּסוֹבֵב: *A woman shall be changed*[2] *into a man*, but after Deut. xxxii. 10, Ps. xxxii. 10 : *shall surround by way of guarding*. Ordinarily it is the man's business to protect the woman, as the bird flutters round its nest in which its mate is brooding. The Lord will make the contrary obtain : The weak, little-esteemed woman shall be the man's guardian. This we understand not of a particular couple, as the Messiah and His mother, but of the antithesis of the humanly strong and weak, the highly and little esteemed within the people and nation. Strength and honour will hereafter lie, not in that in which the people has hitherto sought it, in manly force and will, but in feminine humility and lowliness, which is also receptiveness to the divine. Isaiah and Micah saw the Church as a woman conceiving in weakness and bringing forth in suffering and sorrow —the Church that receives into its heart the word of the Lord; whereas the rulers grounded their confidence on earthly might. Hence Jeremiah designates the defenceless and therefore despised Church of the quiet in the land as he does here. The miracle will be seen, that this Church will form the guard of proud man, who can never find safety in his self-confidence and strength. Here also Jeremiah does not renounce his inward, spiritual aim, which runs counter to the usual order of sense. He foresees in what the world-conquering might lies; he knows the invisible and therefore scarcely noticed power that guards even those who think they ought to guard the weak.[3]

[1] Cf. xxxi. 12, טוֹב יהוה, with Hos. iii. 5.
[2] Ewald, *Ausf. Lehrb. der hebr. Sprache*, § 298*b*.
[3] Cf. Luther's saying, he intends to guard his Elector better than the latter does him.

That time of salvation will contain the opposite both inwardly and outwardly of the present time, xxxi. 27 ff. " Behold, days come" (such is Jeremiah's favourite introduction, when he has something to tell in strongest contradiction to the present) "when I sow the house of Israel and the house of Judah with seed of men and seed of cattle." This implies the abundant degree in which God sows new life, of man and beast, for the wellbeing of His people. And just as earnestly as God has hitherto studied to diminish and destroy this life will He now proceed to multiply and guard it. Hitherto God was the most dangerous foe, a power of terrible cunning, intent on plucking up the life planted, pulling down what was built, shattering, razing to the ground, destroying.[1] What promised to succeed He overthrew. No one had felt this terrible curse so keenly as Jeremiah. " Behold! the Lord will now display the like energy," according to ver. 28, "for the salvation of His people." In those days the heritage of woe burdening the people will be removed (ver. 29). Then the proverb, now so sadly true, will no longer apply : "The fathers ate sour grapes, and the teeth of the sons are set on edge," *i.e.* the acts of the fathers are revenged on the children. This proverb, mentioned also Ezek. xviii. 2 f., has a certain warrant, so far as it is based on Ex. xx. 5, Deut. v. 9, according to which God visits the misdeeds of the fathers to the third and fourth member. But it is an abuse to make the solidarity of generations weaken the moral responsibility of the individual; in opposition to this current view, not in opposition to the Torah, Ezekiel insists that the Lord will reckon with each individual according to his moral conduct. Still less is a polemic against the Mosaic law to be found in Jeremiah's promise that a time will come when the curse,[2] now so palpably lying on all, will be cancelled, so that every one will only be punished for his personal sins done spontaneously. In this sentence we find a high truth uttered in relation to God's perfect revelation.[3] Giving it a more general form, we may say : The curse burdening entire humanity as an inheritance from Adam is cancelled in the New Covenant in such

---

[1] xxxi. 28, שָׁקַד, properly : *to watch over something ;* cf. i. 12.

[2] Lam. v. 7. Cf. Herzog, *Realencykl.* (2nd ed.) vi. 529.

[3] That which is the divine norm for the exercise of human justice (Deut. xxiv. 16 ; 2 Kings xiv. 6) must at last appear in the exercise of divine justice, although for a time it is not to be seen everywhere.

a way that the decision for and against salvation is put into the hand of each individual, and he only is liable to condemnation who continues under the curse by free choice. Hence there are good inner reasons for the prophet now to go on to describe a New Covenant that is to take the place of the one at Sinai:—

xxxi. 31. "Behold, days come, saith Yahveh, when I make a NEW COVENANT with the house of Israel and the house of 32 Judah, not after the manner of the covenant which I made with their fathers on the day when I took their hand to lead them out of Egypt, which covenant of mine they have broken, 33 and I am weary of them,[1] saith Yahveh; for this is the covenant which I will make with the house of Israel after these days, saith Yahveh: I will put my law into their MIND and write it in their HEART, and will be to them a God and 34 they shall become to me a people. And they shall no longer instruct every one his companion and every one his brother in this form: 'Know Yahveh;' for they shall all know me, from the little among them unto the great, saith Yahveh; for I will forgive their guilt and no longer remember their sin."

Jeremiah's prophecy, everywhere, as we saw, aiming at a spiritualizing and deepening of the Church's relation to God, here reaches its climax, where in *one* word the termination of the entire economy of the Old Covenant is announced. The prophet foresees a "*New Covenant*," by which the one resting on the fundamental fact of the exodus from Egypt[2] and announced in the lawgiving on Sinai is made *old!* Thus the kingdom of God is built anew from the very ground. And the basis on which this is done stands in notable contrast with that of the Mosaic covenant. The position of the latter is given in ver. 32*b*: On the part of men a breach of the covenant had intervened, on the part of God weariness with this covenant-breaking people. Thus a dangerous severance had ensued instead of union. That such a dissolution

---

[1] בָּעַל, like the Arabic بَعِلَ, *to feel satiety, disgust* in something, so in the present passage, LXX. Heb. viii. 9; Syr., Abulw., Jos. Kimchi, Schultens, Gesenius (*Thesaurus*, i. 223). Jer. iii. 14 also is to be so taken (against the LXX.). Modern writers have wrongly returned to the usual signification: *whilst I had appropriated, married them*, which does not suit the train of thought.

[2] Cf. Jer. xvi. 14 f., xxiii. 7 f.

of the holy covenant may be impossible henceforth, its nature will be altogether changed. It is true, a Torah, a revelation of God's will, will form the bond joining God and the people—how could it be otherwise, if the Lord is to rule over them?—but the expression of His will will be written by God's finger directly on the heart, not on stone tables, from which God's will scarcely found access to the heart. It is a glimpse of astounding depth that is here granted to the prophet. The efforts and struggles of man to conform to the divine law will never satisfy that law, if the corruption of the human heart be taken into account (xxxii. 30), so long as man's inner nature is not so re-created by a divine act as to make its desires and aims harmonize fully with the divine will. So long as the law stands over against man as something foreign and outward, he will never keep it as he ought. For this reason in the days when the divine covenant is perfected, that covenant cannot be heteronomous; but the human will must be brought into such unison with the divine that it does what is well-pleasing to God of its own native impulse. Then first that relation is really brought about after which the Old Covenant strove with inadequate means: God is theirs, and they are His. This covenanting, which transforms the heart itself, is an act of God's miraculous grace, as Ezekiel also emphasizes in analogous oracles, xi. 19, xxxvi. 26 f.

When in this manner God's will has become immanent in every member of the Church, the Church's full maturity has come, which we found illustrated in Joel under a somewhat different aspect.[1] Then it will no longer be necessary for one member to teach and exhort another to know the Lord, for all will know Him from the least to the greatest, *i.e.* stand in living spiritual fellowship with Him; cf. Isa. liv. 13; John vi. 45; 1 John ii. 20, 27.

What forms the indispensable condition for this whole blessed transformation, and therefore comes first in Ezek. xxxvi. 25, here follows at the close: "For I will forgive their guilt, and remember their sin no more." Even without this statement we must have seen that such a covenant can only be the work of a grace that does away all sin and obliterates all the guilt that has accumulated under the present covenant, xxxiii. 8.

Here also we see everywhere the germs of New Testament

[1] Joel ii. 28 f. See p. 205.

truth. Before the seer stands the covenant of grace, in which God changes sinners into His children, so that they are able to serve Him from holy love to Him and blessed fellowship of spirit with Him.

In xxxii. 39 also the prophet speaks of this work of grace, dwelling especially on the union which must be the fruit of such an implanting of a godly mind and the blessing that must result therefrom, since the Lord will then have unqualified joy [1] in His people and load it ever with benefits.

xxxii. 39. "And I give them ONE heart and ONE way to fear me always for their good and their children's good after them. 40 And I make with them an ETERNAL covenant, so that I turn not away from doing good to them, and will put my fear in 41 their heart, that they depart not from me. And I have my delight in them, to do them good and plant them in this land faithfully with my whole heart and whole soul."

To this statement xxxiii. 9 adds the significant feature that the benefits with which the Lord then gladdens His redeemed Church will make an overpowering impression on all nations, with which iii. 17 (p. 332) is to be compared. Of the city of Jerusalem, at present given up to the destroyers, it is said :—

xxxiii. 9. "And it shall be to me a name of delight, a praise and pride to all nations of the earth that shall hear all the good that I do to them, and they shall tremble and be disquieted for all the good and all the peace that I show to it."

Thus not only the *world-judgment* has a mission to perform in the heathen world; also the unexampled goodness shown by the Lord to Jerusalem will shake the nations out of their self-confident complacency. Jerusalem will be to the Lord a name of delight in the eyes of the heathen, will be a sign of the delight He feels, hence a subject of His praise (bringing praise to Him) and pride before the whole world. The unrest and discomfort, nay, terror[2] of the nations, arises from their learning Yahveh's absolute superiority over them and their gods. But the perception of their own nothingness and of the Lord's uniqueness will lead to their praising Him, blessing themselves in Him, and bestirring themselves to obtain His salvation.

Finally, chap. xxxiii. ff. repeats with slight deviation (see p. 334)

[1] Cf. Zeph. iii. 17, p. 321.   [2] Cf. Ps. ii. 11.

the oracle of the righteous Sprout of David's stem, xxiii. 5 f.[1] But peculiar here is not merely the transference of the name "The Lord our Righteousness" to Jerusalem, which perhaps may be so named as the Church of the divinely righteous, but especially the confirmatory exposition, ver. 17 ff. The emphatic assertion that the seed of David shall never lack one to sit on Israel's throne is based on Nathan's saying,[2] and is to be understood in accordance with it thus: "The kingship of this house can never depart from it, despite any temporary interruption in its rule."[3] And as the Davidic royal house does not expire, neither does the Levitical priesthood, whose functions are established once for all.[4] Despite all appearance to the contrary (xxxiii. 24), these two pillars of the theocracy, a divinely-chosen (the Israelitish) monarchy and priesthood, continue; nay, a greater future lies before them. According to ver. 22, these two orders, the kingly and priestly, will be numberless as the stars of heaven or the sand of the sea. What does this mean? Considering the previous circumstances of the theocracy, national and geographical, a monarchy so strong or a priesthood so immense would not be even conceivable. Prophecy thus contemplates an extraordinary enlargement of the theocracy, transferring the promise[5] made to the entire seed of Jacob to its two most important orders in a moral sense. It is also intimated that the future of Israel rests with these two. Only it is too definite an explication of the assurance here given to make it say, with Hengstenberg and Nägelsbach, that the whole of Israel will attain kingly and priestly

[1] The whole section (xxxiii. 14-26) is wanting in the LXX., and is denied by many to belong to Jeremiah, to whom yet the entire style of these oracles points, as even Ewald maintains.

[2] 2 Sam. vii. 15 f. In the wording Jeremiah follows the form in which David (1 Kings ii. 4), and afterwards Solomon (1 Kings viii. 25), repeated the prophetic testament.

[3] Here also (as in xxiii. 4 f., see p. 333) the temporal relation of the one perfect Son of David to the rest is not more exactly defined. That the Davidic glory will culminate in the One, is confirmed by the statement that eternal dominion is assured to the entirety of David's seed, ver. 17. But ver. 21 f. no longer rises to that one culminating point, but speaks of a measureless, multiple development, which the relation of the people to God begun in David awaits.

[4] With respect also to the Levitical priesthood, it is not stated (xxxiii. 18) how its ministry will assume a new shape through the downfall of the existing temple now in prospect (iii. 16). Only its continuance and growth (ver. 21 f.) are taken into account.

[5] Gen. xxii. 17.

dignity, and that even the heathen will find admittance into this royal priesthood.[1] Later prophetic sayings, like Isa. lxi. 6 f., lxvi. 20 f., certainly indicate this mode of aggrandizement; but here merely the future of the orders, which will survive the judgment and grow to an unexampled extent, is contemplated. In Jeremiah above all an oracle like this, stretching beyond the conceivable from the first, must not be understood in a mere material sense; he insists on a more spiritual sense, taking as its starting-point and goal the inner significance of the Davidic and Levitical order more than its physical state. Like the relation of divine sonship founded in the Davidic monarchy, the priesthood attached to Levi's tribe also will have a vast number of representatives, so that its future will be related to its former state as tree to shoot, harvest to seed-corn, as the nation of Israel to its patriarchs.

Jeremiah foretold the judgment on Jerusalem and Judah as immediately impending, and that in the form of the overthrow of the city and the deportation of the people to Babylon. There the bondage is to continue seventy years according to his oracle;[2] then the judgment on Babylon[3] and the return of the captives occur, of which he says so much, and following thereon the rebuilding of the city.[4] He sees the inward in combination with the outward redemption, like Deutero-Isaiah again.[5] The nation, after its return, enjoys in untroubled peace its fellowship with the Lord, and the blessing accruing to it therefrom, chap. xxxi. No more precise relation of the one true David to the Davidic house generally, that is to rule for ever, is stated. But it is very significant that the same Jeremiah who pronounces an inexorable judgment on the outward and inward form of the national theocracy, and even puts the exodus from Egypt into the shade by a new act of mercy, while superseding the law of Moses with its ethical as well as ritual enactments by a higher kind of revelation and a more spiritual worship,

---

[1] The latter is maintained by Keil only, according to Isa. lxvi. 20 f.

[2] xxv. 12, xxix. 10. To suppose a later interpolation on account of the prediction is without warrant.

[3] Cf. also Jer. l. and li., which at least are Jeremiah's in the main.

[4] Cf. Jer. xvi. 14 f., xxiv. 6, xxix. 14, xxx. 3, 10 f., 18, xxxi. 23 ff., 38 ff., xxxii. 36 ff., xxxiii. 7, xlvi. 27 f., l. 4, 34.

[5] Cf. what was said on p. 33 respecting the one indivisible framework of the prophetic visions.

declares the promises given to the fathers of Israel as well as those to David and his house to be as irreversible as the order of nature, in virtue of which the earth exists.[1] The contents of those divine testaments will only find a far purer and more glorious expression in the life of his people than has hitherto been the case. The new character of the Church, which is the product of God's creative, redeeming act, will, above all, perfectly harmonize with God's holy will, and thus even the outward form of God's covenant will be according to truth, and the life of God's people pure and undisturbed.

§ 37. *Zechariah* xii.–xiv.

The following remarks may serve to justify the insertion of these oracles in this place. As the author of Zech. ix.–xi. appears to be a contemporary of Hosea, so the author of xii.–xiv. appears to be a prophet of the last period before the Babylonian exile. The northern kingdom is here no longer noticed; it has plainly fallen into ruin. The prophecy revolves round Judah-Jerusalem, especially round the siege of the city, which will be invested and taken by the heathen, but yet at last will come out conqueror through the Lord's intervention. On it the hostile efforts of the whole world will be wrecked. Chap. xii. 11 takes us more definitely into the years after Josiah's death at Megiddo, after 610 B.C. Against the post-exilian composition (to say nothing of the style of language and presentation, so widely different from that of the post-exilian Zechariah) tells the prevalence of idolatry and false prophets in the land, xii. 2 ff. The post-exilian messengers of the Lord have no longer to rebuke these two sins, whereas Jeremiah particularly has so much to do with uncalled prophets, chap. xxiii. As to contents, the announcement of a conquest of Jerusalem by the heathen finds no analogy in the field of post-exilian prophecy (leaving Daniel out of sight). Ezekiel, indeed (xxxviii. f.), depicts a final attack of the nations on the newly-built Jerusalem, but it is repelled by the Lord Himself. What Zechariah (xii.–xiv.) combines is there separated, viz. the future conquest (in Ezekiel's eyes belonging to the past), having the exile for its consequence, and the last ineffectual storming of the city of God by

---

[1] Jer. xxxi. 35 ff., xxxiii. 20 ff., 25 f.

the heathen. We therefore hold this *massa* to be an oracle coming from the last years of the old temple.[1] The similarity of Zech. xiii. 7 to xi. 17 has led, as we believe, to the union of the section with ix.–xi., as ix. 9 (cf. ii. 10) brought about its connection with the post-exilian Zechariah (cf. also viii. 20 ff. with xiv. 16 ff.). The name Zechariah is one of the most frequent in the Bible, so that the identity of name may also have had to do with the matter.

Thus even in the days when Jerusalem was in rapid decline, a seer took up Isaiah's assertion of the indestructibleness of the heaven-chosen Zion, and set in clear light its central significance in reference to the world-judgment as seen already by Joel. Not that the author of Zech. xii.–xiv. held the city to be impregnable, in glaring contradiction to the prophecies of the other genuine prophets, especially of his contemporary Jeremiah. On the contrary, he foretells, in the most definite manner, Jerusalem's fall, chap. xiv. What he sees in chap. xii. relates, as the indications of time show (vers. 3, 8, 9), to the more distant future. Then a more general movement of the nations will take place against the city of God, whose cause the Lord espouses.

Then according to xii. 2 f., Jerusalem becomes a cup full of drunkenness and reeling, from which all nations will greedily drink[2] stupefying wine. It becomes a burdensome stone, from which they will suffer hurt, trying their strength on it in vain.[3] For the foundation-stone laid by God in Zion (Isa. xxviii. 16) cannot be thrust aside by the united strength of the whole world. The multitude of well-armed, assailant nations, who have all made God's city the aim of their destroying work, are smitten by God with blindness and reeling (xii. 4 ff.), like Pharaoh's armament, Ex. xiv. 24 f.; on the other hand, the Lord's eye remains open over Judah, so that Jerusalem abides unmoved in its place, and Judah grows so skilled in war, that it expands and burns on every side like a firebrand in corn-

---

[1] So even Ewald. Reuss puts this section in the time of Manasseh; Bleek puts xiii. 7–xiv. 21 under Josiah or Jehoiakim, xii. 1–xiii. 6 (by the same prophet) in the last days of Jehoiakim or under Jehoiakin, Zedekiah.

[2] The figure occurs in Obad. ver. 16, where it expresses the nemesis on the drunken revelling of the plunderers of Jerusalem. Jeremiah uses it more freely, xxv. 15, li. 7.

[3] Jerome rightly reminds of the gymnastic exercises of this kind engaged in by the youth of his day in Palestine, as is the case still in Syria.

sheaves. But while Jerusalem is God's proper seat, He is not bound to castle and temple of stone, or to precedence of race. He proves this by granting deliverance first to the country inhabitants of Judah who are also in distress [1] (xii. 7), that the house of David and citizens of Jerusalem may not be lifted up in carnal conceit. How their martial strength is divinely enhanced is shown in

xii. 8. "On that day Yahveh will defend the dwellers of Jerusalem, and the stumbler among them on that day shall be like David, and the house of David like divine beings, like the angel of Yahveh before them."

The coming of the divine rule, which is also a dwelling of the Lord in the midst of His Church, is made known in the bestowal of special gifts and powers. In the above passage the citizens of the future Jerusalem, who are without exception living members of the Church,[2] enjoy divine protection from all evil, and divinely-given strength fitting them for every heroic act of faith. The stumbler, *i.e.* the feeblest, who is weak of foot, will be a hero like David, the conqueror of the giant, who leaped every wall in the name of his God (Ps. xviii. 29, 33 ff.). But David's house, that was chosen to guide his people, will be like superhuman beings, super-terrestrial *Gibborim* (Ps. ciii. 20), immortal and unconquerable, far superior to all earthly powers. This is further enhanced by the addition: "Like the angel of Yahveh before them," *i.e.* the angel personating God Himself, who once under Moses and Joshua marched before them—a guide to victory. Now David's house, as God's immediate representative, will be able to assume this guiding function. Then the Messianic idea has attained full reality, God's gracious presence is embodied in the king of the nation; for self-evidently this king is presupposed as the one head of the Davidic house, and is compared to the guarding, guiding angel. The Lord, therefore, has a wondrous exaltation of this race and people in mind, little as any prospect of so great a future appears at present. But certainly the nation in its present state

[1] That because of such sympathy with the fate of the country people the prophet cannot have been an inhabitant of the town, is an inference characteristic of modern science. Was the author of Isa. viii. 23 a Galilæan? Hitzig also is wrong in supposing that the Judæans are here thought of as encamped against Jerusalem, which ought not to be imported from xiv. 14. See below.

[2] Cf. Isa. iv. 3, p. 262.

is neither capable nor worthy of such exaltation. The way thither, as the prophet says in a noteworthy manner, lies through deepest humiliation, not merely outward, but chiefly inward.

xii. 9–11. "And it shall come to pass on that day, I will seek to destroy all the heathen who come against Jerusalem. And I will pour out on the house of David, and on the inhabitants of Jerusalem, the spirit of grace and supplication, and they shall look on me, whom they pierced, and mourn for him, like the mourning for the first-born, and be distressed for him, as one is distressed for the first-born. On that day, great will be the mourning in Jerusalem, as the mourning of Hadadrimmon in the vale of Megiddo."

As what precedes reminds us of Joel who described Jerusalem as the target of the hostility of all nations, and placed the judgment in the vale of Jehoshaphat in the immediate vicinity of Zion, so what ver. 10 says of the esoteric salvation of Jerusalem is allied to Joel ii. 28. As there,[1] an "outpouring of the Spirit" takes place, a rich universal dispensing of the Divine Spirit of mercy and grace. But the effect ascribed to this Spirit is strange. The תַּחֲנוּנִים: *precationes, supplicationes*, introduces this effect. The new relation of the Church to God is based on grace on God's side, and penitent prayer for grace on the people's side. The Spirit who brings grace will work repentance as the necessary condition of its reception. The evil they have done they will feel in its entire extent and full weight. Their gaze will be fastened on Him on whom they have inflicted an unmerited fate, and who is no other than the holy God Himself.

Many schemes have been tried to get rid of or render intelligible the monstrous thing here affirmed by the prophet. Apart from unauthorized changes in the reading,[2] דָּקַר has been weakened into *maledicere*,[3] which has no warrant in usage and

---

[1] See p. 206.

[2] A number of codices read אֵלָיו instead of אֵלַי; the former is a decidedly later reading. The old versions read אֵלַי (LXX., Vulg., Targ., Syr.), and even John xix. 37, Rev. i. 7 prove nothing for אֵלָיו, which Ewald and Bunsen prefer. The reading אֵל (= אֶל), desired by Bleek after Michaelis, would be intolerably flat, and on linguistic grounds scarcely comprehensible.

[3] So already Theodore of Mopsuestia. And Calvin: *Metaphorice hic accipitur confixio pro continua irritatione.* Similarly Grotius, Rosenmüller, Gesenius.

does not suit the mourning for the dead that follows. Rather the speaker, the Lord Himself, describes Himself as the One whom they pierced with deadly steel.[1] But how is this conceivable in reference to the living God? The key is found, as even Hitzig confesses, in chap. xi., where we saw that the Lord regards the treatment of His representative as done to Himself. As the Lord in chap. xi. 13 regards the contemptuous dismissal of His servant as befalling Himself, so here He regards the still worse outrage, nay, murder! But the prophet has in view not simply some past murder of a prophet,[2] but, as xiii. 7 especially shows, the future fate of the man of God. He sees that God's most trusty servant, the true Shepherd, who feeds the flock in God's stead, will fall victim to the hate of the house of David and the dwellers in Jerusalem. So hostile in disposition are they now to God. Before the Lord exalts them, they will complete their guilt, and the commencement of a turning to good will be their feeling keenly the crimes which they have committed in incomprehensible blindness.

The sorrow of repentance will express itself in a national mourning like that occasioned by the death of the beloved King Josiah, who in the plain of Megiddo[3] found a hero's death in conflict with Pharaoh Necho. The mourning of Hadadrimmon in the valley of Megiddo cannot well refer to anything else than the country's mourning for that king.[4] This gave the finest example of a universal and yet sincere mourning. Thus distress for the murdered man of God will fill the whole people, and withal be felt as deeply as if every house had lost its best, nay, only son.

[1] "They shall look on me as one whom they pierced." For the construction Köhler rightly refers to Jer. xxxviii. 9.

[2] The traditional martyrdom of Isaiah under Manasseh has been thought of, or that of Uriah under Jehoiakim, Jer. xxvi. 20 ff.

[3] 2 Kings xxiii. 29 f.; 2 Chron. xxxv. 20-24; Herodotus, ii. 159. The place called here Hadadrimmon, whose site Jerome (ad loc.) fixes near Jezreel (under the modern name Maximianopolis), is consequently a more exact designation of the spot where Josiah fell and the mourning ceremony was afterwards presumably celebrated (according to 2 Chron. xxxv. 25), although according to the more precise account of Chronicles the king was brought mortally wounded to Jerusalem before he died.

[4] The ingenious interpretation of Hitzig, that the prophet means the mourning for the god Adonis (= Hadadrimmon), is to be unreservedly rejected. See against this comparison Baudissin's *Studien zur Semit. Religionsgesch.* i. 295 ff. How could a prophet of Yahveh name a feast of this kind, of whose observance in the vale of Megiddo no trace is found, as a type of the profoundest contrite sorrow? Just as little can we think, with Pressel, of the mourning for Sisera (Judg. v. 28 ff.).

Every race will mourn as if it had been specially concerned in that death and had lost its head, first David's royal house and the priestly one of Levi, those two bearers of the promise, who also stand side by side as "races" in Jer. xxxiii. 24;[1] moreover, the other races all follow their example. The participation of the women is expressly noted, not only because they had much to do with mourning for the dead, but also because like the men they had special reason for *this* penitent sorrow, being no less concerned in the guilt (cf. Jer. xliv. 9, 15).

This oracle of the seer foretells a wonderful change in the nation, which will first complete its evil-doing in terrible fashion and then be made conscious of it through the influence of the Divine Spirit. The description of its evil-doing as a piercing of the Lord is not a mere metaphor or to be referred to the future in a typical sense only, as if the matter in hand were the murder of a prophet already past; but it is a prophetic announcement of what lies before the nation's true Shepherd. But by the one thus shamefully murdered in the future does the prophet understand the Son of David promised by Isaiah and Micah, as well as in Zech. ix. 9 ? This might be inferred from the comparison with the mourning for King Josiah, as well as from the fact that this man of God is afterwards described as Shepherd (xiii. 7), which generally points more to a king than a prophet. On the other hand, the house of David here stands not on the side of God, but on that of the people, and is in great need of repentance (cf. also xiii. 1), and the parallel prophecy Zech. xi. shows that a prophet also may fill the shepherd's office. In accordance with this parallel it seems more probable to us that the experiences of the prophet as such gave him a view of the true Shepherd of the people, and he pictured Him to himself in simple prophetic activity, yet still as leading the better portion of the nation, until the enmity of the great inflicted on Him a still worse lot than the one depicted in chap. xi.

The *fulfilment* first put it beyond doubt that the Shepherd

---

[1] It is impossible to state with certainty why the house of Nathan is placed specially beside David's house, and the race of Shimei alongside Levi's, really forming as they do secondary lines belonging thereto. For the Nathan mentioned is not the prophet, since a family in an improper sense (body of prophets) would here be out of place, but the son of David (2 Sam. v. 14 ; Luke iii. 21), and the race of Shimei placed beside Levi's is scarcely a Benjamite one (2 Sam. xvi. 5), but a branch of Levi according to Num. iii. 17 ff., 21.

dying in God's stead is no other than He who in Micah v. 3 feeds the flock in divine majesty. What seems in the prophecy a monstrous anthropomorphism was literally fulfilled in Him who was able to say: "He that sees me sees the Father." And even what is said here of Judah's conversion has through the Spirit of God found its realization, at least initially. When the Spirit of God was poured out on Jerusalem at Pentecost, the eyes of many were opened. Peter cried to the inhabitants of that city: τοῦτον διὰ χειρὸς ἀνόμων προσπήξαντες ἀνείλατε! And it is said, "they were struck to the heart" by this accusation: κατενύγησαν τὴν καρδίαν, Acts ii. 23, 27. What was it they saw when the covering fell from their eyes? That they had pierced the Lord Himself, the Son of God, who is one with the Father. When once all Israel shall learn the truth about this incomparably faithful and loving One who was designed to be its Shepherd and whom in fearful blindness it has put to death, its first gaze on Him will cause it unspeakable terror, its first feeling will be the heart-piercing sorrow of self-accusation. But this terror is health-giving, this sorrow brings salvation; for it is the work of the Spirit of grace. That the heathen also will join in slaying the great Shepherd of the tribe of Judah, and hence will join in the mourning, when they see Him (John xix. 37; Rev. i. 7), is not said in this prophecy.

Chap. xiii. 1–6 is to be joined closely to xii. 9 ff. The work of grace on Jerusalem is further described. It consists, as in Jer. xxxi. 33 f., Ezek. xxxvi. 25 f., in justification and sanctification. The former is promised as the effect of a fountain opened by God and flowing in Jerusalem:—

xiii. 1. "On that day a fountain shall be opened for the house of David and the inhabitants of Jerusalem for sin and uncleanness."

On the penitent cry of the princely house and the people of the city, covered as they are with blood-guiltiness, a fountain of cleansing will be opened at the instance of the same merciful God who by His Spirit produced the repentance. Their penitence itself can only be the subjective precondition of salvation; the objective medium of justifying or cleansing must be provided by God. Whilst Isa. liii. represents the very suffering and death of the Servant of God, which according to Zech. xii. is the sin of the people and forms the subject of its repentance, as the means of expiation, chap. xiii. 1 stops at the wondrous fountain, which according to Joel iii. 18 also will adorn the future Jerusalem, and is content with indicating its effect, which is also mentioned in Joel iii. 21, but not put in express connection with the fertilizing water.[1] It will be a fountain for the use of the house of David and the dwellers in Jerusalem, to wash away sin and uncleanness. The latter word (נִדָּה) applies elsewhere to Levitical defilement, which is to be washed away with pure water, the former (חַטָּאת) to sin proper; but according to the Mosaic law the two stand in intimate connection. Uncleanness is called חטאת (Num. xix. 9), having an ethical background, while sin proper or guilt falls under the idea of defilement,[2] on which account the prophet here mentions it by both names, and promises that it shall be removed by pure water. What the manifold and burdensome Levitical usages of expiation and purifying fail really to accomplish, the Lord will then effect simply and perfectly: the cleansing of His Church from everything that renders it displeasing in His eyes. The divine fountain, flowing abundantly and unceasingly, makes superfluous artificial means of expiation which of necessity are constantly renewed. When, therefore, Jerusalem is cleansed from the sins cleaving to it and made a priestly Church (Num. viii. 7), the Lord will preserve it also from new guilt, sanctify it,—which is especially affirmed in reference to two sources of continual sin, idolatry and false prophets.

xiii. 2. "And it shall come to pass on that day, saith Yahveh of hosts, I will root out the names of the idols from the land, and they shall not be remembered henceforth, and also the prophets and the spirit of uncleanness I will sweep away from the land."

That at the time when the prophet speaks idolatry was practised in Jerusalem, is clear from the fact of his describing first of all the radical destruction of this abominable wickedness as God's sanctifying act. This is quite in keeping with the days of Zephaniah, Jeremiah, and Ezekiel. The Lord will destroy these fictitious gods to the last vestige—to every defilement of the lips

---

[1] In Zech. xiv. 8 the fertilizing effect of this fountain comes out more strongly, in the train of Joel iii. 21. Finally, in the wake of Zechariah comes Ezekiel, who expands into a picture (xlvii. 1 ff.) these outlines, here sketched briefly in the style of the early prophets. No proof is forthcoming that this order of dependence is to be reversed (despite Stade, *Zeitschr. f. altt. Wft.* 1881, p. 81 f.).

[2] Cf. "water of expiation," Num. viii. 7, which expression plainly alludes to the ethical side of uncleanness.

and the heart.[1] The second thing from which He will thoroughly purge the land is the class of vagrant *prophets*, controlled by an impure spirit and partaking of a heathen character, so that it pollutes the nation in God's sight as a hateful stain,—a condemnation again which is quite in place on the lips of a contemporary of Jeremiah. So thoroughly will the Lord wean the people that now assumes, without being called, the prophet's mantle and boasts of divine revelations, from this abuse, that to follow this practice will then be the greatest disgrace, nay, expose to death, and no one will wish to have it said that he belongs to this impure fraternity. Their own parents will accuse the lying prophets, nay, put them to a violent death, as is now done to the true prophets,[2] so alive will the Church then be to all the misery brought upon it by the arts of these fanatics and deceivers. That by the prophets to be swept away (xiii. 2) only the false ones are meant (so rightly LXX., Targ., Syr.), should not have been questioned. How could a prophet describe true prophets as a pollution to the land, to be abolished along with idolatry, and bringing the land into intimate association with the impure spirit?[3] The expression is used in the same sense as in Jeremiah,[4] from whose discourses we see that in his time false prophets were the rule, true prophets a vanishing exception. These prophets are also seen to be thoroughly heathen by their self-inflicted wounds, which are made out to be scars received in conflict, such physical maceration ministering to exaltation of spirit, 1 Kings xviii. 28. But it is a wrong supplement to the prophet's thought to make him prophesy, as many do,[5] that prophecy will cease in the last days, because in the general divine illumination it will no longer be necessary, so that any one claiming to be a prophet would prove himself a deceiver by assuming such a peculiar attitude. What Jer. xxxi. 34 says of the maturity of the Church only comes into view here in so far as the gift of trying the spirits, now altogether absent, will then

---

[1] So in the train of Hos. ii. 19, p. 232.

[2] Cf. xiii. 3, דָּקַר, with xii. 10.

[3] רוּחַ הַטֻּמְאָה, not *unclean mind and spirit* generally, but in antithesis to the Spirit of God: *Spirit of impurity*, proceeding from unclean powers.

[4] Cf. Jer. xxiii. 13 ff.; Lam. ii. 14, iv. 13, etc.

[5] Hitzig, Köhler, Stade, and others. That our Zechariah himself does not profess to be a prophet (Hitzig, Stade), is only to be conceded in the sense that he does not wish to belong to the "wicked caste" (Hitzig) that gives itself this name.

be so general, that a *lying* prophet will find no favour even with his parents. Thus we have here only the negative side, to which Joel ii. 28 f. gives the positive complement.

But the present unhappy condition, in which God's noblest gifts are forced to serve the ungodly spirit, will lead to a most terrible judgment, the Lord renouncing His chosen instrument and so giving up to destruction the good who still adhere to it.

xiii. 7. "Sword, arise[1] over my shepherd and against the man of my fellowship,[2] saith Yahveh of hosts. Smite the shepherd that the sheep may be scattered, and I will turn my hand against the little ones."

To wish to join this oracle (xiii. 7–9) directly to chap. xi., as if it stood here in the wrong place (Ewald, Stade), was only possible through an entire mistaking of its sense. It is true, the Shepherd meant here must take an attitude to God just like that of the prophet there, xi. 1 ff.; but xiii. 7 does not suit the close of that chapter, because there the good Shepherd has meantime been dismissed, and the flock is no longer under him. But it is incomprehensible how any one could confound one whom the Lord so emphatically calls *His* shepherd and man of His intimate fellowship, and who is the protection of the little, defenceless sheep, with the bad, vicious shepherd in xi. 15–17.[3] On the contrary, it is one whose guidance is the last refuge of the poor, faithful Church, a guardian of the Church who stands in intimate relationship to God, certainly none else than He of whose violent death chap. xii. 10 speaks as if in him the Lord Himself were murdered. If chap. xii. 10 traces his death to the violence of the people, and xiii. 7 to divine infliction, this cannot mislead us. Both accounts are correct. His murder is just as much the people's grossest sin as God's heaviest judgment, since the most terrible punishment is for the nation to be violently deprived of the Head, in whom fellowship with God is incarnate.

---

[1] Properly = "Awake!" עוּרִי is *milra*, contrary to rule, as in Judg. v. 12, Zech. ix. 9, because the iambic tone-fall is more appropriate to such a summons. Observe also the rhythm with רֹעִי and עֲמִיתִי.

[2] עָמִית occurs elsewhere in the concrete meaning "companion" (= רֵעַ); here in the more original meaning: *companionship, fellowship*. Very unhappily Ewald: "my Lord-nephew;" so God is said to address the bad monarch, who yet as king stands near Him!

[3] Even Hitzig understands by him a bad although legitimate king.

Thus the difficult question, considering the mystic character of the vision, which the prophet has in view in this heaven-favoured Shepherd, is answered here as in xii. 10. It is to be noted that by his murder, according to xiii. 8 f., the judgment bursting on Judah is completed, since after his removal the nation is two-thirds annihilated, whilst the last third (cf. Ezek. v. 2 f.) is put into the crucible, from which it emerges pure metal, moulded into God's true people (xiii. 9, like Hos. ii. 25). The power of the judgment is consequently released by the fall of the God-chosen shepherd; the seer beholds his fall in conjunction with the dissolution of the theocracy. Whether, then, a pious prince of David's house stands before him, or, which seems more probable to us in accordance with the related chap. xi., a prophetic Head of the Church, in whom God once more directly assumes its guidance, the main element in this prophecy is, that *God's true representative in Judah must suffer and die through the guilt of the nation*, and that the worst catastrophe will be when this divine shepherd succumbs to the hate of his people, hate really directed against God Himself, the nation thus filling up the measure of its enmity against the Lord. Here we have a profound glance into God's plan, which is further unfolded and materially enlarged by Deutero-Isaiah.

If, then, this fearful event presented itself to the prophet in direct connection with the fall of Jerusalem imminent in his own days, still his prophecy was not exhausted either in what befell Judah's God-estranged king, or in what Jeremiah had to suffer as a genuine shepherd of the people. The martyrdom of God's faithful servants could here only be typical, as its use in the second book of Isaiah shows. Only when Judah crucified the prophet of David's house who was entirely one with God, was its destiny completed: it was left without a shepherd, and fell into the hands of thieves and murderers. Therefore did Jesus, who called Himself "*the good Shepherd*" (John x. 11 ff.) with reference to such prophecies, on the last night expressly refer His disciples to Zech. xiii. 7,[1] which saying must now be fulfilled in Him and them. If He alone, in virtue of His unique relation to God, could fully claim for Himself this title at once regal and indicative of love to the people, only His death had all the

[1] Matt. xxvi. 31; Mark xiv. 27; cf. John xvi. 32.

terrible significance for the people, which the seer attributes to the violent end of the true Shepherd. That this image of the suffering and dying friend of God, like the one sketched in Isa. liii., tended strongly towards union with the image of the Davidic Prince of peace formed by the prophets, even the Synagogue felt (of which later); but Jesus Christ first exhibited the union of the two figures which appear to be in irreconcilable contradiction, thus proving the possibility and fact of this union having been intended by the Spirit of prophecy. Springing from David's house, He yet appeared before His people with no other legal title than that of the Good Shepherd sent by God, and submitted without resistance to dismissal, nay, to a martyr's death, without His kingdom of salvation and peace being on this account hindered in its victorious march.

Chap. xiv. of the same prophet presents a new eschatological discourse. The Day of the Lord is here illustrated from a different side than the one in chap. xii. First of all, on it Jerusalem is attacked and *taken* by all the heathen, half of the people being left in the city (xiv. 1, 2). Then the Lord marches forth against the enemies of His city (ver. 3), to smite them down before it by a miraculous pestilence (ver. 12), at the same time making them attack each other in hand-to-hand conflict (ver. 13). These two different acts (xiv. 1 f. and 3 ff.) are combined under the idea of the "Day of Yahveh," ver. 1, which therefore does not represent a strict temporal unity, but, on the other hand, that it may be concentrated in closer unity, is shown in ver. 6 f., where stress is laid on such unity. Here also the seer is marked by the transcendental character, that we found *e.g.* in Isa. xxiv.–xxvii., where the prophet's gaze is less confined within the bounds of the historical present than is the case elsewhere; on the contrary, looking from a lofty perspective, he sees earthly things very concretely indeed, but in spiritual absoluteness, the intermediate points of transition disappearing entirely. Thus in ver. 2 it is all nations, not the Chaldæans alone, who conquer Jerusalem, and the divine judgment upon them is linked immediately to their victory, ver. 3. The image of the new kingdom of God arising out of the judgment thrusts itself into its very midst (vers. 8–11), and the worship of the heathen in Jerusalem follows at once on their destruction (ver. 16 ff.). The description is of a strongly visionary character, so that, while everything takes sensuous forms, these can nowhere be understood in a merely sensuous meaning, the outer framework being merely the veil of the mysterious divine working. Thus in form and contents the seer most closely follows Joel. What has just been said applies equally to the picture of the judgment of the nations, ver. 3 ff.

xiv. 3. "And Yahveh shall march forth and fight against the heathen as on the day when He fought, on the day of hand-
4 to-hand conflict. And His feet shall stand on that day upon Mount Olivet, that lies before Jerusalem eastward. And Mount Olivet shall split from the middle eastward and westward into a very great valley, and half of the mountain shall
5 move northward and half southward. And ye shall flee into the valley of my mountains; for the valley of the mountains shall reach to Azel. And ye shall flee as ye fled before the earthquake in the days of Uzziah, king of Judah. And
6 YAHVEH SHALL COME, my God, all the saints with thee. And it shall come to pass on that day no light shall be, the stars
7 of splendour shall be veiled. And it shall be a definite DAY known to the Lord, not day and not night, but at eventide it shall be LIGHT."

Here, as in Joel iii., the judgment takes place in the immediate neighbourhood of Jerusalem, the heathen having streamed together against the city, and especially swarming in the Kidron valley. Over this valley the Lord, who marches forth as His people's champion, takes His stand on the Mount of Olives commanding the city (cf. Ezek. xi. 23). But the mountain miraculously divides, a broad valley girt by a mountain-wall appearing. Thither, into the "valley of my mountains" (*i.e.* into the valley enclosed by the mountains built by the Lord), the inhabitants of Jerusalem, terrified by the shaking of the earth, spontaneously flee,[1] so that the mountain on which God, the world-judge, stands becomes a fastness for His Church. Thus in the last decisive conflict He brings it unexpected help. Then *He comes*, and on His appearance the words of the seer pass into prayer: "All the saints with Thee!" The angels accompanying the Judge and executing His sentence are meant, as in Joel iii. 11. Ver. 6 f. also adopts

---

[1] That they can pass at once from the city into the valley, is affirmed in the clause by the obscure word אצל, which, according to Micah i. 11, is to be understood of a locality in the immediate neighbourhood of Jerusalem.

the conception of the Day of the Lord usual since Joel's days; mysterious darkness will veil in gloom this baleful day. It is without the clear light of heaven.[1] That *one* day, known to the Lord and fixed by Him, will lack the light of day. But after light and darkness have struggled together the whole day, at eventide it shall be light, as after heavy storm. *Post tenebras lux* is the motto of the whole of prophecy. Even the terrible catastrophe of the final judgment, which is here, as in Joel, at first veiled in impenetrable gloom, leads to light and life. Out of it comes the rejuvenated Jerusalem, from which perennial living waters stream through the land, xiv. 8.

xiv. 9. "And on that day YAHVEH SHALL BE KING OVER THE WHOLE EARTH. On that day YAHVEH SHALL BE ALONE, AND HIS NAME ALONE."

The result of the final judgment is the unlimited rule of the true God revealed in Israel, who is already Lord of the whole earth in a certain sense (Micah iv. 13), but is then acknowledged as king universally, after all the heathen have felt His power. The victory over the whole world of nations necessarily brings with it this universal rule of God, on which account כָּל־הָאָרֶץ is not to be limited, with Köhler, to the land of Judah, as in the next verse, where the residence of this universal ruler is described. Yahveh will be *One, i.e.* acknowledged by all the world as the only God, in which character the law had long ago revealed Him to Israel, and so in very deed He will have no other God beside Him.[2] Even the dangerous manifoldness of His name, which had the effect of multiplying God Himself, the diverse conception of His nature giving rise to an *alter Deus*, will cease among Israel and the nations. His true name, guarded against all misunderstanding, will, in consequence of His perfect revelation, be in every mouth.

In ver. 10 f. the "holy mountain," on which God then takes up His abode, is described with geographical distinctness, but not without ideal transfiguration. It is Jerusalem restored to its full compass and raised to public distinction, encircled by a fertile country, secure against the ban, *i.c.* the extreme judgment of the

---

[1] Cf. Joel ii. 31, iii. 15. In Zech. xiv. 6 the *kethib* יְקָרוֹת יִפָּאוּן, *the splendid ones* (*stars*, cf. Job xxxi. 26) *shall withdraw themselves*, is to be retained, in accordance with Joel iii. 15; the *Keri* reads less suitably: קָרוֹת וְקִפָּאוֹן, *cold and frost*.

[2] Deut. vi. 4, cf. iv. 35, 39, v. 7; Ex. xx. 3.

Lord, because its deadly sins have ceased. But the prophet's gaze falls back once more (xiv. 12 ff.) on the judgment-act of the Lord; now its mode is more precisely indicated for the first time, and in ghastly colours. In consequence of the plague with which the Lord smites the enemy, they will rot away during life, and also slaughter each other, two forms of national judgment such as history furnishes on a smaller scale,[1] and as are constantly recurring among the enemies of God. Thus all that will be left for the defenders of Jerusalem will be the pursuit, in which Judah also takes part,[2] and the division of the spoil.

But all the heathen who escape destruction at the judgment will come up yearly to the residence of King Yahveh to offer worship, and so will form with Israel one great festive Church, celebrating the feast of Tabernacles, xiv. 16 ff., and in keeping with the meaning of the feast will offer thanks for the bounties of nature, and pray for further blessings on the earth. Whoever does not journey thither is excluded from rain, and therefore from blessing, not excepting even Egypt, watered in other ways (p. 215). The prosperity of every land, the welfare of every people, consequently depends on whether they worship the King of the divine kingdom, Yahveh of hosts, or not.

xiv. 20 f. "On that day 'holiness of Yahveh' will stand on the bells of the horses, and the pots in the house of Yahveh will be like the sacrificial bowls before the altar. And every pot in Jerusalem and Judah will be holiness of Yahveh of hosts, and all who sacrifice come and take of them, and cook therein, and there shall no more be any Canaanite in the house of the Lord of hosts in that day."

To the universal extension of God's kingdom over the earth corresponds the extraordinary increase in the holiness of Jerusalem, where what is most profane and worldly in itself will bear the stamp of the holy God. By way of example the bells of the horses are mentioned, which hitherto served merely worldly ends as a resource and luxury of vain princes (ix. 10). On their bells will one day stand the sacred inscription found on the high priest's diadem. There is nothing so earthly and worldly

---

[1] Cf. for the first Isa. xxxvii. 36; for the second, Judg. vii. 22; 2 Chron. xx. 23. See p. 213.
[2] The context shows that ver. 14 cannot, as the majority think, refer to a conflict of Judah *against* Jerusalem. See Köhler here.

that it will not then be consecrated by nearness to God to the
service of the Most High. And what hitherto had possessed the
lowest degree of holiness, such as the vessels used in cooking the
sacrificial flesh, will then be so holy that it may be brought before
the Lord, like the sacrificial bowls filled with blood, and borne to
the altar. Nay, every vessel in Judah-Jerusalem will have the
character of holiness, so that the masses of strangers may use
them without hesitation for purposes of worship. In consequence
of this the unworthy traffic in new vessels and animals for sacrifice that draws traders[1] there will cease in the temple, *i.e.* in its
precincts. This traffic, so repugnant to the prophet, which our
Lord significantly opposed with ardent zeal as a desecration of the
temple,[2] will then be needless and impossible, everything in the
land being holy. We see that as the temple enlarges, so that all
nations appear in its forecourts, so the holiness of the God dwelling
therein gains such intensity that it penetrates everything in the
land. All this did a prophet see and say at a time when, as he
clearly knew, the temple and the holy city were doomed to
destruction!

[1] כנעני is perhaps here to be taken with Hitzig, not in the national, but in the
ethical sense. Cf. Prov. xxxi. 24; Job xl. 30; Isa. xxiii. 8.

[2] Matt. xxi. 12 f.; Mark xi. 15 ff.; Luke xix. 45 f.; John ii. 14 ff.

FIFTH SECTION.

THE PROPHETS OF THE EXILE: EZEKIEL, ISAIAH XL.–LXVI.

§ 38. *Ezekiel's Oracles and Visions.*

COMPARED with previous prophetic discourse, the prophecy of the period of the *exile* shows a notable difference. If hitherto the menace of destroying judgment everywhere stood in the foreground, now when judgment has run its course the promise of the *redemption and new birth of God's people* forms the main subject of prophetic announcement. The transition is represented by *Ezekiel*,[1] a younger contemporary of Jeremiah, who had been deported with King Jehoiakin even before Jerusalem's fall, and called in his banishment to the prophetic office. In the first part of his book (i.–xxiv.), spoken before 588 B.C., the announcement of judgment still predominates. The rebellious house of Israel (Judah), the city of Jerusalem with its temple defiled by heathen abominations, are doomed to destruction; Judah, like Israel, must go into exile. But after all this is done, in the second part (xxxiii.–xlviii.), the oracle of promise, which previously only appeared here and there amid words of condemnation, speaks in clear, full tones.

We have first of all to call attention to these beams of light in the book (i.–xxiv.) full of mourning, lamentation, and woe. The exile inflicted on the nation is to last only a fixed number of years (iv. 5 f.), like the Egyptian bondage; of the nation abandoned in great measure to judgment a small remnant is preserved for the future (v. 3); this remnant will be gathered from all lands, whither it has been dispersed (xi. 17). Just where the departure of the divine Shekinah from the temple is spoken of, a future spiritualizing of the Church's relation to God is foretold, analogous to the one promised by Jeremiah (xxxi. 31 ff.), Ezek. xi. 19 f., an oracle repeated in more complete form in the section of promise, xxxvi. 25 ff.

---

[1] Cf. art. "Ezekiel," in Herzog, 2nd ed. iv. 462 ff.

Also the symbolic description of the history of Jerusalem ends with the promise of unexampled experience of grace after the judgment. The representation is symbolic in a twofold respect, the city being characterized in its course of development, while the Church is typified therein; and just because of this religious, moral character of Jerusalem it is presented in personal form as a woman. It was a helpless foundling, to which Yahveh, out of mere pity, showed tender care, thus securing its life and growth. But it was an ill-starred, graceless foster-child, which, instead of remaining true to its legal lord, gave itself up to whoredom, and therefore must bear its shame. Its history, however, will not end at this point, but at the divine favour shown to the faithless one, with whom the Lord establishes His covenant anew and for ever. Jerusalem certainly behaved worse than Samaria and even Sodom, her sisters (xvi. 49–51). But the Lord will also restore these, in order to be able again to have mercy on Jerusalem (xvi. 53). This linking of the mercy to Jerusalem with that shown to *Sodom*, which stands, of course, typically or representatively for heathendom lost and far from God,[1] is extraordinarily significant in every aspect. It implies that God does not exercise judgment and grace according to party caprice, but that the same mercy which is shown to the covenant people involved in sin and suffering, must also at last be shown to the heathen world condemned for like sins, but more excusable. When Smend asserts (pointing to ver. 47) that Ezekiel does not follow up the thought of a restoration of Sodom, the only inference, certainly a weighty one, to be drawn from the absence in the visions xl.–xlviii. of any account of a converted heathendom outside Canaan is, that the picture does not give the entire image of God's rule upon earth floating before the mind of Ezekiel. That, on the other hand, the oracle does speak in perfect seriousness of the restoration of the condemned heathen cities, cannot reasonably be disputed,[2] when one reads (xvi. 61) in what relation they stand to Jerusalem, and that the highest distinction and also the deepest humiliation of Jerusalem will lie in its being raised to the position of mother-city.

---

[1] So also Hos. xi. 8; Matt. x. 15; Mark vi. 11. In contrast with the first passage (p. 239), the present shows a material advance. The mercy of the Lord, unable to forsake His people, will have mercy on all, in order to save it.

[2] Smend would derive this prospect from a "momentary polemical interest."

xvi. 60. "But I will remember my covenant with thee in the days of thy youth, and establish with thee an eternal cove-
61 nant. And thou shalt remember thy ways, and feel shame when thou takest (to thee) thy sisters, who are greater than thou, to those who are smaller than thou, and I give them to thee for daughters, and that not in virtue of thy covenant.
62 And I will establish my covenant with thee, and thou shalt
63 learn that I am Yahveh, that thou mayest remember this and be ashamed and open the mouth no more[1] for thy feeling of disgrace, when I provide thee with expiation for everything thou hast done, saith Yahveh, Lord of all."

The whole of the expressive picture, given in this chapter of God's ways and those of His Church, is well calculated to set in clear light His unfathomable love and the Church's unworthiness. If the beginning of the history of Jerusalem was a divine election of grace, the end will be pure mercy. The sins which deprived it of the covenant blessing will then stand before it in vivid remembrance. It will see that God's love, which encompasses it continually, has turned again to it only because it is infinite mercy and puts grace in the place of justice. The divine benefits will close its mouth, because it keenly feels how little it has deserved such distinction. Thus the fruit of beneficent grace is the deepest humbling and inward repentance, such as the severest judgment is powerless to produce. But this unmerited divine favour culminates in the fact that this city, which by nature had no privilege above its sisters, and after its traitorous conduct was condemned to the lowest place, acquires the other cities as her own, becoming the mother of the rest, as well of those that surpass her in age and magnitude as of the minor ones. This follows not by covenant right, for this she has lost by breaking the covenant, but by the Lord's free grace.[2] It ought not to be necessary to observe that, by these cities, great

---

[1] "Opening of the mouth" (so again only in Ezek. xxi. 29) is not arrogance, but παῤῥησία, the utterance of exulting self-confidence.

[2] Ver. 61: לֹא מִבְּרִיתֵךְ. Not by a covenant that is thine, in virtue of which thou mightest demand something. Such an attitude, indeed, on the part of Israel is the natural effect of the covenant with Abraham; but that covenant, belonging to the days of its youth (ver. 60), is broken, and therefore no longer belongs to it with its rights. For this reason there is a new covenant, a free dispensation of the grace of God. Schrader erroneously, after John x. 16: "Such as were without law, such as did not belong to thy covenant."

and small, all of which, without regard to the rank they previously held in the world, must be inferior to Jerusalem as the city where God dwells, and through which He gives His revelation, cannot be meant specifically Samaria and Sodom with their surrounding "daughters;" but that here what is affirmed in Ps. lxxxvii. of nations, viz. that they would become the spiritual children of Jerusalem, is affirmed of cities generally, so that the fountain of life there issuing from the living God will stream over them. That Samaria and Sodom are included—those two models representing estrangement from God raised to its highest degree—is undeniable; nowhere in the Old Testament is the Lord's all-pitying grace revealed more gloriously than here.

To obtain a true picture of Ezekiel's prophecy, we must not ignore or unduly weaken such pregnant features. So far from putting the ground of salvation, and consequently the essence of religion, in legal performances, this prophet emphasized most strongly the *grace* of God as the sole and sufficient ground of salvation. Like Jeremiah, he unmercifully exposes the insufficiency of the common theocratic righteousness, with which the carnal mind of the Jews satisfied itself, shattering the claims built on their ancestral covenant and citizenship in Jerusalem. According to him, the covenant of the law was made void through sin; the new eternal covenant, established by God, will have His sovereign grace for its sole ground. And the worst sinner, Jerusalem, will be the channel of such superabounding grace to the cities of the earth, and thus to her own deep humiliation become their spiritual mother.

Ezek. xvii., the allegory of the cedar of Lebanon, *i.e. the house of David*, contains the judgment on the faithless vassal Zedekiah, who relied on Egypt, instead of remaining true to his liege lord, the Babylonian king. But the history of this cedar concludes with honourable exaltation, as vers. 22–24 testify:—

xvii. 22. "Thus saith Yahveh, Lord of all: And I will take from the leafy crown of the high cedar and set—from its highest shoots I break off a tender one, and I plant it on
23 a high and exalted mountain. On the lofty mountain of Israel I will plant it, and it shall bear leaves and form fruit, and become a splendid cedar, and all birds shall nestle under it, every winged thing shall dwell under the
24 shadow of its branches. And all the trees of the field

shall learn that I am Yahveh, and lower the high tree and exalt the low tree, I make the sappy tree dry and the dry tree shoot forth. I, Yahveh, have said and perform it."

The Chaldæan eagle has carried away the crown of the cedar into the land and city of merchants (Babylon). But exaltation to universal rule awaits this exiled kingly house in the future. What God does stands in plain antithesis to what the Chaldæan eagle did. God exalts the humbled. From the lofty cedar transplanted to the lower country, still lofty in the dignity belonging to it in God's sight, the Lord breaks off one of the topmost twigs, the highest in dignity which that house has borne, the production of which was its destiny; and this sappy green twig, still tender, but full of divine vital energy, He plants carefully on a high towering mountain, on the mountain heights of Israel, to which it belongs. The prophet is here thinking chiefly of the high-lying abode of Israel (xxxiv. 14), whose country towers above Babylon as Israel above the nations. But this does not preclude the supposition that in the "high exalted" mountain the future Zion more specifically floated before him (xl. 2; cf. Isa. ii. 2; Micah iv. 1), since even within the land of Israel the cedar takes a commanding position. There the twig, diminutive at first, will grow into a powerful tree, under which all the birds of heaven seek shelter,—a figure of universal rule well known to the Oriental, because the tree rules what it shelters, and everything resorts to the shadow of *this* tree.[1] Ver. 24 states still more definitely that all kingdoms (trees) will acknowledge the superiority of *this* ruler, and of his God who humbles the high and exalts the low kingdom. The high sappy tree, the humbling of which is the Lord's work, refers here chiefly not to the future state of Israel, but to the world-empire, at present powerful, whose humiliation is imminent.

Consequently Ezekiel also foretells a new birth of the Davidic house, which will again rise through *one* twig from the very ground and attain universal dominion, as in Isa. vii. 14 ff., ix. 5 ff., xi. 1 ff.; Micah iv. 1 ff. The low condition, out of which this dominion rises, to his vision is the Babylonian exile. That Zerubbabel, the twig transplanted back from Babylon to Zion, did not exhaust the meaning of this prophecy, is clear; for the univer-

[1] Cf. Ezek. xxxi. 6; Dan. iv. 7 ff.; Matt. xiii. 31 f.; Mark iv. 31; Luke xiii. 19.

sally acknowledged authority here ascribed to him never belonged to him.

Before Ezekiel's prophecy could unfold the coming redemption without hindrance, God's judgment had to take effect on Jerusalem. During the long investment of the city the prophet was dumb. In the gap in his book thus arising he has intercalated (chaps. xxv.–xxxii.) the oracles on foreign nations belonging in part to a later time, and foretelling judgment on these nations, the exaltation of Israel being at the same time brought into conjunction with their humiliation, xxix. 21. The shattered horn of Israel (Lam. ii. 3) will again sprout, a reference to power in general, not to the Messiah specifically;[1] and the harassings of the foe on every side will cease, Ezek. xxviii. 24.

With the fall of Jerusalem, announced in chap. xxxiii., the second chief part of the book begins. As Ezekiel traces everything to the Lord's grace as its ultimate ground, and to the divine honour as its supreme end, so in particular he insists that the happy change now commencing is grounded not in any superiority of Israel, but solely in the holy name of the Lord, which will again be honoured (xxxvi. 22), and in His mercy, in virtue of which He wills not the death of the sinner, but that he repent and live (xxxiii. 11). In chap. xxxiv. the Lord sets Himself to gather anew His smitten, scattered people. This discourse moves in a circle of thoughts of the future already sufficiently known to us from earlier prophets. The wicked prophets, already characterized in Zech. xi. and Jer. xxiii. 1 ff., are rebuked, because they have neglected and mercilessly plundered the flock. The Lord Himself, so He declares, will now gather and feed His sheep (xxxiv. 11 ff.). In a closer specification of His government a human shepherd next appears in His place, who will be a worthy representative of God, namely, David, in the sense of Jer. xxx. 9.

xxxiv. 23 f. "And I raise up over them one shepherd to feed them, MY SERVANT DAVID, who will feed them and be their shepherd. And I, Yahveh, will be their God, and my servant David a prince in their midst. I, Yahveh, have said it."

That it is altogether contrary to the prophetic style of thought and speech to find here a reappearance of the dead David has already been observed (p. 336). But they do too little justice

[1] So, on the other hand, Ps. cxxxii. 17. The primary passage is 1 Sam. ii. 1. Yet the לְ, Ezek. xxix. 21, refers, according to xxiv. 27, to the prophet.

to the definite personal stamp of the prophecy who would see a collective in it and in Jeremiah's righteous Sprout.[1] The one Shepherd, whom the Lord calls with delight His righteous Servant, is he in whom David's virtue will be perfected to the salvation of His Church. This perfecter of the Messianic idea stands before the seer's gaze in personal unity, and the ideal image must be left thus, otherwise it loses in grandeur. Already, in xxi. 32, Ezekiel tore the falsely assumed Davidic crown from the head of the reprobate Zedekiah, which crown perishes until He come to whom it belongs by divine right.[2] This will be One, who is not merely of David's blood, but has his God-fearing, God-trusting mind; according to this passage the true David, whom the Lord acknowledges without reserve, and under whose rule the overflowing abundance of the land, promised long ago by the prophets, will appear and be enjoyed in undisturbed peace (xxxiv. 25-31).

Ezek. xxxvi. 25 ff., where the oracle of xi. 19 f. recurs in enriched form, gives us a most profound glance into this state of untroubled peace with God. To the shepherd whom God approves, a cleansed and sanctified Church will correspond; for when the Lord delivers His people from bondage, He will also redeem it internally:—

xxxvi. 25. "And I sprinkle upon you pure water, for you shall be PURE from all your pollutions; and from all your idols[3] I
26 will cleanse you. And I give you a NEW HEART, and a NEW SPIRIT I put within you, and take away the stony heart out
27 of your body and give you a fleshy heart. And my SPIRIT I put within you and make you to walk in my statutes and
28 keep and do my laws. And you shall dwell in the land that

---

[1] So, e.g., Schrader in Schenkel's *Bibellexikon*, ii. 253 f., according to whom the hope of a personal Messiah cherished by Isaiah and Micah was extended by Jeremiah and Ezekiel to the whole Davidic dynasty, these two prophets thus forming the transition to the exilian Anonymous one, Isa. xl.-lxvi., where this expectation gives place to a still more general one, namely, that the ideal people of God itself as "Servant of Yahveh" will partly introduce the Messianic salvation, partly itself share it.

[2] "Until he comes to whom the government (מִשְׁפָּט, as in Hos. v. 1) is due, and to whom I give it." On the allusion to Gen. xlix. 10, see p. 120. Cf. also Delitzsch, *Messianic Prophecies*, p. 83.

[3] גִּלּוּלִים, very often in Ezekiel as a contemptuous designation of idols; cf. Baudissin, *Studien*, i. 95 f. This passage favours the interpretation "dung-heaps," "dung-gods," rather than the one which makes it mean "blocks." Cf. the closely-related passage, Zech. xiii. 2.

I gave to your fathers, and you shall be to me a people, and I will be to you a God."

This announcement of what the Lord will do to His people is parallel to that of Jer. xxxi. 31 ff. If there a new covenant was spoken of, here a complete remoulding of God's relation to His people is promised, which is carried out in such a way that the Church's inmost nature is transformed by a miraculous act of God. More plainly than in Jeremiah two things may be here distinguished: *cleansing* or justifying (ver. 25), and positive *new-birth* through the Spirit of God (ver. 26 f.), in consequence of which the people will henceforth be both able and willing to keep the divine commands. In the former respect the Lord will sprinkle His Church with pure water, *i.e.*, as in Zech. xiii. 1, provide it with effective means of expiation,[1] to set it free from the defilements cleaving to it. No Levitical ceremony can do this in adequate manner, no human asceticism atone for these offences. The Lord Himself must sprinkle this impure people. But with one such cleansing His work would only be half done. He will also create an entirely new and holy life in His Church. The human heart, the source of all volition and inclination (Deut. xxx. 6), of all desire and effort, is unfit for God's service (Gen. viii. 21), as Israel's whole history shows. It is just as unreceptive to the divine as inclined to all evil. The spirit that rules men is impure, sinful. God will give His accepted people a new heart, related to the former one as flesh to stone, *i.e.* instead of a heart hard, stubborn, unreceptive, one sensitive to God's word and will, receptive to all good, or as Jeremiah says, like a soft table on which God can write His holy law. And the new Spirit that is to fill these receptive hearts will be God's Spirit, who impels to the keeping of the divine commands. Here Jeremiah, who speaks of a transforming of the divine law, and Ezekiel, who speaks of a new creating of the human organs, beautifully supplement each other. That the Lord may be able to write His law in men's hearts, the hearts themselves must be radically changed. In order to this end a fresh, creative act of divine grace is essential.

Here the prophet, who has been accused of superficial Levitical externalism, displays insight of extraordinary depth, insight putting him on a level with Jeremiah as a true evangelist in the

[1] Cf. p. 351 on this metaphor.

Old Covenant. He shows us the sole-sufficiency and all-sufficiency of divine grace in that work of God, from which the new Church will proceed. Every individual member of it is *born again* of water and spirit; else he is unable to stand before the holy God and render the required obedience. The יהוה צדקנו of Jeremiah here undergoes a wonderful expansion. Although the outward bliss, which is the fruit of this inner work of grace, is presented under O. T. limitation (xxxvi. 28 ff.), the act of grace itself, from which peace with God springs, is seen with divine clearness and also in grand divine unity, a clearness and unity which it has not always been easy even for evangelical Christendom to hold fast. That "the Lord our righteousness" does not mean merely "the Lord our justification," but also "our right-doing, our sanctification," that the latter also is not our work, to which "gratitude" is enough to impel us, but the fruit of God's wonder-working grace—this N. T. truth, revealed already to Ezekiel, has not everywhere received its due in Church doctrine, and, moreover, has been far too much overlooked in the Protestant Church.

The *restoration of God's people* is further pictured to us in Ezek. xxxvii. That people has now entered the state of death already foretold by Hosea;[1] only by a resurrection of the dead can it be recalled to life. But the Lord is a God with the power and will to do this. This is shown to the seer in a splendid vision, xxxvii. 1 ff., where he sees a plain sown far and wide with mouldering bones. The Church of the Lord is not even to be compared to a corpse, but consists merely of *disjecta membra*, of scattered, mouldering bones, on which representation chap. xxxvii. gives a commentary. According to this explanation, the purpose of the whole lies not so much in announcing the bodily resurrection of buried members of the Church, as in promising in the most definite terms the raising of the Church out of its present state of outward dispersion and inner estrangement from God, a work to human appearance utterly impossible. Its present state cannot be described in too hopeless terms. It is one of utter corruption. But from the buried relics of His people, the Lord will again raise up to Himself a countless Church. Thus it is certainly declared that He can call even the dead to life. If the prophet had not attributed such power to God, he could not have believed in the revivifying of the holy nation. This is

[1] Hos. vi. 2, xiii. 14 f.; cf. pp. 238-240.

implied in the form of vision deliberately chosen. The vision refers prophet and people to the God who is able to raise the dead, and consequently to reanimate the people, now mouldering in all lands, by His creative Spirit in all its members, and bring them together again. Only here the emphasis does not fall, as in Isa. xxvi. 19 (p. 303), upon the idea that the true members of the Church, dead in a physical sense, rise again to life on earth, though this is certainly not excluded, and is suggested by the description of the rising again of the individual "slain." The chief thing here is, that God's people, forsaken of the spirit of life, is revivified by God's higher Spirit (xxxvii. 14), and again occupies its land.

Chap. xxxvii. 15 ff. then combines what has been foretold of God's "Servant" David with what is said of the Church, xxxvi. 25 ff. The kingdom of Israel-Judah, again united under one prince, will, after its redemption from captivity, represent in every respect what has ever been God's will in respect to it: a nation richly blessed, among whom God has taken up His abode for ever, ruled by His righteous Servant David who has taken possession of it permanently, and, in virtue of the divine cleansing and sanctifying, well-pleasing and absolutely obedient to the Lord.

Of peculiar importance also is the picture of the attack, which *Gog* of the land of *Magog* makes at last on faithful Israel that has long returned from captivity, and of the judgment smiting him and expanding into the general judgment, Ezek. xxxviii. f. The description of this Gog shows plainly that the Scythians are in the prophet's mind, those northern barbarians, distinguished by their rage for plunder, whose enormous hordes of horse, especially skilful at the bow, had not failed by their attacks to make a deep impression on the Israelites (from about the year 630).[1] With this agrees the fact that Magog is thought of as found on the northern horizon (xxxviii. 15, xxxix. 2), and Gog, a name occurring only in Ezekiel as the name of the king of Magog, is called prince of Rosh,[2] Meshech, and Tubal, by which are meant northern populations on the Pontus Euxinus. These ideas are not sharply defined either in a geographical or ethnological respect. The

---

[1] See particulars in Herzog, *Real-Encycl.* v. 263 ff.

[2] xxxviii. 3. רֹאשׁ is scarcely an appellative, along with נָשִׂיא: *chief prince* (Chald., Syr., Aqu., Jer. ; Ewald, Smend), but likewise the name of a people on the northern Taurus, Gesenius, *Thesaurus*, p. 1253. Meshech and Tubal are the ancient Moschi and Tibareni.

conception of Magog, viewed in the passages cited as extending to the farthest north, was as elastic among the Israelites as the idea of the "Scythians" among the ancient Greeks. But this is noteworthy, that from the barbarians of the north, hitherto scarcely visible on the world's stage, a world-convulsing movement will proceed, when the empires now figuring in history have succumbed to their doom.

Moreover, Gog, who comes rolling on like a thunder-cloud, not merely carries along with him, in his fury, the entire north (the Persians, Gomarites, and the house of Togarmah, with all their satellites following in his train), but also sweeps away the peoples of the extreme south — Cush and Put, Ethiopia and Libya [1] — in his terrible violence, which is finally directed against the harmless people of God in Canaan. We have here, then, a final rising of the whole world against Yahveh and His people, in which the nations hitherto veiled in obscurity, whose power is not yet broken at the end of the days (xxxviii. 16), will step into the foreground. Then the general judgment announced long before by the prophets is carried out on them, the Lord unloosing all the powers of destruction upon the nations who invade His inheritance. Earthquake, sword, pestilence, hail, fire, and brimstone slay the invaders in masses, and also devastate their home (xxxix. 6). So vast is the host slain on Israel's mountains that its weapons furnish wood for seven years' burning, as the drastic account of ver. 9 f. says. By this destruction of the foe Yahveh gains honour in the eyes of all the heathen, and proves that Israel's fall and banishment were a punishment imposed on it by its God, whereas now He preserves His sanctuary inviolate.

Thus what Zech. xiv. saw in conjunction — the judgment on Jerusalem, and that on the world of heathen nations — are separated in Ezekiel. The judgment on the city belongs already, in his view, to the past; on the other hand, what the prophets had long before said about an ineffectual storming of Jerusalem by the heathen is still to come. To it the "Day of the Lord" will join on. In the allusion to those prophecies (xxxviii. 17, xxxix. 8), Ezekiel is certainly thinking chiefly of Joel (iii. 2, 9 ff.), and this reference supports the earlier date of Joel's

---

[1] These stand, of course, by way of example. Cf. xxxix. 6, where the "islands" are mentioned as the corresponding western region.

prophecy. Joel had mainly in view the nations engaged in conflict with Israel; Ezekiel sees the nations of the farthest zones drawn into the conflict between God's kingdom and the world-power, and fighting it out. Meantime Joel's vision has been taken up by other prophets, Micah iv. 11 ff.; Zech. xii. 2 ff., xiv. 3 ff. In Ezekiel, this general tempest has reached its widest geographical extension. The Revelation of John (xx. 7 ff.) also gives to what he saw a range going far beyond the Old Covenant. The Church of Christ has yet to endure that last assault of the heathen. After the thousand years' reign of Christ and His Church on earth, Satan, bound so long, is once more unloosed, and leads the nations from all the four ends of the earth, to a final assault on the holy city. This threatening power of the last days is there called "Gog and Magog;" it is destroyed by fire from heaven, after which follows the new-creating of heaven and earth, and the new Jerusalem descends from heaven to earth.

Ezekiel closes his book (chap. xl.–xlviii.) with a picture of the purified city of God, of the temple principally, where God's majesty now dwells permanently, and whence the fountain of blessing pours life and salvation upon all the country round. What renders this passage unique in O. T. prophecy, and makes it difficult for our theological consciousness to enter into it, is the detailed completeness of Ezekiel's style. Whereas the other prophets sketched the Church of the last days, the glorified temple, Jerusalem, Canaan, by characteristic touches on the bright fringe of their circle of vision, in which the filling up could be conceived according to the hearers' or readers' standpoint in O. T. concreteness or N. T. spirituality, Ezekiel here unfolds before their eyes a thoroughly finished picture of quite uncommon breadth, a rigid architectural plan, defining the future temple with special distinctness, and ordaining its forms of worship with the precision of a lawgiver. What picture is this? Is it the Jerusalem of the time of restoration that here presented itself to his prophetic vision with historic fidelity? For this the form is too ideal; the relations described by him are too perfect to allow us to see in his picture a representation beforehand of the redeemed Church of Zerubbabel and Joshua, or of Ezra and Nehemiah, that was afterwards realized historically. Or is it the perfected Jerusalem, the eternal city of

God? For this, again, the relations are too limited, too specifically Jewish. We must say, however, that in the prophecy hitherto considered, even in the oracles of Ezekiel, there are elements which do not find expression to their full extent in this architectural plan framed after the Mosaic pattern.

The twofold character of the picture, by which on the one hand it exhibits the hitherto existing in unattained purity and perfection, and on the other hand is able to exhibit the future only as a purified and improved form of the previous commonwealth, is to be understood from Ezekiel's calling and position. The temple was fallen, the theocracy overthrown, Yahveh's wondrous institutions of law and grace in His temple on Zion had ceased. This was a heavy blow to the theocratic consciousness animating every better Israelite. Was the rule of God among His people, and on earth, at an end? Ezekiel beheld the opposite on the day of the overthrow of Jerusalem, fourteen years after the fall of the temple (xl. 1). Then he discerned in spirit the new temple standing on a very high mountain. This feature, and especially the temple-fountain swelling into a river, shows that the whole is more than a new architectonic plan for the building of God's house, or a new revision of the law on the restoration of the State. It is a prophetic vision in which the temple and Church of the future are presented in glorified form. But, on the other hand, these detailed descriptions of the temple-walls, doors, chambers, etc., are of such a kind that they yield a real architectonic whole, of which a complete plan may be drawn at least as well as of the Solomonic or Herodian temple.[1]

In the same way the encampment of the twelve tribes, who are all quartered on this side Jordan, and the organization of national worship, while influenced by ideal conceptions, are also practically arranged and deliberately framed in every point. The reasons are evident why the old Mosaic Torah is partly departed from, whilst the old demands of the law are still asserted against abuses that have crept in (cf. xliv. 7 f.).

It is Ezekiel's peculiarity, not to picture the days to come in general outlines, but thoroughly to enter into and appropriate such anticipations of the future, both in inward and

---

[1] This has been shown by Thenius, J. F. Böttcher (*Proben A. T. Schrifterklärung*, 1833, p. 218 ff.), J. J. Balmer-Rinck, *Des Propheten Ezechiel Gesicht vom Tempel*, 1858; R. Smend, *Commentar zu Ezechiel*, 1880.

outward respects. Hence he does not simply foretell the re-erection of the temple and holy nation, in whose midst God will take up His abode for ever; but this perfect restoration of God's house, in which nothing that ever belonged to it will be lost, is carried out before his eyes to the least minutiæ. In this process, indeed, the O. T. limitation asserts itself more strongly than in the prophets elsewhere; while often transcended in spirit, it cannot permanently be overcome by the existing power of conception. In great measure the picture is only a prophecy of the true consummation of God's kingdom, in so far as the Mosaic cultus is so also. Here, where prophecy sketches the concrete shape of the future Church, it falls back into the typical. It is a description of God's perfect residence in the imperfect, figurative language of the Old Covenant. Certainly attempts have been made by artificial means to crane up this picture and its separate features to the height of the N. T. revelation, by putting a spiritual meaning into everything;[1] or the outward fulfilment has been claimed for the future, on which view even the institution of bloody sacrifices must again be logically ascribed to converted Israel. Really neither the one nor the other view corresponds to the teaching of the New Testament, which, while adopting the essential features of Ezekiel's picture (Rev. xxii. 1 f.) in describing the perfected city of God, omits all limitations of a national and local character. Thus the form which Ezekiel's vision assumes is only explained by the circumstances of his age, which, as the prophet was informed, had to expect a new establishment of the Mosaic temple-service; and this blended, to the eye of the seer, with the introduction of God's perfected presence among His people.

As Moses once saw the pattern of the tabernacle, so here the prophet sees the model of the new temple altogether in the sacred, expressive style of the old one, but in still greater simplicity, purity, and perfection of form. Just so the administration of the temple, the distribution of space among the tribes, and of privileges among the orders, are seen by him in Mosaic fashion, only with a more complete carrying out of principles. The essential distinction of this temple is that the *glory of the Lord* takes up its abode in it for ever.[2] The

[1] So Hengstenberg and Kliefoth, *Das Tempelgesicht Ezechiel's*, 1865.
[2] Ezek. xliii. 1 ff., 9, xlviii. 35.

secular power comes little into notice; it lies in the hand of a prince (נָשִׂיא), of course of David's house (xvii. 22, xxxiv. 24); but the Anointed of the Lord does not appear in personal prominence; only domestic authority and law is exercised, having nothing of a priestly character (xlvi. 1 ff.).

The inwardness which still constitutes the soul of this picture so outward in character, comes out most strongly in the description of the *temple-fountain* that waters the whole land, giving it fertility and health, chap. xlvii. It is an extended description of the fertilizing, cleansing fountain that springs on Zion, already known to us from Joel iii. 18; Zech. xiii. 1. According to Ezekiel, it bursts forth from the threshold of God's house at the eastern entrance, turns aside south of the altar of burnt-offering in the forecourt, and so finds its way to the wall, under which it flows. A thousand ells' distance from the wall its water is still not a foot high, a thousand ells farther it reaches to the knees, a like distance again to the loins, to become finally a powerful river, too deep to wade through,—a glorious image of the way in which this salvation becomes ever mightier and richer the farther it penetrates into the world. On the two banks of the living stream grow shady trees, bearing fresh fruit every month, and leaves that cure every sickness. The Dead Sea also is healed by the flood of life pouring into it, so that fishers find large catches on its shores. Certain marshes only are left to remind of the former barrenness. But clearly as this transformed physiognomy points to a new spiritual creation, we ought not to adopt this interpretation forthwith, and least of all allegorize the particular traits, *e.g.* understand the fishers of the fishers of men, Matt. iv. 18 f. (Hengstenberg), or of the angels (Kliefoth), the trees of righteous men (Kliefoth), etc. Rather the image stands before the eyes of the seer in concrete reality, apart from all interpretation. A land endowed by the Lord with altogether new forces of blessing, a paradisaic garden of God, in place of former sterility — such is the fit surrounding of the temple. It will be a delight to live in the Lord's land; even the heathen will be made welcome there, and permitted to acquire landed possessions (xlvii. 22 f.).

What of the *fulfilment* of this whole vision, Ezek. xl.-xlviii. ? Delitzsch calls it a prophecy that remained unfulfilled, because the two kingdoms of Israel did not turn to God in true penitence, and did on returning from exile greet Him with their first love; and certainly in this case the nation would have witnessed a far more glorious renewal of the theocracy and of prosperity in its land. At all events, the reason why the prophecy could not be fulfilled in its literal terms lies in its peculiar character, in the interweaving of eternal ideas and temporal, passing forms that distinguishes it. The final form of the divine presence could not be of this kind. According to the prophet's own words, a new, more perfect covenant of grace must come, no longer needing the mediation of salvation by priestly, Levitical apparatus and the former means of divine revelation.[1] So far as the description of God's dwelling in the midst of His people given by Ezekiel belongs to the shadows of the old legal covenant, it is abolished with that covenant. Hence this book is a standing exhortation to Christian theology not to regard the letter of prophecy, apart from its spiritual import, as the essential and eternal part; while it should be a proof to the Jews of the changeableness of the letter of the Torah, since Ezekiel puts himself to a certain extent in contradiction to the latter.[2] So far, on the other hand, as the Lord's dwelling on earth has not yet been perfected in visible reality, this vision points to the future, even as it was taken up again by N. T. prophecy in essential points. What features in Ezekiel's picture will be found in the city of God that is to be seen hereafter on earth (Rev. xxi.), what on the other hand belong only to the perishing image, can only be perfectly and incontestably made clear when God's perfect kingdom is revealed.

§ 39. *The Prophecies of the Servant of Yahveh*, Isa. xl.–lxvi.

The promise of Ezekiel, speaking to us out of the time of exile, receives an exceedingly rich supplement from a prophetic book, likewise originating in the seven decades of captivity, and indeed in their closing period—the time between the opening of the victorious career of Cyrus and the fall of Babylon, although it is now joined to the Book of Isaiah (note A).

---

[1] Cf. with Ezekiel's description of the temple, Jer. iii. 17; Rev. xxi. 22.
[2] The differences between Moses and Ezekiel have caused the Rabbins great distress, and led them in some degree to attack the canonical dignity of the latter. Cf. Mishna, *Schabb.* f. 13, col. 2 (ed. Surenhus. ii. p. 5); J. G. Carpzov, *Introd. ad V. T.*, iii. 214 ff.

The prophet appears towards the end of the exile. The incredible has happened. The apparently unconquerable world-power, Babylon, sustains one defeat after another from a stronger One who rises up against it. Then Israel is summoned joyously to observe what is transpiring. For God, who is now showing Himself so much greater in power than the idols, will redeem all His promises. *Redemption* draws nigh. The new spring of life and love, already foretold by Hosea, is at hand. A sacred year of grace, bringing universal freedom, dawns (lxi. 2). Not for the merits or excellence of His people (xliii. 22 ff.), but, as former prophets have already insisted (Ezek. xxxvi. 22), for His own sake, for His name's sake (xliii. 25, xlviii. 9), the Lord will succour His own. He comes Himself to lead *His* people (xl. 1) from captivity through the desert to desolated Zion. Already one hears in the desert the voice of His heralds, who prepare the way for His glory. He comes, bringing to the city of Zion as a precious gift the reward of His work—a redeemed people, whom He leads homeward with the loving care of a true shepherd.

These features of the coming redemption, appearing already in chap. xl., run through the entire book.[1] Remembrance of the deliverance from the first captivity in Egypt, whence the way lay through the desert to Canaan, gives the keynote. As there the Lord revealed Himself most gloriously in the desert, so now also His glory, which had departed from Zion, will appear there and return thence: "And the glory of Yahveh is unveiled, and all flesh shall see it together; for the mouth of Yahveh has spoken it" (xl. 5). The barren, pathless desert will not merely be levelled, the road becoming easy,[2] but will be changed into well-watered garden-land,[3] as Isa. xxxv. already foretold; which vision, now nearer fulfilment, expands before the eyes of our prophet into rich variety of detail.

Plainly as the account reveals the fatherly care of the Lord, who leads His people on a level, easy road through pleasant pastures, still the metamorphosis does not refer merely to a momentary, physical easing of the march of the home-going pilgrims; but the prophet everywhere with plastic symbolism makes his picture utter spiritual truth. The levelling of the

---

[1] Isa. xl. 3 ff., 10 ff., xliii. 1 ff., lii. 9 ff., lv. 12 ff.; cf. lx. 4, 8 ff.
[2] Isa. xl. 4, xlii. 16, xlix. 11, lvii. 14.
[3] xli. 17 ff., xliii. 19 f., xlviii. 21, xlix. 9 f., lv. 13.

country through which the Lord's host marches, the lowering of the hills and filling up of the valleys, like the drying up of impassable rivers,[1] presents the thought first, that all hindrances opposing the Lord's coming are easily swept aside by Him. All the powers of the world[2] cannot hinder His advent. He so transforms the earth that His glory can be displayed on it. At the same time the Elijah-voice, xl. 3 ff. (cf. Mal. iii. 1), is an exhortation to a moral and spiritual preparation for His coming; proud minds and spirits are to humble themselves deeply before the revelation of the Most High, whilst bowed and oppressed hearts will revive (lvii. 15).

A deeper intention is just as evident in the descriptions of the change of the desert into the garden of God, into paradise. In lv. 13 it is expressly said that this blessed metamorphosis of the landscape is not a transitory but an abiding one, as an eternal monument of divine grace. Thus God's present revelation will leave in the word a miraculous track along the whole of the way it has taken, a track of fertility and blessing such as springs from God's gracious presence. The desert will enjoy this blessing in the fullest degree. But this is true also in another sense. Not only are Zion and its neighbourhood at present like the desert, not only therefore do they need a transformation which they will experience in glorious form (li. 3; cf. lxi. 4); but in the plastic freedom and spiritual animation of these prophetic conceptions the state of the nation itself, above all its spiritual state, is compared to a desert watered by the Lord with blessing from above and turned into a scene of joyful growth, xliv. 3 ff., lviii. 11 f. Such life-giving bounty (cf. lv. 1 f.) as is promised to the holy land and people, certainly cannot point to material prosperity only; but as this revival is out and out of higher origin, so the life resulting therefrom is one permeated by powers of divine grace and hallowed by the Divine Spirit. This is most beautifully shown in xlv. 8:—

"Drop, ye heavens, from above, and let the clouds trickle with well-doing.[3] Let the earth open and salvation blossom and make righteousness shoot forth at once—I, Yahveh, have created it."

---

[1] xliii. 16, xliv. 27; cf. li. 10.   [2] Cf. the heights, xli. 15, xlv. 2.

[3] צֶדֶק passes in this prophet from the fundamental meaning of normal conduct to that of divine favour and grace (pp. 243, 335), cf. xli. 2, xlii. 6. The heavens rain divine goodwill, and thus educe from the earth a healthful harvest of human well-

Thus the conception of faithful guidance through the desert,[1] and that of the redeeming of the desert-Church from its abject condition, constantly interchange. The latter idea ensures a deeper meaning to the former one. Even the captivity, from which the Lord will deliver His people (li. 14), is not the mere outward bondage in which Babylon holds it. It is bound in a darker prison by its own guilt, benighted by its own blindness, enslaved by its own ill-conduct. These captives are in fact kept in bondage by the guilt they have heaped up by sinning against their God (xlii. 22, 24). They pine away in darkness, because with eyes to see, in their unreceptiveness to the divine they are blind where they ought to behold the wonderful ways of the Lord.[2] What hinders them walking with firm step is their moral bondage, their sins being their chains.[3] Hence the Lord must needs speak a redeeming word to set them free in every aspect.[4]

Who is God's *instrument* in effecting this deliverance? This question takes us to the main idea of the book. The outward deliverance, indeed, Cyrus will accomplish;[5] but the incomparably greater and more difficult work of spiritual redemption another must perform, the *Servant of Yahveh*, whose form here emerges more and more out of obscurity in new and mysterious dignity.

The *nation* of Israel had been designed by the Mosaic covenant to *serve* God (Ex. iv. 23; cf. p. 128), to be His peculiar people, obediently rendering Him the service He desired on earth. Hence the greatest distinction is for God to call Israel "His Servant," as in Jer. xxx. 10, where it is said that it shall belong to no master but its rightful lord. On this broad national basis stands the Deutero-Isaianic idea of the Servant of the Lord, as xli. 8 ff. (cf. xliv. 1) proves. There the Lord with tender goodwill addresses Israel-Jacob, the seed of His friend Abraham, as His chosen servant, and assures it of His assistance in all weakness (xli. 14). By this means it will rise victorious above its foes and crush to pieces the proud mountains and hills of the world, after God has redeemed and refreshed His poor, despond-

doing. צְדָקָה must not, on account of the parallel יֶשַׁע, be weakened into "prosperity" and the like, but is the ethical fruit of that bestowal of grace; cf. Ps. lxxxv. 11 ff.

[1] That the desert also is not to be confined to a mere literal meaning, is shown by xlix. 9, where the people itself is the flock feeding.
[2] xlii. 7, 16, 18–20, xliii. 8, xlix. 9.   [3] Cf. lix. 9, 10.
[4] xliii. 8, xlix. 9, lii. 2 f., lxi. 1 ff.   [5] xliv. 26, 28, xlv. 13.

ing people. Chap. xliv. 1 ff., xlviii. 20, return to the same breadth of conception. "Servant of the Lord" is Israel's official name, stamped on it by God's love as a *character indelebilis*. Hence it not only bears the name where in the light of God's grace it appears as His actual instrument, but even where its unfitness for such an office comes out most strikingly, xlii. 19.

But just as little ought it to be overlooked that in O. T. usage this title of honour is usually assigned to individuals, namely, to the greatest instruments selected by God for His service.[1] And indeed *Moses*, the deliverer of the nation from Egyptian bondage and mediator of the Sinaitic covenant, is called עֶבֶד יְהוָֹה far the oftenest, and in the prophetic promises the Lord calls *David* with special preference עַבְדִּי, "My Servant."[2] This idea, like that of Son of God originally given to the whole nation, and first fully developed in the Lord's Anointed, tends toward personal consummation. Such is the case in Deutero-Isaiah in a striking manner. Although he starts from the vocation of the entire nation to be God's servant and recurs to it as an inalienable office of Jacob-Israel, yet in his view, as soon as he begins to speak more precisely of the work of redemption and the instrument chosen for it, the bearer of this office assumes personal definiteness:—

xlii. 1. "Behold MY SERVANT, whom I uphold, mine elect one, in whom my soul delights! I have laid my Spirit upon him,
2 that he may bring out right to the nations. He cries not, and makes no noise,[3] and causes not his voice to be heard in
3 the street. A bruised reed he breaks not, and a glimmering wick[4] he quenches not: assuredly[5] he will bring out the
4 right. He will not faint and break down[6] until he establish right on the earth, and the isles wait for his instruction.
5 Thus saith God Yahveh, who created the heavens and extended them, who spread the earth with its products, who gave breath to the people upon it, and spirit to them that

---

[1] Compare the way in which in the New Testament the apostles assume the title δοῦλος Ἰησοῦ Χριστοῦ as the highest distinction, Jas. i. 1; Jude ver. 1; Rom. i. 1; Phil. i. 1, etc.

[2] Isa. xxxvii. 35; Jer. xxxiii. 21 f., 26; Ezek. xxiv. 23, xxxvii. 25.

[3] That נָשָׂא is meant of ostentatious noise, is plain from the context without reference to the following קוֹלוֹ.

[4] The dull, slow-burning flax-wick, in which the oil is failing.

[5] Properly, according to the rule of fidelity, truly and infallibly.

[6] יָרוּץ from רָצַץ, as in ver. 3.

6 walk on it. I, Yahveh, have called thee in righteousness[1]
and grasp thine hand, and guard thee and make thee a
7 covenant of the people, a light of the nations, to open
blind eyes, to bring captives out of prison, out of the house
of bondage them that sit in darkness."

The figure here presented to the gaze of the seer is the instrument which the Lord uses to accomplish His great redeeming work; and in the description of the medium we learn more definitely in what the work consists and how broad its range. Now not a ruler in God's name is needed, but a *Servant* of the Lord; for the work cannot be accomplished without the deepest condescension, while he to whom it is entrusted must be a Servant of the *Lord* absolutely, One in whom the Lord can feel an unqualified delight, and whom He has endowed with His Spirit in full measure. Thus he is enabled with perfect spontaneity and divine illumination to carry out His mission, which is to impart divine light to the far-off heathen. At the same time He will not shout His doctrine in the market-place of the world, nor force it on any one with violence. Conscious of its mighty truth, He lets His word operate quietly and secretly in those who are not among the eminent of the earth, the lights of the world, or its professed saints. He addresses Himself to the obscure, dull, and desponding, whom He does not overwhelm with strong words and rob of the last spark of courage, but confirms by rekindling their glimmering light of faith. And whilst He breathes strength into the feeble and faint, He Himself is not exhausted by His wearing labour; and His Holy Spirit fails not until He has finished His blessed, world-embracing toil.

The method of His working is the *Word*, which He preaches.[2] The content of this word is on one hand the making known of God's will, the divine law (מִשְׁפָּט and תּוֹרָה, cf. Isa. ii. 3), which the heathen here need not come to Jerusalem to obtain (as in Isa. ii.; Micah iv.), but which is brought to them by the true Servant of the Lord to enlighten them. But at the same time this divine word is in particular a word of grace, in which the Lord's *gracious will* toward all nations, and pre-eminently toward His people, is revealed. Hence the unostentatious Servant, so kind

---

[1] צֶדֶק, again in the sense of Deutero-Isaiah: *in good disposition, i.e.* divine goodwill.
[2] Cf. Isa. xlix. 2, 1. 4 f.

to the feeblest, is its chosen bearer. It was God's favour (ver. 6) that called Him to His work and destined Him to be "a covenant with the people, a light to the heathen." Alongside גוים, עם could only apply to Israel,[1] even if xlix. 6, 8, did not imperatively require this reference. And in this case the sense can only be that God uses His Servant as a means for restoring the covenant with His people. In Him the divine covenant with the latter will be concluded, even as the enlightening of the heathen is His work, who also obtain a part in God's revealed grace. According to xlix. 6, 8, the Servant of Yahveh will be the instrument for again establishing, like Moses and Joshua, the holy nation and settling it in its land. This passage shows most clearly that the people and the Servant of God are here distinguished; the latter is the subject, the former the first and principal object of the redeeming work. And this is also clear from the whole discourse respecting the God-accepted Servant of the Lord, xlii. 1 ff., compared with the description of the people, xlii. 18–22. The latter is the blindest of all peoples, most deeply involved in darkness. Hence more than all it needs healing by the Servant, which is also emphatically promised to it, xlii. 7, xlix. 9. At all events this Servant of Yahveh appears here as a single personal figure in contrast with the people[2]— whether the figure represents a plurality, may be left open at present. He is one who in His being and action really fulfils Israel's vocation, which is now set forth in unprecedented grandeur. The nation, to which the vocation properly pertains, is so little adequate to it, that instead of being able to bring salvation to the heathen world, it must itself first receive salvation. The first and greatest work of the true Servant of God will be done on Israel-Judah, now far from God and sunk in spiritual wretchedness.

At the beginning of the second main part of the book, xlix. 1 ff., this Servant of Yahveh, ideal and yet contemplated in historical and personal concreteness, Himself begins to speak without any preface. His testimony to Himself, like that in lxi. 1 ff., forms to some extent a more detailed parallel to the testimony about Him in xlii. 1 ff. As there He was in a sense introduced and

---

[1] It makes no material difference if we translate: "to be a covenant of a (whole) people." In this case also Israel is meant.

[2] The apostrophe: "Israel" (my chosen one), interpolated, xlii. 1b, in the LXX., is therefore out of keeping; it would have to be understood as in xlix. 3.

described by God, so here He presents Himself addressing His words directly to the heathen, for which we are already prepared by what was said there:—

xlix. 1. "Listen to me, ye isles,[1] and hearken, ye nations from afar. Yahveh called me from the womb, from my mother's
2 lap he mentioned my name. And He made my mouth like a sharp sword, in the shadow of His hand He hid me, and
3 made me a polished arrow, in His quiver He hid me. And he said to me: My Servant art thou, Israel in whom I will
4 gain glory. But I said: 'In vain have I wearied myself, for nothing and again nothing consumed my strength.' But my
5 right is with Yahveh, and my reward with my God. And now saith Yahveh, who formed me from the womb to be His Servant, to bring Jacob back to Him and that Israel may be gathered—and I have been honoured in Yahveh's eyes and
6 my God was my strength—and said to me: 'It is too little that thou art my Servant to establish the tribes of Jacob and to bring back the preserved of Israel, and so I have set thee for a light of the heathen, to be my salvation[2] to the
7 end of the earth.' Thus saith Yahveh, the Redeemer of Israel, His Holy One, to him whose soul is despicable, the abhorred of the people, to the slave of rulers: 'Kings shall see and arise, princes, and fall down for Yahveh's sake, because He is faithful, and because the Holy One of Israel
8 has chosen thee.' Thus saith Yahveh: 'In a time of complacency I hear thee, and on the day of salvation I help thee, and I defend thee and make thee the covenant of the people,
9 to establish the land, to distribute desolate heritages, to say to the captives: Go forth, to those who are in darkness: Come to the light!'"

Here, too, the first impression is that of individual personality. As Cyrus, before he knew, was chosen by God to be an instrument in carrying out a higher plan (xlv. 3-5), so has the Lord called by name (*i.e.* in a personal capacity) and specially equipped His true Servant from the womb for a far more glorious and

---

[1] On this designation of the distant heathen-world, a favourite one with Deutero-Isaiah, see p. 318.

[2] Such is the most natural sense of the words, viz. that the great Servant of God is called the salvation as well as the light of the world (Delitzsch, Nägelsbach). Gesenius, Hitzig, Knobel, Ewald otherwise: "that my salvation may be," etc.

spiritual work. And this organon, with which God intends to glorify Himself, despite the martial images used concerning him, is not like Cyrus a military leader, but a depositary of spiritual force, as is evident from His *mouth* being called an elect weapon. His *word* therefore is the sharp, world-conquering sword,[1] the smooth, heart-piercing arrow, with which he will accomplish great things in God's service.

Thus his work will be that of a *prophet*, and of course will infinitely transcend the limits of what any prophet before had done. Because of this passage it has been thought that the prophet is here speaking of himself, somewhat like Jer. i. 5, and consequently claims to be himself the "Servant of the Lord."[2] But even in this section (apart from chap. liii.) this supposition is untenable. As little as the author can say of himself what is said in xlii. 1 ff., and boast that the isles wait for his instruction, so little can he there and here assume the monstrous position that not only will Israel receive its covenant from him, but also the heathen their light, while princes will do him homage. Moreover, the name Israel so contradicts this view, that Gesenius is forced to expunge it in xlix. 3.

This name compels us to recognise in the person addressed Israel's ideal representative, *i.e.* him in whom the relation into which God desires to enter with Israel is perfectly realized, and through whom the world-wide vocation assigned to that people is fully carried out. Once more, that the Servant is not identical with Israel, is confirmed to us here by exactly the same circumstance that we observed in chap. xlii., but which comes out, if possible, still more strongly here, namely, that the Church of Israel to be converted is, on the contrary, the object of the Servant's toilsome labour, as ver. 5 f. shows unmistakably. It needs to be delivered and led faithfully home by the Servant of the Lord not only in an outward but in an inward sense. When through God's strength He has happily discharged this task, a far greater and more glorious one is reserved for Him, namely, to establish the kingdom of God over the whole heathen world.

And as in chap. xlii. the faithful, Spirit-filled Messenger appeared in obscurity and without reputation in this world, so that He was only sustained on His difficult course through the world by a secret miracle of divine strength, so we see Him now

---

[1] Cf. Heb. iv. 12. [2] So Gesenius in the wake of Kimchi and Ibn Ezra.

doing His work in contempt and shame, apparently without success. According to His human judgment, He sees no fruit at all of His toil; yet in the Lord He is certain of His reward and draws from Him new strength. And as certainly as God is faithful, and will not leave His chosen one to defeat, so certainly will the path of this His true representative lead through deepest dishonour to glory. Now He is personally despised, mocked by the common people, treated with sovereign caprice by the holders of power. One day they will stand, nay, fall down, before Him with reverence, when they see whose ambassador He is. We see plainly that, much as His prophetic calling stands in the foreground, the significance of the Servant of Yahveh is not exhausted in it, but that He is the heir of the entire mission of Israel.

And as the path of all Israel lies through bondage to freedom, through shame to glory, as in particular the Lord's faithful servants—a David, for example—have taken this path, so must he who completely fulfils Israel's vocation, taste pain and shame in fullest measure. None of the true prophets have been without suffering as the badge of the genuineness of their mission; by their martyrdom they stamped the seal of attestation on their word. Thus Jeremiah's whole course was one long martyrdom; and in the exile it was the most faithful on whom hate and persecution fell most heavily.[1] So, according to the view of the great prophet, who now speaks of redemption, this aspect could not be wanting in the image of the true Redeemer. He is quite absorbed in this image of the genuine witness of God in servant-form, speaking again in l. 4 ff., and once more in lxi. 1 ff. from his very soul, of his life of testimony and suffering.

l. 4. "Yahveh, Lord of all, has given me a disciple's tongue,[2] that I may know how to comfort the weary with words; he awakens every morning, awakens my ear to hear after the
5 manner of disciples. Yahveh, Lord of all, has opened my ear,
6 and I have not resisted, not drawn back. My back I offered to the smiters, my cheeks to the pluckers (of hair), my face
7 I have not veiled from revilings and spittle. And Yahveh, Lord of all, helps me, therefore I am not affronted, on this

[1] Cf. Isa. li. 7, lvii. 1.
[2] "Tongue of the experienced, instructed, able to speak well," as the ear of a disciple is accustomed to pay good attention, ver. 4.

account I made my face like flint and know I shall not be put to shame."

As little as the personal description here suits the indocile people (xlii. 18 ff.), so easily may one recognise in it a faithful prophet such as Jeremiah. Only it would be improbable in itself that such a prophet would so praise his own fidelity. Rather here, also, the prophet gives a description of his ideal, whom he would fain imperfectly imitate. He weaves into the image the greatest features of his prophetic models, but is far from confounding it with himself.[1]

The Servant of God, here again the perfect prophet, possesses in highest measure the two attributes which are the most important requisites in every true prophet (p. 4). He is trained to *speak* according to the Lord's will, and indeed his mission is in particular the comforting of the despairing and helpless—that most humble yet most blessed duty of a messenger of God. And, again, he is willing to *hear* when God speaks; without resistance he receives the divine word, which he will appropriate, enjoying every day the intercourse of a true disciple with God. From this second attribute follows of itself the third, willingness to accept in the service of the divine word the shame and abuse always falling on the preachers of divine truth and on this Servant of the Lord in special degree. He does not shun the grossest assaults and reproaches, conscious that enduring them is part of his office, and that neither his strength, which is spiritual and of divine origin, will be weakened, nor his honour, which is internal and acknowledged by the Lord, will be sullied thereby. Thus he whose heart is so full of feeling for the need and suffering of men is altogether passive under the assaults showered upon himself. He knows that he has to bear them for God's sake.

If in chaps. xlix. and l., in comparison with chap. xlii., the lowliness of the faithful Servant appears in more intense form, the

---

[1] Also in lxi. 1 ff., where the decision respecting the person of the speaker depends in our opinion on the explanation of xlviii. 16, we cannot, with Targ., Calvin, Grotius, and most moderns, regard the prophet as speaking of himself, although there can be no doubt that the vocation of the author and that of the *Ebed Yahveh* stand in close connection. The former is quite absorbed in his ideal pattern, which, of course, must take quite another form, as he knows, than is the case with himself. Perhaps the key to the anonymous character of the book lies in this absorption on the author's part in some higher one. The speaker wishes, not himself, but the Servant of Yahveh to be heard, the voice of the approaching Redeemer.

contradiction between divine greatness and deepest human humiliation found there reaches its climax in the next section, in which his image is presented to us, lii. 13–liii. 12. A new discourse begins in lii. 13. It is not indeed unconnected with the foregoing ones. Chaps. li. and lii. 1–12 spoke of the transition of God's Church from the shame of captivity to honourable freedom. But now the Servant of the Lord also is called to take this path through shame to glory, and He in the highest potency. And as we saw above, that in assuming Israel's office he exercises it first on his own people, so here it appears that just by the heavy suffering which he undergoes he brings them deliverance from suffering. But for this very reason it is a notably different stage at which the seer now stands, lii. 13. What he said of Zion's redemption-morn after the night of suffering is seen by him now in glorified form in a higher sphere, where the imperfect gives place to its true archetype. In the place of that many-headed, self-willed servant of God enters the one true, pure Servant of the Lord, whom we have seen as the instrument of divine grace to the whole world, absolutely and perfectly obedient, entirely given up to the will of God. If the Church of God has to traverse its course *per crucem ad lucem*, now before Him who is the perfect representative of divine fellowship in servant-form there opens a whole abyss of suffering, from which He will emerge all the more gloriously. And the imperfection of God's suffering Church, whose sufferings are not unmerited, becomes a high-priestly diadem on the head of Him who without sin must drink the bitterest cup of suffering and death, since He bore it all merely for the sin of the Church. The suffering of the Just One for the salvation of the guilty is the deepest humiliation laid upon Him by God, and at the same time the most glorious distinction that God will reveal in Him.

Chap. lii. 13–15 forms the prelude of the section. It contains in general terms the main thought of the wondrous exaltation of one who was humbled beyond precedent.

lii. 13. "Behold, MY SERVANT will act wisely,[1] will ascend and
14 arise and be very high. Like as many were startled at
thee—so disfigured from man was his look and his appear-

---

[1] Wise dealing is implied as well as good success. הִשְׂכִּיל is often used like הִצְלִיחַ In any case praise is implied, cf. p. 333.

15 ance so unhuman,[1]—so will he make many nations start up;[2] kings shall shut their mouth at him, for what was not told them they have seen, and what they never heard they have learnt."

It is the Lord who here speaks, foretelling the destiny of His Servant. Despite all appearance to the contrary he will have a good end, the good issue which he deserves, and of which he was confident in his God. If he was unspeakably humbled, his position at last will be all the higher. In the same degree in which he was the object of speechless horror, nay, unconquerable aversion on account of the unhuman fate he endured, in the same degree will he attract astonishment and reverence in his exaltation. Men will be unable to contain themselves at the divine honour falling to him. And not only his countrymen, but the nations outside will start up in admiration to behold the glory revealed in him; kings will testify their homage to him by reverential, adoring silence (cf. xlix. 7). For it is a deep, marvellous, incomparable mystery, whose unravelling by the Lord surprises them, when the Servant of Yahveh stands before them at the end of his way and work. What is then unveiled to their gaze is something unheard of, the like of which is not found in the whole world's history.

The connection with liii. 1 is close, inasmuch as the discourse liii. 1–6 also refers to that future, in which the heathen admire the exalted Servant of the Lord. Only it is not these who speak,[3] but the Jews who will then have learnt the truth. They heard indeed of the Lord's plan, and beheld His work long ago, but with deaf ears and blind eyes. Hence now that the veil has at last been taken from their eyes they accuse themselves, saying (to the heathen world?) what follows in vers. 1–6:—

liii. 1. "Who has given credence to our report? And the arm

---

[1] כִּי, 14b, is only subordinate, referring to יִשְׁמְמוּ. Ver. 15 first gives what corresponds to כַּאֲשֶׁר. "Disfiguring from man was his look," means: "He was so disfigured by ill-usage that he could no longer be recognised as human."

[2] הִזָּה is not here to be taken as a Levitical expression: *to sprinkle*, in which case we should expect עַל as well as miss the parallelism and sympathy with the close of ver. 15; but it is to be referred with most moderns to נָזָה : *to spring, lead back*, therefore hiph. : *to make spring up*.

[3] So indeed D. Kimchi, who makes the heathen say: "He has borne our sicknesses," and in this way seeks to make the identification of the Servant with Israel possible. The עַמִּי, liii. 8, among other things, is decisive against this view.

2 of Yahveh, to whom was it revealed? He grew up before
him like a tender shoot, and like a root-sprout out of dry
ground. No form had he and no grace, that we should look
3 on him, and no beauty that we should desire him.[1] Despised
and forsaken of men, a man of sorrows and acquainted with
sickness, and like one before whom one veils his face,[2]
4 despised, that we should not esteem him. Nevertheless our
sicknesses he bore, and our sorrows—he took them on himself.
5 But we regarded him as one judged,[3] smitten of God and
tormented. But he was pierced for our sins, bruised on account
of our misdeeds; the penalty of our welfare lay upon him,
6 and by his wound healing came to us.[4] We all, like sheep
we strayed, we walked every one in his own way, but
Yahveh made to fall on HIM the guilt of us all."

Coming nearer to the mystery, the prophet makes *Israel* speak
and tell what it has witnessed and now learned for the first time
at the end of God's ways. It has to confess that the news of the
Lord's wondrous intention to reveal Himself most gloriously
through the most lowly of men, came to its ears through His
prophets, but found no credence at its hands, that it witnessed
God's dealings in its midst, the aim of which was salvation, but
did not understand them. The questions, ver. 1, require the
answer: *No one* gave credence to the marvellous tidings of God's
patient servant, no one recognised the arm of the Lord working
mysteriously in that instrument!

He, in whom the highest, most blessed revelation to Israel and
the heathen world lay wrapped up, appeared in obscure and
lowly form. He made no show, like a tree overshadowing the
land (cf. Ezek. xvii. 23), as one might expect, but was rather to
be compared to a bare lowly shoot which, springing out of the

---

[1] In ver. 2 the chief distinctive *athnach* should stand under וְנִרְאֵהוּ, which is
used in the sense of רָאָה בְ: *to gaze with pleasure at something*, as also כְּמַרְאֶה
means "pleasing appearance."

[2] כְּמַסְתֵּר, not *part.* (= "one who veils his face before us in sorrow, shame, on
account of impurity"), but *nomen verbale:* "veiling of the face before him," is One
before whom one veils his face.

[3] נָגוּעַ, smitten by God's scourge or plague. נֶגַע especially means the leprosy,
which, as is well known, was regarded as God's judgment, a sign of the divine displeasure in a special degree.

[4] חַבּוּרָה, properly *bandage*, then *wound*, cf. i. 6. The *niph.* stands in the
sense: "healing came to us by means of his wound, accrued to us therefrom."

root, rises but a little above sandy soil, and so lives a wretched existence—a description challenging comparison with Isa. xi. 1,[1] and the oracles of the "י צמח. Thus the elect "Servant of the Lord" had nothing attractive externally, nothing to indicate his unique pre-eminence and the preciousness of the blessings he brought. Therefore the people of his country and age in their superficiality were completely deceived as to his nature and worth by outward seeming, they regarded him as of no account.

Nay, they despised and abhorred him, for he not only looked uninviting to the ordinary mind, but even offensive and terrifying, as ver. 3 affirms; not indeed through harshness of nature or unfriendliness of disposition,—we heard the opposite in chap. xlii.,—but on account of the harsh fate with which God and men visited him. He was a martyr-figure, whose extremity of pain and suffering estranged the people from him, not merely because no one could see a deliverer and helper in a Son of man afflicted with evil beyond all others, but also because the plagues heaped upon him awakened the suspicion that he was an evil-doer chastened and branded by God's scourge, one of those unhappy ones from whom we avert our gaze as if the mere sight of them were defiling.

Vers. 4–6 reveal the deep mystery surrounding the sufferer. His suffering has a unique character. It turns not to his shame, but to his people's salvation. He bore the punishment belonging to the people, *i.e.* due to it, so that in sheer blindness it quite mistook him and condemned him. Observe the emphatic antithesis marked everywhere here by the pronouns (*separata* and *suffixa*). What belonged to *us he* bore, and *we* imputed it to *him*. The speakers, who knew him, of course did not recognise him, thought him so heavily visited by the hand of the Most High on account of his demerit and misdeeds.[2] But his terrible visitation was only punitive in so far as he endured the punishment due to them—the foolish judges.

The penalty of our welfare (שלום), *i.e.* here: *of our impunity*, lay upon him. This affirms most definitely, that he endured the chastisement, through whose endurance by him they themselves go unpunished, an explanation again confirmed to superfluity

---

[1] There also the figure was chosen to set forth the *lowliness* of the Messiah, p. 278.
[2] Observe in ver. 5*a* the strongly passive participles expressing the violent character of the judgment.

by the addition: "By *his* wound healing was effected *for us*." That there was a burden of guilt lying on the whole people, and every member of it, needing to be cancelled, is shown in the confession, ver. 6, in which plainly the entire Church says, that it had forfeited salvation by its sins. As little as sheep, left to themselves, remain in the straight road, so little have they kept the divine path of righteousness. Without exception they have gone, every one at his own will, their self-chosen ways of error, and thus destruction must have overtaken them, unless the Lord had made the guilt of all fall as a penal infliction on the alone Just One.

Thus has the righteous Servant of the Lord, as the Church of the Lord which he saved saw and confessed at last, suffered for its sake. It ought never to have been denied, that here *vicarious expiatory suffering on the part of the Just One for the unjust* is the subject. No exegesis can ever get rid of this thought, expressed here as plainly as human language can put it, and repeated from ver. 4 to the end of the chapter in the most emphatic way. The solution, then, of the dark riddle presented by the form of the devout Sufferer is this, that he bears the sufferings of others, viz. the sufferings which they have incurred by their sins, but which they are to be spared according to God's decree, because the Just One has taken their place. This is the extraordinary tidings, the wondrous secret, which they whose welfare was at stake did not see and believe, so that they wickedly mistook and harshly condemned the Holy One who suffered for them, as they afterwards sorrowfully confess.

With ver. 6 this confession, put into the mouth of the converted Church of Israel, comes to an end, as Ewald rightly saw. The prophet himself now recounts, ver. 7 ff., the wondrous story.

liii. 7. "He was ill treated, whilst yet he humbled himself willingly, and opened not his mouth. Like the sheep that is dragged to the slaughter and the lamb that is dumb before
8 its shearers, so he opened not his mouth. From prison and judgment he was taken away,[1] and among his generation who is concerned?[2] For he was cut off out of the land of

---

[1] לקח has here a sinister meaning as in Prov. xxiv. 11. Like our "leading away" (to death), it is used almost euphemistically of fetching for execution.

[2] דור, not to be confounded with זרע, *posterity*, is rather = *body of contemporaries*.

9 the living, for the sin of my people he was afflicted.¹ And
so they gave him his grave with the evil-doers, and with the
rich his hill of the dead, although he committed no violence
10 and no deceit was in his mouth. But Yahveh was pleased
to bruise him by loading (him) with sickness:² when thou
shalt have made his soul a guilt-offering, he will see posterity,
live many days, and what pleases God will prosper by his
11 hand. Out of the travail of his soul he will see, be satisfied,
by his knowledge will my righteous Servant justify many,
12 and their transgressions he will take on himself. On this
account I will give him a portion among the great, and
with the strong he shall divide spoil, in lieu of his having
poured out his soul unto death and let himself be reckoned
among sinners, whilst he yet bore the sin of the multitude
and made intercession for sinners."

It is now seen more definitely, that the despised Sufferer does
not sink under the burden of affliction laid on him by God,
but that the rejection and condemnation of his generation
grew into gross ill-treatment (cf. l. 6) of the condemned one,
which he accepted with lamb-like patience without complaint
or reply. This willingness which, without cursing the unjust
tormentor, surrenders itself to the penalty of unmerited
suffering and death, discerning its higher necessity, is an
essential element in the sacrifice offered by the Servant to the
Lord.

But such gross injustice, perpetrated on the defenceless one,
was not all. Ver. 8 shows that he was taken through every
form of trial and declared guilty of death. By a flagrant mis-
carriage of human justice he was "led away" to the place of
execution, without any one remonstrating or reflecting on the

---

את we take as preposition, as in vers. 9, 12 (Knobel, Delitzsch differently): "Who in the company of his contemporaries considers it?" Answer: "No one troubles himself about it." Usually it is joined to the following בי נגזר: "Who considers that he was cut off?" but the rhythm in brief measures does not allow this.

¹ למו, sing. = לו, as in xliv. 15. See p. 99, note.

² החלי, not a determined noun (Hitzig), nor yet a Syriasm for חלה (the majority), but according to Klostermann, Delitzsch, hiph. החליא (cf. 2 Chron. xvi. 12), where the last letter is not written on account of the א with which the next word begins, as in 2 Kings xiii. 6. The inf. is more precisely defined by this finitum. What goes before shows that no ordinary sickness is spoken of. The sufferings which men cause him appear in God's plan as sickness inflicted on him.

frightful injustice thereby perpetrated.[1] The prophet repeats more plainly what can scarcely be uttered : " He is violently hurried out of the world," like a criminal defiling or dangerous to mankind, whereupon the prophet is constrained once more to disclose the true cause of this shameful death : " for the sin of my people this divine penalty was executed on him." The prophet is certainly the speaker, and understands by עַמִּי those who in ver. 5 said מִפְּשָׁעֵינוּ, his people Israel.

Thus it came to pass that he was treated as a gross sinner up to the grave, as ver. 9 adds : " His grave was assigned him in the company of evil-doers," an insult which the Hebrew feels keenly (cf. Jer. xxvi. 23). But the second clause is obscure. In accordance with its pointing the Masoretes understand בְּמֹתָיו : *in his death.* We should then have to understand the certainly rare plural of מָוֶת (only found again in Ezek. xxviii. 10), not of different cases of death, but of death struggles, dying agonies, which the rich noble, who parts from his mammon with difficulty, must feel keenly.[2] But serious doubts present themselves against this reading. The pains of death come in strangely after the burial, and the second member lacks syntactical compactness. We must therefore read בָּמוֹתָיו after some codices, in the sense of " sepulchral hill."[3] The plural is the main argument of those who would understand the Servant in a plural sense. But it would be strange in the highest degree for the prophet, who preserves the strict unity of the person both before and after, here suddenly to split it up and to speak of one grave but many sepulchral hills. Rather the plural seems here to denote burial-places more generally. A second difficulty consists in the synonymous use of עָשִׁיר alongside רְשָׁעִים. It is not allowable to assign the former word a signification quite different from the

---

[1] In Isa. lvii. 1 there is a similar reference to the indifference of the people to the death of the just man, but there his end is described as a removal from judgment. Wisd. iv. 10 alludes to this passage, the early death of the just man there also conducing to his preservation. The descriptions of Wisd. iii.-v. generally refer to Deutero-Isaiah, without comprehending its deepest import.

[2] It is untenable to suppose an *antithesis* between the first member and the second : "but with the rich man (he was) in his death," as many current expositions do. Nor does this view supply a direct reference to the history of Jesus, since He, on the contrary, died with evil-doers and was buried with the rich man.

[3] Ezek. xliii. 7 ; cf. also Job xxi. 32, where certainly another phrase is used.

usual one (Hitzig). Still through the juxtaposition and the close of the verse it easily obtains an evil qualification, which, moreover, is not very remote from it according to Hebrew modes of conception; it is one who has become rich through oppression and fraud, whose hill of sepulchre is cursed by the poor who have suffered from him. Thus also the grave of the Just One is regarded after his innocent death. His burial-place is not passed without cursing! And yet no trace of the sins justly visited with such punishment was to be found in him, as is again testified.

Thus before his death, nay, during the whole of his earthly existence (the rest of the grave included), he received no recompense for the grievous injustice done him. And yet such recompense will be given him in ample degree by God's decree, which is to the effect, that the life of this noblest and poorest One will furnish a sacrifice for sin; and afterwards he will live many days and rejoice in a numerous posterity. The discourse here passes altogether from the prophetic vocation of the עֶבֶד ", described previously, to the priestly office he administers in giving himself to a sacrificial death for the salvation of his people. This is the deepest ground and most glorious design of his suffering. The Lord Himself[1] designed His life to be an *offering for sin*, plainly for the offences of the people, in compensation for the obedience which the people had failed to render. For the character of the אָשָׁם is that of a compensatory sacrifice (note B). Only the thing in question here is not, as in the Levitical law, a particular omission easily atoned for, or occasional, unintentional offences against God. Rather here a compensatory sacrifice of the highest kind will be seen, in which all the guilt of the Church will be outweighed by one peerless act—the willing surrender of the Just One to death. Since he does not give the compensatory sacrifice, which is ever a *satisfactio*, for himself, a *satisfactio vicaria* is here implied, which again ought never to have been denied.

This path of heaven-appointed self-sacrifice even to death

---

[1] תָּשִׂים is best taken as 2 sing. masc.—an address to God. If it is taken as 3 sing. fem., "when his soul shall lay down an offering for sin," the object (himself) is wanting. Reuss and Scholten would take אִם as a negative particle of asseveration: "thou verily wilt not," quite perversely and in contravention of everything the prophet has insisted on from ver. 4.

conducts the obedient Servant to life and bliss.¹ Although he died unvindicated, and apparently without hope, this cannot be the end. In this very path he will obtain posterity,—plainly the spiritual Israel, that owes its life to him, is meant,—and see it with his own eyes, rejoicing just as much in prolonged life as in numerous descendants. How it can be possible for one who was hurried off by a violent death in the midst of his days to live surrounded by many children, the prophet himself can scarcely explain. Enough that an inner necessity, such as we found in Job xix. 25 ff. (p. 184), shows this to be God's plan; and the prophet is confident that the counsel of the Lord will prosper in His (God's) hand, will come to a happy result.

Ver. 11. The fruit of his sufferings will be for his own good and the good of many. He himself will see delight in it.² Here and in ver. 10 emphasis is laid on "seeing" in the sense of Job xix. 26 f. His best recompense is that he is the living, actually present witness of the work of salvation which he has accomplished. Thus his coming to life again is certainly presupposed. The fruit accruing to others is this, that through his knowledge, his wise surrender to God's will, he is to many the medium of righteousness, such as he himself enjoys and they have hitherto lacked. He brought about this right relation between them and God by taking their offences on himself, and bearing them in their stead.

Ver. 12. After this heroic act, the most blessed ever accomplished, divine victory and honour justly await him. Although apparently defeated, he receives a lofty place among conquerors, and rich spoil like theirs as a reward for voluntarily emptying himself unto death, and letting himself be reckoned among the worst and meanest. This only happened, because like a sacrificial lamb he assumed the burden of others' sin, and interceded for them as a priest before God. Thus he receives at last the splendid vindication that is his due.

This whole passional moves in a mysterious twilight. Even the language is in part mysteriously obscure, in keeping with the profound contents. And apart from disputable details, the entire

¹ אִם implies that the path of suffering will be the condition of a unique experience of salvation.

² יִרְאֶה יִשְׂבָּע must be joined closely together; כִּי has not a privative sense, but means "out of the travail of his soul," i.e. as its fruit he will see what will delight him.

picture, in which yet many weighty features are sketched with thorough distinctness, fits with difficulty into a frame yet to be discussed. Is it past or present that the prophet depicts? Or is he painting a future tragedy? Is he describing realities at all, or are they ideal abstractions that occupy him and pass before him in such vivid figures? All these questions unite in the one, before which the chamberlain from Ethiopia stood without being able to decide it—a question among those oftenest discussed, and the answer to which is most critical: *Who is this Servant of Yahveh?* And how came the seer to behold him in the form he did?

In entering, after our review of the passages involved, on the former of these questions, we quote some views which, while containing an element of truth, are incorrect, because they fail to do justice to the entire greatness and the full details of this figure. The most comprehensive theory is the one which identifies the "עֶבֶד י״" with the *nation of Israel*.[1] We saw (p. 379) that there is a certain warrant for this view, since in fact the nation is called *Ebed Yahveh*, and the Servant is the true fulfiller of Israel's entire mission. But it is just as certain that this identification does not explain the chief point in question. Not only in the most important sections is the faithful Servant ever spoken of in strict personal unity, so that a collective can never be seen there; not merely does this image of the obedient, receptive, devoted Servant stand in striking contrast to the useless Servant which the Lord has in His people; but we even saw that the Church is first enlightened and enfranchised by the prophetic Servant of God, who is easily distinguished from it (xlii.), and that the Church needs to be first reconciled to God by him, who intercedes for it as priest (liii.).[2]

Some of these fatal objections apply to a second view,[3] to the effect that only *pious Israel*, the better portion of the exiled

---

[1] So Hitzig and Reuss in the wake of most of the Jewish expositors, Ibn Ezra, Jarchi, Kimchi, Abarbanel, the last, however, deciding afterwards in favour of the reference to King Josiah. But even Origen (against Celsus, *True Word*, l. i. 55, Paris 1733) tells of Jews who quoted to him this exposition of Isa. lii., liii.: "It applies to the nation scattered, despised, and ill-used in the world, and yet showing itself superior to the nations and converting many." Origen referred them to liii. 6, and especially liii. 8.

[2] Cf. especially liii. 8. How can this be said of the contemporaries of Israel, or how can the עַמִּי be understood otherwise than of Israel? This proof of Origen remains impregnable. We seek in vain in Hitzig and Reuss (*Gesch. d. heil. Schr. Alten Testaments*, 1881, ii. 434 ff.) for any feasible mode of evading it.

[3] Maintained by v. Cölln, Knobel, Thenius, Anger, and others.

nation, that had to suffer innocently with the rest, nay, was specially exposed to attacks and persecutions by reason of its stedfastness, is presented in this synthesis. To this worthy class belong, according to Knobel, heads of tribes and elders, priests and Levites, as well as the prophets. We cannot, indeed, doubt that the sad experiences of many pious servants of Yahveh, of course not merely exilian, supplied motives and separate features in the origination and working out of this image, as we have already insisted (p. 385); but that a whole class of the prophet's contemporaries as such was characterized by him in such personal terms, is quite untenable. Rather the Servant of Yahveh, individual and unique, is put in contrast with the whole body (cf. especially liii. 6). The best portion of the nation is not without guilt. On the contrary, it is a flock thirsting for salvation, and its longing will be satisfied by the faithful Messenger of grace, who will also certainly die to expiate its guilt.[1]

A third opinion[2] that would see the *prophetic order* in this docile, patient disciple of God must be rejected, although in chaps. xlii., xlix., and again also lxi. 1 ff., his prophetic activity and mission come out so strongly.[3] There the "genuine" Israel is seen already to be made up of many different elements; and, moreover, to take the priestly sacrificial lamb of chap. liii. as a portraiture of the prophetic order is all the more incongruous, as there was no such order in the proper sense.

Apart from prejudice it is impossible to escape the impression that a description so definitely personal cannot be explained as a collective.[4] But while it is undeniable that a personal unity appears, at least in the prophetic vision, there is still a question whether the person is historic, ideal, or belongs to future history. In point of fact, a martyr already dead has been thought of as the object of panegyric here, *e.g.* an Isaiah or Jeremiah.[5] But

---

[1] See also the confessions of lxiv. 5 ff. (lix. 10 ff.), where the prophet confesses himself impure and guilty with the entire Church.

[2] Defended by Gesenius, de Wette, Winer, *et al.*

[3] Chap. xliv. 26 might be best appealed to in favour of this view, where the Servant (*sing.*) is put in line with God's messengers. But even here the perfect prophet is distinguished from the chorus of divine messengers.

[4] Cf. H. Schultz, *A. T. Theologie* (2nd ed.), p. 753 f.

[5] Ewald thought the "Oratorio," xlii. 13–liii., was composed on the solemn leading to martyrdom of a great prophet, perhaps of Isaiah. The author of Isa. xl.–lxvi., he thinks, found it ready to hand, and incorporated it without material alteration in his book. But the piece so obviously grows out of the whole organism of the book (cf. *e.g.*

chap. xlii. 1 ff. is unsuitable as a panegyric of a dead martyr, xlix. 1 ff. absolutely so, while lii. 13–liii. would be very strange.[1] Such a glorifying of the dead is altogether foreign and contrary to the sober Hebrew mind, and especially to the unselfish spirit of prophecy.

The past nowhere furnished the prophet with this perfect image, nor yet the present, although past and present contributed to originate and shape it. Nor again is it an empty ideal, for such things are not at all in the style of the prophets. Rather the prophet definitely expected what he saw : a perfect instrument of the Most High, who, uniting all excellences of the past and passing through its perplexing experiences in full measure, would accomplish the work of internal and external redemption. This work is the new element announced by the prophet "before it springs up." For the rest, in mystic devotion he is absorbed in this wondrous figure of whose intrinsic necessity he is certain, without the time and place of its appearance being indicated.

The advance in knowledge here confronting us is extraordinary. The sufferings and privations of the period of exile have co-operated to this end. They brought clearly out to view the noblest and most powerful elements wrapped up in Israel's life. Not the outward power of the Davidic kingdom and its prosperous development, not the local existence of the ritual was the surest pledge of divine life, but that *Divine Spirit*, who can inspire the most unlikely instrument, and who by His mighty *word* achieves the greatest triumphs in the face of outward weakness and resistance, nay, amid apparent defeat and abandonment by heaven. Precisely in its tribulation the true Church of Israel felt itself nearest to God, and suffering is seen in it to be the true path to glory. David and many psalmists early had experience of this truth and deposited votive songs in the temple, proving that the righteous man does not, nay, cannot escape suffering, because otherwise he will not learn all the greatness of a delivering God to his own profit and others' salvation.[2] But in the suffering of the Isaianic Servant of God, in distinction from all the

---

xlix. 7) that a borrowing of the section in which it culminates is inconceivable, and till less a casual insertion by some one else than the author, as Ritschl supposes (*Rechtfertigung*, ii. 62). Bunsen has revived the hypothesis of Saadya Gaon, that Jeremiah is the "Servant of the Lord" extolled, and conjectures that Baruch his disciple was the composer.

[1] Cf. *e.g.* lii. 15, liii. 10 f., etc.   [2] Cf. Ps. lxix. 32, xxii. 26 ff., p. 176 f.

Passion-psalms, we find an essentially new element. This is the expiatory effect of the Righteous One's suffering, the vicarious satisfaction made by his submission and death for the guilty. Not that this idea was entirely new. The ministry of sacrifice pointed to it from the first. The slain-offering, in which an animal life was given up, often with the declared intention of thereby procuring respite for human life,[1] rests on the same idea, that a vicarious surrender is possible; but after the insufficiency of animal blood to make expiation had long been felt by profounder spirits, now when that ministry was altogether suspended, Deutero-Isaiah spoke of a far higher expiatory sacrifice. That he expressly represents the suffering of the Servant as a vicarious sacrifice, we have seen. Though it may be open to question whether the prophet in liii. 7 was thinking specifically of a sacrificial lamb, at all events he emphasizes that which made the Servant, like the animal, a suitable sacrifice: his unresisting surrender;[2] and the entire section testifies, that the effect of his suffering is that of a perfect sacrifice, efficacious for the whole people. More precisely in liii. 10 it is characterized as a sin-offering which he has to render in accordance with God's will. What the animal sacrifices signified only symbolically, i.e. in inadequate representation, the innocent suffering of a messenger of God does in reality; not only does it make an overwhelming, saving impression on sinners, but God accepts it instead of the punishment of sinners, when the Just One intercedes for them, as Job, the innocent sufferer and victim of wrong, interceded for his culpable friends. While the intercession of the Righteous One avails much, his innocent suffering avails infinitely more in God's sight. It shields the wrong-doers from punishment.

That sin requires expiation, a restoration of the disturbed relation between God and man, by which above all the divine justice will be satisfied, is proclaimed by the whole sacrificial cultus; and what constitutes the really atoning, justifying sacrifice, Isa. liii. declares: The alone pure, absolutely obedient Servant of the Lord is designed to redeem His people by unspeakable pain and

---

[1] See Lev. xvii. 11. The expiatory effect of the blood arises from its being the substratum of the soul or life. Of course the essential element is not the deathagony suffered by the animal, but the surrender of its life, which is also the most painful privation. Through the animal enduring this loss man escapes it.

[2] In John i. 29, 36, at all events, the Baptist connects the lamb, Isa. liii. 7, with an expiatory function, thus viewing it as a sacrificial lamb.

shame. His dying passion has full atoning power, and His honourable exaltation will bring all peoples to know the true God and His salvation. Thus Ps. xxii., with its prophetic conclusion (p. 176), finds here a marvellous climax.

Without doubt it is the true Redeemer, the Saviour of His people, whom the prophet meant to depict under this humble yet honourable name. But another question is, how in his view this figure is related to that of the *Messiah*, who, springing from David's stem and sitting on his throne, appeared in former prophets as Saviour and Mediator of God's salvation. Nowhere is the *Ebed Yahveh* expressly set in relation to that king. He is not called Son of David, or Son of Yahveh, or "Sprout of the Lord," like him. A superficial glance might conceive the two images of the reigning Son of David and the prophetic Martyr to be quite distinct, having nothing to do with each other. And the gulf between the two is the main reason why Israel has rejected the crucified Messiah as a σκάνδαλον to this day.

Nevertheless a deeper look into the prophetic writings should have taught that *the Christ must needs suffer* (Acts iii. 18). And it is significant that the intrinsic connection between the kingly image and the martyr-form forced itself strongly enough on the older *Synagogue*, so long as the synagogue was not yet involved in opposition to Christianity.[1] The older Messianic interpretation is confirmed even by the Jewish scholars of the Middle Ages, who themselves would understand the *Ebed Yahveh* to refer to their nation.

Thus *Ibn Ezra* remarks on Isa. liii.: "Many refer this section to the Messiah, because our forefathers of blessed memory said, that on the same day on which the temple was destroyed, the Messiah was born, and that he is bound in chains" (therefore of a Messiah already come). And *Abarbanel* on the same section: "The first question is, of whom this prophecy treats. For, behold, the wise of the Nazarenes refer it to the man who was executed in Jerusalem about the end of the second temple, in their opinion the Son of God, who took shape in the virgin's womb, as they explain in their doctrine; and in fact Jonathan, son of Uzziel

---

[1] See the instances in the excellent collection of Aug. Wünsche: יְסוֹדֵי הַמָּשִׁיחַ, *The Sufferings of the Messiah*, 1870, and in the lengthy catena published by Neubauer under Pusey's guidance: *The Fifty-third Chapter of Isaiah according to the Jewish Interpreters*, vol. i. 1876, Texts; vol. ii. 1877, Translations.

expounded it of the Messiah who is to come hereafter, and this is also the opinion of the wise of blessed memory in many of their Midrashim." In the same sense *R. Mosheh al Shech*, who lived about the middle of the 16th century in Palestine : " Behold, our masters of blessed memory have unanimously decided and preserved the tradition, that here King Messiah is spoken of," etc. Of older expositions of the chapter, which take it Messianically, the *Targum Jonathan* and *Midrash Tanchuma* may be mentioned.[1] In the Haggada also the suffering Messiah is an accepted idea, a fact which is to be put to the account chiefly of Deutero-Isaiah, and consequently bears witness to the universal Messianic interpretation of this section.[2] Only later, as it seems, attempts were made to place a subordinate Messiah, *Son of Joseph*, side by side with the *Son of David*, assigning to the former the *rôle* of suffering and dying (note C), in order to explain the two images of the Messiah, which were difficult of reconciliation.

But how did it come to pass, that despite the strong contrast between the two prophetic portraits, which at the first glance refuse to combine, the Messiah was involuntarily thought of when Isa. lii. 13–liii. was read, and that even when opposition to Christianity required the identity to be denied, it was given up with difficulty? It is not merely the inner logic of the case, that compels the acceptance of the oneness of the Servant of Yahveh with His beneficent King, both appearing as mediators of salvation. Nor is it merely the circumstance, that the designation "Servant of Yahveh," David's title of honour, was entirely appropriate to the Messiah's dignity, and was applied to Him by the prophet. Even the *lowliness* joined with this title in Deutero-Isaiah was not altogether new in the Messianic image. The Psalms of David, like his history, already testify, as we have seen, not only to the divine greatness reflected in his person and kingdom, but also to deep humiliation and trial of the Righteous One at the hand of God and men,[3] especially trial on men's part out of hostility to God. David took the royal path of the *Ebed Yahveh*,

---

[1] See Wünsche, p. 40, 42 ; Pusey-Neubauer, i. 4 f., 9. Cf. F. Weber, *System der altsynagogalen Theologie*, p. 344 ff.

[2] See Wünsche, p. 55 ff.

[3] Here also we may refer to the psalms of sickness, which show that this affliction also, which, although scarcely to be understood physically, pressed on the *Ebed Yahveh* so heavily, did not spare the old saints, David especially. Job is the classical example of this.

leading through suffering to glory. Again in the prophetic picture of the greater Son of David sketched by the prophets of the Assyrian period, alongside the brightest radiance, shadows are not wanting. The King of peace entering into Jerusalem (Zech. ix. 9) is differenced from other rulers by his mysterious lowliness and poverty. And in Isaiah as in Micah his beginning is marvellously humble. Nay, Isa. liii. 2 characterizes the lowliness of its hero almost in the same words, at any rate by the same figure, as Isa. xi. 1, 10 does. From that passage the name "Sprout of Yahveh" became a standing designation of the Messiah, and in this phrase His marvellous lowliness is chiefly expressed. Besides Zech. xii. 10 (cf. xi. 4 ff.), xiii. 7 ff. forms a bridge between the two ideas, inasmuch as here at any rate a national shepherd clad with divine dignity is spoken of (if not a Davidite expressly), who is at the same time Yahveh's Servant and is shamefully misjudged, nay, *slain* by his people, an act the guilt of which is only recognised afterwards by the inhabitants of Jerusalem.

On the other hand, the *Ebed Yahveh* of Deutero-Isaiah is not without *greatness*. After completing his work he will receive more than princely honours. He will be a father of the people he has delivered, a ruler who again establishes the holy nation in the beloved land, a conqueror rich in spoil, to whom kings and peoples do reverence. Of course the reference here is ever first of all to purely *spiritual* greatness and display of intrinsic power; the *Ebed Yahveh* grows not merely altogether from below upwards, but also altogether from within outwards. And the prophet did not further develop the existing Messiah-image, but his peculiar image of a Saviour is entirely new. It tends, however, unmistakably to unite with the one already existing. The glory of the exalted Servant must be that of a king even outwardly, nay, such as distinguishes him from all princes, converting the old Messiah-image into reality. The proof that the prophet did not consider that image obsolete or superfluous, but the goal of God's ways, is contained in lv. 3 f.:—

"I will make with you an eternal covenant: the MERCIES OF DAVID, which are inviolable: behold, for a witness of the nations I have set him, for a prince and commander of the nations."

After the work of redemption has been accomplished, what was solemnly promised to David by divine grace will be fulfilled (note D); namely, that he, David, will rule over the world in his God's name as a *witness*, namely of God his Lord. Here also, where the ruling Servant of the Lord is spoken of, we see the spiritual character and function belonging to the Servant come out. Were not the two to be one and the same person? Cf. also Isa. xlii. 1 with xi. 2 (p. 280).

If our prophet did not see fit to carry out the synthesis in so many words, he at least suggested it plainly enough. And the fulfilment, which in other things also unites what was divergent in prophecy, has supplied the synthesis. It exhibited a King, claiming to be such, but in a servant's form, the true Son of David, but without empire in this world. The agreement of his person and fate with what is prophesied of the *Ebed Yahveh* is so marvellous that it has already opened the eyes of many in Israel. When the majority of that nation on the appearance of Jesus Christ refused Him the acknowledgment due to Him according to this prophecy, when after His death it saw only an offence in His cross, by this very means it converted the prophetic picture into reality. It proved itself the blind and deaf people that understood not the words of its God, and knew not the wonders done in its midst. By misjudging and condemning the Righteous One, it filled up His cup of suffering, such as our prophet pictured.

The Son of God came in servant form, not to be ministered unto, but to minister, and to give His life a ransom for many. Because He was so willing to fulfil all the good pleasure of His Father (cf. John viii. 29), He received as none else did the testimony of the divine approval, Isa. xlii. 1.[1] His work was the redemption of Israel, whose covenant He established more gloriously than Moses, and the communication to the heathen of the saving[2] revelation and laws of God's kingdom. But compared with the divine greatness and world-wide range of His work, His appearance was strangely humble and free from ostentation. He built His Church up into a kingdom of God altogether from within outwards, from below upwards. His power depended purely on inspired speech, exercising redeeming influence on soul and body.[3] And the most lowly, they who most needed healing, expe-

---

[1] Cf. the divine voice at the baptism of Jesus, where the Spirit of God appeared descending upon Him, Matt. iii. 17; Mark i. 11; Luke iii. 22. Just so Matt. xvii. 5; Mark ix. 7; Luke ix. 35; 2 Pet. i. 17.

[2] The name-giving in Luke i. 31 alludes to passages like Isa. xlix. 6: ישׁעתי (cf. li. 5).

[3] Cf. what was said on xlii. 3, 7 (p. 290) respecting the cures of Jesus.

rienced most richly His self-denying help, and showed themselves most open to and capable of enlightenment by His divine word.[1] Thus His appearance in divine strength and humble servant-form gave the impression in overpowering degree, that He was no other than the *Ebed Yahveh* described by the prophet, as Matthew declares in the citation xii. 17–21, after telling how the Lord indignantly opposed the public glorifying of His work and person. In presence of the Saviour, who assumed all the sickness and infirmities of men, because His calling was to save all, the same evangelist alludes to Isa. liii. 4, not as if he did not know the connection of this chapter with Christ's own bodily sufferings, but because he was aware of a connection between Christ's mediatorial suffering on the cross and the work of healing by which He also delivered men from sickness proper.

For, of course, the violent suffering and death that befell our Lord Himself furnishes the most striking fulfilment of what our prophet says of the Lord's elect Servant. The coincidence is here so unmistakable that no express reference of the evangelist to it was necessary. Who can be meant in Isa. l. 6, lii. 4, but the *Ecce Homo* of John xix. 5? Who can be meant by the Lamb dragged without resistance to slaughter (Isa. liii. 7), but He who is spoken of in 1 Pet. ii. 21 ff.? What history would illustrate to us, as the passion-history of the Gospels does, the words of unspeakable sadness (Isa. liii. 8) respecting the penal judgment, from which the Just One is led to death after the fashion and in the company of common criminals,[2] while princes and people vent on Him their brutal caprice and malice?[3]

Moreover, there can be no doubt that among the testimonies which our Lord found in Scripture to the necessity of His suffering and death,[4] this prophecy of the second part of Isaiah stood in the foremost line; nor that the apostolic Church, primarily the apostles themselves, judged of the inner ground and saving effect of His death, according to His own direction, principally in the light of these oracles, which directly reveal the saving character of the innocent suffering of the Just One for the guilty as the most wondrous of mysteries. Both positions, again, are

---

[1] Matt. xi. 25; Luke x. 21.   [2] Luke xxii. 37, xxiii. 32.
[3] Cf. Acts iv. 27, spoken in reference to this prophecy.
[4] Cf. Matt. xvi. 21; Mark viii. 31; Luke ix. 22; Matt. xx. 18 f., etc., and especially Mark x. 33 f.; Luke xviii. 31 ff. with Isa. l. 6.

confirmed by definite allusions in the words of Jesus and His apostles to the ground and purpose of His guiltless suffering, as stated by Deutero-Isaiah. The passage usually taken in modern days as the classical declaration from Christ's own lips respecting the saving value of His death (Matt. xx. 28; Mark x. 45) has its roots entirely in the revelation of the lowliness of the God-accepted "Servant" found in Isa. liii., and refers specifically to his lowly yet blessed ministry expressed in the words תַּחַת אֲשֶׁר נַפְשׁוֹ, ver. 10.[1] In the same way the testimony of the apostles, nay, even of John the Baptist,[2] respecting the significance of Christ's death is steeped in the idea of expiatory suffering expressed with dogmatic definiteness in Isa. liii.[3] But at the same time the prophecy involved the necessity of the exaltation and glorification of the martyred One, by which he was to receive honour and glory before all the world in the same degree in which previously he had voluntarily descended to shame and death.[4]

Although, then, in the prophet himself the personal union between Son and Servant, King and sacrificial Lamb was not expressly formulated, the apostolic Church, with a unanimity that included all tendencies, discerned in the true Son of David the true Servant of Yahveh, and gave no hesitating or half answer to the question, Who is it that is described in Isa. liii.?[5] And it must be conceded that even if the prophet did not get so far as to concentrate his genuine Israel in one historic personality, the character he drew of the appearance and mission of the true Servant of Yahveh only found its historical realization in one person, and in him found an antitype complete in every point. Thus doubt is impossible respecting the fulfilment of this prophecy.

Having spoken of the Mediator of redemption, we have still to

---

[1] That λύτρον used here corresponds to the Hebrew כֹּפֶר, not אָשָׁם, is correct. But that the אָשָׁם paid to God for sinners has the effect of a λύτρον, that it ransoms from punishment, is taught positively and repeatedly in Isa. liii. Thus the sacrifice offered by the Servant is both. In face of this undeniable connection it is incredible that a scholar like A. Ritschl should write (*Die chr. Lehre von d. Rechtfertigung*, ii. 69): "*In any case*, the utterances of Jesus respecting the saving value of His death have *no relation* to the type of the innocently suffering Servant of God." *Credat Judæus Apella!*

[2] John i. 29, 36.

[3] Cf. especially 1 Pet. ii. 24 f.; 1 John iii. 6; Heb. ix. 28; Rev. v. 6, 9.

[4] Cf. Acts iii. 13, 26, where, as in iv. 27, 30, Jesus is called the παῖς of God, not Son, but Servant, according to Isaiah's prophecy, Phil. ii. 5 ff.

[5] Cf. Acts viii. 35.

glance at the *goal* of redemption, as Deutero-Isaiah conceived it. In what form did the prophet conceive the divine rule, in which it is self-evident history is consummated in his view ? With him, also, the future kingdom of God does not lose its national shape. After Israel has been redeemed from bondage and fitted for its high calling by the Servant of Yahveh, after it has reached a happy condition through the return of its captives and a blessed increase, it remains the Lord's favoured people. Zion-Jerusalem remains the centre of the kingdom, after its God has become King of the world (lii. 7). Then first the city really comes to splendour and honour. Its restoration is dwelt on throughout the book with special love and delight.[1]

Compared with the image of Zion in Ezekiel, the one in Deutero-Isaiah stands on a higher level of spiritual glory. It is not, indeed, exempted from the limits of earthly life; death is not yet abolished; still life is normal, long (far beyond the century!), blessed, free from pain and plague.[2] The neighbourhood of Jerusalem is a true garden of God, where only anthems of praise and psalms of joy are heard (li. 3); the truce of nature promised Isa. xl. 6 ff., has there begun (lxv. 25); the city itself is founded on and adorned with precious stones. Its inhabitants are pure, genuine disciples of the Lord. And this happy state never ends; it rests on a divine dispensation valid for ever. In liv. 9 this dispensation is described as inviolable, like the promise made to Noah in reference to the earth's continuance (p. 94).

liv. 10. "For the mountains shall depart and the hills totter,
       but my favour shall not depart from thee, nor my covenant
11 of peace totter, saith He that pities thee, Yahveh. Thou
       afflicted one, storm-tossed, uncomforted, behold, I place thy
12 stones in stibium,[3] and lay thy foundation in sapphires, and
       make rubies thy wall-pinnacles, and thy doors carbuncles,
13 and thy whole surrounding jewels. And all thy sons shall
       be Yahveh's disciples, and great shall be the welfare of thy
14 sons. By righteousness thou shalt be established. Be far

---

[1] Isa. xl. 2, xliv. 26, xlix. 16 ff., li. 3, lii. 1 ff., liv. 1 ff., 9 ff., lix. 20, lx. 1 ff., lxi. 3 ff., lxii. 1 ff., lxv. 18 ff., lxvi. 10, etc.

[2] lxv. 19 ff., with which cf. xxxiii. 24 and xxxv. 10.

[3] פּוּךְ, *stibium*, denotes the bright black colouring with which Oriental women paint their eyelids to enhance the beauty of their eyes. This powder forming the mortar, the several precious stones shine forth from it like eyes. One is thereby reminded of the architectural bordering common in ancient Palestine.

from anxiety, for thou hast nothing to fear, and from terror, for it cannot come nigh thee. Behold, they assemble in crowds—it proceeds not from me. Who assembles against thee ?—he shall join himself to thee."[1]

Thus Yahveh's grace and favour to His city are firm as the foundation of the earth. Nay, should even the "eternal" mountains and hills begin to totter, His counsel of peace and salvation concerning Zion will not be shaken. The Church, hitherto so terribly tempest-tossed, will form a strong city, built of most costly stone. Isa. xxviii. 16 (p. 286) is here figuratively developed further. The stones of the city being all jewels, it will acquire immense worth. But these precious stones, which reflect God's light in diverse pure, glowing colours, imply something deeper. The whole city is transfigured in light, etherealized by the glory of the Lord. The precious stones, already employed significantly in the Mosaic cultus, express the penetration of the densest mass by the most spiritual element, by ethereal light. Henceforth this feature, transcending empirical reality, is used frequently in depicting the perfect city of God.[2]

But what is said of the glorifying of the walls and gates by the Lord animating and illumining everything, applies also to the persons in God's city. All its dwellers without exception[3] are what their holy calling requires them to be—disciples of Yahveh, docile to divine revelation and well trained in obedience. Thus not merely will One by way of exception bear the character which God's true Servant attributed to himself in distinction from Israel; nor will even a number of prophets be thus distinguished; but the whole Church, now God's willing organ of revelation, will be mature, as former prophets already foretold in reference to the last days.[4] Just so in lx. 21 the whole Church is characterized as without blame: "Thy people are *wholly righteous*, they possess the land for ever."

This illumination of mind and heart, rendering the people

---

[1] את has here a hostile sense: "Whoever assembles in thy vicinity with hostile intent is overcome by thy wondrous force of attraction and must yield to thee." נפל על we take, according to 1 Chron. xii. 9 ff., in the sense of: *to fall to one, join him* (so also Gesenius, Knobel, *et al.*), not: *to be ruined by thee.*

[2] Tob. xiii. 16 f.; Rev. xxi. 18 ff.   [3] Cf. Isa. iv. 3, p. 262.

[4] Joel iii. 1 f.; Jer. xxxi. 34.

obedient, secures also enduring prosperity, peace without and within, on the part of God and men, in one word שָׁלוֹם (liv. 10–13), which reminds us of liii. 5, as the צְדָקָה, ver. 14, does of liii. 11. Both are originally procured for the people by the suffering Servant, and become its abiding inner possession. Such a Church cannot be harmed by any power of the world; it is impregnable, and may live in the joyous confidence that everything which the world may undertake against it will turn to its advantage. What Joel and others[1] said of the future inviolability of Zion is true of the new city of God; cf. also Isa. lii. 1.

In reference to the more spiritual conception of the Church and its vocation in its final state, chap. lix. 21 is especially to be consulted, where it is said, not of the entire nation as it now exists, but "of those converted from sin in Jacob," ver. 20:—

lix. 21. "And I, this is my covenant with them, saith Yahveh: My SPIRIT, which is upon thee, and my WORDS, which I laid in thy mouth, shall not depart from thy mouth nor from the mouth of thy seed, nor from the mouth of thy seed's seed, saith Yahveh, henceforth for ever."

As far as I am concerned, the Lord here declares,[2] "this is the agreement by which I put myself in a relation of grace with them: the irrevocable bestowal of my Spirit and words upon thee and thy posterity." By the latter phrases we are to understand, not the prophet, but the Church now directly addressed. It is no longer, as in previous covenants, an external promise, or the requirement of outward legal observance, which the Lord lays down; but Israel's divine privilege as well as its vocation becomes altogether spiritual. It is designed to be the depositary of God's Spirit and word to all time.

Here, also, we learn more clearly than in Ezekiel's diagram of the future temple why the fulfilment of these prophecies was not seen on the restoration of Judah after the exile. The Church lacked altogether the spiritual preconditions for taking such an attitude to God before the whole world, and for discharging so high a vocation towards the whole world. The internal work of

---

[1] Obad. ver. 17; Joel iii. 20; Jer. xxxi. 40; Zech. xiv. 11, etc.

[2] In exact accordance with the form of the covenant made with Abraham, Gen. xvii. 4. אֹתָם for אֲנִי as above, liv. 15.

redemption, which, according to our prophet's view, must precede the state of favour, was not yet accomplished.

Yet the attitude and vocation of God's exalted Church towards the world appear in his prophecy as the crown of the whole. Wherever he pictures the glory of the future Zion, there also the nations of the world come into the limits of his vision; and by no means merely as a dark foil in judgment being executed upon them. Certainly judgment falls on them all, even as Babylon is at present involved in it. Upon Edom the day of merited vengeance comes in terrible form (lxiii. 1 ff.), and upon all adversaries of the Lord (lix. 18), upon all peoples and tongues, who gather in crowds against Jerusalem, in accordance with Joel iii. 1 ff. (lxvi. 18). But far more frequently he speaks of the *salvation* coming to the *heathen world* also. The judgment upon it is not merely external, but spiritual. It is conquered internally by proofs of the Lord's power, before which the authority of idols sinks into hopeless ruin. Yahveh proves Himself the First and the Last, the sole God.[1] Even the final judgment will bring new members to God's kingdom and contribute to its completion (lxvi. 19 ff.). But even now the heathen world is not inaccessible to the knowledge of the true God. It is ripe to receive the divine light and right, and awaits the messenger who is to bring it these. And this was just the mission of Israel, the nation engaged in Yahveh's service, to communicate to the nations the light given it by divine revelation. Only, the messenger whom the Lord would send to them is utterly unfit for the work; he himself hears and sees nothing (xlii. 19 f.). But the Lord finds an instrument for His purpose; it is the one set forth in xlii. 1 ff., the true Servant of God, in whom his Lord has unqualified delight. He is chosen for this work, as we saw xlii. 4, 6; and, insignificant as his outward strength and appearance may be, will accomplish the incredible, carrying God's right and light to the ends of the earth. Nay, according to xlix. 6 f., the highest distinction coming to him consists in this work being laid upon him by God, a work far grander and more glorious than the new establishment of the Israelitish nation in its own land.

Here everywhere there is a sense of the need of mission-toil, a consciousness of a mission to be accomplished among the heathen, such as never expressed itself with equal force and breadth in

[1] Isa. xl. 25, xli. 1 ff., xlii. 8, xlv. 21, xlvi. 9.

former prophecies. What hitherto had been Israel's sacredly-guarded privilege, the divine Torah and judgment,[1] go forth to the heathen. No doubt Isaiah and Micah have already foretold in similar words the diffusion of the divine light from Zion over the whole world, and the going forth of the Torah from Jerusalem to all nations.[2] But it is not altogether without importance, that there the nations must first take the trouble to go to Jerusalem to obtain their light there, whereas here the enlightening word is first carried forth to them, and so, no doubt, they also learn the way to Jerusalem; for even in our prophet's thoughts Jerusalem remains the centre of God's kingdom. It is a distinction in which the contrast of ruling and serving is reflected. In Isaiah and Micah the Messianic Jerusalem calls the heathen to it by its glory and greatness; while this is also the case in Deutero-Isaiah, he sees also in the lowliness of the Servant of Yahveh a means, and that the mightiest, for winning the heathen to God. In his self-sacrificing ministry this Servant brings the light to them, thus fulfilling the mission entrusted to him by God.

We shall not go wrong in supposing that this insight into God's saving purposes in reference to the heathen, and into His use of the true Israel for their salvation, was a fruit of the sojourn in exile. As Israel there learnt through its conquerors the impotence of idols and consequently of heathenism, so it became aware of a certain hunger after God in the nobler heathen which constitutes the greatness of the human race. And so perhaps the feeling grew deeper in Israel, that despite its insignificance it was called as the people of the true God to give the supreme law to its tyrants, thus by an act of self-denial winning its finest triumph over them. The prophet declares this with divine confidence; but, of course, he regards not the empirical nation, but its ideal representative, as entrusted with this mission.

The thought, intimated already in Obad. ver. 20 f. (p. 322), that a connection exists in God's intention between Israel's bondage and dispersion among the nations, and the conversion of the heathen to God, now takes this energetic shape. The captives dragged to the farthest zones become the occasion of bringing the most unknown nations to worship at Jerusalem. They come with their treasures, bringing the children of Zion for their most

---

[1] תורה and משפט, Isa. xlii. 4, li. 4.

[2] Isa. ii. 3; Micah iv. 2.

precious offering, as described so gloriously in chap. lx., where the city slumbering in impotence is addressed:—

lx. 1. "Arise, grow light, for thy light comes, and the glory of
2 Yahveh rises brightly upon thee! For, behold, darkness covers the earth, and obscurity the nations; but upon thee Yahveh beams forth, and His glory will appear upon thee!
3 And nations walk to thy light, and kings to the rising of thy
4 rays. Lift up thine eyes round about and behold, they all assemble, they come to thee! thy sons shall come from far,
5 and thy daughters be borne on thy side.[1] Then shalt thou behold and shine, and thy heart trembles and enlarges; for the wealth of the sea rolls to thee, the strength of the heathen comes to thee."

What a sight for the orphaned, widowed mother, when she opens her eyes and sees her children being brought from every side! The foreign heathen, who bring the noblest products of their land and themselves[2] as tribute, at the same time bring with reverent care the children of Jerusalem pining in exile in their land, to whom, according to xlix. 22 f., the foremost among them do not disdain to render a nurse's office. This, according to lxvi. 20, is the most acceptable offering they can present to the Lord. Moreover, they themselves—the heathen—experience the full power of divine grace. It is true, they must minister to Zion (lx. 12). According to lxi. 5 f., they have to look after the profane work in the sacred land, the feeding of the herds as well as tillage and vintage, that Israel may be given wholly to the *priesthood*, the service of God. They have also to endow the holy people and land with their riches, lx. 7. And for this end they become members of the holy nation. They subscribe, not without reason, to Yahveh, and name themselves after Jacob's name (xliv. 5); in fact, they are incorporated with the holy nation.

lvi. 3. "Let not the foreigner, who has joined himself to Yahveh, speak thus: 'Verily Yahveh will sever me from His people.' And let not the eunuch say: 'Behold, I am a dry tree.'"

Not in "a very pardonable proselytizing spirit," as Gesenius

---

[1] Properly: *supported on thy side*. Little children in the East are often carried astride on the shoulder, and also, which is meant here and lxvi. 12, on the hip-joint, so that the child's face is turned to the bearer.

[2] So חיל, ver. 5, is perhaps meant: *the strength*, *i.e.* the *élite*, of heathen nations.

supposes, but in the large-hearted spirit that breaks not a bruised reed, access to the Church is thrown open to all, who by observing merely the fundamental commands of the law prove their subjection to the God of Israel. Let no one deem himself too mean to be an accepted member of the Church, not even one labouring under the dishonouring infirmity which according to Deut. xxiii. 2 excluded from the Church. The Lord will know how to richly make up such defects to His faithful ones, giving them an eternal name better than that of fair children. And to all the foreigners, who prove faithful to the covenant, He promises:—

lvi. 7. "I bring them to my holy mountain and make them joyful in my house of prayer; their burnt-offerings and slain-offerings are well-pleasing on mine altar, for my house shall
8 be called a HOUSE OF PRAYER FOR ALL NATIONS. Thus saith Yahveh, Lord of all, who gathers the scattered ones of Israel: 'Still further will I gather beyond it to its gathered ones.'"

This destination of the temple, to receive all nations, is significant enough. Solomon indeed in his consecration-prayer thought of the stranger coming there to worship, 1 Kings viii. 41. But there individuals only are referred to, here a union of nations (lxvi. 23, *all flesh*) to worship in this temple, thus almost doing away with the local limit of the conception, which is felt to be too narrow. The chief point is that the God who dwells on Zion will be acknowledged and invoked by all mankind. As ver. 8 indicates, His flock will be too small for the Lord, even after He has brought together all the scattered sheep of His people; He will yet bring others with like care. The thought is the same as in John x. 16, which even the form of the conception closely resembles.

Chap. lxvi. 20 f. goes a step farther, where that which the heathen offer, namely, the returning Israelites, whom they conduct with respectful mien, is made parallel with the valid Levitical offerings; and then, the heathen having shown themselves competent to offer acceptable gifts to God, entrance into the priestly and Levitical order is thrown open to them. "From them also I will take for priests and Levites, saith Yahveh." Certainly this "from them" is referred not only by Jewish expositors, but also by Knobel, Hitzig, Duhm, and others, to the returning exiles, in favour of which they appeal to ver. 22 [1] with more right than to lxi. 5 f. But this explanation we hold to be untenable. That the Levitical priesthood will be formed out of the captives, among whom at that time the kernel of the order is found, is taken for granted; but here a new election of grace is in question, by which the Lord completes His priesthood from those who did not previously belong to it—according to the connection with ver. 20, undeniably from the heathen—to whom therefore will be assigned, not merely profane labour for God's kingdom and the position of laymen in the Church, but also a fitting representation in the priesthood. This is the new thought meant to be expressed in the sentence complementary to lxi. 5 f.[2] That it is quite in the spirit of our large-hearted prophet, with his kindliness to the heathen, no one will contest.

Thus it is not a mere restoration of ancient Jerusalem that he foretells, but a real rebuilding of the holy city, a new birth of the whole theocracy. The conception, perhaps, still rests on the venerable and significant forms of the past, but the spirit everywhere soars higher. The prophet gives himself no time to linger amid these forms, like Ezekiel. He hastens without pause to the supreme goal. That goal is a genuine Israel, born again inwardly, emancipated and sanctified by God's wonder-working grace, serving Him not only in the outward forms of life, but in spirit and in truth, and in accordance with its high destiny summoning all nations to this service. True, he sees the community of nations, enlarged immeasurably, still performing a locally limited worship on Zion, where the old temple stood. But the new temple of the Lord is no longer specifically Israelitish, but a house of prayer for all nations; for now every knee shall bow before the true God (xlv. 23). Animal sacrifices are still mentioned in the old style, but the prophet is aware of a more

---

[1] Ver. 22 declares the eternal duration of the memory and priesthood of Israel. But according to our explanation, this agrees quite well with ver. 21; for the incorporation of the heathen into God's people, and of its representatives into God's priesthood, is a security for their ever-enduring continuance after the analogy of xliv. 3-5.

[2] The relation to this passage shows that the prophet here is not giving laws, but his great ideas of redemption shape and mould themselves spontaneously. Were lxi. 5 f. taken as legal paragraphs, even the reference of lxvi. 21 to the Jews would be impossible, since there all the Jews are advanced to the priesthood, consequently a selection from them for this dignity could no longer be thought of.

perfect and effectual sacrifice, quite putting in the shade the Levitical ritual which, performed without the true God-pleasing disposition, is, by reason of its common externalism, only a gross offence to the Lord.[1]

Thus everywhere the old gives place to the new, even the previous form of God's kingdom to a living energy that will give it a shape incomparably broader, more true and spiritual. The Lord makes everything new, even nature, heaven and earth. If, according to Isa. lx. 19 f., the new Jerusalem no longer needs light of sun and moon, the Lord illumining it by His glory day and night, this, of course, does not mean that neither sun nor moon will any longer exist. But that a new creating of the universe will actually take place, is proved by lxv. 17 (cf. lxvi. 22): "Behold, I create a *new heaven* and a *new earth.*" The kingdom of God is consummated, when not merely Zion, not merely Israel, not merely the world of nations, humanity, but also the *world*, hitherto the arena of history and judgment, is completely transfigured into a temple of the Lord, resplendent with His glory.[2]

Thus the light of prophetic promise dawned the brightest in the darkest days. The oppressed and humbled nation might contemplate such days without anxiety. Yet even this "Evangelist" among the prophets[3] does not omit the earnest warning, that the salvation which grace offers must not be wickedly scorned and trifled with. Nay, this warning is the *ceterum censeo*, which he repeats[4] after each of the three main parts of his book, and which he strengthens the third time by an alarming picture of the condemned, whose worm dies not and whose fire is not quenched (lxvi. 24). There is no peace, no prosperity for the wicked, who meet the Lord with obstinate resistance.

---

[1] Isa. lxvi. 3. This passage, indeed, does not contain a rejection of every animal sacrifice, which would contradict lvi. 7, lx. 7, but is directed against the overvaluing of the unholy *opus operatum*. But, of course, it declares strongly enough how merely relative the value of sacrifice is, the insufficiency of which is already emphasized in xl. 16. And xliii. 2 ff. proved the dispensability of such ceremonial. God makes His grace independent of it. On the other hand, He deemed the sin-offering of the Righteous Servant necessary and adequate for the salvation of others!

[2] Cf. Rev. xxi. 23 and xxi. 1.

[3] Cf. Augustine, *De civitate Dei*, xviii. 29.

[4] Isa. xlviii. 22, lvii. 20, lxvi. 24; cf. lxv. 11 ff. The appearance of those under divine judgment, which will be a powerful memento to the Church, reminds us of Ezek. xxxix. 11, 15. Cf. with Dan. xii. 2.

NOTE A.—That Isa. xl.–lxvi. was not composed, as tradition says and many moderns still maintain,[1] by the prophet Isaiah previously considered, who was already well advanced in life towards the end of Hezekiah's reign, is made certain to us by the historical environment which the book everywhere[2] presupposes. The exile in Babylon, as well as the destruction of Jerusalem and the temple, are nowhere *foretold*, but *presupposed* throughout. In the same way the prophet speaks of the victorious course of Cyrus as a history of the time familiar to his contemporaries, to which allusion only need be made to be understood. The case certainly is different if, as Nägelsbach still asserts, the prophet (xlv. 3 f.) meant to describe the mention of the name Cyrus found in his book as a divine miracle.[3] But this "I called thee by thy name" is to be understood, according to xliii. 1, xlix. 1, of the personal call whose object Cyrus was, as the elect instrument of the God of whom he knew nothing. Just so אֲכַנְּךָ, "I have surnamed thee, given thee thy title," xlv. 5 (cf. "my shepherd," xliv. 28; "my anointed," xlv. 1), therefore "determined thy honour as well as thy person." Thus the mention of the name Cyrus does not at all bear the character of a mysterious disclosure or prediction. In xlii. 2 ff., 25, this conqueror is spoken of as if his name need not be mentioned, since it is in every mouth. In xliv. 28, where he is first named incidentally, no kind of emphasis is laid on it. In xlv. 1 the discourse turns to him as one who has already appeared. And when in these prophecies it is very often insisted that what was announced long ago by Yahveh is being *now* fulfilled,[4] this, of course, does not mean what is contained in the book itself, but what former prophets predicted.[5] The reference is to their oracles against the powerful empire of Babylon which now, when the exile foretold by Jeremiah was nearing its end, suffered blow on blow, by which means the Lord was preparing for the long-promised deliverance of His people. The prophet supplies this verification of former prophecies, and also announces new things which will just as certainly happen.

[1] Hengstenberg, Hävernick, Stier, Keil, Delitzsch, A. Rutgers (*De Echtheid van het Tweede Gedeelte van Jesaja*, 1866), Nägelsbach, Löhr (*Die Frage über die Echtheit von Jes.* xl.–lxvi., 1878), Himpel (*Tübinger Quartalschrift*, 1878), *et al.*

[2] The question whether lvi. 9–lvii. 11 is pre-exilian, does not here concern us.

[3] So already Josephus, *Ant.* xi. 1. 2, who makes Cyrus proclaim publicly that he found his name in the prophetical writings of the Jews—whereas in Ezra i. 1 f. the piety of the king towards the God of the Jews, which, of course, may have been fostered by the prophecies to be discussed immediately, appears without this addition.

[4] Isa. xli. 26 f., xlii. 9, xliv. 7, xlviii. 3.

[5] This shows that very definite prophecies of the overthrow of Babylon were extant, such as Jer. xxv. 12, xxix. 10, 1. Moreover, Isaiah's oracles, xiii. f., xxxiv., xxxv. (p. 295), receive hereby critical support, and without doubt were present to the mind of the seer, along with those of Habakkuk and Jeremiah.

The purpose of the book also, like its historical situation, corresponds to the exile alone. Those found in captivity and in the misery of those days are urged to take comfort, and, in view of the great events in which God's prophecies were just then beginning to be fulfilled, to revive their confidence in the Lord, since now the time of the fulfilment of all those great promises is coming. This is the practical aim and end of the book, whose tone, almost throughout comforting and cheerful, would not at all suit Isaiah's age and mission.

This twofold character of the book, its uniform presupposal of a state of punishment that has already existed long, and its effort to comfort and encourage the people found among the heathen by the hope of the approach of a glorious future, admits but two explanations. One is, that the former Isaiah belonging to the Assyrian period was so transported by the Spirit into the far future of the Babylonian exile, that he not merely addressed one oracle, like chap. xxxv., to that future generation, but completely identified himself with that age, and thus in the long series of discourses contained in chaps. xl.–lxvi. everywhere had before his eyes, not his contemporaries, but that posterity and their circumstances. He must have written this book as a sealed book (neither intelligible nor useful to his age) for the after-age, which alone could decipher it. The other more intelligent supposition is, that the author was not Isaiah at all, but lived in the age for which he spoke and wrote. In distinction from the first part Isaiah's personality nowhere appears, nor does any heading claim the book for him.

In confirmation of the view that we have to do with another author of unknown name, the difference in style, phraseology, and strain of thought may be adduced as a reason of the second rank. In respect of form it is important that certain expressions characteristic of Isaiah frequently recur even in the second part, and that in him we have an extraordinary diversity of style. But this is not at all the style of the second part. Here the language is calm, uniform, broad, and transparent. There a hundred springs gush forth, here a clear, majestic stream pours along with equable movement; there the prophecy follows the most diverse melodies, here one ground-strain rules the whole composition. As to contents, the second part, altogether of a piece, is pervaded by the same ever-recurring conceptions, which are little seen in i.–xxxix. (opposition to the idolatry of the Babylonians, return of the exiles, transforming of the desert, etc.), and is governed by one main idea, that of the Servant of Yahveh, which is foreign to the first part, but here forms the uniting soul of the whole just as much as that of Immanuel in Isa. vii.–xii.

Further, Deutero-Isaiah is strongly dependent on *Jeremiah*, just as much as on Isaiah. His minute descriptions of idol-manufacturing¹ stand to Jer. x. 1 ff. as exposition to text. In the same way his conception of the Servant of Yahveh has its starting-point in Jeremiah (xxx. 8–11), even as the personal experiences of the latter prophet contributed not a little to the individual shaping of that idea. We cannot help putting Isa. xl.–lxvi. after Jeremiah in the development of prophecy.

Certainly the connection of the book with Isaiah remains an enigma. The enigma finds some explanation in the circumstance that Isaiah's book was collected late, and arranged without fixed principle. The old Talmudic order of the books may be connected with its late conclusion: Jeremiah, Ezekiel, Isaiah, the Twelve. (*Baba Bathra*, f. 14, col. 2.) So grand a prophecy might naturally be regarded as the work of the great prophet, to whose greatness certainly this second part contributed not a little in the eyes of after ages. Cf. already Ecclus. xlviii. 22 ff., which plainly has this book of consolation chiefly in view, ver. 24. Add to this, that among the prophecies of Isaiah some are found to which our prophet refers, or which (like chap. xxxv.) had first struck the airs which he again took up. Still, after all, the enigma lying in the anonymity of this "great Unknown" (Ewald), to whom no prophetic book of approximate extent furnishes an analogy, is not solved satisfactorily. Elsewhere we see the prophets' assuming responsibility for their prophecies by giving their name, and this is done most carefully of all after the exile. That this prophet should wish and be compelled to conceal his name at Babylon, is little in harmony with his triumphant bearing. And what hindered him coming forward after the victory of the Persians? Further, how could the home-coming exiles, in whose hearts his words must have stood uppermost of all prophecies, forget his name?

However this may be, the divine greatness of this prophetic book by no means depends on the answer given to the critical question as to its human author. Its marvellous import lies, not in what it describes as fulfilled, but in what it announces "before it springs up." In significance it leaves the days of Cyrus far behind, moving amid incomparably loftier scenes than the great events of that age.

NOTE B.—אשם (cf. the verb) is *shortcoming*, *debt* (in a moral, not merely pecuniary sense), then *making amends for it*, the *reparation* or *satisfaction* symbolically rendered to God; cf. 1 Sam. vi. 3, 8, 17. Not only is the injury done to men to be repaid them, but a recompense is also to be paid to the Lord, whose justice is likewise violated by such illegal action, Lev. v. 1–26, vii. 1–10. That "no sacrifice of the Old Testament has the force of a legal satisfaction to God," is a preconceived opinion of Ritschl (*Rechtf. u. Versöhn.* ii. 64), which is refuted by the use of אשם in the Torah and by history. The

---

¹ Isa. xl. 19 ff., xli. 6 f., xliv. 9 ff.

fact that the prophet describes the significance of the supreme sacrifice he has in view by the special expression, in which the element of satisfaction comes out most strongly, ought to be carefully observed.

NOTE C.—J. Hamburger (*Encyklopädie für Bibel und Talmud* ii. 5, p. 765; 1880) would derive the entire notion of a suffering Messiah among the Jews (and the Messianic exposition of Isa. liii.) from the death of Bar Cochba, whose Messiahship was afterwards sought to be proved by that exposition, just as Christians sought to prove that of Jesus of Nazareth; but even if particular features in the description of the Messiah ben Joseph originate in the Roman conflicts of that age, the pragmatical connection just stated is opposed by the fact that the Messiah-faith did not remain attached to the person of Bar Cochba; on the contrary, the oldest and most numerous testimonies to the suffering Messiah utterly exclude any reference to him. In the same way we must deny that the two figures of the ruling and suffering Messiah were sharply separated among the Jews from the first, which fact, according to Hamburger, was simply unknown to Christian scholars. The opposite again is proved by the oldest testimonies. For example, in Tract. *Sanhedr.* f. 93, col. 2, the Messiah's suffering is attached to Isa. xi. 2. See Wünsche, *ut ante*, p. 56 ff.

NOTE D.—The exposition that understands the words of a transfer of David's rights of grace to the people founders on the strongly emphatic הַנֶּאֱמָנִים, lv. 3. The moment would be ill chosen to emphasize their unchangeableness, when they were to be severed from David's house. On the other hand, the fulfilment of the mercies assured to David includes rich promise for the people (cf. ver. 5). By David is meant the son of Jesse, who received such assurances of divine favour as Ps. cx. or Ps. ii., in which, as is specially recalled, the position of a true witness for God before all the world was assigned to him, since he had to represent God and so to convey the knowledge of God to it. That this divine testament is inviolable is here confirmed; it will form the contents of the New Covenant that God makes with His people, will therefore redound to the salvation and glory of the latter, which hitherto had been very imperfectly the case; cf. Ps. lxxxix. 28.

SIXTH SECTION.

THE POST-EXILIAN PROPHETS: HAGGAI, ZECHARIAH, MALACHI (PERIOD OF THE PERSIAN RULE), DANIEL.

§ 40. *Haggai and Zechariah.*

SPEAKING generally, the substance and purpose of the prophecies uttered after the Exile are the ratification of the promise after a preliminary fulfilment. The predictions of the former prophets were accomplished in so far as the Jewish nation had undergone a restoration unique in history. A considerable portion at least of the banished people, its spiritual *élite*, had by the permission of the Persian king, Cyrus, returned out of exile to Jerusalem, with Zerubbabel, a representative of the Davidic royal house, and Joshua the high priest, at their head. But just now more than ever the fulfilment of the prophetic word was relegated to the future. How differently the new life in the home-land looked from what might have been expected according to Ezekiel and Isa. xl. ff.! All that could be seen by human eye was a paltry restoration which gave no promise of raising the theocracy to its former grandeur. The means, and consequently even the inclination, were wanting to rebuild the temple itself, so soon as the attempt met with opposition. Moreover, the political circumstances were of such a kind that no hope could be cherished that the people of the Lord could ever, in face of the world-power now tyrannizing over all, regain an independent, to say nothing of a dominant position.[1]

In these circumstances the mission of *Haggai* and *Zechariah*, who spoke to the nation in part contemporaneously, in part alternately,[2] was to encourage it, to revive its confidence in the divine promises, and exhort it not to neglect doing its part, through want of faith

---

[1] Cf. Ezra iii. 12 f.; Hag. ii. 3; Zech. iv. 10.
[2] Ezra v. 1, vi. 14. Cf. the dates of their prophecies.

and selfish worldliness, toward restoring the divine rule. In particular, by re-erecting the temple it was to fulfil the outward condition of God's dwelling in its midst. It is true that according to Ezra iii. 8 ff., a beginning had been made in the second year after the return (534 B.C.) in rebuilding the *temple*. But the work came to a standstill at once, and remained so until the second year of the reign of Darius (519).[1]

First of all, *Haggai* pleads with glowing zeal for the resumption of the work neglected far too long, reminding his people, who were only too moderate and thought more of their own advantage than of God's honour, that they would gain nothing by their parsimony toward the temple. In these years of indifference, he says, they had experienced nothing but misfortune, and indeed they had deserved nothing else, seeing that while declaring the building of the house of God "inopportune," they had held the comfortable, nay, luxuriant, furnishing of their own dwellings opportune. The great moment of deliverance had found a puny race.

By the plea (i. 2) that the time to build the Lord's house was not yet come, the worldly wise are supposed not merely to allege that the time was not favourable for so great an undertaking, but with an indolence that wears the look of piety they direct attention to the hour of God : "Wait till the Lord sets on foot the building He promised!" In opposition to this Haggai declares that God's help and blessing will not be wanting when they are willing to set to work. In particular, to the two high-hearted leaders of the colony, the worthy representatives of the holy kingdom and priesthood, who have clearly waited long for the moment when they could continue the building, he proclaims the divine promise :[2] "*I am with you!* Be of good comfort, my Spirit will be with you, fear not ! Set to work with all the people, and the Lord's miraculous, abundant help will not be wanting."

---

[1] Eb. Schrader (*Stud. und Krit.* 1867, p. 460 ff.) tries to prove that this account of the Book of Ezra is incorrect, and that the temple-building was first begun under Darius at the instance of Haggai and Zechariah (cf. Hag. ii. 18 ; Zech. viii. 9). So Steiner in Hitzig's Comm., 4th ed. p. 321 f. See against this, F. W. Schultz, *Die Bücher Ezra, Nehemia und Esther*, p. 10 ff. Observe especially Hag. ii. 3 (cf. Ezra iii. 12), from which it appears that the outlines of the temple must have been already settled before the foundation-day mentioned in Hag. ii. 18.

[2] Hag. i. 13, ii. 4, 5.

ii. 5. "The word that I established with you, when you marched out of Egypt, and my Spirit abides in your midst;[1] fear ye
6 not! For thus saith Yahveh of hosts: Yet one period it lasts, a brief one, when I will shake the heavens and the earth and
7 the sea and the dry land, and set in commotion all heathen nations, and the preciousness of all the heathen shall come, and I will fill THIS HOUSE with glory, saith Yahveh of hosts.
8 Mine is the silver and mine the gold, saith Yahveh of hosts.
9 Greater shall be the after glory of this house than the former, saith Yahveh of hosts. And in this place I will dispense PEACE, saith Yahveh of hosts."

Little as the present state of the people of Israel seems to answer to these words, the ancient covenant of Sinai, according to which it was the elect nation in which God dwells,[2] remains in force; and in proof of this He makes His *Spirit* dwell still as formerly and for ever in its midst, *i.e.* in the chosen organs of the people,[3] a treasure infinitely more precious than all the outward honours and riches wanting to the impoverished people of God. Moreover, a mighty revolution will soon take place in the whole state of the world, the effect of which will be to transfer the centre of the world's power and glory to the temple on Zion. Thus a new evolution in the world's history approaches. After the passage of a single and brief section of time,[4] the Lord will bring to an end the dead calm now pressing with leaden weight on His people in its despised position in the eyes of the nations. God sets in motion heaven and earth to make His kingdom acknowledged in the world. The chief result of this movement will be to give quite a new direction to the aspirations of the nations. In accordance with Isaiah's numerous oracles, they will

---

[1] Permanent validity is assured to the Word settled in covenant-form at the exodus from Egypt, as well as permanent abode to the Divine Spirit in the midst of the Church. Hence by an easy zeugma the prophet could join עֹמֵד with both word and Spirit, only he had at first a transitive construction in mind, as אֵת proves.

[2] Ex. xix. 5, see p. 128.

[3] Cf. the similar combination of Spirit and word in the same connection, Isa. lix. 21. Of course here the general life-spirit is not meant, but the specifically Divine Spirit; cf. Zech. iv. 1 ff. The work of the Spirit is not to be limited to assistance in building the temple, since His permanent abode in the nation is emphasized.

[4] The LXX. translate ii. 6 incorrectly: "*Yet once* I will shake the heavens" (followed by Heb. xii. 26). There is no reference to former shakings. Cf. Isa. x. 25; Ex. xvii. 5; Hab. ii. 3. The words are accordingly to be explained: *Yet continues it one* (neuter = *a section of time*), *and that a brief one—then will I*, etc.

deem only their best possessions good enough to adorn Yahveh's temple, which will then be filled with glory. As in Isa. lx. 5 (p. 411) one may be doubtful whether in Hag. ii. 7 by the ornament, the *deliciæ* of the nations, are meant mere wares, or the noblest of the heathen themselves. At any rate, what they are and have of greatest value they bring to enrich "this house," all the riches of the earth belonging *à priori* to the Lord.

Thus the former splendour of the temple under Solomon will be excelled by that of the future. Let it be observed that two temples are not distinguished here. The house of Yahveh on Zion is always one and the same, its appointments only differing in the course of ages. But, little favourable as circumstances seem, these appointments will soon attain an unexampled splendour through the universal acknowledgment accorded to the temple of Yahveh in the world. And not in vain do the nations stream together there, bringing their most costly gifts; there they too obtain the best of gifts from God, one they possess not, true *peace*, the divine salvation that includes also earthly well-being (p. 310). The bestowal of this most precious gift, comprehending in itself all others, the Lord has bound to that spot, the scene of His revelation and worship. The glory (כָּבוֹד), with which the Lord fills His temple, ver. 7, is, of course, as the context shows, meant concretely of the presents which men bring thither. All this presupposes that He first fills the house with its former glory,[1] and hence reveals Himself to the world, so that all nations learn that peace and well-being stream to them from here, as promised in so many prophetic oracles.

The oracle of Haggai speaks of the completion of God's house on earth. It is evident that scant justice is done to his language, which points to a world-wide convulsion, turning all eyes to Jerusalem and bringing the homage of all the heathen thither, by a reference to the acknowledgment, which followed soon, of the temple by single non-Israelitish princes, like Darius (Ezra vi. 6–10), Artaxerxes (ibid. vii. 15 ff.), and later ones (2 Macc. iii. 2), Herod who finished the temple in more splendid style than Solomon (Joseph. *Ant.* xv. 11), or to the presents of non-Israelites, who came into the temple in great numbers (Joseph. *Bell. Jud.* ii. 17. 3). These acts of homage were merely isolated, encouraging tokens, pointing to a complete realization of Haggai's utterances.

[1] Cf. 1 Kings viii. 11; Zech. ii. 9.

The shaking of the world foretold by him, comprehensive as creation, followed shortly, taking its start from "this house." We would assign less weight, indeed, than older expositors to the outward relations of Jesus to this temple, *e.g.* His teaching in the structure of which Zerubbabel laid the foundation, though it is significant that God here published the message of peace and salvation designed for all nations through the elect organ of His Spirit. But the temple comes into view, as in Isa. ii. (Micah iii.), as the dwelling of the true God and the seat of His revelation. Israel's great prerogative is that it has God dwelling in its midst. And the greatness of this distinction was to be shown in days to come in a way quite different from what was the case in the past. From His dwelling in Israel God's supreme, world-embracing revelation has gone forth; and to that place (*i.e.* to the revelation of His nature there, appearing in historical realization) all nations learn to direct their gaze and worship. With the appearance of this divine glory certainly the outward temple structure must fall into ruin, or rather undergo a transformation that it may correspond to the grandeur of its purpose and the heathen may be able to enter it. The greatest events of the world's history must subserve the building of this temple, the abode of Yahveh, and men's noblest gifts and possessions are only just good enough to form its adornment. The local and historical limitation of the prophecy explains why Haggai still sees this perfected temple in the form of the stone one about to be built.[1] The stone one was still in his days what the immovable, spiritual one was to be in the New Covenant: "The dwelling of the true God upon earth." Before the glorifying of the temple foretold by him but *one* period had still to run, and that a short one. Of course, where the existence of a temple is in question, no scanty measure of time is to be laid down. But, measured by the religious development of Israel, the last period of the holy nation before the revealing of the New Covenant had in fact dawned. No really new epoch followed before the great one, that brought to completion the history of God's people, and threw open its temple to all the world. Moreover, the world-convulsions, that ushered in this great crisis of time, presented themselves soon enough.

---

[1] In Zechariah we already find the perfect temple-building separated from the present work, p. 440.

The prophet's exhortations to build the dwelling of the Lord fell on receptive soil, not only in the case of the two leaders, but also at last among the people. On the twenty-fourth day of the ninth month of the second year of Darius a new start in building was made.[1] From this day, as the prophet was empowered to promise, the people's state of impurity in God's sight would cease, and the misfortune hitherto experienced turn into blessing (ii. 10 ff.). But Haggai had a still more important promise to address on this same day to the heir of the regal dignity, *Zerubbabel*. To him the word of the Lord came:—

ii. 21. "Speak to Zerubbabel, the governor of Judah, thus: I
22 will shake the heavens and the earth, and will overthrow the throne of the empires,[2] and destroy the strength of the kingdoms of the heathen, and will overthrow the war-chariots and them that ride thereon, and the steeds and their riders shall perish, every one by the sword of his companion.
23 On that day, saith Yahveh of hosts, I will make thee, Zerubbabel, son of Shealtiel, my servant, saith Yahveh, and make thee as a signet ring, for I have chosen thee, saith Yahveh of hosts."

The world-shaking described in ver. 6 is now considered on its political side, in its significance for the *Davidic royal house*, as in ver. 6 in its reflex influence on the position of the *temple*. For this reason the promise is given in altogether personal form to Zerubbabel, on whose person the Messianic dignity rests, and who, a worthy descendant of David, like another Solomon, takes in hand the building of the temple.[3] The divinely-caused convulsion appears here as a judgment on all kingdoms of the earth,

---

[1] It is strange that in Hag. i. 15 this beginning is already announced three months earlier. We explain the matter thus: i. 15 is a gloss, attached in loose grammatical form, which a reader rightly borrowed from ii. 1, 10. But afterwards some one changed the ninth into the sixth month, because all the rest of the first chapter falls into the sixth, and in ii. 1 the seventh follows. Consequently between Haggai's first exhortation and energetic action, not three weeks, but somewhat over three months intervened, in which, of course, various preparations had to be considered.

[2] Not one throne is meant, by which the world-power would be set collectively over against God's people (Köhler), but כִּסֵּא stands just as generally as חֹזֶק.

[3] Quite unwarranted is Hitzig's distinction, that Zerubbabel received this message, not as David's descendant, but as the then leader of the Jews! עַבְדִּי and

in which their martial power, their war-chariots, in which they trust, perish, one destroying the other.[1]

Whilst in this way the Lord involves the heathen kingdoms in turmoil and conflict, so that they destroy each other, just at the time when He brings every crown and throne to the dust He will display His loving care for the Davidite, and crown him with the highest honour. The promise to Zerubbabel is limited to a single figure, but a significant one, a figure susceptible not unintentionally of various interpretations. The *signet-ring*, to which God compares David's heir,[2] expresses in any case the value at which he is estimated by God. Also the element of inseparableness lies in it;[3] only not this exclusively, as some expositors think. For the meaning is not merely that when God destroys the other empires He will not reject this prince, but keep him inseparably with Himself; but that catastrophe will raise this princedom to an exceptionally glorious position; its relation to what is promised is causal, not merely antithetical. Zerubbabel will thus be made a jewel, on which God's eye rests with pleasure, which He reckons His most precious ornament, and therefore takes great care of. Moreover, a signet-ring has not merely a real, but also an ideal value; it is more intimately associated with the person of the possessor than any other ornament; it bears his initial, and is the token attesting the genuineness of his utterances. Hence the thought is suggested, that the Davidite will be to the world the sign of God's acts and utterances. What the world sees of divine action will come through his means; in his person the finger of God and the law of God will be everywhere acknowledged; so inseparable on earth is God's rule from His people.[4]

בְּחַרְתִּי clearly enough recall David, Ps. lxxviii. 70. Here also the point in question is the kingdom in opposition to the heathen empires, not the position of the Jews generally; hence the quite personal address to the representative of the kingly race.

[1] Cf. Judg. vii. 22; Ezek. xxxviii. 21; Zech. xiv. 13.

[2] שִׂים, used absolutely, is not *to put on, lay on*, but : *to set for something, make*.

[3] The signet-ring is so used in Cant. viii. 6; Jer. xxii. 24; Ecclus. xvii. 17.

[4] Von Hofmann, *Schriftbeweis*, ii. 2, p. 600 : "Thereby it is not merely said, that He will hold him true or in honour like a signet-ring, but that He will give him the position of a signet-ring, and use him like one . . . in the sense, that only that and all that has force and validity in God's sight, which bears the seal of His acknowledgment and the stamp of His gracious approval through being put by Him under Zerubbabel." Here the figure is worked out more definitely than its general terms require.

Thus the "unchangeable mercies of David" (Isa. lv. 3) are not forgotten. The Anointed of the Lord towers in personal individuality above the nation, exhibiting to view the nation's intimate union with its God. The aim of the approaching world-crisis is just as much the exalting of the Davidic ruler above all princedoms as the enrichment of the temple by the homage of all nations. Zerubbabel here receives such a promise because he is David's Son, permitted to hear the title "my Servant" from God's lips. He is reserved for a glorious future. *How* the Lord will honour him, is of set purpose not specified more distinctly. We know that he was only the mediator of the promise: as representative of the race chosen to be the salvation of mankind[1] he was also permitted to be the representative of the promise, *i.e.* to receive the great promises referring to the future of this house, which would be fulfilled in after days in a scion of his house. The conscious, typical, representative use of this Davidite by the prophet is confirmed by the analogous significance attributed to him and the high priest Joshua by his contemporary Zechariah. In the history of the fulfilment, which shows, in fact, how the Lord makes all movements among the nations subserve the kingdom of David's Son, and all sceptres and thrones sink down before him, the wonderful figure of the signet-ring attains a realization complete under every aspect. The true Messiah shares the unique honour of a most intimate relation to God, and is to the world the confirming sign of everything divine made known to it, for God's initial is engraven on Him in unique fashion.

§ 41. *The Visions of Zechariah.*

Hand in hand with Haggai, *Zechariah*, belonging to a priestly race,[2] in those days cheered the resuscitated Church in Jerusalem by prophetic confirmation of former divine promises, heartening it for its work of faith. At the same time he described in novel, original style the growth of God's kingdom out of obscure

---

[1] Both the genealogies of Jesus, Matt. i. 12 f. and Luke iii. 27, contain Zerubbabel's name. Cf. Delitzsch, *Die zweifache Genealogie des Messias*, *Luth. Zeitsch.* 1860, p. 460 ff.

[2] Ezra v. 1, vi. 14; Neh. xii. 16. In these passages he is called son of Iddo; on the other hand, in Zech. i. 1, son of Berechiah, the son of Iddo. Cf. Bleek, *Einleitung in's A. T.*, p. 448, 4th ed.

beginnings. This was done chiefly in a series of *night-visions*,[1] received by the prophet in the time when the building of the temple was vigorously going on. These eight visions were seen in one night, and, mutually complementary, form a finished whole. In the first introductory vision (i. 8 ff.) Zechariah sees a *band of horsemen*, led by a rider on a red horse, halting between the myrtle trees in the deep ground, by which is meant a well-known locality at the foot of the temple-hill. The leader is called "the angel of Yahveh" simply, meaning the angel in whom Yahveh revealed Himself from of old pre-eminently and in particular assumed the guidance of His people Israel.[2] After the horsemen have delivered their report before the Lord's dwelling: "We have gone through the earth, and behold the whole earth is quiet and still," the leader begins: "O Lord of hosts, how long wilt Thou not have pity on Jerusalem and the cities of Judah, with which Thou hast been wroth seventy years?" Hereupon the prophet receives from the Lord through His angel joyous, comforting assurances, which testify the awaking of the divine love for His people. On the heathen in their security He will bring retribution for the wrongs done to His people, and cause Jerusalem-Judah to experience His mercy: "Its cities shall again be built and overflow with plenty, Jerusalem shall again appear the chosen city of the Lord."

Here as in Haggai we see that the easy careless calm of the world, that is unconcerned about Israel's God, pressed like an Alpine burden on the Church of the faithful in these days. Was the present wretched state of the sacred cause to last for ever? Were not the prophecies, promising to Zion a central position in the world, soon to be fulfilled? What the seer beholds is an answer to this eager question of the good. Already has the great Covenant-Angel, who in old days showed himself

---

[1] These visions, although received in the night, are no dreams (cf. p. 15); nor are they the clothing of previously conceived ideas, as Jesus clothed His teachings in parables; for they are presented to the prophet quite objectively; he has to inquire and search after their significance, as the disciples of Jesus after the meaning of the parables.

[2] Cf. Ex. xiv. 19, xxiii. 20 f., xxxiii. 15; Josh. v. 14; Judg. v. 23; Isa. lxiii. 9, etc. This angel, who sets forth God's objective revelation to His people and the world, is to be distinguished from the *angelus interpres*, who is the medium of the subjective revelation to the prophets, *i.e.* makes them see visions and hear God's words (against Hitzig). On the other hand, he is identical with the man on the red horse, the leader of the horsemen (Hofmann, Köhler, Keil differently).

the victorious leader of the heavenly as well as earthly hosts, mounted his blood-red steed, already has his motley martial train swept through the earth, reconnoitring the scene of their future activity.[1] And Israel has an eloquent advocate before God in His angel, who reminds Him of the promises given, whose fulfilment can be delayed no longer, since according to the word spoken to Jeremiah[2] the time of the bondage was to last seventy years, and this space has now elapsed (reckoning from 588 B.C., the year of the overthrow).

The twofold purport of the assurance given in Zech. i. 14 ff. then divides, in keeping with the symmetry ruling in the cycle, into two special visions, the first of which (i. 18 ff.) sets forth the judgment on the world-powers, the second (ii. 1 ff.) the divine benefits to Israel. The prophet sees four *horns* rise up. According to the explanation given, these are the world-powers who attacked the people, tribe, and city of God, and scattered them. The horn is a common symbol of power.[3] The number four, taken from the quarters of heaven, denotes the Cosmos in its many-sidedness. Thus the world-power in its entire extent is meant, and to the seer geographical juxtaposition is more important than historical succession. We have not therefore to seek four historical kingdoms (as in Daniel), which attained universal rule in succession. This does not preclude our connecting with the several quarters of heaven the great power found there. Zechariah now sees four smiths[4] come forward fully equipped, and strike off the four threatening horns which prevented any one breathing freely. Here also no historic persons come into view.[5] The importance of the smiths lies simply in what they do, and the great teaching of this vision is that to every arrogant power of the world, setting itself up as a tyrant over God's people, a smith is already appointed to humble and

---

[1] Cf. with this הִתְהַלֶּכְ, Job. i. 7, ii. 2. That these mounted martial hosts of the Lord are copied from the Persian post-riders (Herod. viii. 98, iii. 126; Xen. *Cyr.* viii. 6. 17), as now generally maintained, is more misleading than helpful in explanation, apart from the doubtful poetry of the conception.

[2] Jer. xxv. 11, xxix. 10.

[3] Cf. Amos vi. 13; Jer. xlviii. 25; Ezek. xxix. 21, and often.

[4] Blacksmiths are meant (more fully חרש ברזל, Isa. xliv. 12), not carpenters, (LXX.), since the horns are conceived of as iron (cf. Micah iv. 13).

[5] Many Jewish expositors interpret the four of Zerubbabel, Joshua, Ezra, Nehemiah!

break it. Although this or that power may seem invincible for a long time, it falls; the Church alone, defenceless, sorely tried, severely attacked, endures; whereas all the secular and temporal powers, that try their hostile horn on the Church, are smitten to the ground.

Alongside this thorough humbling of the world-powers the third vision puts the *rebuilding of Jerusalem*, the enlarging and exalting of the city and people of God (ii. 1 ff.). In graphic, dramatic style the prophet is shown that they are in error who conceive the city of God, which is to be newly erected, according to former standards. In i. 16 it was promised that the measuring-line should be stretched over Jerusalem, *i.e.* its rebuilding should take place. But the youth who goes forth full of eagerness to measure must be taught that in the new city of God measurement is superfluous, nay, impossible. The crowd of men and cattle dwelling in it will be so vast that the city cannot be enclosed by walls. But its open position will be no harm to it: "I will be to it, saith Yahveh, a wall of fire round about, and I will be the glory in its midst" (ii. 5). As no respectable city was conceivable in antiquity without walls and gates, we see here again, as in Isa. xxxiii. 23 (p. 293), the city of God lifted above the sphere of experience.[1] It assumes a magnitude incapable of comparison with an ordinary earthly city, and has a defence in God, whose glory inhabits it in a way unheard of hitherto. The prophetic idea of the city of God reaches beyond the geographical, historical Jerusalem, as beyond the temple of stone on Zion.

To this exalted perspective is joined a twofold exhortation: To flee from the heathen country (Babylon), where judgment is beginning (ii. 6 ff.), and to rejoice in Jerusalem, where the Lord enters (ii. 10 ff.).

ii. 10. "Sing and rejoice, daughter of Zion, for behold I come
11 and take up my abode in thy midst, saith Yahveh. And many heathen nations shall join themselves to Yahveh on that day, and they shall be my people, and I will dwell in thy midst, and thou shalt learn that Yahveh of hosts has sent me to thee."

Almost in the same words, in which in Zech. ix. 9 Zion is summoned to receive with joy the Son of David appearing in

[1] Cf. Zech. ix. 8; Isa. iv. 5 f., xxx. 25; Micah v. 10; Ezek. xxxviii. 11.

lowly form, Yahveh here invites Himself, when about to enter his city, to take up His abode there for ever. In this twofold advent-message we have a striking parallel between the coming of the Messiah and the Parousia of the Lord (p. 58). More precisely, it is not the Lord as absolute God who comes into His dwelling on Zion. It is His angel, His manifestation in finite form (p. 105). But so perfectly is the Most High Himself revealed in this "ambassador" of God, that in a sense He is one person with the latter in contrast to men; hence the alternating of identity and self-distinction, vers. 13, 15. The same angel who, according to ii. 8 f., received the mandate to smite the heathen in God's stead, and give rich spoil to his poor people (the rider on the red horse, chap. i.), will take up his abode in Jerusalem, his presence being regarded as that of the Lord Himself. Thus here, also, the Lord's dwelling among His people does not take place apart from finite, creaturely mediation, although no human mediator and representative is spoken of.[1]

In any case this entry of the Lord into His city denotes such a union of God with it as had not existed before. His presence in the Church will be enhanced in a wonderful way; and in consequence of this enhancement His revelation will exert an overwhelming attraction on the nations remote from Him, so that they will voluntarily unite themselves in subject dependence with the God who has His residence and makes His nearness graciously felt there. Here, also, an internal conquest of the heathen, disposing them to the service of the true God, is not wanting. Still, after as before, Judah remains the Lord's heritage, the "holy ground" (v. 12), Jerusalem His elect dwelling-place, whose glory He is. Listening for the approaching Parousia, the prophet cries at the close: "Let all flesh be still before Yahveh, for He has risen up from His holy dwelling."[2]

But this outward establishment of the city of God, however glorious and broad in design, is not all. The two next visions show us the inner life-springs of the newly sanctified Church, the fourth chiefly its *priesthood by divine grace*. The seer

---

[1] Observe that in the course of the visions the Messiah comes more and more into the foreground. We cannot therefore infer from single oracles, in which he does not appear, that a prophet did not share this hope, or laid less stress upon it.

[2] This alludes to Zeph. i. 7; Hab. ii. 20. Not only in the former, but also in the latter passage (p. 327), the warning cry also prepares for the Parousia.

beholds the high priest Joshua accused before the angel of the Lord (iii. 1 ff.), who here again is one with, and yet distinguished from, Yahveh Himself. The high priest is wearing filthy clothes. This symbolizes something more than the condition of an accused person, as was the case among the Romans.[1] The uncleanness of the clothes is a sign of actual guilt, cleaving to the high priest before the Lord, in whose sight His ministering angels are not pure (Job iv. 18).[2] The accusation of Satan, who certainly does not appear as a conscientious advocate, but as a malignant, envious accuser, was therefore not without ground. Yet the Lord (or His angel) gives it no hearing, but orders the "adversary" to be silent, reminding him of the grace which the Lord, who chooses Jerusalem, has shown the high priest, who is like a brand plucked from the fire. It cannot be God's will to accuse at law and persecute the Aaronite who had been so wonderfully delivered. As a sign that his guilt is removed, the angel makes him take off the filthy garments and put on honourable clothing. It is a high-priestly investiture, in which the linen mitre cannot be wanting (Lev. xvi. 4).

Ver. 7 says without metaphor, that the high priest will be qualified to assume this high office and enjoy its highest privilege; while, of course, the keeping of God's prescribed will is made the condition, and the obligation of that will is in a sense assumed afresh. The last clause: "and I grant thee walks[3] among them that stand here," promises him the greatest and most weighty privilege belonging to the high priest: "He may come before God's throne, go in and out among the ministering angels standing there!" In these words the high priest is fully installed in his honours and rights.

The correct appreciation of this act depends on the question, what kind of guilt it is that is represented as lying on Joshua

---

[1] Livy, ii. 54, vi. 20. Also among the Romans the *restis sordida* was merely of dark colour, not filthy, and that as a sign of sorrow, perhaps also of fault that needed to be cleared away. Just so the Israelites, when under accusation, at most wore black clothing, Joseph. *Ant.* xiv. 9. 4.

[2] Cf. Isa. iv. 4; Prov. xxx. 12; Rev. iii. 4, vii. 14.

[3] מַהְלְכִים is subst., not part. (*companions, leaders, guides*, Gesenius, Hengstenberg, Neumann; or intransitively: *walkers*, LXX., Syr., Vulg., Baumgarten, Hofmann), with which, apart from the form, the בֵּין would not agree. From מַהֲלָךְ, *walk, way*, one would certainly expect a plural מַהְלָכִים; so Hitzig would read; whilst others (Ewald, Köhler) assume a form מְהַלֵּךְ in the same signification.

and removed from him. That no offence of extraordinary weight on the part of this priest is meant, is clear, because no personal fault is said to attach to him.[1] Nor is the trespass of his sons in marrying strange women (Ezra x. 18 ; Neh. xiii. 28) to be thought of, as the Targum, Jerome, Rashi, Kimchi think, because those incidents fall much later in time. Far better is the view of Hitzig and Köhler, who see in the guilt resting on the high priest that of the whole people, which it was his office to bear, with special reference to the long interruption in building the temple, which according to Hag. ii. 11 made the whole people unclean. Still even this does not satisfy the meaning of the vision. Here the question does not concern the making of expiation for the people, which is done by the continuance of the high-priesthood of itself, but the rehabilitation of the latter, which Satan tries to hinder in order to rob the people of the office of atonement, and thus of atonement itself. The accusation, indeed, does not apply to Joshua personally, but as the bearer of this sacred office. After the long interruption of the priestly service by the exile the question easily suggested itself, whether this sacred office could continue despite the many sins with which its bearers had stained their robes, whether its present representative, human and imperfect, did not with the dignity inherit the guilt of his predecessors. A new divine institution of the office was therefore necessary at the beginning of the new temple, and brought great comfort to the Church.

With this agrees also the continuation of the Lord's discourse, iii. 8 ff., according to which a future consummation awaits the priesthood established in imperfection, of which consummation the office is a typical pledge.

iii. 8. "Hear then, O Joshua, high priest, thou and thy comrades, who sit before thee ; for men of a miraculous sign are they,

9 for behold, I will bring forth MY SERVANT, SPROUT. For behold, the stone which I have placed before Joshua—on the one stone seven eyes are directed—behold, I will carve its inscriptions, saith Yahveh of hosts, and I blot out the

---

[1] Quite perversely Ewald thinks that a slandering of the high priest at the Persian court is meant, and explains the close of ver. 7 : "He may again go freely about his business among his servants, without being further accused." As if a calumny before the Persian court would inculpate him in God's sight and put his dignity in question !

10 guilt of this land in one day. On that day, saith Yahveh of hosts, ye shall invite one another under the vine and the fig-tree."

That the section iii. 1 ff. treats of the preserving or restoring of the priestly office, is confirmed by this concluding passage, in which the high priest is united with his official comrades, who sit before him in priestly assemblies. They are men who are a miraculous sign.[1] Even the fact that the priesthood, which culminates in the high priest, still exists, after the fire of judgment that has fallen on the people, must be regarded as a miracle.[2] But the miracle is also a sign; it has its significance and aim in the future, as the close of ver. 8 indicates. It refers to the advent of the true, adequate representative of God, the Messiah; for according to Jer. xxiii. 5, xxxiii. 15, none else can be meant by "my Servant, Sprout."[3] The title Sprout has become here, as in vi. 12, a proper name of the great Davidite rising up out of obscurity in mysterious stillness. And the fact of his appearance just here, where the importance of the priesthood is in question, nay, that the whole priesthood is called a miraculous sign and pledge of him, the Lord's true Servant, is specially noteworthy. It is here declared unmistakably that he will be Joshua's perfect successor in the high-priestly dignity. In *his* days, when the bearer of the office is seen to be perfect, the work also of priestly expiation will be consummated according to ver. 9.

The *stone* lying before Joshua, to which the seer is pointed, has given interpreters no slight difficulty. Some have erroneously seen in it the foundation-stone of the temple, by the laying of which the land became pure,[4] or its top-stone (Ewald), which is here just as little intimated (otherwise in iv. 7). The fact also of the stone lying before Joshua, and indeed

---

[1] מוֹפֵת is usually the miracle itself as an inversion of the ordinary state of things; and then also miraculous *sign*, 1 Kings xiii. 3, 5, in which, at all events, the miraculous character which the sign has in itself comes out more strongly than in אוֹת. In the present passage also we cannot pass this by.

[2] See Zech. iii. 2; Ps. lxxi. 7; cf. also Isa. viii. 18.

[3] Cf. on Isa. iv. 2, p. 262.

[4] So Rosenmüller, Hitzig, Neumann. But the present vision falls two months later than the blessed foundation-day, Hag. ii. 18, and yet the Lord speaks still of a future day of expiation. What the beautifying of the foundation-stone now lying before Joshua would signify, it is hard to see; the stone would need, at all events, to be understood in a more spiritual sense.

being placed before him by God, does not accord with either of these views. The reference of the stone to Israel (Köhler), as well as that to the kingdom of God (Keil), have too little support from the context; the ancient reference to the Messiah is too abrupt.

What kind of a stone is meant, in the absence of a more specific description, must be learnt from its position before Joshua (note A). What is laid by divine appointment before the high priest in his official robes must be something standing in close connection with his official function, something essential to it. An altar cannot be thought of; before it the high priest does not exclusively officiate. Yet the object in question must stand in close conjunction with the expiation of the guilt of the land effected by the high priest, since with its completion the expiation will be finally accomplished. By this divinely-laid stone, before which the high priest stands, we can only understand a substitute for the *covenant-ark*, throned on which God was wont to receive the high priest in the act of atonement. It was the vehicle of the divine presence in the temple, the medium of union between God and the people represented by the high priest. Here, where the continuance in uncurtailed form of the priesthood, and thus of intercourse between God and Israel, is ratified, we necessarily expect some explanation in regard to the absent ark of the covenant. It is very possible that such a stone not merely lay in vision before Joshua, but once actually had its place in the Holy of Holies somewhat after the manner of the rock that rises up in the Sakra mosque,[1] which fact would make the statement generally intelligible.[2] At all events two points are essential: First, this stone is placed by God, and is shaped by Him alone, in contrast with stones wrought by men's hands (iv. 7, 9). It is that which God Himself lays and contributes to the completion of the temple, and which accordingly constitutes the Holiest of all.[3] Secondly, the fact that a mere stone takes this place before Joshua—whether

---

[1] The mosque of Omar at Jerusalem.

[2] Thus in fact Mishna Yoma, v. 2, relates, that in the Most Holy Place of the second temple a stone was found from the time of the early prophets, called foundation-stone, rising a height of three fingers above the ground, on which the high priest used to set down the censer.

[3] That the Holiest of all itself will undergo a re-creation, the Lord testifying His presence in the time of consummation far more gloriously than by the ancient ark, we found foretold already, Jer. iii. 16 f. (p. 332).

in vision or reality—implies the imperfect, provisional nature of the apparatus that symbolized the presence of the Most High, and was indispensable for expiating the guilt of His people; the Lord reserves to Himself a glorious transforming of this most holy object in His dwelling.

Let no one on this account think lightly of this imperfect temple. Already over the stone laid before the priest there watch seven eyes; *i.e.* (as in iv. 10) the Spirit of God in His full energy, which assumes a sevenfold form (the number of divine completeness), concentrates His loving, watchful care on this *one* stone, which He intends gloriously to transfigure. He will put on it inscriptions, carvings,[1] such as were engraved on the high-priestly diadem (Ex. xxviii. 36). There will be a divine sign on it, like the initial on a signet-ring. This sign will give the stone its sacred character in a manner universally cognizable. Remaining a mystery for a time, this character contains a saving revelation of God. As the Lord once wrote with His own finger the tables of the law deposited in the ark (Ex. xxxii. 16), so with His own hand He will engrave on the stone the sign of His gracious presence, at the same time wiping out at a stroke all the guilt of the land. Not by oft-repeated sacrifices, such as must now be offered, but by *one* divine act the land and people shall be completely set free from guilt and punishment (Heb. vii. 27). Then the long-promised state of untroubled peace will set in, such as is presented in a lovely figure at the close. Men will invite each other to enjoy in undisturbed quiet the abundance which the Lord has lavishly given (cf. Micah iv. 4).

Although we may not say with the older expositors that the precious stone before Joshua is the Messiah directly, there is still an undeniably close connection between vers. 8 and 9, between the coming of the Divine Sprout and the perfecting of the priestly expiation, of which the divine transfiguring of that most sacred object is the presupposal. When the Lord sends the high-priestly Prince, He will also so constitute the Most Holy Place in His temple, that the true reconciliation of the whole land with Him may be accomplished therein. All guilt being thus abolished, the state of Messianic peace with God begins.

---

[1] פתחים are usually *engraved inscriptions*, such as are put on precious stones, signet-rings, etc. (Ex. xxviii. 11, 21, 36, xxxix. 14, etc.), also *figures*, the outlines of which are cut out (as in 1 Kings vi. 21).

A companion picture to this fourth vision is given in the fifth (iv. 1 ff.), which likewise affords us a glimpse into the Church's innermost life. Alongside the newly sanctified priest appears here the Prince, likewise filled with God's Spirit and mediating Him to the Church, whose sacred work of temple-building will come to happy completion through the *Spirit* of the Lord. It is the most calm and solemn vision,—the seven-branched *lamp*, which can never want oil, because two olive-trees, standing on the two sides, feed all its lights. Noiselessly the pure, golden oil, the symbol of the Divine Spirit, flows through all the pipes of the lamp, that old Mosaic symbol of the Church, to ascend again to God in sevenfold flame of pure adoration. For the perfecting of God's ministering Church is here meant to be set forth; and its Head is to be taught, that in this work no worldly weapons of defence or human energy can effect anything, but the quiet, sacred operation of God's Spirit alone (iv. 6). As he is the soul of everything in his temple, so must he also be the all-effective energy in its erection. But in him is a power that overcomes the whole world. The mountain that towers up before Zerubbabel will be levelled by God's word, *i.e.* all the hindrances put by the world's hostile power in the way of his heaven-approved undertaking must give way before the Divine Spirit vouchsafed to him, and thus he will bring forth the top-stone [1] of the temple amid the jubilant cries of the multitude: "Grace, grace unto it!" This cry of blessing applies to the top-stone, the preservation of which implies that of the whole building.[2]

The symmetry of the passage should not be overlooked. As a dangerous foe stood opposed to Joshua, so to Zerubbabel. Before the former lay a stone with which the priest seems able to effect little; before Zerubbabel towers up a whole mountain to hinder his work. But in both cases the Lord Himself rebukes the hostile power and avows Himself on His Servant's side, for God's loving watchful eye is set with sevenfold intensity on Zerubbabel's plummet as on the yet ungraven stone before Joshua. In iv. 8 f. the assurance is given to the prince in plain words that, as he began the building, so his hands will finish it. Since Zerubbabel

---

[1] Since the reference is to the future, the "headstone" cannot be the foundation-stone, but will be the final stone forming the head of the building.

[2] Ps. cxviii., sung at the consecration of the new temple, gives the fulfilment. Cf. the Hosanna, cxviii. 26, with the above: "Grace unto it!"

cannot be the yet future Servant of the Lord (iii. 8), whose name is Sprout, while the innermost sanctuary is only completed by the latter, a distinction is here made between a nearer and more distant completion. Zerubbabel himself will set the top-stone on the outer building; but the appointments of the Most Holy Place the Lord reserves to Himself in the age of the Messiah soon to begin. But meanwhile He bestows on the Church His Spirit in double measure, through the two sons of oil (iv. 14), *i.e.* the two anointed ones of God (Messiahs), who like the heavenly angels have their station before God's throne. Self-evidently, the Prince and the Priest are meant.[1] More exactly, since the two separate bushes, from which the golden sap flows into the lamp, are distinguished from the olive trees, we have to understand by the trees the regal race and priestly order, by the bushes the actual representatives of the two. The entire vision exhibits in finished beauty the secret life-force that makes Israel God's Church and qualifies it for God's service, which is this people's glory and life-work, and encourages confidence in the attainment of this ideal by the thought of the Divine Spirit, who works in the Church purely and holily, wisely and strongly, calmly and constantly, and whose unfailing presence is secured by the two offices, by which the mediation between God and His people is carried on. Thus, like all the visions, this fifth one is promissory and comforting in high degree.

Nevertheless the land cannot enjoy its blessed future without being purified from sin and guilt. This is taught in the next pair of visions (chap. v.), of which the first exhibits a *curse-roll* flying over the land and causing the extirpation of hardened sinners along with their dwellings (especially thieves and perjurers, of whom a great number now defile the people of God). Still the removal of the worst sinners is not all. *Sin* itself, of which all are more or less guilty,[2] must be abolished from the land. Sin, personified as a woman, is shut up in a corn-measure, the mouth of which is closed with a leaden weight,[3] and is borne through

[1] On the anointing of the king and the high priest, see p. 148; with the form "son of oil" = "richly blessed therewith," cf. Isa. v. 1.

[2] In v. 6 עֵינָם must be read, after LXX., Syr., instead of עֵינָי.

[3] The imprisonment of sin in a corn-measure, which is closed by a weight, reminds us of the form in which it filled the land. It is especially dishonesty, which uses false measure and weight. So rightly Pressel, who in other respects entirely distorts the plain figure.

the air by two female figures furnished with wings of storks[1] to Shinar-Babylon. There in the heathen metropolis let sin have its abode henceforth, in the Lord's land no place is granted it!

The point in hand is primarily the re-establishment of a God-consecrated people on hallowed soil, and the reference of כָּל־הָאָרֶץ, v. 3, 6, to the whole earth is quite inadmissible.[2] But that the Lord will make the world also feel His sway by executing there, not single judgments as in Israel, but national judgments, is taught in the last vision, vi. 1 ff., which forms a closing counterpart to the prefatory first vision. Whereas at the fall of night the divine rider-hosts presented themselves before the Lord's residence to give account of the state of the earth, which they have traversed, now towards daybreak these hosts again go forth into the world to execute God's commands. Two mountains of brass, well known (with article) but not named, are mentioned as their starting-place. The chariots drive out between these mountains, thus coming from "the depth," without doubt the deep ground mentioned in i. 8, where the horsemen arrived. The two mountains are the temple-hill and the Mount of Olives; they are of brass, because in a sense they form the entrance to the dwelling of God. The place from which He sets the whole world in commotion is itself immovable.

The *chariots* which drive out, freighted with divine judgment and wrath, like the horses in chap. i., bear a martial character; they are war-chariots. In the issuing forth, not merely of horsemen who are frequently used as a reconnoitring vanguard, but of the most formidable instrument of war, there is an intentional climax. The seer sees four such teams hurry forth. The number four, as we saw previously, denotes the world with its four regions of space. This is still more evident in vi. 5, where the angel exchanges the figure of the four chariots for that of the four winds, in order to characterize the action of God's power in all four quarters of the earth, while, of course, it may be directed with special intensity to one side. Thus here, in free employ-

---

[1] The wings are those of a migratory bird. Sin must emigrate, and is carried away by these two genii in their secure flight. For the rest, we must not embellish the simple vision with its great leading thoughts by all sorts of additions, as Neumann especially does.

[2] So Hofmann, Kliefoth, Bredenkamp. Chap. v. 4, where abuse of Yahveh's name is in question, and v. 11, according to which sin will really settle in Babylon only, are decisive against this view.

ment of the resources of war at God's disposal, two chariots are sent to the same quarter of the earth, vi. 6, namely, to the north, where the world-empire then strongest had its seat. On the black team, hurrying in that direction, follows another with white, triumphal steeds, since God will there triumph most gloriously. The dappled steeds draw the third chariot to the south, where diverse, although not such dangerous, enemies are to be encountered, such as Edom, Egypt (Dan. xi. 5), Cush. Finally, the fourth team (vi. 7), which is impatient to start forth, but has no definite goal assigned it, is commissioned to wander for a time up and down the earth, plainly until a world-power appears for it to act against. In the west and east, meantime, there are no hostile kingdoms of importance; the north has a double share, the south quite enough. So inexhaustible are God's resources of judgment, that after subduing every world-power He still has at command a full complement for enemies springing up in the future. And scarcely have they departed when the angel shows the seer the result of the chief mission. Those sent to the north have quieted the Spirit of God, *i.e.* according to Ezek. v. 13, satisfied His spirit of revenge. This general statement of God's resources of judgment, unfolding on every side and subjugating the world, must not, as in Daniel, be divided historically into four empires appearing one after another.[1] The point of view is rather geographical, which does not preclude a reference to the dominant world-power in the north, and the chief one in the south, as well as to one on the point of appearing.

The whole cycle of these night-visions has revealed under different aspects how the Lord will show Himself gracious to His cleansed and purified people, whereas the hostile world-power must soon feel God's displeasure operating from Zion. But the inner sanctuary of this revelation is what is said of the relation of the Lord, brought about by His two organs, to His Church. And the most sacred mystery, to which these visions point, is the consummation of this relation, which will be effected by the one Servant of the Lord of David's house, who unites the priestly with the regal dignity. As the outcome in a sense of these

---

[1] So *e.g.* Delitzsch in Herzog, iii. 475. The "strong" horses, Zech. vi. 7, certainly recall the strong beast of Dan. vii. 7. But in the former passage the word is probably a copyist's error.

night-revelations, a symbolic action is next added to them (vi. 9 ff.), which shows how these two offices now standing side by side are united in their perfect possessor.

The action which God's voice enjoins on the prophet is this, to put on the high priest a crown of gold and silver.[1] This altogether unusual adornment of the high priest, who as such wore a linen mitre (iii. 5), is explained by an accompanying statement:—

> vi. 12. "And thou shalt say to him as follows: Thus saith Yahveh of hosts: 'Behold a man, whose name is SPROUT, and he shall sprout from beneath and build the temple of Yahveh.
> 13 Nay, HE shall finish the Lord's temple, and HE shall wear ornaments of honour, and sit and rule on his throne, and shall be priest on his throne, and a counsel of peace shall be between them both.'"

As in iii. 8, so here, where the glorious consummation of the high-priesthood is again referred to, the mysterious "Sprout" appears, who is far from being identical with Joshua or Zerubbabel. On the contrary, in iii. 8, vi. 12, he is announced as still to come, and, indeed, in the latter passage as one who, in keeping with his name, will spring up wondrously out of lowliness as a gift of the Lord's pure grace.[2] One will come to build the temple of the Lord, who, although named so indefinitely, is yet well known from prophecy. In ver. 13 this work is emphatically ascribed to one who is to come, in distinction from one now living and engaged on it. This seems to contradict iv. 7, 9, where Zerubbabel is assured that his hands will finish the work begun. But Zechariah separates what was still combined in Haggai's vision, viz. the completion of the present work now near at hand, occurring in the sixth year of Darius, and the glorious

---

[1] vi. 11. עֲטָרוֹת (cf. ver. 14) refers not to two or several crowns (Jerome, Rosenmüller, Hitzig, Ewald, Bredenkamp, *et al.*), but the plural refers to the silver and golden hoops of the crown; cf. Job xxxi. 36. That two crowns are to be put on Joshua's and Zerubbabel's heads respectively, is an assertion only possible on a complete mistaking of the sense and a violent alteration of the text. Ewald inserts in ver. 11 the words: "and on the head of Zerubbabel" (without warrant), after which licence we should next logically change the אֵלָיו, ver. 12, into אֲלֵיהֶם.

[2] וּמִתַּחְתָּיו יִצְמָח can only be explained according to Ex. x. 23 properly: *from that which lies under him*, thus *from beneath*. It is an expansion of what is wrapped up in the name צֶמַח. Incorrectly Hitzig, after LXX.; Luther: *it will sprout under him*—everything will be green!

finishing of the temple, in which those afar off (*i.e.*, according to ii. 15, viii. 20–23, Hag. ii. 7, the heathen) are to help, that God's dwelling may be adorned with the glory befitting it—a distinction pointing to an impending spiritualizing of the temple,[1] since in its empirical limitation it is as little adequate to its destiny as the present faint image of the city of God to its ideal (ii. 8).

In the same way Zechariah's prophecy no longer stops, like that of Haggai, at the actual representative of the Davidic house, promising him princely dignity and honour, but first definitely indicates the coming One as the true wearer of the dignity,[2] to whom it is granted to sit and rule on David's throne. As the building of the perfect temple in which God will dwell is incumbent on the true Son of David, so lordship in God's new and perfect kingdom belongs to him (Micah v. 3). But the principal point in the oracle, and what the symbolic action chiefly sets forth, follows at the close: "And he shall be priest on his throne." Hitherto the priest's place was not a throne, just as little as a crown adorned him. But the wondrous Sprout, to whom the Lord has reserved the near completion of His kingdom, will unite the priestly with his royal dignity, although sitting on the throne as Lord of the land, nay, of the earth, he will humbly serve *the* God in whose name he rules (note B).

The last words are certainly difficult: "And counsel of peace shall be between them both." Considering the equality implied in the שְׁנֵיהֶם, a reference to God and the Messiah is impracticable. Nor can we suppose that the former is a ruler side by side with the latter. We rather believe that the prophet had in mind the two offices which regularly stood side by side in his days, or the dignitaries, the ruler and the priest. Cf. especially iv. 12–14, where not merely Joshua and Zerubbabel, but also the two lifepowers representing them are contrasted with each other in the form of olive-trees. Only then will the true counsel of peace bind together the two powers, the worldly and spiritual, to the salvation of the whole nation, when both dignities are combined in one person, which will be done in the *Zemach*. The unique

---

[1] Like the temple, so the *building*, spiritually understood, has found in the New Testament rich application.

[2] הוֹד, the royal majesty *upon* one (Num. xxvii. 20; Dan. xi. 21; 1 Chron. xxix. 25), which is therefore worn like a crown.

importance attributed by Zechariah to the true Servant of the Lord, makes it improbable that (despite Ps. cx. 4 and Jer. xxx. 21, cf. p. 337) he would have ascribed to him but one of the two equally warranted powers, and thought of their dualism as continuing in the period of consummation. Moreover, the union is indicated already in iii. 8 by the fact that the regal *Zemach*, undeniably Davidic in origin, appears in order to consummate the high-priesthood. The most probable interpretation is, that the present priest is regarded as the imperfect type of the Zemach. The latter, therefore, will stand before God a high priest without spot and, being perfectly acceptable to the Lord, will perfect the work of expiation. This personal union is brought into view still more strongly in vi. 9 ff. Here, indeed, there is less reference to the leading priestly function assigned to the Messiah in iii. 8. According to that passage, the reconciliation will be accomplished at a stroke. But the priestly dignity continues, nay, only then obtains its glorification. Regal dignity also pertains henceforth to the true high priest.

If the question is asked, with Hitzig, why Zerubbabel rather was not crowned as a type of Messiah, the answer simply is: Because his crowning would express nothing new, and especially would not express what is the gist of the whole section, namely, that the priesthood will be raised to regal honour. The "Sprout" of royal stock will with his rule inherit also this office, as was promised already in Ps. cx. 4 (p. 154). When this climax of development in the history of redemption is reached, the harmony of the two heads of the nation, previously so often wanting, will leave nothing to be desired. There will be a king who lives entirely for the temple, a priest who has the welfare of the kingdom purely in view. This royal priest, as Micah v. 4 says, will himself be the peace, and will think of nothing but his people's peace and welfare.

The remaining words of this prophet also are intended to hearten and comfort Israel by retouching and unfolding the promised redemption. A future of divine splendour is not, indeed, promised to Judah-Jerusalem unconditionally. At the very beginning, i. 2 ff., Zechariah requires thorough repentance as an indispensable condition, and at the close of his visions, i. 7—vi. 15, he makes the fulfilment of the glorious promises given here dependent on the nation's obedience to its God. And in chap.

vii. he explains that the obedience consists, not in outward fasting and the like, but in the observance of righteousness and love of one's neighbour long since enjoined on the Church, vii. 9 ff., as he declared plainly in chap. v., and repeats in viii. 16 ff. If they are not careless as their fathers were, they will be a blessing, as the latter were a curse, among the nations, viii. 13 (cf. Hos. ii. 1). Then will the Lord again take up His abode permanently and openly in Jerusalem; and it will be called the city of the faithful and the mountain of Yahveh (Zion), the holy mountain (viii. 3), in which two things are implied, the upright disposition and holiness of the inhabitants, as well as the fidelity and protection they will enjoy from the Lord, who will keep His sanctuary inviolate.[1] The idyllic picture of the city (viii. 4 f.), distinguished by the long peaceful life of its inhabitants and its teeming aftergrowth of young life, while not soaring to the elevation of Isa. xxv. 6 ff., perhaps reaches that of Isa. xxxiii. 24 or lxv. 20 ff. (p. 406). Finally, this sacred prosperity of Israel will allure the nations around to come to seek the favour of the God who dispenses salvation.

viii. 20. "Thus saith Yahveh of hosts: It still comes to pass that (whole) nations come, and the inhabitants of numerous
21 (populous) cities. And the inhabitants of one city journey to another, saying: We will go to pacify the face of Yahveh,
22 and to seek Yahveh of hosts. 'I also will go.'[2] And numerous peoples shall come, and strong nations, to seek Yahveh of hosts in Jerusalem, and to pacify the face of
23 Yahveh. Thus saith Yahveh of hosts: In that day it comes to pass that TEN men of all tongues of the heathen take hold of ONE Jewish man by the skirt, saying: We will go with you, for we have heard that God is with you."[3]

The heathen world, conscious of the vanity of its worship and the impotence of its gods, needs but an impulse in order to turn its back on these gods and ally itself with the God of Israel. The news of the salvation prepared by the Lord for His city and people will turn their yearning desire for a true gracious God in

---

[1] Cf. Isa. i. 21, and on Isa. iv. 3, p. 263.

[2] "יי חלה פני, properly: *to smooth the face of the Lord*, hence: *to seek His favour*, is used where one comes before the Lord with gifts (1 Sam. xiii. 12). It implies, like בקש, the importunity, urgency of their desire for God.

[3] On the numerical relation, cf. Lev. xxvi. 26.

the direction of Jerusalem.[1] One city shouts to another the signal already heard in Isa. ii. 3, and everywhere the reply is heard: "I also will go!"[2] Nay, *ten* heathen will throw themselves with vehemence on *one* Jew, of whom they catch sight, and cling to him, that he may take and lead them to his God, whose presence is the salvation of every nation. If vers. 20–22 recall the oft-promised national pilgrimage, which may be periodical,[3] in ver. 23 the personal longing of individuals finds expression to enter into abiding communion with the God dwelling on Zion, and to become united with His people. This desire is met already in ii. 15 with encouraging promises, according to which whole peoples will be incorporated with the Lord's people. One Israelite will be a guide to ten heathen, and so the people will be a blessing to the nations in mightily increasing ratio. Thus the discourse concludes, and with it the book of this prophet, who in spirit does not belong to the "minor" ones, his book replacing the antithesis between God's people and heathen peoples, which has hitherto governed everything, by universal harmony and reconciliation with God. How grandly his last saying has been fulfilled since Pentecost, when people of every tongue hung on the apostles with the question: "What shall we do?" *i.e.* with inquiry after the way to God, we scarcely need to recall. The yearning of heathenism after God's salvation, as well as its mediation by the men of Israel to all the world, belong to the facts that have confirmed the truthfulness of the prophetic word in the most striking manner.

The outward success of the discourses of Haggai and Zechariah was seen in the building and completion of the temple. The spiritual fruit of their discourses and prophecies is shown us in many Psalms, which celebrate the return from exile and the rising again of Jerusalem, while at the same time they joyously welcome these divine acts as a beginning and pledge of the future completion of God's kingdom. That the Lord has redeemed His pledged word is thankfully and boldly confessed. He has done great things for His people (Ps. cxxvi. 3, cxviii. 23). This is the ground-tone of these songs, especially of Ps. cxviii., which seems to date from the consecration of Zerubbabel's temple.[4] Not

---

[1] Cf. Jer. xxxiii. 9, p. 342.
[2] In the text this is the answer of the city addressed to the summons.
[3] Zech. xiv. 16 ff.; Isa. lxvi. 23.   [4] Cf. Delitzsch on Ps. cxviii.

without reason he strikes the air of the old song of the Red Sea,[1] for in its deliverance from heathen captivity the nation has experienced a wondrous redemption, like that from Pharaoh's power. The day when it is again permitted to enter the door of His temple, is especially a visible proof of the faithfulness of its God.

cxviii. 20. "This is the gate of Yahveh, the righteous may enter
21 therein. I will praise thee, for thou hast heard me, and art
22 become my salvation. The stone which the builders rejected
23 has become the head corner-stone. By Yahveh is this done;
24 it is marvellous in our eyes. This is the day which Yahveh made; let us exult and rejoice in it!"

This rejoicing is for the newly-risen temple, into whose fore-courts, as the corresponding Ps. xxiv. (p. 186 f.) has already mentioned, the righteous alone may enter. The stone, according to ver. 22 despised by the builders, but now put in the place of honour belonging to it, must stand in close relation to the temple. It cannot be interpreted of Israel, so that the heathen would be meant by the builders, but must be understood from Isa. xxviii. 16 (p. 286), to which the thanksgiving refers as to a promise now fulfilled. It is the God-laid foundation, on which through His prophets He commanded men to build, — the Messianic salvation, consisting in God's dwelling by His Anointed One on Zion, and forming in its previous shape the mere beginning of God's rule on earth, a foundation-stone, which the nation's leaders, like the majority of the nation itself, despised, trusting rather in their own policy and in foreign power, which only brought shame and ruin. Now by the people's redemption from bondage and the new erection of the temple, both accomplished in accordance with the word of the Lord, that divine stone has proved the only true foundation and corner-stone. It is a day of honour to the Lord; He triumphs to-day, having proved the power of His word by putting to shame all unbelief and littleness of faith.

The Messianic salvation was symbolized by the stone of Isaiah with a vagueness appropriate to a first sketch, but not without the prospect of a future completion effected by the person of the Messiah. From sad experience the psalm confesses that God's initial work of founding, by which He sought to assure His people of His protecting presence, was abandoned

---

[1] Cf. Ex. xv. 2 with Ps. cxviii. 14, 21, 28.

and rejected by those who were called to carry on His work. This did not take place by chance. Even the Messiah Himself, the elect foundation-stone, on which the new and true theocracy, the perfect temple, was to be built, must experience similar contradiction of sinners, similar scornful rejection. In Him also God has celebrated a triumph, one far more glorious than in the erection of the temple, and will celebrate it further in the world, the more it becomes clear that He is made the foundation-stone on which the building rests, which alone outlasts time, and further, the corner-stone on which every hostile power is broken to pieces.[1]

If Ps. cxviii. is based on an old saying of Isaiah, others sound like a jubilant echo of the promises of Isa. xl.–lxvi. After redemption experienced they sing a *new song* (Isa. xlii. 10) to the Lord, who has shown Himself the true King, and will now assume dominion over the whole earth, which He comes to judge. So especially Ps. xcvi., xcvii., xcviii., which greet the God of Israel, revealed to all nations by His glorious deeds, as Ruler of the world. So also Ps. lxxxv., which is not, like those just named, a purely triumphal song, but along with experienced redemption from captivity gives expression to the inadequacy of the present fulfilment, a failure certainly to be put to the account of men, whose unworthiness prevents the Lord displaying the fulness of His grace in their midst. Still the singer is sure that the salvation promised by Deutero-Isaiah will come, soon come to them that fear God, ver. 10 ff. He anticipates with exultation the time when love and faithfulness meet together, righteousness and peace kiss each other, faithfulness springs out of the earth and gracious goodwill looks down from heaven. Then will the Lord no longer keep back the fulness of heavenly blessings, and the produce of the earth will be richly blessed.[2]

NOTE A.—Bredenkamp (*Der Prophet Sacharja*, 1879) avoids the objections to the above interpretation by taking the stone as an

---

[1] The Fulfiller is shown in Matt. xxi. 42–46; Mark xii. 10 f.; Acts iv. 11.; 1 Pet. ii. 7. Moreover, the crowd that greeted Jesus with the "Hosanna (to the Son of David), Blessed be He that cometh in the name of the Lord!" (Matt. xxi. 9; Mark xi. 9 f.; Luke xix. 38; John xii. 13), which is taken from this psalm, welcomed Him as the Messiah. These passages show that in the days of Jesus the whole psalm was taken Messianically under the influence of the Messianic stone, ver. 22; especially the בָּרוּךְ הַבָּא בְּשֵׁם יְהוָה was understood of the coming Messiah, whereas originally it was a general greeting of those entering the temple, Matt. xxiii. 39.

[2] Cf. Isa. xlv. 8, xxxii. 15 ff.

ornament of the high priest's breastplate. But decisive against this view is נָתַן לִפְנֵי, which can neither mean that God put this precious stone on his breast, nor that He simply handed it over to Joshua, which latter meaning this expositor cannot support by passages like Ezek. xxiii. 24, or even Josh. x. 12 and the like. The phrase always means: *to place or hand over something* so that it lies or stands before one, but does not at all suit the handing over of a precious stone worn on the person. On the other hand, Bredenkamp rightly objects to the ordinary interpretation of פִּתַּח, that the word (noun and verb) is never used of hewing stones for building purposes, but always of carving, engraving precious stones (also wood).

NOTE B.—Hitzig's translation (cf. LXX.): "and there shall be a priest on His throne," as if here all at once a co-ruler of the Zemach were spoken of, having a throne of his own alongside, besides its formal and intrinsic improbability, has no support from the following words. How strangely the second dignitary would be introduced here; and how well, on the other hand, the sentence agrees with the description of the royal Sprout! Ewald again resorts to an arbitrary interpolation of the name Joshua, in which case the emphasis would lie awkwardly on the consideration that Joshua will be a priest, whilst his throne would be assumed to be well known! Just as impossible is Riehm's interpretation, which at least concedes the identity of the throne, but makes two persons sit thereon, as if the words could mean: *And there shall also be a priest on His* (the Messiah's) *throne!*

§ 42. *Malachi's Sayings respecting the Herald of the Lord.*

That the devout enthusiasm, kindled at the time of the temple-building by the prophets of God, was unable to raise the nation permanently to the height of its mission, is shown by the further unworthy development of the colony in Jerusalem and the reformation which an Ezra and Nehemiah had afterwards to undertake in the Church that had apostatized in many ways from the law. Also the discourses of the prophet *Malachi*, who appeared about a hundred years after Zechariah in the days of Nehemiah, complain of the evident decline in the theocratic spirit and the perilous degeneracy of the whole commonwealth (note A). The temple, indeed, has long been completed, but the Lord can take no pleasure in sacrifices offered half unwillingly and in sordid avarice. Better no worship at all than careless and negligent worship. Moreover, the Lord needs no such forced reverence, He to whom the heathen everywhere joyfully render service and sacrifice :—

i. 11. "For from the rising of the sun to its setting my name is great among the heathen, and in every place incense is offered to my name and pure offerings; for great is my name among the heathen, saith Yahveh of hosts."

This oracle, in which the Lord glories in being worshipped in the whole earth and honoured with acceptable offerings, is of the highest significance,[1] as already cursorily intimated (p. 318). For in any case it declares, in opposition to the Jewish particularism, which imagined God could not dispense with His people and temple, that the world is capable of being sanctified by God's revelation and is fit to worship God. This also is the pith of the saying just quoted, which neither expressly refers to the future nor finds its satisfaction in the present. The hearers or readers might think only of the future. A very intelligible threat lay in the saying. For the first time the thought finds utterance, that God might take away His kingdom from the chosen people and cause the heathen to offer more acceptable service. But at the same time the statement discloses a greatness and large-heartedness on God's part far beyond the thoughts of a narrow-hearted race. God declares that He despises not the offerings of the heathen, nay, He calls them pure in opposition to those brought by the Jews. As His name is known to the heathen, so their incense reaches Him in His heavenly temple.

If the state of the Church, and especially of the priesthood,—according to chap. ii., chiefly to blame for the prevailing religious and moral declension,—is so bad, the day of the Lord cannot enter without one being compelled to think with horror of Israel's fate. That day is really coming, and judgment with it; only, the Lord in His mercy will not let it burst without preparation.

iii. 1. "Behold, I send my messenger and he shall cleanse the way before me, and the Lord whom ye desire will suddenly come to His temple, and the covenant-angel, whom ye long for.

2 Behold, He comes, saith the Lord of hosts. And who is he that can endure the day of His coming, and who is he that can stand when He appears? For He is like the smelter's fire and like the washers' lye."

[1] Of course its use in the Romish Church, as a main support for the doctrine of the Sacrifice of the Mass (Trident. Sess. xxii.), is quite unwarranted.

Here the prophecy of the Day of the Lord receives new enrichment. A preparatory messenger (note B) will precede, and prepare the way for, the coming God or His covenant-angel, who will suddenly enter His temple to fill it with the Shekinah. Whereas in Isa. xl. 3 the forerunner, who cries פַּנּוּ דֶּרֶךְ יְהֹוָה, seemed merely a means of prophetic presentation, here he attains independent significance, he has to fill an office of essential importance in historical reality. And whereas the preparation of the way had more in view the removal of the hindrances that opposed the Lord's advent on the part of the outer world, which, of course, includes the creating of the necessary ethical preconditions (p. 378), here the principal aim is the putting away of the offences among God's people which violate the holiness of the coming ruler, and provoke His wrath against them.

Only too quickly will the Lord, whose advent they cannot endure, appear. This "commander" is God Himself; in the parallel clause stands instead the *angel of the covenant*, who, in virtue of the covenant existing between God and Israel, sets forth the divine presence amid His people.[1] This angel is distinguished from the first-mentioned messenger, who merely warns of God's advent. It is the Mediator through whom the Lord Himself takes up His abode in the temple, since such a revelation of the Godhead is inconceivable without angelic mediation. Before the judgment the Shekinah forsook the temple (Ezek. xi. 23); according to the exilian prophets, it will return thither; but, although according to (Haggai and) Zechariah God's gracious presence hovers over His house, the promises that announce a coming of the Lord with perfect manifestation of His glory are not yet fulfilled.

Since the sacred majesty of the Most High will take up its abode among His people in intensity never witnessed before, the approaching revelation contains a fearful danger for all sinners (cf. Ex. xxxiii. 3). Hence this generation is greatly mistaken in longing for the day of judgment and desiring impatiently the Lord's appearing. The persons addressed here are not unbelieving mockers,[2] who ironically desire that the day threatened may come at once, but, as in Amos v. 18, 20, those weary of life and filled with theocratic ambition, who fancy in their blind-

---

[1] Cf. on Zech. ii. 11, p. 430.
[2] Such *illuminati* were not wanting, according to Mal. iii. 13 ff.

ness that the Lord's Parousia will bring them and their people glory in the eyes of the world. In their illusion they do not reflect that they, hardened sinners, cannot endure the presence of the holy God, which acts like a consuming fire on everything impure and unholy. This judgment will not pass a single individual without causing him pain and bitter woe. There will be a sifting as in a furnace, a searching of men's hearts as with lye. Thus in the best case by terrible heat and all-corroding severity the metal would be severed from the dross, the filth from the garments. According to ver. 3, the judgment would fall specially on the priests, whom the Lord would first purify by cleansing fire before receiving them into His service. Since they are principally attacked throughout the writing of this prophet, we must suppose that they were chiefly to blame for the inner corruption of the people, little suspecting in their self-righteousness the nature of the Lord's judgment upon them. Probably they encouraged themselves with vain hopes of approaching exaltation through the judgment on the nations.

As Malachi has emphatically declared, in opposition to this, that the present generation, estranged from God and His law (iii. 22), has nothing to hope and everything to fear from the Day of the Lord, so he sets his hope on the forerunner, whom God in His grace will send before His face, in order that his advent, with which of necessity judgment will be connected, may not prove entirely destructive to the covenant people. Then at the close Malachi recurs to this salutary monitor:—

iv. 5. "Behold, I send you the PROPHET ELIAS, before the day of
6 Yahveh comes, great and terrible. And he shall turn again the heart of the fathers to their sons, and the heart of the sons to their fathers, lest I come and smite the land with outlawry." [1]

In the sending of the prophet *Elijah* we are not to think of a return of the Tishbite,[2] as the people generally understood and the Jews in the time of Jesus really expected,[3] an expectation which may have been fostered by the fact that Elijah was removed from the earth without dying, 2 Kings. The

---

[1] Cf. Zech. xiv. 11, p. 358.

[2] So still Ewald, Hitzig, *et al.*, after many ancients.

[3] Cf. Matt. xvii. 10; John i. 21. See the detailed notions in Weber, *Altsynagogale Theologie*, p. 337 f.

passage is rather to be understood after the analogy of the
one concerning David, Jer. xxx. 9 (p. 336). A prophet in the
style of the ancient Elijah is necessary to accomplish such
a work as the conversion of Judah, at present sunk in sin.
A man in the spirit and power of Elijah the Lord must and
will send, to bring back this people from the abyss, just as
Elijah with holy violence, so to speak, led back Ephraim, when
entangled in idolatry and hastening to ruin, to the service of the
true God.

The work to be done hereafter by this Elijah in Judah is
described in ver. 24 in peculiar terms. We should expect to
hear that he will convert the people to God. Instead of this, a
reconciling of fathers and sons is spoken of. But, of course, this
must be one that includes such conversion. Fathers and children,
old and young are separated, not merely by domestic quarrels,
but also by a deep gulf of a religious nature. The young
generation has broken with the faith of the fathers and despised
the law held in high esteem by the latter. To this apostasy, it
is true, the fathers have contributed not a little, their piety being
in many respects merely external and apparent. Thus fathers
and sons are at variance with each other. The former will no
longer bless the latter, the latter no longer honour the former.
When Elijah comes, and with new spiritual power brings
home the old law of Moses to the people's hearts, the gulf
will be closed. By teaching the sons again to fear God he
will again incline the fathers to them, and by inspiring the
fathers with a right mind he will again win for them the
hearts of the young.[1] It is thus intelligible how the work of
conversion done by God's herald is presented as a union of
fathers and sons. The supposition that no more is meant than
a restoration of childlike reverence and thus of domestic peace,
is plainly insufficient. Moreover, it is out of place to understand

---

[1] The translation of הֵשִׁיב by "convert" is misleading. Since עַל plainly indicates the direction, and is not = עַם, as some suppose, the awkwardness would
arise, that the parents would be first converted to the children, then the latter to
the parents. The meaning of הֵשִׁיב is obtained from the correct apprehension of
לֵב, which according to Judg. xix. 3, Hos. ii. 15, is to be understood as the seat of
love and confidence. In bringing back all the nation to God that true mentor will
again turn the inclination of the parents, paternal favour, to the sons, and the
childlike confidence of the sons to the fathers.

by the fathers, pious ancestors; for the prophet has living persons in view. These, however, represent, although with little credit, the great sacred past of Israel, to which the young generation, now estranged from it, will learn to look back with reverent love. This will take place when Elijah's fiery zeal and spiritual power shall again hold up before its eyes the now despised Torah of Moses (iv. 4) in its true greatness.

This prophecy of Malachi of the forerunner of the divine Parousia was made specially notable by its *fulfilment*. Our Lord Himself, as is well known, pointed to *John* the Baptist, who was that Elias, if men would think so.[1] There is implied in this, as well as in the reference of Isa. xl. 3 to the same John,[2] a powerful testimony of Jesus Christ to His own Deity. For He thereby designates Himself the manifested Yahveh, or the covenant-angel, in whom God reveals Himself directly.[3] And John, the conscious forerunner of the Messiah, has already assented to this claim of equality, professing to be the voice heard, Isa. xl. 3, that prepared a way for the Lord in the desert.[4] There also he made himself known as the preparer of the way announced by Malachi. When in John i. 21 he denies that he is Elijah, he only renounces the title in the personal sense embodied in the prevailing expectation of an actual return of Elijah.

And, in fact, not merely did John's outward appearance, his hairy prophet's mantle, recall the Tishbite, but his mission most closely resembled the one ascribed in our text to Elijah. A last representative of the entire Old Covenant, he preached repentance, return to the commands of Moses, in order to pave the way for a greater One, in whom God would reveal Himself most perfectly. This Greater One certainly came in human form and gentle loving condescension, but judgment, sifting was connected with His coming (cf. John ix. 39). This John the Baptist knew. It is observable that in the Messiah he principally emphasizes the work of judging and sifting. He has the winnowing-fan in His hand, and baptizes with fire.[5] And indeed the

---

[1] Matt. xi. 14, xvii. 11; cf. Luke i. 17.
[2] Matt. xi. 10; Luke vii. 27.
[3] The covenant-angel forms a natural middle term between the manifestation of the Lord Himself and His revelation in a human Messiah; cf. Zech. xii. 8.
[4] John i. 23; cf. Mark i. 2 f.; Luke iii. 4 f.
[5] Matt. iii. 11 f.; Luke iii. 16 f.

Messiah's advent, finding the people unprepared, became a judgment to them. On that Day of the Lord, only they were able to stand who had been converted by the testimony of His messenger.

Thus the last prophet of the Old Covenant joins hand with the forerunner of the New. The latter once more summed up in his person the whole testimony of the Old: the law of Moses, which is a trainer for Christ, the prophetic allusion to the Day of the Lord, when Yahveh will appear for judgment and salvation, the saying about the Messiah as the Greater One coming from of old, whose shoe-latchet he is not worthy to unloose, and finally the mystery of the God-chosen Lamb which takes away sin (John i.). Thus did he lead back to the true understanding of the Old Covenant those who were estranged from its spirit and letter, and vindicate the truth of the glorious revelations of the past as a preparation for the approaching most glorious one, in which all will be consummated.

NOTE A.—The prediction of this prophet, without date, is most probably to be placed (with Nägelsbach, Köhler, Schrader) in the time between the first and second presence of Nehemiah in Judea (between 433 and 424 B.C., the year of Artaxerxes' death). Like the latter, he combats the marrying of foreign women (cf. Neh. xiii. 23 ff.; Mal. ii. 11) as a cancer threatening to eat up all family and public life, in Mal. ii. 14 also the thoughtless putting away of Israelitish wives; further, the latter rebukes the offering of imperfect sacrifices, i. 6 ff., with which the obligation assumed in Neh. x. 32 ff. and the rebuke of Neh. xiii. may be compared. On the other hand, it is far from probable that Malachi would have spoken of the governor as he does, i. 8, if Nehemiah were then in this office, since the latter could boast that he had demanded no taxes from his people, Neh. v. 14 ff. These discourses, therefore, probably fall within the time before Nehemiah's return, after which he reformed these and other abuses.

NOTE B.—The prophet perhaps uses this מַלְאָכִי with a play on his own name. He is himself a messenger, whose mission is to warn of the Lord's approach. Yet in ver. 23 it appears that he sees a still stronger One coming after him, whose preaching will bear more fruit. The prophet may have viewed his own mission in relation to that of God's messenger, as the author of Isa. xl.–lxvi. viewed his in relation to that of God's Servant (p. 386). That our prophet also wrote anonymously, or prefixed the merely assumed name Malachi to his oracles (Hengstenberg, Ewald, et al.), is not probable after the simple בְּרִי, i. 1. See Caspari, *Micha der Morasthite*, p. 27 ff.; Nägelsbach in Herzog, ix. 177 ff.

§ 43. *The Apocalypse of Daniel.*

The Book of *Daniel* occupies quite a peculiar position among or alongside the prophetic books of the Old Testament. Its isolated character is indicated by its outward separation from the rest of the books in the Hebrew canon, whether this separation be due to the intrinsic peculiarity of Daniel's official work, or, as the criticism of our day supposes, to the late origin of the book, which is alleged to have been written after the close of the prophetic canon (acknowledged as the standard in Ecclus. xlix.).

In the former respect it cannot be denied that Daniel's visions are essentially different in form and contents from those of the other biblical prophets, a feature harmonizing with his position as a statesman at the court of various heathen rulers. His prophecy on the whole is more *exoteric*, directed more to the development of the world-power and the conflict of God's kingdom with it. With a glance that takes in universal history, the seer gives a vast panorama of the world's history, in which one power displaces another, a definite period being assigned to each (vii. 12). This development of grand politics takes place according to a fixed divine programme, and advances systematically in well-defined periods to the goal fixed by God, which will be inevitably reached, although after severe and ever severer crises. This goal is the rule of God on earth, which is brought about by His chosen people and its elect Head. Thus Daniel, like Balaam's oracles, standing of course on higher vantage-ground at an advanced point of time, supplements the prophets who see things from the standpoint of the temple on Zion and are chiefly occupied with the internal events of their own nation. From the centre of the world of nations, he follows the course of the two kingdoms—the world-kingdom and God's—up to the end, and discloses the movement of the entire world-development toward the triumph of the divine rule.

If this universal tendency, giving the Book of Daniel a final character in several respects, is perhaps enough in itself to justify its being placed at the close of the chain of O. T. prophecy, there is a second element which directly assigns this position to it. Even if the seer's standpoint be the exile, the goal of the book is a far later period, for which alone it is written (xii. 4), and the illustration of which is so much part of its plan, that it can only be understood from this period, in which all the rays of the book converge as in their focus. It is the period of the oppression of God's people by the Syrian ruler *Antiochus Epiphanes* (reigned 175–164 B.C.). As Isa. xl.–lxvi. was written for the exiles, the Book of Daniel was written for those persecuted by the ruler mentioned. Certainly there is a noteworthy difference. Whereas the former unnamed prophet professes to be nothing but a comforter sent to that generation, and speaks to it as to contemporaries, in the Book of Daniel an exilian prophet may be heard beyond the age of the Seleucids.

Modern criticism would regard this difference as nothing more than a form artificially assumed, the exilian standpoint of the seer in "Daniel's" visions being as truly fictitious as the history given of him in the first part of the book (i.–vi.). The author, it is said, invented the former like the latter, about the year 167 B.C., to encourage his people to stedfastness under the harsh tyranny of the world-power; in the pious, faithful Daniel, they were to find an example, and learn how the Lord will not disappoint them that confess Him; under the name of the wise Daniel (since the gift of prophecy had now vanished, and there would be no slight danger to a patriot uttering such truths without disguise) they were to use words of confident hope in regard to the speedy end of the world-power that now ruled with unexampled violence and hostility to God.

Although the design of the book is here rightly indicated, we hold this account of its origin to be impossible. Neither of the narratives of Dan. i.–vi., nor of the visions vii.–xii., can we allow that they owe their origin to the Maccabæan age. As to the former, which we do not here examine, we are of opinion that they contain history handed down from the time of the exile and were merely compiled by a late author, who to all appearance, especially according to linguistic indications, belonged to the Maccabæan age (note A). We come to a similar conclusion in respect to the apocalyptic visions. That these also did not originate at *one* stroke, is easily seen. How the several visions are to be combined together, is not everywhere evident. The order of the world-empires, chaps. ii., vii., does not seem adapted to the Maccabean period; the reference of the 70 weeks to it encounters unsolved difficulties. On the other hand, it is certain that the most elaborate delineations refer to Antiochus Epiphanes and his age, the political circumstances of which are unfolded with a detail to which nothing at all analogous can be shown in the whole field of biblical prophecy elsewhere. We think that even here traditional visions of the ancient Daniel, renowned for his prophetic keenness of sight (Ezek. xxviii. 3), form the real kernel, but that these visions were not merely collected and redacted by an author living under Antiochus, but also set by illustrative explanations in intimate relation to the oppression of that age. It is no doubt impossible to discriminate in detail what belonged to the ancient Daniel. Yet the attitude of the reviser is evidently such that, in an age forsaken by the spirit of prophecy,[1] he does not dare to predict, but, taking his stand entirely on existing revelations, seeks to make them intelligible and useful to his contemporaries. The fundamental ideas undoubtedly go back to Daniel; it is so with the development of the world-kingdom in four figures and the triumph of God's kingdom following thereupon; so again with the climax of the resistance of the world-power in its last representative, and the period of the 70 weeks running on to the setting up of the divine rule. Let us consider these main ideas.

The antithesis of world-kingdom and God's kingdom meets us in the dream of the world-ruler, ii. 31 ff., which the seer interprets to him, ii. 36 ff., as well as in the latter's vision in a different way, vii. 1 ff. In both cases, in distinction from the prophecies found elsewhere,[2] the world-power is contemplated in its course of historical development, and that in *four* phases, which it runs through in succession. *Four* stands here as the number of the Cosmos, as in Zech. ii. 1 ff., vi. 1 ff.[3] Therefore the power of the world in its entire development is meant. But this development is plainly viewed, in distinction from Zechariah, as a series of world-rulers appearing one after another. That in reality it is one and the same power, of which the several great powers are merely different manifestations, is shown in chap. ii., where they are simply members of *one* colossal image. It is observable that

---

[1] Cf. 1 Macc. iv. 46, ix. 27, xiv. 41.
[2] Num. xxiv. 20 ff. supplies an attempt at such a delineation.
[3] Cf. the four winds, Dan. vii. 2, with Zech. vi. 5.

the material degenerates continuously (gold, silver, brass, iron), while at the same time growing stronger and more dangerous, until at last in the case of the most dangerous power its strength is coupled with the greatest weakness (iron and clay).

There the colossus is struck in the most sensitive part by another power, and collapses in consequence. The fourth world-power, the harshest and strongest, succumbs to the kingdom of God, which by this victory triumphs over the whole world-power. It is prefigured by a stone, which, detached by invisible hand, falls on the feet of the statue, crushing it to pieces; whereupon the stone becomes a great mountain filling the whole earth. The stone, which recalls Isa. xxviii. 16, exhibits the divine kingdom in its unpromising, incomplete beginning, in which, however, it proves itself superior to all the power and glory of this world; the mountain exhibits the perfected, world-ruling kingdom of God in accordance with the interpretation :—

ii. 44. "And in the days of these kings the God of heaven will set up an eternal kingdom, which shall never be destroyed, and its dominion shall not be delivered to another people. It will crush and destroy all these kingdoms, but it shall last for ever."

This kingdom, set up at last by God's hand to conquer the whole world, and, in distinction from the previous alternation of supremacy, to maintain its position for ever, can only be God's kingdom, in which the Lord Himself is king. In Obad. ver. 21 (cf. Ps. xxii. 28) it was said already that the מְלוּכָה pertains to Him, and the setting up of His kingly rule was often enough described as the goal of His plans and ways.[1] In point of fact this kingdom was founded by the "God of heaven;" it springs from above in contrast to the world-colossus towering up on the earth, which it grinds to pieces by invisible, spiritual, divine authority. We have here the O. T. basis of the expression βασιλεία τῶν οὐρανῶν, found so frequently in Matthew on the lips of Jesus. But it is to be observed that this rule of God is thought of as brought about by human means. Over against the "other peoples" ruling hitherto stands the people of the Lord now ruling by the favour of God. From it the authority shall not again be taken away. In this O. T. national form the truth is expressed, that the

[1] Cf. Isa. xxiv. 23, lii. 7; Ps. xlvii. 9, xcvi. 10, xcvii. 1, xcix. 1, and similar passages.

Lord will rule for ever on earth by means of men, and indeed of His elect Church.

The same triumph of God's kingdom over the world-power is exhibited in Dan. vii. 2 ff. with new and significant traits. In this dream-vision the same four world-kingdoms unmistakably appear, this time as four beasts ascending in succession out of the storm-tossed sea (the unquiet element of the world of nations), to exercise their authority and dominion up to the limit of time assigned them. After their time has run out and a horn (ruler) belonging to the fourth beast has filled up its measure of heaven-defying arrogance, the "Ancient of days" holds the world-judgment, by which all earthly power is abolished and the heaven-defying one condemned. Then He who is destined to indestructible dominion appears:—

vii. 13. "I beheld in visions of the night, and behold, one came like a SON OF MAN with the clouds of heaven, and came to
14 the Ancient of days,[1] and was brought before him. And authority was given him, and glory and kingship, and all peoples and nations and tongues shall serve him. His authority is an everlasting authority, which passes not away, and his kingship one that is not destroyed."

The distinction between the human mediator of the divine rule and God, the Most High, comes out here more strongly than in chap. ii. After God, who has always determined the fate of nations and men, has held the final judgment on the powers, in which they lose all their dominion, which is of perishable nature, the true ruler approaches, for whom the kingdom is designed. In opposition to the beasts (not to the angels, cf. Ezek. i. 26; Dan. x. 16, 18), he appears in *human* form, human in aspect. This implies his spiritual and ethical elevation above those world-monarchs. Whereas the world-power is animal, *i.e.* governed by savage, sensuous, impure and sinful impulses and passions,[2] the future belongs to a power not threatening in aspect, like the world-powers grim with horns and teeth, but uniting true dignity and greatness with superior spiritual energy, a ruler who, as true Son of man, thoroughly and truly fulfils man's proper and highest

---

[1] Even this appellation of God, vii. 9, 13, 22, with which the description vii. 9 agrees, corresponds to the more exoteric and historical standpoint of Daniel. It is God in the aspect in which He is presented in common human history.

[2] Cf. p. 282.

destiny of ruling in God's name on earth as God's image.[1] Here at the end prophecy acquires the vast range it had at the beginning. The Messiah, the God-chosen ruler, will not only be the true David, exhibiting the God-anointed One in His consummation, not merely the true Israel (Isa. xl.–lxvi.), realizing fully and finally the vocation of this people, but the true Son of man, verifying in full both the high vocation of humanity and the position assigned it by God.

Or was this person, moving along in human form, not meant, in accordance with the interpretation of vii. 18, 22, 27, to be taken personally, but to be understood of the *nation* of the saints = Israel? This is contradicted by the "coming with the clouds of heaven," in which the heavenly origin of the ruler of the future is expressed (more strongly than in the falling stone, ii. 34); he is of supramundane extraction.[2] In any case, we should have to conceive the "nation of the saints of the Most High" in a glorified spiritual form, going far beyond the national reality. It would be the Church made wholly the Lord's and forming in a manner His heavenly host.[3] But there is no intimation of such an exaltation of God's people to heaven before the end, and it is even excluded by vii. 21, 22. Moreover, the personal portraiture, vii. 13, is opposed to every collective interpretation. Also the antithesis to the earthly powers requires that this divine kingdom, now entering into visibility, should have its visible Head. And this can be no other than the long-expected *Messiah* appearing at the right time.[4] So the passage has been unanimously understood by Judaism.[5] Certainly this ruler must also have a people exercising dominion in conjunction with him. In the application of the vision to present historical circumstances (vii. 18, 22, 27) only the people is spoken of, *i.e.* the saints who have remained faithful will receive dominion; for the approaching ruler is their

---

[1] Cf. on Gen. i. 26, p. 83, on Gen. iii. 15, p. 87, 91.

[2] The scene of judgment, vii. 9 ff., is not in heaven (Ewald), but the Ancient of days comes to the earth, vii. 22; there the judgment-thrones are set, vii. 9. But the Son of man descends on the clouds of heaven.

[3] This expression is used of the heavenly retinue of the Judge, Zech. xiv. 5; cf. Dan. iv. 10, 20. But throughout Dan. vii. the faithful Church on earth is understood thereby, vii. 18, 21 f., 25, 27.

[4] See Ewald, *Jüngste Propheten*, 1868, p. 404 ff.; Riehm, *Messianic Prophecy*, p. 132.

[5] *Buch Henoch*, 46 ff., 69; *Tract. Sanhedr.* f. 98*a*; Jarchi, Saadia, etc.

own, the Head given them by heaven, in whom they are concentrated, and to whom they stand in reciprocal relation, as in Deutero-Isaiah the people to the true Servant of God.

That this chapter is the proper source of a certain N. T. phrase, *i.e.* of the name, which Jesus was fond of applying to Himself according to the four Gospels, scarcely needs remark. That He chose the appellation "Son of man" in allusion to Dan. vii. 13, follows from the sayings of Jesus in which He expressly refers to this passage, like Matt. xvi. 27, xxiv. 30 ;[1] Mark xiv. 62 ; Matt. xxvi. 64, with which also John i. 52, iii. 13, should be compared, which also put the Son of man in relation to heaven. At the same time it ought certainly to be said, that in the teaching of Jesus this idea, in comparison with the one in Daniel, is just as much deepened and enriched as that of the kingdom of heaven. Also in the time of Christ this "Son of man" was not one of the current names of the Messiah.[2] This simple appellation was therefore pre-eminently adapted, in accordance with the intention of Jesus, to conceal His eminence and yet to reveal to instructed eyes the divine greatness of His person. To the receptive disciples it implied that He was the Messiah, while claiming to be more than the national Messiah whom the Jews expected in those days.

An essential feature in Daniel's prophecy, which is also again taken up by the New Testament, is the knowledge that before the appearance of God's kingdom the resistance of the heaven-opposing world-power will burst forth in all its magnitude and force ; and this not merely in the form of an attack of heathen nations on Jerusalem, as in Joel iii. 9 ff., Ezek. xxxviii. f., but concentrated in a person who will reign a long time as a tyrant over the people of God and persecute them for their religious fidelity. This ruler, exhibited in viii. 9 ff. as a horn, there issues directly from one of the four kingdoms of the Diadochi. It is the same in chap. xi., where Alexander's victory over the Persians is referred to, while next the conflicts between the Seleucids (kings of the north) and the Ptolemies (kings of the south) are described, and from the former arises a ruler, who in his campaigns against Egypt shall also ill-treat the land of "ornament"

---

[1] The combination of Dan. iii. 17 with Zech. xii. 10 here is observable.

[2] The Book of Henoch so uses it exceptionally in the section xxxvii.-lxxi., whose pre-Christian character is certainly contested.

(ver. 41), *i.e.* Canaan, his fierce hatred turning more and more against the Most High God and His people. All this is described with such historical plainness, that the corresponding parts of the Maccabæan books, especially 1 Macc. i., almost form a parallel account to it.[1]

If, then, in these chapters without doubt none but *Antiochus Epiphanes* is meant, we cannot help also understanding the horn, described in Dan. vii. 8, 11, 20 f., of him, the description of whom agrees with the description in chap. viii. ff. just as exactly as with historic reality. It is a horn having eyes, a human mouth, speaking presumptuous things and bold enough to war against the saints of God, setting itself in the place of the Most High. In fact it acquires authority over the Holy Land for a brief period ($3\frac{1}{2}$ years according to xii. 25, exactly as in Dan. vii. 7), and abuses it to lay waste the temple of the Lord, to abolish the daily sacrifice and alter the sacred seasons and ordinances.[2] No doubt this portrait has peculiar features. The eyes of the horn, its human aspect, its insolent words, are meant to intimate that here we have to do, not with savage, brutal violence, such as belongs to the brutish world-kingdoms, but with a more rational enemy of God, who undertakes the war against His kingdom with full consciousness, and with equal cunning and violence tries to uproot it.

Such a diabolical personality was Antiochus, the pre-Christian Nero, a tyrant in whom coarseness blended with lofty ideals in a wonderful way.[3] He was the first heathen ruler who sought not merely the conquest of Canaan and the political annihilation of the Israelitish nation, but quite deliberately and in the first place the destruction of that which constituted Israel's distinction above all nations, its worship. Keil rightly observes on 1 Macc. i. 10, that in reference to such an energetic and consistent policy as Antiochus pursued in order to accomplish this end, we have no

---

[1] Cf. with Dan. xi. 25, 1 Macc. i. 17 ff. ; with Dan. xi. 28, 1 Macc. i. 20 ff. ; with Dan. xi. 29-35, 1 Macc. i. 29 ff. ; with Dan. viii. 9 ff., 1 Macc. i. 22 ff. With reference to Dan. xi. 31, xii. 11, in 1 Macc. i. 54 (see Grimm and Keil) the small idol-altar set on the altar of burnt-offering is called "abomination of desolation." Cf. also Schürer, *N. T. Zeitgeschichte*, p. 71 ff.

[2] Cf. with the blaspheming mouth, 1 Macc. i. 21 ; with the conflict about the sacred seasons (Sabbaths, feasts) and ordinances (circumcision, laws as to food, etc.), 1 Macc. i. 41 f., 51, ii. 21 ; 2 Macc. iv. 11, vi. 1, etc.

[3] See his character in Diodorus, xxxi. 16 ; Polybius, xxvi. 10.

right to refer the hostility of this prince against the Lord of hosts to a mere despot's caprice, having no deeper ground. The daring pride of the human heart, that fills the world with enmity to the Most High, found in him a conspicuous representative.

If, then, we take this horn, which connects the four kingdoms (chaps. ii., vii.) with the visions (chap. viii. ff.), as a guide, the kingdoms would have to be fixed as the Babylonian, the Median, the Persian, the Greek. (*a*) Nebuchadnezzar is the head of gold (ii. 32, 38), the lion with eagle's wings (vii. 4). (*b*) Darius the Mede would be meant by the weaker follower (ii. 39), represented in the colossus by breast and arms of silver, in the animal-group by the bear with three ribs (three satrapies?) in its mouth, established in a one-sided manner. (*c*) The Persian kingdom would be presented (ii. 32) as a belly and loins of brass, according to ii. 39 ruling over the whole earth, in vii. 6 as a leopard with four wings and four heads (cf. the four Persian kings, xi. 2). In viii. 3 *b* and *c* would be combined in the Medo-Persian ram. Finally (*d*) Alexander's kingdom, established from the west and issuing in the reigns of the Diadochi, would correspond to the legs of iron, ii. 33, terminating in feet of iron and clay. Cf. ii. 40 ff., according to which it is made up of strong and weak elements, and is dismembered. In vii. 7 ff. it appears as a specially terrible beast with ten horns, in viii. 5 as a he-goat with one horn, in the place of which four grow up, out of one of which the little bad horn proceeds.

This division, according to which the Græco-Macedonian kingdom with its offshoots would form the horizon of the book, is in opposition to the traditional one, which found the fourth kingdom in Rome, and which is generally accepted in modern days. Taking the book in its present form as a single whole, one cannot escape the above division. In a theological aspect also there is no objection to this limit of the circle of vision. This limit was afterwards left behind, the last oppression by the enemy of God being pushed into the future, when one should come, of whom Antiochus was only a type. But in comparing the visions themselves doubts arise as to the correctness of the former interpretation of chaps. ii. and vii., which we cannot pass over.[1] Incontestably as the visions of chap. viii. ff. point to the

---

[1] Cf. also Hofmann, *Weissagung und Erfüllung*, i. 278 ff., 283 ff. H. Ewald, *Jüngste Propheten*, 1868, p. 314 f.; F. Godet, *Bibelstudien*, i. 257 ff.

reign of Antiochus, those of chaps. ii. and vii. seem just as little adapted thereto. In chap. ii. the ominous horn is entirely wanting, in chap. vii. it springs out of a number ten, not ascertainable historically, instead of a number four. An unprejudiced comparison, moreover, suggests as far more probable the reference of the second empire to the Medo-Persian rule. To this points the dualism in breast and arms, ii. 32, as well as in the bear more strongly established on one side, vii. 5. Both symbols have their counterpart in the ram with two unequal horns, viii. 3. The swift leopard with four wings and four heads excellently suits Alexander typified by the active he-goat (viii. 5), who subjugated the west as well as the east (ii. 39). The form and description of the fourth beast without name, crushing everything with iron force, more terrible than any that had preceded, will not square with the fleet-footed Alexander; nor can it be referred to his successors in distinction from himself (Zöckler). On the other hand, it agrees excellently with the iron rule of Rome.

We are therefore of opinion that the traditional conception of the four world-kingdoms, viz., (*a*) Babylon, (*b*) Medo-Persia, (*c*) Macedonia, (*d*) Rome, corresponds at least to the original plan of Daniel's visions; that, on the other hand, their editor, from whose hand we receive them in a redacted form, referred their aim everywhere to his own age, and sought to make this reference evident to his contemporaries by the explanations given in chap. xi.[1] Considering the epoch-making significance of the Seleucid struggle, this application of the prophetic word was not unwarranted; but the range of Daniel's prophecy was not exhausted therein.

The same, in our opinion, holds good of the seventy weeks and their calculation, Dan. ix. In allusion to the seventy years of Babylonian captivity predicted by Jeremiah,[2] it is made known to the seer Daniel, that not seventy years, but seventy weeks will elapse before the consummation of God's glorious kingdom seen by the prophet in conjunction with the return from exile.

ix. 24. "Seventy weeks are settled respecting thy people and

---

[1] The God-resisting horn, in which at last the hostility of the world to the God of heaven culminates, must be acknowledged as belonging to the ancient Daniel; on the other hand, it cannot be certainly indicated where it had its place originally, the redactor having made some adjustment just here.

[2] Dan. ix. 2. Cf. Jer. xxv. 11 f., xxix. 10.

thy holy city, to abolish sin and seal[1] transgressions and expiate guilt and bring in eternal righteousness, and seal vision and prophet and anoint the most holy (place)."

The penal time of seventy weeks must be endured before full redemption comes, such as the prophets beheld in immediate connection with the return from exile,—entire deliverance from sin and guilt, the first being made an end of, the latter expiated, —the fulfilment of all the glory predicted by them, the perfecting of the innermost sanctuary on Zion (Zech. iii. 9, p. 433). These "weeks" are spaces of seven years, as is seen by comparing ix. 27 with vii. 25, xii. 7. But the period of seventy weeks = 490 years, is again divided into $7 + 62 + 1$, the year of the summons to return being named as the starting-point, therefore 536 B.C. The meaning, however, is that the seven weeks first mentioned had already elapsed, since the years of exile are certainly included in the time of punishment.[2] With this also agrees the historical duration, these seven weeks counting from c. 588 to c. 536 B.C. On the seven weeks of exile, which as already well known are not specially noticed, follows the paltry restoration and the undisturbed continuance of Jerusalem in limited circumstances during many years (sixty-two weeks). At the close of this period the "Anointed One" appears, or rather is violently put to death in that moment, ix. 26. Then the last week of heaviest tribulation begins. In this מָשִׁיחַ a Christian reader can only see the Messiah, especially when in ix. 25 He is called מָשִׁיחַ נָגִיד, *princely, kingly, Anointed One*. Thus He is the same as the one in vii. 13, where He is to return in triumph after having suffered death on earth. Here the combination with Zech. xiii. 7, xii. 10, suggests itself, such as we find carried out in Matt. xxiv. 30. The historical fulfilment certainly would not fit exactly in a chronological point of view, since 536–434 (sixty-two weeks) would only bring us down to c. 100 B.C., which is little improved by dating the seven weeks also from 536. Hengstenberg does better in referring the saying about the rebuilding of Jerusalem to Artaxerxes. But these typical weeks

---

[1] So at least the *Kethib* in the sense of *to complete, finish*. In the same sense the *Keri* reads לְהָתֵם. See Gesenius, *Thesaurus*, i. p. 533. Isa. xl. 2 should be compared as to the idea.

[2] Otherwise Hofmann, Wieseler, Delitzsch (Herzog, iii. 477), who make the seven weeks follow the 62 + 1, which would have needed to be expressly said.

in prophecy are not to be taken at all as mere mathematical quantities.

However, it can scarcely be denied that the editor and redactor of the Book of Daniel has identified the last week, following the 62 and beginning with the killing of the "Messiah," with his own time, and the second half of the same with the desecration of the temple by Antiochus (ix. 27). How he reckoned in order to obtain 62 (52 instead) weeks from c. 536 to c. 170, has not been satisfactorily shown. On the other hand, in the murder of the high priest Onias III., in whom the guardian spirit of the nation seemed taken away, he thought he saw the fateful murder of the "Anointed One" (note B). This, in connection with his reckoning of the 70 weeks and the fearful events of his days, inspired him with confidence that the last week had already begun, and only half of it had yet to be endured before full redemption came. Nor in this brief period of $3\frac{1}{2}$ years was he deceived, thereby proving that something of the spirit of prophecy lived in him also. But what he was permitted to learn from prophecy respecting those days of heroic struggle for freedom did not exhaust its meaning. The last week really began when the true Anointed One was put to a violent death. Then the powers of desolation were let loose upon Judah and its temple,[1] while at the same time the kingdom of the Son of man, in which all guilt is cancelled and the Most Holy Place is perfected, began its course. But its outward, complete and final triumph over the world-kingdoms, which Daniel so triumphantly foretold, will only take place on the return of the Crucified in the clouds of heaven.

Then also will be realized the great things which Daniel said (xii. 2) respecting the *consummation of the Church*:—

xii. 1b. "And there shall be a time of tribulation, such as has not occurred since there has been a people up to this time. And at the same time thy people shall be delivered, every
2 one written in the book. And many of those who sleep in the dust of the ground shall awake, these to eternal life, and
3 those to shame, to everlasting abhorrence. And they who have made (others) wise[2] shall shine like the glory of the heavenly vault, and they who have pointed many to righteousness, like the stars for ever and ever."

---

[1] Matt. xxiv. 15 ; Mark xiii. 14.
[2] הִשְׂכִּיל stands here in the transitive sense : *to teach, instruct*, as in ix. 22.

As already in Isa. xxvi. 19 (p. 303) we heard that to a full restoration of the Church the bodily resurrection of its members sleeping in God is necessary, so here a twofold resurrection of the dead is foretold as the end of the world. The one class, those entered in God's book of life, awake to eternal life in God; and in particular, they who were not merely themselves righteous and pleasing to God, but also by word and example led others to fear God and work righteousness, like Daniel himself (xii. 13), shall be made partakers of heavenly glory; while others rise from the dead to receive their doom, which is a further expansion of what is said in Isa. lxvii. 24 (cf. xxiv. 22). A universal resurrection of the dead is not indeed taught in this passage; for "many of them that sleep" (despite Hofmann, Oehler) is different from "all that sleep;" but the emphasis lies not on the partial character inherent in the expression, but on the multitude of those who shall arise, some because they are found in God's book of life and therefore cannot remain for ever in the power of death, others because God's retributive justice must yet overtake them.

This prophecy also was taken up again by Christ and the apostles, and its fulfilment is still to come, like what is said in this book of the establishment of a word-ruling kingdom of God. Still the world's history goes on its course, still the colossus stands, still the beasts ascend from the sea of nations. Still also the greatest tribulation of the Christian Church is to come. For as under the Old Covenant hostility to God embodied itself at last in *one* all-powerful ruler, so according to apostolic prophecy resistance to Christ culminates finally in an "Antichrist," who tries to strike a deadly blow at the kingdom of the Lord. But when the need is greatest and the cause of the "saints" is apparently lost, then the Exalted One will appear and gather His Church from among the living and the dead. To the Church the kingdom will fall at the final judgment.

The Book of Daniel, whatever the conjectures respecting its origin, puts the crown on Old Testament prophecy, giving utterance with unequalled grandeur to ideas of the divine kingdom, which entered into the basis of the revelation of the New Covenant.

NOTE A.—On the one side these visions, considering their loosely-connected state, give the impression of having arisen out of oral tradition, by which many inaccuracies may be explained; while the highly-coloured style of narrative, approximating somewhat to the apocryphal, and markedly different from the Biblical style generally, is made intelligible. On the other hand, both generally and in detail these visions, as modern investigation has proved, bear so much the stamp of the age and the reigns from which they profess to come, that their critical rejection is unsatisfactory on scientific grounds. See F. Lenormant, *Magie der Chaldäer*, 1878, p. 525 ff. As concerns the Maccabæan age, it, of course, perfectly explains the interest felt in bringing forward these traditional histories. The abstinence from unclean meats (Dan. i. 8 ff.) was a chief point in the creed of that age, 1 Macc. i. 62 (Fritzsche's ed. 1871), 2 Macc. vi. 18 ff., vii. 1 ff.; just so the refusal to worship idols at the command of tyrants, 1 Macc. i. 47, 51, with which Dan. iii. 1 ff. should be compared. In the time of the Seleucids the Jews witnessed (1 Macc. i. 23; 2 Macc. v. 16) something analogous to the desecration of the temple-vessels, Dan. v. 2 ff. But why should the narrator, to whom the gift of invention could not be denied, omit to illustrate and commend other chief acts of his creed by means of "Daniel's" narratives, such as the observance of the Sabbath (1 Macc. i. 39, 43, 45, ii. 32 ff.; 2 Macc. vi. 6), and of circumcision (1 Macc. i. 15, 48, 60 f.; 2 Macc. vi. 10), which would have been all the more easy since both customs were observed in the exile?

NOTE B.—See 2 Macc. iii. 1, iv. 1 ff. Were Dan. ix. 25 f. written originally of Onias, the way in which he is spoken of would be hard to understand. How is it that of all the high priests of the whole period he only is called מָשִׁיחַ נָגִיד, Dan. ix. 25? Also, to pass by the statement of Josephus, *Ant.* xii. 5, according to which on his (natural) death he was simply succeeded in office by his brother, he was according to 2 Macc. iv. (vers. 7, 23 f., 29, 34), at the time of his murder no longer high priest, of which there is no intimation in Daniel. But considering the reverence felt for him, a Messianic oracle already existing in that age might well be referred to him.

CONCLUSION.

Thus we find in the Old Testament an abundance of life-germs striving after union and mutual completion. These prophecies, while still of an isolated character (1 Cor. xiii. 9), yet tend to become a whole. They are not free from limitation of form and indistinctness of colour, due to the circumstances of the age, on which Delitzsch aptly remarks,[1] that the human short-sightedness of the prophets is made to subserve the divine plan just as much as their far-sightedness which was the gift of the Spirit. Their conception of the kingdom of God in general is still bound to the people of Israel, the land of Canaan, the House of God on Zion, the Mosaic ceremonial. As a rule they are only able to set forth the perfecting of God's future kingdom as a perfecting of these forms, an enhancement of the blessings already experienced in nature and national life. But everywhere the Spirit seeks to burst through this veil, which fails to satisfy Him; in many passages the veil falls aside, at least for a moment.

Still Old Testament prophecy first received its unity and completion in the New Covenant. Remove the latter, and what is left of the former? A harvest withering on the eve of maturity, a struggle of the holiest saints continued for centuries —without result; travail painful enough, but no new-birth! The fate of prophetic Israel would be a tragedy, powerless to give comfort to any people. The noblest hopes would have proved the vainest. We should despair of the Divinity of the Spirit who inspired them.

But the fulfilment has taken place in unanticipated glory. We saw that in the beginning prophecy had the establishment of God's kingdom for its chief subject, afterwards the redemption of the nation. The fulfilment conversely first brought illumination and redemption by the Servant of the Lord, the Messiah of David's stock in a state of lowliness, the insignificant Son of man. Although everything spoken by the prophets of the glory of God's people and kingdom was wrapped up in His person, His immediate work was the ministry of redemption, carried out in deepest lowliness and privacy. The effect of this work of His was that He did not remain alone, but became the foundation-stone of a whole temple, the king of a whole people, the type of a whole new-born humanity. True, this work was begun and was meant to be carried on primarily in a spiritual form, whilst at the same time a more radical judgment than the Babylonian was executed on the existing theocracy, receptive hearts being thus impelled to a refinement, a freedom and spiri-

[1] *Messianic Prophecies*, p. 94.

tuality of view altogether different from what was the case in the time of Jeremiah. To-day the building still continues, the Spirit produces His life quietly, where He wills. But one day His work will be revealed to all the world.

As certainly as redemption came the hour of consummation also will strike. Our Lord, who spoke to men as God's Messenger and made Himself known to His own as High Priest, will one day reveal Himself to the world as King. In Him, by whom every yearning of man's heart is stilled and all its woe healed, all the world's contradictions will find their solution, all divine ideas their consummation.

Thus the prophecies speak, not merely of the most glorious and precious contents of the history of mankind in the past, but also of the highest bliss which the future carries in its bosom, bearing witness as they do to Him (John v. 39) "who is, and who was, and who is *to come!*"

INDEX.

PRINCIPAL PASSAGES OF SCRIPTURE DISCUSSED OR REFERRED TO.

GENESIS.		EXODUS.		JUDGES.	
CHAP.	PAGE	CHAP.	PAGE	CHAP.	PAGE
i. 1–ii. 3,	80, 82	iii. 14,	127	i. 1,	119
i. 26,	78, 83	iv. 6,	7	v. 11,	273
iii.,	80, 87	iv. 22,	128, 229, 236	v. 24,	92
iii. 15,	78	iv. 23,	379	xiii. 18,	274
iv. 7,	89	vi. 3,	109, 127		
iv. 26,	126, 209	vi. 7,	128	1 SAMUEL.	
viii. 21,	94	vii. 1,	7	ix. 9,	5
ix. 8,	93	xiv. 19,	263	xiii. 14,	149
ix. 25–27,	79, 96, 126	xix. 6,	263	xv. 22,	178
xii. 1, 3, 7,	106, 113	xx. 5,	339	xvi. 14,	9
xii. 8,	209	xxxii. 32,	262	xviii. 26,	16
xiii. 14–17,	108	xxxiv. 15,	229	xix. 24,	17
xv.,	109			xxviii.,	18, 25
xv. 5,	236	LEVITICUS.			
xv. 6,	288	xxvi. 5,	227	2 SAMUEL.	
xvi. 10,	112			vi. 12,	186
xvi. 11,	265	NUMBERS.		vii. 1,	150
xvii. 1,	109	xiv. 14,	263	vii. 3, 4,	10, 156
xvii. 7, 8,	110	xxi. 18,	118	vii. 11–16,	150
xviii. 18,	112	xxiii. 7–10,	135	xxii.,	155
xvii. 19, 21,	110	xxiii. 18–24,	136, 140 f.	xxiii. 1–7,	164
xviii. 18,	108	xxiv. 3–9,	138, 141	xxiii. 5,	151
xx. 7,	107	xxiv. 3,	17		
xxi. 12,	112	xxiv. 15–24,	140, 318	1 KINGS.	
xxii. 17, 18,	108, 111, 114, 237	xxv. 1,	215	v. 9,	280
xxv. 1,	110	xxxv. 34,	100	xiv. 25,	215
xxv. 29,	112			xxi. 29,	52
xxvi. 3–6,	108, 112	DEUTERONOMY.			
xxvi. 26,	114	v. 9,	339	2 KINGS.	
xxvii. 27–29,	113, 117, 122	xiii. 1–3,	26	xiii. 23,	124
		xiii. 16,	273	xiv. 25,	226
xxvii. 33,	114	xvii. 14,	179		
xxviii. 13, 14,	108, 112	xviii. 15, 18,	132	1 CHRONICLES.	
xxxv. 9, 11,	110, 112	xviii. 22,	50	v. 1,	116
xxxvi. 31,	110	xxxi. 16,	229	xvii. 1,	150
xlvi. 1–4,	112	xxxii. 4,	325		
xlviii.,	116	xxxii. 6,	128	2 CHRONICLES.	
xlviii. 20,	108	xxxiii. 7,	122	xx. 16,	210
xlix. 1,	115	JOSHUA.			
xlix. 8–12,	117, 138	ix. 23,	99	JOB.	
xlix. 24, 25,	122	xviii. 1,	119	ix. 17,	92

INDEX.

JOB—continued.
CHAP.	PAGE
xix. 25-27,	184
xxxviii. 4,	80

PSALMS.
CHAP.	PAGE
ii.,	158, 163, 309
viii. 3,	85
xvi. 8-11,	181
xviii.,	155, 162
xxii.,	174, 180
xxiv.,	186
xxvii. 12,	160
xl.,	177, 180
xli.,	174
xlv. 6,	169
li. 17,	178
lv.,	174
lxviii.,	170
lxix.,	179
lxxii.,	170, 246 f., 281
lxxxv.,	446
lxxxvii. 3,	304
lxxxix.,	151
xcvi.-xcviii.,	446
cx.,	153, 156, 187, 226, 442
cxviii.,	444 ff.

PROVERBS.
CHAP.	PAGE
vi. 23,	129
xi. 25,	107
xii. 17,	325
xxviii. 4,	129

CANTICLES, 172

ISAIAH.
CHAP.	PAGE
i. 8,	225
ii. 2,	256, 318
ii. 3,	444
iv. 2,	334
vii. 9,	326
vii. 14, 265, 279, 309, 334
viii. 8, 9,	160, 268
ix. 1, 2,	271
ix. 3,	246
ix. 5,	268, 279
xi. 1-10,	278, 284
xix. 16-24,	296
xxiv. 5,	317
xxiv. 21,	300
xxv. 6,	301, 443
xxvi. 19,	303, 370, 466
xxviii. 16,	286, 326, 407
xxix. 14,	274
xxix. 17-19,	290
xxx. 7,	304
xxx. 18-26,	291
xxxii. 1 ff.,	292
xxxiii. 5, 17,	293

ISAIAH—continued.
CHAP.	PAGE
xxxiii. 21,	429
xxxiii. 24,	443
xxxiv. 4,	294
xxxv. 10,	294
xli. 8,	379
xlii. 1-7,	380, 403
xlv. 21,	245
xlix. 1-9,	383
l. 4-7,	385
lii. 13-15,	387
liii. 1-6,	388
liii. 7-22,	391
liv. 10-15,	406
lv. 3,	151, 402
lix. 21,	408
lx. 1-5,	411
lxiii. 1,	213
lxv. 20,	443
lxv. 25,	88, 92
lxvi. 3, 7, 8,	411 f.
lxvii. 24,	466

JEREMIAH.
CHAP.	PAGE
iii. 16, 17,	331
xvi. 60-63,	363
xvii. 22-24,	364
xxiii. 5,	333, 336, 433
xxvi. 18 f.,	52
xxx. 9,	336, 451
xxx. 15,	66
xxx. 21,	337, 442
xxxi. 22,	338
xxxi. 27,	339
xxxi. 31-34,	340, 368
xxxii. 39-41,	342
xxxiii. 9,	342
xxxiii. 15,	336, 433
xxxiii. 16,	335
xxxiii. 17,	343
xxxiv. 23,	367
xxxvi. 25-28,	367
xlix. 12,	198

EZEKIEL.
CHAP.	PAGE
xi. 19,	341
xviii. 2,	339
xxi. 32,	120
xxxiv. 23,	123
xxxvi. 25,	335
xxxvi. 26,	341
xxxvii.,	303, 369 f.
xxxviii.,	370, 460
xlvii. 1,	215

DANIEL.
CHAP.	PAGE
ii. 44,	457
vii. 13, 14,	458
ix. 24,	463
xii. 1,	465

HOSEA.
CHAP.	PAGE
i. 10,	236
ii. 1,	236
ii. 18,	232
ii. 19,	233
ii. 20,	282
ii. 21,	235
iii. 5,	161, 262
vi. 1,	237
vi. 2,	303
xi. 1,	236
xi. 8,	239
xi. 10,	161
xii. 13,	126
xiii. 12,	239
xiii. 13,	269, 309
xiii. 14,	240

JOEL.
CHAP.	PAGE
ii. 28,	205, 348, 354
ii. 30,	208
ii. 32,	209
iii. 1,	210, 409
iii. 9,	211, 460
iii. 11,	357
iii. 16,	187
iii. 18,	352, 375

AMOS.
CHAP.	PAGE
i. 2,	187
iii. 8,	6
ix. 11,	123, 225
ix. 13-15,	215, 225

OBADIAH.
CHAP.	PAGE
ver. 15-21,	197
ver. 17,	187, 226
ver. 18-21,	213

JONAH, 253
CHAP.	PAGE
iv. 2,	52

MICAH.
CHAP.	PAGE
iii. 12,	52, 257
iv. 1,	261, 318
iv. 2-6,	260
iv. 4,	123
iv. 6-8,	305
iv. 11,	212, 372
iv. 13,	310
v. 2-5,	307
v. 7, 8,	311
v. 9,	216

NAHUM, 311

HABAKKUK.
CHAP.	PAGE
ii. 2-4,	323
ii. 16,	198

INDEX.

HABAKKUK—*continued.*

CHAP.	PAGE
iii. 2,	327
iii. 18, 19,	328

ZEPHANIAH.

i. 2,	315
i. 7,	316
ii. 1, 11,	317
ii. 3,	326
iii. 8–10,	319
iii. 11–13,	320
iii. 14–17,	321

HAGGAI.

ii. 5–9,	421
ii. 7,	441
ii. 21–23,	424

ZECHARIAH.

ii. 10 f.,	429
iii. 8 ff.,	432
vi. 12, 13,	440
viii. 20–23,	443
ix. 8, 10,	311
ix. 9,	123, 245, 350
ix. 13,	247
xi.,	248, 354
xi. 7,	246
xii. 2,	372
xii. 8,	347
xii. 9–11,	348, 354, 402
xiii. 1,	215
xiii. 2,	352
xiii. 1–6,	351, 375
xiii. 7,	59, 354, 402
xiv.,	356 f.
xiv. 9,	358
xiv. 20,	359

MALACHI.

i. 3,	200
i. 11,	319, 448
iii. 1,	448
iv. 5, 6,	449

MATTHEW.

ii. 2,	141
ii. 18,	66
iv. 13,	271
iv. 18,	375
v. 3–5,	291
v. 17,	57
xiii. 47,	32
xvi. 16,	163

MATTHEW—*continued.*

CHAP.	PAGE
xvi. 27,	460
xx. 28,	405
xxi. 4, 5,	248
xxi. 9,	446
xxi. 42–46,	446
xxi. 30,	460
xxiv.,	208
xxvi. 31,	59
xxvii. 9,	250
xxvii. 35, 43,	176
xxvii. 46,	175
xxviii. 18,	163

MARK.

x. 45,	405
xiv. 61,	58
xv. 24, 29,	176
xv. 34,	175

LUKE.

vi. 20,	291
xix. 14,	163
xix. 41,	53
xxiii. 35,	176
xxiv. 44–46,	186

JOHN.

i. 21,	132
i. 52,	460
iii. 13,	460
iii. 18,	55
iv. 23,	319
v. 45–47,	132 f.
vii. 40,	132
x. 11,	355
xii. 14–16,	248
xii. 48,	55, 132
xiv. 7, 9,	163
xix. 24, 28,	176
xix. 37,	351

ACTS.

ii. 16,	217
ii. 23, 27,	351
ii. 25,	182
iii. 22,	132 f.
iv. 25,	163
vii. 37,	132 f.
xiii. 33,	163
xiii. 34,	182

ROMANS.

i. 17,	326
ii. 14,	299

ROMANS—*continued.*

CHAP.	PAGE
viii. 19,	91, 284
x. 13,	219
xi. 12,	65

1 CORINTHIANS.

x. 4,	63
xv. 54,	302

GALATIANS.

iii. 7,	65
iii. 11,	326
iv. 21,	63
iv. 24–26,	187
v. 22,	233

EPHESIANS.

ii. 14,	310

HEBREWS.

i. 5,	163
i. 13,	157
ii. 6,	85
v. 6,	157
vii. 7,	103
vii. 17, 21,	157
vii. 27,	435
viii. 1,	157
x. 5,	179
x. 12,	157
x. 37,	324
x. 38,	326

JAMES.

i. 17,	303

1 PETER.

ii. 21,	404
iv. 17,	192

2 PETER.

i. 19,	65

REVELATION.

i. 7,	351
i. 16,	281
v. 5,	123
vi. 12,	208
xiv. 15,	213
xxi.	332
xxii. 1,	374

www.ingramcontent.com/pod-product-compliance
Lightning Source LLC
Chambersburg PA
CBHW051855300426
44117CB00006B/411